# TRADE, THEORY AND ECONOMETRICS

This volume brings together cutting edge essays to mark the achievement of American economist John S. Chipman. The selection of work from international experts offers the latest in research in four of the fields to which Chipman has made major contributions:

- international economics
- micro theory
- welfare economics
- econometrics

*Trade, Theory and Econometrics* not only celebrates the career of John S. Chipman but demonstrates the ongoing importance of his work for current and future research in each of his areas of interest.

**James R. Melvin** is Professor of Economics at the University of Waterloo, Ontario, Canada.

**James C. Moore** is Professor of Economics at Purdue University, Indiana, USA.

**Raymond Riezman** is Professor of Economics at the University of Iowa, USA.

# ROUTLEDGE STUDIES IN THE MODERN WORLD ECONOMY

1 INTEREST RATES AND BUDGET DEFICITS
A study of the advanced economies
*Kanhaya L. Gupta and Bakhtiar Moazzami*

2 WORLD TRADE AFTER THE URUGUAY ROUND
Prospects and policy options for the twenty-first century
*Edited by Harald Sander and András Inotai*

3 THE FLOW ANALYSIS OF LABOUR MARKETS
*Edited by Ronald Schettkat*

4 INFLATION AND UNEMPLOYMENT
Contributions to a new macroeconomic approach
*Edited by Alvaro Cencini and Mauro Baranzini*

5 MACROECONOMIC DIMENSIONS OF PUBLIC FINANCE
Essays in honour of Vito Tanzi
*Edited by Mario I. Blejer and Teresa M. Ter-Minassian*

6 FISCAL POLICY AND ECONOMIC REFORMS
Essays in honour of Vito Tanzi
*Edited by Mario I. Blejer and Teresa M. Ter-Minassian*

7 COMPETITION POLICY IN THE GLOBAL ECONOMY
Modalities for co-operation
*Edited by Leonard Waverman, William S. Comanor and Akira Goto*

8 WORKING IN THE MACROECONOMY
A study of the US labor market
*Martin F.J. Prachowny*

9 HOW DOES PRIVATIZATION WORK?
*Edited by Anthony Bennett*

10 THE ECONOMICS AND POLITICS OF INTERNATIONAL TRADE
Freedom and Trade: Volume II
*Edited by Gary Cook*

11 THE LEGAL AND MORAL ASPECTS OF INTERNATIONAL TRADE
Freedom and Trade: Volume III
*Edited by Asif Qureshi, Hillel Steiner and Geraint Parry*

12 CAPITAL MARKETS AND CORPORATE GOVERNANCE IN JAPAN, GERMANY AND THE UNITED STATES
Organizational response to market inefficiencies
*Helmut M. Dietl*

13 COMPETITION AND TRADE POLICIES
Coherence or conflict
*Edited by Einar Hope*

14 RICE
The primary commodity
*A.J.H. Latham*

15 TRADE, THEORY AND ECONOMETRICS
Essays in honor of John S. Chipman
*Edited by James C. Moore, Raymond Riezman and James R. Melvin*

16 WHO BENEFITS FROM PRIVATIZATION?
*Edited by Moazzen Hossain*

17 TOWARDS A FAIR GLOBAL LABOUR MARKET
Avoiding the new slavery
*Edited by Ozay Mehmet, Errol Mendes and Robert Sinding*

18 MODELS OF FUTURE MARKETS
*Edited by Barry Goss*

19 VENTURE CAPITAL INVESTMENT
*Gavin C. Reid*

# TRADE, THEORY AND ECONOMETRICS

## Essays in honor of John S. Chipman

*Edited by James R. Melvin,*
*James C. Moore and*
*Raymond Riezman*

Routledge
Taylor & Francis Group
LONDON AND NEW YORK

First published 1999
by Routledge
2 Park Square, Milton Park, Abingdon, Oxfordshire OX14 4RN
Simultaneously published in the USA and Canada
by Routledge
711 Third Avenue, New York, NY 10017
First issued in paperback 2016

*Routledge is an imprint of the Taylor and Francis Group, an informa business*



Typeset in Garamond by
J&L Composition Ltd, Filey, North Yorkshire



*British Library Cataloguing in Publication Data*
A catalogue record for this book is available from the British Library

*Library of Congress Cataloging in Publication Data*
Moore, James C.
Trade, theory, and econometrics: essays in honour of John S. Chipman/
James C. Moore, Raymond Riezman, and James R. Melvin.
p. cm.
A collection of 21 essays by the author-editors and others.
Includes bibliographical references and index.
1. International trade—Econometric models. 2. Free trade—Econometric models. 3. Equilibrium (Economics)—Econometric models. 4. Welfare economics—Econometric models. 5. Econometrics. I. Riezman, Raymond Glenn. II. Melvin, James R. III. Chipman, John Somerset, 1926– . IV. Title.
HF1379.M664 1999
382—dc21
98–3068 CIP

ISBN 13: 978-1-138-98593-3 (pbk)
ISBN 13: 978-0-415-14831-3 (hbk)

**Publisher's Note**

The publisher has gone to great lengths to ensure the quality of this reprint but points out that some imperfections in the original may be apparent

*On September 26th and 27th, 1992, a very distinguished group of economists gathered at the University of Minnesota to honor an admired colleague, John Somerset Chipman. Many of the papers appearing in this volume were presented at the two-day conference honoring Chipman, and most of the papers presented at the conference do appear in this volume; although other commitments have prevented the appearance of one or two of the papers presented.*

*The editors would like to take this opportunity to thank the contributors for the splendid cooperation which we have received in preparing this volume. We would also like to share with the readers of this volume some of the atmosphere of the conference by including the text of two toasts and some remarks which were presented at the banquet the first night of the conference, and which follow.*

*James Melvin*
*Ray Riezman*
*and*
*James Moore*

# TOAST FOR JOHN S. CHIPMAN

Author of over 105 articles, books, reviews, notes, and comments;
advisor to over 25 Ph.D. students;
recipient of numerous honors and awards;
colleague and university citizen of the first rank.
All in all, more than full measure of contributions and achievements and, best of all, one that continues to grow.
It is with appreciation and affection that we gather tonight to recognize and honor John Somerset Chipman.

*Craig Swan, University of Minnesota*
26 September 1992

# SALUTE TO JOHN SOMERSET CHIPMAN

Good Americans, when they die, go to Paris. Good American economists, when they are born, are born in Canada. I have in mind Simon Newcomb. And Stephen Leacock. And Jacob Viner. Of course on this occasion I make reference to John Chipman. Indeed some sage – it may even have been I – defined Chipman as Viner without claws. Profundity and erudition but this time erudition along with knowledge of generalized matrix inverses.

John and I, and many of you present, come from a special, special circle of scholars. When my son's first child was born his mother-in-law was heard to say, "Couper is the most wonderful grandchild that ever was." Susan Stobaugh Samuelson reprimanded her: "Now, Mother, all grandmothers say that." Beverly Stobaugh replied impatiently, "Of course. I know that. But *this time* it's really true!"

Those are my sentiments. The generation of American economists born between 1914 and the Great Depression have all been my friends and companions at arms. It is not sentimental memory that makes me recall Lloyd Metzler as a Sir Galahad. And it will be a long waiting time before we meet another Lionel McKenzie or Tjallings Koopmans.

Most people are born very young. That was especially true of John Somerset Chipman. I knew his first paper when he was still 22. In Our Crowd Chipman stood out. Once upon a time American economists came off the farm – Frank Knight and Wesley Mitchell come to mind. After that, more of us came from Gary, Indiana, or Brooklyn. Judge Potter Stewart said he couldn't define pornography, but he knew it when he saw it. So it is with being a gentleman. Ian Little tells me gentlemen go to private schools; they have middle names of indeterminate gender. Maybe their families served in the diplomatic service.

The young Chipman was guilty on every count. But that didn't mean he sucked eggs or divided by zero. He recognized when complex roots had to have coefficients that got outweighed by the real.

It is perfectly possible to be brilliant and prolific without being generous. After John Chipman invents new theorems, he invariably scours the literature to see where it might already have appeared. His publications are a model of careful citation. Thus, if I wanted to refresh my memory on an obscure wartime multiplier theorem of mine, I could probably do so as well by paging through Chipman's published Hopkins thesis as by looking up my collected papers. Ramseys', Kahns', and Chipmans' – we may hope – will get their reward in heaven for the selfless refereeing and consultings that they do here on earth.

Sir Thomas Gresham was wrong. It is *good* money that drives out bad in the end. Leo Durocher was wrong. It is the good guys who end up first. John Chipman is living proof of these lemmas.

John, we all say, with love and affection:

Hail Apollo!

*Paul A. Samuelson, MIT*
26 September 1992

# REMARKS FOR JOHN CHIPMAN

I first met John Chipman in Chicago in 1950–51 when we were both visitors to the Cowles Commission. It was a glorious time for Cowles with Tjalling Koopmans and Jacob Marschak there as Professors, and Gerard Debreu and the mathematician Morton Slater among the researchers, and Harry Markowitz among the graduate students, and visitors who included Martin Beckman, Karl Brunner, Edmond Malinvaud, and ourselves. The volumes on activity analysis and econometrics were in the late stages of publication. We studied activity analysis with Koopmans and choice under uncertainty with Marschak. Koopmans' class was taught for the first few weeks by Leo Hurwicz before he left for Minnesota. Jimmy Savage was in the statistics group in the mathematics department and writing his book on personal probability. Milton Friedman and Lloyd Metzler were in the economics department although we had little time for their courses. Much of our time was taken up with mathematics, which John audited and I took for credit since officially I was a graduate student and needed to have registrations. It was also a great time for mathematics at Chicago with young professors like Paul Halmos, Irving Kaplansky, and Saunders MacLane within the circuit of our interests. There were also giant senior figures that I at least did not attempt. I recall that John attended a mathematicians' party where he reported that Irving Kaplansky looked at a table littered with liquor bottles and glasses and described it as a compact Hausdorff space.

John was working on the material of his Johns Hopkins thesis which included a study of the properties of Metzler matrices, where he had found that economic intuition could lead to correct theorems in mathematics. I succeeded in having my first paper of substance, which was concerned with Ideal Output, published in the *Economic Journal*. John assured me that this meant that I was "made." I remember John in two particular contexts. One was when we were walking back to the social sciences building with Martin Beckmann and Tjalling Koopmans. The subject arose of the existence of equilibrium and Koopmans in his grave manner emphasized the great difficulty of the problem. The other is from the class of Marschak on choice under uncertainty, where I reported on Frank Ramsey's version of personal probability and John on Marschak's derivation of von Neumann–Morgenstern utility. John was my closest friend that year and he has occupied a special place in my affections ever since. John is the archetype of the quiet Canadian with strong beliefs which lie deceptively underneath the quiet exterior.

In subsequent years we have met often at meetings of the Econometric Society, which we faithfully attended for many years. I especially remember the meetings in Montreal where Debreu presented his treatment of uncertainty in his forthcoming book on value theory and the discussant Nat Wolfe commented "Whew" and little else. John also visited Rochester for a year, where he inspired the thesis of Yasuo Uekawa on factor price equalization and Stolper–Samuelson theory. We attended the Formula II races at Watkins Glen that year. John narrowly escaped being run down by a car in the hurly-burly. Then I had the pleasure of being with John and his family when the National Academy of Sciences awarded him the Luck Prize for his masterful articles on the literature of economics.

John has one of the broadest spectra of contributions in economics. Much of his work I am quite unqualified to appreciate, particularly the econometrics. However I can give my plaudits with some assurance to his monumental survey with extensions of the theory of international trade which was done for *Econometrica*, and his numerous contributions in collaboration with his student Jim Moore to welfare economics,[1] and his classic article in the QJE on competitive equilibrium with increasing returns to the scale of the industry. His work is distinguished by careful scholarship and meticulous accuracy. My congratulations, John, on what you have already accomplished. We will await the maturity of the many projects you are embarked on now. I very much doubt that my paper on Ideal Output was the making of me, although it has brought me so far forty-one years of the *Economic Journal*. On the other hand, I am sure, John, that what you have done since those early days has left you the distinguished scholar that you are recognized everywhere to be. It has been a pleasure for me and an advantage to me to know you over these years.

*Lionel McKenzie, University of Rochester*
26 September 1992

1 (Note added by editor, J.C. Moore.) While it is certainly true that I am in many ways a student of John Chipman's, it should be noted that it was Leo Hurwicz who suffered through the principal advisor's role in the writing of my dissertation.

# CONTENTS

# TABLES

# SYNOPSES OF CHAPTERS

## Papers on international economics

**J. Bhagwati and D. Davis "Intraindustry trade: issues and theory"**
This paper reviews John Chipman's contribution to the intraindustry trade debate and argues that his important contributions have not received the attention they deserve. The authors begin by noting that the existence of intraindustry trade is often believed to be inconsistent with the basic Heckscher–Ohlin model, and that this led to a concentration on the new trade theory emphasizing internal scale economies and the resulting imperfect competition. The authors review earlier work by Chipman, Bhagwati and Davis and conclude that, when properly interpreted, the standard Heckscher–Ohlin model easily allows for intraindustry trade. The argument depends on the question of how commodities are aggregated to industries, and indeed they show that in the standard general version of the Heckscher–Ohlin model there will always exist an allocation of world endowments such that 100 percent of trade is intraindustry trade. They also discuss the issues of intraindustry trade as it relates to technological differences between countries and the relationship between the volume of trade and differences in factor endowments.

**M. Ho and D. Jorgenson "Trade policy and US economic growth"**
This is an empirical paper that estimates the effects of trade liberalization. They use an explicit dynamic model in which agents optimize over time. Their main result is that the benefits of trade liberalization are several times greater than they are estimated to be in the static case. This result is in line with other work in this area, but buttresses the argument that free trade has important intertemporal benefits.

**T. Inoue "On the mutual imposition of tariffs with free capital mobility"**
This paper derives conditions under which mutual tariff reduction can increase every country's welfare in a $2 \times 2 \times 2$ model. The innovation in

this paper is that international capital movements are permitted. Theorem 1 solves for the Nash equilibrium tariffs. Theorem 2 solves for conditions under which a mutual tariff reduction benefits all countries. These results are shown to hold regardless of the pattern of specialization and not to depend on the assumption of no specialization.

**K. Kletzer and T. Srinivasan "The importance of price normalization for models of international trade under imperfect competition"**
This paper argues that in imperfect competition models with positive profits, the choice of the numéraire good affects the outcome of the equilibrium. The authors begin with a careful review of the literature, followed with a theoretical discussion of the relationship between profit maximization and the choice of the numéraire. They then provide an example to show that the choice of the numéraire fundamentally affects the outcome of the model. They argue that computable general equilibrium models are particularly vulnerable to the kinds of difficulties they identify. In particular, the calculated effects of policy changes on welfare and resource allocation are very sensitive to the choice of numéraire.

**K. Krishna and M. Thursby "Flexibility: a partial ordering"**
An important but often neglected topic in international trade is the ability of countries to adjust to exogenous shocks. This paper develops certain criteria for ranking the adjustment ability of economies. They show that restrictions on factor mobility and production reduce the flexibility of small economies to adjust to such things as price changes, endowment changes, and technological shocks. These distortions are shown not only to reduce the level of GNP but also to reduce the ability of a country to adjust to external shocks. They conclude that although generally economies cannot be ranked in terms of their ability to adjust, partial orderings based on factor mobility are available.

**A. Krueger "Free trade agreements as protectionist devices: rules of origin"**
Free Trade Agreements are analyzed taking into account rules of origin (ROOs). ROOs are shown to allow countries to extend the effects of their protection, thus making an FTA more protectionist than it first appears. Here is how it works. Suppose Mexico exports cloth to the US and the cloth is produced with imported textiles. Suppose the US is less efficient in textiles than the rest of the world. By imposing strict ROOs the US can essentially force Mexico to buy its expensive textiles (thereby further protecting the US textile industry) in order to be able to export its cloth to the US. Some specific examples are computed in the paper.

**J. Melvin "Demand conditions in international trade theory"**
Although demand conditions are present in all international trade models, the implications of different demand assumptions are not always fully recognized. This paper takes up the issue of demand and investigates the role that demand plays in the classical model, the Heckscher–Ohlin model, the specific-factor model and models with increasing returns to scale. The discussion of the classical model extends earlier work by Chipman to show that the assumptions concerning demand may be at least as important as the production assumptions in determining final equilibrium prices. It is shown that in the Heckscher–Ohlin model assumptions about demand essentially determine whether or not factor prices will be equalized and in the specific-factor model demand is again important in determining the pattern of international trade. With increasing returns to scale it is argued that it is the different assumptions about demand that produce different results when models of external and internal economies are compared.

**T. Mitra and R. Jones "Factor shares and the Chipman condition"**
An early contribution of John Chipman in the international trade area was a discussion of the generalization of the Stolper–Samuelson Theorem. Chipman provided a condition on distributed factor shares by which factors could be assigned to commodities in such a way as to guarantee that an increase in the price of that commodity would increase the return of the factor. Chipman showed, however, that this condition did not extend beyond the $3 \times 3$ model. The present paper takes up the issue of the generalization of the Stolper–Samuelson Theorem and both reviews and extends the earlier work of Chipman and Kemp and Wegge. They showed that both the Kemp–Wegge and Chipman conditions can be strengthened. They argue that the weak form of the Stolper–Samuelson Theorem discussed may be more relevant in policy analysis since presumably factors of production will not generally care whether they are the sole benefactor of a commodity price increase.

**R. Riezman "Oligopoly and customs unions"**
This paper analyzes a model of international oligopoly when customs unions are possible. It is shown that importer–exporter customs unions are pro-competitive in the sense that internally they will tend to have industries produce at their competitive output level, but will tend to exclude imports from non-member countries. Exporter customs unions are anti-competitive and will produce the monopoly output. The core concept is used to determine which unions would form. With one firm in each country the importer will form a union with the low cost exporter. With identical costs, but variable numbers of firms, when the number of firms is small an importer–exporter customs union forms. A union of the exporters will form if there are four or more firms in the world.

## Papers on micro theory, welfare economics, and econometrics

**A. Dixit "Competitive industry equilibrium with firm-specific uncertainty"**
Dixit constructs a model incorporating firm-specific uncertainty, along the general lines of Hopenhayn's 1992 *Econometrica* paper. However, Dixit is able to exhibit the structure of the industry equilibrium in a much simpler way; which allows him to obtain an explicit solution of the long-run stationary distribution of firms.

**K. Kadiyala and D. Oberhelman "Estimation and inference in simultaneous equations"**
Consider the general problem of estimation and inference in stochastic simultaneous equations. They introduce a class of modified limited information maximum likelihood estimators and show that these estimators possess finite moments. They then use unbiased estimator results, which they prove to hold for these estimators, to derive new asymptotic tests of hypotheses. Simulation results indicate that these tests perform better than traditional tests.

**M. Kemp and H. Wan "On lumpsum compensation"**
As has long been known, perturbations or structural changes in an economy (for example, the institution of free trade agreements) will generally benefit some agents, but harm others. As has also been known for some time, it is often possible in such a context for the gainers to compensate the losers in such a way as to make everyone better off after the change than before. However, in recent years the usual procedure in policy analysis conducted in a general equilibrium setting has been to avoid arguments or mechanisms which make use of lump-sum taxes; leaving the status of some of the earlier analysis (for example, of the gains from trade) somewhat ambiguous. On the other hand, as Kemp and Wan point out, the compensation scheme developed by Grandmont and McFadden in their 1972 *Journal of International Economics* paper (and which was later expanded by Grinols (1981, 1984) has the advantage of not requiring information about preferences and technologies, but only about trades and production vectors chosen *before* the change; assuming nothing else has changed in the economy except for the disturbance or perturbation under scrutiny.

In order to formally analyze the efficacy of the Grandmont–McFadden–Grinols (GMG) scheme, Kemp and Wan develop the concept of an **essentially repetitive economy**, which is, among other things, a two-period model in which some disturbance takes place at the beginning of the second period. In the context of such a model, the authors develop a formal expression of the GMG scheme, and prove, for example, a existence result in which the GMG compensation scheme is used in the second period. They analyze a number of other properties of the GMG scheme in the context of an essentially repetitive economy; and show how their results apply to an overlapping-generations model as a special case.

**M. Ali Khan "A result on large anonymous games: an elementary and self-contained exposition"**

Presents an existence result (of Cournot–Nash equilibrium) of a large anonymous game. Remarkably, the exposition of the result is entirely self-contained; in fact, in principle at least, a prospective reader need have no background at all in either advanced mathematics or game theory to follow Khan's development of the result. Khan also shows how this result is related to Chipman's 1970 article on external economies of scale and competitive equilibrium (*Quarterly Journal of Economics* (1970) 84: 347–85), and uses the theoretical problems investigated in Chipman's article to motivate and to help explicate the theorem and constructs which he develops.

**M. Majumdar "Complicated behavior in models with two commodities: a review"**

In his 1987 *New Palgrave* article, John Chipman notes that "a good definition of international-trade theory as it has evolved would be 'general equilibrium theory with structure'." The need for structure arises, in particular, because in trade theory one is generally interested in comparative statics results, which are generally not obtainable, at least not in a very precise form, in the general case. Consequently, the two-by-two case is the most often studied; with the interest in comparative statics results tacitly being dependent upon the general feeling that in this simple case, equilibrium is generally stable, and thus the results of comparative statics analysis were meaningful.

The belief that two-commodity systems would generally exhibit a globally stable equilibrium has, however, stemmed from differential equation analyses; whereas it would appear that a discrete time analysis is generally more appropriate in economics. Consequently, a difference equation analysis becomes the appropriate mode for the study of stability of equilibrium systems; and here, as was pointed out by Samuelson in his *Foundations*, and emphasized by Chipman in his trade survey, things become quite different.

Majumdar shows that things become very different indeed when one takes into account modern work on chaotic behavior in non-linear systems. He extends and refines earlier results by Bala and Majumdar (1992), Day and Pianigiani (1991), and Saari (1985, 1987, 1991) to more precisely delineate the possibilities for both topological and ergodic chaotic behavior in simple (real-valued) systems, such as arise in two-commodity models. He shows that such behavior is both pervasive and robust in such a context. More original and startling, however, is Majumdar's demonstration that a two-agent exchange economy in which both agents have Cobb–Douglas utility functions may exhibit topological chaos; and worse yet, that such behavior may be robust.

**D. McFadden "Computing willingness-to-pay in random utility models"**

McFadden's piece focuses on calculating mean willingness-to-pay (WTP) for a change in resource allocation in an economy where consumers have a distribution of preferences. This type of calculation is particularly useful when evaluating public policies, such as environmental policies, in circumstances where consumer choices are discrete. In the second section, McFadden defines WTP and shows how to compute bounds for it that hold for general distributions of preferences. In some policy applications, these bounds will be adequate to identify preferred social policies without placing further assumptions on the distribution of preferences. The third section considers the case of additively separable indirect utility functions. When indirect utility is linear in income, with a coefficient that does not vary over consumers or alternatives, the Chipman–Moore conditions for the existence of a "representative" consumer are met, and WTP can be expressed in terms of a change in expected utility. Absent this restriction on the effects of income, there is no representative consumer representation: it is still possible to calculate expected utility for the population, but it is not possible to estimate WTP by adjusting mean income to keep expected utility constant. The fourth and fifth sections look at WTP in Generalized Extreme Value (GEV) models, which include multinomial logit and nested multinomial logit models. Here, an analytic formula for mean WTP is available when indirect utility is linear in income with a constant coefficient. However, when indirect utility does not have this structure in income, there is no closed formula for calculation of WTP. The final section of the paper deals with this difficulty by developing a simulation method that can obtain accurate estimates of mean WTP in GEV models when there is no representative consumer representation of community preferences.

**L. McKenzie "The core and competitive equilibria in finite economies"**

McKenzie shows the way in which results regarding the core and the equivalence between the core and competitive equilibrium can be sharpened by considerations based upon his notion of an irreducible economy, while at the same time dropping the assumptions of transitive and convex preferences. He presents interesting refinements and new results concerning (1) the relationship between the core and competitive equilibrium, and (2) the existence (non-emptiness) of the core or an economy, as well as non-emptiness of the equal treatment core. He is able to establish the first of these two existence results under significantly weaker conditions than the known sufficient conditions for the existence of a competitive equilibrium. Thus it appears, as McKenzie emphasizes, that the core is truly a notion intermediate in generality between that of Pareto efficiency and competitive equilibrium.

**J.C. Moore "Quasi-equivalent variation analysis in the Gorman Polar case"**

Moore introduces a new interpretation of a "valid indicator of welfare change," introduces a stronger condition ("a valid ranking") for indicators of welfare change, and explores the relationship between the two concepts. He develops a simplification of the "quasi-equivalent variation analysis" technique developed by John Chipman and Moore for the case of the Gorman Polar Form (Chipman and Moore [1990]); and provides a greatly simplified discussion of why the technique works. A number of examples are developed showing how the technique works in some useful special cases. A beginning is also made in the direction of analyzing the simplifications made possible in the situation wherein only a subset of the prices are expected to change. The claim is made, and defended, that this "quasi-equivalent variation analysis" is as practical and easily done as is the theoretically indefensible Marshallian consumer's surplus analysis.

**T. Negishi "Marshallian demonstration of a tax-subsidy scheme under variable returns to scale"**

Considers the Marshallian welfare proposition that increasing cost industries should be taxed, and decreasing cost industries subsidized; and finds reason to vindicate Marshall's claims within the context of his (Marshall's) life-cycle view of a firm and of the life-cycle composition of the firms within a competitive industry.

**Y. Otani "The envelope theory in a smooth constrained optimization problem with applications in economics"**

Otani presents a new look at the relationship between comparative statics results, the envelope theorem, the LeChatlier principle, and the properties of the optimum value function. Using techniques of differentiable topology, he presents a much more sophisticated and general presentation of this topic than has appeared in print heretofore. Moreover, he goes on to show how the general formulation which he is using can be applied to characterize the set of Pareto efficient allocations. Interestingly enough, in this latter investigation Otani develops (in a much more general context) an extension of earlier work co-authored by Chipman himself

(Chipman J.S. and Moore, J.C. [1971] "The Compensation Principle in Welfare Economics," in *Papers in Quantitative Economics*, 2nd edn., by Arvid M. Zarley, University Press of Kansas, Lawrence, Kansas).

**P. Samuelson "A classical theorem for John Chipman: maximal and minimal Malthusian population; a sweeping non-substitution theorem at the core of the canonical classical model"**

In the Malthusian–Ricardian economic models, wage is driven toward the subsistence level, with any rise in the real wage above this level causing increases in population, which in turn drives real wages back downward. What has been left out of the story historically is what determines the equilibrium level of population. Samuelson shows that this missing link is supplied, in the context of a closed linear model of the Malthusian–Ricardian type, by landlords' tastes for luxury goods. More specifically, "population is *maximal* (*minimal*) when [landlords'] consumption concentrates on good(s) with maximum (minimum) ratio of *augmented embodied labor* relative to *augmented embodied land* – where 'augmented' means we count in for each good both its required direct and indirect primary inputs *and* those same primary inputs required for the subsistence fodder of its labor inputs." From this and other considerations, Samuelson also derives a fundamental non-substitution theorem in production for this model.

**J. Silvestre "External diseconomies in the commons"**

Silvestre's paper extends the Chipman approach to parametric external economies and diseconomies of scale to the problem of a common resource pool exploited by many independent firms. Thus, the problem of returns to scale is analyzed in a dynamic model of renewable resources. The basic question asked is when does many firms exploiting a common resource pool generate external diseconomies of scale? Silvestre shows that many cases of external diseconomies of scale can be explained by looking at the renewable resource as an implicit input subject to natural growth laws.

# 1

# INTRAINDUSTRY TRADE: ISSUES AND THEORY

*Jagdish Bhagwati and Donald R. Davis*

## Introduction

In a recent issue of the *Journal of Economic Perspectives*, two Stanford graduate students, Joshua Gans and George Shepherd (1993), wrote about the difficulties that eminent economists had in getting their ideas published in the mainstream professional journals. They focused on papers containing unfamiliar ideas that have yet no resonance for the profession trapped in "conventional wisdom." But they ignore the difficulty that sometimes attends publishing papers that challenge an orthodoxy that is newly established, no matter how penetrating and persuasive the critique is, simply because the challenge is seen as emanating from the "old and obsolete school."

This latter has been the fate of John Chipman's important work on intraindustry trade which refuted the new orthodoxy among the younger trade theorists working with models of imperfect competition; that perfectly competitive models could not generate intraindustry trade. Rejected by referees on grounds that Chipman's results were "uninteresting" or "wrong" or "obvious" or attacking "straw men," and published in consequence in volumes and exotic journals, this work remains a major contribution. This *festschrift* provides an appropriate place and occasion to resurrect that work, put it into context, and to reshape and extend it analytically.[1]

## The issues

### *Two different concepts of intraindustry trade*

The phenomenon of intraindustry trade, which was propelled into center stage by the seminal empirical work of Grubel and Lloyd (1975), has been taken in the analytical literature to raise two wholly different questions.

*1. Close substitutes in consumption* One set of theorists has taken the phenomenon to mean that there is two-way trade in "similar products" across countries, obviously thinking of intraindustry trade therefore as trade in products which are close substitutes in *consumption*, much the way industrial-organization theorists implicitly and typically define an industry prior to undertaking the analysis of oligopolistic or large-group market structure in partial-equilibrium.[2]

When Staffan Linder (1961) initiated the analysis of intraindustry trade, noting that countries at similar stages of development had a high degree of trade, evidently he had in mind trade in similar products, so defined. So did Bhagwati's (1964) survey of the theory of international trade where Linder's theory of trade was set alongside Ricardo's and the Heckscher–Ohlin theory as an alternative approach of significance.

In fact, while some of the writers on intraindustry trade have dismissed this trade in similar products by asserting that it simply reflects "categorical aggregation" (where the word "categorical" is used, not in the sense of the Kantian Imperative but simply as defined by categories of the SITC variety) and that therefore there is nothing more to be said about the matter, this is surely wrong. Linder himself attempted to explain why such two-way trade would arise (as with countries trading different varieties of cars, small and large), arguing basically from the demand side, allowing demand differences to obtain across countries and for there to be greater overlap between countries with closer per capita incomes than across poor and rich countries, and hence greater trade in similar products and in trade per se. Of course, this demand-side explanation is complete only when paired with a theory of location that accounts for the need for trade.

In a similar vein, Bhagwati (1982) also produced the outlines of a theory, based on differences in tastes and demands across countries which reflect essential differences in country "environment," which then lead to similar product developments, with characteristics differentiated so as to reflect the different country "tastes," in countries endowed with similar resources and broad know-how.[3] With tastes diffusing quickly, and translating into demand for most such similar products, trade in similar products will break out. This was described as a "biological" theory of trade in similar products and its "dynamic" essentials detailed as follows (Bhagwati, 1982: 175–176):

> just as in biological theorizing the "environment" interacts with "genetic factors" to produce a phenotype, we can think of an economic process whereby a specific choice of a product type emerges within a nation-society. Thus, think of the income level and the level of R&D in manufacturing as defining the capacity of the society to come up technologically with a given set of characteristic product combinations, e.g. small, medium, and large cars. The United States and Japan share this "genetic" set of traits

> . . . But which phenotype is selected in the market depends on the interaction of this common set of "genetic" traits with the specific "environment" of Japan and the United States. Thus the land–man ratios, the size and structure of the family, etc. may lead to the evolution of "gas guzzlers" in the United States and of smaller, fuel-economy cars in Japan, as, in fact, has been the case. At the next stage . . . the successful development of small cars in Japan and of gas guzzlers in the United States gets reinforced by localized technical change in precisely these types of cars with the result that one is now dealing with a situation of *ex ante* differentials in the know-how of producing and selling different types of cars. Next, since "cars" represent a generic product, representing a certain manner of transportation, the taste for cars diffuses to the United States and for gas guzzlers to Japan as part of the Schumpeterian process of dynamic capitalism, aided by advertising in search of new markets. Thus, trade in similar products arises.

Subsequently, Feenstra (1982) and Dinopoulos (1988) have formalized the essential elements of this "biological" theory.

2. *Similar factor-intensity in production* In contrast to this way of thinking about intraindustry trade as trade in similar products, however, trade theorists in the 1980s defined intraindustry trade from the *production* side, as two-way trade in commodities whose production was *similar in factor-intensity*.

From an empirical, as against a theoretical, point of view, the latter definition does not seem to correspond to the way that the bureaucrats and experts who devised the SITC categories down to five digits at the United Nations were grouping commodities. There is no evidence of ex ante intention to do so, and research by Michael Finger (1975) shows in fact that capital to labor ratios varied less between 3-digit industries than within them.[4]

Why did this factor-intensity-based definition arise and come to dominate the analysis and arguments which Chipman and others have addressed? The principal reason is the dominance in this period of the Heckscher–Ohlin–Samuelson model, whose analytic framework emphasized factor proportions. Equally, it was believed that trade in goods of similar (or especially *identical*) factor intensity posed a genuine puzzle that could not be accounted for in this model (Helpman and Krugman, 1985: 2).[5]

Any other way of getting to two-way trade in commodities of identical factor intensities, such that (say) homothetic symmetry of tastes or production functions across countries was abandoned while perfect competition was maintained, was not considered. In fact, many claims that imperfect competition was *necessary* to generate intraindustry trade may be found in the literature of the 1980s; and this gave a significant boost to the imperfectly-competitive theory of international trade (which, of course, is a major scientific achievement whose credentials do not depend on invalid arguments).[6]

### *The aggregation issue*

Before we turn to a fuller analysis of the theoretical issues, it is necessary to note an altogether different, aggregation-based, critique of intraindustry trade that Chipman has done most to advance, which is orthogonal to the analytical issues as posed above.

Chipman (1992) has argued that the SITC-data-generated estimates of intraindustry trade reflect aggregation of different goods, and statistically demonstrates that disaggregation, carried down to multiple digits as far as is necessary, virtually eliminates such intraindustry trade. Note that this exercise simply fits an equation to the existing SITC categories, which have no clear correspondence to either of the two criteria which we discussed earlier, and which go down to five digits. Chipman shows that carrying the disaggregation down to 18 digits would reduce the share of intraindustry trade to negligible levels.

How should we look on this demonstration? Given the doubts that we have noted above about the correspondence between the SITC division into industries and the theoretical categories, which require aggregation by factor intensities, we find these results more interesting than compelling. Extrapolating by fitting an equation to SITC-groupings-generated data, where there is no identifiable principle by which these data are generated, seems to lack the necessary theoretical rationale on which to base any theoretically interesting conclusions.

Moreover, the theoretical work of Chipman and others, reviewed below, which shows that properly-defined intraindustry trade (i.e. aggregated by factor intensities, in contrast to the SITC data) is compatible with the conventional competitive Heckscher–Ohlin–Samuelson (H–O–S) theory, also suggests that empirical questions about the share of intraindustry trade are less pertinent.

### *Key theoretical questions*

In any event, the key theoretical questions are the following:

- How do we account for trade in goods of similar factor proportions; and

- Why is there such a large volume of trade between countries with similar endowments?

The primary presumption of the new trade theorists that these phenomena – correctly observed or not – require that the constant returns to scale and perfectly competitive HOS model must be abandoned, and the secondary presumption that this requires a turn to increasing returns to scale and imperfect competition (rather than alternative formulations) need to be reexamined. This is the task to which we now turn, in the spirit of Chipman's major theoretical contributions.[7]

## The theory

### *Introduction*

In the remainder of this chapter, we will review theoretical models of intraindustry trade in a competitive setting.[8]

1 First we focus on Chipman's (1988, 1991) demonstration that intraindustry trade can be generated in a competitive HOS model. We proceed, however, to re-prove his principal theorem in a simpler and more transparent way by resort to a generalized version of the celebrated Lerner diagram of trade theory.
2 Next we extend this argument to show, as did Chipman (1992) and Rodgers (1988), that a large share of trade in this model being intraindustry is not anomalous.
3 Then we review the contributions of Bhagwati (1964) and Davis (1992, 1995) which account for intraindustry trade instead by departing from the conventional HOS model, not by allowing imperfect competition, but by allowing for international differences in production functions.
4 Finally we address a different, but related, issue which was considered by Chipman (1992) and has been addressed more fully by Davis (1997): in a multilateral world, with the competitive HOS model in place, would one be able to account for the presumed fact that there is more trade between countries that are similar rather than dissimilar in factor proportions? The answer again is in the affirmative.

In combination, therefore, these contributions present a powerful argument that the competitive trade theory in general, and the HOS factor proportions theory in particular, cannot be rejected based on evidence of the large share of intraindustry trade in world trade, or the large share of the major developed countries in world trade.

### *Intraindustry trade and the theory of aggregation: proving the compatibility of the HOS model with intraindustry trade*

Chipman (1988, 1991) argues that the oft-cited statistics on the large share of intraindustry trade in total trade provide no basis for rejecting the HOS factor proportions model of trade, and develops a theorem that it is always possible to find endowments for which 100 percent of trade is intraindustry trade. In this section, we will provide an intuitive development of his theorem, and discuss its importance for the broader problem of intraindustry trade.

It proves convenient to think about the Chipman argument in a framework that focuses on trade as the implicit exchange of factors. Accordingly, we develop two points of analysis. The first reviews the conception of trade in the Samuelson–Dixit–Norman–Helpman–Krugman "integrated equilibrium" framework. The second develops what we call the Lerner technology matrix, which generalizes the familiar Lerner diagram to a many-dimensional setting.

The integrated equilibrium is defined to be the allocation of resources that would occur if there were barriers neither to the movement of goods nor factors. We then ask what divisions of factors between countries is consistent with replicating this equilibrium via trade in goods alone. The set of such partitions of the world endowments is referred to as the Factor Price Equalization (FPE) set. In the conventional setting with two countries, goods, and factors, this is represented as a parallelogram in factor space (see Figure 1.1). The slopes of the sides of the parallelogram reflect the factor intensities employed in the integrated equilibrium in the respective sectors. The lengths of the sides of the parallelogram reflect the allocation of factors to each of the sectors in the integrated equilibrium.

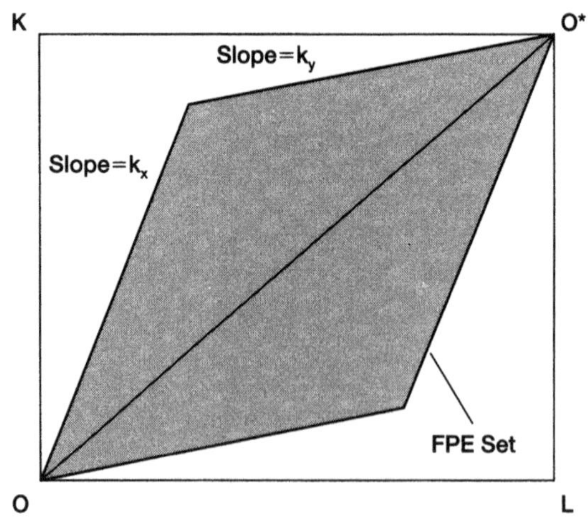


*Figure 1.1*

In this setting, the implicit trade in factors is simply the difference between the factor content of production, given by the endowment, and the factor content of consumption. The latter is proportional to the world endowment (so on the diagonal of the factor box), with the factor of proportionality being the country's share in world spending. Under balanced trade, the endowment and the factor content of consumption lie on an isoincome line, whose slope is minus the factor rental ratio. The crucial point for our purpose is that trade here consists of the export of factor services in the proportion that they are used in the exportable sector, and the import of factor services in the proportion that they are used in the importable sector, subject to meeting the previously described net factor trade (see Figure 1.2).

Now we turn to thinking about this in a setting that will be convenient for problems that require higher dimensionality of goods, factors, and perhaps countries. We develop a tool that we call the Lerner technology matrix,[9] which generalizes the Lerner diagram to many dimensions:

$$A^L(w) = \left[A_1^L A_2^L \ldots A_N^L\right] = \left[a_{ij}^L\right]$$

Columns of this matrix represent the factor input coefficients for the respective goods sufficient to trade at integrated equilibrium prices for a unit of the numéraire. The utility of this construct – following our earlier discussion – is that trade then consists of the one-for-one exchange of columns of this matrix.

We will now use this framework to prove a theorem developed in a more general setting in Chipman (1988, 1991).

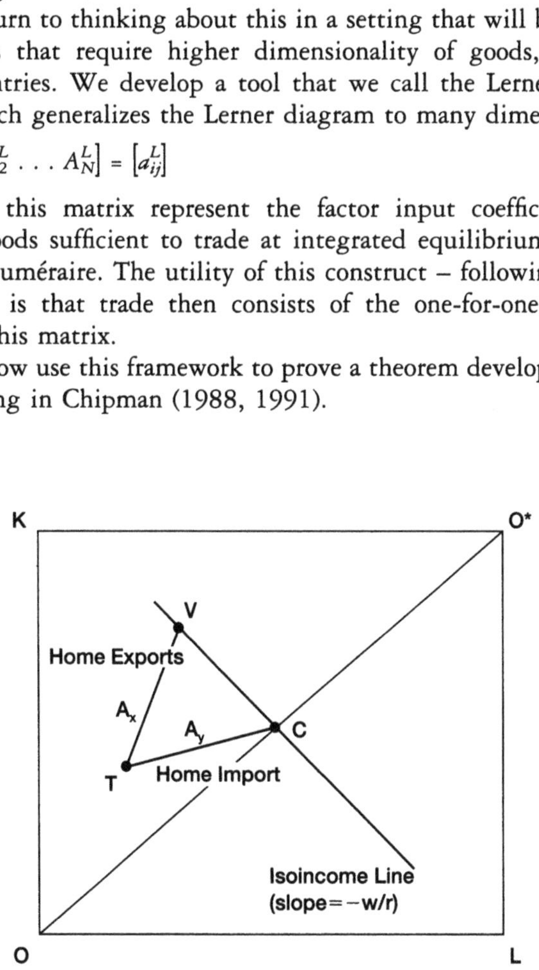


*Figure 1.2*

*Theorem (Chipman)*

> Given an $N$-good, $N$-factor, $K$-country world, that satisfies the conventional assumptions of the Heckscher–Ohlin model, and in which the production techniques employed in the integrated equilibrium are linearly independent, and given *any* aggregation of the $N$ goods into $\bar{N} < N$ industries, there exists an allocation of world factor endowments such that one hundred percent of trade is intraindustry trade.

The proof of this statement follows the suggestion of Chipman (1991), and is made more direct by the use of the Lerner technology matrix. We show this for the case of two countries; the extension to more countries is straightforward.

*Proof*

Suppose, first, that the two countries have identical factor proportions, so $V^1 = \mu\bar{V}$ and $V^2 = (1 - \mu)\bar{V}$, where $\mu \in (0, 1)$ is a scalar reflecting country one's share in world income, and $\bar{V}$ is the vector of world factor endowments. The assumption that the techniques employed in the integrated equilibrium are linearly independent insures the determinacy of production patterns. Since each country has a fixed share of each of the endowments, it undertakes that same share of the production of every good, which is also the share of that good consumed. No trade occurs.

We now construct factor endowments that meet the requirements of the theorem. First, consider the Lerner technology matrix. It is an $N \times N$ matrix of the input coefficients consistent with the integrated equilibrium techniques, where the quantities are chosen so that they yield equal value at integrated equilibrium prices. The theorem assumes that the $N$ goods have been aggregated into some smaller number $\bar{N}$ of industries. Thus some industry has at least two goods. Consider such an industry, with goods we will label X and Y. $A^L_X$ and $A^L_Y$ are columns in the Lerner technology matrix. Consider the effect of taking factors measured by $\theta A^L_X$ from country one and giving this to country two, while taking factors measured by $\theta A^L_Y$ from country two and giving this to country one. The induced endowments would be:

$$V^1_\theta = V^1 + \theta(A^L_Y - A^L_X)$$

$$V^2_\theta = V^2 + \theta(A^L_X - A^L_Y)$$

So long as both goods are consumed in the integrated equilibrium, any $\theta$ less than the minimum of the number of X produced initially in country one or Y in country two will leave the new endowments in the FPE set. Moreover, this exchange leaves incomes, so consumption patterns, unchanged. The only change is a shift in the location of production of $\theta$ units of X from two to one, and $\theta$ units of Y from one to two. With consumption unchanged, and initially no trade, the only trade that will exist is the export by country one of $\theta$ units of good X in exchange for $\theta$ units of good Y from country two. That is, this endowment pattern has generated trade, 100 percent of which is intraindustry trade. This completes the proof.

It is evident from the construction of the proof that it is likewise always possible under the same conditions to find endowments for which zero percent of the trade is intraindustry trade. In fact, we can always find endowments for which the share of intraindustry trade is at any level that we desire. The implication, then, is that the share of intraindustry trade per se can provide no evidence for or against the factor proportions model.

The remarkable fact about this theorem is that it holds irrespective of the criterion used to aggregate goods into industries. It holds equally well whether actual aggregation is based on production attributes (such as similar factor intensity), consumption attributes, or even arbitrary characteristics such as color.

Recall that we have assumed that the number of goods equals the number of factors, and that the technologies employed in equilibrium were linearly independent (so that our technology matrix was non-singular). This excludes the case in which two goods use identical (as against similar) factor intensities. If we continue to hold the number of goods to equal that of factors, but want to allow two or more of the goods to use identical factor intensities, then it is no longer possible to use the integrated equilibrium framework, as the FPE set will have less than full dimension in factor space. This is effectively the same as the case in which the number of goods is smaller than the number of factors, since in production terms some of the goods are identical. We can also consider the case in which there are sufficiently more and technologically diverse goods that, in spite of some using identical factor proportions, the FPE set has full dimension. So long as there is some industry that has goods with diverse technical coefficients, the theorem will continue to hold without modification. Of course, in this case the level of trade in the goods with identical factor proportions will be indeterminate (there potentially being other indeterminacies as well).

### *The share of intraindustry trade in the pure HOS model*

Chipman (1988, 1992) and his former student, Joan Rodgers (1988) have also gone on to demonstrate that a large share of intraindustry trade is compatible with the HOS model. Chipman (1992) addresses this problem by exploring the relations between similarity of factor endowments across countries. similarity of technologies, and the ratio of exports to output-of-the-exportable within a country. He develops his analysis within an example that restricts both technologies and preferences to be Cobb–Douglas, in addition to satisfying exact symmetry conditions. These strong restrictions are amply rewarded by the transparency of the results. Given these assumptions, he shows that as technologies symmetrically become more similar, there is a rise in the ratio of exports to output-of-the-exportable. This result flows principally from the production relations. As demonstrated by Lizondo, Johnson and Yeh (1981), making the technologies more similar tends to make the production possibility frontier "flatter," or linear in the limit. As this suggests, this tends to promote greater specialization in production, and so for fixed consumption shares, both a greater level of exports and a larger share of the exportable actually exported. In fact, he shows that the sensitivity of the export to output ratio to growing similarity of technologies increases as the technologies become more and more similar. Or more plainly, as the goods come more and more to have similar input proportions, the share of the exportable actually exchanged rises. This suggests very strongly that a large share of intraindustry trade – particularly in goods of similar factor content – should not be surprising.

Rodgers (1988) extends Chipman's (1992) demonstration to a world with four goods and factors. While Chipman's paper is very much to the point in stressing the link between similar factor intensity of goods and the likely share of the exportable actually exported, one must strain to think of a two-good model as one of intraindustry trade. To make progress on the question in the four by four model, Rodgers is obliged to impose a fairly stringent set of conditions on the set of technologies available and the way in which the two countries' endowments are allowed to differ. She groups the goods into industries based on a Euclidean metric operating on the Cobb–Douglas production elasticities, as developed by Chipman (1992). Granted these assumptions, she is able to develop three propositions. The first states that the industry in which the technologies are closer by the metric will have a larger share of trade which is intraindustry. This is interesting, as it again suggests that in a factor proportions world, important cross hauling of factor services may be the rule rather than the exception. Her second result relates more directly to Chipman (1992), and establishes that as the technologies within an industry become more similar in a specific way, the fraction of that industry's trade which is intraindustry rises. Finally, she shows that the same exercise also raises the share of total trade which is intraindustry.

The one caution we would raise about Rodgers' results is that the assumptions on which they are based are very restrictive. It is straightforward to demonstrate that proposition one fails once we remove the restrictions on the endowments of the countries. We simply use the Lerner matrix developed above to construct endowments for which the only intraindustry trade is in the industry whose technologies are further apart by the metric. This would also seem to cast doubt on the generality of the remaining propositions. Nevertheless, the examples she develops remain strongly at odds with the proposition that intraindustry trade is puzzling in a factor proportions setting.

Rodgers also sought to demonstrate that the possibility of substantial intraindustry did not depend on "cooked" assumptions on the pattern of endowments or technologies. In a separate exercise, she considered three varied patterns of endowments among three countries, and ran 500 simulations in which the Cobb–Douglas constant-returns-to-scale production elasticities were selected randomly. Based on these elasticities, the goods were grouped into industries, and the Grubel–Lloyd index was calculated. The results verified that, depending on the particular technologies at work, and the specific pattern of endowments, both very high and very low indices of intraindustry trade could arise. In any case, the exercise did not suggest that high intraindustry trade in a factor proportions setting is an anomaly.

### *Relaxing assumptions of HOS, while maintaining perfect competition*

Since the central concern was whether competitive constant-returns-to-scale models could generate intraindustry trade, it was natural to consider a relaxation of other assumptions of the conventional HOS model. For reasons that will be clarified below, the natural assumption to relax is that of identical technologies.

In fact the textbook one-factor Ricardian model should itself be considered as a paradigmatic model of intraindustry trade. With but a single factor, trade is necessarily in goods with identical factor "intensity." Of course, with constant returns to scale, this gives rise to flat production surfaces, so that even small technical differences suffice to drive the intraindustry trade. In fact, within this simple example lies much of the intuition of what drives intraindustry trade in a competitive constant returns setting.

While accounting for intraindustry trade was not his intent, Bhagwati (1964: 9–10) contributed to this line of argument.[10] In surveying the literature on tests of the Ricardian theory of the pattern of trade, which had used comparative labor productivity ratios, he suggested generalizing the Ricardian theory to Hicks-neutral differences in production functions across countries. If one then assumes that both countries have identical factor endowment ratios, equal in turn to the non-substitution-theorem-implied unique factor intensity observed in each country we again generate a Ricardian "flat" production possibility curve in each country but with different slopes.[11] It is immediately obvious that both goods in each country would be characterized in production by the same factor intensity, equal to the common factor-endowment ratio of both countries, and trade with complete specialization by each country in commodities with identical factor intensities would be observed. The generalized[12] Ricardian model used here then generates 100 percent intraindustry trade: each of the two countries exports a unique commodity that has the same factor intensity in equilibrium. This demonstrates that giving up perfect competition is not necessary to generate intraindustry trade; giving up the assumption of identical production functions is sufficient.

The paper by Davis (1992) also departs from the conventional HOS setting by introducing Ricardian cross-country technical differences. He argues that this departure is not only defensible, but eminently reasonable given central characteristics of the problem of intraindustry trade. Two points are emphasized: first, the characterization of intraindustry trade as trade in goods of similar factor intensity; and second, the emphasis within this literature on the large number of goods being traded (large here being understood as large relative to the number of primary factors).[13] Both characteristics tend to make production possibility surfaces have "flats" – precisely the setting in which Ricardian technical differences matter.

The approach of Davis has two advantages. First, it dramatically simplifies the demonstration of the consistency of intraindustry trade with a factor-proportions view of the world. Second, since it is developed within the Dixit–Norman–Helpman–Krugman FPE framework, it facilitates direct comparison with the alternative hypothesis of increasing returns as the source of intraindustry trade. This includes a full graphic mapping of endowment patterns within the FPE set into trade patterns. Among the results is a demonstration in a factor proportions setting of 100 percent intraindustry trade among countries with identical endowment proportions. In the two-country setting, intraindustry trade is encouraged by two characteristics: (1) similarity of endowments, so that the countries will have the same general industrial structure; and (2) specialization within industries. Increasing returns at the firm level offers one reason for specialization, but it need not be the only reason. Ricardian technical differences offer an alternative.

### *The volume of trade in a multilateral world*

Chipman (1992) also breaks ground on a fascinating problem, that of the volume of bilateral trade in a factor-proportions world with more than two countries. He notes that it is often claimed that if world trade were driven by factor differences, then most trade should be between dissimilar countries. He disputes this, and develops a counterexample based on a model with three goods, factors and countries. Technologies and preferences are again Cobb–Douglas. Two of the countries are designed to be broadly similar in their endowments, and a third different from the first two. Two of the goods are designed likewise to be similar technically, while the third is more distinct. In order to judge the similarity of technologies and endowments, he develops metrics for each. While the metric developed for the similarity of technologies is broadly plausible, there are greater difficulties with the metric on the similarity of endowments. Unfortunately, ordering by the metric is sensitive to the units in which factors are measured, and so the particular example developed is not compelling. Nonetheless, Chipman makes two important contributions here, first to recognize the importance of the problem of bilateral trade volume, and second to see intuitively that a large volume of trade between "similar" countries is not inherently problematic for a factor-proportions model.

Davis (1997) likewise addresses the problem of bilateral trade patterns in a world of many countries. He begins by articulating the features of the conventional factor-proportions models that apparently have convinced many that it would be surprising to find large volumes of trade between similarly endowed countries. In the case where factor prices fail to equalize, he shows that the conventional argument rests on the idea that countries in different cones will produce virtually disjoint sets of goods. He shows that this rests crucially on the conventional restriction to two factors. He also considers the argument in the case where factor prices are equalized. He extends the conventional argument, as per Helpman and Krugman (1985), to a world with many countries, factors and goods, demonstrating the robustness of the conventional exercise. Yet he also demonstrates that the conventional argument fails to address the right question, as is suggested by the fact that this account provides no measure of which countries are most similar. He suggests that the conventional accounts falter by confounding the net and gross factor content of trade. The traditional Heckscher–Ohlin–Vanek theorem gives results on the net factor content of trade, while trade volume is a measure of gross factor flows weighted by the competitive rentals. The possibility of significant implicit cross-hauling of factors in intraindustry trade can lead trade volumes to be large even when net factor trade is small. He illustrates these possibilities with a pair of striking examples, each with four goods, factors and countries. The examples developed are not vulnerable to the criticism that similarity of endowments depends on the units in which factors are measured. As elsewhere, strong symmetry assumptions are imposed to make the analysis transparent. In one case, trade patterns are conventional, the two northern countries trading primarily with southern counterparts. In the second example, trade patterns defy the conventional logic, each of the northern countries having the other as the largest trading partner, and similarly for countries of the south.

## Conclusions

Is a large share and volume of intraindustry trade surprising in a factor proportions setting? The theoretical arguments developed here strongly suggest that it is not. Chipman's aggregation theorem demonstrates that in principle any proportion of intraindustry trade can be reconciled with a factor-proportions model. The work of Chipman, Davis, and Rodgers goes further in exploring the characteristics of factor-proportions models that facilitate a large share of intraindustry trade in total trade. Finally, Chipman and Davis likewise suggest in a many-country setting, neither is it anomalous to find a large volume of trade between similarly endowed countries.

## Notes

1 In doing so, we draw extensively also on the research of Donald Davis (1992) on intraindustry trade as part of his dissertation at Columbia University and subsequently (Davis, 1995, 1997).

2 We may recall the questions raised by this procedure, unresolved to this date, when the Chamberlin–Robinson revolution broke out in the early 1930s, and particularly Robert Triffin's (1940) argument that there was no persuasive way to break and segment the chain of commodities into industry groups and that it was best to abandon the concept of industry. Evidently, while theorists are aware of this problem, they have had to proceed as if there was a satisfactory definition of industry as an agglomerate of commodities that are close substitutes in consumption whereas outside-of-industry commodities are less close substitutes with the intraindustry commodities.

3 This emphasis on localized technical change, based on local market conditions, as a source of advantage resonates in the current business school literature, as in Michael Porter's (1990) *The Competitive Advantage of Nations*. Of course, his aim was to account for concentration of activity, but is easily adapted to account for several centers, each based on local characteristics, with intraindustry exchange.

4 This finding of Finger's raises serious difficulties also for the economists who have used the factor-intensity definition of intraindustry trade while also citing SITC data to argue that there is a great deal of intraindustry trade today.

5 To our knowledge, however, any formal demonstration of a "larger" volume of trade between countries with dissimilar rather than similar endowments is not to be found in the literature for the simple reason that the theory of bilateral trade in a multi-country world is practically non-existent.

6 The first author of this paper recalls an argument with the research leadership of the World Bank some years ago when the Bank appeared to be embracing the new trade theory (of imperfect competition) as more compelling, and this theory was even then being cited by the pro-import-substitution lobbies and intellectuals in some developing countries as justifying their protectionist preferences. The main argument advanced in favor of the new theory then was precisely the existence of substantial intraindustry trade as shown by SITC data: an assertion that is both empirically irrelevant (as argued in the text) since the SITC data are not aggregated by factor-intensity similarities, and theoretically invalid if it is implied that such trade can be explained only by abandoning the perfectly competitive assumption in the HOS model. Chipman (1991) has made the latter criticism trenchantly.

7 We may note here that, as analyzed in the first theoretical model below, Chipman's (1992) major contribution has been to show that it is indeed possible to account for intraindustry trade even while maintaining all of the assumptions of the HOS framework, denying this core presumption of the new theorists.

8 The most elegant and insightful treatment of intraindustry trade in an imperfectly competitive setting is Helpman and Krugman (1985).

9 A similar exposition of this result appears in Davis (1992).

10 This aspect of the generalized Ricardian model was not remarked on by Bhagwati simply because no one at the time would have thought of defining intraindustry trade (which Bhagwati discussed in the context of Linder's 1961 work in the same survey) as trade in commodities using identical factor intensities in production.

11 Thus, for example, in the Edgeworth–Bowley box diagram, the box would be identical between countries, the contract curve would be on the diagonal, and one country (say) had a Hicks-neutral absolute and comparative advantage in good X, leading to its production advantage in good X and its exports thereof, if all other fundamentals were identical across countries.

12 It is generalized in the sense that, instead of one factor, we allow for two factors, as in the 2 × 2 × 2 HOS model.

13 As suggested by the classic, but neglected, analysis of Vanek and Bertrand (1971).

## Bibliography


Bhagwati, Jagdish N. (1964) "The Pure Theory of International Trade: A Survey," *Economic Journal* 74, March, pp. 1–84.

—— (1982) "Shifting Comparative Advantage, Protectionist Demands, and Policy Responses" in *Import Competition and Response*. Chicago: University of Chicago Press, pp. 153–195.

Chipman, John S. (1988) "Intra-Industry Trade in the Heckscher–Ohlin–Lerner–Samuelson Model," mimeo, University of Minnesota.

—— (1991) "Intra-Industry Trade in a Loglinear Model," mimeo, University of Minnesota.

—— (1992) "Intra-Industry Trade, Factor Proportions and Aggregation," in *Economic Theory and International Trade: Essays in Memoriam, J. Trout Rader*. New York: Springer-Verlag.

Davis, Donald R. (1992) "Essays in the Theory of International Trade and Economic Growth," PhD thesis, Columbia University.

—— (1995) "Intraindustry Trade: A Heckscher–Ohlin–Ricardo Approach," *Journal of International Economics* 39(3/4), pp. 201–226.

—— (1997) "Critical Evidence on Comparative Advantage? North-North Trade in a Multilateral World," *Journal of Political Economy*, October, 105: 5.

Deardorff, Alan V. (1987) "Weak Links in the Chain of Comparative Advantage," in Jagdish Bhagwati (ed.) *International Trade: Selected Readings*, 2nd edn. Cambridge: MIT.

Dinopoulos, Elias (1988) "A Formalization of the 'Biological' Model of Trade in Similar Products," *Journal of International Economics* 25, pp. 95–110.

Feenstra, Robert C. (1982) "Product Creation and Trade Patterns: A Theoretical Note on the 'Biological' Model of Trade in Similar Products," in *Import Competition and Response*. Chicago: University of Chicago Press.

Finger, J.M. (1975) "Trade Overlap and Intra-Industry Trade," *Economic Inquiry* 13, pp. 581–589.

Gans, Joshua S. and Shepherd, George B. (Winter 1994) "How Are the Mighty Fallen: Rejected Classic Articles by Leading Economists," *Journal of Economic Perspectives* 8(1), pp. 165–179.

Grubel, Herbert G. and Lloyd, Peter J. (1975) *Intra-Industry Trade*. London: Macmillan.

Helpman, Elhanan and Krugman, Paul (1985) *Market Structure and Foreign Trade*. Cambridge: MIT.

Linder, S. (1961) *An Essay on Trade and Transformation*. New York: Wiley.

Lizondo, S., Johnson, H. and Yeh, Y. (1981) "Factor Intensities and the Shape of the Production Possibility Frontier," *Economica* 48.

Porter, Michael (1990) *The Competitive Advantage of Nations*. New York: Free Press.

Rodgers, Joan R. (1988) "Intra-industry Trade, Aggregation, and the HOS Model," *Journal of Economic Studies* 15: 5.

Triffin, Robert (1940) *Monopolistic Competition and General Equilibrium Theory*. Cambridge: Harvard University Press.

Vanek, B. and Bertrand, T. (1971) "Trade and Factor Prices in a Multi-Commodity World," in J. Bhagwati, R. Jones, R. Mundell and B. Vanek (eds) *Trade, Balance of Payments, and Growth*. Amsterdam: North-Holland.

2

# TRADE POLICY AND US ECONOMIC GROWTH

*Mun S. Ho and Dale W. Jorgenson*

## Introduction

One of the most striking developments in the postwar US economy is the increasing role of international trade. Imports were only 4.4 percent of the national product in 1960, but rose to 10 percent of the national product by 1985. There have also been large shifts in the sectoral composition of output. The shares of agriculture and manufacturing in the national product were 4.7 and 31.4 percent, respectively, in 1960, but only 2.6 and 22.8 percent in 1985. Finally, the annual growth rate of the national product has declined from 3.7 percent in 1947–73 to 2.3 percent in 1973–85.

The purpose of this chapter is to present an intertemporal general equilibrium model for analyzing the impact of changes in trade policy on US economic growth. Traditional approaches to estimating the economic impact of trade restrictions are purely static. The first of these is based on detailed partial equilibrium models, such as that of Hufbauer, Berliner, and Elliott (1986). The second approach uses multi-country general equilibrium models, such as the "Michigan Model" of Deardorff and Stern (1986) and the world trade model of Whalley (1985).[1] Each of these approaches has many desirable features, but both ignore the effects of trade policy on capital formation and productivity growth.

Recently, Jorgenson and Yun (1990) have presented an intertemporal general equilibrium model for analyzing the impact of tax policy on US economic growth. However, this model is too highly aggregated to be useful for analyzing the impact of trade policy. In this chapter we combine the intertemporal features of tax modeling with the detailed disaggregation by commodity and industrial sector employed in models of international trade. This enables us to capture the impact of trade policy on US imports and exports, the sectoral composition of output, capital formation, and productivity growth.

If tariffs in the US and the rest of the world had been eliminated in 1980, we find that US consumption of goods and services would have risen by only 0.16 percent in the first year. This is similar to the results reported by Deardorff and Stern (1986) and Whalley (1985). However, consumption would have been 0.82 percent higher in the long run. The mechanism underlying this substantial growth in consumption is that trade liberalization reduces the price of capital goods relative to other prices. This leads to an increase in investment and more rapid growth of capital stock, thereby expanding both output and consumption.

Over recent decades the focus of trade policy in the US and the rest of the world has shifted from tariffs to quantitative restrictions. Tariff revenue as a percentage of the value of US commodity imports has declined steadily in the postwar period. However, the scope and stringency of quotas and "voluntary" export restrictions have increased dramatically. We model these restrictions by means of "equivalent" tariffs. If the most significant quotas had been eliminated along with tariffs in 1980, the consumption of goods and services would have been 1.08 percent higher in the long run, compared to a first year increase of only 0.36 percent. Our estimates of the first year effects of trade liberalization are very similar to those obtained from static general equilibrium models. Over time, however, our estimates increase by several times. The difference is due to the impact of trade liberalization on US capital formation and productivity growth.

In the first section below we outline the structure of our model and our key assumptions. Jorgenson and Wilcoxen (1990b) have described our models of producer and consumer behavior in considerable detail. We emphasize the features that are critical in capturing dynamic adjustments by households and businesses to changes in trade policy. We then describe our treatment of US demand for imports and rest of the world demand for exports from the US. We conclude with a description of the exogenous and endogenous elements in our model of the US current account balance.

In the next section we estimate the impact of trade barriers on US economic growth. We first examine the effects of US trade restrictions still in effect after the Tokyo round of negotiations under the General Agreement on Trade and Tariffs (GATT). These negotiations were finally concluded in 1979 and have been analyzed by Cline et al. (1978). We estimate the effects of a multilateral agreement abolishing all remaining tariffs in the US and the rest of the world. We then estimate the impact of also eliminating quantitative restrictions on trade. Finally, we compare our results with those of Deardorff and Stern (1986) and Whalley (1985). The last section concludes the chapter.

## The structure of the model

We divide the US economy among four sectors: businesses, households, governments, and the rest of the world. Since trade policy differs substantially among industries, we subdivide the business sector into the thirty-five industries listed in Table 2.1 below. These industries correspond approximately to two-digit industries in the Standard Industrial Classification. Our model distinguishes the same number of commodities as industries. Each industry produces a primary product; this is the commodity group in which the industry is predominant. Industries also produce secondary products, the primary products of other industries.

### *Producer behavior*

We represent producer behavior by means of econometric models for each of our thirty-five industries. We first express the output of each industry as a function of inputs of intermediate goods, capital services, and labor services. These production functions are characterized by constant returns to scale. The rate of productivity growth in each industry is endogenous and can be expressed as a function of the input prices.[2] The intermediate inputs include the thirty-five commodities produced within the US business sector. Each commodity group is allocated among intermediate demands by the thirty-five industries and final demands for private and public consumption, investment by households and businesses, and exports to the rest of the world.

To implement our econometric approach to modeling producer behavior we have constructed a consistent time series of interindustry transactions tables for the US economy, covering the period 1947–85 on an annual basis. An alternative approach would be to characterize substitution among inputs by calibration from a single data point.[3] For example, Deardorff and Stern (1986) and Whalley (1985) characterize producer behavior in the US economy by means of fixed "input–output" coefficients for intermediate goods, estimated from a single interindustry transactions table. The possibility of substitution among intermediate goods, such as energy and materials, is ruled out by assumption.

Empirical evidence on substitutability among inputs is essential in analyzing the impact of trade restrictions. A high degree of substitutability implies that the cost of these restrictions is relatively low, while a low degree of substitutability implies high costs of trade restrictions. Although a calibration approach avoids the burden of estimation, it also specifies the substitutability among inputs by assumption rather than relying on empirical evidence. This defeats one of the major purposes of modeling the impact of trade policy changes.

In our model of the US economy a single stock of capital is allocated among the thirty-five industries and the household sector. We assume that capital is perfectly malleable and mobile among sectors, so that the price of capital services in each sector is proportional to a single capital service price for the economy as a whole. The supply of capital available in every year is the result of past investment. This relationship is represented by an accumulation equation, giving capital at the end of each year as a function of investment during the year and capital at the beginning of the year. This backward-looking equation incorporates the whole past history of investment and constitutes the first component of our dynamic model of adjustment to changes in trade policy.

Our model of producer behavior also includes an equation giving the price of capital services in terms of the price of investment goods at the beginning and end of each period. The current price of investment goods incorporates expectations about future prices of capital services and discount rates through the assumption of perfect foresight or rational expectations. Under this assumption the price of investment goods is based on expectations that are fulfilled by the solution of the model. This forward-looking equation incorporates expectations about all future prices and is the second component of our dynamic model of adjustment to trade policy changes.

### *Consumer behavior*

Our model of consumer behavior is based on full consumption, comprised of goods and services and leisure time. Full consumption is allocated over time to maximize an intertemporally additive utility function, subject to an intertemporal budget constraint. The necessary conditions are expressed as an Euler equation, giving the growth rate of full consumption as a function of the discount rate and the growth rate of the price of full consumption.[4] This forward-looking equation embodies the same rational expectations assumption as our model of producer behavior. Current full consumption incorporates expectations about all future prices that are fulfilled by the solution of the model. This is the third component of our dynamic model of adjustment to changes in trade policy.

In our model of the US economy there is a single, exogenously given, time endowment. The US population grew substantially during our sample period, 1947–85. For later periods we project the population and transform it into a projection of the time endowment. In each period this endowment is divided between leisure time and the labor market. Our model of consumer behavior allocates full consumption between goods and services and leisure. Time in the labour market is allocated among the thirty-five industries; labor services are also included in final demands for personal consumption expenditures and public consumption. We assume that labor is perfectly mobile among sectors so that the wage rate in each sector is proportional to a single wage rate for the US economy as a whole.

Finally, total expenditure on goods and services by the household sector includes expenditures on the thirty-five commodities represented in the model, capital services, and labor services. We estimate price and total expenditure elasticities econometrically for each of 672 types of households.[5] An alternative approach would be to assume that preferences for all types of households are homothetic, so that all total expenditure elasticities are set equal to unity. However, this assumption is strongly contradicted by empirical evidence.

Introducing nonhomothetic preferences into a dynamic general equilibrium model of the US economy raises issues not confronted by static models. If productivity growth were to continue indefinitely, equal rates of productivity growth would be required for all industries, at least in the limit. Otherwise, relative prices would not converge to a steady state. Even if productivity growth rates converged to the same limit, total expenditure per capita would rise indefinitely, so that at least one of the expenditure shares for the household sector would become negative. Accordingly, we require that the productivity level in each industry converges to an upper limit. Our projection of the future US population reaches a maximum, so that aggregate expenditure approaches an upper limit in the steady state.[6]

### *Total supply and imports*

We next describe the features of the rest of the world sector of our model. The total supply of commodities in the US economy comes from the output of domestic industries and "competitive" imports. Competitive imports are defined in the US national income and product accounts as commodities produced in the US. In our model purchasers of these commodities regard them as imperfect substitutes for the domestically produced counterparts.[7] Noncompetitive imports enter directly into the production functions for each industry in the same way as other inputs. They also enter final demands for consumption by households and governments and investment by businesses and households.

We model the allocation of total supply of the *i*th commodity $QS_i$ between domestic production $QC_i$ and competitive imports $M_i$ by means of the translog price function:

$$\ln PS_{it} = \ln p_{it}' \alpha_{it} + \tfrac{1}{2} \ln p_{it}' B_i \ln p_{it}, \tag{1}$$

where $PS_{it}$ denotes the price of total supply and in period $t$ and:

$$\ln p_{it} = (\ln PC_{it}, \ln PM_{it})$$

is a vector of logarithms of prices of the domestic commodity, $PC_{it}$, and competitive imports, $PM_{it}$.

The shares of the domestic commodity and competitive imports in the value of total supply are denoted $v_{it}$, where:

$$v_{it} = \begin{bmatrix} PC_{it}\, QC_{it}/PS_{it}\, QS_{it} \\ PM_{it}\, M_{it}/PS_{it}\, QS_{it} \end{bmatrix}.$$

These value shares can be expressed in terms of logarithmic derivatives of the price function with respect to logarithms of the input prices:

$$v_{it} = \alpha_{it} + B_i \ln p_{it}, \tag{2}$$

where $B_i$ is a matrix of share elasticities, defined as derivatives of the value shares with respect to logarithms of the prices.

A novel feature of our model is that the vector $\alpha_{it}$ in equation (2) is treated as a function of time. This permits us to represent the large increases in import penetration experienced by the US economy during the postwar period without resorting to implausible values of the price elasticities. The phenomenon of "unexplained imports" is noted by Petri (1986), who observed that the postwar US demand for imports cannot be explained by price variations alone. According to Petri's estimates, such an explanation would have required a price elasticity of demand for US steel imports of thirty-two. By comparison the Michigan Model's assumed price elasticity is only 1.4.[8]

A common approach to modeling import demands has been to use a measure of aggregate economic activity as an explanatory variable for imports. We have employed a time trend instead, since we concur with Petri's conclusion that the high elasticities of imports with respect to aggregate activity estimated from time series data are probably spurious.[9] The limiting behavior of the time trends $\alpha_{it}$ presents a potential problem for our model of supply. Unless these functions remain bounded, one of the value shares must eventually become negative. Accordingly, we take these trends to be logistic in form, so that:

$$v_{it} = \alpha_i + \frac{\beta_i}{1 + e^{-\mu_i(t-\tau_i)}} + B_i \ln p_{it}, \tag{3}$$

where $\alpha_i$, $\beta_i$, $\mu_i$, $\tau_i$ are parameters that differ among commodities. We find that these time trends greatly simplify the model and fit the historical data reasonably well.

We model dynamic adjustments by producers to changes in trade policy through the backward-looking accumulation equation for capital and the forward-looking asset pricing equation for the price of investment goods. We estimate the import demand functions (2) by applying nonlinear two-stage least squares to annual data for the sample period 1964–85.[10] We present the implied price elasticities of demand for imports in Table 2.1. For comparison we also present elasticities employed in previous studies. Imports of most manufactured commodities are price elastic, while imports of most primary commodities are price inelastic. For eighteen of our twenty-five commodity groups the values of $R^2$ are greater than 0.8.

Our model is limited to the US economy, so that we do not model production by the rest of the world.[11] Accordingly, we take the prices of competitive and noncompetitive imports into the US as exogenously given; during our sample period, 1947–85, we set these prices equal to the actual data. Since our model determines prices, both domestic and foreign, relative to a numéraire given by the US wage rate, we allow prices of imports from the rest of the world to change through the terms of trade, say $e_t$, and through tariffs levied on imports by the US government, say $\theta_{it}$ and $\theta^n_{it}$:

$$PM_{it} = (1 + \theta_{it})\, e_t\, PM^*_{it}, \tag{4}$$

$$PNCI_{it} = (1 + \theta^n_{it})\, e_t\, PNCI^*_{it},$$

where $PM_{it}$ and $PNCI_{it}$ are prices for competitive and noncompetitive imports paid by the US and $PM^*_{it}$ and $PNCI^*_{it}$ are prices received by the rest of the world. The terms of trade $e_t$ is the price of goods in the US relative to the price of goods in the rest of the world.

### *Exports*

Since we do not model production in the rest of the world, we express the demand for US exports, say $X_{it}$, as a function of rest of the world output $Y^*_t$ and the price of exports $PC_{it}$:

$$X_{it} = EX_{i0}(Y^*_t)\, [(1 + \theta^*_{it}) \frac{PC_{it}}{e_t}]^{\eta_i}, \tag{5}$$

where $EX_{i0}(Y^*_t)$ represents actual US exports during the sample period, 1947–85, and projected exports outside this period, $\theta/^*_{it}$ is the rest of the world tariff rate on US exports, and the term in square brackets is the price for US exports faced by the rest of the world. We do not have the data on rest of the world imports from the US required for estimation of the export price elasticities $\eta_i$. We take these elasticities as averages of import price elasticities of major trading partners of the US.

A number of alternative estimates of price elasticities of demand for US exports are presented in Table 2.2. Petri (1984) has estimated rest of the world demand for US exports. Petri's export elasticities are remarkably low; however, his sectors are relatively highly aggregated, including only ten manufacturing industries. By contrast, our thirty-five industries include twenty-one manufacturing industries. The remaining estimates are based on imports into a single country with the rest of the world treated as a single supplier. Cline et al. (1978), have presented composite elasticities of demand for US exports that are similar to those estimated by Stone (1979), so that we adopt these elasticities.

In projecting the functions $EX(Y^*_t)$ we first estimate the following equation for each commodity from annual data for the period 1947–85:

$$\ln X_{it} = \gamma_i + \lambda_i \ln Y^*_t, \tag{6}$$

*Table 2.1* Import demand elasticities

| *Industry* | *Substitution elasticities* | | | *Import price elasticities* | | | | |
|---|---|---|---|---|---|---|---|---|
| | *Stern* | *Shiells* | *Ours* | *Stern* | *Shiells* | *Petri* | *Cline* | *Ours* |
| Agriculture | | | 0.70 | | | | −0.90 | −0.68 |
| Metal mining | | | 0.11 | | | | −0.22 | −0.09 |
| Coal mining | | | | | | | −0.22 | |
| Oil & gas mining | | | | | | | −0.22 | |
| Non-metal mining | | | 0.34 | | | | −0.22 | −0.34 |
| Construction | | | | | | | | |
| Food & kindred | 1.13 | 0.31 | 0.65 | −1.13 | −0.21 | | −1.13 | −0.62 |
| Tobacco | 1.13 | −16.27 | 2.60 | −1.13 | −7.57 | | −1.13 | −2.59 |
| Textile mill | 1.15 | 2.58 | 1.62 | −1.14 | −1.41 | −1.2 | −2.43 | −1.54 |
| Apparel | 4.27 | 1.62 | 1.27 | −3.92 | −0.52 | −1.2 | −2.43 | −1.01 |
| Lumber & wood | 1.76 | 0.26 | 1.76 | −0.69 | −1.32 | −1.4 | −0.96 | −1.60 |
| Furniture | 3.10 | 12.13 | 1.49 | −3.00 | −9.56 | −1.4 | −0.96 | −1.36 |
| Paper | 1.58 | 1.80 | 1.16 | −0.55 | −1.80 | −1.4 | −1.44 | −1.07 |
| Printing & publishing | 3.01 | 2.72 | 1.22 | −3.00 | −1.46 | −1.4 | −1.44 | −1.20 |
| Chemicals | 2.61 | 9.85 | 1.20 | −2.53 | −6.82 | −0.8 | −0.97 | −1.10 |
| Petroleum refining | 2.36 | −0.34 | 1.09 | −1.96 | −0.79 | −0.8 | −0.97 | −1.00 |
| Rubber & plastic | 5.71 | 2.67 | 1.76 | −5.26 | −1.32 | −0.8 | −3.57 | −1.65 |
| Leather | 1.81 | 4.11 | 1.86 | −1.58 | −2.01 | | −2.46 | −1.11 |

| | | | | | | | | |
|---|---|---|---|---|---|---|---|---|
| Stone, clay & glass | 1.63 | 4.29 | 1.86 | −1.60 | −2.86 | −0.8 | −1.37 | −1.72 |
| Primary metal | 1.45 | 3.05 | 1.48 | −1.42 | −2.28 | −1.6 | −1.99 | −1.29 |
| Fabricated metal | 3.67 | 1.54 | 1.13 | −3.59 | −0.94 | −1.1 | | −1.08 |
| Machinery | 1.02 | 3.34 | 1.72 | −1.02 | −0.88 | −0.9 | −0.87 | −1.53 |
| Electrical machinery | 2.11 | 7.46 | 1.45 | −1.00 | −3.08 | −0.6 | −0.87 | −1.23 |
| Motor vehicles | 3.59 | 2.01 | 1.52 | −3.28 | −1.24 | −2.5 | −2.53 | −1.16 |
| Transport equipment | 3.59 | 2.01 | 1.35 | −3.28 | −1.24 | −2.5 | −1.70 | −1.28 |
| Instruments | 1.98 | 0.45 | 0.86 | −1.08 | −0.44 | −0.9 | | −0.77 |
| Misc manufactures | 1.98 | 3.55 | 1.52 | −2.06 | −2.37 | −0.8 | −4.44 | −1.14 |
| Transportation | | | | | | | | |
| Communications | | | | | | | | |
| Electric utilities | | | | | | | | |
| Gas utilities | | | | | | | | |
| Trade | | | | | | | | |
| Finance, insurance | | | | | | | | |
| Services | | | | | | | | |
| Govt enterprises | | | | | | | | |

*Notes*
The industrial classification system is different for each study. All entries correspond to the categories used in this study.
Stern: Central tendencies in Stern, Francis and Schumacher (1976), sample period before 1974.
Shiells: Shiells, Stern and Deardorff (1986), sample period 1962–78.
Petri: Petri (1984), US imports from rest of the world, excluding Japan, 1960–80.
Cline: Cline *et al.* (1978: 58).
Ours: Elasticities evaluated at 1983 shares, sample period 1964–85.

*Table 2.2* Export price elasticities

| *Industry* | *Petri* | *Stone* | *Cline* |
|---|---|---|---|
| Agriculture | | −0.72 | −0.61 |
| Metal mining | | −0.92 | |
| Coal mining | | −0.92 | |
| Oil & gas mining | | −0.92 | |
| Non-metal mining | | −0.92 | |
| Construction | * | | |
| Food & kindred | | −1.975 | −0.63 |
| Tobacco | | −1.975 | −0.63 |
| Textile mill | −1.6 | −1.18 | −1.57 |
| Apparel | −1.16 | −1.18 | −1.57 |
| Lumber & wood | −1.0 | −1.5 | −1.43 |
| Furniture | −1.0 | −1.5 | −1.43 |
| Paper | −1.0 | −1.41 | −1.53 |
| Printing & publishing | −1.0 | −1.41 | −1.53 |
| Chemicals | −0.5 | −0.98 | −1.47 |
| Petroleum refining | −0.5 | −1.72 | −1.47 |
| Rubber & plastic | −0.5 | −2.10 | −2.14 |
| Leather | −1.6 | −0.62 | −1.49 |
| Stone, clay & glass | −0.7 | −1.26 | −1.56 |
| Primary metal | −1.1 | −1.65 | −1.97 |
| Fabricated metal | −1.1 | −1.06 | −1.59 |
| Machinery | −0.9 | −1.04 | −1.59 |
| Electrical machinery | −1.2 | −1.05 | −1.59 |
| Motor vehicles | −0.9 | −2.49 | −1.55 |
| Transport equipment | −0.9 | −2.49 | −1.55 |
| Instruments | −0.9 | −1.18 | −1.85 |
| Misc manufactures | −1.0 | −1.55 | −1.62 |
| Transportation | * | | |
| Communications | * | | |
| Electric utilities | * | | |
| Gas utilities | * | | |
| Trade | * | | |
| Finance, insurance | * | | |
| Services | * | | |
| Govt enterprises | * | | |

*Notes*
* Sectors assumed to have zero price elasticities. Trade and transportation exports are margins on exported goods; other service sectors have only negligible exports.
Petri: Petri (1984).
Stone: Stone (1979), average of import elasticities for EEC and Japan.
Cline: Cline *et al.* (1978), average of Canada, EEC, Japan.

where $X_{it}$ is US exports of the $i$th commodity in year $t$ and $Y_t^*$ is gross world product in that year. We employ the estimated rest of the world output elasticity for US exports $\lambda_i$ in projecting US exports.[12] Our estimates of these elasticities are reported in Table 2.3. These estimates have plausible magnitudes and are consistent with the view that aircraft, computers and

*Table 2.3* Export demand functions

$\log X_{it} = \gamma_i + \lambda_i \log Y_t^*$

| *Industry* | *Exports 1982 billion $* | $\alpha^x$ | $\lambda^x$ | $R^2$ |
|---|---|---|---|---|
| Agriculture | 22.03 | 9.9053 | 1.1158 | 0.97 |
| Metal mining | 0.70 | 6.5874 | 0.3464 | 0.47 |
| Coal mining | 4.98 | 8.1475 | 1.0020 | 0.90 |
| Oil & gas mining | 0.79 | 6.6248 | 1.6037 | 0.40 |
| Non-metal mining | 0.68 | 6.4517 | 0.4769 | 0.85 |
| Construction | 0.06 | 4.0946 | 1.0857 | 0.47 |
| Food & kindred | 11.00 | 9.2225 | 1.0963 | 0.99 |
| Tobacco | 3.05 | 7.9161 | 0.5584 | 0.98 |
| Textile mill | 1.82 | 7.4994 | 1.2599 | 0.92 |
| Apparel | 1.33 | 7.0451 | 1.3368 | 0.91 |
| Lumber & wood | 2.74 | 7.9231 | 1.8252 | 0.93 |
| Furniture | 0.60 | 5.9395 | 1.9033 | 0.84 |
| Paper | 4.09 | 8.3103 | 1.2732 | 0.96 |
| Printing & publishing | 1.37 | 7.0587 | 0.9823 | 0.99 |
| Chemicals | 15.64 | 9.7205 | 1.5350 | 0.99 |
| Petroleum refining | 8.08 | 8.8938 | 0.3972 | 0.97 |
| Rubber & plastic | 7.26 | 8.8071 | 1.5698 | 0.96 |
| Leather | 0.52 | 6.0303 | 0.90191 | 0.90 |
| Stone, clay & glass | 1.82 | 7.5123 | 1.0974 | 0.98 |
| Primary metal | 5.68 | 8.7869 | 0.7946 | 0.78 |
| Fabricated metal | 6.88 | 8.6473 | 1.2608 | 0.97 |
| Machinery | 37.20 | 10.4400 | 1.7359 | 0.99 |
| Electrical machinery | 18.03 | 9.6417 | 2.2744 | 0.98 |
| Motor vehicles | 11.91 | 9.6537 | 1.8583 | 0.97 |
| Transport equipment | 23.34 | 9.9396 | 1.9255 | 0.95 |
| Instruments | 8.03 | 8.9174 | 1.8918 | 0.99 |
| Misc manufactures | 2.67 | 7.5453 | 1.6481 | 0.91 |
| Transportation | 21.93 | 9.8604 | 0.8761 | 0.98 |
| Communications | 1.55 | 7.2877 | 1.3805 | 0.95 |
| Electric utilities | 0.21 | 5.5175 | 1.5862 | 0.57 |
| Gas utilities | 0.35 | 6.1484 | 1.6575 | 0.36 |
| Trade | 24.94 | 9.8189 | 1.5746 | 0.97 |
| Finance, insurance | 6.90 | 8.8025 | 1.9184 | 0.91 |
| Services | 7.83 | 8.7675 | 1.4544 | 0.96 |
| Govt enterprises+ | 0.25 | 5.6493 | | |
| Travel* | 14.10 | 9.4316 | 1.5810 | 0.71 |

*Notes*
+ Most exports in this category are military.
* Travel is expenditures by tourists in the US.

pharmaceuticals are the leading industries in the growth of US exports. In projecting exports after 1985, we assume that the growth rate of world product is initially 2 percent per year and gradually declines to zero, as required for the existence of a steady state of our model.

### *Noncommodity flows*

To complete the current account for the US economy we must determine factor income and payments to the rest of the world. These are interest and dividends on net US private claims on the rest of the world, say $BF_t$, and net US official liabilities, say $BG_t^*$. These net factor incomes, denoted by $i_t^* BF_{t-1}$ and $-\ i_t BG_{t-1}^*$, where $i$ and $i^*$ are domestic and rest of the world rates of return, are set exogenously. The final exogenous flow is net unilateral transfers or foreign aid, denoted *transfers*.

The allocation of savings among domestic capital formation, acquisition of foreign assets, and investment in government bonds is exogenous in our model. This implies that the public sector deficit and current account balance are exogenous. We allow the public sector deficit to decline gradually to a steady state value in the year 2025, equal to the inflationary gain on the stock of outstanding government debt, which has the effect of holding per capita debt constant in real terms. The current account deficit is allowed to fall to zero by the year 2000. These projections are expressed in terms of the numéraire for our model, the US wage rate.

Adding foreign trade and noncommodity flows, we obtain the US current account surplus in year $t$, say $CA_t$:

$$CA_t = \sum PC_{it}X_{it} - \sum PM_{it}M_{it} - \sum PNCI_{it}NCI_{it} + i_t^* BF_{t-1} - iBG_{t-1}^* - transfers. \tag{7}$$

From equations (3)–(5) we see that US exports $X_{it}$ and imports $M_{it}$ are functions of the terms of trade $e_t$. This variable is endogenous in our model and adjusts the purchasers' prices of US imports and exports so that the exogenously given current account balance (7) is maintained.

## Effects of trade barriers

In this section we estimate the impact of trade policy on US economic growth. We construct a base case for growth of the US economy under actual trade policies, incorporating historical data for all exogenous variables. We then simulate the US economy with a change in trade policy. To evaluate the economic impact of the policy change, we compare the results of the two simulations. We initiate both simulations in 1980, immediately after the conclusion of the Tokyo round negotiations in 1979. Deardorff and Stern (1986) and Whalley (1986) have provided simulations of the impact of trade policy for the same period, using static general equilibrium models.

### *Tariff reductions*

We first describe the effects of multilateral reductions in tariffs with no change in quantitative restrictions on trade. In Table 2.4 we present tariff

*Table 2.4a* Tariff rates and quota equivalents in 1980

| No. | Sector | Tariff rates | | Tariff equivalent |
|---|---|---|---|---|
| | | ROW | US | |
| 1 | Agriculture | | 0.035 | |
| 2 | Metal mining | | 0.000 | |
| 3 | Coal mining | | 0.000 | |
| 4 | Oil & gas mining | | 0.000 | |
| 5 | Non-metal mining | | 0.003 | |
| 6 | Construction | | 0.000 | |
| 7 | Food & kindred | | 0.027 | |
| 8 | Tobacco | | 0.111 | |
| 9 | Textile mill | 0.107 | 0.108 | 0.030 |
| 10 | Apparel | 0.207 | 0.218 | 0.063 |
| 11 | Lumber & wood | 0.027 | 0.020 | |
| 12 | Furniture | 0.103 | 0.035 | |
| 13 | Paper | 0.058 | 0.005 | |
| 14 | Printing & publishing | 0.029 | 0.008 | |
| 15 | Chemicals | 0.094 | 0.041 | |
| 16 | Petroleum refining | | 0.000 | |
| 17 | Rubber & plastic | 0.058 | 0.067 | |
| 18 | Leather | 0.045 | 0.097 | 0.056 |
| 19 | Stone, clay & glass | 0.105 | 0.091 | |
| 20 | Primary metal | 0.058 | 0.030 | 0.048 |
| 21 | Fabricated metal | 0.090 | 0.057 | |
| 22 | Machinery | 0.067 | 0.041 | |
| 23 | Electrical machinery | 0.096 | 0.055 | |
| 24 | Motor vehicles | 0.077 | 0.023 | 0.047* |
| 25 | Transport equipment | 0.077 | 0.026 | |
| 26 | Instruments | 0.078 | 0.065 | |
| 27 | Misc manufactures | 0.078 | 0.058 | |
| 28 | Transportation | | | |
| 29 | Communications | | | |
| 30 | Electric utilities | | | |
| 31 | Gas utilities | | | |
| 32 | Trade | | | |
| 33 | Finance, insurance | | | |
| 34 | Services | | | |
| 35 | Govt enterprises | | | |

*Notes*
US tariff rates are calcualted from International Trade Commission data. Rest of the world (ROW) tariff rates are from Deardorff and Stern (1986). See Table 2.4b below for tariff equivalents of quotas.
* 1981 data.

rates on US imports in 1980, following several rounds of tariff reductions under GATT that culminated in the Tokyo round. The most highly taxed commodity imports were textiles, apparel, leather (mainly footwear), glass, and primary metals (mainly iron and steel). Total customs duties collected

*Table 2.4b* Tariff equivalents of selected quotas

| | *Textiles* | *Apparel* | *Leather* | *Metals* | *Autos* |
|---|---|---|---|---|---|
| 1973 | 0 | 0 | 0 | 0.032 | 0 |
| 1974 | 0.030 | 0.063 | 0 | 0.032 | 0 |
| 1975 | 0.030 | 0.063 | 0 | 0 | 0 |
| 1976 | 0.030 | 0.063 | 0 | 0 | 0 |
| 1977 | 0.030 | 0.063 | 0.056 | 0 | 0 |
| 1978 | 0.030 | 0.063 | 0.056 | 0.048 | 0 |
| 1979 | 0.030 | 0.063 | 0.056 | 0.048 | 0 |
| 1980 | 0.030 | 0.063 | 0.056 | 0.048 | 0 |
| 1981 | 0.030 | 0.063 | 0.056 | 0.048 | 0.047 |
| 1982 | 0.071 | 0.095 | 0 | 0.048 | 0.047 |
| 1983 | 0.071 | 0.095 | 0 | 0.048 | 0.047 |
| 1984 | 0.071 | 0.095 | 0 | 0.048 | 0.047 |
| 1985 | 0.071 | 0.095 | 0 | 0.048 | 0 |

*Notes*
Tariff equivalents of "voluntary" export restrictions are calculated from Hufbauer, Berliner, Elliott (1986) by aggregation to our model's industry classification.

*Table 2.4c* Tariff equivalents of quotas on US imports from Japan

| *Sector* | *1970* | *1980* |
|---|---|---|
| Textiles, apparel | 3.5 | 1.3 |
| Primary metal | 6.0 | 7.0 |
| Electrical machinery | – | 0.8 |

*Source*: Petri (1984: 138).

on US imports amounted to $7.2 billion or about 2.9 percent of total commodity imports of $251 billion. For comparison the US gross national product in 1980 was $2,732 billion in prices of that year.[13]

To evaluate the economic impact of tariffs, we eliminate all domestic and foreign tariffs, beginning in 1980. This is not equivalent to free trade, since quotas and other quantitative restrictions remain in effect. In both the base case and alternative case simulations, we set the US capital stock and all other state variables at the beginning of 1980 equal to their historical values. We then simulate the growth of the US economy from 1980 to the year 2100. This provides ample time for the economy to converge to a steady state. In the base case the government deficit and tax rates are exogenous, but government spending outside the sample period is endogenous. With all tariffs removed we set government expenditures equal to values from the base case. Government transfers and interest payments are exogenous in both simulations.[14]

The economic impact of eliminating tariffs is summarized diagrammatically in Figures 2.1a and 2.1b. The vertical axis in these figures gives the percentage change in each variable from the elimination of tariffs. The impact of the tariff cut is to raise consumption of goods and services by 0.16 percent in the first year. From the first panel of Figure 2.1b we see that

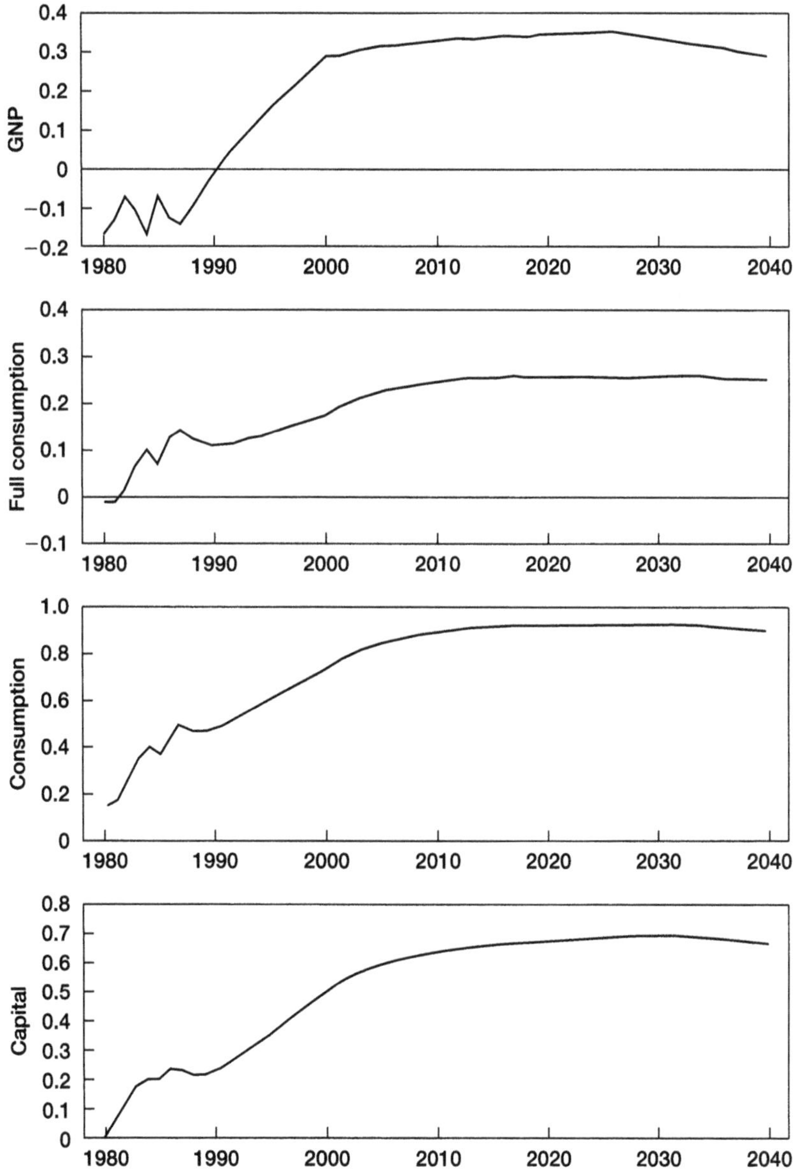


*Figure 2.1a* Dynamic effects of tariff elimination (% change).

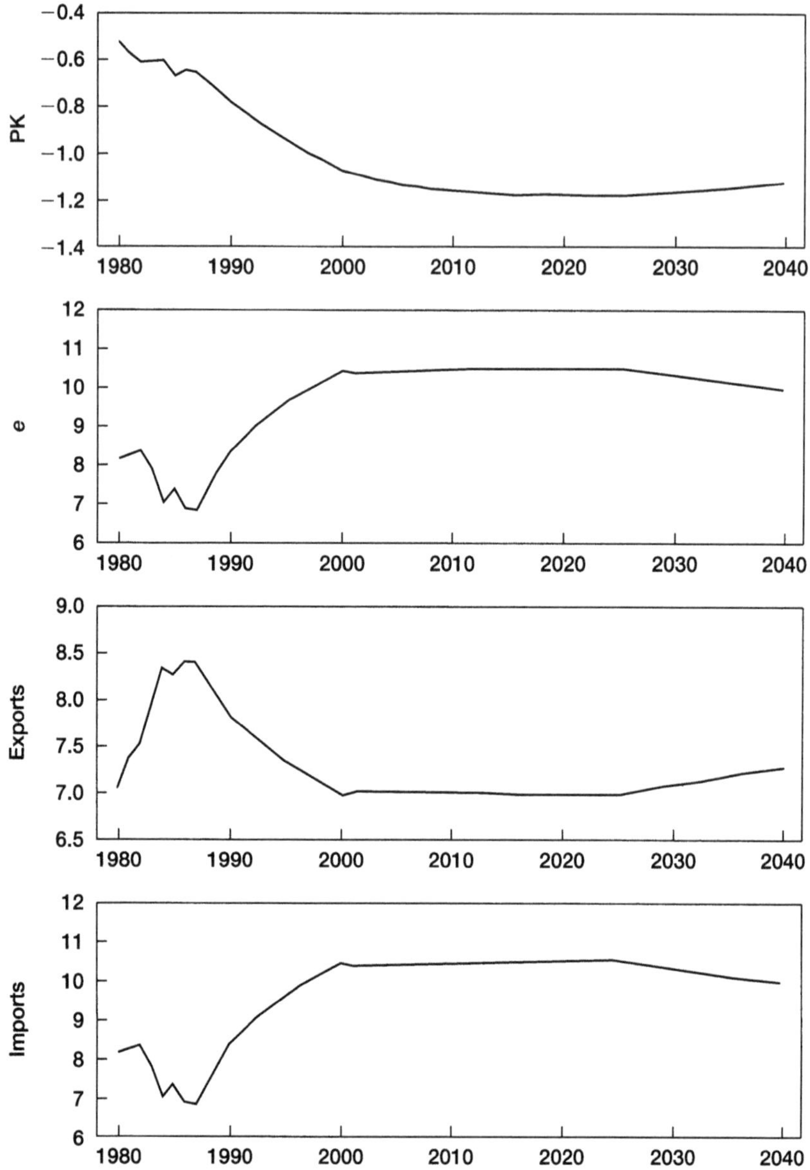


*Figure 2.1b* Dynamic effects of tariff elimination.

the price of capital goods is lower than in the base case and keeps falling. A falling price of capital goods leads to an increase in investment and boosts the growth of capital stock, as shown in Figure 2.1b. By the year 2000 the capital stock is 0.49 percent higher than in the base case.

Lower commodity prices and an investment boom induce higher import demands. US exports also increase with reduced tariffs in the rest of the world. From Table 2.4 we see that these tariffs are generally higher than those in the US. Given the elasticities we have employed, the initial impact is greater for exports than for imports. Since the current account balance is exogenous, the terms of trade $e_t$ must fall to stimulate higher imports. The required decrease of 0.6 percent in the terms of trade is very substantial. The quantity of exports increases by 6.7 percent while the quantity of imports rises by 7.5 percent.

Over time the difference between the two simulations increases, due to the growth in capital stock resulting from the elimination of tariffs. By the year 2000 full consumption is 0.17 percent higher; this is comprised of an increase of 0.74 in consumption of goods and services and a decrease of 0.6 percent in leisure. The terms of trade decline over time, since US prices fall but rest of the world prices remain constant, implying an increase in US international competitiveness. As a consequence, the quantity of exports is only 6.5 percent higher in the year 2000, while the quantity of imports is 9.7 percent higher.

Table 2.5 gives the sectoral effects of tariff elimination in the initial year, while Table 2.6 shows the effects after 20 years. Raw material industries such as mining have small trade flows; the small decreases in exports are due to the fall in the terms of trade. Agricultural trade is largely governed by quantitative restrictions, including trade embargoes, that we do not explicitly model. The small changes in trade should be interpreted with this in mind. Similarly, the industries producing nontradables – trade, finance, and services – have small declines in exports, due mainly to the terms of trade. Commodities with the highest tariff levels – textiles, apparel, rubber, leather, and glass – show the largest gains in imports. Chemicals, electrical machinery (which includes computers), and instruments have the highest rest of the world tariffs and the most substantial increases in exports.

The output and employment effects of tariff reductions largely parallel the shifts in imports and exports. Chemicals, primary metals, machinery, electrical machinery, and instruments show the largest gains in output and employment. Since the capital stock is initially fixed in supply, capital must be drawn from other sectors to these export-oriented industries. Import penetration is so high in the food, furniture, and leather industries that domestic output actually falls. Capital and labor shift from these sectors to sectors that are more competitive internationally.

## *Quantitative restrictions*

With successive reductions in tariff rates, trade policy has shifted away from tariffs to quantitative restrictions like quotas and "voluntary" export restraints on suppliers of US imports. As a concrete example, world trade

*Table 2.5* Sectoral effects of eliminating all tariffs in 1980

| *Sector* | *Output* | *Capital* | *Labor* | *Exports* | *Imports* |
|---|---|---|---|---|---|
| Agriculture | −0.32 | −0.44 | −0.47 | −0.34 | 2.09 |
| Metal mining | 2.17 | 2.08 | 2.04 | −0.43 | 2.31 |
| Coal mining | 0.36 | 0.26 | 0.17 | −0.44 | 0.84 |
| Oil & gas mining | 0.08 | 0.00 | 0.16 | −0.56 | 0.69 |
| Non-metal mining | 0.75 | 0.59 | 0.35 | −0.42 | 0.97 |
| Construction | 0.23 | 0.05 | 0.22 | −0.14 | |
| Food & kindred | −0.34 | −0.45 | −0.44 | −0.31 | 1.62 |
| Tobacco | −0.42 | −0.47 | −0.52 | −0.30 | 20.56 |
| Textile mill | 1.42 | 0.88 | 0.17 | 18.94 | 20.23 |
| Apparel | 1.71 | −0.26 | 0.09 | 29.07 | 31.06 |
| Lumber & wood | 0.25 | −0.06 | −0.35 | 3.39 | 4.59 |
| Furniture | −0.51 | −0.66 | −0.72 | 16.25 | 6.03 |
| Paper | 0.85 | 0.71 | 0.69 | 8.64 | 1.98 |
| Printing & publishing | 0.70 | 0.70 | 0.57 | 3.57 | 2.27 |
| Chemicals | 2.47 | 2.39 | 2.36 | 14.58 | 8.01 |
| Petroleum refining | 0.17 | 0.10 | 0.12 | −0.62 | 0.75 |
| Rubber & plastic | 1.71 | 1.58 | 1.45 | 12.74 | 15.07 |
| Leather | −1.40 | −2.17 | −1.75 | 5.93 | 16.93 |
| Stone, clay & glass | 0.37 | 0.23 | 0.00 | 18.04 | 20.38 |
| Primary metal | 2.34 | 1.74 | 1.74 | 11.80 | 7.48 |
| Fabricated metal | 1.63 | 1.17 | 1.24 | 15.56 | 8.67 |
| Machinery | 2.51 | 1.94 | 1.87 | 11.11 | 10.52 |
| Electrical machinery | 2.29 | 1.84 | 2.06 | 16.77 | 11.17 |
| Motor vehicles | 1.84 | 1.44 | 0.85 | 13.08 | 5.76 |
| Transport equipment | 2.93 | 2.30 | 2.38 | 12.65 | 7.09 |
| Instruments | 3.78 | 3.62 | 3.50 | 15.35 | 9.81 |
| Misc manufactures | 1.44 | 1.23 | 1.07 | 12.94 | 11.23 |
| Transportation | 0.26 | 0.15 | 0.15 | −0.01 | 0.78 |
| Communications | 0.28 | 0.26 | 0.24 | −0.05 | |
| Electric utilities | 0.22 | 0.21 | 0.13 | −0.06 | 0.09 |
| Gas utilities | 0.40 | 0.32 | 0.34 | −0.03 | |
| Trade | 0.26 | 0.22 | 0.22 | −0.02 | |
| Finance, insurance | 0.08 | 0.08 | 0.07 | −0.07 | 0.65 |
| Services | 0.02 | −0.01 | −0.09 | −0.11 | 0.61 |
| Govt enterprises | 0.30 | 0.31 | 0.27 | −0.10 | |
| Household | | −0.54 | −0.27 | | |
| Government | | 0.00 | −0.82 | | |

*Notes*
Entries are percentage change in the first period from the base case. Output is industry output, not commodity supply. Imports are competitive imports only.

in apparel is governed by Multi-Fiber Agreements that allocate quotas to each exporting country. The quotas are highly detailed, covering many categories of apparel. Some countries attain these limits while others are constrained in only a few or even none of the categories. Another example is

*Table 2.6* Sectoral effects of tariff cuts in 2000

| *Sector* | *Value $82 billion* | | | *% change from base* | | |
|---|---|---|---|---|---|---|
| | *Output* | *Exports* | *Imports* | *Output* | *Exports* | *Imports* |
| Agriculture | 296.73 | 26.75 | 5.33 | −0.52 | −1.40 | 2.53 |
| Metal mining | 19.43 | 1.01 | 3.16 | 3.03 | −1.62 | 3.06 |
| Coal mining | 31.63 | 5.75 | 0.15 | 0.07 | −2.07 | 2.40 |
| Oil & gas mining | 278.60 | 0.89 | 40.23 | 0.02 | −1.52 | 2.76 |
| Non-metal mining | 26.00 | 0.60 | 2.11 | 1.42 | −1.75 | 2.60 |
| Construction | 691.57 | 0.16 | 0.00 | 0.25 | −0.46 | 0.00 |
| Food & kindred | 290.25 | 14.88 | 15.41 | −0.70 | −1.02 | 3.23 |
| Tobacco | 33.03 | 3.27 | 0.22 | −0.72 | −1.26 | 18.88 |
| Textile mill | 74.28 | 2.81 | 2.38 | 1.21 | 16.06 | 26.52 |
| Apparel | 125.52 | 2.92 | 40.94 | 2.58 | 34.46 | 26.14 |
| Lumber & wood | 63.22 | 4.70 | 4.82 | 0.15 | 1.04 | 6.86 |
| Furniture | 38.44 | 0.97 | 4.63 | −0.10 | 13.81 | 6.93 |
| Paper | 148.53 | 6.81 | 9.79 | 1.03 | 6.02 | 4.40 |
| Printing & publishing | 214.63 | 2.12 | 2.06 | 0.95 | 1.09 | 4.39 |
| Chemicals | 277.97 | 35.17 | 24.56 | 3.37 | 12.46 | 10.05 |
| Petroleum refining | 340.84 | 19.40 | 16.03 | 0.54 | −2.49 | 3.28 |
| Rubber & plastic | 131.93 | 19.31 | 7.50 | 2.04 | 9.02 | 16.33 |
| Leather | 18.80 | 0.97 | 13.10 | −1.47 | 8.42 | 16.54 |
| Stone, clay & glass | 91.21 | 3.14 | 7.61 | 0.61 | 15.46 | 15.44 |
| Primary metal | 236.17 | 9.92 | 32.89 | 2.72 | 8.71 | 10.40 |
| Fabricated metal | 165.97 | 9.13 | 9.88 | 1.94 | 12.62 | 8.00 |
| Machinery | 434.94 | 96.62 | 25.92 | 3.18 | 8.33 | 13.59 |
| Electrical machinery | 217.47 | 42.98 | 43.60 | 3.38 | 14.54 | 12.63 |
| Motor vehicles | 213.08 | 36.81 | 45.83 | 2.75 | 11.25 | 10.34 |
| Transport equipment | 202.95 | 46.70 | 6.81 | 3.66 | 9.51 | 9.06 |
| Instruments | 81.53 | 20.91 | 9.81 | 4.80 | 12.36 | 11.23 |
| Misc manufactures | 36.83 | 3.18 | 17.55 | 1.92 | 12.05 | 10.26 |
| Transportation | 272.90 | 19.59 | 3.53 | 0.46 | 0.02 | 2.87 |
| Communications | 295.22 | 1.81 | 0.00 | 0.60 | −0.12 | 0.00 |
| Electric utilities | 158.29 | 0.65 | 1.24 | 0.74 | 0.24 | 1.16 |
| Gas utilities | 230.99 | 0.51 | 0.00 | 0.91 | 0.18 | 0.00 |
| Trade | 908.17 | 29.95 | 0.00 | 0.25 | −0.07 | 0.00 |
| Finance, insurance | 689.19 | 9.43 | 0.26 | 0.26 | −0.12 | 2.73 |
| Services | 910.16 | 12.14 | 0.07 | 0.05 | −0.26 | 2.62 |
| Govt enterprises | 150.18 | 0.51 | 0.00 | 0.50 | −0.15 | 0.00 |

*Notes*
Entries in the last three columns compare variables in the year 2000. Output is industry output. Imports are competitive imports only.

motor vehicles, where Japanese exports to the US are under "voluntary" export restrictions, while European exports are not.

We have modeled all quantitative restrictions by assuming that the realized import prices reflect the full effects. The primary justification for this approach is simplicity. More specifically, we assume that quotas result in a higher world price of imports $PM_{it}^*$. Hufbauer, Berliner and Elliott (1986) have provided estimates of the tariff equivalents of quantitative restrictions on US imports. While bearing in mind the many limitations of the concept of a tariff equivalent, these tariff rates are consistent with the assumptions of constant returns to scale and perfect competition employed in our model for all industries.

We next consider the economic impact of eliminating all domestic and foreign tariffs and the tariff equivalents of quantitative restrictions for textiles, apparel, shoes, steel and automobiles given in Table 2.4. These are the most significant restrictions, but do not exhaust US quotas. We have ignored restrictions on agricultural products and motor vehicles other than autos. We simulate the elimination of quantitative restrictions by reducing the rest of the world price of US imports $PM_{it}^*$. Under this change in trade policy foreigners lose rents that accrue to them under quotas.

As before, we begin our simulation in 1980 and continue through the year 2100. We have combined tariffs with quantitative restrictions to provide an estimate of the impact of eliminating both types of trade barriers. The results given in Figures 2.2a and 2.2b are similar but more substantial in magnitude than those for tariff reductions alone. The only exception is the terms of trade $e_t$. In our simulations the elimination of quantitative restrictions is unilateral. Given the exogenous trade balance, the terms of trade must rise in some years to cover the increased US imports of textiles, steel, autos, and shoes. In the initial year the fall in the terms of trade is only 0.53 percent compared with 0.61 percent for tariffs alone.

By the year 2000 the economic impacts of eliminating all trade barriers are considerably greater than the effects of tariff cuts alone. The percentage changes at the aggregate level are:

| | *No tariffs* | *No barriers* |
|---|---|---|
| Capital | 0.50 | 0.54 |
| Full consumption | 0.17 | 0.26 |
| Consumption | 0.74 | 0.96 |
| CPI | 1.00 | 1.25 |
| Exports | 6.54 | 7.19 |
| Imports | 9.72 | 10.68 |
| Price of capital | −0.72 | −1.30 |

These impacts arise from reductions in import prices for all the five quota items and the implied reduction in the price of investment goods. Investment goods industries are large consumers of steel; automobiles are included among these industries.

The sharp drop in the price of investment goods due to the elimination of

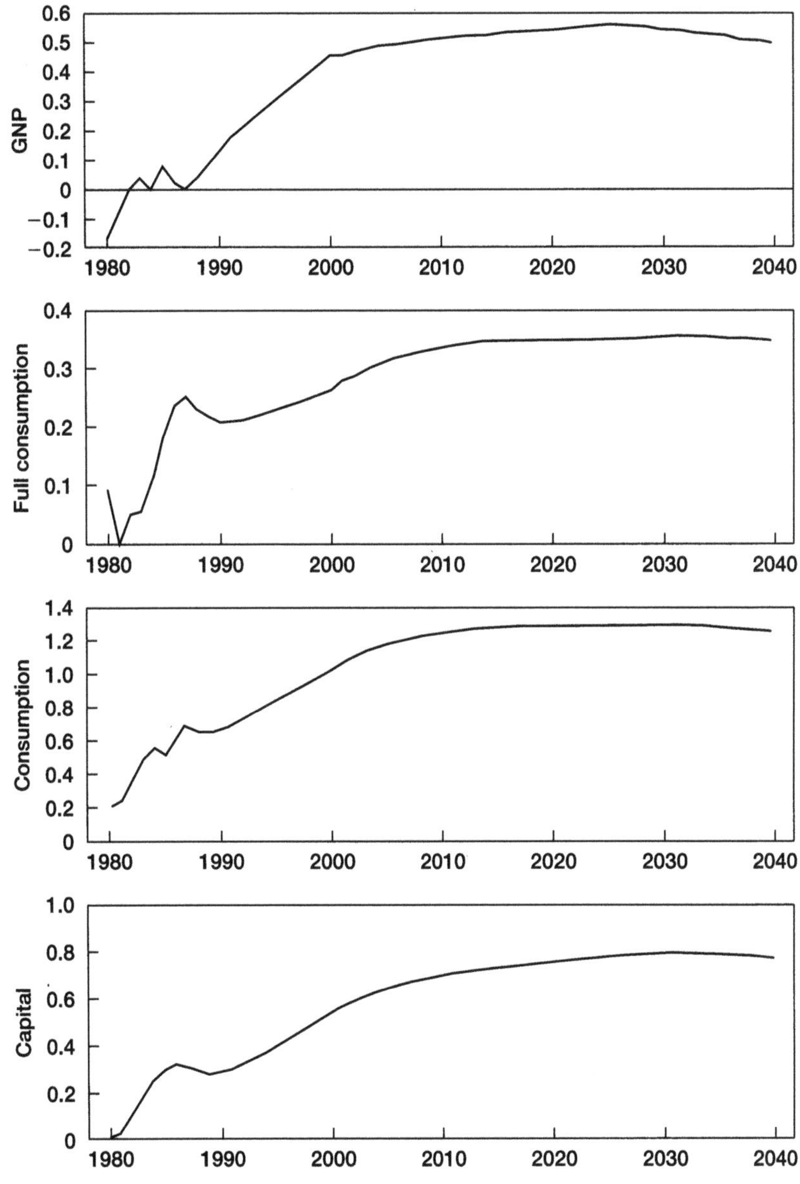


*Figure 2.2a* Dynamic effects of eliminating tariffs and quotas.

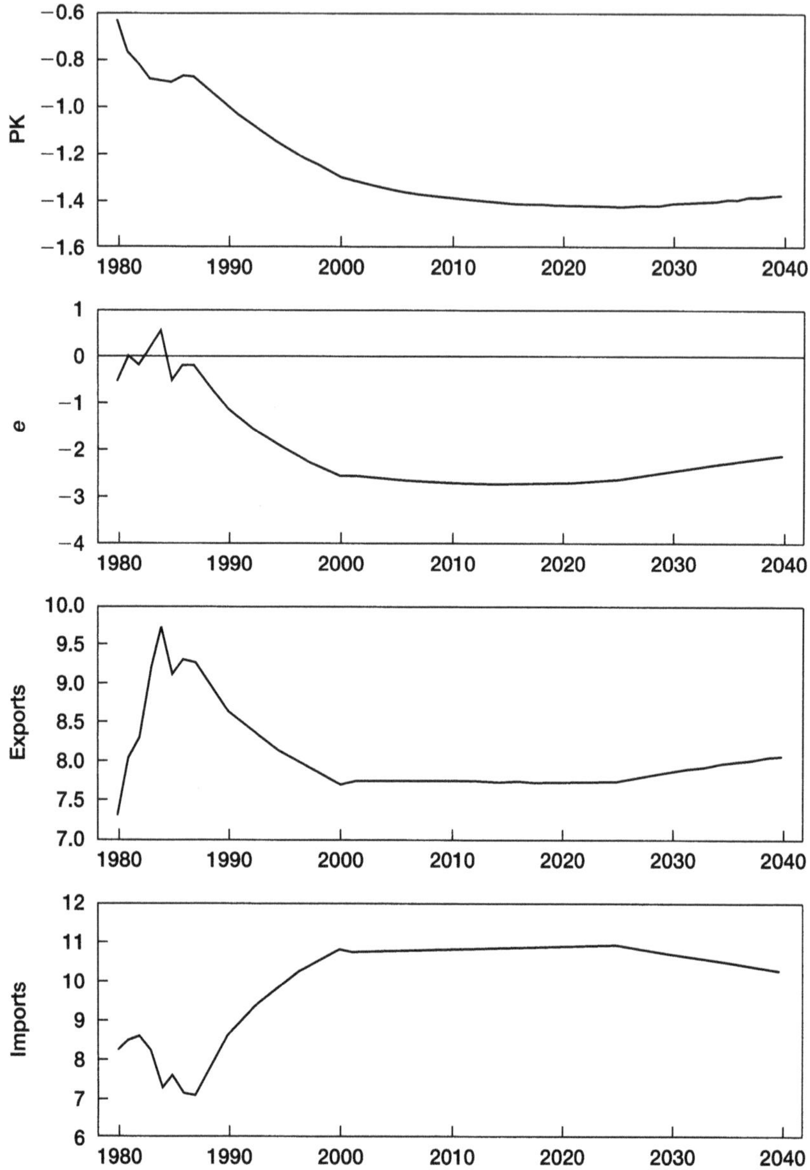


*Figure 2.2b* Dynamic effects of eliminating tariffs and quotas.

auto quotas raises the US investment level and economic growth rate. These quotas were eliminated in 1985, so that the impact on the growth rate fell. The effects of the elimination of all tariff barriers on growth of the US gross national product is summarized in the following table:

| | Annual GNP growth rate % | | |
|---|---|---|---|
| | Base case | No tariffs | No barriers |
| 1980:1990 | 3.47 | 3.48 | 3.50 |
| 1980:2000 | 2.34 | 2.37 | 2.38 |

The sectoral effects of eliminating all trade barriers are given in Table 2.7. This can be compared with Table 2.5 for tariff cuts alone. The sectoral effects are quite similar, except for the commodities subject to quotas. Apparel imports, for example, rise by 42 percent, compared to a gain of only 31 percent for tariff cuts alone. For iron and steel the gain is 15 percent versus only 7 percent; for leather the gain is 28 percent versus 17 percent. These shifts translate into parallel output changes. The leather industry's output falls by 2.5 percent by comparison with 1.4 percent with tariff cuts alone, while textile output rises by only 1.2 percent compared to 1.4 percent. Resources move out of apparel; since textiles, its main intermediate input, also falls in price, the output of apparel actually rises.

In summary, the economic impact of quantitative restrictions is substantial, even though only a few commodities are affected by them. Elimination of these restrictions on the five items we have considered would produce a gain in US consumption that exceeds the gain from abolishing all remaining tariffs. A multilateral reduction of nontariff barriers would probably have had an even greater impact, given the likelihood that quantitative restrictions in the rest of the world are even higher than those in the US.

## *Comparisons with other studies*

For a multilateral elimination of all tariffs in 1980, Deardorff and Stern (1986) have reported a static gain of 0.1 percent of the US gross national product, based on a 1976 reference year.[15] Whalley (1985) reports a 0.05 percent gain for a 50 percent multilateral tariff cut using 1977 as a reference year. By comparison, our model generates a change in consumption equal to 0.16 percent of the US gross national product in 1980, which is closely comparable to previous results.

The sectoral effects of multilateral trade reductions are broadly similar, despite important differences in assumptions among the models. Tariff

*Table 2.7* Sectoral effects of eliminating tariffs and selected quotas

| *Sector* | *Output* | *Capital* | *Labor* | *Exports* | *Imports* |
|---|---|---|---|---|---|
| Agriculture | −0.34 | −0.43 | −0.51 | −0.14 | 1.97 |
| Metal mining | 2.10 | 2.09 | 1.86 | −0.18 | 2.20 |
| Coal mining | 0.30 | 0.24 | 0.02 | −0.27 | 0.60 |
| Oil & gas mining | 0.07 | 0.00 | 0.15 | −0.32 | 0.56 |
| Non-metal mining | 0.50 | 0.32 | 0.03 | −0.23 | 0.68 |
| Construction | −0.15 | −0.30 | −0.17 | −0.21 | |
| Food & kindred | −0.50 | −0.56 | −0.62 | −0.13 | 1.37 |
| Tobacco | −0.54 | −0.54 | −0.73 | −0.09 | 20.06 |
| Textile mill | 1.19 | 0.61 | −0.24 | 19.91 | 25.64 |
| Apparel | 2.01 | −0.46 | −0.09 | 33.60 | 42.31 |
| Lumber & wood | −0.12 | −0.45 | −0.83 | 3.81 | 3.91 |
| Furniture | −1.20 | −1.35 | −1.49 | 16.81 | 4.93 |
| Paper | 0.81 | 0.67 | 0.62 | 8.94 | 1.75 |
| Printing & publishing | 0.90 | 0.93 | 0.72 | 3.89 | 2.29 |
| Chemicals | 2.45 | 2.38 | 2.31 | 15.13 | 7.74 |
| Petroleum refining | 0.18 | 0.19 | 0.09 | −0.44 | 0.62 |
| Rubber & plastic | 1.30 | 1.21 | 1.01 | 13.44 | 14.38 |
| Leather | −2.52 | −3.59 | −3.04 | 11.27 | 27.56 |
| Stone, clay & glass | −0.04 | −0.16 | −0.47 | 18.83 | 19.56 |
| Primary metal | 2.40 | 1.33 | 1.32 | 13.57 | 15.09 |
| Fabricated metal | 1.66 | 0.86 | 0.95 | 16.42 | 8.23 |
| Machinery | 2.36 | 1.59 | 1.45 | 11.96 | 9.87 |
| Electrical machinery | 2.02 | 1.46 | 1.72 | 17.94 | 10.52 |
| Motor vehicles | 1.58 | 1.13 | 0.29 | 13.95 | 5.02 |
| Transport equipment | 2.87 | 2.15 | 2.10 | 13.15 | 6.70 |
| Instruments | 3.56 | 3.40 | 3.21 | 16.41 | 9.42 |
| Misc manufactures | 1.50 | 1.28 | 1.02 | 14.58 | 10.89 |
| Transportation | 0.10 | −0.01 | −0.03 | 0.00 | 0.49 |
| Communications | 0.21 | 0.20 | 0.14 | −0.07 | |
| Electric utilities | 0.23 | 0.25 | 0.05 | −0.02 | 0.12 |
| Gas utilities | 0.35 | 0.31 | 0.25 | −0.03 | |
| Trade | 0.10 | 0.06 | 0.05 | −0.04 | |
| Finance, insurance | 0.04 | 0.09 | −0.01 | −0.09 | 0.46 |
| Services | −0.01 | −0.04 | −0.15 | −0.15 | 0.45 |
| Govt enterprises | 0.23 | 0.28 | 0.18 | −0.14 | |
| Household | | −0.40 | −0.50 | | |
| Government | | | −0.99 | | |

*Notes*
Entries are percentage change from base case in 1980. Imports are competitive imports only.

reductions induce movements of factors of production from the nontradable sectors to manufacturing. Our model allows for an increase in investment, which has a strong positive impact on industries like primary metals. This counteracts the effects of lower import prices from foreign competitors.[16]

## Conclusion

In this chapter we have implemented an intertemporal general equilibrium model of trade policy and US economic growth. By incorporating the dynamic adjustments of business and households to changes in trade policy, we have successfully captured the impacts on savings and investment ignored by static models. These effects predominate in the long run, so that economic impacts estimated from static models may be substantially understated.

For example, we find that the multilateral elimination of tariffs alone beginning in 1980 raised long run consumption by 0.82 percent, compared to an initial gain of only 0.16 percent. When both tariffs and major quotas are lifted the long run gain in consumption is estimated to be 1.08 percent. By comparison the first year gain is only 0.36 percent. These results illustrate the importance of including dynamic adjustments by households and businesses in estimating the impact of changes in trade policy.

In our model dynamic adjustments are the consequence of intertemporal optimization by households and businesses. With forward-looking consumer behavior, savings and labor supply respond to changes in trade policy. With forward-looking producer behavior investment is affected by the reduction in the relative price of capital goods. Our model can thus be used to analyze the impact on US economic growth of many other economic policies, such as capital taxation and environmental regulation, as well as exogenous disturbances to the US economy like the oil shocks of the 1970s.

## Notes

We are deeply indebted to Peter Wilcoxen for his work on the model presented in this chapter and to Richard Goettle and Edward Hudson for their collaboration on the initial phases of the research. Barbara Fraumeni, Daekeun Park, Andrew Parks, and Daniel Slesnick generously provided essential data. The authors retain sole responsibility for any remaining deficiencies.

1 Srinivasan and Whalley (1986) have summarized the features of nine general equilibrium models of world trade.
2 Our methodology for modeling the demand for inputs and productivity growth is discussed by Jorgenson (1984, 1986). Additional details on our econometric models of producer behavior are given by Jorgenson and Wilcoxen (1990b).
3 The calibration approach is discussed by Mansur and Whalley (1984).
4 Our application of the Euler equation approach to full consumption follows Jorgenson and Yun (1990).
5 Our methodology for modeling the allocation of total expenditure is discussed by Jorgenson (1984, 1990). The model we have employed was constructed by Jorgenson and Slesnick (1987) and is described in detail by Jorgenson and Wilcoxen (1990b).
6 Additional details are presented by Ho (1989, Appendix C) and Jorgenson and Wilcoxen (1990a, 1990b).
7 This approach was introduced by Armington (1969).
8 See Petri (1986: 227).

9 See Petri (1984: 51).
10 Details are given by Ho (1989, Chapter 4).
11 Goulder and Eichengreen (1989) present a two-country model with the US and the rest of the world represented as individual countries. In characterizing the behavior of producers, consumers, and governments in the rest of the world, this approach places heavy reliance on estimates derived from US data.
12 The sign of the bias from omitting export prices is not obvious. If growth of world product were due to productivity growth, then prices in the rest of the world would fall relative to US prices, imparting a downward bias to our estimates of the output elasticities. If growth of world product were due to population growth, the bias would be upward.
13 Tariff rates given in Table 2.4 were calculated from data generously provided by Andrew Parks of the US International Trade Commission, described in detail by Ho (1989, Appendix H). Tariff rates for the rest of the world are taken from Deardorff and Stern (1986).
14 Further details on our simulation techniques, projections of the exogenous variables, and existence of a steady state are provided by Ho (1989, Appendix F), and Jorgenson and Wilcoxen (1990a, 1990b).
15 See Deardorff and Stern (1986: 68).
16 More detailed comparisons among results from different models are available from the authors.

## Bibliography

Armington, P.S. (1969) "The Geographic Pattern of Trade and the Effects of Price Changes," *IMF Staff Papers* 16: 176–199.

Cline, W., Kawanabe, N., Kronsjo, T. and Williams, T. (1978) *Trade Negotiations in the Tokyo Round.* Washington: The Brookings Institution.

Deardorff, A. and Stern, R.M. (1986) *The Michigan Model of World Production and Trade.* Cambridge: The MIT Press.

Goulder, L.H. and Eichengreen, B. (1989) "Savings Promotion, Investment Promotion, and International Competitiveness," in R. Feenstra (ed.) *Tax Policies for International Competitiveness.* Chicago: University of Chicago Press.

Ho, M.S. (1989) "The Effects of External Linkages on U.S. Economic Growth," unpublished PhD thesis, Harvard University.

Hufbauer, G., Berliner, D.T. and Elliott, K.A. (1986) *Trade Protection in the United States*, Washington: Institute for International Economics.

Jorgenson, D.W. (1984) "Econometric Methods for Applied General Equilibrium Analysis," in H. Scarf and J. Shoven (eds) *Applied General Equilibrium Analysis.* Cambridge: Cambridge University Press.

—— (1986) "Econometric Methods for Modeling Producer Behavior," in Z. Griliches and M.D. Intriligator (eds) *Handbook of Econometrics*, vol. 3. Amsterdam: North-Holland.

—— (1990) "Aggregate Consumer Behavior and the Measurement of Social Welfare," *Econometrica* 58: 1007–1040.

Jorgenson, D.W. and Slesnick, D.T. (1987) "Aggregate Consumer Behavior and Household Equivalence Scales," *Journal of Business and Economic Statistics* 5: 219–232.

Jorgenson, D.W. and Wilcoxen, P.J. (1990a) "Environmental Regulation and U.S. Economic Growth," *Rand Journal of Economics* 21: 314–340.

—— and —— (1990b) "Intertemporal General Equilibrium Modeling of U.S. Environmental Regulation," *Journal of Policy Modeling* 12: 1–30.

Jorgenson, D.W. and Yun, K.Y. (1990) "Tax Reform and U.S. Economic Growth," *Journal of Political Economy* 98: 151–193.

Mansur, A.H. and Whalley, J. (1984) "Numerical Specification of Applied General Equilibrium Models: Estimation, Calibration and Data," in H. Scarf and J. Shoven (eds) *Applied General Equilibrium Analysis*. Cambridge: Cambridge University Press.

Petri, P.A. (1984) *Modelling Japanese-American Trade*. Cambridge: Harvard University Press.

—— (1986) "Comments," in T.N. Srinivasan and J. Whalley, *General Equilibrium Trade Policy Modelling*. Cambridge: The MIT Press.

Shiells, C., Stern, R.M. and Deardorff, A. (1986) "Estimates of the Elasticities of Substitution between Imports and Home goods for the U.S.," *Weltwirtschaftliches Archiv* 3: 497–519.

Srinivasan, T.N. and Whalley, J. (1986) *General Equilibrium Trade Policy Modelling*. Cambridge: The MIT Press.

Stern, R.M., Francis, J. and Schumacher, B. (1976) *Price Elasticities in International Trade: An Annotated Bibliography*. London: Macmillan.

Stone, J.A. (1979) "Price Elasticities of Demand for Imports and Exports: Industry Estimates for the U.S., the EEC and Japan," *Review of Economics and Statistics* 61: 117–123.

Whalley, J. (1985) *Trade Liberalization among Major World Trading Areas*. Cambridge: The MIT Press.

# 3

# ON THE MUTUAL IMPOSITION OF TARIFFS WITH FREE CAPITAL MOBILITY

*Tadashi Inoue*

Based on the standard two countries, two goods and two primary factors model with neo-classical technology and free capital mobility between the two countries; the Nash equilibrium tariff formula is derived first. The mutual tariff reduction is shown to be beneficial for both countries, irrespective of the patterns of specializations of both countries.

## Introduction

This chapter aims at analyzing the welfare effects on the home and foreign countries (the world) of a mutual imposition of tariffs on imports when free capital mobility is allowed between the two countries. In particular the focus is on the structure of the Nash equilibrium tariff and the welfare effects of trade liberalization (a reduction of tariff rates) when the world economy is on or not on the Nash equilibrium.

The welfare effects with factor mobility when both countries can take various policy measures were discussed by a few authors; Hamada (1966) discussed the case where taxation on foreign investment is the only decision variable for both countries. Miyagiwa and Young (1988) discussed the welfare effects when both countries levy different tariffs, assuming fixed commodity prices and factor-specific capital. This chapter has several points in common with Miyagiwa and Young's work in the sense that the welfare effects of mutual tariffs with free capital mobility are discussed. However, in this chapter, capital is not sector-specific. Capital is assumed to be employed in any industry in both countries and the international prices of goods are not fixed, rather they are determined by the world equilibrium.[1] Furthermore, the Nash equilibrium with bilateral tariffs is considered explicitly here.

The welfare effects of bilateral tariffs without factor mobility have been one of the most popular topics of international trade theory. Earlier discussions of tariff retaliation have been made by Kaldor (1940), Scitovsky (1941), Robinson (1950), Johnson (1953) and Gorman (1958). Harsanyi (1965) suggested that the game theory can be used to analyze international conflicts. Kuga (1973) and Otani (1980) demonstrated the existence of a general equilibrium with strategic tariff imposition. Weymark (1980) treated the case where each country uses tariff revenue rather than tariff levels to maximize its welfare. Mayer (1981) considered the case of negotiated tariff reductions where the negotiating parties have different strengths in negotiation and different negotiation rules. Markusen (1981) discussed the distributional effects of mutual tariff reductions. Riezman (1982) discussed both the cases of non-cooperation and cooperation games. Hamilton and Whalley (1983) estimated the numerical values of the Nash equilibrium tariff rates. McMillan (1986) provided a thorough survey of the welfare effects of tariff imposition from the viewpoint of game theory. Chan (1988) treated the Nash equilibrium bargaining model of trade. Cheng and Wong (1990) analyzed the strategies of income taxes and quotas of two countries which choose between capital and labor mobility under one commodity case and generalized Ramaswami's (1968) results that a country is better off by becoming larger than becoming smaller. Turunen-Red and Woodland (1991) discussed a model of many countries trading arbitrary numbers of commodities and examined the possibilities of the strict Pareto improvement of tariff reforms. Yet no one has explicitly considered the welfare effects of bilateral tariffs with free capital mobility.

In the next section our model and the results are explained. The chapter works within the standard two countries, two traded goods, two primary factors (labor and capital) model encompassing with free capital mobility, neo-classical technology and bilateral tariffs on imports, and it provides three main new results. First, with complete diversificaton of both countries the positive tariff rates of both countries constitute the Nash equilibrium tariff with free capital mobility (Theorem 1). Second, the mutual tariff reduction is beneficial for both countries as far as initial tariff combination is restricted to a certain area containing the Nash equilibrium tariffs (Theorem 2), generalizing the results known for the case without capital mobility. (For these points without capital mobility see, e.g., McMillan (1986).) Third, Theorems 1 and 2 are generalized to the case of specialization of one country (Theorem 3) and of each country (Theorem 4).

## Models and results

Let there be two countries – the home country and the foreign country – and two goods. For the home country let $c_i$ be the amount of consumption for good $i$, $i = 1, 2$; $y_i$ be the amount of production of good $i$; $x_i = c_i - y_i$ be the excess demand for good $i$; $x_i > 0$ be the imports of good $i$; $-x_i > 0$ be its exports; and $u = f(c_i, c_2)$ be the social utility function. Further, $p_i$ is the international price of good $i$. Goods are produced by two primary factors – the immobile one is called labor and mobile one is called capital – under neo-classical technology with constant returns to scale. The home country is assumed to import good 1, export good 2, and capital $k > 0$ as far as the complete diversification or specialization of both countries prevails. However if the specialization of the home country occurs, then while its trade pattern of goods remain unchanged, it may either export capital or import it, i.e. $k \gtrless 0$. $t$ is the tariff rate on good 1 so that $(t + 1)p_1$ is the domestic price of good 1 for the home country whereas the foreign country is assumed to levy tariff $T$ for good 2 (foreign imports) so that $(T + 1)p_2$ is the domestic price of good 2 for the foreign country.

$n = (t + 1)p_1c_1 + p_2c_2$ is the gross national income (gni) for the home country whereas $N = p_1C_1 + (T + 1)p_2C_2$ is that for the foreign country. Henceforth small letters are used for the variables and parameters for the home country and capital letters are used for the foreign country. $\pi = (t + 1)p_1y_1 + p_2y_2 = g((t + 1)p_1, p_2, k)$ is the gross domestic product (gdp) where $g$ is the revenue function. By definition $g_i = \partial g/\partial P_i = y_i$, $i = 1, 2$; $P_1 = (t + 1)p_1$; $P_2 = p_2$; and $g_k = \partial g / \partial k = -r = -r((t + 1)p_1, p_2, k)^2$, where $r$ is the rental price of capital. $n$ is expressed as $n = g((t + 1)p_1, p_2, k) + tp_1x + Rk$, where $R$ is the foreign rental price of capital. By definition of gni, it is rewritten as $p_1x_1 + p_2x_2 = Rk$. Similarly, $N$ is expressed as $N = G(p_1, (T + 1)p_2, k) + Tp_2X_2 - Rk$, which is rewritten as $p_1X_1 + p_2X_2 = -Rk$. By definition, $G_i = \partial G / \partial P_i = Y_i$, $i = 1, 2$; $P_1 = p_1$; $P_2 = (T + 1)p_2$; and $G_k = R = R(p_1, (T + 1)p_2, k)$. Free capital mobility is assumed so that in equilibrium $R = r$.

### *Complete diversification of both countries*

First the complete diversification of both countries is considered. For this case, price of capital depends only on commodity prices. Then $R = R(p_1, (T + 1)p_2)$, and $r = r((t + 1)p_1, p_2)$. $x_W = x_1 + X_1$ is the world excess demand for good 1. $h_i$ is the ordinary demand function for good $i$ so that $c_1 = h_i((t + 1)p_1, p_2, n)$, $i = 1, 2$. The same letters are used to express variables and their functions; $y_i = y_i((t + 1)p_1, p_2, k)$, $c_i = c_i(p_1, p_2, t, T, k)$, $x_i = x_i(p_1, p_2, t, T, k)$, $n = n(p_1, p_2, t, T, k)$, $Y_i = Y_i(p_1, (T + 1)p_2, k)$, $C_i = C_i(p_1, p_2, T, k)$, $X_i = X_i(p_1, p_2, T, k)$ and $x_W = x_W(p_1, p_2, t, T, k)$.[3] The equilibrium conditions for world commodity and capital markets

$$x_W(p_1, p_2, t, T, k) = 0 \tag{1}$$

and

$$R(p_1, (T + 1)p_2) = r((t + 1)p_1, p_2) \tag{2}$$

define $p_1$ and $k$ implicitly to be functions of $t$ and $T$ so that $p_1 = p_1(t, T)$ and $k = k(t, T)$. Good 2 is the numéraire so that $p_2 = 1$. Let the matrix $A$ be:

$$A = \begin{bmatrix} x_{W1} & x_{Wk} \\ R_1 - (t+1)r_1 & R_r - r_k \end{bmatrix},$$

where $R_1 = \partial R / \partial p_1$, $r_1 = \partial r / \partial P_1$, $P_1 = (t+1)p_1$ and $x_{W1} = \partial x_W / \partial p_1$. Then from equations (1) and (2) we observe

$$P_{1t} = -x_{Wk} r_1 p_1 / |A|, \tag{3}$$

$$P_{1T} = x_{Wk} R_2 p_2 / |A|, \tag{4}$$

$$k_t = \{x_{W1} r_1 p_1 + x_{Wt}(R_1 - (t+1)r_1)\} / |A| \tag{5}$$

and

$$k_T = \{-x_{W1} R_2 p_2 + x_{WT}(R_1 - (t+1)r_1)\} / |A|, \tag{6}$$

where $R_2 = \partial R / \partial P_2$, $P_2 = (T+1)p_2$, $x_{Wk} = \partial x_W / \partial k$, $x_{Wt} = \partial x_W / \partial t$, $k_t = \partial k / \partial t$, $k_T = \partial k / \partial T$ and

$$|A| = -x_{Wk}\{R_1 - (t+1)r_1\}, \tag{7}$$

here $r_k = R_k = 0$ due to the complete diversification of both countries. ($r_k > 0$ (respectively $R_k < 0$) iff (if and only if) the home (respectively foreign) country specializes.)

Since $p_1 h_{1n} / (1 - t^*) + p_2 h_{2n} / (1 - t^*) = p_1 H_{1N} / (1 - T^*) + p_2 H_{2N} / (1 - T^*) = 1$ holds by definition where $t^* = tp_1 h_{1n}$ and $T^* = Tp_2 H_{2N}$, $p_i h_{in} / (1 - t^*)$ (respectively $p_i H_{iN} / (1 - T^*)$) can be interpreted as the marginal propensity to consume good $i$ for the home country (respectively foreign country) evaluated at the price, $p_i / (1 - t^*)$ (respectively $p_i / (1 - T^*)$). Further we denote $m_i = p_i h_{in} / (1 - t^*)$ and $M_i = p_i H_{in} / (1 - T^*)$ to be the effective marginal propensity to consume good $i$ for the home country and for the foreign country, $i = 1, 2$. By definition, $m_1 + m_2 = M_1 + M_2 = 1$ holds. Both goods are assumed to be normal in either country so that $0 < m_1, M_1 < 1$ holds. Let $s_{ij} = h_{ij} + c_j h_{in}$, $i, j = 1, 2$ be the Slutsky substitution term where $h_{ij} = \partial h_i / \partial P_j$, $P_1 = (t+1)p_1$ and $P_2 = p_2$. $s_{11} < 0$ and $y_{11} = \partial y_1 \partial P_1 > 0$ ($P_1 = (t+1)p_1$) are assumed. Similarly $S_{11} < 0$ and $Y_{11} = \partial Y_1 / \partial p_1 > 0$ are assumed. Furthermore the following are assumed to obtain the regular results for the signs of the Nash equilibrium tariffs:

**A.1** Each country exports capital intensive goods so that $r_1 < 0$ and $R_1 > 0$ under complete diversification.

**A.2** $x_1 - R_1 k > 0$ as far as $x_1 > 0$, i.e. intuitively the amount of capital trade is below a certain level as far as trade in goods is concerned.

**A.3** $m_1 \geq M_1$, i.e. the marginal propensity to consume good 1 (home imports) of the home country is not less than that of the foreign country.

One of the sufficient condition for the existence of the complete diversification for the case of factor intensity reversal between countries (**A.1**) is given by Uekawa (1972) in the following:

*(Simplified) Uekawa's condition (4)*

Let $f_i$ and $F_i$ be the labor productivity functions of good $i$ of the home and the foreign countries respectively, $i = 1, 2$. Then for given $t$ and $T > 0$, there exist $p_1 > 0$, $\bar{v} > 0$ and $\bar{V} > 0$ such that

$f_2(v) > p_1(t + 1)f_1(v)$ iff $v < \bar{v}$

and

$F_1(V) > p_1(T + 1)F_2(V)$ iff $V > \bar{V}$.

Uekawa's sufficient condition is assumed for the case of incomplete diversification of both countries. Under **A.1**, $R_1 - (t + 1)r_1 > 0$, $x_{Wk} < 0$ and $|A| > 0$ are easily seen (see Appendix I). Furthermore:

**Lemma 1** Under A.1, an increase in a tariff on imports in either country improves terms of trade of its own country, i.e. $p_{1t} < 0$ and $p_{1T} > 0$.

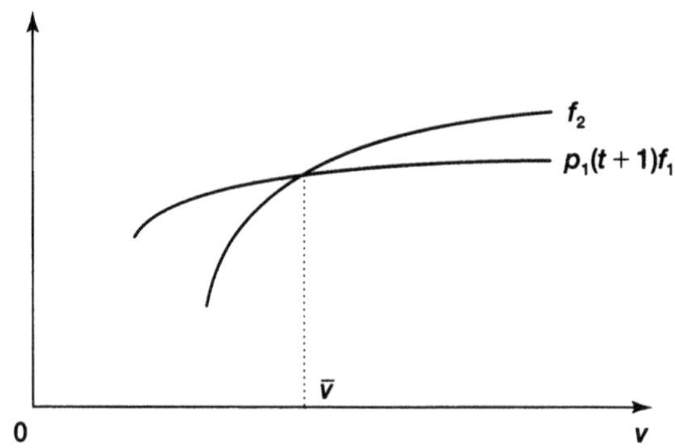


*Figure 3.1*

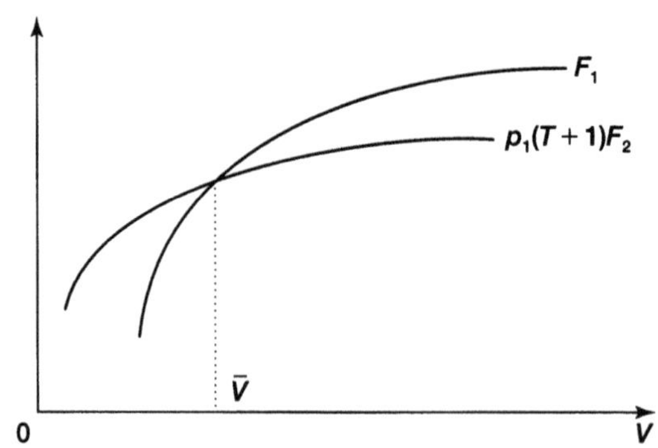


*Figure 3.2*

In view of Lemma 1, A.1 is seen to be reasonable. In fact without A.1, $p_{1t} > 0$ or $p_{1T} < 0$ may occur, which may lead to the negative Nash equilibrium tariffs as is seen later in **Theorem** 1.

**A.2** is general in the sense that it covers the case of no capital mobility. Furthermore, though A.2 seems restrictive, it is required to assure the home optimal tariff $\hat{t}$ will be positive given foreign tariff $T$, as is seen later in Theorems 1 through 4. In fact, as for example equation (10) of Theorem 1 shows, $x_1 - R_1k \leq 0$ would imply that the optimal home tariff $\hat{t}$ would be non-positive given foreign tariff $T$, thus the *positive* Nash equilibrium tariff combination could not exist.[4]

Henceforth A.1, 2 and 3 are assumed to hold irrespective of the patterns of specialization of each country.[5]

Next we consider the effects on social welfare of an increase in tariffs in both countries. Hereafter the marginal utility of income of each country is assumed to be unity without loss of generality. Denote:

$\tilde{x}_i(t, T) = x_i(p_1(t, T), k(t, T), t, T)$, $\tilde{X}_i(t, T) = \tilde{X}_i(p_1(t, T), k(t, T), T)$, $\tilde{x}_{it} = \partial\tilde{x}_i / \partial t$, $\tilde{x}_{iT} = \partial\tilde{x}_i / \partial T$, $\tilde{X}_{it} = \partial\tilde{X}_i / \partial t$ and $\tilde{X}_{iT} = \partial\tilde{X}_i / \partial T$, $i = 1, 2$.

To determine the signs of $\tilde{X}_{1t}$ and $\tilde{x}_{2T}$ it is assumed that:

**A.4** In the case of diversification of both countries, the amounts of foreign trade both in goods and capital are below a certain level so that $x_1 - R_1k(> 0)$ and $x_1 - (t + 1)r_1k(> 0)$ are small enough to assure that both $\tilde{x}_{1t}$ and $\tilde{x}_{2T}$ are positive. (See Appendix II.)

A.4 implies that an increase in tariff on imports of either country decreases the exports of the other country. We can then obtain:

*Theorem 1*

1. $$u_t = -(x_1 - R_1k)p_{1t} - p_1\tilde{X}_{1t}t \tag{8}$$
   $$U_T = (x_1 - (t + 1)r_1k)p_{1T} - p_2\tilde{x}_{2T}T. \tag{9}$$
2. Let $\hat{t}$ and $\hat{T}$ be the values of $t$ and $T$ which satisfy $u_t = 0$ and $U_T = 0$ for given $T$ and $t$ respectively. The Nash equilibrium tariffs $N = (t_N, T_N) = (\hat{t}, \hat{T})$ are given by $t$ and $T$ which satisfy simultaneously $u_t = 0$ and $U_T = 0$, i.e.
   $$\hat{t} = -(x_1 - R_1k)p_{1t} / p_1\tilde{X}_{1t} > 0, \tag{10}$$
   $$\hat{T} = (x_1 - (t + 1)r_1k)p_{1T} / p_2\tilde{x}_{2T} > 0 \tag{11}$$
   under A.4.

*Proof*

See Appendix II.

As is well known, as far as the export elasticities of both countries are positive, the Nash equilibrium tariffs are positive without capital mobility (for this, see e.g. McMillan (1986) pp. 26–31). Theorem 1 is seen to be a generalization of this result.

By setting $u_t = 0$ and $U_T = 0$ in equations (8) and (9), the response curves of the home country and the foreign country are derived. In Figure 3.3, the response curves of the home country and the foreign country are given by the line segments $(0, T_a)$ and $(t_0, 0)$, and $(0, T_0)$ and $(t_a, 0)$ respectively. The intersection of the two line segments, $N$ is the Nash equilibrium. The slope of the response curve of the home country is assumed to be steeper than that of the foreign country for stability, though it is not necessary so in general.

Since $x_1 \geq 0$, $x_2 \leq 0$ and $k \geq 0$ hold for the case of complete diversification of both countries, the budget constraint $p_1x_1 + p_1x_2 = Rk$ implies that $x_1 = 0$ leads to $x_2 = k = 0$, i.e. autarky. Hence tariff combination $(t, T)$ satisfying $\tilde{x}_1(t, T) = 0$ is the curve on which autarky prevails. Furthermore, under A.2, $x_1 - R_1k = 0$ or under A.1, $x_1 - (t + 1)r_1k = 0$ implies $x_1 = k = 0$. Hence we observe at $T = T_a$ and $t = t_a$, the tariff rate of either country is so high that autarky prevails, and that more generally for $(t, T)$ on the curve $T_at_a(\tilde{x}_1(t, T) = 0)$ autarky prevails. Furthermore since the change in trade patterns is assumed away for simplicity, for tariff rates $(t, T)$ higher than the values on the curve $T_at_a$ autarky still prevails.[6] $t = t_0$ and $T = T_0$ are so-called optimal tariffs of the home country and the foreign country respectively, given the tariff rates of the foreign country and the home country are zero.

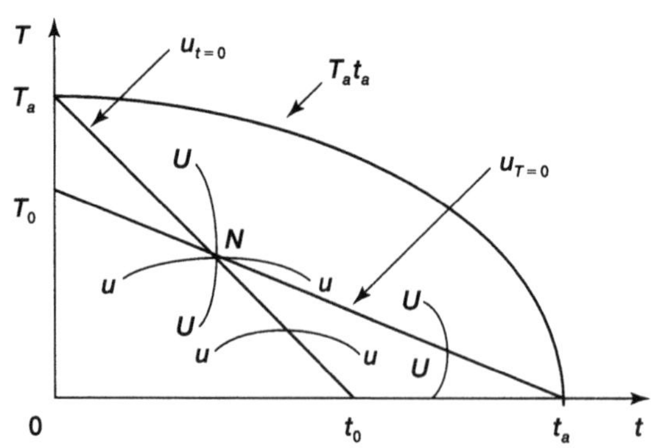


*Figure 3.3*

By the calculations similar to those used in equations (8) and (9), it can be shown that (see Appendix III):

$$u_T = -(x_1 - (t+1)r_1k)p_{1T} - p_1\tilde{X}_{1T}t \tag{12}$$

and

$$U_t = (x_1 - R_1k)p_{1t} - p_2\tilde{x}_{2t}T. \tag{13}$$

Since $\tilde{X}_{1T}$ and $\tilde{x}_{2t} > 0$, and hence $u_T < 0$ and $U_t < 0$ under **A**.4 (see Appendix IV), the indifference curves of the home country $uu$, and those of the foreign country $UU$ are drawn as in Figure 3.3, i.e. $dT / dt|_{u = \bar{u}} = -u_t / u_T > 0$ (resp. $< 0$) for $t < \hat{t}$ (resp. $> \hat{t}$) and $dT / dt|_{U = \bar{U}} = -U_t / U_T > 0$ (resp. $< 0$) for $T < \hat{T}$ (resp. $> \hat{T}$). Furthermore it is easily seen that as the indifference curve $uu$ (resp. $UU$) of the home (resp. foreign) country moves downward (resp. leftward), its utility goes up. As a result, it follows that:

*Theorem 2*

1. For tariff combination $(t, T)$ contained in the area encircled by the curves $T_at_a$, $T_aN$ and $t_aN$, especially for the Nash equilibrium tariff $N = (tN, TN)$, the mutual reduction of tariff rates (i.e. trade liberalization) causes the increase in the utility levels of both countries.
2. For tariff combination $(t, T)$ contained in the triangle $Nt_at_0$ (resp. $NT_aT_0$), such a reduction causes the increase in the welfare of the home (resp. foreign) country.

### *Specialization of one country*

Next, we consider the case of specialization in either country. Although there exist two cases of specialization, i.e. home specialization and foreign diversification, and home diversification and foreign specialization, the latter case is formally the same as the former with the home country importing foreign capital. Hence the latter case can be treated by the same method as the former with $k < 0$. In short, the home country specializes and either exports or imports capital, while the foreign country always diversifies. For the latter case ($k < 0$), since **A.2** holds automatically it is deleted.

For both these cases of home country is specialization, A.4 is slightly changed to:

**A.4′** The amounts of foreign trade both in goods and capital are below a certain level so that $x_1 > 0$, $x_1 - R_1k(> 0)$ and $k(\lesseqgtr 0)$ are small enough to assure $\tilde{X}_{1t}$, $\tilde{x}_{2T}$ and $\tilde{X}_{1T}$ to be all positive. (See Appendix V.)

Here note that equations (8), (9), (12) and (13) remain unchanged. For the case of the home country's specialization, $r = r(p_2, k)$ holds so that we observe:

$$|A| = x_{W1}(R_k - r_k) - x_{Wk}(R_1 - (t + 1)r_1) > 0, \quad (7\text{-}1)$$

where $r_1 = 0$, $R_k = 0$, $r_k > 0$, $x_{W1} < 0$ and $x_{Wk} < 0$. Hence it follows from equations (1) and (2) that:

$$p_{1t} = x_{Wt}r_k \,/\, |A| < 0, \quad (3\text{-}1)$$

$$p_{1T} = (x_{WT}r_k + R_2p_2x_{Wk}) \,/\, |A|, \quad (4\text{-}1)$$

$$k_t = x_{Wt}R_1 \,/\, |A|, \quad (5\text{-}1)$$

and

$$k_T = (-\, x_{W1}R_2p_2 + x_{WT}R_1) \,/\, |A|. \quad (6\text{-}1)$$

By a similar calculation as in equations (8), (9), (12) and (13) we obtain:

$$u_t = -\,(x_1 - R_1k)p_{1t} - p_1\tilde{X}_{1t}t \quad (8\text{-}1)$$

$$U_T = (x_1 - R_1k)p_{1T} - R_2p_2k - p_2\tilde{x}_{2T}T, \quad (9\text{-}1)$$

$$u_T = -\,(x_1 - R_1k)p_{1T} + R_2p_2k - p_1\tilde{X}_{1T}t, \quad (12\text{-}1)$$

$$U_t = (x_1 - R_1k)p_{1t} - p_2\tilde{x}_{2t}T. \quad (13\text{-}1)$$

It is shown that:

$$(x_1 - R_1k)p_{1T} - R_2p_2k > 0$$

holds for small $k \lesseqgtr 0$,[7] and here again that $\tilde{X}_{1t}$, $\tilde{x}_{2T}$ and $\tilde{X}_{1T}$ are positive by A.4′ and that $\tilde{x}_{2t}$ is always positive (see Appendix V).

Furthermore, $p_{1T} > 0$ for small $k > 0$ and for any $k < 0$,[8] and $p_{1t} < 0$ show that an increase in tariff on imports of each country improves its terms of trade.

To generalize Theorem 2, it is necessary to show that tariff combination $(t, T) = (0, T_a)$ (resp. $(t_a, 0)$) satisfying $x_1 - R_1k = 0$ (resp. $(x_1 - R_1k)p_{1T} - R_2p_2k = 0$) implies $x_1 = k = 0$, i.e. autarky. In fact, if $x_1 - R_1k = 0$ holds, then $x_1 = k = 0$ follows for $k \geq 0$ from A.2, and for $k \leq 0$ due to the assumptions of $x_1 \geq 0$ and $R_1 > 0$. On the other hand, if $(x_1 - R_1k)p_{1T} - R_2p_2k = 0$ holds, then $x_1 - R_1k = 0$ and $k = 0$, i.e. autarky follows for $k \geq 0$ from $p_{1T} > 0$, A.2 and $R_2 < 0$, but does not necessarily so for $k \leq 0$. To overcome this ambiguity:

the equation $f(t) = (x_{1T} - R_1k)p_{1T} - R_2p_2k = 0$ given $T = 0$ is assumed to have a *unique* solution $t = t_a$ for $k \leq 0$ (so that $f(t) = 0$ implies $t = t_a$ and hence $x_1 = k = 0$).

We then observe:

*Theorem 3*

Assume that either country specializes in the production of exported goods. Let the level of foreign trades both in goods and capital be below a certain level in the sense of A.4′. Then the conclusions of Theorems 1 and 2 still hold. Here $\hat{T}$ is slightly changed to $\hat{T} = \{(x_1 - R_1k)p_{1T} - R_2p_2k\} / p_2\tilde{x}_{2T} > 0$.

Theorem 3 generalizes the characteristics of the Nash equilibrium tariff, and the Pareto improvement effects of the trade liberalization into the case of specialization of either country assuming the trade-deterring effects of tariff hike (i.e. $\tilde{x}_{2t}$, $\tilde{x}_{2T}$, $\tilde{X}_{2t}$ and $\tilde{X}_{2T}$ are all positive). Especially the Pareto improvement property of tariff reductions seems vital in view of the prevalence of trade protectionism by means of tariff (higher than the Nash equilibrium level). (For this, see Hamilton and Whalley (1983).)

## *Specialization of both countries*

Lastly we consider the case of complete specialization of both countries with the home country exporting capital. Noting that both $r$ and $R$ depend on $k$, we observe that

$$|A| = x_{W1}(R_k - r_k) - R_1x_{Wk} > 0, \tag{7-2}$$

where $x_{Wk} < 0$ (see Appendix VI),

$$p_{1t} = - x_{Wt}(R_k - r_k) / |A| < 0, \tag{3-2}$$

$$p_{1T} = - x_{WT}(R_k - r_k) / |A| > 0, \tag{4-2}$$

where $x_{WT} > 0$ (see Appendix VI). Equations (3-2) and (4-2) show a generalization of Lemma 1.

$$k_t = x_{Wt}R_1 / |A| < 0, \tag{5-2}$$

$$k_T = x_{WT}R_1 / |A| > 0. \tag{6-2}$$

Here we obtain that equations (8), (9), (12) and (13) are rewritten as

$$u_t = - (x_1 - R_1k)p_{1t} + R_kkk_t - p_1\tilde{X}_{1t}t, \tag{8-2}$$

$$U_T = (x_1 - R_1k)p_{1T} - R_kkk_T - p_2\tilde{x}_{2T}T, \tag{9-2}$$

$$u_t = - (x_1 - R_1k)p_{1T} + R_kkk_T - p_1\tilde{X}_{1T}t, \tag{12-2}$$

$$U_t = (x_1 - R_1k)p_{1t} - R_kkkt - p_2\tilde{x}_{2t}.^9 \tag{13-2}$$

Utilizing the definitions of $p_{1t}$, $p_{1T}$, $k_{1t}$ and $k_{1T}$ above, it is easy to observe

$$- (x_1 - R_1k)p_{1t} + R_kkk_t > 0 \text{ and } (x_1 - R_1k)p_{1T} - R_kkk_T > 0,$$

in view of $x_{Wt} < 0$ and $x_{WT} > 0$. Here the equalities $- (x_1 - R_1k)p_{1t} + R_kkk_t = 0$ and $(x_1 - R_1k)p_{1T} - R_kkk_T = 0$ respectively are seen to imply autarky. From the above two inequalities it follows that if $\tilde{X}_{1t}$, $\tilde{x}_{2T}$, $\tilde{X}_{1T}$ and $\tilde{x}_{2t}$ are all positive, then Theorems 1 and 2 are generalized. The following assumption is made instead of A.4 and A.4′ above:

A.4″ The amounts of foreign trade both in goods and capital are below a certain level so that $x_1 - R_1 k(> 0)$ and $k(> 0)$ are small enough to assure that $\tilde{X}_{1t}$ and $\tilde{x}_{2T}$ are positive.

Furthermore, observing that $\tilde{X}_{1T}$ and $\tilde{x}_{2t}$ are always positive (for these and A.4″, see Appendix VI), we then obtain:

*Theorem 4*

Assume that each country specializes in the production of exported goods. Let the level of foreign trade both in goods and capital be below a certain level in the sense of A.4″. Then the conclusions of Theorems 1 and 2 still hold. Here $\hat{t} = -\{(x_1 - R_1 k)p_{1t} - R_k k k_t\} / p_1 \tilde{X}_{1t} > 0$, and $\hat{T} = \{(x_1 - R_1 k)p_{1T} - R_k k k_T\} / p_2 \tilde{x}_{2T} > 0$.

*Proof*

See Appendix VI.

Theorems 1 through 4 show that the Nash equilibrium tariffs are positive and that trade liberalization with free capital mobility benefits both countries, under all possible patterns of specialization of production as far as the trade-deterring effects of tariff increases are assumed.

## Concluding remarks

The factor intensity reversal assumption, A.1, though it seems strange, is seen to be necessary to obtain the normal effects of the tariff increase on terms of trade, and the positive Nash equilibrium tariffs. Without this intensity assumption the Nash equilibrium tariff of either country could be negative. Though such an occurrence cannot be denied logically, it seems hardly plausible to put the negative tariff into force. Hence the analysis of the negative Nash equilibrium tariffs are omitted because of its lack of implementability.

Furthermore A.1, 2, 3, and especially 4 (4′ or 4″ in case of specialization) are required to derive the trade-reducing effects of tariff increases of either country. Thus, if such effects are assumed from the beginning, then A.4, 4′ and 4″ are unnecessary.

One alternative model would be to assume free good trade but restricted capital mobility, or more generally restricted trade both in goods and capital. Such extensions could be done by similar methods.

## APPENDIX I

By partially differentiating $x_i = h_i - y_i$ with respect to $p_1$, we obtain

$$x_{i1} = \partial x_i / \partial p_1 = h_{i1}(t+1) + h_{in}n_1 - (t+1)y_{i1},\ i = 1, 2, \tag{A-1}$$

where $n_1 = \partial n / \partial p_1$, which is obtained by partially differentiating the identity

$$n = g + tp_1x_1 + RK \tag{A-2}$$

with respect to $p_1$;

$$n_1 = (t+1)y_1 + tx_1 + tp_1x_{11} + R_1k. \tag{A-3}$$

Then $x_{11}$ is expressed as

$$x_{11} = \{t_{11}(t+1) - h_{1n}(x_1 - R_1k)\} / (1 - t^*) < 0, \tag{A-4}$$

where $h_{ij} = s_{ij} - c_jh_{in}$ and $t_{11} = s_{11} - y_{11} < 0$ is the sum of the substitution effects of consumption and production. The term $x_{21}$ is obtained by partially differentiating the identity

$$p_1x_1 + p_2x_2 = Rk \tag{A-5}$$

with respect to $p_1$, as

$$x_{21} = (R_1k - x_1 - p_1x_{11}) / p_2. \tag{A-6}$$

Observing $n_t = p_1y_1 + p_1x_1 + tp_1x_{1t} = p_1c_1 + tp_1x_{1t}$ and $n_T = p_1x_{1T} + R_2p_2k$, we obtain

$$x_{1t} = h_{11}p_1 - y_{11}p_1 + h_{1n}n_t = t_{11}p_1 + t^*x_{1t} = t_{11}p_1 / (1 - t^*) < 0 \tag{A-7}$$

and

$$x_{1T} = h_{1n}n_T = h_{1n}R_2p_2k / (1 - t^*) < 0. \tag{A-8}$$

Similarly from $n_k = -r + tp_1x_{1k} + R = tp_1x_{1k}$, it follows from $r_i = -y_{ik}$ that

$$x_{1k} = h_{1n}n_k - y_{1k} = r_1 + r_1t^* / (1 - t^*) = r_1 / (1 - t^*) < 0. \tag{A-9}$$

Similarly for the foreign country employing the identities $X_i = H_i - Y_i$, $i = 1, 2$,

$$N = G + Tp_2X_2 - Rk, \tag{A-10}$$

and

$$p_1X_1 + p_2X_2 = -Rk, \tag{A-11}$$

it follows that[10]

$$X_{11} = \partial X_1 / \partial p_1 = \{T_{11} / (T+1) + (x_1 - R_1k)H_{1N}\} / (1 - T^*) \tag{A-12}$$

where $T_{ij} = S_{ij} - Y_{ij}$, $i, j = 1, 2$ and $T_{11} = S_{11} - Y_{11} < 0$, $Y_{11} = \partial Y_1 / \partial p_1$,

$$X_{1k} = -R_1 - Tp_2R_2H_{1N} / (1 - T^*) = -R_1 - Tp_2R_2M_1 / p_1$$

$$= -(p_1R_1 + Tp_2R_2M_1) / p_1 < 0, \quad \text{(A-13)}$$

from $R = p_1R_1 + (T + 1)p_2R_2 < p_1R_1 + Tp_2R_2M_1$,

$$X_{1T} = -(p_2^2T_{22} + R_2p_2kp_1H_{1N}) / (1 - T^*)p_1$$

$$= \{-p_1T_{11} / (T + 1)^2 - R_2p_2kH_{1N}\} / (1 - T^*) > 0, \quad \text{(A-14)}$$

where $R_i = \partial Y_i / \partial k$, $p_1T_{1i} + (T + 1)p_2T_{2i} = 0$, $i = 1, 2$, $T_{12} = T_{21}$ and hence $(T + 1)^2p_2^2T_{22} = p_1^2T_{11}$ are employed.

Also it is easy to observe $x_{W1} < 0$ and $x_{WT} > 0$ if $m_1 \geq M_1$.

## APPENDIX II

1 and 2 By definition, $c_1 = y_1 + x_i = y_i - X_i$, $i = 1, 2$. Hence $u_t = (\partial u / \partial c_1)\{y_{11}((t + 1)p_{1t} + p_1) + y_{1k}k_t - X_{11}p_{1t} - X_{1k}k_t\} + (\partial u / \partial c_2)\{y_{21}((t + 1)p_{1t} + p_1) + y_{2k}k_t - X_{21}p_{1t} - X_{2k}k_t\} = (t + 1)p_1\{y_{11}((t + 1)p_{1t} + p_1) + y_{1k}k_t - X_{11}p_{1t} - X_{1k}k_t\} + p_2\{y_{21}((t + 1)p_{1t} + p_1) + y_{2k}k_t - X_{21}p_{1t} - X_{2k}k_t\} = -rk_t - (t + 1)p_1(X_{11}p_{1t} + X_{1k}k_t) - p_2(X_{21}P_{1t} + X_{2k}k_t)$ where $(t + 1)p_1y_{11} + p_2y_{21} = 0$, $X_{it} = 0$, $y_{ik} = -r_i$ and $r = (t + 1)p_1r_1 + p_2r_2$. Then by partially differentiating the identity

$$p_1X_1 + p_2X_2 = -Rk \quad \text{(A-15)}$$

with respect to $p_1$ and $k$ respectively it follows that $p_1X_{11} + p_2X_{21} = x_1 - R_1k$ and $p_1X_{1k} + p_2X_{2k} = -R$. Hence $u_t = -rk_t - tp_1(X_{11}p_{1t} + X_{1k}k_t) - (x_1 - R_1k)p_{1t} + Rk_t = -(x_1 - R_1k)p_{1t} - tp_1(X_{11}p_{1t} + X_{1k}k_t) = -(x_1 - R_1k)p_{1t} - tp_1\tilde{X}_{1t}$.

Similarly since $C_i = Y_i - x_i$, $i = 1, 2$, $U_T = p_1(Y_{11}p_{1T} + Y_{12}p_2 + Y_{1k}k_T - x_{11}p_{1T} - x_{1k}k_T - x_{1T}) + (T + 1)p_2(Y_{21}p_{1T} + Y_{22}p_2 + Y_{2k}k_T - x_{21}p_{1T} - x_{2k}k_T - x_{2T})$. Observing $p_1Y_{1i} + (T + 1)p_2Y_{2i} = 0$, $Y_{ik} = R_i$, $i = 1, 2$, and $R = p_1R_1 + (T + 1)p_2R_2$, the above is rewritten as $U_T = Rk_T - p_1(x_{11}p_{1T} + x_{1k}k_T + x_{1T}) - (T + 1)p_2(x_{21}p_{1T} + x_{2k}k_T + x_{2T}) = Rk_T + (x_1 - R_1k)p_{1T} - Rk_T - R_2p_2k - p_2(x_{21}p_{1T} + x_{2k}k_T + x_{2T})T$ from $p_1x_{11} + p_2x_{21} = -x_1 + R_1k$, $p_1x_{1k} + p_2x_{2k} = R$ and $p_1x_{1T} + p_2x_{2T} = R_2p_2k$ (obtained from partial differentiation of $p_1x_1 + p_2x_2 = Rk$). In short, $U_T = (x_1 - R_1k)p_{1T} - R_2p_2k - p_2(x_{21}p_{1T} + x_{2k}k_T + x_{2T})T = R_2p_2x_{Wk}(x_1 - (t + 1)r_1k) / |A| - p_2(x_{21}p_{1T} + x_{2k}k_T + x_{2T})T$ (from Equations (5) and (8)) $= (x_1 - (t + 1)r_1k)p_{1T} - p_2\tilde{x}_{2T}T$.

3 Let

$$w = (X_{11}p_{1t} + X_{1k}k_t)|A| = -X_{11}p_1r_1x_{Wk} + X_{1k}\{x_{W1}r_1p_1 + x_{Wt}(R_1 - (t + 1)r_1)\} \text{ (from equations (3) and (5))}$$

$$= X_{1k}[p_1r_1\{t_{11}(t + 1) - h_{1n}(x_1 - R_1k)\} + (R_1 - (t + 1)r_1)t_{11}p_1] / (1$$

$- t^*) - p_1 r_1 X_{11} x_{1k}$ (from equations (A-4) and (A-7)) $= X_{1k} p_1 R_1 t_{11} / (1 - t^*) - X_{1k} p_1 r_1 h_{1n}(x_1 - R_1 k)/(1 - t^*) - p_1 r_1 x_{1k} T_{11} / (T + 1)(1 - T^*) - p_1 r_1 x_{1k}(x_1 - R_1 k) H_{1N} / (1 - T^*)$ (from equation (A-12)) $= X_{1k} R_1 t_{11} p_1 / (1 - t^*) - (X_{1k} m_1 + x_{1k} M_1)(x_1 - R_1 k) r_1 - p_1 r_1 x_{1k} T_{11} / (T + 1)(1 - T^*) > 0$ if $x_1 - R_1 k (> 0)$ is small in view of $X_{1k}$, $x_{1k}$ and $r_1 < 0$ and $R_1 > 0$.

4 Let

$z = (x_{21} p_{1T} + x_{2k} k_T + x_{2T})|A| = x_{21} x_{Wk} R_2 p_2 + x_{2k}\{-x_{W1} R_2 p_2 + x_{WT}(R_1 - (t + 1) r_1)\} - x_{2T} x_{Wk}(R_1 - (t + 1) r_1)$ (from equations (4), (6) and (7)) $= R_2 p_2 \,[\{(R_1 k - x_1 - p_1 x_{11}) / p_2\} (x_{1k} + X_{1k}) - (R / p_2 - p_1 x_{1k} / p_2)(x_{11} + X_{11})] + (x_{2k} x_{WT} - x_{2T} x_{Wk})(R_1 - (t + 1) r_1)$ (from (A-6)) and $(p_1 x_{1k} + p_2 x_{2k} = R) = R_2 p_2 [\{(R_1 k - x_1) / p_2\} x_{1k} + \{(R_1 k - x_1 - p_1 x_{11}) / p_2\} X_{1k} - (R / p_2)(x_{11} + X_{11}) + (p_1 x_{1k} / p_2) X_{11}] + \{(R / p_2 - p_1 x_{1k} / p_2)(x_{1T} + X_{1T}) - (x_{1k} + X_{1k})(R_2 p_2 k - p_1 x_{1T}) / p_2\} (R_1 - (t + 1) r_1)$ (from $x_{2T} = (R_2 p_2 k - p_1 x_{1T}) / p_2$) $= -(R_2 p_1 X_{1k} + R_2 R) x_{11} + (-R_2 R + R_2 p_1 x_{1k}) X_{11} + R_2(R_1 k - x_1)(x_{1k} + X_{1k}) + \{(R / p_2 + p_1 X_{1k} / p_2) x_{1T} + (R / p_2 - p_1 x_{1k} / p_2) X_{1T} - (x_{1k} + X_{1k}) R_2 k\}(R_1 - (t + 1) r_1) = R_2 p_2 X_{2k} x_{11} - R_2 p_2 x_{2k} X_{11} - R_2 (x_1 - (t + 1) r_1 k)(x_{1k} + X_{1k}) + (-X_{2k} x_{1T} + x_{2k} X_{1T})(R_1 - (t + 1) r_1)$ (from $p_1 X_{1k} + p_2 X_{2k} = -R$ and $p_1 x_{1k} + p_2 x_{2k} = R$) $= R_2 p_2 X_{2k}(t + 1) t_{11} / (1 - t^*) - \{R_2 p_2 (T + 1) x_{2k} + x_{2k} (R_1 - (t + 1) r_1) p_1\} T_{11} / (T + 1)^2 (1 - T^*) + \{-R_2 p_2 X_{2k}(x_1 - R_1 k) - X_{2k}(R_1 - (t + 1) r_1) R_2 p_2 k\} h_{1n} / (1 - t^*) - \{R_2 p_2 x_{2k}(x_1 - R_1 k) + x_{2k}(R_1 - (t + 1) r_1) R_2 p_2 k\} H_{1N} / 1 - T^*) - R_2(x_1 - (t + 1) r_1 k) x_{Wk}$ (from (A-4), (A-8), (A-12) and (A-14)) $= R_2 p_2 X_{2k} (t + 1) t_{11} / (1 - t^*) - x_{2k} r_2 T_{11} / (T + 1)^2 (1 - T^*) - R_2 p_2 X_{2k}(x_1 - (t + 1) r_1 k) h_{1n} / (1 - t^*) - R_2 p_2 x_{2k} (x_1 - (t + 1) r_1 k) H_{1N} / (1 - T^*) - R_2(x_1 - (t + 1) r_1 k) x_{Wk}$, from $R = p_1 R_1 + (T + 1) p_2 R_2 = r = (t + 1) p_1 r_1 + p_2 r_2$.

The first two terms are positive.[11] Let $B = -p_2 X_{2k} p_1 h_{1n} / (1 - t^*) - p_2 x_{2k} p_1 H_{1N} / (1 - T^*) - p_1 x_{Wk} = -p_2 X_{2k} m_1 - p_2 x_{2k} M_1 - p_1 x_{Wk} = (p_2 x_{2k} + p_1 x_{Wk}) m_1 - p_2 x_{2k} M_1 - p_1 x_{Wk}$ (from $X_{2k} + x_{2k} = -(R + p_1 X_{1k}) / p_2 + (R - p_1 x_{1k}) / p_2 = -p_1 x_{Wk} / p_2$) $= p_2 x_{2k} (m_1 - M_1) - p_1 x_{Wk} (1 - m_1)$. Thus $B > 0$ in view of $m_1 \geq M_1$ noting $x_{Wk} < 0$ and $x_{2k} > 0$ in general. Hence $z > 0$ if $x_1 - (t + 1) r_1 k (> 0)$ is small.

## APPENDIX III

As is shown in Appendix II, it is immediate to obtain $u_T = (t + 1) p_1 (y_{11}(t + 1) p_{1T} + y_{1k} k_T - X_{11} p_{1T} - X_{1k} k_T - X_{1T}) + p_2(y_{21}(t + 1) p_{1T} + y_{2k} k_T - X_{21} p_{1T} - X_{2k} k_T - X_{2T}) = -r k_T - (t + 1)\, p_1\, (X_{11} p_{1T} + X_{1k} k_T + X_{1T}) - p_2(X_{21} p_{1T} + X_{2k} k_T + X_{2T})$ (from $(t + 1) p_1 y_{11} + p_2 y_{21} = 0$, $y_{ik} = -r_i$, $i = 1, 2$ and $r = (t + 1) p_1 r_1 + p_2 r_2$) $= -(x_1 - R_1 k) p_{1T} - p_1 (X_{11} p_{1T} + X_{1k} k_T + X_{1T}) t$

+ $R_2p_2k$ (observing $p_1X_{11} + p_2X_{21} = x_1 - R_1k$, $p_1X_{1k} + p_2X_{2k} = -R$ and $p_1X_{1T} + p_2X_{2T} = -R_2p_2k$ by partial differentiation of $p_1X_1 + P_2X_2 = -Rk$) $= -R_2p_2x_{Wk}(x_1 - (t + 1)r_1k) / |A| - p_1(X_{11}p_{1T} + X_{1k}k_{1T} + X_{1T})t = -(x_1 - (t + 1)r_1k)p_{1T} - p_1\tilde{X}_{1T}t$, from equations (4) and (7).

Similarly $U_t = p_1(Y_{11}p_{1t} + Y_{1k}k_t - x_{11}p_{1t} - x_{1k}k_t - x_{1t}) + (T + 1) \times p_2(Y_{21}p_{1t} + Y_{2k}k_t - x_{21}p_{1t} - x_{2k}k_t - x_{2t}) = Rk_t - p_1(x_{11}p_{1t} + x_{1k}k_t + x_{1t}) - (T + 1)p_2(x_{21}p_{1t} + x_{2k}k_t + x_{2t})$ (from $p_1Y_{11} + (T + 1)p_2Y_{21} = 0$, $Y_{ik} = R_i$, $i = 1, 2$ and $R = p_1R_1 + (T + 1)p_2R_2$) $= (x_1 - R_1k)p_{1t} - p_2(x_{21}p_{1t} + x_{2k}k_t + x_{2t})T$, observing $p_1x_{11} + p_2x_{21} = -x_1 + R_1k$, $p_1x_{1k} + p_2x_{2k} = R$ and $p_1x_{1t} + p_2x_{2t} = 0$.

## APPENDIX IV

1 Let

$\alpha = |A|(X_{11}p_{1T} + X_{1k}k_T + X_{1T}) = X_{11}x_{Wk}R_2p_2 + X_{1k}\{-x_{W1}R_2p_2 + x_{WT}(R_1 - (t + 1)r_1)\} - x_{WK}(R_1 - (t + 1)r_1)X_{1T}$ (from equations (4), (6) and (7)) $= (X_{11}x_{1k} - X_{1k}x_{11})R_2p_2 + X_{1k}x_{1T} - x_{1k}X_{1T})(R_1 - (t + 1)r_1)$ (A-16)

$= -X_{1k}R_2p_2(t + 1)t_{11} / (1 - t^*) + \{x_{1k}R_2p_2 / (T + 1) + x_{1k}(R_1 - (t + 1)r_1)p_1 / (T + 1)^2\}T_{11} / (1 - T^*) + \{X_{1k}R_2p_2(x_1 - R_1k) + X_{1k}R_2p_2k(R_1 - (t + 1)r_1)\}h_{1n} / (1 - t^*) + \{x_{1k}R_2p_2(x_1 - R_1k) + x_{1k}(R_1 - (t + 1)r_1)R_2p_2k\}H_{1N} / (1 - T^*)$ (from (A-4), (A-8), (A-12) and (A-14)) $= -X_{1k}R_2p_2(t + 1)t_{11} / (1 - t^*) + x_{1k}(r_2p_2 / (T + 1)^2)T_{11} / (1 - T^*) + X_{1k}R_2p_2(x_1 - (t + 1)r_1k)h_{1n} / (1 - t^*) + x_{1k}R_2p_2(x_1 - (t + 1)r_1k)H_{1N} / (1 - T^*)$ (from $R = p_1R_1 + (T + 1)p_2R_2 = r = (t + 1)p_1r_1 + p_2r_2$). Hence $\alpha > 0$ since $X_{1k}$, $x_{1k}$ and $R_2 < 0$, and $r_2 > 0$.

2 Let $\beta = |A|(x_{21}p_{1t} + x_{2k}k_t + x_{2t}) = x_{21}(-x_{Wk}r_1p_1) + x_{2k}\{x_{W1}r_1p_1 + x_{Wt}(R - (t + 1)r_1)\} - x_{2t}x_{Wk}(R_1 - (t + 1)r_1)$ (from equations (3), (5) and (7)) $= \{(R_1k - x_1 - p_1x_{11}) / p_2\}(-x_{Wk}r_1p_1) + x_{2k}\{x_{W1}r_1p_1 + x_{1t}(R_1 - (t + 1)r_1)\} + (p_1 / p_2)x_{1t}x_{Wk}(R_1 - (t + 1)r_1)$ (from (A-6) and $p_1x_{1t} + p_2x_{2t} = 0$) $= \{(p_1 / p_2)x_{Wk}r_1p_1(t + 1) + x_{2k}r_1p_1(t + 1) + x_{2k}(R_1 - (t + 1)r_1)p_1 + (p_1 / p_2)x_{Wk}(R_1 - (t + 1)r_1)p_1\}t_{11} / (1 - t^*) + x_{2k}r_1p_1(T_{11} / (T + 1)) / (1 - T^*) + \{-(p_1 / p_2)x_{Wk}r_1p_1 - x_{2k}r_1p_1\}(x_1 - R_1k)h_{1n} / (1 - t^*) + x_{2k}r_1p_1(x_1 - R_1k)H_{1N} / (1 - T^*) - (R_1k - x_1)x_{Wk}r_1p_1 / p_2$ (from (A-4), (A-7) and (A-12)) $= \{x_{2k}R_1p_1 + (p_1 / p_2)x_{Wk}R_1p_1\}t_{11} / (1 - t^*) + x_{2k}r_1p_1(T_{11} / (T + 1)) / (1 - T^*) - r_1p_1((p_1 / p_2)x_{Wk} + x_{2k})(x_1 - R_1k)h_{1n} / (1 - t^*) + x_{2k}r_1p_1(x_1 - R_1k)H_{1N} / (1 - T^*) - (R_1k - x_1)x_{Wk}r_1p_1 / p_2 = R_1p_1(R / p_2 + p_1X_{1k} / p_2)t_{11} / (1 - t^*) + x_{2k}r_1p_1(T_{11} / (T + 1)) / (1 - T^*) - r_1p_1(R / p_2 + p_1X_{1k} / p_2)(x_1 - R_1k)h_{1n} / (1 - t^*) + x_{2k}r_1p_1(x_1 - R_1k)H_{1N} / (1 - T^*) + (x_1 - R_1k)x_{Wk}r_1p_1 / p_2$ (from $p_1x_{1k} + p_2x_{2k} = R$). First two terms are positive, observing $R / p_2 + p_1X_{1k} / p_2 = (R + p_1X_{1k}) / p_2 = -X_{2k} = R_2 / (1 - T^*) < 0$ and $x_{2k} = R / p_2 - p_1x_{1k} / p_2 > 0$. Furthermore, from $x_{Wk} < 0$,

we see that $\beta = |A|\tilde{x}_{2t} > 0$ if $s = ((R + p_1X_{1k}) / p_2)h_{1n} / (1 - t^*) - x_{2k}H_{1N} / (1 - T^*) - x_{Wk} / p_2 > 0$.

Here notice that if $m_1 \geq M_1$, then $s = ((R + p_1X_{1k}) / p_2)h_{1n} / (1 - t^*) - x_{2k}H_{1N} / (1 - T^*) - x_{Wk} / p_2 = \{(R + p_1X_{1k} / p_2) - p_1x_{Wk} / p_2\}h_{1n} / (1 - t^*) - x_{2k}\, H_{1N} / (1 - T^*) - (1 - m_1)x_{Wk} / p_2 > 0$ because $(R + p_1X_{1k}) / p_2 - p_1x_{Wk} / p_2 - x_{2k} = (R - p_1x_{1k} - p_2x_{2k}) / p_2 = 0$ (i.e. the coefficients of $h_{1n} / (1 - t^*)$ and of $H_{1N} / (1 - T^*)$ are respectively $x_{2k}$ and $-x_{2k}$), and $x_{Wk} < 0$ and $x_{2k} > 0$.

## APPENDIX V

**Home country's specialization with $k \lesseqgtr 0$.** From (A-2) and (A-9), noting $y_1 = 0$, we observe $x_{1k} = n_k = 0$. Note also that (A-1) through (A-15) remain true with $r_1 = 0$. Furthermore from equations (3-1) and (5-1), it follows that

1 $w = (X_{11}p_{1t} + X_{1k}k_t)|A| = X_{11}x_{Wt}r_k + X_{1k}x_{Wt}R_1 = x_{Wt}\,(X_{11}r_k + X_{1k}R_1)$. (A-17)

Noting $x_{Wt} = x_{1t} = s_{11}p_1 / (1 - t^*) < 0$ from (A-7), $r_k > 0$, $R_1 > 0$, $X_{1k} < 0$ and $X_{11} = T_{11} / (T + 1) + (x_1 - R_1k)M_1 / p_1$ ((A-12)), we observe

$X_{11}r_k + X_{1k}R_1 < 0$, and hence $w > 0$ if $x_1 - R_1k(>0)$ is small.

2 $z = (x_{21}p_{1T} + x_{2k}k_T + x_{2T})|A| = \{(R_1k - x_1 - p_1x_{11}) / p_2\}(x_{WT}r_k + R_2p_2x_{Wk}) + (R / p_2)\,(-x_{W1}R_2p_2 + x_{WT}R_1) + R_2km_2(-x_{W1}r_k - x_{Wk}R_1)$ from equations (4-1), (6-1), (7-1), $x_{21} = (R_1k - x_1 - p_1x_{11}) / p_2$, $x_{2k} = R / p_2$, (from $p_1x_{1k} + p_2x_{2k} = R$ with $x_{1k} = 0$) and $x_{2T} = (R_2p_2k - p_1x_{1T}) / p_2 = R_2km_2$ (from $p_1x_{1T} + p_2x_{2T} = R_2p_2k$, and equation (A-8)). Hence we observe

$$z = r_k\, \{(R_1k - x_1 - p_1x_{11})x_{WT} / p_2 - x_{W1}R_2km_2\} + (R / p_2)\,(-x_{W1}R_2p_2 + x_{WT}R_1) - R_2km_2x_{Wk}R_1 + (R_1k - x_1 - p_1x_{11})R_2x_{Wk}. \qquad \text{(A-18)}$$

The sign of the inside of the curly bracket is shown to be positive if $x_1 - R_1k(>0)$ and $k(\lesseqgtr 0)$ are both small, observing that

$$p_2x_{21} = R_1k - x_1 - p_1x_{11} = -p_1t_{11}(t + 1) / (1 - t^*) - m_2\,(x_1 - R_1k) \qquad \text{(A-19)}$$

and

$$x_{WT} = -p_1T_{11} / (T + 1)^2 + R_2p_2k(m_1 - M_1) / p_1 \qquad \text{(A-20)}$$

can be positive.

The sum of the second, third and fourth terms equals $x_{21}x_{Wk}R_2p_2 + x_{2k}\,\{-x_{W1}R_2p_2 + x_{WT}\,(R_1 - (t + 1)r_1\} - x_{2T}x_{Wk}(R_1 - (t + 1)r_1)$ in

Appendix II with $r_1 = x_{1k} = 0$. This is shown to be positive if $x_1$ (>0) is small. Hence $z>0$ follows.

3 $\alpha = |A|(X_{11}p_{1T} + X_{1k}k_T + X_{1T}) = X_{11}(x_{WT}r_k + R_2p_2x_{Wk}) + X_{1k}(-x_{W1}R_2p_2 + x_{WT}R_1) + X_{1T}(-x_{W1}r_k - x_{Wk}R_1)$ (from equations (4-1), (6-1) and (7-1)) $= r_k(X_{11}x_{WT} - X_{1T}x_{W1}) + \{X_{11}R_2p_2x_{Wk} + X_{1k}(-x_{W1}R_2p_2 + x_{WT}R_1) - X_{1T}x_{Wk}R_1\}.)$ (A-21)

The inside of the curly bracket equals $X_{11}x_{Wk}R_2p_2 + X_{1k}\{-x_{W1}R_2p_2 + x_{WT}(R_1 - (t+1)r_1)\} - x_{Wk}(R_1 - (t+1)r_1)X_{1T}$ with $r_1 = 0$. This is known to be positive in Appendix IV.

Furthermore, observing $x_{1T} < 0$, $X_{1T} > 0$ and $x_{11} < 0$, we see that

$d = X_{11}x_{WT} - x_{1T}x_{W1} = X_{11}x_{1T} - X_{1T}x_{11} > 0$ if $X_{11} < 0$ (i.e. $x_1 - R_1k(>0)$)

is small, or

$d = \{T_{11} / (T+1) + (x_1 - R_1k)M_1 / p_1\}R_2p_2km_1 / p_1 + \{p_1T_{11} / (T+1)^2(1 - T^*) + R_2p_2kM_1 / p_1\}\{t_{11}(t+1)(1 - t^*) - (x_1 - R_1k)m_1 / p_1\} > 0$ (from (A-4), (A-8), (A-12) and (A-14)) if $k(\lesssim 0)$

is small.

Hence $\alpha > 0$ follows.

4 $\beta = |A|(x_{21}p_{1t} + x_{2k}k_t + x_{2t}) = x_{21}x_{Wt}r_k + x_{2k}x_{Wt}R_1 + x_{2t}(-x_{W1}r_k - x_{Wk}R_1)$ (from equations (3-1), (5-1) and (7-1)) $= (x_{21}x_{Wt} - x_{2t}x_{W1})r_k + x_{2k}x_{Wt}R_1 - x_{2t}x_{Wk}R_1$. (A-22)

The sum of the second and third terms equals $(x_{2k}x_{Wt} - x_{2t}x_{Wk})R_1$. Here $x_{2k}x_{Wt} - x_{2t}x_{Wk} = (R / p_2)x_{1t} + (p_1x_{1t} / p_2)X_{1k} = (x_{1t} / p_2)(R + p_1X_{1k}) = (x_{1t} / p_2)(1 + TM_2)R_2p_2 = (1 + TM_2)x_{1t}R_2 > 0$ from (A-7), $x_{2k} = R / p_2$, $p_1x_{1t} + p_2x_{2t} = 0$, $x_{1k} = 0$, (A-13) and $R = p_1R_1 + (T+1)p_2R_2$. Next we observe that $x_{21}x_{Wt} - x_{2t}x_{W1} = x_{21}x_{1t} + p_1x_{1t}x_{w1} / p_2 = (p_2x_{21} + p_1x_{W1})x_{1t} / p_2 = (R_1k - x_1 - p_1x_{11} + p_1x_{11} + p_1X_{11})x_{1t} / p_2 = (R_1k - x_1 + p_1X_{11})x_{1t} / p_2 > 0$ since $R_1k - x_1 + p_1X_{11} = p_1T_{11} / (T+1)(1 - T^*) - m_2(x_1 - R_1k) < 0$ from (A-12). Hence $\beta > 0$ follows.

## APPENDIX VI

First we observe that (A-1) through (A-15) except (A-9) and (A-13) remain true with $R_2 = 0$. Furthermore, noting $R = R(p_1, k)$ and $Y_2 = 0$, we obtain

$N_k = Tp_2X_{2k} - R_kk$, $X_{2k} = H_{2N}H_k$, $X_{1k} = H_{1N}N_k - Y_{1k}$, $R_1 = R / p_1 = Y_{1k} > 0$

where $Y_{1k}$ is the marginal product of capital in the foreign country.

From these it follows that

$$X_{1k} = -R_1 - M_1 R_k k / p_1. \qquad \text{(A-13')}$$

Similarly for the home country noting $y_1 = 0$, we observe $n_k = tp_1 x_{1k} + R_k k$, $x_{1k} = b_{1n} n_k$, and hence

$$x_{1k} = R_k k m_1 / p_1 < 0. \qquad \text{(A-9')}$$

From (A-13′) and (A-9′), we observe

$$x_{Wk} = -R_1 + R_k k(m_1 - M_1) / p_1 < 0. \qquad \text{(A-23')}$$

$x_{1T} = 0$ from (A-8) with $R_2 = 0$, and hence $x_{WT} = X_{1T} = -p_1 T_{11}/(T + 1)^2 (1 - T^*) > 0$ from (A-14) with $R_2 = 0$.

1 $w = (X_{11} p_{1t} + X_{1k} k_t)|A| = X_{11}\{-x_{Wt}(R_k - r_k)\} + X_{1k} x_{Wt} R_1 = x_{Wt}\{-X_{11}(R_k - r_k) + X_{1k} R_1\}$. Here $v = -X_{11}(R_k - r_k) + X_{1k} R_1 = -\{T_{11} / (T + 1) + (x_1 - R_1 k) H_{1N}\}(R_k - r_k) / (1 - T^*) + (-R_1 - M_1 R_k k / p_1) R_1$ (from (A-12) and (A-13′)). Hence we obtain that if $x_1 - R_1 k (> 0)$ and $k(>0)$ are both small, then $v < 0$ and hence $w > 0$.

2 $z = (x_{21} p_{1T} + x_{2k} k_T + x_{2T})|A| = -x_{21} x_{WT}(R_k - r_k) + x_{2k} x_{WT} R_1$ (from equations (4-2), (6-2) and $x_{1T} = x_{2T} = 0$) $= x_{WT} \{-x_{21}(R_k - r_k) + x_{2k} R_1\}$. Here we observe that from (A-19), $x_{21} > 0$ if $x_1 - R_1 k(> 0)$ is small, and $x_{2k} = (R_k k + R - p_1 x_{1k}) / p_2 = (m_2 R_k k + R) / p_1 > 0$ if $k(> 0)$ is small.

Hence in short, if both $x_1 - R_1 k(> 0)$ and $k(> 0)$are small, then $z > 0$.

3 $\alpha = (X_{11} p_{1T} + X_{1k} k_T + X_{1T})|A| = X_{11}\{-x_{WT}(R_k - r_k)\} + X_{1k} x_{WT} R_1 + X_{1T}\{x_{W1}(R_k - r_k) - R_1 x_{Wk}\}$ (from equations (4-2), (6-2) and (7-2)) $= (R_k - r_k)(-X_{11} x_{WT} + X_{1T} x_{Wk}) + R_1(X_{1k} x_{WT} - X_{1T} x_{Wk})$. Note that

$-X_{11} x_{WT} + X_{1T} x_{Wk} = -X_{11} x_{1T} + X_{1T} x_{11} = X_{1T} x_{11} < 0$, and that

$- X_{1k} x_{WT} - X_{1T} x_{Wk} = X_{1k} X_{1T} - X_{1T} x_{Wk} = -X_{1T} x_{Wk} > 0$. Hence $\alpha > 0$ follows always.

4 $\beta = (x_{21} p_{1t} + x_{2k} k_t + x_{2t})|A| = x_{21} \{-x_{Wt}(R_k - r_k)\} + x_{2k} x_{Wt} R_1 + x_{2t} \{x_{W1}(R_k - r_k) - R_1 x_{Wk}\}$ (from equations (3-2), (5-2) and (7-2)) $= (R_k - r_k)(-x_{21} x_{Wt} + x_{2t} x_{W1}) + R_1(x_{2k} x_{Wt} - x_{2t} x_{Wk})$. Note that

$-x_{21} x_{Wt} + x_{2t} x_{W1} = -x_{21} x_{1t} - x_{1t} x_{W1} p_1 / p_2 = -x_{1t}(x_{21} + x_{W1} p_1 / p_2)$. Here we observe that

$x_{21} + x_{W1} p_1 / p_2 = (p_2 x_{21} + p_1 x_{11} + p_1 X_{11}) / p_2 = (R_1 k - x_1 + p_1 X_{11}) / p_2 < 0$, and that

$x_{2k} x_{Wt} - x_{2t} x_{Wk} = x_{1t} (x_{2k} + x_{Wk} p_1 / p_2)$, and

$x_{2k} + x_{Wk} p_1 / p_2 = (p_2 x_{2k} + p_1 x_{1k} + p_1 x_{1k}) / p_2 = (R + R_k k - p_1 R_1 - M_1 R_k k) / p_2 = M_2 R_k k / p_2 < 0$. Hence $\beta > 0$ follows always.

## Notes

1 In fact their model is partial in the sense that international prices of goods are assumed to be fixed because the equilibrium in the world market is not explicitly taken into consideration.

2 Hereafter a subscript indicates the partial derivative with respect to its variable.

3 $n = \pi + tp_1x_1 + Rk$, $\pi = g((t+1)p_1, p_2, k)$, $x_i = h_i((t+1)p_1, p_2, n) - y_i$, $\partial g / \partial P_i = y_i$, $i = 1, 2$, $(P_1 = (t+1)p_1, P_2 = p_2)$ and $R = R(p_1, (T+1)p_2)$ define $n$, $x_i$ and $c_i$, $i = 1, 2$ to be functions of $p_1, p_2, t, T$ and $k$. The same is true for $N$, $X_i$ and $C_i$, $i = 1, 2$.

4 If $x_1 - R_1k \leq 0$ were allowed, then $\tilde{X}_{1t} > 0$ and hence $\hat{t} \leq 0$ would result as is seen from point 3 of Appendix II.

5 Under A.2 and 3, the generalized Lange–Lerner condition $x_{W1} < 0$ holds irrespective of the patterns of specialization of each country from (A-4) and (A-12), and under A.1 and 3, $x_{Wk} < 0$ for specialization of both countries holds from (A-23). (For the other types of specializations $x_{Wk} < 0$ holds without A.3 as is seen from (A-9) and (A-13).) Furthermore, under A.1, 2 and 3 the following dynamic adjustment system $\dot{p} = x_W$, $\dot{k} = R - r$, where $\dot{p}$ and $\dot{k}$ are time rates of change of $p$ and $k$ respectively, satisfies the Routh–Hurwitz condition for stability; $|A| > 0$ and $x_{W1} + R_k - r_k < 0$ because $x_{W1} < 0$, $R_1 - (t+1)r_1 > 0$ and $x_{Wk} < 0$ hold. Hence A.1, 2 and 3 seem reasonable also from these considerations. Here for such an adjustment system, see Das and Lee (1979), and the Routh–Hurwitz condition is found in Gantmacher (1960).

6 Figure 3.3 is essentially the same as the one obtained by Dixit (1987) for the case of no capital mobility.

7 $|A|\{(x_1 - R_1k)p_{1T} - R_2p_2k\} = r_k\,\{(x_1 - R_1k)x_{WT} + R_2p_2kx_{W1}\} + R_2p_2x_{Wk}x_1$ (from equations (7–1) and (4–1)). Here observing that $x_{WT} > 0$ for small $k \geq 0$ and any $k < 0$ from (A-20), and that $x_{W1} < 0$ for any $k$ from (A-4) and (A-12), the sign of the inside of the curly bracket is seen to be positive for small $k \geq 0$ and small $k < 0$. Furthermore, $x_{Wk} = X_{1k} < 0$ from (A-13). The above is shown to be positive for small $k \geq 0$ and small $k < 0$.

8 This is seen from $x_{WT} > 0$ for small $k \geq 0$ and for any $k < 0$, and $x_{Wk} = X_{1k} < 0$ as is shown in 7 above.

9 Noting $p_1x_{1k} + p_2x_{2k} = R + R_kk$ and $p_1X_{1k} + p_2X_{2k} = -R - R_kk$ for this case, these four equations are derived by the same methods as the case of complete diversification of both countries. (See Appendices II and III.)

10 (A-12) is obtained from $X_{21} = \partial X_2 / \partial p_1 = H_{21} + H_{2N}N_1 - Y_{21} = S_{21} - C_1H_{2N} + H_{2N}N_1 - Y_{21} = T_{21} + (N_1 - C_1)H_{2N}$, and $N_1 = \partial N / \partial p_1 = Y_1 + Tp_2X_{21} - R_1k$ where $Y_{21} = \partial Y_2 / \partial p_1$, by observing $X_{21} = \{T_{21} + (x_1 - R_1k)H_{2N}\} / (1 - T^*)$ and $X_{11} = (x_1 - R_1k - p_2X_{21}) / p_1$ which is obtained by partially differentiating (A-11) with respect to $p_1$ and from $X_1 = -x_1$. Here $1 = p_1H_{1N} + (T+1)p_2H_{2N}$ and $p_2T_{21} = -p_1T_{11} / (T+1)$ are also used. Similarly (A-13) is obtained from $X_{ik} = H_{iN}N_k - Y_{ik}$, $p_1X_{1k} + p_2X_{2k} = -R$ and $N_k = R + Tp_2X_{2k} - R = Tp_2X_{2k}$. $X_{1T}$ is obtained from $X_{2T} = H_{22}p_2 + H_{2N}N_T - Y_{22}P_2 = T_{22}p_2 - p_2C_2H_{2N} + H_{2N}N_T$, $N_T = Y_2p_2 + Tp_2X_{2T} + p_2X_2 - R_2p_2k$, by observing $X_{2T} = (T_{22}p_2 - H_{2N}R_2p_2k) / (1 - T^*)$ and $X_{1T} = (-R_2p_2k - p_2X_{2T}) / p_1$.

11 $X_{2k} = (-R - p_1X_{1k}) / p_2 = -R_2 / (1 - T^*) > 0$, from (A-13) and $p_1H_{1N} + p_2H_{2N} = 1 - T^*$, and $x_{2k} = (R - p_1x_{1k}) / p_2 = R / p_2 - r_1p_1 / (1 - t^*) > 0$ from (A-9).

## Bibliography

Batra, R.N. and Casas, F.R. (1976) 'A Synthesis of the Heckscher–Ohlin and the Neo-Classical Model of International Trade', *Journal of International Economics* 6: 21–38.

Chan, K.S. (1988) 'Trade Negotiations in a Nash Bargaining Model', *Journal of International Economics* 25: 353–63.

Cheng, L.K. and Wong, K. (1990) 'On the Strategic Choice between Capital and Labor Mobility', *Journal of International Economics* 28: 291–314.

Das, S.P. and Lee, S.D. (1979) 'On the Theory of International Trade with Capital Mobility', *International Economic Review* 20: 119–32.

Dixit, A. (1987) 'Strategic Aspects of Trade Policy', in T.R. Bewley (ed.) *Advances in Economic Theory – Fifth World Congress: Econometric Society Monographs No. 12*, ch. 9, pp. 329–62. Cambridge, England: Cambridge University Press.

Gantmacher, F.R. (1960) *The Theory of Matrices*, vol. II, New York: Chelsea Pub. Co.

Gorman, W.M. (1958) 'Tariffs, Retaliation, and the Elasticity of Demand for Imports', *Review of Economic Studies* 33: 133–62.

Hamada, K. (1966) 'Strategic Aspects of Taxation on Foreign Investment Income', *Quarterly Journal of Economics* 80: 361–75.

Hamilton, B. and Whalley, J. (1983) 'Optimal Tariff Calculations in Alternative Trade Models and Some Possible Implications for Current World Trading Arrangements', *Journal of International Economics* 15: 323–48.

Harsanyi, J.C. (1965) 'Game Theory and the Analysis of International Conflicts', *Australian Journal of Politics and History* 11: 293–304.

Johnson, H.G. (1953) 'Optimum Tariffs and Retaliation', *Review of Economic Studies* 21: 142–53.

Kaldor, N.A. (1940) 'A Note on Tariffs and the Terms of Trade', *Economica, N.S.* 7: 377–80.

Kuga, K. (1973) 'Tariff Retaliation and Policy Equilibrium', *Journal of International Economics* 3: 351–66.

McMillan, J. (1986) *Game theory in International Economics*. Chur, Switzerland: Harwood Academic Publishers.

Markusen, J.R. (1981) 'The Distribution of Gains from Bilateral Tariff Reductions', *Journal of International Economics* 11: 553–72.

Mayer, W. (1981) 'Theoretical Considerations on Negotiated Tariff Adjustments', *Oxford Economic Papers* 33: 135–53.

Miyagiwa, K.F. and Young, L. (1986) 'International Capital Mobility and Commerical Policy in an Economic Region', *Journal of International Economics* 20: 329–41.

Otani, Y. (1980) 'Strategic Equilibrium of Tariffs and General Equilibrium', *Econometrica* 48: 643–62.

Ramaswami, V.K. (1968) 'International Factor Movement and the National Advantage', *Economica* 35: 309–10.

Riezman, R. (1982) 'Tariff Retaliation from a Strategic Viewpoint', *Southern Economic Journal* 48: 583–93.

Robinson, J. (1950) 'Beggar-My-Neighbour Remedies for Unemployment', in *Readings in the Theory of International Trade*. Homewood, Ill: Irwin.

Scitovsky, T.A. (1941) 'A Reconsideration of the Theory of Tariffs', *Review of Economic Studies* 9: 89–110.

Turunen-Red, A.H. and Woodland, A.D. (1991) 'Strict Pareto-Improving Multilateral Reforms of Tariffs', *Econometrica* 59: 1127–52.

Uekawa, Y. (1972) 'On the Existence of Incomplete Specialization in International Trade with Capital Mobility', *Journal of International Economics* 2: 1–23.

Weymark, J.A. (1980) 'Welfare Optimal Tariff Revenues and Maximum Tariff Revenues', *Canadian Journal of Economics* 13: 615–31.

# 4

# THE IMPORTANCE OF PRICE NORMALIZATION FOR MODELS OF INTERNATIONAL TRADE UNDER IMPERFECT COMPETITION

*Kenneth M. Kletzer and T.N. Srinivasan*

## Introduction

The application of models of imperfectly competitive industries from the industrial organization literature to international trade theory and the analysis of commercial policy gained widespread attention in the late 1970s and early 1980s. Models of imperfectly competitive industries continue to serve as workhorses of international trade analysis, most notably in the study of the relationship between international trade and endogenous economic growth with induced innovation by Grossman and Helpman (1991) and others. From the viewpoint of positive economics, this literature provided analytical models of intra-industry international trade based on increasing returns to scale and imperfectly competitive producer behavior. On the normative side, several papers sought to demonstrate that imperfect competition in international markets provided a rationale for national governments to intervene to increase the profits of national firms participating in international oligopolies. A growing literature applies models of imperfectly competitive world markets to the quantitative analysis of trade policy changes in computable general equilibrium versions.

For some time, general equilibrium theorists have recognized that major difficulties are encountered by introducing oligopoly and monopolistic competition into general equilibrium analysis. Although these problems are well-known among theoreticians, their implications for the theoretical and quantitative analysis of international trade policies under imperfect competition has not been acknowledged in the trade literature. The purpose of this chapter is to point out the potential importance of these pitfalls for the analysis of trade with imperfect competition.

The difficulties that arise for the theory of monopolistic competition and oligopoly in general equilibrium originate in the optimization problem for non-price-taking firms. When a monopolistic or oligopolistic firm takes account of the income effect generated by its profit on the demand for its output, convexity can fail for both the choice set and the best response for the profit-maximizing firm, and existence of equilibrium cannot be proved in general. The possibility of non-existence of an equilibrium in which some firms behave in Cournot fashion and other agents act as price-takers (defined as a Cournot–Walras equilibrium by Gabszewicz and Vial (1972)) has been shown in examples by Dierker and Grodal (1986) and proven to be a generic property by Bohm (1990).

It is also known that the set of equilibria is sensitive to the manner in which relative prices are normalized. That is, the equilibrium allocation and vector of relative prices change with the price normalization, and equilibrium may fail to exist for some choices of normalization and not for others. This is a consequence of the assumption that firms maximize profits and take account of the effect their decisions have on market prices. Typical partial equilibrium models of oligopoly set the nominal wage equal to one, implicitly assuming that labor serves as the numéraire. The firm then maximizes the purchasing power of profits in units of labor. If the firm's product is chosen as numéraire, then the oligopolist would maximize the purchasing power of profits in terms of that good. Changing the numéraire has no effect on Walrasian equilibria since the objective function for profit-maximizing firms is unaffected if all prices are taken as given. Changing price normalization typically leads price-setting firms to choose different production plans.

Two types of models have gained popularity in the literature on international trade under imperfect competition. The first consists of general equilibrium versions of the Chamberlin model of monopolistic competition for a large group of firms with free entry. Krugman (1979, 1980, 1981), Dixit and Norman (1980), Ethier (1979) and several others adopt the specific general equilibrium model of Chamberlinian monopolistic competition due to Dixit and Stiglitz (1977), while Helpman (1981) and Lancaster (1980) use a variant based on Lancaster's model of demand for product characteristics. The second set of models is based on the partial equilibrium analysis of oligopoly. This approach is well-represented by the simple duopoly model presented in the critical analysis of the literature by Eaton and Grossman (1986).

We show how the choice of price normalization affects equilibrium relative prices and allocations in a simple general equilibrium model in the spirit of the Dixit–Stiglitz and Eaton–Grossman models. Production technologies display constant returns to scale in one case and increasing returns to scale in the other. Firms behave as Cournot oligopolists while households act as price-takers. We argue that the dependence of equilibria on the choice of a numéraire is an important problem for theoretical models of international trade under imperfect competition and their empirical implementation.

Once it is established that equilibria are sensitive to the specification of the numéraire, it is a straightforward conclusion that estimates of the effects on welfare and resource allocation of changes in indirect or direct tax rates, tariff rates or quantitative restraints on international or national trade from computable general equilibrium models incorporating imperfect competition should be treated with suspicion. Since imperfect competition is included in these models, policy reforms take place in a second-best world. Trade liberalization or the reduction of a distortionary tax has an ambiguous effect on welfare so that simulation using a computable model based on estimated equations is a useful tool for assessing the impact of trade and fiscal reforms under such market structures.[1] The analyses of trade reforms using computable general equilibrium with monopolistically competitive or oligopolistic industries by Harris (1984a, b), Cox and Harris (1985), de Melo and Roland-Holst (1990a, b) and Devarajan and Rodrick (1989a, b), among others, are all subject to the criticism that the results depend upon the arbitrary choice of price normalization made.[2] Changing the numéraire in a computable general equilibrium version can affect the size and even sign of the effects of policy changes on welfare and the allocation of factors across industries.

## The importance of numéraire choice for equilibrium

Consider an economy in which there are at least two price-setting firms. There are $n$ goods and a single price-taking representative household. The production function for each produced good is continuously differentiable and is given by $f_j(x_1, x_2, \ldots, x_n)$. The vector of absolute (not normalized) prices is denoted by $(p_1, p_2, \ldots, p_n)$.The profit for a price-setting firm producing good $j$ in absolute prices is given by

$$\Pi_j = p_j f_j(x_1, \ldots, x_n) - \sum_{i=1}^{n} p_i x_i.$$

If good 1 is chosen as the numéraire, the firm's profit function is given by

$$\pi_j = \frac{p_j}{p_1} f_j(x_1, \ldots, x_n) - \sum_{i=1}^{n} \frac{p_i}{p_1} x_i$$

Alternatively, if good $n$ is taken to be the numéraire, the firm's profit function becomes

$$\hat{\pi}_j = \frac{p_j}{p_n} f_j(x_1, \ldots, x_n) - \sum_{i=1}^{n} \frac{p_i}{p_n} x_i,$$

so that

$$\hat{\pi}_j = \frac{p_1}{p_n} \pi_j.$$

The first-order conditions for profit maximization by firm $j$ under these two choices of numéraire are related by the equation

$$\frac{\partial \hat{\pi}_j}{\partial x_j} = \frac{p_1}{p_n} \frac{\partial \pi_j}{\partial x_j} + \pi_j \frac{\partial (p_1/p_n)}{\partial x_j}, \text{ for each } j = 1, \ldots, n,$$

where $\frac{\partial (p_1/p_n)}{\partial x_j}$ is firm $j$'s conjecture of the effect of an increase in firm $j$'s output on the relative price, $p_1/p_n$.

Note that if $\pi_j = \hat{\pi}_j = 0$, then $\frac{\partial \hat{\pi}_j}{\partial x_j} = \frac{p_1}{p_n} \frac{\partial \pi_j}{\partial x_j}$. This implies that the necessary conditions for profit maximization by firm $j$ are identical under these two choices of relative price normalization only if the relative price, $p_1/p_n$, is taken as given by the firm, or the profit expressed in terms of either numéraire is zero in *the particular equilibrium.*

In general, the objective function and supply correspondence for a profit-maximizing oligopolist depend upon the normalization chosen for relative prices. Whenever the profit of some non-price-taking firm is not zero in equilibrium, changing the numéraire changes equilibrium relative prices and allocations. If the profits of all firms are zero in a particular equilibrium for one choice of normalization for relative prices, then that equilibrium will survive a change in the method of normalizing prices.

Below we assume that the firm recognizes the income effect of its own profit on demand, and we restrict our attention to Cournot conjectures for simplicity. In the literature on monopolistic competition and oligopoly in general equilibrium, this is called the objective demand approach (see Hart (1985)). Under Cournot conjectures, each firm includes the effect of its output level on profit income in its calculation of the effect of its decision on demand.

## Some examples

A simple example economy is used to demonstrate the importance of numéraire choice for models of international trade and policy under monopolistic competition and oligopoly. This model is a simple general equilibrium version of that used by Eaton and Grossman (1986) to show the dependence of optimal national policies on the conjectures assumed to be held by firms. It also is recognizably close to the Dixit–Stiglitz model for a small group of firms.

There are three commodities and two firms. There is a single representative household. For the sake of simplicity, we neither identify countries nor discuss international trade explicitly. It is straightforward to envision that one firm operates in each country and that households have identical tastes across the border.

The endowment of the representative household consists of a supply of only one commodity, leisure, denoted $z$. Production of each of the other two goods, $x$ and $y$, requires an input of labor. The amount of labor needed to produce one unit of good $x$ is $\alpha_1 + \beta_1 \cdot x$, and the labor requirement per unit of good $y$ is $\alpha_2 + \beta_2 \cdot y$. The household has an initial endowment of leisure equal to unity. The preferences for the household display constant elasticity of substitution and are represented by the utility function:

$$U = x^\theta + y^\theta + z^\theta, \text{ for } 0 < \theta < 1.$$

The household behaves as a perfect competitor choosing how much of goods $x$ and $y$ to purchase and how much labor to supply. Each of the two firms behaves as a Cournot duopolist, taking into account how its production decision affects equilibrium prices under the assumption that the other firm's output is fixed. That is, the firm does not take the wage rate, as well as the price of its output, as given.

Maximization of utility subject to the household's budget yields the following first-order conditions:

$$\left(\frac{z}{x}\right)^{1-\theta} = \left(\frac{p_1}{w}\right) \tag{1}$$

$$\left(\frac{z}{y}\right)^{1-\theta} = \left(\frac{p_2}{w}\right) \tag{2}$$

$$w + \Pi_1 + \Pi_2 = p_1 \cdot x + p_2 \cdot y + w \cdot z, \tag{3}$$

where $p_1$, $p_2$ and $w$ are the absolute prices of goods $x$, $y$ and $z$, respectively. $\Pi_1$ and $\Pi_2$ are the profits in terms of absolute prices for firm 1 and firm 2, respectively.

If leisure is chosen as the numéraire, then the profits for the two firms are given by:

$$\pi_1 = \left(\frac{z}{x}\right)^{1-\theta} \cdot x - (\alpha_1 + \beta_1 x)$$

and

$$\pi_2 = \left(\frac{z}{y}\right)^{1-\theta} \cdot y - (\alpha_2 + \beta_2 y),$$

where

$$z = 1 - (\alpha_1 + \beta_1 x) - (\alpha_2 + \beta_2 y).$$

Note that the inverse demand function for good $x$ is given by

$$q_1(x, y) \equiv \frac{p_1}{w}(x, y) = \left[\frac{1 - (\alpha_1 + \beta_1 x) - (\alpha_2 + \beta_2 y)}{x}\right]^{1-\theta}.$$

The first-order conditions for profit maximization under the Cournot assumption subject to the equilibrium condition are

$$\frac{\partial \pi_1}{\partial x} = \theta q_1 - \beta_1(1 - \theta)q_1^{\theta/(\theta - 1)} - \beta_1 \leq 0 \tag{4}$$

and

$$\frac{\partial \pi_2}{\partial x} = \theta q_2 - \beta_2(1 - \theta)q_2^{\theta/(\theta - 1)} - \beta_2 \leq 0, \tag{5}$$

where $q_1 \equiv \frac{p_1}{w}$ and $q_2 \equiv \frac{p_2}{w}$ are the relative prices of goods $x$ and $y$ in terms of leisure, respectively.

If good $x$ is chosen as the numéraire, then the profit for each firm is given by:

$$\hat{\pi}_1 = x - \left(\frac{x}{z}\right)^{1-\theta} (\alpha_1 + \beta_1 x)$$

and

$$\hat{\pi}_2 = \left(\frac{x}{y}\right)^{1-\theta} y - \left(\frac{x}{z}\right)^{1-\theta} (\alpha_2 + \beta_2 y).$$

The first-order condition for an interior solution to firm 1's profit-maximization problem is

$$\frac{\partial \hat{\pi}_1}{\partial x} = 1 - \left[\frac{\alpha_1}{z} + \beta_1 q_1^{1/(\theta-1)}\right] q_1^{\theta/(1-\theta)}(1-\theta)\left[1 + \beta_1 q_1^{1/(\theta-1)}\right] - \beta_1 q_1^{-1} \leq 0. \tag{6}$$

The first-order condition for an interior solution for firm 2 is

$$\frac{\partial \hat{\pi}_2}{\partial x} = q_1^{-1}\left[\theta q_2 - \beta_2(1 - \theta)\left(\frac{\alpha_2}{z} + \beta_2 q_2^{1/(\theta-1)}\right) - \beta\right] \leq 0. \tag{7}$$

A Cournot-Walras equilibrium when leisure is the numéraire is found by solving inequalities 1, 2, 4, 5 and

$$z \leq 1 - (\alpha_1 + \beta_1 x) - (\alpha_2 + \beta_2 y). \tag{8}$$

When good $x$ is chosen to be the numéraire, then the general equilibrium relative prices and allocation solve inequalities 1, 2, 6, 7 and 8. Clearly, these two sets of necessary conditions differ in general. As noted by Dierker and Grodal (1986) and Hart (1985), Cournot–Walras equilibria may not exist for some price normalization rules.

We give the following numerical example to illustrate that the sets of equilibria can differ when neither is non-empty.

*Example 1*

Let $\alpha_1 = \alpha_2 = 0$ and $\beta_1 = \beta_2 = 1/3$, and let $\theta = 0.5$. When leisure is chosen to be the numéraire, there is a single equilibrium. This is

$$q_1 = q_2 = 1$$

and

$$x = y = z = 3/5 = 0.6$$

This allocation yields utility, $U = 3(3/5)^{0.5} \cong 2.3228$.

If good $x$ is chosen as the numéraire, then the solution to the first-order conditions that satisfies the second-order conditions for profit-maximization of the Cournot-duopolists is

$$q_1 = 0.6369, \quad q_2 = 0.8285,$$

$$x = 1.0684, \quad y = 0.6314, \quad \text{and} \quad z = 0.4334.$$

This allocation yields utility, $U = 2.4866$.

The unique Pareto optimum (the Walrasian equilibrium allocation) is by

$$x = y = 9/7, \quad \text{and} \quad z = 1/7.$$

This allocation gives the household utility, $U = 7^{0.5} \cong 2.6458$.

*Example 2*

As a second example, we allow fixed costs to be positive. Keeping the rest of the example the same, let $\alpha_1 = \alpha_2 = 0.2$. The solution for the unique Cournot–Walras equilibrium when leisure is

$$q_1 = q_2 = 1 \quad \text{and} \quad x = y = z = 9/25 = 0.36.$$

Utility for the household is equal to $U = 1.8$.

When good $x$ is chosen to be the numéraire, the equilibrium is given by

$$q_1 = 0.9050, \quad q_2 = 0.9779$$

$$x = 0.4173 \quad y = 0.3574, \quad \text{and} \quad z = 0.3418.$$

The equilibrium level of utility for the household and profits for each firm are given by $U = 1.8284$, $\hat{\pi}_1 = 0.3450$ and $\hat{\pi}_2 = 0.0336$. The unique Pareto optimal (and Walrasian equilibrium) allocation is $x = y = 27/35$, and $z = 3/35$, resulting in a level of utility, $U = 2.0494$.

In these examples, the free entry and exit of firms can be allowed by letting the utility function be given by

$$U = z^{\theta} + \sum_{i=1}^{n} x_i^{\theta},$$

as in Dixit and Stiglitz (1977), where $n$ is the equilibrium number of product types under free entry. Firms enter until the addition of one more firm results in negative equilibrium profits for that firm. In the second example, it is easily checked that entry by a third firm is not profitable. The addition of another Cournot oligopolist producing either a new product or one of goods $x$ or $y$ leads to an equilibrium in which at least one firm earns negative profit for both numéraire choices.

Applications of models of monopolistic competition to international trade assume that the profits of every firm are zero as a condition for equilibrium (see, for example, Krugman (1979, 1980 and 1981), Helpman (1981) and Helpman and Krugman (1985)). When the condition that every firm must realize zero profits in equilibrium is arbitrarily imposed, the particular price normalization rule chosen has no effect on any firm's decision problem so that the set of equilibrium relative prices and allocations are the same for all such rules. However, free entry is not the same as assuming that profits are zero for every active firm in equilibrium when technologies display increasing returns to scale. It is only true in exceptional cases that imposition of the zero profit condition along with the standard equilibrium conditions leads to an equilibrium with an integer number of firms in these models.

## Alternative objectives for the firm

In a Walrasian equilibrium, the supply correspondence for a profit-maximizing firm that takes relative prices as given does not depend upon the numéraire choice so that price normalization does not affect equilibrium relative prices and allocations. There is no difference between maximizing profit and maximizing the purchasing power of profits in terms of any commodity bundle. In Cournot–Walras equilibria the objective for the firm is to maximize profit in terms of the bundle of goods specified by the price normalization. When the firm recognizes its effect on prices, this objective varies with the numéraire.

As Marshall (1922) pointed out, profit maximization may not be the appropriate objective for imperfectly competitive firms, since owners care about what their profits can purchase, implying a tradeoff between monetary profit and the cost of the consumption bundle owners desire. When the firm can influence prices, it is natural to substitute utility maximization by the owners for profit maximization.

Suppose that there is a single owner for each of the two firms in our examples. Replacing profit maximization with utility maximization for this single shareholder eliminates the dependence of the firm's optimal production plan on price normalization. Suppose that the owner of firm $j$ has preferences satisfying standard properties and that these yield the indirect utility function $V_j(p_1, p_2, \ldots, p_n, w, w + \Pi_j)$. We assume that household $j$

owns all of firm $j$ and no shares in other firms for simplicity only. Since this indirect utility is homogenous of degree zero in prices, the optimal production plan is independent of the numéraire.

The large group Chamberlinian monopolistic competition model used by Krugman (1979, 1980, 1981), Helpman (1981) and others assumes that $p_j$ has no direct effect on $V_j$. Under this assumption, the owner's utility is maximized if the firm maximizes its income expressed in any price normalization. In this case, maximizing profit with leisure as the numéraire is the same as maximizing indirect utility for household $j$. However, maximizing the profit of firm $j$ for other choices of numéraire is not identical to maximizing its income. We do not need to worry about the profit maximization assumption in the monopolistic competition models offered in the international trade literature because they impose zero profits as an equilibrium condition and assume that utility is broad-based in the sense that the first-order effect of a rise in the price of any commodity on shareholder utilities is null.

Difficulties for modeling general equilibrium under imperfect competition are not easily solved by the substitution of shareholder utility for profit. Dierker and Grodal (1986) show that a Cournot–Walras equilibrium need not exist when there is a single shareholder with regular preferences over consumption bundles in an example economy in which there are two firms with strictly convex production sets. If there are many shareholders, each having different tastes, then the well-known problem of aggregating these preferences to derive an objective function for the firm in the absence of stockholder unanimity arises.

## Conclusion

The difficulties encountered by theorists for extending general equilibrium analysis to economies with monopolistic competition and oligopoly have been ignored in the literature on international trade under imperfect competition. Under the large group assumptions made in the applications of the Dixit–Stiglitz model of Chamberlinian monopolistic competition to international trade, these problems do not arise. When these are relaxed the assumption of profit maximization becomes problematic. Utility maximization for the owners does not provide a thoroughly adequate remedy.

Computable general equilibrium models of trade with imperfect competition are especially vulnerable to the critique that the results can be very sensitive to the arbitrary choice of price normalization. Our examples of how price normalization matters in a model representative of those used in the trade literature with oligopoly imply that the effects of policy changes on welfare and resource allocation are sensitive to the arbitrary choice of numéraire in these models. The computable general equilibrium versions proposed by Harris (1984a, b), Cox and Harris (1985), Burniaux and

Waelbroeck (1992), de Melo and Roland-Holst (1990a, b) and Devarajan and Rodrick (1989a, b) are all subject to the criticism that the estimated effects of trade reforms depend on the price normalization chosen by the authors with no guidance from economic theory.

## Notes

1 Ginsburgh (1990) shows the possibility that elimination of a consumption tax in a simple general equilibrium model with oligopoly can lead to an increase in utility for a representative household under one choice of numéraire and a decrease under another. He uses an input–output model with Leontief technology for two firms that violates the 'no free lunch' axiom, so that the technologies are specified with exogenous bounds on outputs.

2 Alternatively, Smith and Venables (1988, 1989) present computable partial equilibrium industry models with imperfect competition. These follow the spirit of oligopoly models in the trade theory literature, such as Eaton and Grossman (1986), in making an implicit assumption about the numéraire and an explicit one about firms not perceiving the income effect of their own profit on demand.

## Bibliography

Bohm, V. (1990) "General Equilibrium with Profit Maximizing Oligopolists," Discussion Paper No. 414/90, University of Mannheim, January.

Burniaux, J.-M. and Waelbroeck, J. (1992) "Preliminary Results of Two General Equilibrium Models with Imperfect Competition," *Journal of Policy Modelling* 14: 65–92.

Cox, D. and Harris, R. (1985) "Trade Liberalization and Industrial Organization: Some Estimates for Canada," *Journal of Political Economy* 93: 115–45.

de Melo, J. and Roland-Holst, D. (1990a) "Industrial Organization and Trade Liberalization: Evidence from Korea," Centre for Economic Policy Research Discussion Paper No. 399, May.

—— and —— (1990b) "Tariffs and Export Subsidies when Domestic Markets are Oligopolistic," The World Bank, manuscript, February.

Devarajan, S. and Rodrick, D. (1989a) "Pro-competitive Effects of Trade Reform: Results from a CGE Model of Cameroon," National Bureau of Economic Research Working Paper No. 3176, November.

—— and —— (1989b) "Trade Liberalization in Developing Countries: Do Imperfect Competition and Scale Economies Matter?," *American Economic Review Papers and Proceedings* 79: 283–87.

Dierker, H. and Grodal, B. (1986) "Nonexistence of Cournot–Walras Equilibrium in a General Equilibrium Model with Two Oligopolists," in W. Hildenbrand and A. Mas-Colell (eds) *Contributions to Mathematical Economics in Honor of Gerard Debreu*. Amsterdam: North-Holland: 167–85.

Dixit, A. and Norman, V. (1980) *Theory of International Trade*. Cambridge: Cambridge University Press.

Dixit, A. and Stiglitz, J.E. (1977) "Monopolistic Competition and Optimum Product Diversity," *American Economic Review* 67: 297–308.

Eaton, J. and Grossman, G. (1986) "Optimal Trade and Industrial Policy Under Oligopoly," *Quarterly Journal of Economics* 101: 383–406.

Ethier, W. (1979) "Internationally Decreasing Costs and World Trade," *Journal of International Economics* 9: 1–24.

Gabzsewicz, J.J. and Vial, J.-P. (1972) "Oligopoly 'a la Cournot' in General Equilibrium Analysis," *Journal of Economic Theory* 4: 381–400.

Ginsburgh, V. (1990) "In the Cournot–Walras Model, there may be 'More to Gain' by Changing price Normalization than by Eliminating Imperfections: A Two-goods Economy Example," paper presented at Applied General Equilibrium and Economic Development Workshop, University of Montreal, February.

Grossman, G. and Helpman, E. (1991) *Innovation and Growth in the Global Economy*. Cambridge, MA: MIT Press.

Harris, R. (1984a) "Applied General Equilibrium Analysis of Small Open Economies with Scale Economies and Imperfect Competition," *American Economic Review* 74: 1016–32.

—— (1984b) *Trade, Industrial Policy and Canadian Manufacturing*. Toronto: Ontario Economic Council.

Hart, O.D. (1985) "Imperfect Competition in General Equilibrium: An Overview of Recent Work," in K. Arrow and S. Honkapohja (eds) *Frontiers of Economics* Oxford: Basil Blackwell and Co: 100–49.

Helpman, E. (1981) "International Trade in the Presence of Product Differentiation, Economies of Scale and Monopolistic Competition: A Chamberlinian–Heckscher–Ohlin Approach," *Journal of International Economics* 11: 305–40.

—— and Krugman, P. (1985) *Market Structure and Foreign Trade*. Cambridge, MA: MIT Press.

Krugman, P. (1979) "Increasing Returns, Monopolistic Competition and International Trade," *Journal of International Economics* 9: 469–79.

—— (1980) "Scale Economies, Product Differentiation and the Pattern of Trade," *American Economic Review* 70: 950–59.

—— (1981) "Intra-Industry Specialization and the Gains from Trade," *Journal of Political Economy* 89: 959–73.

Lancaster, K. (1980) "Intra-industry Trade under Perfect Monopolistic Competition," *Journal of International Economics* 10: 151–75.

Marshall, A. (1992) *Principles of Economics*, 8th Edn. London: Macmillan.

Smith, A. and Venables, A. (1988) "Completing the Internal Market in the European Community: Some Industry Simulations," *European Economic Review* 32: 1501–25.

—— and —— (1989) "Trade Policy Modelling with Imperfectly Competitive Market Structures," Centre for Economic Policy Research, June.

# 5

# FLEXIBILITY: A PARTIAL ORDERING

*Kala Krishna and Marie Thursby*

We use an approach developed by Krishna and Young to examine the ability of economies to adjust to exogenous shocks. While, in general, economies cannot be ranked in terms of their flexibility, we provide a partial ordering for certain types of economies. In particular, properties of the revenue function are used to show that placing restrictions on factor mobility and on production in certain sectors reduces the flexibility of a small open economy with respect to all price, endowment, and technology shocks of small enough magnitude. Since one can think of these restrictions as distortions, we would expect them to reduce the level of GNP in the economy. The insight provided by the analysis of flexibility is that, not only is the level of GNP affected, but also the intrinsic ability of the economy to adjust to shocks is reduced.

## Introduction

The term "flexibility" in the Oxford English dictionary is defined as adaptability to various purposes. In economic usages it carries connotations of an *ability* to adjust. The flexibility of an economy is often thought of as a desirable characteristic as a flexibile economy is thought of as being able to adapt its resource use, and change its production patterns, in response to exogenous shocks more than an inflexible one. The presumption is that this responsiveness to exogenous shocks would then result in greater national income and could foster growth. For example, Young (1989) argues that it was the ability of Hong Kong to adapt to changing opportunities in the world market that enabled it to grow much faster than other similar countries.

Yet, the term is relatively badly defined in the literature. In common usage, there is a tendency to confuse actual adjustment of an economy, as reflected in changes in its resource allocations and thereby in its production composition, with the *ability* to adjust. For example, Young (1989) measures flexibility by computing an index of change in value of output from different sectors. In labor economics, a measure of actual adjustment often used is an index of gross job creation and destruction as in Davis and Haltiwanger (1992). While such measures are related to *actual* adjustment, it says little about the *ability* to adjust. The adjustment may have occurred because the economy was subjected to shocks. Another economy with less actual adjustment may really be more intrinsically flexible if it was not subject to significant shocks and hence did not *need* to adjust. Moreover, one economy may respond more than another to a *given* shock, under one set of base conditions, and less under some other set of base conditions. Thus, flexibility must, in general, be defined *relative* to a given shock and at some *given* existing situation.

This distinction between ex ante and ex post measures is essential. We shall refer to measures of the former as measures of flexibility, and the latter as measures of adjustment. In this chapter we are concerned with measures of flexibility.

We adopt an approach to flexibility recently developed by Krishna and Young (1992) in our analysis of the ability of different types of economies to adjust to external shocks. Their approach is a dual one in which flexibility can only be defined relative to given shocks and for given initial conditions. Their definition is based on a metric which defines the distance from a baseline economy which is either perfectly flexible or perfectly inflexible. It provides a microeconomically well based definition of flexibility. It is appealing because it relates flexibility to the responsiveness of the economy, as measured by the derivatives of the revenue function, to exogenous shocks.[1] They develop measures of flexibility in response to price, factor endowment, and technology shocks, and they point out that an economy can be flexible in response to one kind of shock and not another. For example, they show that the standard Heckscher–Ohlin 2 × 2 × 2 model with fixed coefficients in production and incomplete specialization provides an example of an economy which is perfectly inflexible in its response to price shocks, but perfectly flexible in response to endowment shocks. It is empirically implementable by estimating the revenue function, and so provides a basis for empirical estimates of flexibility that are easily interpreted. The approach is particularly fitting for this chapter since Chipman (1972) was one of the early papers examining the properties of the revenue function.

However, since Krishna and Young's measure is dependent on the shock itself as well as the initial conditions, an implication is that economies cannot in general be ordered in terms of their flexibility. We build on their work and show that some *kinds* of economies can be so ordered. We thus provide a *partial* ordering of such economies in terms of their flexibility. In particular, we argue that permitting capital mobility in a baseline economy enhances the flexibility of an economy in response to all price, endowment, or technology shocks, which are "small enough" in magnitude. We then argue that in command economies, target production levels in some, but not in all, sectors similarly reduce the flexibility of the baseline economy.

It is worth emphasizing at the outset that the approach used here and in Krishna and Young (1992) is static and atemporal. The measure of flexibility does not capture another common usage of the term, namely that a flexible economy *adjusts faster* to any given shock than an inflexible one. This interpretation of flexibility is certainly a valid one, but to our knowledge is not well based as yet in terms of the technology underlying it.

It is certainly possible to capture slow or incomplete adjustment to shocks by reduced form estimates such as in Hammermesh (1988). However, it is not quite clear what the estimated parameters measure and how they can be interpreted in terms of a general underlying technology. In contrast, the measures of Krishna and Young (1992) are related to the matrix of the relevant own and cross elasticities. For example, flexibility in response to price shocks is shown to depend on price elasticities of supply and so is intuitively appealing.

It is worth noting that some temporal aspects can be incorporated into the static approach used here. Revenue functions in the short run, when some factors of production are fixed, as well as revenue functions in the long run, when all factors of production are mobile, can both be estimated using the appropriate restrictions in the estimation process. This would permit measures of short run and long run flexibility in response to given shocks.

There is also a large literature relating flexibility to adjustment costs which is microeconomically well based. Fixed adjustment cost models lead to $s$, $S$ type models where adjustment occurs once pressures are sufficient to warrant the cost of adjustment. Variable adjustment models, which have the property that adjustment costs are bounded away from zero at the origin also lead to such regions of inaction.[2] Variable adjustment cost models, which use quadratic adjustment costs, have zero adjustment costs at the origin and result in slow adjustment over time. Increasing hazard models, such as Caballero and Engel (1992) relate the probability of adjustment to the level of pressure for adjustment.

There are even models which aggregate to the macro level in remarkably clever ways, and provide insights into macroeconomic behavior such as Caplin (1985) and Caplin and Leahy (1991) among others. However, the cost of such aggregation is the special assumptions that need to be made to permit it. For this reason, they are not well suited as a base for empirical work as yet.

Another strand in the literature focuses on the value of flexibility for a firm in the face of uncertainty. Stigler (1939) in a classic paper describes one plant as being more flexible than another if it has a flatter average cost curve. He points out that with uncertainty, a firm may well choose a technology which is not efficient for any given level of output, but is optimal for the uncertain environment it faces. Jones and Ostroy (1984) provide a masterful summary of the history of flexibility as an economic concept and formalize the notion of flexibility in a sequential decision context and relate its value to the amount of information an agent expects to receive. Fuss and McFadden (1978) argue that neglecting uncertainty in estimating revenue or cost functions can seriously bias the resulting estimates. They distinguish between ex ante and ex post technological possibilities and provide econometric specifications which permit this distinction to be made in practice. Their work is of great importance in refining and developing ways of implementing the definitions of Krishna and Young (1992) which neglect uncertainty.

The section that follows develops the results on capital mobility. The next section contains the main results for a command economy, while the final section has some concluding remarks and directions for future research.

## Capital mobility and flexibility

It turns out to be convenient to use the dual approach and describe technology using the revenue function. We will first define the revenue functions we use and then derive some properties we will rely on in the following sections.[3]

The revenue function is denoted by $r(P,V)$ where $P$ and $V$ denote exogenously given vectors of prices and endowments, respectively. There are $n$ goods and $m$ factors. The revenue function is defined to be:[4]

$$r(P,V) = \max_{X} P'x \text{ subject to } (X,V) \text{ being in the feasible set.} \quad (1)$$

The reader is reminded that, given constant returns to scale, the revenue function is homogeneous of degree one in both prices and endowments. It is convex in prices and concave in endowments. Its derivative with respect to prices equals the vector of equilibrium outputs, $r_P(P,V) = X(P,V)$, while its derivative with respect to endowments equals the shadow prices (i.e. equilibrium returns) of the factors of production, $r_V(P,V) = W(P,V)$. Of course, these derivatives are homogeneous of degree zero in both prices and endowments.

The revenue function can also be defined as the value function for the program that minimizes factor payments subject to the constraint that price weakly falls short of costs:

$$r(P,V) = \min_{W} W'V \text{ such that } P \leq c(W).^{5} \quad (2)$$

In Theorems 1 and 2 below, we examine the effect of permitting capital mobility on flexibility. In this we build on the work of Neary (1985). For this purpose we will divide the factor endowment vector $V$ into two component vectors, $K$ and $L$, of dimensions $m_K \times 1$ and $m_L \times 1$, respectively.

The $m_K$ factors in $K$ are mobile internationally and so can be acquired at given world factor prices denoted by the vector $\rho$. In this case factors can be thought of as negative traded intermediate goods.

Define:

$$R(P,\rho,L) = \max_{X,K} P'X - \rho'K \text{ subject to } (X,K,L) \text{ being feasible.} \tag{3}$$

It is convenient to think of this as a two-stage process where $X$ is chosen first and $K$ is chosen afterwards. Let $X(\cdot)$ denote the solution to the first stage, that is, for a given $K$. Note that $P'X(\cdot) = r(P,K,L)$. At the second stage, $K$ is chosen. Thus:

$$R(P,\rho,L) = \max_{K} r(P,K,L) - \rho'K. \tag{4}$$

Let $K(P,\rho,L)$ solve this problem. The work of Neary (1985) shows that when $m_L \geq n$, these choices are well behaved functions of their arguments.[6] National income therefore equals:

$$G(P,\rho,K,L) = r(P,K(\cdot),L) - \rho'\{K(\cdot) - K\} = R(P,\rho,L) + \rho'K, \tag{5}$$

where $K(\cdot)$ denotes the choice of $K$ in (3) and $K$ denotes the vector of domestic owned factors which are mobile. The first equality shows that GNP equals GDP less factor payments for net imports of mobile factors.

We will call $K(\cdot)$ the virtual quantity vector for the mobile capital since having a capital stock of $K(\cdot)$ will generate the same output choices as having availability to factor markets at the factor price vector $\rho$ or $X(P,K(\cdot),L) = X(P,\rho,L)$.

The measure of flexibility with respect to price changes in Krishna and Young (1992) is related to the matrix of second-order derivatives of the GNP function with and without capital mobility. Our results will be valid for comparisons of the same baseline economy, with and without capital flexibility. Thus, we wish to relate the matrix of second-order derivatives with and without capital mobility at the capital stock, $K$, given by the virtual quantity $K(P,\rho,L)$. At this point, GNP equals:

$$G(P,\rho,K,L) = r(P,K(\cdot),L). \tag{6}$$

Therefore:

$$G_P(P,\rho,K,L) = R_P(P,\rho,L) \quad \text{and} \quad G_{PP}(P,\rho,K,L) = R_{PP}(P,\rho,L). \tag{7}$$

However, by definition:

$$R(P,\rho,L) \equiv r(P,K(P,\rho,L),L) - \rho'K(P,\rho,L) \tag{8}$$

so that

$$\begin{aligned} R_P(P,\rho,L) &\equiv r_P(P,K,(P,\rho,L),L) + r_K(\cdot)'K_P(\cdot) - \rho'K_P(\cdot) \\ &= r_P(P,K(P,\rho,L),L) \end{aligned} \tag{9}$$

and

$$R_{PP}(P,\rho,L) = r_{PP}(P,K(\cdot),L) + r_{PK}(P,K(\cdot),L)K_P(\cdot). \tag{10}$$

Moreover, by definition of $K(\cdot)$, $r_K(P,K(P,\rho,L),L) = \rho$, so that $r_{KP}(P,K(P,\rho,L),L) + r_{KK}(P,K(P,\rho,L),L)K_P(\cdot) = 0$. Hence:

$$K_P(\cdot) = -r_{KK}^{-1}(P,K(\cdot),L)r_{KP}(P,K(\cdot),L). \tag{11}$$

Substituting back gives:

$$R_{PP}(P,\rho,L) - r_{PP}(P,K(\cdot),L) = -r_{PK}(\cdot)r_{KK}^{-1}(\cdot)r_{KP}(\cdot). \tag{12}$$

This is the key result relied on in Theorem 1. This result is not new by any means. It is identical to that obtained in Neary (1985) and reproduced here for completeness. Neary points out that since (12) defines a positive definite matrix,[7] it implies that the baseline economy with capital mobility has a greater own supply elasticity than the one without capital mobility. In this way it is more flexible than the other. Below, we go further and use this result in conjunction with the definition of Krishna and Young (1992) to generalize this insight of Neary's.

Krishna and Young (1992) define flexibility in response to price changes as:

$$I(P^0) = \frac{r(P^0,V) - r(P^1,V) - (P^0 - P^1)'r_P(P^1,V)}{r(P^0,V)}. \tag{13}$$

The index is the actual change in nominal national income less the change in income that would have occurred if the economy had kept on producing base period outputs (that is, if it had been totally inflexible), divided by first period income. The numerator can be interpreted as the error from a first order approximation of the revenue function. By the mean value theorem, the numerator of this index is also equal to the second-order terms evaluated at some point, $P^{**}$, between the two prices:

$$I(P^0) = \frac{(P^0 - P^1)'r_{PP}(P^{**},V)(P^0 - P^1)}{2r(P^0,V)} \tag{14}$$

for $P^{**} \in (P^0,P^1)$.

Their measure of flexibility is thus fully defined by the price changes and the matrix of second order derivatives with respect to price of the revenue function at some point between the two prices.

Using this definition of flexibility in conjunction with the definitions of national income above gives the indices of flexibility with and without capital mobility to be:

$$I^m(P^0) = [(P^0 - P^1)'\{R_{PP}(P^*,\rho,L)\}(P^0 - P^1)]/2G(P^0,\rho,K,L) \tag{15}$$

and

$$I(P^0) = [(P^0 - P^1)'\{r_{PP}(P^{**},K,L)\}(P^0 - P^1)]/2r(P^0,K,L) \tag{16}$$

respectively at $K = K(\cdot)$, the virtual quantity, and $P^*$ and $P^{**}$ somewhere in the open interval $(P^0,P^1)$.

Using (6) and (12) gives the difference in the two, $\Delta(P^*,P^{**})$, evaluated at $P^* = P^{**} = P^0$ to be:

$$\Delta(P^0,P^0) = [(P^0 - P^1)'\{-r_{PK}(\cdot)r_{KK}^{-1}(\cdot)r_{KP}(\cdot)\}(P^0 - P^1)]/2r(P^0,K,L). \tag{17}$$

This expression is positive since $r_{KK}(\cdot)$ is negative definite. Since $P^*$ and $P^{**}$ lie in the open interval $(P^0,P^1)$, by continuity, $\Delta(P^*,P^{**}) > 0$ for $P^1$ close to $P^0$. This results in Theorem 1.

### *Theorem 1*

> International factor mobility increases the flexibility of the baseline economy with respect to all small price changes.

Similarly, flexibility with respect to factor endowment changes will be related to the matrix of second-order derivatives with respect to factor availability of the baseline economy, with and without factor mobility. Again we use the identity given in (8). Differentiating gives:

$$\begin{aligned} R_L(P,\rho,L) &\equiv r_L(P,K(P,\rho,L),L) + r_K(\cdot)'K_L(\cdot) - \rho'K_L(\cdot) \\ &= r_L(P,K(P,\rho,L),L) \end{aligned} \tag{18}$$

and

$$R_{LL}(P,\rho,L) = r_{LL}(P,K(\cdot),L) + r_{LK}(P,K(\cdot),L)K_L(\cdot). \tag{19}$$

Again by definition of $K(\cdot)$, $r_K(P,K(P,\rho,L),L) = \rho$, so that $r_{KL}(P,K(P,\rho,L),L) + r_{KK}(P,K(P,\rho,L),L)K_L(\cdot) = 0$. Hence:

$$K_L(\cdot) = -r_{KK}^{-1}(P,K(\cdot),L)r_{KL}(P,K(\cdot),L). \tag{20}$$

Substituting back gives:

$$R_{LL}(P,\rho,L) - r_{LL}(P,K(\cdot),L) = -r_{LK}(\cdot)r_{KK}^{-1}(\cdot)r_{KL}(\cdot). \tag{21}$$

This is the key fact used in Theorem 2. Again, this result is due to Neary (1985) and provided for completeness.

Krishna and Young (1992) define the flexibility with respect to factor endowment changes in terms of the ability of the economy to absorb additional factors without the need for factor price adjustments. Consider the function:

$$I(V^0) = \frac{-[r(P,V^0) - r(P,V^1) - (V^0 - V^1)'r_V(P,V^1)]}{r(P,V^0)}. \tag{22}$$

This function can be interpreted as the difference in the response of an economy which is perfectly flexible (that is, an economy which can absorb factors at given wages so that the change in national income is the change in endowments times original wages), and that of an economy which can only fully absorb factors of production if wages change. Note that it is not an index of structural flexibility, but of the loss due to imperfect flexibility. It is easily seen that it is the error from a first-order expansion of the revenue function, i.e. it equals the negative of the second-order terms evaluated at some endowment, $V^*$, between $V^1$ and $V^0$ and hence corresponds to a positive definite quadratic form:

$$I(V^0) = -\left[\frac{1}{2}\,\frac{(V^0 - V^1)' r_{VV}(P,V^*)\,(V^0 - V^1)}{r(P,V^0)}\right] \geq 0. \tag{23}$$

The indices of inflexibility with respect to endowment shocks, with and without capital mobility, are thus given by:

$$I^m(V^0) = -\,[(L^0 - L^1)'\{R_{LL}(P,\rho,L^*)\}(L^0 - L^1)]/2G(P^0,\rho,K,L^0) \tag{24}$$

and

$$I(V^0) = -\,[(L^0 - L^1)'\{r_{LL}(P,K,L^{**})\}(L^0 - L^1)]/2r(P^0,K,L^0) \tag{25}$$

respectively at $K = K(\cdot)$, the virtual quantity, and $L^*$ and $L^{**}$ somewhere in the open interval $(L^0,L^1)$.

Using (6) and (21) gives the difference in the two, $\Delta(L^*, L^{**})$, evaluated at $L^* = L^{**} = L^0$ to be:

$$\Delta(L^0,L^0) = [(L^0 - L^1)'\{r_{LK}(\cdot)r_{KK}^{-1}(\cdot)r_{KL}(\cdot)\}(L^0 - L^1)]/2r(P,K,L^0). \tag{26}$$

This expression is negative since $r_{KK}(\cdot)$ is negative definite. Since $L^*$ and $L^{**}$ lie in the open interval $(L^0,L^1)$, by continuity, $\Delta(L^*,L^{**}) < 0$ for $L^1$ close to $L^0$. This results in Theorem 2.

### *Theorem 2*

> International factor mobility reduces the loss from inflexibility of the baseline economy with respect to all small endowment changes.

Note that Theorems 1 and 2 can also be interpreted as dealing with technical change as the exogenous shock as in Krishna and Young (1992). The effects of technology changes which are Hicks Neutral are equivalent to those of price changes, while factor augmenting technical change is equivalent to factor endowment changes.

Caution should be exercised in interpreting the above results. They deal with comparisons between economies at a given baseline. At this baseline, there would be *no* capital inflows or outflows actually occurring. All we get is the pure effect on flexibility which is related to the curvature of the revenue function.

The intuition behind our results is easily understood by looking at them in terms of the Le Chatelier principle. Note first that in our model of a small country, the absence of capital mobility is the only distortion. Thus, removing the distortion must raise GNP. Formally, GNP without capital mobility is given by $r(P,K,L)$. Also, approximating this about $K = K(P,\rho,L)$, the virtual quantity defined above gives:

$$\begin{aligned} r(P,K,L) &= r(P,K(\cdot),L) + (K-K(\cdot))'r_K(P,K(\cdot),L) \\ &\quad + (1/2)(K-K(\cdot))'r_{KK}(P,K^*,L)(K-K(\cdot)) \\ &= r(P,K(\cdot),L) + (K-K(\cdot))'\rho \\ &\quad + (1/2)(K-K(\cdot))'r_{KK}(P,K^*,L)(K-K(\cdot)) \end{aligned} \tag{27}$$

for $K^*$ in the interval $(K,K(\cdot))$. Thus:

$$G(P,\rho,K,L) - r(P,K,L) = -(1/2)(K-K(\cdot))'r_{KK}(P,K^*,L)(K-K(\cdot)) > 0. \tag{28}$$

Hence, GNP must rise when capital mobility is permitted. Since it is the same when $K = K(\cdot)$, the GNP function without capital mobility is tangent to that with capital mobility at this point and lies below it everywhere else. The GNP function is convex in prices and concave in endowments. This results in the curvature relations depicted in Figures 5.1(a) and 5.1(b) which are at the heart of our results.

## Command economies and flexibility

In this section, we examine the effect of targeting the level of production in some, but not all, sectors of the economy. To do this we divide the output

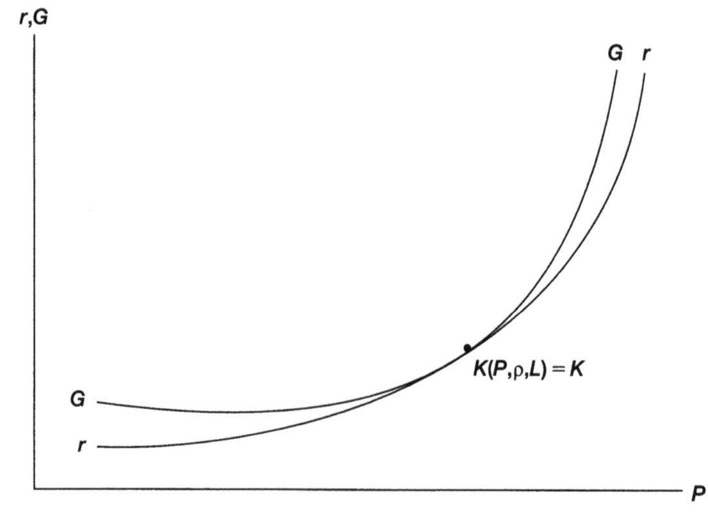


*Figure 5.1a*

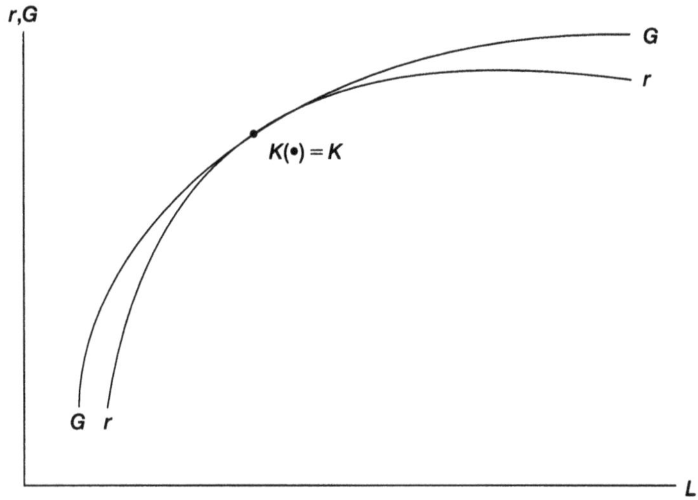


*Figure 5.1b*

vector, $X$, into two component vectors, $Y$ and $Z$ of size $n_y$ and $n_z$, respectively. Competitive behavior determines the levels of outputs in $Y$, while the levels of output in $Z$ are exogenously determined and are denoted by $\bar{Z}$. How or why these levels are determined is unimportant for our purposes, but it is natural to think of their being set to satisfy development goals or more general political objectives.

Before considering the command economy, it is useful to rewrite the revenue function when all outputs are competitively determined as:

$$r(P,Q,V) = \max_{Y,Z} P'Y + Q'Z \text{ subject to } (Y,Z,V) \text{ being feasible,} \tag{29}$$

where $P$ and $Q$ denote exogenously given vectors of prices for $Y$ and $Z$, respectively. As usual this function is convex in prices and concave in endowments. Its derivatives with respect to prices, $r_P(P,Q,V) = Y(P,Q,V)$ and $r_Q(P,Q,V) = Z(P,Q,V)$, give equilibrium output choices, and these derivatives are homogeneous of degree zero in prices and endowments.

We define the revenue function for the command economy as:

$$R(P,Q,\bar{Z},V) = \max_{Y} P'Y + Q'\bar{Z} \text{ subject to } (Y,\bar{Z},V) \text{ being feasible,} \tag{30}$$

where production targets determine outputs in $\bar{Z}$. In this case, $R_P(P,Q,\bar{Z},V) = Y(P,Q,\bar{Z},V)$ gives equilibrium outputs in $Y$ and $R_Q(P,Q,\bar{Z},V) = \bar{Z}$.

We want to examine the economy's flexibility with and without production targets, and, as before, our measures of flexibility are those defined in

Krishna and Young (1992). Thus we need to relate $R(\cdot)$ to $r(P,\bar{Z},V)$, where $Q(P,\bar{Z},V)$ denotes virtual prices for $Z$. $Q(P,\bar{Z},V)$, is implicitly defined as the solution in $Q$ to $\bar{Z} = Z(P,Q,V)$. It is called the virtual price vector for the command economy since the competitive economy would choose to produce the targeted levels of $Z$ at prices given by $P$ and $Q(P,\bar{Z}, V)$.[8]

Using the definition of virtual prices, (29) can be written as

$$R(P,Q,Z^*,V) = P'Y(P,Q(P,\bar{Z},V),V) + Q'Z(P,Q(P,\bar{Z},V),V). \tag{31}$$

Adding and subtracting $Q(P,\bar{Z},V)'Z(P,Q(\cdot),V)$ and using the fact that $Z(P,Q(\cdot),V) = \bar{Z}$, this expression becomes:

$$R(P,\bar{Z},V) = r(P,Q(\cdot),V) + (Q - Q(\cdot))'\bar{Z}. \tag{32}$$

Thus for $Q = Q(\cdot)$, GNP is the same in the competitive and command economies:

$$R(P,\bar{Z},V) = r(P,Q(\cdot),V). \tag{33}$$

As in the preceding section, our results on flexibility rely on the second-order derivatives of the revenue function, with and without targeted production, at this point. Theorem 3 states that targeting production in some, but not all, sectors reduces the economy's flexibility in response to price changes in the nontargeted sector. The result relies on:

$$R_{PP}(P,\bar{Z},V) - r_{PP}(P,Q(\cdot),V) = -r_{PQ}(\cdot)r_{QQ}^{-1}(\cdot)r_{QP}(\cdot) \tag{34}$$

which follows from differentiating (32) and using the definition of the virtual price vector. That is,

$$\begin{aligned} R_P(P,\bar{Z},V) &= r_P(P,Q(\cdot),V) + r_Q(P,Q(\cdot),V)'Q_P(\cdot) - \bar{Z}'Q_P(\cdot) \\ &= r_P(P,Q(\cdot),V) \end{aligned} \tag{35}$$

since $r_Q = Z(P,Q(\cdot), V) = \bar{Z}$. Therefore,

$$R_{PP}(P,\bar{Z},V) = r_{PP}(P,Q(\cdot),V) + r_{PQ}(\cdot)Q_P(\cdot). \tag{36}$$

But $Q(P,\bar{Z},V)$ is the solution to $\bar{Z} = Z(P,Q,V)$, so that

$$\begin{aligned} Q_P(\cdot) &= -Z_P(\cdot)/Z_Q(\cdot) \\ &= -r_{QP}(\cdot)r_{QQ}^{-1}(\cdot). \end{aligned} \tag{37}$$

Substituting gives $R_{PP}(P,\bar{Z},V) = r_{PP}(P,Q(\cdot),V) - r_{PQ}(\cdot)r_{QQ}^{-1}(\cdot)r_{QP}(\cdot)$ and hence (34).

We use these results in conjunction with our earlier definitions of price and endowment flexibility. With and without production targets, these indices are

$$I^c(P^0) = [(P^0-P^1)'\{R_{PP}(P^*,\bar{Z},V)\}(P^0-P^1)]/2R(P,\bar{Z},V) \tag{38}$$

and

$$I(P^0) = [(P^0-P^1)'\{r_{PP}(P^{**},Q(\cdot), V)\}(P^0-P^1)\}/2r(P,Q(\cdot),V) \tag{39}$$

respectively, where $P^*$ and $P^{**}$ are both in the open interval $(P^0,P^1)$.

Using (33) and (34) gives the difference in the two, $\Delta(P^*,P^{**})$, evaluated at $P^* = P^{**} = P^0$ to be:

$$\Delta(P^0,P^0) = [(P^0-P^1)'\{-r_{PQ}(\cdot)r_{QQ}^{-1}(\cdot)r_{QP}(\cdot)\}(P^0-P^1)]/2r(P^0,Q(\cdot),V). \tag{40}$$

This expression is negative since $r_{QQ}(\cdot)$ is positive definite. Since $P^*$ and $P^{**}$ lie in the open interval $(P^0,P^1)$, by continuity, $\Delta(P^*,P^{**}) < 0$ for $P^1$ close to $P^0$. This results in Theorem 3.

### *Theorem 3*

> Setting production targets in some sectors decreases the flexibility of the baseline economy with respect to all small price changes.

Theorem 4 states that the command economy is also less flexible with respect to endowment changes. Again the result relies on differentiating (32). Differentiating with respect to $V$ gives:

$$\begin{aligned} R_V(P,\bar{Z}, V) &= r_V(P,Q(\cdot),V) + r_Q(P,Q(\cdot),V)'Q_V(\cdot)-\bar{Z}'Q_V(\cdot) \\ &= r_V(P,Q(\cdot),V) \end{aligned} \tag{41}$$

and

$$R_{VV}(P,\bar{Z},V) = r_{VV}(P,Q(\cdot),V) + r_{QV}(\cdot)Q_V(\cdot). \tag{42}$$

But $Q_V(\cdot) = -\ Z_V(\cdot)Z_Q(\cdot) = -r_{QV}(\cdot)r_{QQ}^{-1}(\cdot)$.

Substituting gives

$$R_{VV}(P,\bar{Z},V) - r_{VV}(P,Q(\cdot),V) = -r_{VQ}(\cdot)r_{QQ}^{-1}(\cdot)r_{QV}. \tag{43}$$

The indices of inflexibility with respect to factor endowment changes, with and without production targets are given by

$$I^C(V^0) = -\ [(L^0-L^1)'\{R_{VV}(P,\bar{Z},L^*)\}(L^0-L^1)]/2R(P,\bar{Z},L^0) \tag{44}$$

and

$$I(V^0) = -\ [(L^0-L^1)'\{r_{VV}(P,Q(\cdot),L^{**})\}(L^0-L^1)]/2r(P,Q(\cdot),L^0) \tag{45}$$

respectively for $Q = Q(\cdot)$ and $L^*$ and $L^{**}$ in the open interval $(L^0,L^1)$.

Using (33) and (43) gives the difference in the two, $\Delta(L^*,L^{**})$, evaluated at $L^* = L^{**} = L^0$ to be:

$$\Delta(L^0,L^0) = (L^0-L^1)'\{r_{QV}(\cdot)r_{QQ}^{-1}(\cdot)r_{QV}(\cdot)\}(L^0-L^1)]/2r(P,Q(\cdot),V). \tag{46}$$

This expression is positive since $r_{QQ}(\cdot)$ is positive definite. Since $L^*$ and $L^{**}$ lie in the open interval $(L^0,L^1)$, by continuity, $\Delta(L^*,L^{**}) > 0$ for $L^1$ close to $L^0$. This results in Theorem 4.

*Theorem 4*

Setting production targets in some sectors increases the loss from inflexibility of the baseline economy with respect to all endowment changes.

Theorems 3 and 4 are subject to the same types of qualifications and interpretation as Theorems 1 and 2. In particular, our comparisons are made at a given baseline, where the economy faces prices for $Z$ given by the virtual price vector. Thus we are comparing the curvature of the revenue function with and without production targets in certain sectors. Introducing production targets places additional constraints on the economy's resource allocation problem. In terms of the Le Chatelier principle, introducing production targets cannot increase GNP. Formally, GNP without targets is given by $r(P,Q,V)$. Approximating this about $Q(P,\bar{Z},V)$, the virtual price vector, gives:

$$r(P,Q,V) = r(P,Q(\cdot),V) + (Q - Q(\cdot))'\bar{Z} + \tfrac{1}{2}(Q-Q(\cdot))'r_{QQ}(P,Q^*,V)(Q - Q(\cdot))$$

for $Q^* \in (Q,Q(\cdot))$. Thus

$$R(P,Q,\bar{Z},V) - r(P,Q,V) = -\tfrac{1}{2}(Q - Q(\cdot))'r_{QQ}(P,Q^*,V)(Q - Q(\cdot)) < 0.$$

Since $r(P,Q,V) = R(P,Q,\bar{Z},V)$ at $Q(P,\bar{Z},V)$, the GNP function for the command economy is tangent to $r(\cdot)$ at that point and lies below it elsewhere.

## Concluding remarks

In general, economies cannot be ranked in terms of their ability to adjust to exogenous shocks. None the less, properties of the revenue function can be used to provide a partial ordering in which certain types of economies are compared. In this chapter we showed that placing restrictions on factor mobility and on production in certain sectors reduces the flexibility of a small open economy with respect to all price, endowment, and technology shocks of small enough magnitude. Since one can think of these restrictions as distortions, we would expect them to reduce the level of GNP in the economy. The insight provided by the analysis of flexibility is that, not only is the level of GNP affected, but also the intrinsic ability of the economy to adjust to shocks is reduced.

Our results are straightforward applications of the Le Chatelier Principle in that we examine the impact of restrictions when the constraints were just binding. They are more general than the usual Le Chatelier applications since they deal with small but noninfinitesimal changes. In future work we plan to examine other Le Chatelier applications, such as the effect of quotas, which have more complex effects than the simple restrictions considered here. We also plan to examine flexibility in non Le Chatelier contexts, that is, when the relevant distortions are substantial (as, for example, in the literature on piecemeal policy reform).[9] In the applications above, the effects on GNP and the effects on flexibility are in the same direction. An additional question of interest is under what conditions these effects are opposing. Finally, we have assumed differentiability throughout, and it is of interest to know if this assumption can be relaxed.

## Notes

This paper was prepared for the *festschrift* conference in honor of John Chipman, Minneapolis, Minnesota. We wish to thank John Chipman, Ron Jones, Vijay Krishna, Dan McFadden, Jim Moore, Jerry Thursby, and Henry Wan for useful comments.

1 Another strand of literature examines the response of domestic prices to external price shocks. For example, Jones and Purvis (1983) relate the divergence of equilibrium exchange rates from purchasing power parity to the ability of an economy to adjust to external shocks, Chipman (1981) examines the responses of domestic prices to external price shocks for the West German economy.

2 Kemp and Wan (1974) provide an early analysis.

3 A good reference source for those unfamiliar with the general approach is Dixit and Norman (1980).

4 Note that this specification is valid only when there is no joint production.

5 Throughout we define vectors as column vectors, and the notation $'$ denotes transpose.

6 Throughout we assume the revenue function is differentiable, so that we invoke the required conditions on the number of goods and factors (mobile and immobile, constrained and unconstrained).

7 Note that $\bar{Z}R_{PK}]R_{KK}^{-1}[R_{KP}Z] = -Z'R_{PK}R_{KK}^{-1}R_{KK}R_{KK}^{-1}R_{KP}Z > 0$.

8 In this we owe an intellectual debt to Neary and Roberts (1980) who used the concept of virtual prices in their analysis of consumer behavior in the face of quantity constraints.

9 See Milgrom and Roberts (1992) for a general approach to comparing equilibria of models when changes are discrete.

## Bibliography

Caballero, R.J. and Engel, E.M.R.A. (1992) "Microeconomic Adjustment Hazards and Aggregate Dynamics," Mimeo, MIT.

Caplin, A. (1985) "The Variability of Aggregate Demand with *(S,s)* Inventory Policies," *Econometrica* 53: 1395–1410.

—— and Leahy, J. (1991) "State-Dependent Pricing and the Dynamics of Money and Output," *Quarterly Journal of Economics* 106: 3, pp. 682–708.

Chipman, J.S. (1972) "The Theory of Exploitative Trade and Investment Policies: A Reformulation and Synthesis," in L.E. Di Marco (ed.) *International Economics and Development*. New York: Academic Press, pp. 209–242.

—— (1981) "Internal–External Price Relationships in the West German Economy, 1958–79," in R. Richter and W.F. Stolper (eds) *Zeitschrift für die gesamte Staatswissenschaft* 137: 612–637.

Davis, S.J. and Haltiwanger, J. (1992) "Gross Job Creation, Gross Job Destruction, and Employment Reallocation," *Quarterly Journal of Economics* 107: 819–863.

Dixit, A. and Norman, V. (1980) *Theory of International Trade*. Cambridge: Cambridge University Press.

Fuss, M. and McFadden, D. (1978) "Flexibility Versus Efficiency in Exante Plant Design," in M. Fuss and D. McFadden (eds) *Production Economics: A Dual Approach to Theory and Applications*, vol. 1. New York: North-Holland Publishing, pp. 311–364.

Hammermesh, D. (1988) "Labor Demand and the Structure of Adjustment Costs," NBER Working Paper #2572.

Jones, R.A. and Ostroy, J.M. (1984) "Flexibility and Uncertainty," *Review of Economic Studies* 51: 13–32.

Jones, R.W. and Purvis, D.D. (1983) "International Differences in Response to Common External Shocks: The Role of Purchasing Power Parity," in E. Claassen and P. Salir (eds) *The Theory of Flexible Exchange Rates*. Amsterdam: North Holland, pp. 33–55.

Kemp, M.C. and Wan, H.Y. Jr (1974) "Hysteresis of Long-Run Equilibrium from Realistic Adjustment Costs," in G. Horwich and P.A. Samuelson (eds) *Trade Stability, and Macroeconomics*. New York: Academic Press, pp. 221–242.

Krishna, K. and Young, A. (1992) "Conceptually Based Measures of Structural Adaptability," NBER Working Paper #4039.

Milgrom, P. and Roberts, J. (1992) "Comparing Equilibria," Mimeo, Stanford University.

Neary, J.P. (1985) "International Factor Mobility, Minimum Wage Rates, and Factor Price Equalization: A Synthesis," *Quarterly Journal of Economics* 100: 551–569.

—— and Roberts, K.W.S. (1980) "The Theory of Household Behavior Under Rationing," *European Economic Review* 13: 25–42.

Stigler, G. (1939) "Production and Distribution in the Short Run," *Journal of Political Economy* 47: 305–357.

Young, A. (1989) "Hong Kong and the Art of Landing on One's Feet: A Case Study of a Structurally Flexible Economy," unpublished PhD thesis, Fletcher School of Diplomacy.

# 6

# FREE TRADE AGREEMENTS AS PROTECTIONIST DEVICES: RULES OF ORIGIN[1]

*Anne O. Krueger*

Until recently, little attention was paid to free trade agreements (FTAs), and most theory regarding preferential trading arrangements focused on customs unions (CUs). With the recent negotiation of the NAFTA treaty, however, attention is turning to FTAs. Most analysts have regarded FTAs as being little different in their trade effects from CUs, and the NAFTA has mostly been analyzed in the traditional CU framework. For example, it has been argued that the US–Mexican FTA is probably "natural" and hence likely to be trade creating, increasing economic efficiency[2] and thus enhancing welfare.[3]

It is the purpose of this chapter to argue that there is an important protectionist bias inherent in FTAs which is not present in CUs. To make the case, it is first necessary to sketch the traditional analysis of the welfare effects of the CUs and FTAs. Thereafter, attention turns to the fact that external tariffs differ among countries in FTAs, and that rules of origin (ROOs) can therefore automatically extend the protection of one trading partner to another FTA member. A straightforward model of incentives under an FTA is then presented, along with an arithmetic example of "exported protection" via an FTA.

Conventional wisdom has been that a country can avoid the potential trade-diversion losses of an FTA if it has very low, or no, trade barriers when it enters into an FTA. Examination of the implications of ROOs, however, suggests that not only must a country's trade barriers be low, but so also must its partner's, to insure that these costs are avoided. A final section then considers some aspects of the political economy of FTAs and of protection via ROOs.

## Traditional CU–FTA theory

It has long been recognized that the net welfare effects of customs unions and free trade areas are ambiguous. To analyze the problem of the welfare effects of CU, theorists have abstracted from the question of changes in the effects of average protection relative to excluded countries by assuming that a CU is formed among countries which then set a common external tariff equal, in some sense, to the average tariff in place in the individual countries pre-union.

Under these assumptions, a CU could be trade creating or trade diverting. Trade creation would take place when producers in member countries reduced the output of their industries previously protected against imports from CU partners and the rest of the world, and instead imported from lower-cost member countries. Trade diversion would occur when countries replaced imports from low-cost non-member countries with higher-cost production from member countries.[4]

When trade creation predominates sufficiently, there is a strong presumption that welfare of the member country or countries for which trade is "created" will improve. This is because the "created" trade shifts production from the higher-cost home country to the lower-cost partner country.[5] When trade diversion dominates for a given country, there is a presumption of welfare loss for the country in question, as the country shifts from low-cost sources of imports in the rest of the world to sourcing its imports from its partner country, whose production is protected by the external tariff. Unless consumption gains from the arrangement are large enough (because of lower prices to consumers) to offset the trade diversion effects, trade diversion leads to a welfare loss to the importing country.

To be sure, trade diversion could represent a welfare loss for one CU/FTA country and a welfare gain for another. An assessment of overall welfare effects for individual members of the CU could require a weighting of trade diversion, trade creation, and consumption effects, as well as the effects of any terms of trade gain achieved by the trading partners vis-à-vis the rest of the world.[6]

The general view has been that CUs and FTAs are equivalent in these effects: that while CUs differ from FTAs in having a common external tariff, the trade diversion and trade creation effects can be analyzed in similar fashion. Because countries retain their pre-existing external tariffs in the case of FTAs, however, it was not thought necessary to assume that the average tariff remained the same after CU as before: since no tariff was changed, it was *assumed* that that happened. Moreover, that implied that a country that itself practiced free trade could only benefit from forming an FTA with another country: it would gain access to the other country's markets and pay no costs, since its zero tariffs would lead producers to choose the low-cost source.

## Rules of origin and the average height of tariffs[7]

In any CU or FTA negotiation, one of the critical issues concerns "rules of origin" (ROOs). The ROOs specify a criterion, or criteria, under which commodities imported by one CU or FTA partner will be deemed to have originated from within the CU or FTA and thus be eligible for duty-free treatment.

For a CU, ROOs determine eligibility for duty-free entry from the partner; the tariff is common to members.[8] In an FTA, however, ROOs have an important additional function. Without a ROO, each imported commodity would enter through the country with the lowest tariff on each commodity. If the rule were simply that some value should have been added in the country of origin, anything – the addition of a label, the final assembly or even the painting of a product – would qualify an item for duty-free entry to the other country.

The criteria adopted in ROOs can take a variety of forms. One simple and frequently-used ROO is that, in order to qualify as originating in the partner country, the item must change tariff classifications. Another is that a specified percentage of the commodity's sales price must consist of value added in the partner country. A fourth ROO specifies a percentage of purchased parts and components that must be purchased from CU or FTA members.

The criterion for the duty-free treatment is important in determining the economic effects of the ROO. The incentives provided to producers hoping to export to their trading partners obviously vary with the ROO as well as with the structure of tariffs: if materials, but not labor, are counted in establishing origin, there is an incentive to substitute materials. If domestic labor, but not capital, is included in the calculation, the incentive to substitute labor for capital is evidently present.

Even in these relatively simple cases, further elaboration of the ROO is needed. When the ROO is stated in terms of fraction of parts and components, for example, the question then is shifted back one step to determining how much domestic value added there must be in a given part or component for it to count as domestic.[9] When domestic value added is the criterion, the precise criterion for attributing capital costs must be specified.[10] Even accounting practices for allocating joint costs must be agreed upon.

Until negotiation of the NAFTA agreement, the United States used the percentage of domestic value added as its criterion for duty-exempt eligibility under the US–Canada FTA, but counted only labor costs, and not any imputed capital costs.[11]

ROOs agreed upon in forming an FTA in fact extend the protection accorded by each country to producers in other FTA member countries. As such, ROOs can constitute a source of bias toward economic inefficiency in

FTAs in a way they cannot do with customs union.[12] Moreover, a country with a zero-tariff level pre-FTA could find its producers post-FTA diverting their imports from low-cost third-country sources to the partner country in order to be eligible for FTA treatment of their exports to the partner country. ROOs governing treatment of Mexico's exports to the United States, for example, can induce efficient Mexican producers to shift their imports from low-cost third country suppliers to higher-cost United States sources, EVEN IF THERE ARE NO MEXICAN TARIFFS ON THE IMPORTS OF THOSE COMMODITIES.[13]

The United States can, at least in theory, therefore use an FTA agreement to gain protection for its industries in Mexican markets! Rather than inducing Mexican firms to switch to US tariff-free sources because they are then cheaper than low-cost but tariff ridden world sources – the traditional trade diversion case – an FTA could induce Mexican producers to shift their purchases of intermediate inputs knowingly from a low-cost world supplier to a higher cost US supplier in order to qualify for duty-free importation of the final product into the US market. Additional Mexican imports to the US might be incorrectly regarded as trade-creating when in fact they would result from the protection in US tariffs being extended to Mexican products entering the US. An FTA can also induce the development of production facilities in an FTA partner, even when the partner's own external tariff would make such facilities uneconomic.

ROOs can thus provide protection to one country's higher-cost producers in another country's markets even when the latter's tariff structure, when taken by itself, results in imports from the rest of the world being lower cost.

## Profit-maximizing behavior under ROOs

Customs unions have rules of origin[14] but when there is an FTA, the issue is especially important because, by definition, external tariffs differ between partner countries. A ROO may make it profitable to establish production facilities in Mexico, even though at pre-existing Mexican tariff rates such facilities are uneconomic. Alternatively, it may benefit Mexican producers to pay more for some or all of their intermediate goods from higher-priced US sources than to pay less to lower-cost world sources. The choice will clearly depend on relative costs in Mexico and the US and analysis is straightforward.

The interesting case is when the US has a significant cost advantage relative to Mexico but a cost disadvantage vis-à-vis the rest of the world in an intermediate commodity, and is able implicitly to extend its tariffs (or other protective devices) to the Mexican market through a ROO. The exact specification of the ROO was one of the last sticking points of the NAFTA agreement.[15] In those negotiations, the United States was supporting a more stringent ROO while Canada and Mexico were in favor of a lower percentage and a broader definition. It therefore seems evident that the

United States was indeed attempting to provide protection to some US producers in the Mexican market, thus "exporting" American protection despite low Mexican tariff rates.

This can readily be seen. Profit-maximizing producers of cloth in Mexico choose $f$, the fraction of textiles purchased from the US, to maximize:

$$\pi_m = P^c_{us} - P^x_{us} fy - P^x_w (1 - f)y, \tag{1}$$

where:

$p$ is price
$t$ is the tariff rate (or tariff equivalent)
$w$ and $us$ subscripts denote the world and the US
$c$, $x$ superscripts denote clothing and textiles
$f$ = fraction of textiles purchased from US sources
$y$ = international value of textiles purchased per dollar of clothing at international prices ($y < 1$)
$r$ = rule of origin stated as a proportion of sale price of clothing
$P^x_{us} = (1 + t^x_{us}) P^x_w$
$P^c_{us} = 1$ if $P^c_{us} - P^x_w (1 - f)y < r$
$P^c_{us} = 1 + t^c_{us}$ if $P^c_{us} - P^x_w (1 - f)y \geqslant r$.

The world price of textiles, $P^x_w$, can be used as a numéraire and set equal to one. Then, it is evident that producers in the FTA partner country will choose to satisfy the rule of origin whenever

$$1 + t^c_{us} - (1 + t^x_{us}) fy > 1 - fy. \tag{2}$$

But the left-hand side of equation (2) is nothing other than the protection to domestic value added in the United States; while the right-hand side is value added per unit of cloth output at international prices. Dividing through by the right-hand side yields:

$$\frac{1 + t^c_{us} - (1 + t^x_{us}) fy}{1 - y} > 0 \tag{3}$$

which is the criterion for positive effective protection in the United States.

The higher the effective rate of protection in the United States for a given commodity, the more it will pay Mexican producers to buy intermediate goods from US sources despite lower foreign (Mexican tariff-inclusive) prices. To be sure, as Mexican producers increase their sales in the US, the price of their export in the US will fall while the marginal cost of production in Mexico will rise. An equilibrium eventually will be reached in which the ex ante profits are eliminated, but it may well be an equilibrium in which Mexican producers continue to buy from US sources to enable them to sell at tariff-inclusive prices.

This result can be illustrated with an arithmetic example. It is assumed that the United States is exporting its protection on intermediate goods to Mexico, although a similar example could readily be constructed for Mexico to be doing the same thing: indeed, it is possible that rules of origin in an FTA could export protection in some markets in each country to the other country. Table 6.1 gives some hypothetical numbers for Mexican and US tariffs and inputs of intermediates before and after an FTA comes into effect.

The assumptions are all listed at the top of Table 6.1. It is assumed that the ROO is set in terms of a percentage of purchased parts and components.

*Table 6.1* Hypothetical rule-of-origin induced shift to higher-cost US suppliers

*Assume*: Motors, brakes, tires, and batteries are used in fixed proportions in making automobiles.

| *World prices of these items are*: | | |
|---|---|---|
| | auto | $1,000 |
| | motor | 250 |
| | brakes | 200 |
| | tires | 100 |
| | battery | 50 |

Hence, international value added in assembling an auto is $400. Assume that Mexico has zero tariffs on autos and on each component, and assembles autos, importing all components pre-FTA.

| *Let US nominal tariffs be as follows*: | | |
|---|---|---|
| | auto | 50% |
| | motor | 40 |
| | brakes | 40 |
| | tires | 50 |
| | battery | 50 |

Note that the effective rate of protection for auto producers in the US is 125 percent. Let the ROO be that 80 percent of components, valued at purchasers' prices, must be produced within NAFTA. Then Mexican producers will be confronted with the following choices:

| | *Import parts* | *Buy parts in US to meet 80 percent ROO* | |
|---|---|---|---|
| Selling price of auto in US | 1,000 | 1,500 | |
| Cost of components | 600 | motor | 350 (from US) |
| | | brakes | 280 (from US) |
| | | tires | 100 (imported) |
| | | battery | 50 (imported) |
| | | Total components $780 | |
| Return to domestic labor and capital | 400 | 720 | |

Note that a 90 percent ROO would protect American tire manufacturers. But even with a 100 percent ROO, it clearly pays Mexican producers to purchase parts from higher-cost US sources than to import duty-free from non-NAFTA members, unless it is cheaper to produce those parts in Mexico than to buy them in the US.

To assume a value added criterion would complicate the example needlessly, but the principle would remain unaltered.

It is assumed that, pre-FTA, Mexico imports all components duty-free from the rest of the world (ROW) at international prices, and assembles autos, using $600 of components (valued at either world or domestic prices) to make an auto. In the United States, automobiles are subject to a 50 percent tariff, while brakes and motors are subject to 40 percent nominal tariff and tires and batteries 50 percent. This gives rise to a 61.25 percent effective rate of protection for American automobile manufacturers: they must pay $855 for their components, or 42.5 percent more than the world price but they receive 1.5 times the world price for their output.

After the formation of an FTA, Mexican producers have two choices. On the one hand, they can continue to buy all their inputs in the world market; if they do so, they do not meet the ROO. Hence their product is subject to a 50 percent duty on entry into the US, and they receive $1,000 per auto exported. On the other hand, they can shift from purchasing components from the ROW to purchasing enough of them in the US to meet the ROO.

The right-hand side of Table 6.1 shows ex ante profits from shifting components purchased from the ROW to the US in response to a ROO of 80 percent. At that ROO, Mexican auto assemblers could sell in the US market at $1,500 buying motors and brakes from the US at prices 40 percent above that of their foreign suppliers. That would meet the ROO, even though batteries and tires (with a 50 percent duty) were still purchases abroad. At a 90 percent ROO, tires purchases would be shifted toward FTA-member origin. And, at 100 percent ROO, it would pay Mexican producers to purchase all components in the US in order to be eligible for duty-exemption on auto exports to the US.

To see how a higher rule of origin is more protective, note that an 80 percent ROO extends the 40 percent nominal rate of protection to the Mexican market, but leaves batteries and tires unprotected. With a 90 percent ROO, tires are subject to 50 percent nominal protection in Mexico as well as in the US. Clearly also, a higher rate of protection on intermediate goods, or a lower nominal rate of protection on the final commodity in the US market would be consistent with inducing Mexican producers to shift from world sources to higher-cost (to them, as well as to the country) US sources.

Rules of origin can have similar effects even if there is positive effective protection in Mexico prior to the FTA, provided that the Mexican price of the final good is below the US price pre-FTA.

If one ex ante attempted to assess the trade creation and trade diversion aspects of the FTA with respect to textiles and clothing, from a US perspective, there would appear to have been trade creation as Mexican exports of clothing to the US increased. From a Mexican perspective, there might appear to have been trade creation if total imports of textiles increased (because the volume of clothing production increased as exports to the US expanded) or trade diversion (despite the absence of an external tariff).

More generally, producers of a final good in an FTA would find it advantageous to purchase higher-cost (protected) inputs from other FTA members than to purchase from lower cost ROW sources whenever: (1) the effective rate of protection in the partner country was greater than in the home country; and (2) the rule of origin would not be satisfied without such purchases.

## How protectionist is the NAFTA?

It has often been argued that such a high fraction of Mexico's trade is with the United States that Mexico is bound to gain by an FTA. That judgment may well be correct. But there are some indications that American intent was to secure as much advantage for US producers in the Mexican market as possible. One piece of evidence is the report that American negotiators evidently tried to insist that Mexico should not lower its tariff structure any further from its present average of about 9 percent.[16] The higher are Mexican tariffs, the more advantage US firms have relative to foreign competitors in the Mexican market, and the more trade diversion is likely to occur.

But ROOs were also a major issue in the negotiations. The full text of the NAFTA agreement has not yet been made public, but enough details are known to be suggestive. In at least two key sectors, ROOs are clearly important and were a major point of contention until the final hours of negotiations. First, for automobiles and parts, the ROO was set at 62.5 percent, a number which will be reached gradually over eight years starting at 50 percent (the number in the US–Canada Agreement[17]) when the pact goes into effect.[18] Both Mexico and Canada had attempted to bargain for lower numbers.[19] Expectations evidently are that Volkswagen will locate more operations in Mexico in order to comply with the requirement, while Japanese firms will have greater difficulty in meeting it, and potential new Mexican producers will be greatly discouraged from entry.[20] It is noteworthy that Canada agreed to the higher ROO only after the United States accepted a revision of the way in which FTA value added is calculated: the US agreed to include interest and other capital costs, as well as labor costs.[21]

In textiles and clothing, as well, ROOs were an important issue. There, the agreement calls for duty-free treatment of Mexican garments only if the yarn is made, the cloth woven, and all cutting and sewing is done in North America.[22]

To be sure, there are other sectors of the American economy that will be opened, at least to some degree, as a result of the NAFTA agreement. US restrictions on Mexican fruit and vegetables appear to have been relaxed considerably, and that will almost certainly result in trade creation. Financial liberalization, tariff reductions, and other measures will also move in that direction.

Overall, however, it is clear that there are some fairly strong measures designed to provide protection to US producers in the NAFTA agreement. Despite Mexico's position as a "natural" trading partner, one must question the extent to which the NAFTA is truly a step toward a more open, multilateral trading system, or whether it is a step toward greater US protectionism encompassing not only the United States but all of North America.

## What is the political economy of rules of origin?

There remains a political economy puzzle. That is, conventional wisdom is that tariffs are escalated, with higher nominal rates of protection of final commodities than of intermediate goods, and higher nominal rates on intermediate goods than on raw materials. Yet, at first sight it would appear that the chief gainers in the United States from ROOs would be US producers of intermediate goods. Why should US producers of final products, such as automobiles, be "gleeful"[23] at higher ROOs for eligibility for entry into the US market? For that matter, why was it widely believed that a higher ROO would exclude Japanese automobile producers, such as Nissan, from the US market?

The answer must lie, at least in part, in production relations, and the ways in which parts and components must be "designed in" to final products. To the extent that Nissan, for example, is designed with specifications of Japanese parts and components, an attempt to shift to a Mexican, Canadian, or US supplier would involve the start-up of a new production facility. Such a facility may not be able to produce at the same costs as are incurred in Japan; moreover, if there is monopolistic competition, and fixed costs to be covered in the production of parts and components, the North American market for Nissan autos may not be large enough to permit averaging fixed costs and still be profitable. If any of these speculations are correct, the ROO does protect producers of the final product in avoiding competition from those with access to cheaper intermediate goods. The price to the final producers of receiving that protection, however, is that they must share part of it with producers of intermediate goods in the FTA.[24]

As producers of final commodities avoid some competition and receive protection, they are presumably willing to pay higher prices for purchased inputs to continue to enjoy that protection. Once that is recognized, a rule of origin may be a device through which producers of final goods and those of intermediate goods can be induced to support an FTA. If so, then the political economy of FTAs suggests that they are as likely to be protectionist as they are to be trade creating.

## Notes

1 I am indebted to Martin Bronfenbrenner, Peter Dohlman, Omer Gokcekus, Bernard Hoekman, Kala Krishna, Richard Snape and members of the International Economics Workshop at Duke for helpful comments on an early version of this chapter.

2 Throughout, economic efficiency will be used to describe the relationship between marginal rates in domestic production in trade in value added terms. A situation will be regarded as economically more efficient when resources are combined in ways that produce greater value added evaluated at international prices. It is well known that IVA is maximized, and hence the economy economically most efficient, when the international marginal rates of transformation (IMRTs) (which equal international price ratios in the absence of monopoly power in trade) among commodities equal the domestic marginal rates of transformation (DMRTs). However, welfare also increases when consumers are enabled to attain larger consumption bundles. It is well known that one might have a customs union where the divergence between the IMRT and DMRT increased, but consumer welfare improved because of the lower post-FTA prices. For that reason, it is important to distinguish between economic efficiency and economic welfare. If economic efficiency increases, welfare must increase. If efficiency decreases, welfare could either increase or decrease.

3 See Summers (1991) for an application of this analysis to the proposed Western Hemisphere Free Trade Agreement (WHFTA).

4 The classic analysis is by Lipsey (1960). There is considerable evidence emerging in developing countries that increased competition subsequent to trade liberalization may result in increases in X-efficiency. That can surely happen as well subsequent to the formation of CUs and FTAs, but if ROOs do increase protection to some industries, there is no increase in competition in those cases, and the issue is therefore not pertinent to the analysis in this chapter.

5 If the partner's costs are none the less above costs in the rest of the world, the gain to the home country would be even greater if it liberalized multilaterally.

6 Kemp and Wan (1976) have shown that it is always possible for a pattern of tariffs to be established post-union which would insure at least the same level of imports and exports from the CU with the rest of the world; in that case, the CU would clearly be trade-creating.

7 The considerations discussed here are relevant for Canada, the US and Mexico. However, the argument that much support for the FTA with Mexico is protectionist in intent is based on the Mexican case. Hence, to simplify discussion, only the ramifications of US–Mexican trading relations are considered here.

8 The European Community, for example, has protected its semiconductor industry by determining that origin is assigned to the country where "a product has been wholly obtained or where it has undergone its last substantial working or processing". It then defined the "last substantial processing" to have taken place with diffusion. Diffusion, however, is such an early stage that it is not technically feasible to initiate fabrication in any place other than where diffusion is performed. The net impact was that non-EC producers had to invest in fabrication facilities within the EC to avoid border duties. See *Official Journal of the European Community*, vol. 32, February 1989, p. 23.

9 This was the issue in the now-famous Honda case where the US challenged the eligibility of Canadian-produced Hondas to qualify for duty-free treatment in the American market.

10 Under NAFTA, it has evidently been agreed that a part or component that is more than 50 percent domestic value added will be counted as domestic value added, and interest costs on machinery used in production will also constitute domestic value added.

11 How rules of origin are actually administered may also affect their protective content. If, for example, the US authorities take the average value added within the FTA over all a firm's output of a product in question, there could even be a reduction in earlier Mexican exports to third countries as it was no longer profitable to export when purchasing intermediate goods from the US. It is reported that EFTA producers appear willing to pay duties averaging at least 6 percent of price in order to avoid the paperwork needed to establish origin. See Hoekman and Leidy (1992b: p. 19).

12 Rules of origin are also present in customs union and can, of course, bias production decisions. But since external tariffs are similar across countries, they cannot generate the sort of bias discussed here. They then become equivalent to domestic content requirement. See Grossman (1981) for an analysis.

13 This could not happen in the case of a customs union because the external tariff would be common.

14 However, the phenomenon noted here, i.e. the ability of a rule of origin to make it profitable to switch from a lower-cost source to a higher-cost source, could not happen under a customs union because the external tariff rates would be common to both countries. While a Mexican producer might therefore find himself with higher input costs after a customs union than before, any shift to a US source would be the normal trade diversion variety. Under an FTA, it is the difference in tariff rates, combined with the rule of origin, that gives rise to the possibility of a profitable shift to a source which is higher-cost to the buyer.

15 The chapter on ROOs of the NAFTA was 193 pages long in the draft of September 6, 1992.

16 *Financial Times*, June 9, 1992, p. 14.

17 To see how important administration can be, the United States is reported to have achieved the 62.5 percent rule, but to have conceded on how it is calculated. The full cost of processing materials, and interest costs on machinery and equipment had not been counted as part of domestic value added under the earlier US–Canada interpretation and would be under the new ruling. This, in effect, would mean that Honda had met the 50 percent FTA origin rule and would not be liable for duties, as it would have been had the old US formula continued to prevail. *New York Times*, August 15, 1992, p. 26.

18 *New York Times*, August 13, 1992, p. C3. The ROO for new contracts is somewhat more restrictive. See Hufbauer and Schott (1992) for a discussion.

19 See *Financial Times*, July 24, 1992, p. 4.

20 *Financial Times*, June 18, 1992, p. 6.

21\. The Honda dispute with Canada was over interpretation of rules of origin. The US Customs Department "found that the engine blocks, produced in Marysville, Ohio, and exported to Canada for re-export to the US, did not contain sufficient North American content." It was further reported that

Canadian and American authorities were still in disagreement over what constituted domestic content. See *Financial Times*, March 3, 1992.

22 *New York Times*, August 13, 1992, p. C3. Canada evidently won a partial exemption from this "bottoms up" rule for clothing.

23 *Financial Times*, August 18, 1992, p. 4.

24 See Hoekman and Leidy (1992a) for an alternative interpretation, focusing upon sharing rents between producers at various stages of production.

## Bibliography

Grossman, Gene (1981) "The Theory of Domestic Content Protection and Content Preference," *Quarterly Journal of Economics* 96: 583–603.

Hoekman, Bernard M. and Leidy, Michael P. (1992a) "Cascading Contingent Protection," *European Economic Review* 36: 883–892.

—— and —— (1992b) "Holes and Loopholes in Alternative Trade Agreements; History and Prospects," *Aussenwirtschaft* 47.

Hufbauer, Gary C. and Schott, Jeffrey (1992) *North American Free Trade: Issues and Recommendations*. Washington, DC: Institute for International Economics.

Kemp, Murray C. and Wan, Henry Jr (1976) "An Elementary Proposition Concerning the Formation of Customs Unions," *Journal of International Economics* 6: 95–97.

Lipsey, Richard G. (1960) "The Theory of Customs Unions: A General Survey," *Economic Journal* 70: 496–513.

Summers, Lawrence H. (1991) "Regionalism and the World Trading System," in Federal Reserve Bank of Kansas City, *Policy Implications of Trade and Currency Zones*, March, pp. 295–302.

# 7

# DEMAND CONDITIONS IN INTERNATIONAL TRADE THEORY

*James R. Melvin*

## Introduction

In 1964 I was a student in John Chipman's Graduate International Trade course at the University of Minnesota, and I wrote a paper, entitled "The Role of Demand Conditions in International Trade Theory". Professor Chipman was good enough to give me an A on the paper and he also made the comment that the topic was worth developing. This chapter can be seen as a follow-up to his suggestion made over thirty years ago.

Demand conditions have had a rather enigmatic role in the theory of international trade. The demand side of the market is clearly important in any general equilibrium model, whether it be in international trade or elsewhere, and thus all of the international trade models explicitly make assumptions about demand. But while demand is always there, it has not always received the attention it deserves, and in some cases the importance of the specific demand assumptions made has not always been recognized. Thus specific results in some lines of inquiry can be seen to depend for their validity on the specific demand assumptions assumed, and this is not always recognized. There would also seem to have been a neglect of the importance of demand assumptions. Certainly there has been much less attention paid to the issue of differences in demand conditions compared to the attention received by differences in production functions, differences in endowments, distortions, or returns to scale.

In the present chapter I will draw specific attention to demand assumptions and their use in a variety of international trade models. We begin with a discussion of the classical model, and in particular with the demand assumptions associated with Mill and Graham, and then move on to a discussion of the role of demand in the Heckscher–Ohlin framework. I will then consider the role of demand in the specific factor model, particularly as it relates to the neo-classical ambiguity, and finally will turn to a discussion of the role of demand in models of increasing returns to scale.

## The classical model

The originators of what has come to be known as the classical trade model, namely Torrens (1815) and Ricardo (1817), were not explicit about the demand assumptions in their models. It is clear that Ricardo assumed that equilibrium prices would lie somewhere between the slopes of the cost ratios for the two trading countries, and indeed in some of his examples he assumed that the price line would be halfway between these limiting cost ratios. No particular attention was paid to the assumptions that would be required of demand to produce such results, however. The first explicit introduction of demand conditions in the classical international trade model seems to have been Mill (1844), and as Chipman (1965) has noted and analysed with some care, Mill essentially assumed that both countries had utility functions of the form $U = X^{\alpha}Y^{\beta}$, where $\alpha = \beta$. With these demand assumptions, equilibrium price lines lying strictly between the limiting cost ratios of the two countries are possible and the conditions under which this will occur have been analysed by Chipman (1965) for the case where $\alpha = \beta$ and by Melvin (1969b) for the case where $\alpha \neq \beta$.

The sharpest critic of Mill was Graham, who claimed that "limbo prices" (prices lying strictly between the cost ratios of the two countries) were not to be expected and that in general extreme prices would prevail.[1] It was Graham's view that the limiting cost ratios (that is, the slope of the production possibility curve) for one or the other of the countries would be the equilibrium price ratio. It can be shown that the validity of Graham's claims will depend on such things as the relationship between the number of goods and the number of countries, the relationship between the relative cost conditions in the countries, and in particular on the demand assumptions.

A complication in Graham's analysis is that he used two quite different demand assumptions at various points in his analysis. These can be characterized as follows:

A1 Consumers in an economy spend an equal proportion of their total income on both commodities regardless of price.

A2 Consumers in an economy allocate half their expenditure to the two goods in autarchy and continue to purchase goods in this ratio at all other price ratios.

Although these two conditions are superficially similar, they can be shown to produce quite different equilibria. Assumption A1 is the demand condition associated with Mill and implies that utility functions are Cobb–

Douglas with exponents equal.[2] Under these circumstances, own-price elasticities are unity, cross-price elasticities are zero, and income elasticities are unity. Assumption A2, on the other hand, implies that indifference curves are Leontief so that commodities are always consumed in the same proportion. As Chipman has pointed out, this assumption "practically guaranteed the extreme solution" (Chipman 1965: 493–494).

To illustrate the role of demand we follow Chipman and assume two countries, H and F, producing two commodities, *X* and *Y*, with a single factor of production (labor) under conditions of constant returns to scale. The outputs of *Y* and *X* in H are $a'$ and $b'$, while the outputs of *Y* and *X* in F are $a''$ and $b''$. Thus the limiting cost ratios in countries H and F are $a'/b'$ and $a''/b''$ respectively. It is assumed that $a'/b' > a''/b''$. As Chipman has shown, the world production possibility set can be constructed by adding together the production sets of the two countries to obtain TET′ in Figure 7.1. Graham's limbo prices will occur if there is an equilibrium at point E and a price line lying somewhere between the slopes of TE and ET′, while extreme prices will prevail if the equilibrium consumption point lies along either TE or ET′. Which of these outcomes is to be expected depends, at least in part, on the demand assumptions made. To illustrate, consider two extreme cases. First, suppose that there is zero elasticity of substitution between the two commodities so that all indifference curves are linear. An

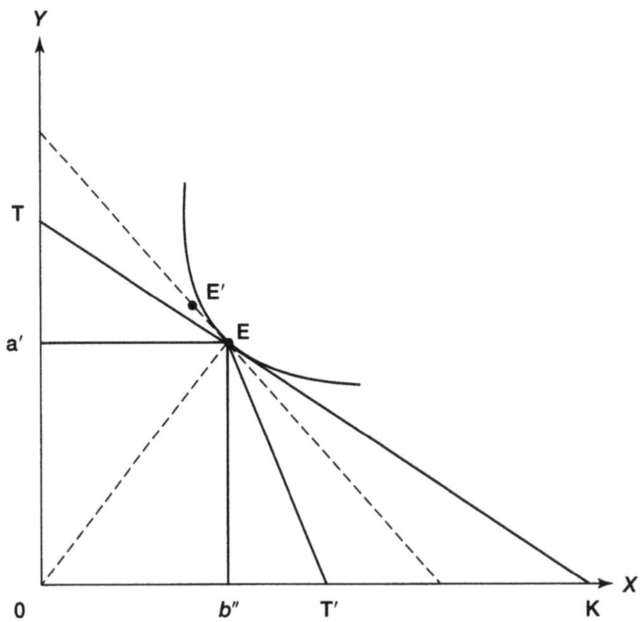


*Figure 7.1*

arbitrary choice of an indifference curve, that is, any arbitrarily sloped straight line, will, with probability 1, lead to complete specialization. Of the infinite number of arbitrary straight lines only two could possibly result in production along either TE or ET′. If one insists that both goods are produced in the world in the final equilibrium, then all equilibrium price ratios, with the exception of TE and ET′, will lead to consumption at E with limbo prices. In this circumstance, then, one would always expect to observe limbo prices.

As another extreme, assume that utility functions for all consumers in the world are Leontief so that both goods are always consumed in the same proportion.[3] The range of demand conditions will then be the infinite number of straight lines emanating from the origin in Figure 7.1. Only one of this infinite array of demand conditions could give limbo price, namely consumption along the ray OE. Thus with probability 1 the price line will be extreme in the sense that it will lie along the cost ratio of either country H or F. Note also that for the special case where consumption is at E, the equilibrium price ratio is indeterminate except that it must lie between the slope of TE and ET′. Although Graham did not generally assume conditions that would allow the existence of community indifference curves, for he assumed that demands differed in the two countries, we will show subsequently that his demand assumptions guaranteed his extreme results.

Graham did not always assume Leontief-type demand conditions however, and in some of his analysis he made the demand assumptions first introduced by Mill. Chipman has shown that, given Mill's assumption that $U = XY$, a necessary and sufficient condition for specialization by both countries is that we have the inequality

$$\frac{a'}{b'} \geq \frac{a'}{b''} \geq \frac{a''}{b''}.$$

Furthermore, $a'/b''$ will be the equilibrium price ratio. Thus in Figure 7.1 the price line tangent to the community indifference curve at E has a slope $a'/b''$, which is the slope of line OE.[4]

Although Mill considered only the case where the same proportion of income is spent on each good, and Chipman followed Mill in this regard, Melvin (1969b) showed that the analysis can be extended to the case where the exponents on the utility function differ. Thus it seems natural to ask how different $\alpha$ and $\beta$ could become and still result in complete specialization in both countries. In Figure 7.1 it is clear that if we were to change the demand assumption by making $\beta$ slightly larger than $\alpha$ then E would no longer be in equilibrium, for at the price ratio shown consumers would wish to be at a point such as E′. At E′ there is excess demand for Y and excess supply of X and the relative price of X would therefore fall until equilibrium is re-established. Clearly if the distance EE′ is small, this change in demand would still result in an equilibrium at E. The question then is how different $\alpha$ and $\beta$ can be made and still result in an equilibrium at E. It is clear that the equilibrium will remain at E as long as the price line remains steeper than the slope TE. As we continue to increase $\beta$ the equilibrium price line will rotate counter-clockwise through E until it becomes equal to the slope of TK. Any further increase in $\beta$ will leave the equilibrium price line equal to the slope of TE, the cost ratio for country F. Thus the limiting price line is the slope of TK and at this point the ratio $\alpha/\beta$ = TE/EK.[5] This in turn is equal to $a''/a'$. Thus as we increase $\beta$ we will continue to have limbo prices as long as $\alpha/\beta > a''/a'$.

A similar argument can be made for increases in the ratio of $\alpha/\beta$ and it can be shown that specialization will occur as long as $\alpha/\beta < b''/b'$. In Figure 7.2 we show these ratios and we can conclude that limbo prices will exist as long as

$$\frac{b''}{b'} > \frac{\alpha}{\beta} > \frac{a''}{a'}.$$

If we were to make the assumption that all possible ratios of $\alpha$ and $\beta$ are equally likely, then the probability of specialization, or limbo prices, is simply the relationship between the size of the "cone of specialization", and the positive quadrant.

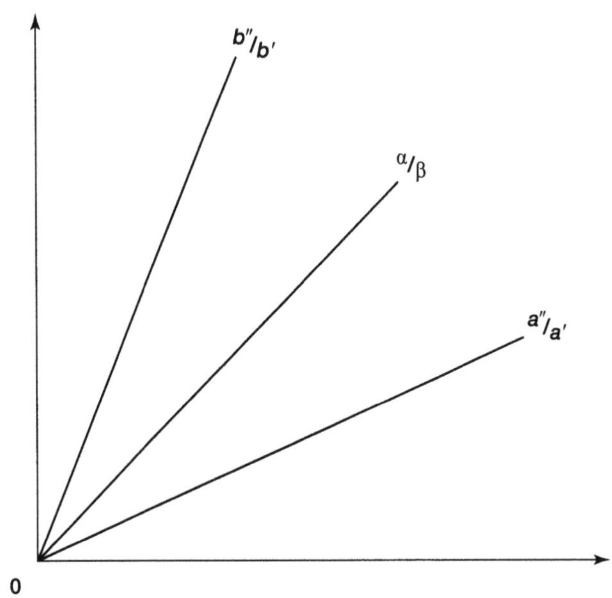


*Figure* 7.2

The above analysis has been carried out under the assumption that tastes are identical in both countries, for this is the only circumstance under which the community indifference curves that we have used can be defined. In situations where Graham assumed that commodities were assumed in fixed proportions, however, this assumption was not employed, and it therefore seems useful to examine the issue of the possibility of specialization for the case where tastes differ. Figure 7.3 shows an alternative method of constructing world production for the case where specialization by both countries is assumed.[6] Again, *a′* and *b′* are the outputs of *Y* and *X* in country H and *a″* and *b″* the outputs of *Y* and *X* for country F. Under the assumption that country F specializes in *X* and country H specializes in *Y*, world output can be found by placing the two production points for countries H and F together at *a′* (or *b″*) so that $0_H$ gives world output as measured from $0_F$. If F and H represent the mid-points of the two production possibility curves, then Graham's demand assumptions imply that all consumption points will lie along FG extended for country F and along HG extended for country H. As Melvin (1969a) has shown, in Figure 7.3 point G is the only limbo equilibrium price, and it is clear that this price is unstable. Furthermore, it is easily shown that given this particular demand assumption all possible limbo price ratios are unstable. Thus one would expect equilibrium to be either at J or K where one of the two countries enjoys all of the gains from

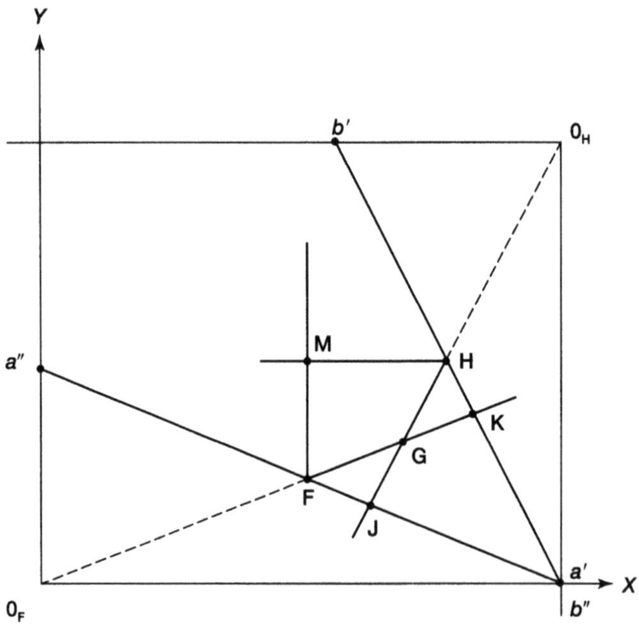


*Figure 7.3*

trade. Since there can be no general presumptions as to whether J or K will prevail, it is impossible to tell which country will gain and which will not.

Notice that quite a different situation occurs for the demand assumption associated with Mill. Here the offer curve for country F becomes $a'$FM extended and the offer curve for country H is $b''$HM extended, and the equilibrium will be at point M. In this case if there is an intermediate or limbo price it will necessarily be stable. Note finally that for the case of identical Leontief preferences in both countries, and with equilibrium at point E from Figure 7.1, the locus of consumption points for H and F in Figure 7.3 would be the straight line joining $0_F$ and $0_H$ and all price lines between the limiting cost ratios would be equilibrium price lines.

As mentioned earlier, another assumption which Graham often made was that the number of countries was larger than the number of commodities. World production sets similar to that of Figure 7.1 can be constructed for several countries and one could again ask, given utility functions of the form $U = X^{\alpha}Y^{\beta}$, which choices of $\alpha$ and $\beta$ would result in specialization and limbo prices. A procedure similar to that used to derive Figure 7.2 can be used to construct a series of cones of specialization and then the issue of whether specialization will take place is settled by the question of whether or not $\alpha/\beta$ falls in one of these cones. Thus suppose there are three countries such that

$$\frac{a'}{b'} > \frac{a''}{b''} > \frac{a'''}{b'''}.$$

Then with $U = X^{\alpha}Y^{\beta}$, specialization will occur if either

$$\frac{b'' + b''}{b'''} > \frac{\alpha}{\beta} > \frac{a'''}{a' + a''} \quad \text{or} \quad \frac{a'' + a'''}{b'} > \frac{\alpha}{\beta} > \frac{b'}{b'' > b'''}.$$

These "cones of specialization" are reminiscent of what Chipman (1966) referred to as "cones of diversification" in his analysis of the conditions for factor price equalization in the Heckscher–Ohlin model. While our cones of specialization have been developed in quite a different model it is of interest to note that there is a sense in which being within a "cone" in either the Heckscher–Ohlin or Ricardian model has a similar interpretation. Being in a cone of diversification in the Heckscher–Ohlin model implies that factor prices are equalized, and as we will argue in the next section, this is equivalent to saying that with trade, and without the necessity of factor movements, commodity trade results in full efficiency for the world as a whole.

Now consider the implications of being in a cone of specialization for the Ricardian model. With $\alpha/\beta$ in a cone of specialization we have limbo prices, and this is a necessary and sufficient condition for both countries to gain from international trade. Note also from the Mill's law inequality that for specialization we have $a' > a''$ and $b'' > b'$. Thus in a sense each country enjoys absolute advantage in the production of one of the goods.[7] With absolute advantage, trade exhausts all possible world gains, and thus even if labor were free to move between countries no mobility would take place. Thus, with absolute advantage, being in the cone of specialization is efficient in the sense that both countries gain from trade, and trade exhausts all possible gains without the need of factor mobility. Of course cones of specialization and limbo prices will exist when both countries do not enjoy absolute advantage. But if one country has an absolute production advantage in both goods, then trade can never produce efficient world output. Full efficiency can only be achieved by allowing all labor to move to the most efficient country.

Graham was adamant in his position that limbo prices were not to be expected. Given his demand assumption A2, this result is practically guaranteed, but clearly must be recognized as being a consequence of this rather peculiar demand assumption. Even for the more general case of assumption A1 we have seen that the probability of specialization depends on the relationship between demand assumptions and production conditions.

## The Heckscher–Ohlin model

Demand conditions have always played a prominent role in the Heckscher–Ohlin model. All formal statements of the Heckscher–Ohlin Theorem make it clear that the existence of identical homothetic preferences for all citizens in both countries is necessary for the proof of the theorem. Most discussions of the model show that differences in demand conditions could offset the effects of endowment differences and some illustrate the fact that differences in preferences themselves could be a determinant of international trade. Indeed, it could be argued that the upfront nature of the demand assumptions in the endowment model has been something of a millstone for international trade theorists. Critics of simple trade models often point to the severe demand assumptions, arguing that a model that assumes that all citizens of the world have identical and homothetic preferences cannot be of much value in policy-making discussions. It is seldom recognized that the assumptions for the existence of community indifference curves are identical to those necessary for the existence of any aggregate demand relationship in macroeconomics. Thus, for example, it is easily shown that the existence of community indifference curves is equivalent to the existence of an aggregate consumption function.[8]

There is, however, a sense in which trade theorists themselves are at fault for the criticism that has been levelled againts the demand assumption. While it is often convenient from a heuristic point of view to assume the existence of community indifference curves, it is almost always the case that the results from international trade models do not depend on such an assumption. For most situations the determination of equilibrium commodity prices depends only on the existence of well-defined offer curves, and contrary to a common perception, the construction of offer curves does not depend on the existence of community indifference curves. The supposed link between community indifference curves and offer curves is probably due to the geometric constructions of Meade (1952) and to early textbooks that used the community indifference approach to derive offer curves. In fact, offer curves depend for their existence only on the ability to determine, for each and every commodity price ratio, a unique production point and a unique consumption point. In the standard Heckscher–Ohlin model with constant returns to scale the existence of the production point is never in question. The existence of a unique consumption point that corresponds to such a production point is almost equally easy to demonstrate, however. Note, first, that any equilibrium production point implies a well-defined vector of commodity outputs, which in turn uniquely determines prices for all factors of production. Factor prices along with information on the resource ownership of factors will allow one to define unique income endowments for all factor owners. With these endowments, and knowing commodity prices, the consumption vector for any individual is easily determined in the usual microeconomic way. These individual consumption vectors can be aggregated and produce a unique aggregate consumption vector. It should be noted that in this approach no assumptions whatsoever need be made about individual preferences; that is they need be neither identical nor homothetic. The only assumption required is that they satisfy the usual microeconomic conditions familiar from any intermediate textbook.[9]

Although demand conditions are often discussed in terms of the Heckscher–Ohlin model, not much attention has been paid to the nature of demand. Certainly there has been very little discussion of the issue of changes in demand and indeed this still remains a forbidden topic in much of economics. However, even simpler questions, such as the effect of differences in preferences among citizens within a country, have not been extensively examined. Some work has been done by Kenen (1959), Johnson (1959), and Melvin (1985), but it is not clear that all of the issues concerning differences in demand have received the attention they deserve.

One of the principal theorems associated with the Heckscher–Ohlin model in which demand conditions have not received much attention is the factor price equalization theorem. In some respects the absence of discussions of demand in this theorem is quite natural, for formal proofs of the theorem need make no mention of demand conditions. At the same time it is quite clear that whether or not factor prices will in fact be equalized may very well depend crucially on demand conditions. The reason for this seemingly paradoxical result is easy to discover. While demand conditions are not explicitly identified, they are nevertheless crucial to the issue of whether one of the other assumptions is satisfied, namely the assumption that all goods are produced in all countries. Thus in situations where the production of all goods in all countries is possible, the issue of whether all goods will in fact be produced depends crucially on demand.

It is possible to gain some insight into the general question of factor price equalization, and in particular to focus attention on the general importance of this theorem, by casting the whole issue of the equalization of factor prices in a somewhat different form. To illustrate, consider a world with any number of factors, any number of commodities, any number of countries, and with any assumptions whatsoever about production functions. Now consider the following two organizations of this world:

> W1 All factors of production, including all consumers, are found at one location where efficient production of all commodities takes place – the integrated economy.
> W2 All factors of production and consumers are identified with specific countries that have their own production technology, and where there is no factor mobility – the world with trade but no factor mobility.

Initially we will assume for simplicity that all individuals in the world have identical homothetic preferences. In W1 consider the equilibrium E1 associated with full maximization by all economic units. Define the equilibrium price vector so generated as $P^1$. Now confront all countries in W2 with $P_1$ and obtain the individual vectors of equilibrium outputs. Sum these outputs to obtain a world equilibrium output vector called E2. I now hypothesize the following:

> **PROPOSITION 1** In the world just described the equalization of world commodity prices through trade will equalize real factor prices among countries if and only if the vector of outputs E2 is exactly equivalent to the vector of outputs E1.[10]

We note that this proposition can be interpreted as a strong result for two reasons. First, it contains none of the traditional assumptions associated with the proof of the factor price equalization theorem. Indeed, it makes no assumptions at all. Second, it provides necessary and sufficient conditions. Of course, the "strength" of this statement is misleading, for while none of the traditional assumptions have been specified they clearly must hold if the factor prices are to be equalized. Thus the failure of any of the traditional assumptions must be reflected in the fact that the equilibrium E1 is not identical to E2. Clearly our reinterpretation of the factor price equalization theorem has treated all of the traditional assumptions in the same way that the more standard treatment has dealt with the assumptions of demand. They have been swept under the rug in the sense that although important, their relevance shows only indirectly through other aspects of the model.

An illustration of this proposition can be given through reference to Figure 7.4. Here we assume the traditional Heckscher–Ohlin model and include all of the traditional assumptions, implying that the two countries differ only through differences in relative factor endowments. The locus $W_1ABW_1'$ represents E1 where all factors of production and consumers are located at a single location. In other words, this represents a world in which there is complete and costless factor mobility for all factors of production. Using a procedure first introduced by Purvis (1972) we now construct the aggregate world output set for the countries of the world, assumed in this simple example to be two. This produces set $W_2ABW_2'$ where sections $W_2A$ and $BW_2'$ represent boundaries of the sum of the production sets where one or the other of the two countries is specialized in production at the relevant price ratio. If preferences are represented by a community indifference curve, then aggregate world consumption could be at a point such as C. Alternatively, with different preferences, consumption on the locus $W_1CW_1'$ could be at a point such as $C_1$. For prices associated with equilibrium at $C_1$, equilibrium consumption on $W_2CW_2'$ would be at $C_2$.

With preferences associated with C the world output vector is the same in W1 as in W2, or in other words E1 = E2. Thus factor prices are equalized. When tastes give rise to production at $C_1$ on the sector $W_1A$ for the integrated economy, then for a trading world E1 ≠ E2 and factor prices

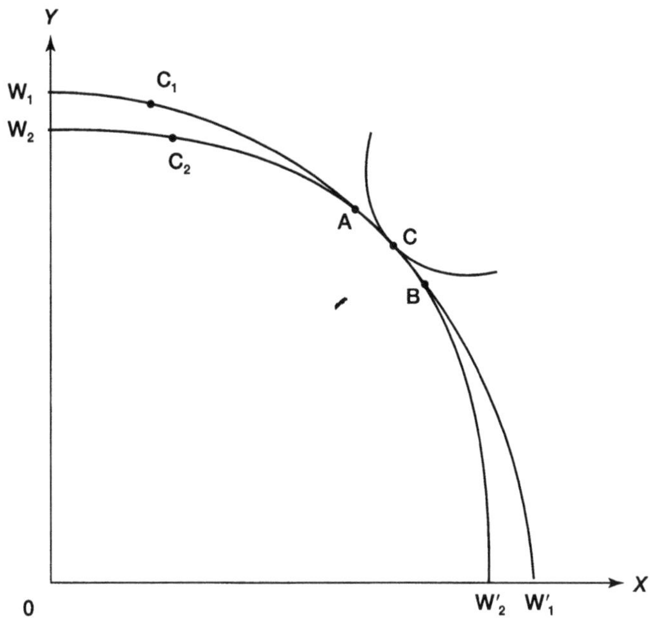


*Figure* 7.4

are not equalized. Of course in the second case the failure of factor prices to be equalized stems from the fact that for these demand conditions both countries are not producing both commodities in equilibrium, and consequently production cannot be efficient. This leads to a production point that is strictly inside the world efficient production frontier.

As a further example consider the case where a factor intensity reversal occurs. Of course if the endowment rays for both countries lie on the same side of the factor intensity reversal ray, then no difficulties will arise, and the situation will be exactly as described in Figure 7.4. Thus we consider the case where the factor intensity reversal ray lies between the endowment rays for the two countries. In the standard analysis, as described for example by Chipman (1966), this produces the possibility of two distinct cones of diversification. Two situations are possible. If one or both countries specialize then again the case is similar to the example described in Figure 7.4 where any consumption point in W2 would have a lower value than a consumption point for W1. It is possible, however, that the endowment rays of the two countries each lie in different cones of diversification. In this case both countries will produce both goods at a given world price ratio. The question now is whether the joint production vector for the two countries will be coincident with a section of the world production possibility set. That is, will production lie in some section such as AB of Figure 7.4? The answer is clearly no. It can be shown that with two countries in different cones of diversification, which necessarily implies different wage–rental ratios, a transfer of capital and labor between the two countries would allow a larger value of output, at given commodity prices, for both countries. This clearly implies that the vector of outputs in W2 must lie strictly below the surface $W_1CW_1'$ in Figure 7.4. In other words, with a factor intensity reversal the world production set found from summing the production sets of the two countries will lie *everywhere* below the world production set for the integrated economy. Factor prices are not equalized because the vector of outputs can *never* be the same in W1 and W2.

A similar argument can be made for the case of increasing returns to scale. It is easy to show that the world output vector for two countries facing the same prices can never be as large as the vector of world output if unlimited factor mobility is permitted. Again factor prices are not equalized because the consumption vectors in W1 and W2 cannot be the same. We are now in a position to state a proposition that emphasizes the role of demand.

> **PROPOSITION 2** For situations where factor price equalization is possible, demand conditions will determine whether or not factor prices are equalized by trade.

Perhaps the most important implication of Proposition 1 is that it makes clear what the factor price equalization theorem is really about. The conditions under which the factor price equalization theorem hold are conditions in which free trade alone can provide full optimality for the world. And in the situations where factor prices are not equalized by trade then full optimality for the world can only be achieved through mobility of some factors of production. It would seem important to know whether a world optimum can be achieved through commodity trade or whether factor movements are also required.

## The specific factor model

Demand conditions have always played a prominent role in the discussions of the specific factor model. A principal result from this model is the neo-classical ambiguity which shows that, while commodity price changes have well-defined effects on the prices of the specific factors, in general one cannot determine how the real return to labor will be affected. But while there is this general ambiguity about the effects on the real return to labor, Ruffin and Jones (1977) have argued that in certain circumstances this ambiguity can be removed, and that there is a presumption that tariffs will reduce the real return to labor. In this section we will briefly examine both the neo-classical ambiguity and the presumption about the effects of tariffs as presented by Ruffin and Jones.

Figure 7.5 presents a four-quadrant diagram familiar from the specific factor literature but with a difference. Whereas the typical diagram has the total product curve in the first and third quadrants, Figure 7.5 has, instead, the marginal product curves for these two industries. Of course this figure is easily derived from the standard one since the marginal product curves shown are simply the slopes of the total product curves. As usual, the third quadrant represents the total labor supply available for division between the two industries.

Now consider the allocation of labor between the two industries given by point A in Figure 7.5. The marginal product of labor function for the *Y* industry shows that with this allocation of labor to *Y* the marginal product will be Q. Similarly the marginal product of labor in the *X* industry will be Q′. Note that the line QQ′, the ratio of marginal products for the two industries, is simply the price ratio line, $p_x/p_y$, and this price ratio must be exactly the one that gave rise to the production of *X* and *Y* that resulted in the allocation of factors between the two industries associated with point A.

A similar procedure can be used for other commodity prices that produce other allocations of labor between the two industries. Thus with a relatively higher price of *Y* we obtain price line NN′ and the associated allocation of labor, and with a relatively lower price of *Y* we get price line MM′. The price lines in quadrant I show the marginal products earned by a unit of labor in the *X* or *Y* industries, and since factors are paid their marginal products, these price lines also represent the budget constraint for a

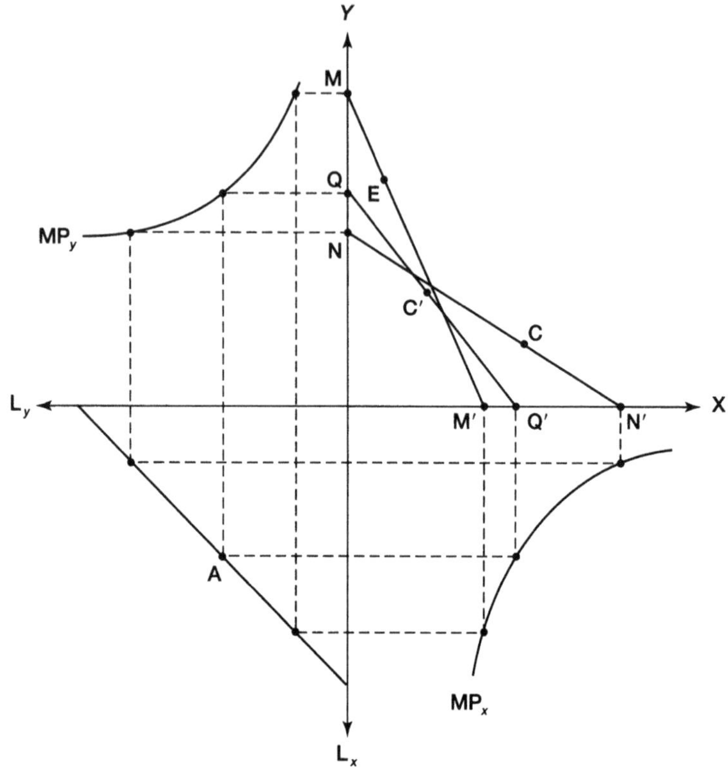


*Figure 7.5*

representative laborer. The exact consumption bundle chosen by a worker can thus be found by introducing a set of indifference curves for the worker and finding where the highest indifference curve is tangent to the budget constraint. Thus, for example, with prices NN′ an indifference curve could be tangent at C.

Figure 7.5 suggests some interesting cases of ambiguity. Consider, for example, consumption at Point C′ on prices QQ′. It is clear that for almost *any* choice of preferences, either increasing the price of *Y* to NN′ or reducing the price of *Y* to MM′ would increase welfare, since both NN′ and MM′ must intersect the indifference curve tangent at C′. Thus there is a price ratio (or price ratios) where the welfare of labor is at a minimum and such that movements of price in *any* direction will improve welfare.[11] Similarly, with an initial equilibrium at E and with an indifference curve that passes below C, increases in the relative price of *Y* will first reduce welfare as we move to C′ and then increase welfare as we move to C. This result would seem to be of interest, since it suggests that, at least for the production and consumption conditions implicit in Figure 7.5, it would be hard to form a presumption about how an increase in the price of a commodity would affect the welfare of labor.

The results from Figure 7.5 do not seem consistent with the conclusions of Ruffin and Jones, and it is therefore useful to review the procedures used by them. Their analysis can be represented in Figure 7.6, which is reproduced from Figure 1 of Ruffin and Jones (1977). The curve $\beta_{Lj}$ shows the percentage change in money wages for a one percent change in the price of commodity *j*, while $\theta_j^L$ represents the fraction of workers' expenditure devoted to commodity *j*. The neutral case described by Ruffin and Jones has the autarchy price at $P_j^0$ in Figure 7.6. An increase in the price, moving the price to the right of point $P_j^0$, increases the money wage rate relative to the share of expenditure on commodity *j*. If, in an initial trading situation commodity *j* were imported, the equilibrium price $P_j$ would be to the left of $P_j^0$ and then "any attempt to raise $P_j$ would hurt workers more via the increase in the cost of living than they would gain through a higher money wage" (Ruffin and Jones 1977: 341).

The Ruffin–Jones results do not seem to admit the possibilities indicated in our Figure 7.5. While the Ruffin–Jones results are certainly possible, there do seem to be other possibilities that they have not considered. In discussing the demand conditions of their model Ruffin and Jones say "no special assumptions as to demand or elasticities of workers for commodity *j* are made, save that consumption of all commodities is always positive and the two curves only intersect once." In a footnote they further claim that a

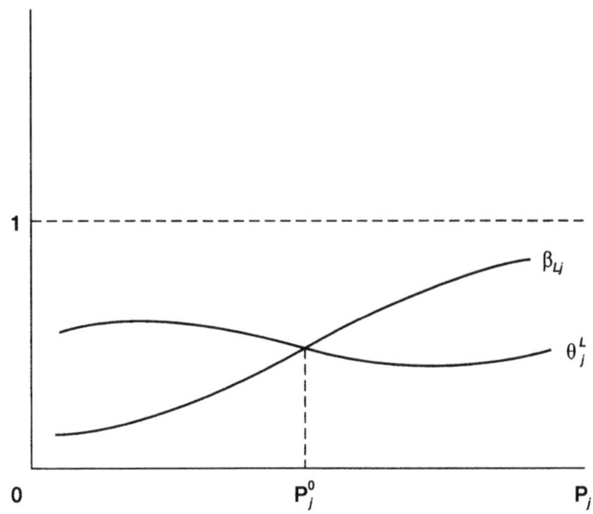


*Figure 7.6*

single intersection would "follow from the standard assumption that taste patterns for the community can be represented by a set of nonintersecting community indifference curves" (Ruffin and Jones 1977: 341).

There are two questions that can be asked about the demand assumption employed in the Ruffin–Jones paper. In Figure 7.6, do the two curves intersect only once and if they do intersect only once do they intersect as shown? The Ruffin–Jones results seem to depend on the type of intersection shown, namely that $\beta_{Lj}$ lies above $\theta_j^L$ to the right of the intersection. Putting aside the question of the shape of $\beta_{Lj}$ we consider the possible shapes of $\theta_j^L$. If preferences were Cobb–Douglas, then the share of income spent on any commodity is a constant and $\theta_j^L$ will be linear and positioned somewhere between 0 and 1 depending on the coefficients of the utility function. This is certainly consistent with the Ruffin–Jones result. But now suppose utility functions are Leontief, with the elasticity of substitution equal to zero. Since a constant amount of each good is consumed, at very low prices of commodity $j$ the share spent is small, this share rises as price rises, and approaches 1 as price gets very high. This produces curve $\theta_1$ in Figure 7.7a, and it certainly seems possible that the curves intersect as shown. Alternatively, if the two goods have a high degree of substitutability, such that the isoquants intersect both axes, then we could have $\theta_2$ of Figure 7.7b. Indeed, with a little work, and even assuming that all individuals have identical and homothetic preferences, it is possible to construct curves for $\theta$ that have a wide variety of shapes. Certainly the $\theta_3$ shown in Figure 7.7b is easy to construct. In this case whether an increase in the price of commodity $j$ will improve or reduce welfare will clearly depend on where the initial price is located.

Nor does it seem necessary that the two curves intersect at all. It is quite possible that $\theta_3$ in Figure 7.7c could lie everywhere below $\beta_{Lj}$, for example. The existence of such an intersection is not important, for intersections do not describe equilibria but are simply points defining ranges where utility changes differ for changes in $P_j$. Thus consider the case similar to Figure 7.7c where $\theta_3$ lies everywhere below $\beta_{Lj}$. In this case the price at which the two curves are closest together represents the minimum utility for the workers, and a movement in either direction would result in a larger gap between $\beta_{Lj}$ and $\theta$. According to the Ruffin–Jones analysis either such change would increase utility. This case is consistent with my Figure 7.5, although the demand conditions necessary to produce this result in the Ruffin–Jones model are more restricted than seem necessary from Figure 7.5.[12]

While the result derived by Ruffin and Jones is clearly correct for the particular demand assumptions implicitly assumed by them, their suggestion that demand assumptions were not important for the result seems to overstate the case. Of course the issue of whether the different forms of $\theta$

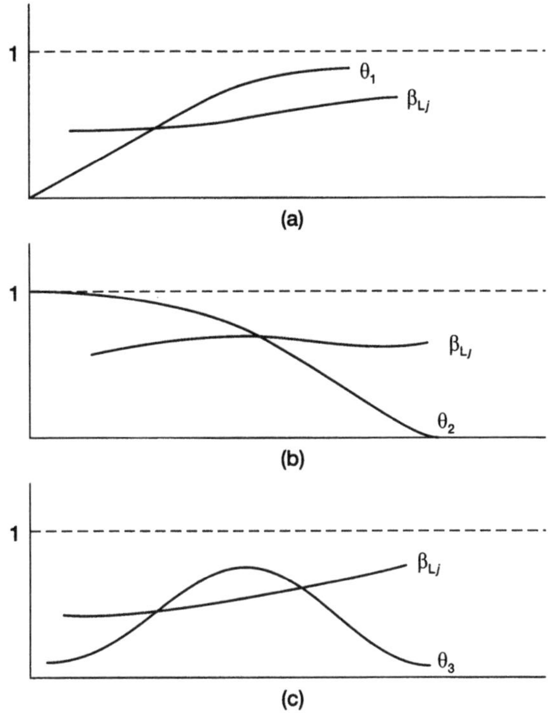


*Figure 7.7a–c*

shown in Figure 7.7 are to be expected is not a question that can be answered from a theoretical analysis.

## Increasing returns to scale

There are two models of increasing returns to scale in the trade literature, both of which have received a good deal of attention. The first to be developed was the model of external economies where individual firms are assumed to be perfectly competitive and the scale economy effects are at the industry level. The example of this model that we will focus attention on is Melvin (1969c).[13] The other model of increasing returns to scale has the economies at the level of the firm, and it is typically assumed that there are fixed costs and constant marginal cost associated with producing any commodity. The original formulation of this model was by Krugman (1979 and 1980) and we will focus our attention on his model.

In both of these models demand conditions have always played a prominent role, so that it is certainly not the case that the influence of demand has been neglected. On the other hand the two models, explicitly or implicitly, make quite different demand assumptions, and the point we wish to make here is that these specific demand assumptions are very crucial for the results derived. To illustrate we will summarize the two-country, two-commodity version of both models and then illustrate how the results will change if the demand conditions are changed.[14]

In panels a and b of Figure 7.8 the simple versions of these two models are shown with the external-economy version in a and the internal-economy version in b. The underlying assumptions for Figure 7.8a are that there are two countries with identical technologies and identical endowments of capital and labor, and that tastes are represented by identical homothetic preferences in the two countries. Thus in autarchy we have a community

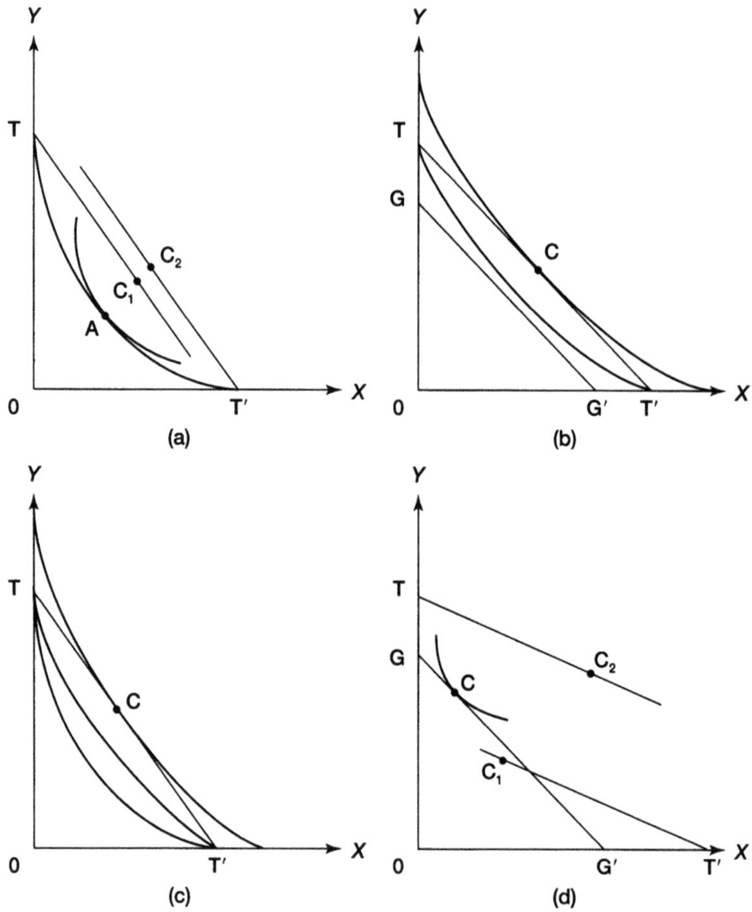


*Figure 7.8a–d*

indifference curve tangent to both of the identical production possibility curves at point A. Although the exact form of the utility function is usually not specified it could well be Cobb–Douglas, and so for the purposes of this discussion we will make that assumption.

For the internal-economy model of Figure 7.8b it is assumed that two goods, $X$ and $Y$, can be produced with identical production functions using a single factor labor, where both industries have identical fixed costs and identical constant marginal costs. This will give the production set made up of points T and T′ along with the straight-line segment GG′. The utility functions are of the form $U = \Sigma\, c_j^{\theta}$, where $0 < \theta < 1$. This utility function is completely symmetric, and a representative indifference curve must pass through both T and T′ in Figure 8.8b. Autarchy in this model will have consumers at either T or T′ consuming only one of the two goods. We can now summarize the implications of trade for these two models.

**EXTERNAL ECONOMIES**

1 Trade can result in gains for both countries but need not.
2 All goods are produced before and after trade.

**INTERNAL ECONOMIES**

1 Trade will result in gains for both countries.
2 There are two reasons for gains, namely "Welfare in both countries will increase, both because of higher w/p and because of increased choice" (Krugman 1979: 476).

It should also be noted that there are some differences in the implications for factor mobility and factor prices, but these are not comparable between the two models since the external model assumes two factors of production while the only factor of production in the internal economy's model is labor.

To illustrate the influence of demand assumptions we have, in panels c and d of Figure 7.8, assumed the same production structure as in panels a and b but now have reversed the assumptions about demand. Thus for the external-economies model of Figure 7.8c, consumption will be at either T or T′ in autarky with both countries consuming only one good. With free trade consumption will be at C, where both goods will be consumed, and both countries will unambiguously gain. With Cobb–Douglas utility functions for the model with internal economies of scale, and with asymmetric tastes so that preferences are biased towards $Y$, we could have an autarky equilibrium at point C where both goods are produced and consumed in both countries. With free trade both countries would specialize and the two consumption points would be $C_1$ and $C_2$, so that whichever country is specializing in commodity $X$ will not gain from trade.

It is clear from Figure 7.8 that switching the demand assumptions between the two models also exactly switches the conclusions. Thus the results listed above for external economies now apply to the internal-economy model and vice versa. There is, therefore, a significant sense in which the differences in the conclusions of the two models are entirely the consequence of the differing demand assumptions.

## Conclusions

We have investigated the effects of demand assumptions in a variety of international trade models beginning with the classical model associated with Ricardo, then considering the Heckscher–Ohlin model, the specific factor model, and concluding with a discussion of increasing returns to scale. In all of these models the effects of demand assumptions are important and their influence sometimes overlooked. It seems justifiable to conclude that although demand assumptions play an important role in all of these general equilibrium models, as of course they must in any type of economic analysis, demand assumptions have not received the same attention as have assumptions on the production side. In certain cases this has resulted in a neglect of certain interesting questions and in others has resulted in some overstatement of the novelty of the results. As an example of the latter, we noted that all of the results associated with trade from the internal-economy model can be derived from the traditional external-economy model by using a different demand assumption. This is not, of course, to suggest that the internal-economy model is not an important addition to the trade literature, for in many circumstances the existence of internal economies is much easier to justify than are external economies. The point is that the conclusions for trade policy do not differ much for the two models, at least for the two-good case.

## Notes

1 A discussion of "limbo prices" and the criticisms of Mill can be found in Graham (1932, 1948).
2 For a proof of this proposition and a complete analysis of the Mill condition, see Chipman (1965).
3 We are assuming here that all individuals in the world have identical Leontief preferences with some unspecified ratio of consumption of the two goods $X$ and $Y$. This is quite a different assumption than made by Graham who assumed that demand conditions differed among countries.
4 For utility functions $U = XY$, it will always be the case that $P_xX = P_yY$, or in other words that $P_x/P_y = Y/X$. Thus the ratio of commodity prices is equal to the ratio in which the two goods are consumed.
5 Note that here TE and EK refer to distances. These distances give the ratios in which the two goods are consumed.
6 This method was employed by Melvin (1969b) to analyze the situation where preferences differ for the Mill condition.

7 Absolute advantage in the sense that $a' > a''$ and $b' > b''$ conforms strictly to the usual notion of absolute advantage only for the case where the labor supplies for the two countries are the same. This condition can, however, be relaxed. It can be shown that if both countries have an absolute advantage in the traditional sense of the comparison of the productivity of a unit of labor, and if Mill's inequality holds, then we have efficiency in the sense described. Thus, the labor supplies for the two countries can differ as long as the difference is not so large as to preclude absolute advantage in one good by each of the countries.

8 For a discussion of this equivalence see Melvin (1974).

9 For a simple demonstration of this fact see Courchene and Melvin (1988). Of course without the assumptions of identical and homothetic preferences, offer curves need not be "well behaved".

10 There has been discussion of the relationship between the integrated economy and the factor price equalization theorem. An early example is Dixit and Norman (1980: 108ff.). Also related is the paper by Blackorby, Schworm and Venables (1993).

11 While for many choices of production functions there will be a point such as C′ that minimizes the utility of labor, we cannot claim that C′ of Figure 7.5 is this point. It is possible that slight changes in price could further reduce utility in Figure 7.5, depending on demand conditions and the shapes of the marginal product curves. It will be the case, however, that sufficiently large changes in prices in either direction in Figure 7.5 will increase utility.

12 The minimum utility for consumers depicted in Figure 7.5 would seem to depend on both the demand conditions and the production conditions. This raises the issue of possible shapes of $\beta_{Lj}$, an issue which we have not addressed.

13 There is extensive literature in this area. For a survey see Helpman (1984).

14 The analysis here is an extension of section 5 of Markusen and Melvin (1984). It should also be noted that the Krugman model, because it is a model of monopolistic competition, considers the case of many commodities. Thus a two-commodity version of his model is not completely true to the spirit of his analysis.

## Bibliography

Blackorby, C., Schworm, W. and Venables, A. (1993) "Necessary and Sufficient Conditions for Factor Price Equalization", *Review of Economic Studies* 60: 413–434.

Chipman, J.S. (1965–66) "A Survey of the Theory of International Trade", *Econometrica* 33: 477–519; 33: 685–760; 34: 18–76.

Courchene, T.J. and Melvin, J.R. (1988) "A Neoclassical Approach to Regional Economics", *Regional Economic Development: Essays in Honour of Francois Perroux*, CIRRD Conference Volume.

Dixit, A.K. and Norman, V.D. (1980) *Theory of International Trade*. Cambridge: Cambridge University Press.

Graham, F.D. (1932) "The Theory of International Values", *Quarterly Journal of Economics* 46: 581–616.

—— (1948) *The Theory of International Values*. Princeton, NJ: Princeton University Press.

Helpman, E. (1984) "Increasing Returns, Imperfect Markets, and Trade Theory", in R.W. Jones and P.B. Kenen (eds) *Handbook of International Economics* 1, ch. 7. Amsterdam: North-Holland.

Johnson, H.G. (1959) "International Trade, Income Distribution and the Offer Curve", *Manchester School* 27: 241–260.

Kenen, P.B. (1959) "Distribution, Demand, and Equilibrium in International Trade: A Diagrammatic Analysis", *Kyklos*: 629–638.

Krugman, P.R. (1979) "Increasing Returns, Monopolistic Competition and International Trade", *Journal of International Economics* 9: 469–479.

—— (1980) "Scale Economies, Product Differentiation and the Pattern of Trade", *American Economic Review* 70: 950–959.

Markusen, J.R. and Melvin, J.R. (1984) "The Gains from Trade Theorem with Increasing Returns to Scale", in H. Kierzkowski (ed.) *Monopolistic Competition in International Trade*, ch. 2, pp. 10–33. Oxford: Oxford University Press.

Meade, J.E. (1952) *A Geometry of International Trade*. London: George Allen and Unwin.

Melvin, J.R. (1969a) "On a Demand Assumption Made by Graham", *Southern Economic Journal* 36: 36–43.

—— (1969b) "Mill's Law of International Value", *Southern Economic Journal* 36: 107–116.

—— (1969c) "Increasing Returns to Scale as a Determinant of Trade", *Canadian Journal of Economics* 3: 389–402.

—— (1974) "On the Equivalence of Community Indifference and the Aggregate Consumption Function", *Economica* 41: 442–445.

—— (1985) "Domestic Taste Differences, Transportation Costs and International Trade", *Journal of International Economics* 18: 65–82.

Mill, J.S. (1844) *Essays on Some Unsettled Questions of Political Economy*. London: John W. Parker, West Strand.

Purvis, D.D. (1972) "Technology, Trade and Factor Mobility", *Economic Journal* 82: 991–999.

Ricardo, D. (1817) *On the Principles of Political Economy, and Taxation*. London: John Murray, Albemarle Street.

Ruffin, R.J. and Jones, R.W. (1977) "Protection and Real Wages: The Neoclassical Ambiguity", *Journal of Economic Theory* 14: 337–348.

Torrens, R. (1815) *An Essay on the External Corn Trade*. London: J. Hatchard.

# 8

# FACTOR SHARES AND THE CHIPMAN CONDITION

*Tapan Mitra and Ronald W. Jones*

## Introduction

Counterexamples often prove to be daunting obstacles to further research. Such was the case for two independent enquiries a quarter of a century ago as to the impact of price changes in commodity markets on the distribution of income. In the October 1969 issue of the *International Economic Review*, John Chipman provided a condition on distributive factor shares which, if satisfied for an economy with three factors of production engaged in producing in non-joint fashion three distinct commodities, sufficed to guarantee that any single commodity price rise would cause the return to the productive factor uniquely assigned to that sector to increase by relatively more than the commodity price. This he dubbed the weak form of the Stolper–Samuelson Theorem. However, Chipman also provided a counterexample to show that his condition would not be sufficient if the number of factors and goods were to equal four (Chipman 1969). A scant seven pages further on in this issue of the *Review* Murray Kemp and Leon Wegge (1969) also exhibited a counterexample for the case $n = 4$ to the proposition that their condition on ratios of factor shares would suffice to guarantee the strong form of the Stolper–Samuelson condition – a form in which a price rise causes all factors save the "intensive" one assigned to that sector to suffer losses in their returns.

In reacting to counterexamples it is sometimes appropriate to abandon the approach taken in the initial conjecture. However, there are occasions in which the criteria originally suggested prove to be useful, but need somewhat to be strengthened to yield the sought-for results. This, we would argue, is indeed the case for these two propositions. In Jones, Marjit and Mitra (1993) a condition sufficient to establish the strong Stolper–Samuelson (1941) result was derived, building upon the earlier criterion of Kemp and Wegge. In this chapter we establish that the original Chipman criterion can also be strengthened to yield conditions which suffice to guarantee the weak form of the Stolper–Samuelson result. Indeed, we go further in establishing conditions which ensure a "strong version" of the weak form: The factor identified with a commodity will have its return increased by relatively more than any other factor if the price of the commodity rises.

The following section of this chapter presents more formally the original criteria suggested in these two papers, as well as the statement of the revised Kemp–Wegge condition. In the next section we prove the sufficiency of a revised form of the Chipman condition. As the proof illustrates, even this revised form can be weakened somewhat. This alteration is noted in the fourth section in order to confirm that Chipman's original condition indeed is sufficient for the 3 × 3 case. That even this revised condition is not necessary if $n$ equals 4 is illustrated in the fifth section for a special class of production structures in which each industry displays a distribution of factor shares (a share rib) that has the same shape as every other industry (with an appropriate permutation of factors). Finally we argue in the concluding section that the form of the Stolper–Samuelson Theorem with which Chipman was particularly concerned (the "weak" form) is perhaps of more interest and relevance than the strong form.

## The two propositions

Both Chipman (1969) and Kemp and Wegge (1969) examine an economy producing $n$ commodities in independent non-joint linearly homogeneous activities using $n$ distinct primary inputs in competitive markets so that market prices reflect unit costs. They each were concerned to establish criteria defining what was meant by the assertion that every industry was associated with a unique factor of production which it used most intensively. Let $\theta_{ij}$ denote the distributive share of factor $i$ in industry $j$. Kemp and Wegge made the strong assumption that industry $i$ so intensively utilized factor $i$ that the ratio of $i$'s share in industry $i$ to that of any other input in industry $i$ (say $\theta_{ri}$) would exceed the corresponding share ratio in any other industry (say $j$). Thus their factor intensity condition (FI) stated:

$$\text{(FI)}: \frac{\theta_{ii}}{\theta_{ri}} > \frac{\theta_{ij}}{\theta_{rj}} \quad \forall i, r, j, \text{ with } i \neq r, j \tag{1}$$

Chipman's condition was less severe and, indeed, is implied by condition (1) (as proved by Kemp and Wegge). It only requires that factor $i$'s share in industry $i$ would exceed its share in any other industry. Call this the Factor Share condition (FS):

$$\text{(FS)}: \theta_{ii} > \theta_{ij} \quad \forall i, j, \text{ with } i \neq j \tag{2}$$

Jones, Marjit, and Mitra (1993) established that a strengthened version of Kemp and Wegge's condition (1) (labeled the Strong Factor Intensity condition – SFI) would suffice to guarantee the strong form of the Stolper–Samuelson Theorem:

$$\text{(SFI): } \left(\frac{\theta_{ii}}{\theta_{ri}} - \frac{\theta_{ij}}{\theta_{rj}}\right) > \sum_{s\neq i,j} \left|\frac{\theta_{si}}{\theta_{ri}} - \frac{\theta_{sj}}{\theta_{rj}}\right| \quad \forall i, r, j, \text{ with } i \neq r, j \text{ and } r \neq j \tag{3}$$

For $n \geq 4$ Kemp and Wegge illustrated in their counterexample that the positivity of the left-hand side of (3) would not suffice. Additionally, bounds must be put on the discrepancy among purely off-diagonal ratios of factor shares.[1] Thus *two* features of factor intensity comparisons emerge as important – each industry must use a unique factor most intensively, and there must not be too much variation among the shares of the unintensively-used factors in any industry compared with the extent of intensity of the most intensive factor. In this chapter we consider a strengthened form of Chipman's Factor Share condition (2) (which we label SFS, the Strong Factor Share condition):

$$\text{(SFS): } (\theta_{ii} - \theta_{ij}) > \sum_{r\neq i,j} |\theta_{ri} - \theta_{rj}| \quad \forall i, j, \text{ with } i \neq j \tag{4}$$

As we prove now, this condition is sufficient to establish the weak form of the Stolper–Samuelson Theorem.

## Implications of the strengthened Chipman condition

We start by assuming condition (4) and letting the price of some commodity, $k$, rise with all other commodity prices constant. Our object is to prove that $\hat{w}_k$ exceeds $\hat{p}_k$, where a "^" over a variable indicates a relative change ($\hat{x} \equiv dx / x$). Let $Q$ denote the set of all $i \neq k$, and given $\hat{p}_k > 0$ let $s$ be the factor in $Q$ which has experienced the greatest relative price rise and $t$ be the factor in $Q$ which has experienced the least relative price rise. Thus

$$\hat{w}_s \equiv \max_{i\in Q} \hat{w}_i \ ; \ \hat{w}_t \equiv \min_{i\in Q} \hat{w}_i$$

If we can prove that $\hat{w}_k$ exceeds $\hat{w}_s$, we are finished, for $\hat{p}_k$ must be a positive weighted average of all the $\hat{w}_j$, and therefore less than the largest of them. In proving this proposition we take a smaller step first – establishing that $\hat{w}_k$ must be larger than $\hat{w}_t$. That is, we start with the more modest aim of showing that when $p_k$ rises, factor $k$'s return is not lowered more than any other. Furthermore, just as set $Q$ denotes all $i \neq k$, let set $I$ be the set of all $i \neq k, s, t$.

Throughout our proofs we eschew formal matrix manipulations in favor of the heuristically more satisfying repeated use of the competitive profit equations of change whereby any relative commodity price change must equal the distributive share weighted average of all relative factor price changes. For industry $k$ this is shown as

$$\theta_{kk}\hat{w}_k + \theta_{sk}\hat{w}_s + \theta_{tk}\hat{w}_t + \sum_{i\in I} \theta_{ik}\hat{w}_i = \hat{p}_k \tag{5}$$

Now subtract $\hat{w}_t$ (equal to $\Sigma_{i=1}^{n} \theta_{ik}\hat{w}_t$) from both sides:

$$\theta_{kk}(\hat{w}_k - \hat{w}_t) + \theta_{sk}(\hat{w}_s - \hat{w}_t) + \sum_{i \in I} \theta_{ik}(\hat{w}_i - \hat{w}_t) = \hat{p}_k - \hat{w}_t \tag{6}$$

In a representation similar to (5) we could also write the competitive profit equations of change for industry $s$ – but the right-hand side would be zero since $p_s$ is being held constant when $p_k$ rises. Suppose we subtract $\hat{w}_t$ from each side of this equation (just as we did in going from (5) to (6)). That is,

$$\theta_{ks}(\hat{w}_k - \hat{w}_t) + \theta_{ss}(\hat{w}_s - \hat{w}_t) + \sum_{i \in I} \theta_{is}(\hat{w}_i - \hat{w}_t) = -\hat{w}_t \tag{7}$$

Finally, subtract term-by-term (7) from (6) to yield (8):

$$(\theta_{kk} - \theta_{ks})(\hat{w}_k - \hat{w}_t) + (\theta_{sk} - \theta_{ss})(\hat{w}_s - \hat{w}_t) + \sum_{i \in I} (\theta_{ik} - \theta_{is})(\hat{w}_i - \hat{w}_t) = \hat{p}_k \tag{8}$$

The next step in the proof involves setting upper bounds on $\sum_{i \in I}(\theta_{ik} - \theta_{is})(\hat{w}_i - \hat{w}_t)$. Since factor $t$ fares worse by the rise in $p_k$ than any other $i \in Q$, each $(\hat{w}_i - \hat{w}_t)$ is non-negative. Therefore,

$$\sum_{i \in I} (\theta_{ik} - \theta_{is})(\hat{w}_i - \hat{w}_t) \leq \sum_{i \in I} |\theta_{is} - \theta_{ik}|(\hat{w}_i - \hat{w}_t) \tag{9}$$

Since $\hat{w}_s$ is the $\max_i \hat{w}_{i \in Q}$, this latter term is $\leq$

$$\{\sum_{i \in I} |\theta_{is} - \theta_{ik}|\} \cdot (\hat{w}_s - \hat{w}_t) \tag{10}$$

which, by the Strong Factor Share condition (4) is less than or equal to $(\theta_{ss} - \theta_{sk})(\hat{w}_s - \hat{w}_t)$. If the resulting inequality,

$$\sum_{i \in I} (\theta_{ik} - \theta_{is})(\hat{w}_i - \hat{w}_t) \leq (\theta_{ss} - \theta_{sk})(\hat{w}_s - \hat{w}_t) \tag{11}$$

is inserted into (8), it follows that

$$(\theta_{kk} - \theta_{ks})(\hat{w}_k - \hat{w}_t) \geq \hat{p}_k > 0 \tag{12}$$

so that (since $\theta_{kk}$ exceeds $\theta_{ks}$ by the FS condition (2)), $\hat{w}_k$ must at least exceed $\hat{w}_t$.

To proceed, we now show that $\hat{w}_k$ is greater than the largest $\hat{w}_i$ (for $i \in Q$), i.e. $\hat{w}_s$. To do so, follow the procedure used in establishing (6) and (8), except consider the competitive profit equations of change for industries $t$ and $s$ (instead of $k$ and $s$), and subtract $\hat{w}_k$ from both sides (instead of $\hat{w}_t$). This yields:

$$\theta_{tt}(\hat{w}_t - \hat{w}_k) + \theta_{st}(\hat{w}_s - \hat{w}_k) + \sum_{i \in I} \theta_{it}(\hat{w}_i - \hat{w}_k) = -\hat{w}_k$$

$$\theta_{ts}(\hat{w}_t - \hat{w}_k) + \theta_{ss}(\hat{w}_s - \hat{w}_k) + \sum_{i \in I} \theta_{is}(\hat{w}_i - \hat{w}_k) = -\hat{w}_k$$

Subtract the second equation from the first to get:

$$(\theta_{ss} - \theta_{st})(\hat{w}_s - \hat{w}_k) + (\theta_{tt} - \theta_{ts})(\hat{w}_k - \hat{w}_t) + \sum_{i \in I} (\theta_{is} - \theta_{it})(\hat{w}_i - \hat{w}_k) = 0 \tag{13}$$

At this stage of the argument nothing has been established about the ranking of any $\hat{w}_i$ ($i \in I$) with $\hat{w}_k$, prompting us to split set $I$ ($i \neq s, t, k$) into two components. Thus let

$$I_1 \equiv \{i \in I \mid (\hat{w}_i - \hat{w}_k) > 0\}\ ;\ I_2 \equiv \{i \in I \mid (\hat{w}_i - \hat{w}_k) \leq 0\} \tag{14}$$

Rewrite (13) to separate $I_1$ from $I_2$:

$$\left\{(\theta_{ss} - \theta_{st})(\hat{w}_s - \hat{w}_k) - \sum_{i \in I_1} (\theta_{it} - \theta_{is})(\hat{w}_i - \hat{w}_k)\right\}$$
$$+ \left\{(\theta_{tt} - \theta_{ts})(\hat{w}_k - \hat{w}_t) - \sum_{i \in I_2} (\theta_{it} - \theta_{is})(\hat{w}_i - \hat{w}_k)\right\} = 0 \tag{15}$$

Once again we use SFS to work on the terms behind the summation signs. We shall proceed by contradiction, assuming $\hat{w}_s \geq \hat{w}_k$ and showing that equation (15) must be violated in such a case.

Examine, first, $\sum_{i \in I_1} (\theta_{it} - \theta_{is})(\hat{w}_i - \hat{w}_k)$. This must be less than or equal to $\sum_{i \in I_1} | \theta_{it} - \theta_{is} | (\hat{w}_i - \hat{w}_k)$ since $\hat{w}_i$ exceeds $\hat{w}_k$ in $I_1$. Since $\hat{w}_s$ is maximal in $Q$, this sum in turn is less than or equal to

$$\{\sum_{i \in I_1} | \theta_{it} - \theta_{is} |\} (\hat{w}_s - \hat{w}_k) \leq \{\sum_{i \in I} | \theta_{it} - \theta_{is} | \} (\hat{w}_s - \hat{w}_k)$$

which, by the SFS condition (4), must fall short of $(\theta_{ss} - \theta_{st})(\hat{w}_s - \hat{w}_k)$. Therefore the first bracketed term in (15) must be non-negative.

Next, consider $\sum_{i \in I_2} (\theta_{it} - \theta_{is})(\hat{w}_i - \hat{w}_k)$. Since in $I_2$, $\hat{w}_i$ is less than or equal

to $\hat{w}_k$, this sum is less than or equal to:

$$\sum_{i \in I_2} | \theta_{it} - \theta_{is} | (\hat{w}_k - \hat{w}_t) \leq \{ \sum_{i \in I_2} | \theta_{it} - \theta_{is} | \} (\hat{w}_k - \hat{w}_t)$$

since $\hat{w}_t$ is the smallest element. This expression in turn is less than or equal to $\{\sum_{i \in I} | \theta_{it} - \theta_{is} | \} (\hat{w}_k - \hat{w}_t)$ which, by the SFS condition, is less than

$(\theta_{tt} - \theta_{ts})(\hat{w}_k - \hat{w}_t)$. This implies that the second bracketed expression in (15) is strictly positive, which establishes the contradiction. Therefore $\hat{w}_k$ must exceed $\hat{w}_s$, and perforce must be larger than $\hat{p}_k$.

The strengthened Chipman condition (4) suffices to establish the weak version of the Stolper–Samuelson Theorem for any value of $n$ even though the original FS condition (2) proved insufficient for $n \geq 4$. Furthermore, we have proved an extra result not stated in the original weak form of the Stolper–Samuelson Theorem: Not only does the $k$th factor gain in real terms ($\hat{w}_k > \hat{p}_k$), but it gains more than any other factor ($\hat{w}_k > \hat{w}_s$) even though some other factor returns might rise.

## The Chipman condition in the 3 × 3 case

A consideration of the proof we just concluded reveals that the Strong Factor Share Condition (4) can be weakened. Condition (4) was invoked to compare terms like $(\theta_{ss} - \theta_{sk})$ with $\sum_{i \in I} | \theta_{is} - \theta_{ik} |$ or $(\theta_{ss} - \theta_{st})$ with $\sum_{i \in I} | \theta_{is} - \theta_{it} |$. But the set $I$ contains only $(n - 3)$ terms, whereas condition (4) involves $(n - 2)$ terms. Clearly if (4) is satisfied, so also will it be if any of the absolute values on the right-hand side is deleted. Thus a weaker form of (4) could be stated as

$$\text{(SFS}'\text{)}: (\theta_{ii} - \theta_{ij}) > \sum_{r \neq i,j,k} | \theta_{ri} - \theta_{rj} | \ \forall i, j, \text{ with } i \neq j \text{ and } k \neq i, j \qquad (4')$$

The somewhat more awkward statement (4′) is relevant in confirming Chipman's observation that the dominance of factor *i*'s share in industry *i* over *i*'s share in any other sector is sufficient if $n = 3$ to establish the weak form of the Stolper–Samuelson Theorem. Such confirmation is immediate, for if $n = 3$ the right-hand side of (4′) vanishes since it has no elements.

The case of $n = 3$ can also be used to illustrate an asymmetry between Chipman's treatment of the weak Stolper–Samuelson Theorem and the Kemp–Wegge analysis of the strong form of the theorem. Kemp and Wegge show that the factor intensity condition (FI, (1)) is a *necessary* consequence if an economy throughout exhibits strong Stolper–Samuelson properties.[2] The analogous question can be raised: If an economy displays weak Stolper–Samuelson properties, is the factor share condition (FS), inequality (2), necessarily satisfied? The answer is in the negative as the following share matrix reveals:

$$\theta' = \begin{bmatrix} 0.31 & 0.3 & 0.39 \\ 0.3 & 0.4 & 0.3 \\ 0.3 & 0.315 & 0.385 \end{bmatrix}$$

Here, $\theta_{31}$, with a value of 0.39, exceeds the $\theta_{33}$ value of 0.385. Computation of $(\theta')^{-1}$, however, reveals that diagonal elements all exceed unity. (The example clearly also shows that condition SFS – which is stronger than condition FS – is not necessary for an economy to display weak Stolper–Samuelson properties.)

If the weak form of the Stolper–Samuelson Theorem does not imply the Chipman FS condition, what can be said about factor shares if the *strong version* of the weak form is assumed to hold? Once again what is true for small values of $n$ ($\leq 3$) fails to hold for $n \geq 4$. The following counter-example suffices: Let

$$\theta' = \begin{bmatrix} 0.28 & 0.24 & 0.24 & 0.24 \\ 0.24 & 0.28 & 0.24 & 0.24 \\ 0.22 & 0.23 & 0.28 & 0.27 \\ 0.24 & 0.25 & 0.25 & 0.26 \end{bmatrix}$$

The inverse of this $4 \times 4$ share matrix,

$$(\theta')^{-1} = \begin{bmatrix} 16.12 & -5.52 & -4.80 & -4.80 \\ -8.88 & 19.48 & -4.80 & -4.80 \\ 15.12 & 15.48 & 35.20 & -64.80 \\ -20.88 & -28.52 & -24.80 & 75.20 \end{bmatrix}$$

satisfies the strict version of the weak form of the Stolper–Samuelson Theorem, but the original share matrix violates the FS condition. However, it can be shown that for $n = 3$ the FS condition follows from the assumption that the strict version is satisfied.[3]

## An example when $n = 4$

A special class of production relationships imposes a kind of strict symmetry among sectors, in which factors are numbered such that the array of distributive shares in the first industry is non-increasing and the shape of this "share rib" is replicated for all other sectors with a permutation such that $\theta_{ii}$ always is the dominant share in industry $i$. (In matrix form this is known as a circulant matrix.) In particular suppose the share rib for sector 1 is composed of:

$$\frac{1}{\Delta}\{1, \alpha, \alpha\beta, \alpha\beta^2\}$$

where $\Delta$ is defined as the sum of the elements in brackets, thus ensuring that distributive shares add to unity. (For example, $\theta_{31}$ is $\alpha\beta/\Delta$.) The terms $\alpha$ and $\beta$ are assumed to be positive fractions. These parameter restrictions imply that the factor share condition (2) is satisfied.

Elsewhere we have examined in detail the properties of an $n \times n$ economy displaying share ribs of this type.[4] There we show that the weak form of the Stolper–Samuelson Theorem is always satisfied for restrictions on $\alpha$ and $\beta$ noted above. Here we illustrate that the Strong Factor Share condition, even in form (4′), is not always satisfied, so that the condition is not necessary, even when condition FS is satisfied.

Consider the term $(\theta_{11} - \theta_{14})$ which, for this case,[5] is $(1 - \alpha)/\Delta$. Condition (4′) would require this to exceed, inter alia, the term $|\theta_{21} - \theta_{24}|$ or $(\alpha - \alpha\beta)/\Delta$. Such a condition reduces to requiring $\beta > 2 - (\frac{1}{\alpha})$. For values of $\alpha$ less than $\frac{1}{2}$ this is clearly satisfied, so suppose $\frac{1}{2} < \alpha < 1$. The accompanying diagram illustrates in the shaded area those values of $\beta$ which do not satisfy the inequality required by (4′). The weak version of the Stolper–Samuelson Theorem is none the less valid (and condition FS is satisfied) so that condition (4′) (much less the SFS condition (4)) is not necessary.

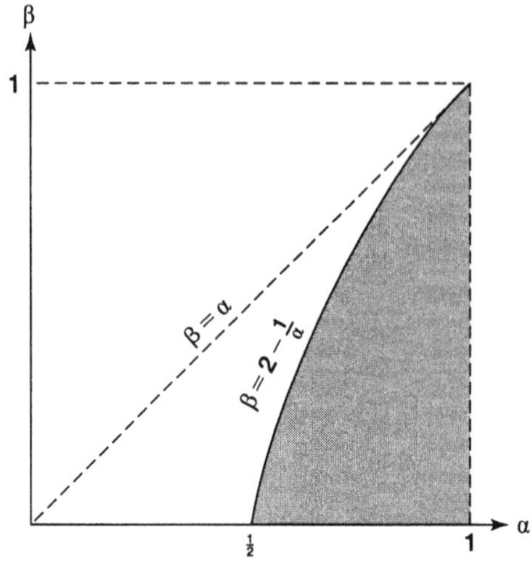


## Concluding remarks

In his 1969 article John Chipman was on the right track in suggesting that a comparison of a factor's distributive share in the industry in which it is uniquely associated with its share in any other industry is of relevance in establishing the weak form of the Stolper–Samuelson Theorem. But the dominance of $\theta_{ii}$ over all other $\theta_{ij}$ proved, as he recognized, not to suffice for economies with large numbers of goods and factors. In this chapter we have pursued the search for sufficient conditions. In our Strong Factor Share condition (4), or somewhat weaker version (4′), we display the requirement that the dominance of factor *i*'s share in industry *i* over its share anywhere else in the economy be large enough to exceed the aggregate absolute value of discrepancies of other factor shares in these two sectors. Thus if variation among shares of unintensive factors is sufficiently limited, the weak Stolper–Samuelson Theorem emerges. In our proof we established the extra property that a single price rise not only results in an increase in the real return to the associated intensively-used factor, but no other factor gains in percentage terms by more.

The weak form of the Stolper–Samuelson Theorem seems more relevant than the strong form from the point of view of the motivation of any particular factor to lobby for a commodity price change which will improve its real reward. Such a factor might either not care about what happens to other income earners or, indeed, may welcome the chance for disguise provided by the possibility that some other factors also gain. In the strong form of the Theorem there is only one winner who unambiguously and nakedly emerges from such a price change.

## Notes

1 Note that the SFI condition (as well as the strong Stolper–Samuelson result) must be violated if there is any factor that is not used in positive amounts in every industry.

2 A proof of the necessity of (FI), making use of competitive profit equations of change, is found in Jones (1993).

3 Although a proof is not provided here, it makes use of the fact that the off-diagonal elements of the inverse of a share matrix can be written as the appropriate diagonal entry minus a term related to the FS condition, e.g. $(\theta_{33} - \theta_{32})$. It can be shown that a stochastic matrix with a "dominating" diagonal (i.e. $\theta_{ii} > \theta_{ij}$ along the *i*th row) has an inverse which is also stochastic and, as well, has a "dominating diagonal" in the $3 \times 3$ case.

4 See Jones and Mitra (1995).

5 The share rib for sector 4 is shown by $\frac{1}{\Delta}\{\alpha, \alpha\beta, \alpha\beta^2, 1\}$.

## Bibliography


Chipman, John (1969) "Factor Price Equalization and the Stolper–Samuelson Theorem," *International Economic Review* (October): 399–406.

Jones, Ronald W. (1993): "Reflections on the Stolper–Samuelson Theorem," in H. Herberg and N. VanLong *Trade, Welfare and Economic Policies*, pp. 21–36. Michigan: University of Michigan Press.

Jones, Ronald, Marjit, Sugata and Mitra, Tapan (1993) "The Stolper–Samuelson Theorem: Links to Dominant Diagonals," in R. Becker et al. *General Equilibrium, Growth and Trade II*, pp. 429–444. New York: Academic Press.

Jones, Ronald and Mitra, Tapan (1995): "Share Ribs and Income Distribution," *Review of International Economics*: 36–52.

Kemp, Murray C. and Wegge, Leon (1969): "On the Relation Between Commodity Prices and Factor Rewards," *International Economic Review* (October): 407–413.

Stolper, Wolfgang and Samuelson, Paul (1941) "Protection and Real Wages," *Review of Economic Studies* (November): 58–73.

# 9

# OLIGOPOLY AND CUSTOMS UNIONS

*Raymond Riezman*

In this chapter we analyze a model of international oligopoly when customs unions are possible. We show that importer–exporter customs unions are pro-competitive in the sense that internally they will tend to have industries produce at their competitive output level, but will tend to exclude imports from non-member countries. Exporter customs unions are anti-competitive and will produce the monopoly output. We apply core theory to determine which unions would form. With one firm in each country the importer will form a union with the low cost exporter. With identical costs, but variable numbers of firms, when the number of firms is small an importer–exporter customs union forms. A union of the exporters will form if there are four or more firms in the world.

## Introduction

Although there has been extensive research analyzing international trade with oligopolistic firms[1] and customs unions,[2] until recently the profit-shifting literature has ignored the effects of customs unions and the customs union literature has assumed perfect competition. We have a dual purpose in combining these topics. First, to see how the possibility that countries can form customs unions changes our views about profit shifting. Second, how does the existence of imperfectly competitive firms alter our thinking about customs unions?

We find that customs unions change the way profit shifting is manifest in the world economy. If an importer–exporter customs union forms then the exporter produces the competitive output and imports from the outside are very small (in some cases zero). If both exporters form a customs union they produce the monopoly output. Despite the fact that world welfare is higher when an importer–exporter union forms we show that the exporter union will sometimes emerge as the equilibrium. Thus, customs unions change profit-shifting behavior.

A central motivation for customs union formation that comes out of the literature is that unions form to enable member countries to compete more effectively on world markets. That motivation is present here, but new motivations emerge. With imperfect competition, customs unions also function as a coordination device in the case of the exporter customs union. Through customs union the world's exporters are able to monopolize the world market by not only coordinating the firms within countries, but also coordinating across countries. The importer–exporter union also is able to use the customs union to counteract the distortion caused by the oligopolistic market structure. This suggests that profit-shifting behavior is different when customs unions can form and that the existence of oligopolistic market structures presents new motivations for customs unions to form.

There has been some recent work on customs unions with imperfectly competitive markets. Gatsios (1987) and Gehrig (1990) have developed models somewhat different than the one here. Unlike the model presented below, they assume segmented markets, do not allow side payments within a customs union, and have only one firm in each country. The results they obtain have a different flavor. Gatsios (1987) finds that either free trade or a customs union between the high cost countries will be the only core allocations. In our model free trade is never in the core and the importer will prefer the country with the most efficient firms as its partner. Gehrig (1990) analyzes a two period model and finds that customs unions may form as a "protection union" so that inefficient firms can eliminate their cost disadvantage.

## The model

We consider a market for a homogeneous good produced by a relatively small number of firms, $F$, $n_1$ of which are located in country 1 and $n_2$ of which are in country 2. Consumers are located in country $C$. For simplicity we ignore domestic consumption in countries 1 and 2 and assume that the good is not produced in country $C$.[3] Firms in country $i$ produce at constant marginal cost $c_i$, so profits of a country $i$ firm are

$$\pi_i = (p_i - c_i)q_i$$

where $p_i$ is the price received by producers in country $i$ and $q_i$ is the output produced by a country $i$ firm.

Assume that the inverse demand in country $C$ is

$$p = a - bQ \tag{1}$$

where $p$ is the price consumers pay and $Q$ is total production. The parameters $a$ and $b$ are both positive. With no government intervention, the Cournot–Nash equilibrium level of firm output is

$$q_1 = \frac{a - (1 + n_2)\, c_1 + n_2 c_2}{b\,(1 + n_1 + n_2)}$$

Total world production is

$$q_2 = \frac{a - (1 + n_1)\, c_2 + n_1 c_1}{b\,(1 + n_1 + n_2)}$$

$$Q = \frac{n_1\,(a - c_1) + n_2\,(a - c_2)}{b\,(1 + n_1 + n_2)} \tag{2}$$

The producer price is

$$p = \frac{a + n_1 c_1 + n_2 c_2}{1 + n_1 + n_2}$$

Per firm profits in the producing countries are

$$\pi_1 = \frac{(a - (1 + n_2)\, c_1 + n_2 c_2)^2}{b\,(1 + n_1 + n_2)^2}$$

$$\pi_2 = \frac{(a - (1 + n_1)\, c_2 + n_1 c_1)^2}{b\,(1 + n_1 + n_2)^2}$$

Welfare in each country is just total profits. In the consuming country, welfare given by total consumer surplus is

$$W_c = \frac{(n_1\,(a - c_1) + n_2\,(a - c_2))^2}{2b\,(1 + n_1 + n_2)^2}$$

We now consider government intervention in a three stage game. In the first stage the government decides which countries, if any, it will cooperate with. Given the first stage decisions, the government chooses optimal export subsidies/taxes and tariffs, and in the third stage firms and consumers make their decisions, taking government policies as fixed. The novel element of the game is the first stage, which is typically ignored in this literature.[4]

As usual, we solve the third stage first. Given firm reaction functions we next determine how countries set export subsidies/taxes and import tariffs for each possible coalition structure. Given this we determine which coalition structures are equilibria.

## Nash equilibrium – no customs unions

In this section we determine what happens if no customs unions form. Countries 1 and 2 set export subsidies/taxes, $s_1$ and $s_2$ respectively, and country $C$ sets its tariff, $t$ (which is allowed to be negative), taking into account how firms and consumers will react. Consumer demand is

$$p = a - bQ - t \tag{3}$$

Solving the firm reaction functions, we determine what firms will produce for a given set of government policies.

$$q_1 = \frac{a - t - (1 + n_2)(c_1 - s_1) + n_2 (c_2 - s_2)}{b (1 + n_1 + n_2)} \quad (4)$$

$$q_2 = \frac{a - t - (1 + n_1)(c_2 - s_2) + n_1 (c_1 - s_1)}{b (1 + n_1 + n_2)} \quad (5)$$

These expressions have the expected properties. Higher tariffs reduce output in both countries. Higher subsidies increase output in the subsidizing country and reduce output in the other country.

Governments use these relationships in computing their optimal policies. Countries 1 and 2 choose export subsidies/taxes which maximize profits net of subsidies for their firms.

$$\max_{s_i} (p - c_i)q_i$$

Using (3), (4) and (5) solving these maximization problems we get reaction functions for countries 1 and 2. For country 1 we have

$$s_1 = -\frac{(n_1 - n_2 - 1)(a - c_1 (n_2 + 1) + c_2 n_2 - n_2 s_2 - t)}{2n_1 (n_2 + 1)} \quad (6)$$

Country 2's reaction function is

$$s_2 = \frac{(n_1 - n_2 + 1)(a + c_1 n_1 - c_2 (n_1 + 1) - n_1 s_1 - t)}{2n_2(n_1 + 1)} \quad (7)$$

Country $C$ chooses its tariff to maximize its welfare, consumer surplus plus tariff revenue.

$$\max_{t} .5bQ^2 + tQ$$

Solution of this problem using (4) and (5) yields country $C$'s reaction function

$$t = \frac{a (n_1 + n_2) - (n_1 c_1 + n_2 c_2) + n_1 s_1 + n_2 s_2}{(n_1 + n_2)(n_1 + n_2 + 2)} \quad (8)$$

Solve (6), (7) and (8) to obtain equilibrium values of $s_1$, $s_2$ and $t$

$$s_1 = -\frac{(n_1 - n_2 - 1)(a (n_1 + n_2) - c_1 (n_1^2 + n_1 (n_2 + 3) + 2n_2 + 1) + c_2 (n_1 + n_2 + 1)(n_1 + 1))}{n_1 A} \quad (9)$$

$$s_2 = \frac{(n_1 - n_2 + 1)(a (n_1 + n_2) + c_1 (n_2 + 1)(n_1 + n_2 + 1) - c_2 (n_2^2 + n_2 (n_1 + 3) + 2n_1 + 1))}{n_2 A} \quad (10)$$

$$t = \frac{a (n_1 + n_2 + 2) - c_1 (n_2 + 1) - c_2 (n_1 + 1)}{A} \quad (11)$$

where $A = n_1^2 + n_2^2 + 4(n_1 + n_2) + 2(n_1 n_2 + 1)$.

Notice that whether exporting countries tax or subsidize depends on the relative number of firms in each country and on relative costs. To see this consider the special case, $c_1 = c_2$. Then, sign $s_1$ = sign $(1 - n_1 + n_2)$, the exporter will subsidize if it has few firms relative to the other country and will tax if it has a relatively large number of firms. To see the effects of relative costs let $n_1 = n_2 = 1$. Then,

$$s_1 = \frac{a - 4c_1 + 3c_2}{7}$$

Country 1's subsidy will be higher the higher country 2 cost is relative to country 1 cost. If country 1 firms are inefficient enough, then country 1 will actually tax its firms. Thus, exporters are more likely to subsidize the more efficient its own firms are relative to its rival.

For the case of Nash equilibrium with no customs unions one can calculate equilibrium prices, quantities, profits, and country welfare (profits net of subsidies) by substituting (9), (10), and (11) into the appropriate expressions. As expected, countries with lower costs and fewer firms do better at Nash equilibrium than those with high costs and many firms. To save space we do not report the details of these calculations. We next turn to the consideration of importer–exporter customs unions.

## Importer–Exporter customs union

In customs unions between importers and exporters there is a conflict of interest since importers want low prices and exporters do better with high prices. We deal with this problem by allowing side payments within the customs union. In particular, we assume that the union sets production subsidies and tariffs jointly and that the Nash bargaining solution determines each country's payoff. In this case there is no conflict of interest and subsidies and tariffs will be set to maximize the joint surplus.

### *Union with the high cost firm {C,1}*

Two types of importer–exporter customs unions could form. The importer could form a customs union with either the high cost or the low cost country. For concreteness we assume that country 1 is the high cost country, that is, $c_1 > c_2$. We first analyze a customs union between countries $C$ and 1.

With this type of customs union it is no longer true that producers in countries 1 and 2 face the same prices. Let $p_i$ be the price faced by producers in country $i$, then

$$\begin{aligned} p_1 &= a - bQ \\ p_2 &= a - bQ - t \end{aligned} \tag{3'}$$

Since only country 2 firms now face the tariffs, the firm reaction functions are

$$q_1 = \frac{a + n_2 t - (1 + n_2)(c_1 - s_1) + n_2(c_2 - s_2)}{b(1 + n_1 + n_2)} \tag{4'}$$

$$q_2 = \frac{a - (1 + n_1)t - (1 + n_1)(c_2 - s_2) + n_1(c_1 - s_1)}{b(1 + n_1 + n_2)} \tag{5'}$$

Notice that $q_1$ is now positively related to the tariff since it is only levied on country 2, and the tariff now has a larger negative effect on country 2's output than it did in the Nash equilibrium case.

We assume that the customs union chooses the tariff rate and subsidy on good 1 to maximize total welfare of both countries and redistributes income in accordance with the Nash bargaining solution, using Nash equilibrium welfare as the security level. This gives rise to the following optimization problem

$$\max_{t,s_i} 5bQ^2 + tn_2q_2 + (p_1 - c_1)n_1q_1$$

The union chooses values for $t$ and $s_1$ to maximize consumer surplus in country $C$ plus profits in country 1. What each country gets is their security value (welfare at Nash equilibrium) plus one-half of the remaining surplus left at the customs union equilibrium. For purposes of determining policy the union tries to maximize the total surplus accruing to the union. Solving this optimization problem we get two reaction functions for the customs union

$$s_1 = \frac{a(2n_2 + 1) + c_1(n_1n_2 - (n_2 + 1)^2) - c_2n_2(n_1 - n_2) - tn_2(2n_1 + 1) - s_2n_2(n_2 - n_1)}{n_1(2n_2 + 1)} \tag{12}$$

$$t = \frac{a(2n_1 + 1) + c_1n_1(n_1 - n_2) - c_2((n_1 + 1)^2 - n_1n_2) - s_1n_1(2n_1 + 1) + s_2(n_1n_2 - (n_1 + 1)^2)}{2(n_1 + 1)^2 + n_2} \tag{13}$$

The non-member country chooses $s_2$ taking $t$ and $s_1$ as given to maximize profits net of subsidies for its firms yielding

$$s_2 = \frac{(n_1 - n_2 + 1)a + c_1n_1 - c_2(n_1 + 1) - t(n_1 + 1) - s_1}{2n_2(n_1 + 1)} \tag{14}$$

Comparing (12) and (13) with (6) and (8) the formation of the union has changed the reaction functions of the member countries in that $s_1$ and $t$ are now negatively related; higher tariffs mean larger subsidies for union firms. The non-member's reaction function is essentially the same as before.

The next step is to solve (12)–(14) to get equilibrium values for $s_1$, $s_2$, and $t$.

$$s_1 = \frac{a(n_1 + n_2 + 1) - c_1(n_1(n_2 + 1) + 2n_2 + 1) + c_2n_2(n_1 + 1)}{n_1(n_1 + n_2 + 1)} \tag{15}$$

$$t = \frac{(n_1 + 1)(c_1 - c_2)}{n_1 + n_2 + 1} \tag{16}$$

$$s_2 = \frac{(n_1 - n_2 + 1)(c_1 - c_2)}{n_1 + n_2 + 1} \tag{17}$$

The union subsidy is higher the more efficient union firms are relative to non-union firms, but the tariff is higher the more *inefficient* union firms are relative to their rivals. The non-member subsidy is higher the more efficient its own firms are. Using (15)–(17) one can compute that $p_1 = c_1$, $Q = (a - c_1)/b$. What the union does is to set subsidies and tariffs to get the competitive output for a market with country 1 costs. Country 2 firms supply more output to the union the more cost efficient its firms are, as $q_2 = (n_1 + 1)(c_1 - c_2)/b(n_1 + n_2 + 1)$. In the limit, as country 2's cost advantage goes to zero, they are squeezed completely out of the market.

### *Union with the low cost country {C,2}*

We now look at the case of union between the importer and the efficient country, country 2. Equations (3′), (4′) and (5′) are modified as follows.

$$\begin{aligned} p_1 &= a - bQ - t \\ p_2 &= a - bQ \end{aligned} \tag{3''}$$

$$q_1 = \frac{a - (1 + n_2)t - (1 + n_2)(c_1 - s_1) + n_2(c_2 - s_2)}{b(1 + n_1 + n_2)} \tag{4''}$$

$$q_2 = \frac{a + n_1 t - (1 + n_1)(c_2 - s_2) + n_1(c_1 - s_1)}{b(1 + n_1 + n_2)} \tag{5''}$$

We follow the same procedure as in the above subsection, and derive reaction functions for the union and the non-member country. To save space we only report the solution to the reaction functions, keeping in mind the restriction that quantities must be non-negative. The solution is $s_1 = t = 0$ and $s_2 = (a - c_2)/n_2$. Total industry output $Q = (a - c_2)/b$, the competitive level with country 2 costs. Foreign firms are completely shut out, $q_1 = 0$. The price in both countries is country 2's cost, $p_1 = p_2 = c_2$.

So if the non-member is a less efficient producer than the member country, the optimal policy is to exclude the non-member completely from the market. Then, the union internally produces the competitive output. Since members' welfare depends only on total union welfare under customs union and the security levels (Nash equilibrium welfare), this policy makes sense despite zero firm profits (net of subsidies). What the union is able to do is not only to coordinate member firms to play effectively against the outside firms, but also it is able to counteract the distortion caused by the oligopolistic industry structure. To summarize: in a union between an exporter and an importer, what the union does is to subsidize union firms to produce the competitive output (relative to the member firm's cost). At the same time, the union sets the tariff to exclude all non-union products, unless foreign firms have a cost advantage over union firms (in which case some imports will be allowed).

Welfare levels can also be computed using the equilibrium tariff and subsidy levels. One interesting question is, will the importing country prefer a union with the high or low cost country? We put off answering that question until the section on welfare comparisons.

## Exporter customs union {1,2}

A customs union between the two exporters implies a model similar to that of the section on Nash equilibrium with no customs unions. Demand is given by (3) and firm reaction functions by (4) and (5). The problem for the customs union is to maximize joint profits. Given constant marginal costs, the solution to the custom union's problem is quite simple: have the firms in the efficient country produced the monopoly level of output and have the inefficient firms produced nothing. Setting $n_2q_2 = (a - c_2 - t)/2b$, and $q_1 = 0$ we get the two reaction functions for the customs union

$$s_1 = -\frac{a - c_1(n_2 + 1) + n_2(c_2 - s_2) - t}{n_2 + 1} \tag{18}$$

$$s_2 = \frac{a(n_1 - n_2 + 1) - 2c_1n_1n_2 + c_2(2n_1n_2 - n_1 + n_2 - 1) + 2n_1n_2s_1 - t(n_1 - n_2 + 1)}{2n_2(n_1 + 1)} \tag{19}$$

The importer faces the same problem as in the Nash equilibrium case and hence has a reaction function given by equation (8). We solve (18), (19), and (8) to get equilibrium values for $s_1$, $s_2$ and $t$.

$$s_1 = -\frac{a(n_1 + n_2) - c_1(2n_1 + 2n_2 + 1) + c_2(n_1 + n_2 + 1)}{(2n_1 + 2n_2 + 1)} \tag{20}$$

$$s_2 = -\frac{(n_2 - 1)(n_1 + n_2)(a - c_2)}{n_2(2n_1 + 2n_2 + 1)} \tag{21}$$

$$t = \frac{a - c_2}{2n_1 + 2n_2 + 1} \tag{22}$$

This yields an equilibrium price and quantity of

$$p = \frac{a(n_1 + n_2) + c_2(n_1 + n_2 + 1)}{2n_1 + 2n_2 + 1} \qquad Q = \frac{(n_1 + n_2)(a - c_2)}{b(2n_1 + 2n_2 + 1)} \tag{23}$$

The payoffs are computed the same way as before. Each customs union member receives its Nash equilibrium payoff plus one-half the remaining surplus. In the next section we discuss welfare comparisons among different customs unions.

## Welfare comparisons

To determine which customs unions will form, we need to be able to compare welfare across different customs union structures. Here we solve for welfare levels and make some preliminary comparisons. The problem we face is that the expressions for welfare are very complicated since the exporters differ both in cost and number of firms. To simplify, we consider two special cases, one in which there is only one firm in each country, $n_1 = n_2 = 1$, and second, the case in which costs are the same in each country, $c_1 = c_2 = c$.

Recall that country 1 has the high cost firms so, $c_1 > c_2$. Let $W^i\{jk\}$ be the welfare of country $i$ when there is a customs union between countries $j$ and $k$. $W^i\{\text{FT}\}$ and $W^i\{\text{NE}\}$ represent the welfare of country $i$ when there is free trade (FT) or at Nash equilibrium (NE), respectively. We report each of these welfare measures for both special cases in the appendix at the end of this chapter.

First examine the $n_1 = n_2 = 1$ case. The Nash equilibrium is important because it determines the security values used in determining the customs union payoffs. Notice that $W^1\{\text{NE}\} < W^2\{\text{NE}\}$, i.e. the low cost country does better than the high cost country at Nash equilibrium. Also note that $W^c\{\text{NE}\} > W^c\{\text{FT}\}$, i.e. the importing country prefers the Nash equilibrium to free trade. This result is consistent with the profit-shifting literature.

Exporters also prefer to be in a union with the importer than excluded from such a union, $W^1\{C1\} > W^1\{C2\}$ and $W^2\{C2\} > W^2\{C1\}$. This result is not surprising. Likewise, the importer prefers union with either exporter to having the exporter's union form, $W^c\{12\} < \min\,[W^c\{C1\}, W^c\{C2\}]$.

There are two comparisons that are not so straightforward. First, does the importer prefer union with the low or high cost country? The advantage of the low cost country is that more output gets produced, giving higher total welfare. However, the low cost country has a higher security value since it does better at Nash equilibrium than the high cost country, so the importer keeps a smaller share of the total payoff to the union. To determine the answer, taking (A15)–(A12) we have

$$\text{sgn}\,(W^c\{C2\} - W^c\{C1\}) = \text{sgn}\,(54a\,(c_1 - c_2) - 83c_1^2 + 112c_1c_2 - 29c_2^2) \qquad (24)$$

Assuming that quantities are always non-negative, we have the constraint that $c_2 \leq c_1 \leq (a + 3c_2)/4$. Given this condition it is easy to show that the right-hand side of (24) is always non-negative and hence the importer will always prefer a union with the low cost country. The intuition is that the gain from union with the low cost country, in terms of increased total welfare for the union, outweighs the smaller share country $C$ gets in such a union.

The second interesting issue concerns whether or not the exporting countries prefer a union with each other to a union with the importer. One would expect that both exporters would prefer a union with the importer since the total surplus is largest in that case, and that indeed turns out to be the case as the reader can easily verify by computing (A7)–(A10) and (A8)–(A14). Given these welfare results, in the next section we can determine what the outcome will be by formulating the problem of coalition choice.

The second set of special cases examines what happens when costs are the same, $c_1 = c_2 = c$, but the number of firms in each country varies. Equations (A16)–(A30) give the appropriate welfare values. If we consider Nash equilibrium, the country with the smaller number of firms does better, $W^1\{NE\} > W^2\{NE\}$ as $n_2 > n_1$. This is consistent with earlier work (see Cooper and Riezman (1989)) on the effects of the number of firms. Also note that, as in the previous case, the importing firm does better at Nash equilibrium than free trade $W^c\{NE\} > W^c\{FT\}$.

Also, as in the previous case, exporters prefer to be in a union with the importer than excluded from such a union, $W^1\{C1\} > W^1\{C2\}$ and $W^2\{C2\} > W^2\{C1\}$. Likewise, the importer prefers union with either importer to having the exporter's union form, $W^c\{12\} < \min [W^c\{C1\}, W^c\{C2\}]$.

Which exporter will the importer want a union with? It will prefer a union with the country that has the most firms, $W^c\{C1\} > W^c\{C2\}$ as $n_1 > n_2$. The intuition is clear; both countries have the same costs and production will be identical, the only difference will be in how the surplus gets shared. Since the country with the large number of firms does worse at Nash equilibrium, it has a lower security value and gets less of the surplus, hence is the preferred partner for the importing country.

The final comparison of interest concerns whether exporters prefer union with each other or the importer. Here the results are sharply different than before. Recall that when costs differed but there was only one firm in each country exporters always preferred union with the importer. Here exporters prefer union with each other provided that the total number of firms in the world exceeds three. In other words, if there are four or more firms in the world exporters will prefer a union with each other to one with the importer. This result is surprising since total surplus is maximized when an importer and an exporter form a union. However, as the number of firms grows the distribution of the surplus in the importer–exporter customs union becomes so unfavorable to the exporter that it prefers an exporter customs union.

Using these welfare results in the next section we turn to determining what customs union will actually form.

## Customs union choice

We use the results of previous sections to determine which customs unions will be chosen. To model the choice of customs unions we use the core solution concept. This approach was first used in Riezman (1985) for a model with competitive industries. The essential idea is that one would expect to observe customs unions that are in the core. A customs union is in the core if it cannot be blocked by any coalition. The notion of blocking is a bit complicated.

There are five possible coalition (customs union) structures,

| | |
|---|---|
| Free Trade (FT) | $(\{1,2,C\})$ |
| Nash Equilibrium (NE) | $(\{1\},\{2\},\{C\})$ |
| $\{1,2\}$ Customs Union | $(\{1,2\},\{C\})$ |
| $\{C,1\}$ Customs Union | $(\{C,1\},\{2\})$ |
| $\{C,2\}$ Customs Union | $(\{C,2\},\{1\})$. |

FT could be blocked by NE if any single country is better off at NE, or it could be blocked by a customs union if both member countries are better off. NE is blocked by FT if each country is better off at FT, or by any customs union in which all members are better off than NE. Any customs union can be blocked by NE or FT if any member country is better off at NE or FT. A customs union can also be blocked by another customs union if both members of the blocking customs union are better off than they are when the blocked customs union forms.

Using these definitions we analyze the two special cases considered to this point. First, suppose $n_1 = n_2 = 1$ and recall we have assumed that $c_1 > c_2$. FT is blocked by NE since $W^c\{\text{NE}\} > W^c\{\text{FT}\}$, and NE is clearly blocked by any customs union. The $\{1,2\}$ customs union is blocked by the $\{C,2\}$ customs union because $W^c\{C,2\} > W^c\{1,2\}$ and $W^2\{C,2\} > W^2\{1,2\}$ and the $\{C,1\}$ customs union is blocked by $\{C,2\}$ since $W^c\{C,2\} > W^c\{C,1\}$ (recall the importer prefers union with the low cost country) and $W^2\{C,2\} > W^2\{C,1\}$. The $\{C,2\}$ customs union is unblocked and therefore the unique core solution. Thus, in the special case in which there is one firm in each country, a customs union between the importer and the exporter with the efficient firms will be the outcome.

The solution is different in our other special case, $c_1 = c_2 = c$. As before, FT and NE are blocked by NE and any customs union, respectively. When $n_1 + n_2 > 3$ then $W^i\{1,2\} > W^i\{C,i\}$ for $i = 1,2$. This means that $\{1,2\}$ blocks both $\{C,1\}$ and $\{C,2\}$ and is itself unblocked. Hence, when the total number of firms in the world is larger than three, a customs union among the exporters is the outcome. This is somewhat surprising since the total surplus available is larger when an importer–exporter union forms, but the distributional advantages outweigh the efficiency considerations in this case.

When the total number of firms is three or less then an importer–exporter union will emerge. In the case $n_1 = n_2 = 1$ both $\{C,1\}$ and $\{C,2\}$ are unblocked and either could form. If $n_1 = 1$ and $n_2 = 2$, the importer prefers a union with 2 and the $\{C,2\}$ union will form. Conversely, if $n_1 = 2$ and $n_2 = 1$ the solution will be the $\{C,1\}$ union.

## Conclusion

We have analyzed importer–exporter and exporter customs unions when industries are imperfectly competitive. Importer–exporter customs unions will be pro-competitive in the sense that internally they will tend to have industries produce at their competitive output level, but will tend to exclude imports from non-member countries. Exporter customs unions are anti-competitive and will produce the monopoly output.

We allowed costs and the number of firms to vary across countries. Countries with lower costs and fewer firms fared better at Nash equilibrium. This means that high cost and large number of firm countries have lower security values and hence less bargaining power within any customs union. However, from the importer's point of view, the low cost country is a more desirable coalition partner because the increased efficiency in terms of lower cost outweighs the benefit of a partner with less bargaining power. Importers always prefer a union with the country with a large number of firms since there is no difference in efficiency and it can take advantage of the weaker bargaining power.

From the exporting countries' point of view, in the case where there is one firm in each country, exporters will prefer union with the importer to union with each other. The total surplus for the coalition is higher with an importer–exporter customs union, and in this case the exporter gets a big enough share of the surplus to make it more attractive than the exporter customs union. When the number of firms vary but both exporters have the same costs, exporters prefer union with each other if the number of firms in the world is larger than three. Here the problem is that when the number of firms increases exporters fare so poorly in the bargaining game with the importer that the lower surplus exporters customs union is better for them.

Finally, we applied core theory to determine which unions would form. With one firm in each country, the importer will form a union with the low cost exporter. With identical costs but variable numbers of firms, when the number of firms is small an importer–exporter customs union will form. A union of the exporter's will form if there are four or more firms in the world.

# APPENDIX

## Welfare for $n_1 = n_2 = 1$

$$W^1\{\mathrm{FT}\} = (a - 2c_1 + c_2)^2/9b \tag{A1}$$

$$W^2\{\mathrm{FT}\} = (a + c_1 - 2c_2)^2/9b \tag{A2}$$

$$W^c\{\mathrm{FT}\} = (2a - c_1 - c_2)^2/18b \tag{A3}$$

$$W^1\{\mathrm{NE}\} = 2(a - 4c_1 + 3c_2)^2/49b \tag{A4}$$

$$W^2\{\mathrm{NE}\} = 2(a + 3c_1 - 4c_2)^2/49b \tag{A5}$$

$$W^c\{\mathrm{NE}\} = 4(2a - c_1 - c_2)^2/49b \tag{A6}$$

$$W^1\{12\} = (14a^2 - 2a(25c_1 - 11c_2) + 25c_1^2 - 11c_2^2)/175b \tag{A7}$$

$$W^2\{12\} = (14a^2 + 2a(25c_1 - 39c_2) - 25c_1^2 + 39c_2^2)/175b \tag{A8}$$

$$W^c\{12\} = 4(a - c_2)^2/25b \tag{A9}$$

$$W^1\{C1\} = (27a^2 - 18a(7c_1 - 4c_2) + 191c_1^2 - 256c_1c_2 + 92c_2^2)/252b \tag{A10}$$

$$W^2\{C1\} = 2(c_1 - c_2)^2/9b \tag{A11}$$

$$W^c\{C1\} = (99a^2 - 18a(7c_1 + 4c_2) + 47c_1^2 + 32c_1c_2 + 20c_2^2)/252b \tag{A12}$$

$$W^1\{C2\} = 0 \tag{A13}$$

$$W^2\{C2\} = (3a^2 + 2a(4c_1 - 7c_2) + 4c_1^2 - 16c_1c_2 + 15c_2^2)/28b \tag{A14}$$

$$W^c\{C2\} = (3a^2 + 2a(4c_1 - 7c_2) + 4c_1^2 - 16c_1c_2 + 15c_2^2/28b \tag{A15}$$

## Welfare results for the case $c_1 = c_2$

$$W^1\{\mathrm{FT}\} = n_1(a - c)/b(1 + n_1 + n_2)^2 \tag{A16}$$

$$W^2\{\mathrm{FT}\} = n_2(a - c)/b(1 + n_1 + n_2)^2 \tag{A17}$$

$$W^c\{\mathrm{FT}\} = (n_1 + n_2)^2(a - c)^2/2b(1 + n_1 + n_2)^2 \tag{A18}$$

$$\begin{aligned} W^1\{12\} = {} & (n_1 + n_2)^2(n_{14} + 4n_1^3(n_2 + 1) + 2n_1^2(3n_2^2 + 10n_2 + 8) + \\ & n_1(4n_2^3 + 28n_2^2 + 40n_2 + 15) + n_2^4 + 12n_2^3 + 24n_2^2 + 17n_2 + 4) \\ & \times (a - c)^2/(2b(n_1^2 + 2n_1(n_2 + 2) + n_2^2 + 4n_2 + 2)^2 \\ & \times (2n_1 + 2n_2 + 1)^2) \end{aligned} \tag{A19}$$

$$\begin{aligned} W^2\{12\} = {} & (n_1 + n_2)^2(n_1^4 + 4n_1^3(n_2 + 3) + 2n_1^2(3n_2^2 + 14n_2 + 12) + \\ & n_1(4n_2^3 + 20n_2^2 + 40n_2 + 17) + n_2^4 + 4n_2^3 + 16n_2^2 + 15n_2 + 4) \\ & \times (a - c)^2/(2b(n_1^2 + 2n_1(n_2 + 2) + n_2^2 + 4n_2 + 2)^2 \\ & \times (2n_1 + 2n_2 + 1)^2) \end{aligned} \tag{A20}$$

$$W^c\{12\} = (n_1 + n_2)(n_1 + n_2 + 2)(a - c)^2/(2b(2n_1 + 2n_2 + 1)^2) \tag{A21}$$

$$W^1\{NE\} = (n_2 + 1)(n_1 + n_2)^2(a - c)^2/(b(n_1{}^2 + 2n_1(n_2 + 2) + n_2{}^2 + 4n_2 + 2)^2) \quad (A22)$$

$$W^2\{NE\} = (n_1 + 1)(n_1 + n_2)^2(a - c)^2/(b(n_1{}^2 + 2n_1(n_2 + 2) + n_2{}^2 + 4n_2 + 2)^2) \quad (A23)$$

$$W^c\{NE\} = (n_1 + n_2)(n_1 + n_2 + 2)^3(a - c)^2/(2b(n_1{}^2 + 2n_1(n_2 + 2) + n_2{}^2 + 4n_2 + 2)^2) \quad (A24)$$

$$W^1\{C1\} = (n_1{}^3 + n_1{}^2(4n_2 + 5) + n_1(5n_2{}^2 + 10n_2 + 4) + 2n_2{}^3 + 5n_2{}^2 + 4n_2 + 2)(a^2 - 2ac + c^2)/(2b(n_1{}^2 + 2n_1 \times (n_2 + 2) + n_2{}^2 + 4n_2 + 2)^2) \quad (A25)$$

$$W^2\{C1\} = 0 \quad (A26)$$

$$W^c\{C1\} = (n_1{}^4 + n_1{}^3(4n_2 + 7) + n_1{}^2(6n_2{}^2 + 20n_2 + 15) + n_1(4n_2{}^3 + 19n_2{}^2 + 30n_2 + 12) + n_2{}^4 + 6n_2{}^3 + 15n_2{}^2 + 12n_2 + 2) \times (a^2 - 2ac + c^2)/(2b(n_1{}^2 + 2n_1(n_2 + 2) + n_2{}^2 + 4n_2 + 2)^2) \quad (A27)$$

$$W^1\{C2\} = 0 \quad (A28)$$

$$W^2\{C2\} = (2n_1{}^3 + 5n_1{}^2(n_2 + 1) + 2n_1(2n_2{}^2 + 5n_2 + 2) + n_2{}^3 + 5n_2{}^2 + 4n_2 + 2)(a - c)^2/(2b(n_1{}^2 + 2n_1(n_2 + 2) + n_2{}^2 + 4n_2 + 2)^2) \quad (A29)$$

$$W^c\{C2\} = (n_1{}^4 + 2n_1{}^3(2n_2 + 3) + n_1{}^2(6n_2{}^2 + 19n_2 + 15) + 2n_1(2n_2{}^3 + 10n_2{}^2 + 15n_2 + 6) + n_2{}^4 + 7n_2{}^3 + 15n_2{}^2 + 12_2 + 2) \times (a - c)^2/(2b(n_1{}^2 + 2n_1(n_2 + 2) + n_2{}^2 + 4n_2 + 2)^2) \quad (A30)$$

## Notes

1 See Brander and Spencer (1985), Eaton and Grossman (1986), and Cooper and Riezman (1989).
2 See Riezman (1985) and Kennan and Riezman (1990).
3 Allowing for domestic consumption will not alter the qualitative results as long as countries 1 and 2 are net exporters for all parameter values.
4 For exceptions see Gatsios (1987) and Gehrig (1990).

## Bibliography


Brander, J.A. and Spencer, B.J. (1985) "Export Subsidies and International Market Share Rivalry", *Journal of International Economics* 18: 83–100.

Cooper, R. and Riezman, R. (1989) "Uncertainty and the Choice of Trade Policy in Oligopolistic Industries", *Review of Economic Studies* 56: 129–140.

Eaton, J. and Grossman, G. (1986) "Optimal Trade and Industrial Policy Under Oligopoly", *Quarterly Journal of Economics* 101: 383–406.

Gatsios, K. (1987) "Customs Unions and the Core: A Reciprocal Dumping Model", Economic Theory Discussion Paper, University of Cambridge.

Gehrig, A. (1990) "Customs Unions Versus Free Trade: A Two-Period Model with International Cournot-Oligopoly", Discussion Paper No 90–18, University of Munich.

Kennan, J. and Riezman, R. (1990) "Optimal Tariff Equilibria with Customs Unions", *Canadian Journal of Economics* 23: 70–83.

Riezman, R. (1985) "Customs Unions and the Core", *Journal of International Economics* 19: 355–365.

# 10

# COMPETITIVE INDUSTRY EQUILIBRIUM WITH FIRM-SPECIFIC UNCERTAINTY

*Avinash Dixit*[1]

This chapter considers the long-run stationary equilibrium of a competitive industry whose firms experience independent cost shocks. New firms enter by incurring a sunk expenditure to obtain an initial cost realization, and old firms exit if their cost rises to a threshold where the current losses exceed the option value of staying active. The gross turnover rate that underlies the aggregate equilibrium is characterized, and its response to various parameter changes is examined.

## Introduction

It is very easy to find a suitable topic for a chapter in a volume honoring John Chipman. He has made major contributions to so many areas of economic theory – utility and demand theory, general equilibrium, international economics, and much more – that one can just write about one's own current research interest and be quite sure it will fit. That is what I have done.

A growing literature has demonstrated the importance of firm-specific uncertainty in understanding aggregate dynamics; for example Davis and Haltiwanger (1990) on gross and net employment flows, and Olley and Pakes (1996) on industries with entry, exit, investment and R&D. Theoretical models include Ericson and Pakes (1990) and Hopenhayn (1992). These are general theoretical models focusing on issues of existence. The models are too complex to permit analytical solutions. Both papers conduct some numerical simulations, but more is needed to develop adequate intuition.

In this chapter I consider a model similar to Hopenhayn's, but one that exhibits the structure of the industry equilibrium in a much simpler way. This allows explicit solution of the long-run stationary distribution of firms and of the gross turnover rate underlying the net constant numbers. Thus the intuition behind the empirically important phenomena stands out more clearly. The model is solved numerically with much richer parametrization than was considered by Hopenhayn, and the effect of various parameter changes is examined. This again helps improve our understanding of the structure of the equilibrium, and should ultimately help bring the theoretical literature closer to the empirical.

A separate strand of theoretical modelling has elucidated the parallel between real investment decisions and financial options. At an industry equilibrium level, most of this work deals with only aggregate uncertainty. Examples are Lippman and Rumelt (1985), Edleson and Osband (1989) and Leahy (1993); see also the recent surveys by Pindyck (1991) and Dixit (1992). My model considers the opposite extreme of purely firm-specific uncertainty, and shows how the "real options" idea emerges in that context.

A fuller treatment needs both kinds of uncertainty. Aggregate uncertainty on its own does not generate the kind of simultaneous entry and exit (or hiring and firing) that is observed. Firm-specific uncertainty on its own cannot generate a persistent non-trivial stochastic process for the aggregate price or quantity, although we will see that it can affect the levels of these variables in the long-run stationary equilibrium. A recent exploration of the joint effects of the two kinds of uncertainty is in Caballero and Pindyck (1996).

## The model

The industry demand function is known and non-stochastic:

$$Q = D(P). \tag{1}$$

There is a continuum of actual and potential firms. They are all risk-neutral; the idiosyncratic uncertainty can be fully diversified by the shareholders. The discount rate is $\rho$.

Potential firms arrive at a rate $n$, which will be determined endogenously in the equilibrium. Each arriving firm pays the sunk "entry fee" $k$ to get a draw of its initial variable cost $c$ from a known cumulative probability distribution $F(c)$; if $F(c)$ is differentiable, the density is $f(c) = F'(c)$. Then, and thereafter at any instant, the firm can decide to be active or to exit the industry. Exit is permanent, in the sense that re-entry requires that the sunk amount be paid again for a fresh cost draw. While active, the firm produces a unit flow of output, and its cost evolves as a geometric Brownian motion:

$$dc/c = \nu\, dt + \sigma\, dW, \tag{2}$$

where $W$ is a standard Wiener process. Both the initial cost draw and the subsequent evolution of cost are independent across firms.

There are two types of cost uncertainty: the pre-entry distribution $F(c)$

and the post-entry evolution (equation (2)). Each can have many conceivable firm-specific sources. Pre-entry uncertainty can be unknown entrepreneurial skills or imperfectly understood technology; post-entry uncertainty can represent changing entrepreneurial skills, failure of machines, and so forth. The trend $\nu$ of the post-entry cost represents a balance between learning by doing on the one hand, and technological or economic obsolescence on the other.

The two kinds of uncertainty serve different purposes. Firms are symmetrically placed with regard to the ex ante uncertainty; it basically helps enforce the zero net worth condition of competitive equilibrium. But each firm observes its own ex post shock when making its production or exit decisions; this is what generates the gross flows underlying the stationary industry equilibrium.

We will later need two conditions for a nontrivial stationary distribution of firms to exist in a long-run stochastic equilibrium: $\rho > \nu$ to ensure convergence, and $\nu > \frac{1}{2}\sigma^2$ to prevent the mass of firms from piling up at zero cost. The latter amounts to assuming that obsolescence dominates learning in the post-entry evolution of cost. I shall later comment on how the model can be extended or modified to allow the opposite case.

I will look for a long-run stationary equilibrium. With a continuum of firms and no aggregate uncertainty, the price $P$ will be constant; of course its actual value in equilibrium is endogenous. Each firm will take $P$ as given and decide its own optimal policy. This will take the form of a cost threshold $C$ such that the firm is active if $c < C$. A new entrant never becomes active if its initial draw exceeds $C$; an active firm exits if its $c$ rises to hit the threshold $C$.

As well as the price $P$ and the arrival rate $n$, the equilibrium will be characterized by (1) the distribution of active firms by their current cost, say the cumulative distribution of numbers (not probabilities) $\psi(c)$, over $0 \leq c \leq C$, and (2) the value function $V(c)$ for each active firm over the same interval. Then the turnover rate $\tau$ is the ratio of the gross entry or exit rate to the population of active firms, $nF(C)/\psi(C)$.

Important exogenous variables are (1) the entry fee $k$, (2) parameters of the initial cost distribution $F(c)$, (3) parameters of subsequent cost evolution, especially $\sigma$. The aim is to find the effect of changes in these exogenous parameters on the equilibrium.

## Value of an active firm

I begin by finding the value function and the exit threshold for a firm that has already paid its entry fee $k$ and has a current cost realization $c$. Over the interval of activity, the firm is an asset valued at $V(c)$, which pays a dividend flow of $(P - c)$ and experiences a capital gain or loss as $c$ evolves stochastically. The dividend and the expected capital gain must sum to the normal return if the firm is willing to stay active. Therefore

$$\rho V(c) = P - c + E[dV]/dt.$$

Using Itô's Lemma to expand the right-hand side, this becomes the differential equation

$$\tfrac{1}{2}\sigma^2 c^2 V''(c) + \nu c V'(c) - \rho V(c) + P - c = 0. \quad (3)$$

The non-homogeneous linear equation has a particular solution $P/\rho - c/(\rho - \nu)$. This is just the expected value of a firm that stays active for ever. For it to be economically meaningful, we need $\rho > 0$ and $\rho > \nu$.

For the general solution of the homogeneous part of equation (3), we need the auxiliary quadratic equation

$$q(\xi) \equiv \tfrac{1}{2}\sigma^2 \xi(\xi - 1) + \nu\xi - \rho = 0. \quad (4)$$

Using $\rho > 0$ and $\rho > \nu$, it is easy to verify that this has a negative root $-\alpha$ and a positive root $\beta$, which moreover satisfy

$$-\alpha < 0 < 1 < \beta < \rho / \nu. \quad (5)$$

Then the general solution of the homogeneous part is

$$Ac^{-\alpha} + Bc^{\beta},$$

where $A$ and $B$ are constants to be determined. To keep $V(c)$ finite as $c$ becomes small, we discard the term in the negative power of $c$, that is, set $A = 0$. This yields the general solution of equation (3)

$$V(c) = Bc^{\beta} + P/\rho - c/(\rho - \nu). \quad (6)$$

The last two terms give the value of a firm that must stay active for ever; therefore the first term must be the value of the option to choose the exit threshold optimally.

The constant $B$ and the exit threshold $C$ are determined jointly from conditions that hold at the threshold. Arbitrage by holders of the active firm ensures value matching

$$0 = V(C) \equiv BC^{\beta} + P/\rho - C/(\rho - \nu), \quad (7)$$

and the optimal choice of $C$ implies smooth pasting,

$$0 = V'(C) \equiv \beta BC^{\beta-1} - 1/(\rho - \nu). \quad (8)$$

These conditions are now well known from the parallel theory of financial call options; see Merton (1973: fn. 60). For a simple exposition in the context of irreversible real investment, see Dixit (1992).

These conditions complete the solution:

$$B = \frac{[(\beta - 1)\rho]^{\beta-1}}{[\beta(\rho - \nu)]^{\beta}} P^{1-\beta}, \quad (9)$$

and

$$C = \frac{\beta}{\beta - 1} \frac{\rho - \nu}{\rho} P. \tag{10}$$

Using the condition (5) it is easy to verify that $C > P$; the firm is willing to accept some operating loss to keep alive its option, given the positive probability of a favorable cost shock in the future.

Figure 10.1 shows the shape of the value function. It is determined by the underlying parameters $\sigma$, $\nu$, $\rho$ and the price $P$ which is parametric to each firm.

An entering firm will become active if it draws an initial $c$ less than $C$, whereupon it will have value $V(c)$. Free entry then requires

$$\int_0^C V(c)\, dF(c) = k. \tag{11}$$

This condition fixes the equilibrium price $P$. As $P$ rises, equation (10) shows that $C$ rises in proportion. Also, the value function shifts up over its entire range. This is intuitive from Figure 10.1 and can be formally verified by differentiation of equation (6) using equation (9). Therefore the left-hand side is monotonic in $P$. Further, as $P$ goes to 0 and $\infty$ respectively, so does the left-hand side of equation (11). Therefore existence and uniqueness are assured. Of course the equilibrium is meaningful if and only if the associated quantity $D(P)$ is positive; otherwise the industry as a whole is inactive in the long run.

Explicit solution for $P$ is generally not possible. Even in the simplest conceivable case, where the distribution of the initial cost is concentrated at a single point $c^*$ and equation (11) reduces to $V(c^*) = k$, the left-hand side involves $P^{1-\beta}$ and $P$, precluding a closed form solution unless $\beta$ happens to

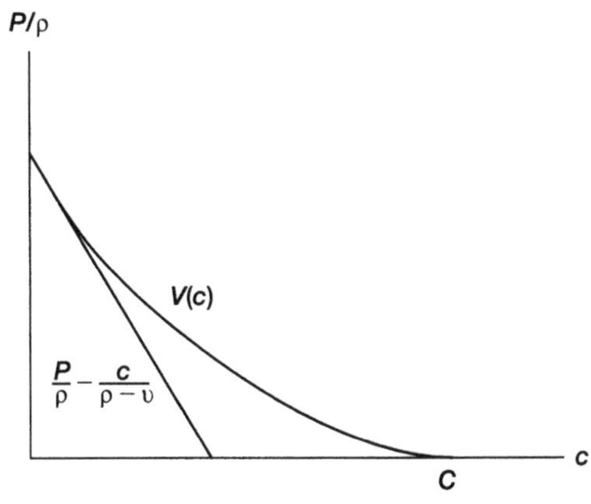


*Figure 10.1* Value function of an active firm.

be an integer between 2 and 4. The section after next considers some numerical solutions in a more interesting case where the distribution of the initial cost is lognormal. But some qualitative comparative static results are available even without an explicit solution.

The simplest such result concerns an increase in the entry fee. A higher $k$ increases the right-hand side of equation (11). To restore equality, $P$ must increase to raise $C$ and shift the value function upward.

A generally higher pre-entry cost can be represented by a rightward shift of the distribution $F(c)$ in the sense of first-order stochastic dominance. Since $V(c)$ is decreasing, at given $P$ and $C$ this lowers the left-hand side of equation (6). To restore equality we need a higher $P$.

Pre-entry uncertainty can be represented by a mean-preserving spread of the distribution $F(c)$. Since $V(c)$ is convex, this raises the left-hand side of equation (6) at unchanged $P$ and $C$. To restore equality, we need a lower $P$.

The analysis of changes in the post-entry uncertainty parameter $\sigma$ is somewhat more complicated. First consider the effect of $\sigma$ on $\beta$: differentiating the quadratic equation $q(\beta) = 0$, we get

$$(\delta q/\delta\beta)(\delta\beta/\delta\sigma) + \sigma\beta(\beta - 1) = 0.$$

At $\beta$ the larger root, $\delta q/\delta\beta > 0$; therefore a higher $\sigma$ implies a lower $\beta$. Now consider the effect of a lower $\beta$ on the value function. In (6), only the option value term depends on $\beta$. Using the expression (9) for $B$, we find

$$\begin{aligned}\delta \ln(Bc^{\beta})/\delta\beta &= [\ln(\beta - 1) + \ln\rho - 1] - [\ln\beta + \ln(\rho - \nu) - 1] + \ln c - \ln P \\ &< [\ln(\beta - 1) + \ln\rho - 1] - [\ln\beta + \ln(\rho - \nu) - 1] + \ln C - \ln P = 0.\end{aligned}$$

Therefore a lower $\beta$ raises the whole value function. To restore equality in (11), we need a lower $P$, which will lower the value function and in the process lower the exit threshold $C$. Thus greater volatility of post-entry cost shocks leads to a lower long-run industry price.

The intuition concerning these effects of increased uncertainty is by now familiar. Greater uncertainty increases the value function of the firm, by increasing the value of the option to choose the exit threshold optimally. This makes entry more attractive. To restore the zero pure profit condition of equilibrium, the value function must be lowered by a reduction in the price. This is how firm-specific uncertainty affects the equilibrium *level* of the price, even though there is no aggregate uncertainty and no long-run stochastic price *process*.

## Long-run distribution of firms

To characterize the industry's long-run stationary equilibrium, it proves more convenient to work with the logarithm of cost, $x = \ln c$. The range

$(0, C)$ for $c$ corresponds to the range $(-\infty, X)$ for $x$, where $X = \ln C$. Applying Itô's Lemma to (2), we see that $x$ follows the Brownian motion

$$dx = \mu \, dt + \sigma \, dW, \tag{12}$$

where $\mu = \nu - \frac{1}{2}\sigma^2$.

We want to find the stationary distribution of firms over $(-\infty, X)$. Write the cumulative function as $\Phi(x)$, and let $\phi(x) = \Phi'(x)$ be the corresponding density. Note these are numbers of firms and not probabilities.

Firms arrive at rate $n$ and pick their costs according to the cumulative distribution function $F(c)$. Therefore the rate of new arrivals at points $x$ or below is given by

$$G(x) = nF(c); \tag{13}$$

let $g(x) = G'(x) = nf(c)c$ be the corresponding density function.

The locations of existing firms in $(-\infty, X)$ shift according to equation (12), and the firms whose $x$ hits the threshold $X$ exit. The stationary distribution is found by balancing the effects of entry, movement and exit.

Such distributions, dynamically as well as in a stationary long run, arise in the theory of heat flow in physics – e.g. Guenther and Lee (1988: 6–7) – and the Fokker–Planck equation with sources or sinks in the theory of stochastic processes – e.g. Bhattacharya and Waymire (1988: 78, 478). But since these are not very well known in economics, I offer an elementary derivation in the Appendix.

The result is the density function (with $\lambda = 2\mu/6^2$)

$$\phi(x) = \frac{2}{\sigma_2} e^{\lambda x} \int_x^X e^{-\lambda\xi} G(\xi) \, d\xi. \tag{14}$$

Integrating this gives the total mass of active firms as

$$\Phi(X) = \frac{1}{\mu} \int_{-\infty}^X (X - x) g(x) \, dx. \tag{15}$$

Note that we now need $\mu > 0$, or in terms of the parameters of the $c$ process, $\nu > \frac{1}{2}\sigma^2$. This was mentioned when the $c$ process was defined in equation (2).

Market clearing in the stationary equilibrium implies $\Phi(X) = D(P)$. Since the arrival rate $n$ enters multiplicatively in $g(x)$, its equilibrium value is fixed by this equation. Of greater interest is the rate $\tau$ of gross turnover of firms (entry and exit) that underlies the zero net change in the stationary equilibrium. It is given by

$$\tau = \frac{G(X)}{\Phi(X)} = \frac{\mu \int_{-\infty}^X g(x) \, dx}{\int_{-\infty}^X (X - x) g(x) \, dx} = \frac{\mu}{X - E[x|x \leq X]} . \tag{16}$$

To interpret this, note that starting at a position $x < X$, the expected first passage time to $X$ for the Brownian motion equation (12) is $(X - x)/\mu$; see e.g. Harrison (1985: 52). Then equation (16) shows that the turnover rate is just the reciprocal of the average first passage time to $X$, taken over the stationary distribution of positions $x$ of active firms.

Since a closed-form solution for $P$ is not generally available, neither is that for $X$. Further, it is not clear how $X$ will affect the denominator in equation (16): if the distribution $g(x)$ has local peaks, the conditional expectation can change quite erratically. Therefore most of our inferences from (16) must rely on numerical solutions. I will do this in the next section for an appealing parametrization, where $x$ is normal (initial cost is lognormal).

We can say a little more in a special case. Suppose the initial cost distribution is concentrated at the single point $c^*$, and $x^* = \ln c^*$. So long as the industry is active, we will have $c^* < C$, so $x^* < X$. Then the turnover rate is

$$\tau = \mu/(X - x^*). \tag{17}$$

Now the effect of $X$ is very direct. We saw above that a higher $k$ implies a higher $X$, and therefore lower turnover. The effects of $\sigma$ are more complicated. A higher $\sigma$ implies a lower $P$, but it raises the multiple by which $C$ exceeds $P$ in equation (10). The net effect on $C$ and thus on $X$ is ambiguous.

A second effect depends on whether we hold $\nu$ (the trend of $c$) fixed as $\sigma$ increases, thereby decreasing $\mu$ (the drift of $x = \ln c$), and therefore contributing to a lowering of the turnover rate $\tau$. It is by no means clear whether $\nu$ or $\mu$ is the more basic parameter that should be kept fixed when $\sigma$ changes. Therefore it is worth examining the effects of changes in $\sigma$ under both conditions, and that is what the numerical work of the next section does.

## Numerical solution

A natural and quite rich specification of the initial cost distribution is the lognormal. Suppose the initial $x = \ln c$ is normal with mean $x^*$ and standard deviation $\gamma$; thus $\gamma$ is a measure of the initial uncertainty. The expectation of the initial cost is $\exp(x^* + \frac{1}{2}\gamma^2)$. The density of the entering firms is

$$g(x) = \frac{n}{\sqrt{2\pi}\,\gamma} \exp\left[ -\frac{(x - x^*)^2}{2\gamma^2} \right]. \tag{18}$$

The interesting magnitudes in the long-run stationary equilibrium are the price, the exit threshold, and the turnover rate. (The size of the demand affects only the arrival rate $n$, which is a matter of choice of scale.) The interesting questions are the effects of the uncertainties in the initial cost and the subsequent cost evolution on these endogenous magnitudes.

Tables 10.1 and 10.2 show the calculations that help answer such questions. The parameters common to both are as follows. The mean of the initial $x$ is $x^* = 0$; this is in effect a choice of units. The sunk cost (entry fee) is $k = 1$, and the interest rate $\rho = 0.05$. For the range of $\gamma$ considered, the expectation of the initial cost is only just above 1. Thus the interest on the sunk cost is only about 5 percent of the average variable cost. One would think this quite a small sunk cost.

Table 10.1 holds the trend parameter of $c$ fixed at $\nu = 0.025$, while Table 10.2 holds the drift parameter of ln $c$ fixed at $\mu = 0.020$. Since $\mu = \nu - \frac{1}{2}\sigma^2$, the two values match when $\sigma = 0.1$; thus the fourth columns of the two tables are identical.

The lowest value of $\gamma$ is sufficiently small to make it a good approximation to the case where the distribution of the initial cost is concentrated at the single point $c^*$. Then the turnover rate in the first row of the tables should approximate the formula (17). This provides a useful check on the numerical calculation.

Turn to the effects of changes in $\sigma$ and $\gamma$. I begin by confirming an analytical result of the section on the value of an active firm. As either $\sigma$ or $\gamma$ increases, the industry price $P$ decreases. With an exit option available, more firms are willing to enter the industry in response to the increased uncertainty.

The exit threshold $C$ increases as the post-entry cost uncertainty $\sigma$ increases; this is also the standard intuition from the option idea. But note that we have a net balance of two effects: a higher $\sigma$ lowers $P$, but

*Table 10.1* Price, exit threshold and turnover rate as functions of cost uncertainty parameters (with drift of $c$ kept constant)

| $\sigma$ / $\gamma$ | *0.01* | *0.05* | *0.10* | *0.20* |
|---|---|---|---|---|
| *0.01* | $P = 1.248$<br>$C = 1.251$<br>$\tau = 0.112$ | $P = 1.204$<br>$C = 1.262$<br>$\tau = 0.102$ | $P = 1.100$<br>$C = 1.292$<br>$\tau = 0.078$ | $P = 0.869$<br>$C = 1.376$<br>$\tau = 0.016$ |
| *0.05* | $P = 1.244$<br>$C = 1.246$<br>$\tau = 0.113$ | $P = 1.201$<br>$C = 1.258$<br>$\tau = 0.103$ | $P = 1.098$<br>$C = 1.289$<br>$\tau = 0.079$ | $P = 0.867$<br>$C = 1.373$<br>$\tau = 0.016$ |
| *0.10* | $P = 1.230$<br>$C = 1.233$<br>$\tau = 0.117$ | $P = 1.188$<br>$C = 1.245$<br>$\tau = 0.107$ | $P = 1.088$<br>$C = 1.277$<br>$\tau = 0.081$ | $P = 0.861$<br>$C = 1.364$<br>$\tau = 0.016$ |
| *0.20* | $P = 1.175$<br>$C = 1.178$<br>$\tau = 0.106$ | $P = 1.137$<br>$C = 1.192$<br>$\tau = 0.098$ | $P = 1.046$<br>$C = 1.228$<br>$\tau = 0.077$ | $P = 0.837$<br>$C = 1.326$<br>$\tau = 0.016$ |

Fixed parameters (see text for definition): $x^* = 0$, $\nu = 0.025$, $k = 1.0$, $\rho = 0.05$

Variable parameters: $\sigma$, $\gamma$

*Table 10.2* Price, exit threshold and turnover rate as functions of cost uncertainty parameters (with drift of log $c$ kept constant)

| $\gamma$ \ $\sigma$ | *0.01* | *0.05* | *0.10* | *0.20* |
|---|---|---|---|---|
| *0.01* | $P$ = 1.223<br>$C$ = 1.226<br>$\tau$ = 0.098 | $P$ = 1.181<br>$C$ = 1.246<br>$\tau$ = 0.091 | $P$ = 1.100<br>$C$ = 1.292<br>$\tau$ = 0.078 | $P$ = 0.959<br>$C$ = 1.403<br>$\tau$ = 0.059 |
| *0.05* | $P$ = 1.218<br>$C$ = 1.221<br>$\tau$ = 0.100 | $P$ = 1.178<br>$C$ = 1.242<br>$\tau$ = 0.092 | $P$ = 1.098<br>$C$ = 1.289<br>$\tau$ = 0.079 | $P$ = 0.957<br>$C$ = 1.400<br>$\tau$ = 0.059 |
| *0.10* | $P$ = 1.204<br>C = 1.207<br>$\tau$ = 0.103 | $P$ = 1.165<br>$C$ = 1.229<br>$\tau$ = 0.095 | $P$ = 1.088<br>$C$ = 1.277<br>$\tau$ = 0.081 | $P$ = 0.951<br>$C$ = 1.391<br>$\tau$ = 0.061 |
| *0.20* | $P$ = 1.146<br>C = 1.148<br>$\tau$ = 0.090 | $P$ = 1.112<br>$C$ = 1.174<br>$\tau$ = 0.086 | $P$ = 1.046<br>$C$ = 1.228<br>$\tau$ = 0.077 | $P$ = 0.925<br>$C$ = 1.354<br>$\tau$ = 0.061 |

Fixed parameters (see text for definition): $x^*$ = 0, $\mu$ = 0.020, $k$ = 1.0, $\rho$ = 0.05
Variable parameters: $\sigma$, $\gamma$

raises the multiple by which $C$ exceeds $P$ in (10). The latter effect turns out to dominate in this example.

The threshold decreases as the initial cost uncertainty $\gamma$ increases. This is simply the translation of the decrease in $P$, because the multiple by which $C$ exceeds $P$ is independent of $\gamma$.

As explained above, changes in $\sigma$ can have conflicting effects on the turnover. The numerical results show the net effect for the lognormal case: turnover rates *decrease* as $\sigma$ increases. This goes against the intuition that greater firm-specific uncertainty should imply faster turnover. In Table 10.1 $\nu$ is held constant so $\mu$ decreases as $\sigma$ increases. Since $\mu$ appears in the numerator of the expression for the turnover rate, one might suspect that the counterintuitive result is a consequence of this feature. But the same happens, although on a more modest scale, in Table 10.2 where $\mu$ is held fixed as $\sigma$ changes. Thus the result must come from the effect of $\sigma$ on $X$.

The intuition is simplest when the initial uncertainty parameter $\gamma$ is small, so the initial $x$ is concentrated at $x^*$, and when $\mu$ is held fixed as $\sigma$ changes. In this case, since $X$ increases in our numerical calculation as $\sigma$ increases, so does the average first passage time to $X$ starting from the fixed $x^*$. Therefore the turnover rate falls. In the more general case, the stationary distribution of active firms also changes as $\sigma$ changes, but in the numerical example the effect of that is not sufficiently large to reverse the result. In the alternative interpretation where $\nu$ is held constant and $\mu$ falls as $\sigma$ increases, the turnover rate falls even faster.

Of course the result is specific to the lognormal case and may be reversed for other initial cost distributions. But the above findings do suggest that the intuitive link between larger firm-specific uncertainty and faster turnover is not robust. Some firm-specific uncertainty is essential for this story of a stochastic stationary equilibrium with gross turnover, but its effects may not be monotonic.

A larger $\gamma$ lowers the turnover rate, but this effect seems quantitatively minor. The point is that with the right tail cut off at $X$, an increase in $\gamma$ puts the average entering firm further to the left of $X$ and therefore increases the expected time to exit.

Finally, the actual numbers for the turnover rates are quite small. In no case can we find them much above 10 percent, and in several cases they go as low as 1 percent. On an annual time-scale, these pertain to a very stable long-run industry. Once again a concentrated initial cost distribution provides the intuition. Take the case of $\gamma = 0.01$ and $\sigma = 0.1$, when $C = 1.292$ and therefore $X = 0.256$. With $\mu = 0.02$ and $x^*$ normalized at 0, the expected first passage time is 12.81, and the turnover rate is its reciprocal, 0.0781. Halving the sunk cost raises the turnover rates generally by a factor of 1.5, but even a 15 percent turnover is not very large. Perhaps a different kind of uncertainty is required. An exogenous Poisson death process would be an obvious solution, but it seems somewhat unsatisfactory to explain large turnover rates simply by assuming large hazard rates for the Poisson process.

## Concluding comments

The above model allows a reasonably rich specification of firm-specific cost uncertainty, both at entry and after entry. The numerical solutions offer some insights into the nature of the industry equilibrium, and suggest some questions for further research.

It is worth emphasizing that a nontrivial long-run stochastically stationary equilibrium will not exist unless the evolution of the logarithm of the cost has a positive drift. For this, learning or other forms of post-entry improvement must be dominated by cost-increasing developments like physical depreciation or economic obsolescence. To allow negative drift, one must either switch the focus to short-run dynamics, using the dynamic form of the Fokker–Planck equation initially derived in the Appendix before specializing to the stationary long run, or introduce some other form of forced exit, such as an exogenous Poisson process, that will prevent a pile-up of firms at zero cost. These are possible extensions for future research.

## APPENDIX

Here I derive the distribution of active firms, considering entry, cost shocks, and exit. To facilitate this, I take a discrete approximation to Brownian motion. For details of this, see Cox and Miller (1965, Sections 2.2 and 5.2), Bhattacharya and Waymire (1988, Chapter 1) or Dixit (1993, Section 1).

Recall that $x = \ln c$ follows the Brownian motion (12). The range $(0, C)$ of $c$ translates into the range $(-\infty, X)$ for $x$, where $X = \ln C$.

Split time into discrete periods of length $\Delta t$ and the $x$-axis into discrete locations of size $\Delta h$, where $\Delta h = \sigma\sqrt{\Delta t}$. Figure 10.2 shows the arrangement. Each row represents a location. The location at $x$ has the mass of firms $\phi(x)\Delta h$. In the unit period of length $\Delta t$, a fraction $p$ of this mass moves down to the adjacent location $x + \Delta h$, and the fraction $q = 1 - p$ moves similarly up to the location $x - \Delta h$, where

$$p = \tfrac{1}{2}\left[1 + \frac{\mu}{\sigma^2}\,\Delta h\right]. \tag{19}$$

Entry and exit are described in the obvious way. In the unit period, the location $x$ receives the mass $g(x)\,\Delta h\Delta t$ of new entry. And from the location $X-\Delta h$, the mass $p\phi(X-\Delta h)\,\Delta h$ moves to the threshold location $X$ and so exits.

### *The Fokker–Planck equation*

To begin with, I shall not restrict the calculation to the long-run stationary state. Then the density function can depend on time as well as location, $\phi(x, t)$. In the unit period from $t$ to $(t + \Delta t)$, the location $x$ gets inflows from its right and left neighbors and from new entry. Therefore

$$\phi(x, t + \Delta t)\,\Delta h = q\phi(x + \Delta h, t)\,\Delta h + p\phi(x - \Delta h, t)\,\Delta h + g(x)\,\Delta h\Delta t.$$

Cancel $\Delta h$ from all terms, and expand in a Taylor series using the above formula (19) for $p$. This gives

$$\begin{aligned}
\phi(x, t) &+ \phi_t(x, t)\,\Delta t \\
&= \tfrac{1}{2}\,[1 - \mu\,\Delta h/\sigma^2][\phi(x, t) + \phi_x(x, t)\,\Delta h + \tfrac{1}{2}\,\phi_{xx}(x, t)(\Delta h)^2 + \ldots] \\
&\quad + \tfrac{1}{2}\,[1 + \mu\,\Delta h/\sigma^2][\phi(x, t) - \phi_x(x, t)\,\Delta h + \tfrac{1}{2}\,\phi_{xx}(x, t)(\Delta h)^2 + \ldots] \\
&\quad + g(x)\,\Delta t \\
&= \phi(x, t) - [\mu(\Delta h)^2/\sigma^2]\phi_x(x, t) + \tfrac{1}{2}\,(\Delta h)^2\,\phi_{xx}(x, t) + g(x)\,\Delta t + \ldots.
\end{aligned}$$

Now cancel $\phi(x, t)$ from both sides, use $(\Delta h)^2 = \sigma^2\,\Delta t$, divide by $\Delta t$ and take limits as $\Delta t \to 0$. This gives the Fokker–Planck (forward Kolmogorov) equation with $g(x)$ as a source:

$$\phi_t(x, t) = \tfrac{1}{2}\sigma^2\,\phi_{xx}(x, t) - \mu\phi_x(x, t) + g(x). \tag{20}$$

| *Location* | *Number of firms* | *Transition probabilities* | *Entry or exit* | *Number of firms* |
|---|---|---|---|---|
| ⋮ | ⋮ | ⋮ | ⋮ | ⋮ |
| $x - \Delta h$ | $\phi(x - \Delta h)\,\Delta h$ | $\begin{cases} q \\ p \end{cases}$ | ← | $g(x - \Delta h)\,\Delta h \Delta t$ |
| $x$ | $\phi(x)\,\Delta h$ | $\begin{cases} q \\ p \end{cases}$ | ← | $g(x)\,\Delta h \Delta t$ |
| $x + \Delta h$ | $\phi(x + \Delta h)\,\Delta h$ | $\begin{cases} q \\ p \end{cases}$ | ← | $g(x + \Delta h)\,\Delta h \Delta t$ |
| ⋮ | ⋮ | ⋮ | ⋮ | ⋮ |
| $X - \Delta h$ | $\phi(x - \Delta h)\,\Delta h$ | $\begin{cases} q \\ p \end{cases}$ | ← | $g(X - \Delta h)\,\Delta h \Delta t$ |
| $X$ | 0 | 1 | → | $p\phi(X - \Delta h)\,\Delta h$ |

*Figure 10.2* Entry, movement, and exit of firms.

Next consider the threshold $X$. The location $(X - \Delta h)$ does not get any input from the right, so

$$\phi(X - \Delta h, t + \Delta t)\,\Delta h = p\phi(X - 2\Delta h, t)\,\Delta h + g(X - \Delta h)\,\Delta h \Delta t.$$

Expanding and simplifying as above, this becomes

$$\phi(X - \Delta h, t) = O(\Delta h),$$

where $O(\Delta h)$ denotes terms of the order $\Delta h$ whose exact form is unimportant. Letting $\Delta h$ go to zero, we get the boundary condition

$$\phi(X, t) = 0. \tag{21}$$

## *The stationary distribution*

In the text I require only the long-run stationary state, where the distribution does not depend on time. Then the Fokker–Planck equation (20) becomes an ordinary differential equation

$$\tfrac{1}{2}\sigma^2\phi''(x) - \mu\phi'(x) + g(x) = 0,$$

or

$$\phi''(x) - \lambda\phi'(x) + (2/\sigma^2)g(x) = 0, \tag{22}$$

where $\lambda = 2\mu/\sigma^2$.

The boundary condition at the threshold becomes

$$\phi(X) = 0. \tag{23}$$

Actually I need a more precise analysis at the boundary to determine the rate of exit. At the threshold, in the stationary state, we have

$$\begin{aligned}\phi(X - \Delta h) &= p\phi(X - 2\Delta h) + g(X - \Delta h)\,\Delta t \\ &= \tfrac{1}{2}[1 + \mu\,\Delta h/\sigma^2][\phi(X - \Delta h) - \Delta h\phi'(X - \Delta h) + \ldots] + g(X - \Delta h)\,\Delta t \\ &= \tfrac{1}{2}\,\phi(X - \Delta h) + \tfrac{1}{2}\,(\mu\,\Delta h/\sigma^2)\phi(X - \Delta h) - \tfrac{1}{2}\,\Delta h\phi'(X - \Delta h) + O(\Delta h^2).\end{aligned}$$

Therefore

$$\phi(X - \Delta h) = [(\mu/\sigma^2)\phi(X - \Delta h) - \phi'(X - \Delta h)]\,\Delta h + O(\Delta h^2)$$

and

$$p\phi(X - \Delta h)\,\Delta h = \tfrac{1}{2}\,[(\mu/\sigma^2)\phi(X - \Delta h) - \phi'(X - \Delta h)]\,(\Delta h)^2 + O(\Delta h)^3.$$

This mass of particles exits in the unit period of length $\Delta t = (\Delta h)^2/\sigma^2$. Dividing by the period length and letting $\Delta h \to 0$, the rate of exit is

$$\tfrac{1}{2}\,[\mu\phi(X) - \sigma^2\phi'(X)] = -\,\tfrac{1}{2}\,\sigma^2\phi'(X).$$

In the long-run stationary equilibrium, this must equal the total rate of entry over the whole interval $(-\infty, X)$, namely the cumulative $G(X)$. This gives us another boundary condition for the differential equation:

$$\phi'(X) = -\,(2/\sigma^2)G(X). \tag{24}$$

## *Solution*

Multiply the equation (22) by the integrating factor $e^{-\lambda x}$ to write it as

$$\frac{d}{dx}\,[e^{-\lambda x}\,\phi'(x)] + \frac{2}{\sigma^2}\,e^{-\lambda x}\,g(x) = 0.$$

Integrate this from a general position $x$ to the threshold $X$ to write

$$e^{-\lambda X}\,\phi'(X) - e^{-\lambda x}\,\phi'(x) + \frac{2}{\sigma^2}\int_x^X e^{-\lambda \xi}\,g(\xi)\,d\xi = 0,$$

where $\xi$ is a dummy variable of integration.

In this, we know $\phi'(X)$ from equation (24). We can also evaluate the integral by parts:

$$\int_x^X e^{-\lambda\xi}\,g(\xi)\,d\xi = e^{-\lambda X}\,G(X) - e^{-\lambda x}\,G(x) + \frac{2\lambda}{\sigma^2}\int_x^X e^{-\lambda\xi}\,G(\xi)\,d\xi.$$

Substituting these and simplifying,

$$\phi'(x) = -\,\frac{2}{\sigma^2}\,G(x) + \frac{2\lambda}{\sigma^2}\,e^{\lambda x}\int_x^X e^{-\lambda\xi}\,G(\xi)\,d\xi. \tag{25}$$

Integrate this from $x$ to $X$. Using the boundary condition (23), the left-hand side integrates to $-\phi(x)$. The second term on the right-hand side involves a double integral, which we evaluate by changing the order:

$$\int_{\eta=x}^{X} \int_{\xi=\eta}^{X} e^{\lambda\eta} e^{-\lambda\xi} G(\xi)\, d\xi\, d\eta = \int_{\xi=x}^{X} \int_{\eta=x}^{\xi} e^{\lambda\eta}\, d\eta\, e^{-\lambda\xi} G(\xi)\, d\xi$$
$$= \frac{1}{\lambda} \int_{\xi=x}^{X} [e^{\lambda\xi} - e^{\lambda x}]\, e^{-\lambda\xi} G(\xi)\, d\xi$$
$$= \frac{1}{\lambda} \left[ \int_{x}^{X} G(\xi)\, d\xi + e^{\lambda x} \int_{x}^{X} e^{-\lambda\xi} G(\xi)\, d\xi \right].$$

Therefore the integration of (25) gives

$$\phi(x) = \frac{2}{\sigma^2} e^{\lambda x} \int_{x}^{X} e^{-\lambda\xi} G(\xi)\, d\xi. \tag{26}$$

We will need $\phi(x)$ to cumulate to a finite function over the range $(-\infty, X)$. As $x$ decreases to $-\infty$, the integral on the right-hand side in (26) increases, because the integrand is everywhere positive and the range is increasing. Now if $\lambda$ were negative, the factor $e^{-\lambda x}$ would go to $\infty$ as $x$ went to $-\infty$. Then $\phi(x)$ would also go to $\infty$, and its integral could not converge. Roughly speaking, if $\lambda$, or equivalently $\mu$, were negative, the drift of the $x$-process would be negative, and its long-run distribution would drift off to $-\infty$. Correspondingly in terms of $c$, the mass of firms would pile up at zero. A long-run stationary distribution with entry and exit would not exist.

Therefore we assume $\lambda > 0$. This means $\mu > 0$, or in terms of the parameters of the $c$-process, $\nu > \frac{1}{2}\sigma^2$. This requirement was stated in the text when the $c$-process was defined.

Now integrate equation (26) from $x$ to $X$. We get a double integral on the right-hand side. Reversing order as above, and simplifying, we find

$$\int_{x}^{X} \phi(\xi)\, d\xi = \frac{2}{\lambda\sigma^2} \int_{x}^{X} G(\xi)\, d\xi - \frac{1}{\lambda}\phi(x).$$

Now let $x$ go to $-\infty$. If the cumulative distribution function $G(x)$ goes to zero sufficiently fast as $x$ goes to $-\infty$, then we see from (26) that $\phi(x)$ will go to zero there. The condition is satisfied for the common distributions, including the cases of uniform and lognormal initial costs. Assuming it, and noting that $2/(\lambda\sigma^2) = 1/\mu$, we finally have

$$\Phi(X) = \int_{-\infty}^{X} \phi(x)\, dx$$
$$= \frac{1}{\mu} \int_{-\infty}^{X} G(x)\, dx$$
$$= \frac{1}{\mu} \int_{-\infty}^{X} (X - x)\, g(x)\, dx$$

This completes the solution.

## Notes

1 I thank Robert Pindyck for comments on a preliminary version, and the National Science Foundation for financial support.

## Bibliography

Bhattacharya, Rabi N. and Waymire, Edward C. (1988) *Stochastic Processes with Applications*. New York: Wiley.
Caballero, Ricardo J. and Pindyck, Robert S. (1996) "Uncertainty, Investment, and Industry Evolution," *International Economic Review* 37: 641–662.
Cox, D. R. and Miller, H. D. (1965) *The Theory of Stochastic Processes*. London, UK: Chapman and Hall.
Davis, Steven J. and Haltiwanger, John (1990) "Gross Job Creation and Gross Job Destruction: Microeconomic Evidence and Macroeconomic Implications," in Olivier Blanchard and Stanley Fischer (eds) *NBER Macroeconomics Annual 1990*, Cambridge, MA: MIT Press.
Dixit, Avinash (1992) "Investment and Hysteresis," *Journal of Economic Perspectives* 6: 107–132.
—— (1993) *The Art of Smooth Pasting*. Reading, UK and Chur, Switzerland: Harwood Academic Publishers.
Edleson, Michael and Osband, Kent (1989) "Competitive Markets with Irreversible Investment," working paper. Santa Monica, CA: Rand Corporation.
Ericson, Richard and Pakes, Ariel (1990) "An Alternative Model of Firm and Industry Dynamics," working paper. New Haven, CT: Yale University Press.
Guenther, Ronald B. and Lee, John W. (1988) *Partial Differential Equations of Mathematical Physics and Integral Equations*. Englewood Cliffs, NJ: Prentice-Hall.
Harrison, J. Michael (1985) *Brownian Motion and Stochastic Flow Systems*. New York: Wiley.
Hopenhayn, Hugo (1992) "Entry, Exit and Firm Dynamics in Long Run Equilibrium," *Econometrica* 60: 1127–1150.
Leahy, John (1993) "Investment in Competitive Equilibrium: The Optimality of Myopic Behavior," *Quarterly Journal of Economics* 108: 1105–1133.
Lippman, Steven A. and Rumelt, R. P. (1985) "Industry-Specific Capital and Uncertainty," discussion paper. Graduate School of Business, UCLA.
Merton, Robert C. (1973) "The Theory of Rational Option Pricing," *Bell Journal of Economics and Management Science* 4: 141–183.
Olley, G. Steven and Pakes, Ariel (1996) "The Dynamics of Productivity in the Telecommunications Industry," *Econometrica* 64: 1263–1297.
Pindyck, Robert S. (1991) "Irreversibility, Uncertainty, and Investment," *Journal of Economic Literature* 29: 1110–1152.

# 11

# ESTIMATION AND INFERENCE IN SIMULTANEOUS EQUATIONS

*K. Rao Kadiyala and Dennis Oberhelman*

In this chapter we consider the general problem of estimation and inference in stochastic simultaneous equations.[1] We introduce a class of modified limited information maximum likelihood estimators and show that these estimators possess finite moments. One of these estimators is asymptotically unbiased to order $\sigma^2$ and a second one is minimum mean square to order $\sigma^4$. Based on the unbiased estimator, asymptotic tests of hypotheses are proposed. Simulation results indicate that these tests perform better compared to traditional tests.

## Introduction

In this chapter we consider the general problem of estimating the coefficients of a structural equation and the associated problem of testing hypotheses concerning the coefficients. In most applications, standardized statistics based on limited information maximum likelihood (LIML), or two stage least squares (TSLS) estimators are used to test these hypotheses. The standardized ratios are formed by computing the differences between the estimated coefficients and their hypothesized values and dividing by the estimated asymptotic standard errors. It is well known that the null distributions of these standardized statistics are asymptotically N(0,1), and it is commonly assumed that student's $t$ distribution provides a reasonable approximation of the null distributions in finite samples. Consequently, the standardized statistics are referred to as $t$-ratios and they are compared to the appropriate percentile values of the $t$ distribution to determine the significance of the coefficients.

There have been few investigations into the finite sample properties of these statistics.[2] The purpose of this chapter, therefore, is to explore the finite sample properties of the $t$-ratios computed using modified LIML estimators, and determine which members of this class might be preferred when testing hypotheses about structural coefficients.

The chapter is divided into four parts. In the first and second parts we present the formal model and provide a general discussion of the problem of estimation. In the third part, the problem of testing for parameters is considered. In the fourth part we use Monte Carlo experiments to investigate the finite sampling properties of the classical $t$ tests for structural coefficients (i.e. those based on TSLS and LIML) and present results concerning an alternative statistic. Our results suggest that the alternative test developed in this chapter is preferred to the classical tests based on TSLS and LIML.

## 1 The model

Let

$$y = Y_1\beta + X_1\gamma + u_1 \tag{1.1}$$

be one of $G$ simultaneous equations where $y$ is a $T \times 1$ vector of observations on an endogenous variable, $Y_1$ is a $T \times G_1$ matrix of observations on $G_1$ additional endogenous variables, $X_1$ is a $T \times K_1$ matrix of observations on $K_1$ exogenous variables. $\gamma$ and $\beta$ are, respectively, $K_1 \times 1$ and $G_1 \times 1$ vectors of parameters to be estimated. Finally, $u_1$ is a $T \times 1$ vector of independently and identically normally distributed errors with mean 0 and variance equal to $\sigma^2$.

It is assumed that equation (1.1) is part of a system of $G \geq G_1 + 1$ equations which are characterized by, in addition to the variables appearing in (1.1), a $T \times (G - G_1 - 1)$ matrix of observations on $G_2 = (G - G_1 - 1)$ endogenous variables and a $T \times (K - K_1)$ matrix of observations on $K_2 = K - K_1$ exogenous variables. Let the $T \times K$ matrix of observations on the exogenous variables be denoted by $X_*$ and let the $T \times K_2$ matrix of observations on the exogenous variables excluded from (1.1) be denoted by $X_2$, so that $X_* = [X_1 \mid X_2]$. Define $Y = [y \mid Y_1]$.

The reduced form of the endogenous variables equals $Y = X_* (\pi_1 \mid \Pi_2) + (v_1 \mid V_2)$ where $\pi_1' = (\pi_{11}' \mid \pi_{21}')$ and $\Pi_2' = (\Pi_{12}' \mid \Pi_{22}')$ are, respectively, $1 \times (K_1 + K_2)$ and $G_1 \times (K_1 + K_2)$ matrices of reduced form coefficients. The rows of $(v_1 \mid V_2)$ are independently normally distributed errors, with each row having mean 0 and nonsingular covariance matrix

$$\Omega = \begin{pmatrix} \omega_{11} & \omega_{12} \\ \omega_{12}' & \Omega_{22} \end{pmatrix}$$

The least squares estimators of $\Pi$ and $\Omega$ are

$$\hat{\Pi} = (X_*' X_*)^{-1} X_*' Y$$

and

$$\hat{\Omega} = \frac{\hat{V}'\hat{V}}{T - K} \qquad (1.2)$$

where

$$\hat{V} = (\hat{V}_1 | \hat{V}_2) = Y - X_* \hat{\Pi}$$

We make the usual assumptions concerning the identifiability and estimability of (1.1). In particular, we assume that $X_*$ has full rank, $K$, and that $K_2 > G_1$. Then, the $k$-class estimator, $b(k)$ of $(\beta' | \gamma')'$ is given by

$$b(k) = [Z'(I - kM)Z]^{-1} Z'(I - kM)y \qquad (1.3)$$

where

$$Z = [Y_1 \mid X_1]$$

and

$$M = I - X_*(X_*'X_*)^{-1} X_*'$$

Many of the single equation estimators used in practice fall within the set of $k$-class estimators. For example, the two stage least squares estimator (TSLSE) has $k = 1$, the ordinary least squares estimator (OLSE) has $k = 0$, and the limited information maximum likelihood estimator (LIMLE) suggested by Anderson and Rubin (1949) has $k = \lambda_0$ where,

$$\lambda_0 = \underset{\beta}{\text{Min}} \frac{(y - Y_1\beta)' M_1(y - Y_1\beta)}{(y - Y_1\beta)' M(y - Y_1\beta)}$$

and

$$M_1 = I - X_1(X_1'X_1)^{-1} X_1'$$

It is well known that the LIMLE does not possess moments and that if $k$ is nonstochastic, the integral moments of $b(k)$ exist up to order $M^*$ where

$$M^* = \begin{cases} T - K_1 - G_1 & \text{for } 0 \leq k < 1 \\ L & \text{for } k = 1 \end{cases}$$

and $L = K_2 - G_1$, the number of overidentification restrictions. (See Kinal (1980) for details.)

Fuller (1977) introduced modifications to the LIML and fixed $k$-class estimators which ensure that the new estimators possess finite moments. Specifically, Fuller modified the LIMLE by defining $k = \lambda_0 - \alpha/(T - K)$ and showed that as long as $\alpha > 0$, this modification will yield an estimator which possesses finite moments in small samples. He also showed that when $\alpha = 1$ the resulting $k$-class estimator is unbiased to $0(T^{-1})$ and demonstrated that setting $\alpha = 4$ yields an estimator whose mean-squared error to $0(T^{-2})$ is uniformly smaller than that associated with any smaller $\alpha$.

Rothenberg (1984) shows that the results proved by Fuller under the assumption of normality hold for any symmetric error distribution possessing higher order moments.

In a comprehensive paper on single equation estimators, Anderson, Kunitomo, and Morimune (1986) use small $\sigma$ expansions of the distributions of the Fuller estimators to show that the Fuller modification improves the LIML estimator in terms of asymptotic mean-squared error and asymptotic probability of concentration. Kadiyala and Oberhelman (1992) consider modified LIML estimators in which $k$ is a general linear function of $\lambda_0$, and use small $\sigma$ asymptotics to define a class of estimators that have lower asymptotic mean-squared error than comparable Fuller estimators. A discussion of the specific results in these papers and their implications concerning the estimation and testing of simultaneous equation models is presented in the following sections.

## 2 Estimation of structural equations

Kadiyala and Oberhelman (1992) consider a subclass of single $k$-class estimators in which

$$k = \left(1 - \frac{\chi_1}{L + T - K}\right)\lambda_0 + \frac{\chi_2}{T - K} \tag{2.1}$$

This class of estimators includes most single $k$-class estimators of practical importance: the OLS, TSLS, LIML, and Fuller estimators. For this reason we refer to the class of estimators, $b(k)$ with

$$k = \left(1 - \frac{\chi_1}{L + T - K}\right)\lambda_0 + \frac{\chi_2}{T - K}$$

as general $k$-class estimators (GKE).

Since the LIML and fixed $k$-class estimators with $k > 1$ are included in this family of estimators, it is clear that the moments of the GKE need not exist. However, a modification of the argument given by Fuller (1977: 944) establishes that the first two moments of the $k$-class estimator will exist if $k$ has the form $k = \lambda_0 - \varepsilon$ where $\varepsilon > 0$. Therefore, we have the following theorem:

Theorem 2.1 The general $k$-class estimators have finite moments if

$$\frac{\chi_1}{L + T - K} - \frac{\chi_2}{T - K} > 0$$

Proof: Proof follows immediately by noting that

$$k = \left(1 - \frac{\chi_1}{L+T-K}\right)\lambda_0 + \frac{\chi_2}{T-K} = \lambda_0 - \frac{\chi_1\lambda_0}{L+T-K} + \frac{\chi_2}{T-K} < \lambda_0 - \frac{\chi_1}{L+T-K} + \frac{\chi_2}{T-K}$$

$$= \lambda_0 - \left(\frac{\chi_1}{L+T-K} - \frac{\chi_2}{T-K}\right) = \lambda_0 - \varepsilon, \text{ where } \varepsilon = \frac{\chi_1}{L+T-K} - \frac{\chi_2}{T-K} > 0$$

Defining $e_k = b(k) - (\beta' | \gamma')'$ and $\Delta\chi = \chi_1 - \chi_2$, Kadiyala and Oberhelman (1992) state the following lemmas concerning the bias and mean-squared error of $b(k)$:

Lemma 2.1 The bias of the general $k$-class estimator to order $\sigma^2$ is given by:

$$E(e_k) = (\Delta\chi - 1)\sigma^2 Qq + 0(\sigma^3) \tag{2.2}$$

Lemma 2.2 The mean-squared error of the general $k$-class estimator to order $\sigma^4$ is given by:

$$\begin{aligned} E(e_k e'_k) &= \sigma^2 Q + \sigma^4 TR(QC_2)Q + \sigma^4(3 - 2\Delta\chi)TR(QC_1)Q \\ &+ \sigma^4 \left[\left(\frac{L+T-K+2}{L+T-K}\right)(\Delta\chi)^2 - 6(\Delta\chi - 1) + \frac{2\chi_2{}^2 L}{(L+T-K)(T-K)}\right] QC_1\, Q \\ &+ \frac{\sigma^4}{(T-K-2)}[(L+T-K-2)(L+2) - 2(L+T-K-2)\Delta\chi \\ &+ \frac{T-K-2}{T-K}(\Delta\chi)^2 + \frac{4\Delta\chi L}{(T-K)} - \frac{4\chi_1 L}{(T-K)} + \frac{2\chi_1{}^2 L}{(L+T-K)(T-K)}\Bigg] QC_2\, Q + 0(\sigma^5) \end{aligned} \tag{2.3}$$

where $q$, $Q$, $C_1$, and $C_2$ are as defined in Kadane (1971). That is,

$$Q = \begin{bmatrix} \Pi_2{}' X_*{}' X_* \Pi_2 & \Pi_2{}' X_*{}' X_1 \\ X_1{}' X_* \Pi_2 & X_1{}' X_1 \end{bmatrix}^{-1}$$

$$q' = (1/\sigma^2)(\omega_{12} - \beta' \Omega_{22} \mid 0')$$

$C_1 = qq'$ and

$$C_2 = \frac{1}{\sigma^2}\begin{bmatrix} \Omega_{22} & 0 \\ 0 & 0 \end{bmatrix} - qq'$$

The asymptotic mean-squared error (AMSE) in equation (2.3) provides the following criteria for choosing between alternative $k$-class estimators, $b(k_1)$ and $b(k_2)$: $b(k_1)$ is preferred to $b(k_2)$ if AMSE($b(k_1)$) $\leq$ AMSE($b(k_2)$). In addition to the above criterion, the asymptotic probability of concentration is frequently used to compare alternative $k$-class estimators. The asymptotic probability of concentration, APC $= \lim_{\sigma\to 0} \frac{1}{\sigma} \Pr(e_k\ \varepsilon S)$ is obtained by integrating the asymptotic density of $e_k$ to $0(\sigma^3)$ over set $S$. When comparing two $k$-class estimators $b(k_1)$ and $b(k_2)$ on the basis of APC, $b(k_1)$ is said to be preferred to estimator $b(k_2)$ if $\lim_{\sigma\to 0} \frac{1}{\sigma} (\Pr(e_{k_1} \varepsilon S) - \Pr(e_{k_2} \varepsilon S)) \geq 0$ for every convex set $S$ that contains the origin.

Using APC and asymptotic mean-squared error as criteria of estimation we state the following two theorems concerning the admissibility of the LIML and Fuller estimators. The proofs of these theorems are contained in the Appendix.

Theorem 2.2 Let $k_1 = \left(1 - \frac{h}{L + T - K}\right) \lambda_0$ and $k_2 = \lambda_0 - \frac{h}{(T - K)}$ where $h < 2(L + T - K)$ so that estimators $b(k_1)$ and $b(k_2)$ have the same asymptotic bias to $0(\sigma^2)$. Then, estimator $b(k_1)$ has lower AMSE to $0(\sigma^4)$ than estimator $b(k_2)$ and for symmetric $S$, APC $(b(k_1)) \geq$ APC$(b(k_2))$.

Theorem 2.3 Consider $k$-class estimators $b(k_h)$ with $k_h = \left(1 - \frac{h}{L + T - K}\right)$ $\lambda_0$. Let $h_* = \frac{L + T - K}{L + T - K + 2}$. Then estimator $b(k_h)$ with $h = h_*$ has greater APC for symmetric $S$ than any other estimator $b(k_h)$ with $h < h_*$, and estimator $b(k_h)$ with $h = 4h_*$ has lower AMSE than any other estimator $b(k_h)$ with $h < 4h_*$.

The above theorems define a set of modified LIML estimators, $b(k_h)$, which dominate the Fuller and LIML estimators in terms of AMSE and APC. Since the estimators in this class are obtained by reducing the scale of the LIML root $\lambda_0$ we refer to them as scaled down LIML estimators. Thus, Theorem 2.2 implies that the Fuller estimators are inadmissible because a scaled down LIML estimator of comparable bias will always have lower AMSE and higher APC, and Theorem 2.3 implies that a scaled down LIML estimator with $h = \frac{L + T - K}{L + T - K + 2}$ has lower AMSE and higher APC than the LIML estimator. A Monte Carlo study in Kadiyala and Oberhelman (1992) found that the scaled down LIML estimators are more efficient in small samples than comparable Fuller estimators and that the relative efficiency of the scaled down estimators becomes more pronounced as the number of overidentification restrictions increases. In section 4 we will investigate whether or not the large sample comparisons between the LIML and scaled down estimators hold in small samples.

Following a procedure similar to that of Nagar (1959), $\chi_1$ and $\chi_2$ can be chosen to minimize the determinantal value of the moment matrix $E(e_k e_k')$. The GKE which satisfies the above criterion has

$$k = k_* = \left(1 - \frac{\hat{\chi}_1}{L + T - K}\right) \lambda_0 + \frac{\hat{\chi}_2}{(T - K)}$$

where

$$\hat{\chi}_1 = \frac{L + T - K - 2}{A} + L + T - K$$

$$\hat{\chi}_2 = \frac{L + T - K - 2}{(T - K - 2)A} \left(\frac{\mathrm{TR}(QC_2)}{\mathrm{TR}(QC_1)}\right)$$

and

$$A = \left[\frac{L + T - K + 2}{L + T - K} + \frac{\mathrm{TR}(QC_2)/\mathrm{TR}(QC_1)}{T - K - 2} + \frac{(\mathrm{TR}(QC_2)/\mathrm{TR}(QC_1))^2}{(T - K)(T - K - 2)}\right]$$

The values of $\hat{\chi}_1$ and $\hat{\chi}_2$ are parameter dependent. Therefore, the optimal GKE, $b(k_*)$, can not be directly implemented. It is possible, however, to identify a subclass of the GKE which contains $b(k_*)$. In this regard, notice that $\mathrm{TR}(QC_2)/\mathrm{TR}(QC_1) \geq 0$ implies that $A \geq \frac{L + T - K + 2}{(L + T - K)}$ and it follows that $\hat{\chi}_1 \geq 4 - \frac{8}{(L + T - K + 2)}$ and $\hat{\chi}_2 \geq 0$. Therefore, if the objective is to minimize the MSE of the GKE, then $k$ in equation (2.1) should be restricted so that $\hat{\chi}_1 \geq 4 - \frac{8}{(L + T - K + 2)}$ and $\hat{\chi}_2 \geq 0$. Any other $k$-class estimator is dominated by a member of this family (note that the TSLS, LIML, and Fuller estimators are *not* within this family of estimators).

Fuller (1977) obtained a similar result under the restriction that $\chi_1 = 0$, and he recommended that if one wishes to minimize the mean-squared error of the estimator, setting $\chi_2 = -4$ is appropriate. The above discussion leads us to suggest that $b(k)$ with $k = \left(1 - \frac{4}{L + T - K}\right)\lambda_0$ be used as a replacement for Fuller's recommendation. This estimator is smaller in MSE to $0(\sigma^4)$ than the Fuller estimator when $L + T - K > 2$.

We can obtain an operational version of $b(k_*)$ obtained by estimating $\hat{\chi}_1$ and $\hat{\chi}_2$. This involves estimating $\mathrm{TR}(QC_2)/\mathrm{TR}(QC_1)$. To estimate this ratio we use the following estimates of $Q$ and $q$:

$$\hat{Q} = \begin{pmatrix} \hat{\Pi}_2'(X_*'X_*)\hat{\Pi}_2 & \hat{\Pi}_2'X_*'X_1 \\ X_1'X_*\hat{\Pi}_2 & X_1'X_1 \end{pmatrix}^{-1}$$

where $\hat{\Pi} = (X_*'X_*)^{-1} X_*'Y$

and

$$\hat{q} = 1/\hat{\sigma}^2 (\hat{\omega}_{12} - \hat{\beta}_{LI}'\hat{\Omega}_{22}|0')$$

where

$$\hat{\Omega} = \frac{Y'MY}{T - K}$$

$$\hat{\beta}_{LI} = \text{LIML of } \beta$$

and

$$\hat{\sigma}^2 = (y - Y_1\hat{\beta}_{LI} - X_1\hat{\gamma})'(y - Y_1\hat{\beta}_{LI} - X_1\hat{\gamma})/T$$

Using $\hat{Q}$ and $\hat{q}$ we can define as estimate for $A$, $\hat{A}$, which provides

$$\tilde{\chi}_1 = -\frac{(L + T - K - 2)}{\hat{A}} + (L + T - K)$$

$$\tilde{\chi}_2 = \frac{L + T - K - 2}{(T - K - 2)\hat{A}} \left(\frac{\mathrm{TR}(\hat{Q}\hat{C}_2)}{\mathrm{TR}(\hat{Q}\hat{C}_1)}\right)$$

and

$$\hat{k}_* = \left(1 - \frac{\tilde{\chi}_1}{L + T - K}\right)\lambda_0 + \frac{\tilde{\chi}_2}{T - K}$$

In a Monte Carlo study investigating the efficiency of $b(\hat{k}_*)$, Kadiyala and Oberhelman (1992) estimated the mean-squared error of $b(\hat{k}_*)$ for models with $G = 2$ and compared it to the MSE of the TSLS estimator. They found that when the correlation between $Y_1$ and $\mu_1$ is low, a moderate increase in MSE results if $b(\hat{k}_*)$ is used instead of the TSLS estimator. On the other hand, sizeable reductions in MSE relative to TSLS are possible if $b(\hat{k}_*)$ is used when the correlation between $Y_1$ and $\mu_1$ is high. Thus, $b(\hat{k}_*)$ provides a viable alternative to classical estimators like TSLS when MSE is the criterion for judging an estimator.

The above discussion has reviewed several modified LIML estimators which can be used in place of classical estimators like TSLS and LIML under a mean-squared error criterion. In the remainder of the chapter we consider the properties of large sample tests based on $b(k)$.

## 3 Testing in structional equations

Let $b_i(k)$ represent the $k$-class estimator for $\delta_i$, the $i$th component of the coefficient vector $\delta = (\beta' | \gamma')'$, and let $V_{ii}(k)$ be the consistent estimator for the $i$th diagonal element of $\sigma^2 Q$ obtained from $\hat{\sigma}_k{}^2\hat{Q}_k$ where

$$\hat{\sigma}_k^2 = (y - Zb(k))'(y - Zb(k))/(T - G_1 - K_1) \tag{3.1}$$

and

$$\hat{Q}_k = (Z'(I - kM)Z)^{-1} \tag{3.2}$$

If $k$ is chosen so that $\mathrm{p}\lim \sqrt{T}\cdot(k - 1) = 0$, then it is well known that $b(k)$ is asymptotically efficient and that it converges to a normal random vector with mean $\delta$ and variance covariance matrix $\sigma^2 Q$. Consequently, the ratio

$$t_i(k) = \frac{b_i(k) - \delta_i}{\sqrt{V_{ii}(k)}} \text{ is asymptotically } N(0,1).$$

In practical applications it is often assumed that the $t$ distribution with $(T - G_1 - K_1)$ degrees of freedom adequately approximates the distribution of this statistic and that standard methods can be used to compute confidence interval statements and test hypotheses concerning $\delta_i$. For instance, it is a common procedure to use the $100(1 - \alpha/2)$ percentile point of the $t$ distribution with $(T - G_1 - K_1)$ degrees of freedom to construct the interval

$$b_i(k) \pm t_{1-\alpha/2} \sqrt{V_{ii}(k)} \tag{3.3}$$

and to report it as a $100(1 - \alpha)$ percent confidence interval for $\delta_i$. Evidence of the general acceptance of this type of analysis is found in the fact that it has been incorporated into conventional software packages used to analyze simultaneous equation models. For example, the SAS/ETS program generates the ratio $t_i(k)$ under the hypothesis that $\delta_i = 0$, and computes the $p$-value of this statistic using a $t$ distribution with $(T - G_1 - K_1)$ degrees of freedom – the implication being that these $p$-values can be used to determine the statistical significance of the estimated coefficients. Traditionally, TSLS and LIML estimators are used to generate the $t$ statistics and confidence intervals just described.

Although these procedures are widely applied, there has been relatively little work done on evaluating their performance. Anderson, Kunitomo, and Sawa (1982) found that the distribution of the LIML estimator generally approaches normality faster than the distribution of the TSLS estimator, due primarily to the bias of the latter. This led them to infer that conventional tests based on the LIML estimator would be preferable to those based on TSLS. In a subsequent study Morimune (1989) used Monte Carlo methods to investigate the null distributions of $t$ statistics based on the TSLS and LIML estimators ($t_{\text{TSLS}}$ and $t_{\text{LIML}}$). He found that the null distribution of $t_{\text{LIML}}$ is generally closer in distribution to a $t$ random variable than the null distribution of $t_{\text{TSLS}}$. There was no investigation of the power of $t_{\text{LIML}}$.

The purpose of this chapter is to identify an estimator $b(k_0)$ whose $t$ statistic, $t_i(k_0)$, will provide more dependable inferences about $\delta_i$ than those based on $t_{\text{TSLS}}$ and $t_{\text{LIML}}$. We discuss a potential candidate below and compare its power to that of $t_{\text{LIML}}$.

In general when testing hypotheses or generating confidence interval statements concerning $\delta_i$, it is desirable to use a $k$-class estimator that has minimal bias and high probability of concentration. Thus, the theorems discussed in section 2 can be used to find an alternative estimator which may be preferable to the TSLS and LIML estimator. Specifically, we propose that a modified LIML estimator, $b(k_0)$, with $k_0 = \left(1 - \dfrac{1}{L + T - K}\right) \lambda_0$ be used when the purpose is to test hypotheses or set approximate confidence intervals for $\delta_i$.

Notice that this estimator has the following desirable properties:

1 from Theorem 2.1, it has finite moments;
2 from Lemma 2.1, it is unbiased to $0(\sigma^2)$; and
3 from Theorem 2.3, it has greater APC and smaller AMSE than the LIML estimator.

Because of the second of these properties we will refer to $b(k_0)$ as the scaled down unbiased (SDUNB) estimator.

The above small $\sigma$ properties suggest several practical implications. First, referring to the results of Anderson, Kunitomo, and Sawa (1982) we would expect the SDUNB estimator to approach normality at a faster rate than the TSLS estimator. This implies that conventional tests based on the SDUNB estimator should be preferable to those based on TSLS. Second, points (1) and (3) imply that the distribution of the LIML estimator has longer tails than that of the SDUNB estimator. This suggests that a $t$ test based on SDUNB should have greater power for comparable levels of significance than a test based on the LIML estimator.

Since the exact distribution of $t_i(k)$ depends on the unknown parameters of the model, we use Monte Carlo simulation to evaluate the validity of the above claims in finite samples. Specifically, in the following section of the chapter we investigate the sampling properties of various $t$ statistics for $\beta$ (the coefficient of $Y_1$) in models in which $G = 2$. The results are presented below together with detailed descriptions of the simulation experiments.

## 4 Monte Carlo results

In order to investigate the finite-sample properties of the SDUNB estimator and the power of its associated $t$ statistic ($t_{\text{SDUNB}}$), we conducted a series of Monte Carlo experiments. The experiments are based on a model which has two endogenous variables (i.e. $G = 2$). This allows us to make use of the results obtained by Anderson and Sawa (1979) and Anderson, Kunitomo, and Sawa (1982) who found that the distribution functions of the TSLS and LIML estimators for $\beta$ depend on $K_2$, $T - K$, the correlation between $Y_1$ and $\mu_1$ (denoted by $\rho$), and noncentrality parameter $\delta^2 = \dfrac{\Pi_2' X_2' M_1 X_2 \Pi_2}{\Omega_{22}}$. Thus by changing the values of these parameters during the course of our simulation, we can systematically investigate the distributional properties of the SDUNB estimator and $t_{\text{SDUNB}}$ under a variety of conditions.

Since our interest lies in the finite sampling properties of the modified LIML estimator, we set $T - K$ equal to 17 and used Anderson, Morimune, and Sawa (1983) as a guide for choosing moderate to low values of $\delta^2$. For each value of $\delta^2$ we generated the distributions of the SDUNB estimator for $\beta$ and its $t$ statistic for values of $\rho = .1, .5$, and $.9$ and for values of $K_2$ ranging from 3 to 15. This provides information on the properties of these statistics for low, medium, and high levels of the correlation between $Y_1$ and $\mu_1$ and for various levels of overidentification. The results of the simulation are summarized in Tables 11.1–11.10. The results in Tables 11.1–11.8 are based on 10,000 replications while those in Tables 11.9 and 11.10 are based on 20,000 replications.

The data in Tables 11.1–11.4 provide general information on how the distribution of the SDUNB estimator compares with those of the LIML and TSLS estimators. Specifically, using the true asymptotic standard error (ASYSDEV) we standardized each $k$-class estimator, $\hat{\beta}_k$, to obtain

$$Z_k = \frac{\hat{\beta}_k - \beta}{\text{ASYSDEV}} \quad k = \text{TSLS, LIML, SDUNB}$$

and computed the relative frequency with which $Z_k$ fell within a predetermined interval.

Three intervals were selected: interval $A$ which corresponds to $[-.32, .32]$, interval $B$ which corresponds to $[-.67, .67]$ and interval $C$ which corresponds to $[-2.0, 2.0]$. Recall that the probability that a normal random variable falls within intervals $A$, $B$, and $C$ is roughly .25, .50, and .95. Thus, in addition to providing measures of the probability of concentration for the various estimators, Tables 11.1 to 11.4 contain information on the speed of convergence to normality.

As might be anticipated the distribution of $Z_{\text{SDUNB}}$ and $Z_{\text{LIML}}$ have certain similarities. In particular, for smaller values of $\delta^2$ the distributions of both estimators tend to have longer tails than the standard normal distribution, and for given values of $\delta^2$, the sampling distributions of both $Z_{\text{SDUNB}}$ and $Z_{\text{LIML}}$ tend to become more concentrated as $\rho$ increases and less concentrated as $K_2$ increases. Notice, however, that because the SDUNB estimator has moments while the LIML estimator does not, the distribution of the standardized SDUNB estimator is more concentrated than that of the standardized LIML estimator; and although for larger values of $\delta^2$ the differences in concentration tend to be marginal, there are significant differences in concentration for smaller values of $\delta^2$. This implies that the asymptotic result established in Theorem 2.3 extends to finite samples and that adjusting the LIML estimator would be particularly appropriate in smaller samples.

Casual inspection of the bottom portions of Tables 11.1 to 11.4 indicates that the sampling distributions of the standardized SDUNB and LIML estimators tend towards normality at a faster rate than the standardized TSLS estimator. This is in agreement with Anderson, Kunitomo, and Sawa's (1982) findings concerning the LIML estimator and suggests that using the normal or $t$ distribution to approximate the distributions of the $t$ ratios should be more accurate for the SDUNB estimator than the TSLS estimator.

In this regard Tables 11.5 to 11.10 provide data on the adequacy of large sample confidence intervals and tests of hypotheses based on the $t$ ratios of the SDUNB, LIML, and TSLS estimators. Specifically, Tables 11.5 to 11.8 contain the relative frequencies with which the $t$ ratios for the SDUNB, LIML, and TSLS estimators fall below (bel), within (with), and above (abv) the interval $[t_{.025}, t_{.975}]$ where $t_{.025}$ and $t_{.975}$ are respectively 2.5 and 97.5 percentile points of a $t$ distribution with $(T - G_1 - K_1)$ degrees of freedom. Thus, Tables 11.5 to 11.8 provide results concerning the coverage of the

*Table 11.1* Probability of concentration for $K_2 = 3$

| $\delta^2$ | $\rho$ | TSLS A | TSLS B | TSLS C | LIML A | LIML B | LIML C | SDUNB A | SDUNB B | SDUNB C |
|---|---|---|---|---|---|---|---|---|---|---|
| 10 | .1 | .266 | .524 | .940 | .220 | .438 | .853 | .246 | .491 | .921 |
| | .5 | .251 | .512 | .953 | .223 | .451 | .870 | .253 | .503 | .942 |
| | .9 | .223 | .463 | .969 | .245 | .486 | .891 | .263 | .546 | .978 |
| 25 | .1 | .256 | .500 | .950 | .238 | .461 | .917 | .247 | .484 | .935 |
| | .5 | .250 | .497 | .954 | .238 | .469 | .923 | .249 | .491 | .944 |
| | .9 | .233 | .485 | .964 | .247 | .489 | .927 | .256 | .509 | .959 |
| 75 | .1 | .250 | .494 | .952 | .244 | .479 | .943 | .247 | .487 | .948 |
| | .5 | .249 | .493 | .955 | .246 | .482 | .946 | .250 | .491 | .952 |
| | .9 | .249 | .487 | .958 | .247 | .490 | .947 | .250 | .497 | .957 |
| 150 | .1 | .249 | .493 | .954 | .246 | .483 | .951 | .247 | .489 | .953 |
| | .5 | .250 | .492 | .956 | .247 | .486 | .951 | .248 | .490 | .954 |
| | .9 | .248 | .490 | .955 | .249 | .491 | .952 | .248 | .493 | .956 |

*Table 11.2* Probability of concentration for $K_2 = 6$

| $\delta^2$ | $\rho$ | TSLS A | TSLS B | TSLS C | LIML A | LIML B | LIML C | SDUNB A | SDUNB B | SDUNB C |
|---|---|---|---|---|---|---|---|---|---|---|
| 10 | .1 | .301 | .571 | .969 | .195 | .385 | .795 | .216 | .437 | .881 |
| | .5 | .231 | .475 | .964 | .199 | .401 | .820 | .227 | .453 | .902 |
| | .9 | .110 | .277 | .977 | .238 | .470 | .883 | .262 | .525 | .977 |
| 25 | .1 | .269 | .517 | .960 | .218 | .431 | .881 | .228 | .452 | .908 |
| | .5 | .236 | .480 | .960 | .226 | .448 | .899 | .238 | .464 | .925 |
| | .9 | .179 | .376 | .972 | .243 | .483 | .924 | .252 | .493 | .957 |
| 75 | .1 | .252 | .496 | .957 | .240 | .470 | .936 | .241 | .475 | .941 |
| | .5 | .242 | .482 | .959 | .241 | .475 | .940 | .245 | .480 | .946 |
| | .9 | .221 | .445 | .963 | .247 | .487 | .944 | .250 | .488 | .955 |
| 150 | .1 | .248 | .489 | .958 | .243 | .480 | .950 | .245 | .481 | .950 |
| | .5 | .244 | .480 | .957 | .244 | .480 | .948 | .245 | .481 | .952 |
| | .9 | .232 | .465 | .960 | .247 | .489 | .951 | .249 | .488 | .956 |

confidence intervals defined in equation (3.3) and data on the percentage of times these intervals fall below and above the true value of $\beta$. Ideally, the confidence intervals should be "unbiased" in the sense that when the interval does not cover the true value, it is equally likely to be above as

*Table 11.3* Probability of concentration for $K_2 = 10$

| | | *TSLS* | | | *LIML* | | | *SDUNB* | | |
|---|---|---|---|---|---|---|---|---|---|---|
| $\delta^2$ | $\rho$ | *A* | *B* | *C* | *A* | *B* | *C* | *A* | *B* | *C* |
| 10 | .1 | .339 | .630 | .985 | .169 | .343 | .728 | .190 | .386 | .816 |
| | .5 | .182 | .412 | .968 | .174 | .360 | .758 | .202 | .407 | .857 |
| | .9 | .028 | .088 | .923 | .223 | .453 | .864 | .247 | .509 | .968 |
| 25 | .1 | .290 | .556 | .971 | .198 | .398 | .838 | .209 | .419 | .871 |
| | .5 | .208 | .431 | .955 | .209 | .415 | .867 | .218 | .436 | .899 |
| | .9 | .084 | .199 | .918 | .242 | .475 | .915 | .243 | .493 | .949 |
| 75 | .1 | .263 | .518 | .963 | .233 | .452 | .923 | .238 | .461 | .928 |
| | .5 | .228 | .463 | .955 | .237 | .465 | .930 | .240 | .470 | .937 |
| | .9 | .167 | .351 | .940 | .243 | .492 | .942 | .246 | .496 | .952 |
| 150 | .1 | .254 | .501 | .959 | .240 | .475 | .941 | .243 | .479 | .944 |
| | .5 | .237 | .473 | .956 | .244 | .482 | .944 | .244 | .484 | .948 |
| | .9 | .202 | .416 | .946 | .246 | .497 | .949 | .245 | .497 | .953 |

*Table 11.4* Probability of concentration for $K_2 = 15$

| | | *TSLS* | | | *LIML* | | | *SDUNB* | | |
|---|---|---|---|---|---|---|---|---|---|---|
| $\delta^2$ | $\rho$ | *A* | *B* | *C* | *A* | *B* | *C* | *A* | *B* | *C* |
| 25 | .1 | .302 | .584 | .979 | .176 | .354 | .767 | .188 | .376 | .804 |
| | .5 | .156 | .341 | .934 | .186 | .375 | .805 | .198 | .396 | .843 |
| | .9 | .020 | .060 | .753 | .230 | .454 | .901 | .228 | .473 | .938 |
| 75 | .1 | .263 | .526 | .967 | .212 | .424 | .895 | .219 | .433 | .902 |
| | .5 | .204 | .412 | .940 | .221 | .437 | .907 | .225 | .447 | .916 |
| | .9 | .096 | .222 | .855 | .241 | .477 | .936 | .240 | .482 | .949 |
| 150 | .1 | .253 | .508 | .963 | .231 | .453 | .927 | .233 | .458 | .932 |
| | .5 | .219 | .441 | .946 | .233 | .462 | .934 | .233 | .467 | .939 |
| | .9 | .153 | .324 | .900 | .243 | .482 | .945 | .242 | .488 | .952 |

below the true value. If the confidence intervals defined in equation (3.3) are "unbiased" and adequately approximate the specified coverage, then the probability values recorded in Tables 11.5 to 11.8 should be close to .025, .95, and .025. In addition to the probability values, Tables 11.5 to 11.8 contain data on the length of the confidence intervals. The recorded lengths were obtained by computing for each case considered the average length (LGTH) of the 10,000 intervals generated by the SDUNB, LIML, and TSLS estimators.

*Table 11.5* Coverage and tail probability $K_2 = 3$

| $\delta^2$ | $\rho$ | TSLS *bel* | *with* | *abv* | *lgth* | LIML *bel* | *with* | *abv* | *lgth* | SDUNB *bel* | *with* | *abv* | *lgth* |
|---|---|---|---|---|---|---|---|---|---|---|---|---|---|
| 10 | .1 | .007 | .972 | .022 | 4.41 | .007 | .972 | .021 | 22420 | .007 | .972 | .021 | 4.70 |
| | .5 | .000 | .927 | .073 | 4.34 | .000 | .943 | .057 | 93.41 | .000 | .934 | .064 | 4.60 |
| | .9 | .000 | .830 | .170 | 4.15 | .000 | .916 | .085 | 31.24 | .000 | .889 | .112 | 4.43 |
| 25 | .1 | .012 | .961 | .027 | 4.22 | .014 | .959 | .028 | 5.33 | .013 | .960 | .027 | 4.39 |
| | .5 | .003 | .940 | .057 | 4.19 | .003 | .949 | .047 | 4.65 | .003 | .946 | .051 | 4.37 |
| | .9 | .000 | .895 | .105 | 4.14 | .000 | .936 | .064 | 4.72 | .000 | .920 | .080 | 4.35 |
| 50 | .1 | .016 | .955 | .029 | 4.17 | .018 | .953 | .029 | 4.32 | .017 | .955 | .028 | 4.24 |
| | .5 | .006 | .944 | .050 | 4.16 | .009 | .949 | .042 | 4.32 | .008 | .948 | .045 | 4.24 |
| | .9 | .002 | .920 | .078 | 4.13 | .003 | .942 | .055 | 4.37 | .002 | .934 | .064 | 4.23 |
| 150 | .1 | .020 | .951 | .030 | 4.14 | .021 | .950 | .029 | 4.18 | .020 | .951 | .029 | 4.16 |
| | .5 | .013 | .948 | .040 | 4.14 | .015 | .949 | .036 | 4.18 | .014 | .948 | .038 | 4.16 |
| | .9 | .008 | .936 | .056 | 4.12 | .010 | .946 | .044 | 4.20 | .008 | .943 | .049 | 4.16 |
| 250 | .1 | .022 | .949 | .029 | 4.14 | .022 | .949 | .029 | 4.16 | .022 | .950 | .029 | 4.15 |
| | .5 | .015 | .948 | .037 | 4.13 | .017 | .949 | .034 | 4.16 | .016 | .949 | .035 | 4.15 |
| | .9 | .011 | .941 | .049 | 4.13 | .013 | .948 | .039 | 4.17 | .012 | .944 | .044 | 4.15 |

*Table 11.6* Coverage, tail probabilities, and length $K_2 = 6$

| $\delta^2$ | $\rho$ | TSLS *bel* | *with* | *abv* | *lgth* | LIML *bel* | *with* | *abv* | *lgth* | SDUNB *bel* | *with* | *abv* | *lgth* |
|---|---|---|---|---|---|---|---|---|---|---|---|---|---|
| 25 | .1 | .015 | .952 | .027 | 3.91 | .018 | .949 | .033 | 35.8 | .017 | .950 | .033 | 4.50 |
| | .5 | .003 | .904 | .094 | 3.79 | .005 | .940 | .055 | 14.09 | .004 | .936 | .060 | 4.42 |
| | .9 | .000 | .791 | .209 | 3.53 | .000 | .932 | .067 | 4.67 | .000 | .917 | .083 | 4.31 |
| 75 | .1 | .018 | .950 | .032 | 4.03 | .022 | .948 | .031 | 4.23 | .021 | .948 | .031 | 4.19 |
| | .5 | .007 | .933 | .060 | 3.99 | .013 | .945 | .042 | 4.22 | .012 | .943 | .045 | 4.17 |
| | .9 | .001 | .891 | .108 | 3.89 | .006 | .943 | .051 | 4.24 | .005 | .935 | .060 | 4.16 |
| 250 | .1 | .021 | .948 | .032 | 4.08 | .022 | .949 | .030 | 4.13 | .021 | .949 | .030 | 4.12 |
| | .5 | .013 | .942 | .045 | 4.06 | .017 | .949 | .034 | 4.13 | .016 | .947 | .037 | 4.11 |
| | .9 | .008 | .927 | .065 | 4.03 | .014 | .946 | .041 | 4.13 | .012 | .943 | .046 | 4.11 |

Referring to Tables 11.5 to 11.8 we can make the following comparisons concerning the approximate 95 percent confidence intervals generated by the SDUNB and TSLS estimators. First, for low values of $\rho$ and $\delta^2$ the TSLS intervals tend to be preferable because they are tighter at comparable levels

*Table 11.7* Coverage, tail probabilities, and length $K_2 = 10$

| | | TSLS | | | | LIML | | | | SDUNB | | | |
|---|---|---|---|---|---|---|---|---|---|---|---|---|---|
| $\delta^2$ | $\rho$ | *bel* | *with* | *abv* | *lgth* | *bel* | *with* | *abv* | *lgth* | *bel* | *with* | *abv* | *lgth* |
| 25 | .1 | .013 | .955 | .032 | 3.61 | .024 | .936 | .040 | 320.7 | .023 | .938 | .039 | 4.73 |
| | .5 | .001 | .858 | .139 | 3.43 | .005 | .928 | .067 | 31.06 | .003 | .926 | .071 | 4.57 |
| | .9 | .000 | .590 | .410 | 3.02 | .000 | .932 | .068 | 4.76 | .000 | .919 | .081 | 4.35 |
| 75 | .1 | .017 | .950 | .033 | 3.90 | .028 | .938 | .034 | 4.25 | .027 | .940 | .034 | 4.20 |
| | .5 | .004 | .913 | .083 | 3.82 | .014 | .942 | .044 | 4.23 | .011 | .942 | .047 | 4.17 |
| | .9 | .000 | .819 | .181 | 3.66 | .005 | .946 | .049 | 4.23 | .003 | .940 | .056 | 4.14 |
| 250 | .1 | .021 | .948 | .031 | 4.02 | .025 | .945 | .029 | 4.11 | .025 | .946 | .029 | 4.10 |
| | .5 | .010 | .938 | .052 | 3.99 | .019 | .947 | .034 | 4.11 | .018 | .946 | .036 | 4.09 |
| | .9 | .004 | .911 | .085 | 3.94 | .015 | .947 | .038 | 4.11 | .013 | .946 | .042 | 4.09 |

*Table 11.8* Coverage, tail probabilities, and length $K_2 = 15$

| | | TSLS | | | | LIML | | | | SDUNB | | | |
|---|---|---|---|---|---|---|---|---|---|---|---|---|---|
| $\delta^2$ | $\rho$ | *bel* | *with* | *abv* | *lgth* | *bel* | *with* | *abv* | *lgth* | *bel* | *with* | *abv* | *lgth* |
| 25 | .1 | .011 | .949 | .040 | 3.32 | .037 | .907 | .057 | 143.2 | .034 | .912 | .054 | 5.00 |
| | .5 | .001 | .762 | .237 | 3.12 | .007 | .901 | .092 | 60.46 | .005 | .897 | .097 | 4.83 |
| | .9 | .000 | .314 | .686 | 2.61 | .000 | .925 | .075 | 5.03 | .000 | .909 | .091 | 4.67 |
| 75 | .1 | .015 | .951 | .035 | 3.76 | .034 | .926 | .041 | 4.46 | .031 | .930 | .039 | 4.25 |
| | .5 | .003 | .870 | .127 | 3.66 | .015 | .930 | .055 | 4.26 | .012 | .931 | .057 | 4.20 |
| | .9 | .000 | .668 | .332 | 3.42 | .006 | .943 | .051 | 4.22 | .004 | .938 | .059 | 4.13 |
| 250 | .1 | .018 | .950 | .032 | 3.95 | .026 | .945 | .029 | 4.10 | .025 | .946 | .029 | 4.09 |
| | .5 | .007 | .925 | .068 | 3.92 | .020 | .946 | .034 | 4.10 | .018 | .945 | .037 | 4.08 |
| | .9 | .002 | .861 | .137 | 3.83 | .013 | .950 | .038 | 4.09 | .011 | .947 | .042 | 4.07 |

of coverage. This is the only situation in which the TSLS intervals are clearly preferable. For the larger values of $\rho$, the fact that the SDUNB estimators provide better coverage compensates for the observed differences in length. This is particularly true as $K_2$ increases. Notice for $K_2 = 6$, 10, and 15 that (except when the value of $\rho$ is low) the intervals generated by the TSLS estimator tend to be highly asymmetric and the coverage is often well below 95 percent. In particular, when $\delta^2/K_2 \leq 5$ the TSLS intervals provide grossly misleading results when compared to the SDUNB intervals.

As $\delta^2$ increases the SDUNB intervals more quickly approach 95 percent normal confidence intervals than do the TSLS intervals. Specifically, notice in Tables 11.5 to 11.8 that for the larger values of $\delta^2$ the differences between the length of the TSLS and SDUNB intervals become negligible. However, the TSLS intervals are still noticeably asymmetric and the coverage of these intervals is appreciably lower than that of the SDUNB intervals. In summary, the simulation results presented in Tables 11.5 to 11.8 imply that the SDUNB intervals are generally preferred to the TSLS intervals unless there is reason to believe that $\rho$ is small.

With regards to the relative performance of the SDUNB and LIML intervals, notice for the most part that there are only minor differences in the coverage rates and symmetry of these intervals. The most significant difference between the LIML and SDUNB intervals concerns their length. In particular notice in Tables 11.5 to 11.8 that for smaller values of $\delta^2$ the lengths of the LIML intervals are unusually large. This occurs because in general the estimated standard error of the LIML estimator based on equations (3.1) and (3.2) does not have finite moments. As a result it is possible that in some instances the estimates of the asymptotic standard error of the LIML estimator can be quite large. Consequently, using the LIML estimator to generate $100(1 - \alpha)$ percent confidence intervals as defined by equation (3.3), can result in extremely long intervals. The data in Tables 11.5 to 11.8 indicate that this is most likely to occur in smaller samples.

In order to better investigate the relative efficiencies of the LIML and SDUNB estimators in making inferential statements about $\beta$, we used Monte Carlo methods to compute power functions for the large sample $t$ tests based on the SDUNB and LIML estimators. Specifically, defining $\beta_0$ as the hypothesized value for the structural coefficient $\beta$ and $\text{ESTSDEV}_k$ as the estimated asymptotic standard error of $\hat{\beta}_k$ obtained from equations (3.1) and (3.2), we computed the power of

$$t_k^* = \frac{\hat{\beta}_k - \beta_0}{\text{ESTSDEV}_k} \quad k = \text{LIML, SDUNB}$$

for various values of $\Delta = \dfrac{\beta - \beta_0}{\text{ASYSDEV}}$.

With regards to $t^*_{\text{SDUNB}}$ we estimated the power for given $\Delta$ by calculating the relative frequency with which $|t^*_{\text{SDUNB}}| > t_{.975}$ where $t_{.975}$ equals the 97.5 percentile point of a $t$ random variable based on $T - G_1 - K_1$ degrees of freedom. Thus, the nominal level of significance for a two-tailed test using $t^*_{\text{SDUNB}}$ is .05. The actual level of significance associated with $t^*_{\text{SDUNB}}$ is given in Tables 11.9 and 11.10 in the rows corresponding to $\Delta = 0$.

In order to make the power comparisons between $t^*_{\text{LIML}}$ and $t^*_{\text{SDUNB}}$ meaningful we adjusted the power of $t^*_{\text{LIML}}$ so that its significance level equalled the significance level observed for $t^*_{\text{SDUNB}}$.

Tables 11.9 and 11.10 provide data on the relative power of $t^*_{\text{LIML}}$ and $t^*_{\text{SDUNB}}$ for various levels of $\delta^2$ and $\rho$. Notice that the power of $t^*_{\text{SDUNB}}$

*Table 11.9* Power functions for $\rho = .5$ and $K_2 = 3$

| $\Delta$ | $\delta^2 = 10$ LIML | SDUNB | $\delta^2 = 20$ LIML | SDUNB | $\delta^2 = 30$ LIML | SDUNB | $\delta^2 = 50$ LIML | SDUNB |
|---|---|---|---|---|---|---|---|---|
| −6 | .944 | .983 | .992 | .997 | .998 | .999 | 1.000 | 1.000 |
| −4 | .884 | .927 | .958 | .970 | .977 | .982 | .985 | .987 |
| −3 | .754 | .800 | .823 | .840 | .841 | .851 | .850 | .855 |
| −2 | .372 | .400 | .396 | .405 | .410 | .418 | .427 | .432 |
| −1 | .036 | .039 | .057 | .057 | .072 | .072 | .090 | .090 |
| 0 | .062 | .062 | .055 | .055 | .053 | .053 | .052 | .052 |
| 1 | .274 | .296 | .246 | .258 | .232 | .240 | .218 | .222 |
| 2 | .513 | .564 | .505 | .537 | .503 | .525 | .500 | .513 |
| 3 | .684 | .750 | .713 | .752 | .730 | .759 | .749 | .767 |
| 4 | .786 | .859 | .837 | .872 | .864 | .887 | .893 | .905 |
| 6 | .886 | .948 | .940 | .962 | .963 | .975 | .982 | .987 |

*Table 11.10* Power functions for $\delta^2 = 25$ and $K_2 = 6$

| $\Delta$ | $\rho = .10$ LIML | SDUNB | $\rho = .50$ LIML | SDUNB | $\rho = .90$ LIML | SDUNB |
|---|---|---|---|---|---|---|
| −6 | .969 | .980 | .989 | .994 | .998 | .999 |
| −4 | .891 | .910 | .954 | .963 | .990 | .996 |
| −3 | .745 | .767 | .812 | .827 | .937 | .955 |
| −2 | .452 | .468 | .402 | .410 | .284 | .312 |
| −1 | .140 | .143 | .066 | .066 | .009 | .011 |
| 0 | .048 | .048 | .062 | .062 | .079 | .079 |
| 1 | .183 | .190 | .245 | .256 | .286 | .298 |
| 2 | .476 | .497 | .502 | .528 | .528 | .553 |
| 3 | .727 | .756 | .710 | .743 | .711 | .742 |
| 4 | .865 | .891 | .833 | .863 | .826 | .857 |
| 6 | .960 | .974 | .938 | .959 | .934 | .953 |

always exceeds that of $t^*_{\text{LIML}}$. The greatest gains in power from using $t^*_{\text{SDUNB}}$ appear to be realized at smaller values of $\delta^2$. In these situations it appears that moderate gains in power can be realized by using $t^*_{\text{SDUNB}}$ in lieu of $t^*_{\text{LIML}}$.

## Conclusion

In this chapter we consider several modified LIML estimators. We pick one optimal estimator among these and call it the SDUNB estimator. This estimator has finite moments, is unbiased to $0(\sigma^2)$, and has greater asymptotic probability of concentration and lower asymptotic MSE than the LIML estimator and the Fuller unbiased estimator.

Monte Carlo methods were used to study the distribution of the SDUNB estimator in finite samples, and determine how it compares with the distributions of the TSLS and LIML estimators. The main findings of the simulation study are:

1 When the sample size is small, the distribution of the SDUNB estimator is significantly more concentrated than that of the LIML estimator.
2 When intervals of the type presented in equation (3.3) are used to estimate confidence intervals for the components of $\beta$, the intervals generated by the SDUNB estimator are preferred over those generated by the TSLS estimator. In particular, for large values of $\rho$ and $K_2$, it is found that the coverage rates of the confidence intervals generated by the TSLS estimator were grossly overstated.
3 When the sample size is small, moderate gains in power are possible by using $t$ tests based on the SDUNB estimator in lieu of those based on the LIML estimator.

Overall, therefore, the findings of this chapter concerning the asymptotic and small sample properties of the SDUNB estimator suggest that conventional tests and confidence intervals based on the SDUNB estimator are preferred to those based on the classical TSLS and LIML estimators.

## APPENDIX

The results in Anderson, Kunitomo, and Morimune (1986) can be used to establish Theorems 2.2 and 2.3.

### Proof of Theorem 3.2

Consider $b(k_1)$ with $k_1 = \left(1 - \frac{h}{L + T - K}\right) \lambda_0$ and $b(k_2)$ with $k_2 = \lambda_0 - \frac{h}{T - K}$ where $h < 2\,(L + T - K)$. Refer to equations A.33 and A.34 in Anderson, Kunitomo, and Morimune (1986) and take $\hat{e}_1 = e_{k1}$ and $\hat{e}_2 = e_{k2}$. Referring to equation (2.3) in Kadiyala and Oberhelman (1992) and equation (A.34) it can be seen that $d_1 = 0$, $d_2 = \frac{-h^2 L}{(L + T - K)\,(T - K)}$ and $d_3 = \frac{h^2 L}{(L + T - K)\,(T - K)\,(T - K - 2)} - \frac{2hL}{(T - K)\,(T - K - 2)}$. Since $d_2 < 0$ and $d_3 < 0$ if $h < 2(L + T - K)$ it follows that $\mathrm{APC}_\sigma(b(k_1)) > \mathrm{APC}_\sigma(b(k_2))$ and $\mathrm{AMSE}(b(k_1)) < \mathrm{AMSE}(b(k_2))$.

## Proof of Theorem 3.3

Consider $b(k_1)$ with $k_1 = \left(1 - \frac{\chi_1}{L + T - K}\right) \lambda_0$ and $b(k_2)$ with $k_2 = \left(1 - \frac{h}{L + T - K}\right) \lambda_0$ where $0 \leq \chi_1 \leq h$. Refer to equations A.33 and A.34 in Anderson, Kunitomo, and Morimune (1986) and take $\hat{e}_1 = e_{k1}$ and $\hat{e}_2 = e_{k2}$. Referring to equation (2.3) in Kadiyala and Oberhelman (1992) and equation (A.34) it can be seen that $d_1 = \frac{1}{2}(\chi_1 - h)$, $2d_2 = \left(\frac{L + T - K + 2}{L + T - K}\right) \times (\chi_1^2 - h^2) - 2(\chi_1 - h)$, and $2(T - K - 2)d_3 = -2(L + T - K - 2)(\chi_1 - h) + \left(\frac{L + T - K - 2}{L + T - K}\right) (\chi_1^2 - h^2)$. Note that $d_1 < 0$ and $2d_3 = (\chi_1 - h) \times \left[- 2 (L + T - K - 2) + \left(\frac{L + T - K - 2}{L + T - K}\right)(\chi_1 + h)\right] \geq 0$.

Since $2d_2 = (\chi_1 - h)\left[\frac{L + T - K + 2}{L + T - K}(\chi_1 + h) - 2\right]$ implies that $d_2 > 0$ if $\chi_1 < \frac{L + T - K}{L + T - K + 2}$, it follows that $\mathrm{APC}_\sigma(b(k_1)) < \mathrm{APC}_\sigma(b(k_2))$ when $\chi_1 < \frac{L + T - K}{L + T - K + 2} = h_x$. The results concerning AMSE follow directly from the discussion of the optimal estimator, $b(k_*)$.

## Notes

1 This chapter is a paper prepared for a special volume to honor John S. Chipman on his sixty-fifth birthday. The findings in this paper are preliminary and are not to be quoted without the authors' written permission.

2 See Basmann, Richardson, and Rohr (1947), Dhrymes (1969), Maddala (1974), Morimune (1989), and Richardson and Ruhr (1971).

## Bibliography


Anderson, T.W. and Rubin, H. (1949). "Estimation of the Parameters of a Single Equation in a Complete System of Stochastic Equations," *Ann. Math. Statist.* 20: 46–63.

Anderson, T.W. and Sawa, T. (1979) "Evaluation of the Distribution Function of the Two-Stage Least Squares Estimate," *Econometrica* 47: 163–182.

Anderson, T.W., Kunitomo, N. and Sawa, T. (1982) "Evaluation of the Distribution Function of the Limited Information Maximum Likelihood Estimator," *Econometrica*, 50: 1009–1027.

Anderson, T.W., Kunitomo, N. and Morimune, K. (1986) "Comparing Single Equation Estimators in a Simultaneous Equation System," *Econometric Theory* 2: 1–32.

Anderson, T.W., Morimune, K. and Sawa, T. (1983) "The Numerical Values of Some Key Parameters in Econometric Models," *Journal of Econometrics* 21: 229–243.

Basmann, R.L., Richardson, D.H. and Rohr, R.J. (1974) "An Experimental Study of Structural Estimators and Test Statistics Associated with Dynamical Econometric Models," *Econometrica* 42: 717–730.

Dhrymes, D.J. (1969) "Alternative Asymptotic Tests of Significance and Related Aspects of 2SLS and 3SLS Estimated Parameters," *Review of Economic Studies* 36: 213–226.

Fuller, W.A. (1977) "Some Properties of a Modification of the Limited Information Estimator," *Econometrica* 45: 939–953.

Kadane, J. (1971) "Comparison of *k*-class Estimators When the Disturbances are Small," *Econometrica* 39: 723–737.

Kadiyala, K.R. and Oberhelman, D. (1992) "Optimizing in the Class of Fuller Modified Limited Information Maximum Likelihood Estimators," *Journal of Multivariate Analysis* 43: 218–236.

Kinal, T.W. (1980) "The Existence of Moments of *k*-class Estimators," *Econometrica* 48: 241–249.

Maddala, G.S. (1974) "Some Small Sample Evidence on Tests of Significance in Simultaneous Equation Models," *Econometrica* 42: 841–850.

Morimune, K. (1989) "*t* Test in a Structural Equation", *Econometrica* 57: 1341–1360.

Nagar, A.L. (1959) "The Bias and Moment Matrix of the General *k*-class Estimators of the Parameters in Structural Equations," *Econometrica* 27: 575–595.

Richardson, D.H. and Ruhr, R.J. (1971) "Distribution of a Structural *t*-statistic For the Case of Two Included Endogenous Variables," *Journal of the American Statistical Association* 66: 375–382.

Rothenberg, T.J. (1984) "Asymptotic Properties of Some Estimators in Structural Equations," in S. Karlin, T, Amemiya and L.A. Goodman (eds) *Studies in Econometrics Time Series and Multivariate Statistics*. San Diego: Academic Press.

Takeuchi, K. and Morimune, K. (1985) "Third-Order Efficiency of the Extended Maximum-Likelihood Estimator in a Simultaneous Equation System," *Econometrica* 53: 177–199.

# 12

# ON LUMPSUM COMPENSATION

*Murray C. Kemp and Henry Y. Wan Jr*[1]

The focus of theoretical welfare economics has recently drifted away from lumpsum towards non-lumpsum compensation. Implicit in the trend is the perception that the implementation of non-lumpsum compensation requires less information or more accessible information than does the implementation of lumpsum compensation. It is here argued to the contrary that there can always be found a scheme of lumpsum compensation which is preferred to any scheme of non-lumpsum compensation. However it is noted that there are deeper difficulties which have their origin in changing preferences and technologies and which are common to all schemes of compensation.

## Introduction

Almost any disturbance to an economy benefits some individuals and harms others. Following Pareto we may then ask concerning any particular disturbance whether there is a scheme of compensation such that, after compensation, all individuals are better off than they would have been in the absence of the disturbance. Going beyond Pareto, we may want to know in addition the types of information needed to implement the scheme.

From Pareto until quite recently the focus has been on questions of the first kind and on schemes of *lumpsum* compensation. Implicitly, it has been assumed that the authorities have all the information needed for implementation of such schemes.

However there is now a widespread belief among economists that the implementation of lumpsum compensation requires detailed and reliable information about the preferences of individuals and the technical capabilities of firms; information which, practically speaking, is unattainable and is likely to remain so. It is believed also that there are preferred alternatives to lumpsum compensation. In this connection, the demonstration by Diamond and Mirrlees (1971), that schemes of *non*-lumpsum compensation can be both feasible and compatible with efficiency in production, has been influential. Since the appearance of their paper, the focus of theoretical work has shifted away from lumpsum towards non-lumpsum compensation; see, for example, the well-known texts by Atkinson and Stiglitz (1980) and Dixit and Norman (1980). Implicit in the trend is the perception that the implementation of non-lumpsum compensation requires less information, or more accessible information, than does the implementation of lumpsum compensation.

It has been shown elsewhere that, in a context of international trade, this perception is mistaken; see Kemp and Wan (1993). In particular, it has been shown that if the disturbance to the economy fails to yield a production gain, that is, an increase in the value of output at post-disturbance prices, then schemes of non-lumpsum compensation like those proposed by Dixit and Norman (DN) (1980) are inapplicable; that if the Weymark (1979) condition for a welfare-enhancing direction of price change is not satisfied then DN non-lumpsum compensation is infeasible; and, most important, that DN compensation for a finite disturbance can be implemented only if the authorities have global information about individual preferences, information that is not and never will be available to them. Taken together, or one at a time, these observations imply that DN non-lumpsum compensation is not generally implementable. It has been shown also that there is a scheme of lumpsum compensation which is successful over a wider domain, and the implementation of which relies on more accessible information than any of its competitors, lumpsum or non-lumpsum. This is the Grandmont–McFadden–Grinols (GMG) scheme of compensation, so named after Grandmont and McFadden (1972) and Grinols (1981, 1984) which accords to each individual the value at cum-disturbance prices of trades that would have been chosen in the absence of the disturbance and to each firm the value at cum-disturbance prices of the net inputs that would have been chosen in the absence of the disturbance. In particular, it has been shown that, in contrast to earlier schemes of lumpsum compensation, like the *princeps* scheme of Vanek (1965, Appendix to Chapter 4) and Kemp and Wan (1972), the GMG scheme of compensation incorporates detailed instructions for implementation; that the scheme can handle discrete disturbances characteristic of institutional rearrangements such as the opening of trade or the formation of a customs union; and that, whatever the extent of the disturbance, the scheme is relatively modest in its informational needs – specifically, it requires information about individuals' pre-disturbance trades and shareholdings and about firms' pre-disturbance production vectors, but it does not require further knowledge of preferences or technologies. Moreover the GMG scheme of compensation may be feasible even when there is no production gain and even when the Weymark condition is not satisfied. Thus it is free of some of the weaknesses that we have attributed to schemes of non-lumpsum compensation.[2]

Kemp and Wan (1993) focused on disturbances to the conditions of international trade. However the above appraisal of GMG and alternative schemes of compensation is valid in a broader context; indeed, it is quite general. Thus, in comparison with alternative schemes, GMG compensation is both *more powerful* (has a wider domain) and *informationally less oppressive.*

In the present chapter we provide a proposition which marks out a broad field within which GMG compensation is feasible. Specifically, it is shown that if the technical capabilities of some firms unexpectedly expand, and those of no firm contracts, then GMG compensation is feasible.[3] The proposition is then fitted into a two-stage, two-period allocation mechanism which accommodates both the social decision to accept or reject the additional technical capabilities as well as the allocation of resources contingent on that decision. It is noted that the implementation of compensation requires historical information and that therefore compensation can be sensibly discussed only in a dynamic context. Ironically, it is shown also that the relevant historical information is available for a finite economy only if the economy is "essentially repetitive" and that it is available for an economy with overlapping generations only if, before the disturbance, the economy is in a steady state. Thus the allowed dynamics is severely limited.

In summary, lumpsum compensation of GMG type is a preferred alternative to any scheme of non-lumpsum compensation. However, deeper difficulties do exist for both lumpsum and non-lumpsum schemes, and in fact for any welfare analysis based on comparative statics. These difficulties flow from the possibility of changing preferences and technologies, which make observable data from the past irrelevant to decisions concerning the future.

For the most part (that is, in the "Analysis" section), we work with a finite economy of Arrow–Debreu–McKenzie type. However the analysis is briefly reworked (in the "Reformulation" section) to accommodate overlapping generations and an infinite horizon. Moreover, recent work by Kemp and Wong (1995) on the gains from international trade suggests that our conclusions are valid for economies with an incomplete set of markets.

## Analysis

To effect GMG compensation the authorities must know the trade vectors of firms as they would have been in the absence of a disturbance. Since they relate to a hypothetical situation, the vectors cannot be directly observed. However, for a restricted class of economies it suffices to observe choices in an earlier period. This is the class of *essentially repetitive economies* (EREs), that is, economies which decompose into one-period economies which are identical except for the disturbance or perturbation under scrutiny. We proceed to describe a two-period ERE for the case in which there is an optional expansion of the aggregate production set. At least two periods must be accommodated; for, otherwise, the economy will lack the minimum dynamics specified in the Introduction. On the other hand, longer lasting

EREs can be built up straightforwardly from one-period and two-period economies.

## *Essentially repetitive economies*

Let there be $m$ individuals, $n$ firms and $H$ goods in each of two adjacent and equal intervals of time (periods); and let $I \equiv \{1, . . ., m\}$ and $J \equiv \{1, . . ., n\}$. The two periods are indicated by the superscripts 0 and 1. The disturbance occurs at the end of period 0.

A two-period ERE is then an array

$$\varepsilon = \left((X_i, \succsim_i, e_i)_{i \in I}, (Y_j)_{j \in J}, (\theta_{ij})_{i \in I, j \in J}\right) \tag{1}$$

where

$X_i \subset R_+^{2H}$ is the consumption set of individual $i$
$\succsim_i \subset R_+^{2H} \times R_+^{2H}$ is the preference pre-ordering of $i$
$e_i \in R_+^{2H}$ is the endowment vector of $i$
$Y_j \subset R^{2H}$ is the production set of firm $j$
$\theta_{ij} \geq 0$ is the share of $i$ in the ownership of $j$ ($\Sigma_i \, \theta_{ij} = 1$)

and where the essentially repetitive structure of $\varepsilon$ is captured in the following specifications.

$$X_i = X_i^0 \times X_i^1, X_i^0 = X_i^1 \subset R_+^H \tag{2}$$

where $X_i^k$ is the component consumption set for period $k$, $k = 0,1$.

$$\succsim_i^0 = \succsim_i^1 \subset R^{2H} \tag{3}$$

is the component preference ordering for periods 0 and 1.

$$\succsim_i^0 = \succsim_i^1 \subset \succsim_i \tag{4a}$$

$$\left((X_i^0)^2 \setminus \succsim_i^0\right) \times \overline{\left((X_i^1)^2 \setminus \succsim_i^1\right)} \subset (X_i)^2 \setminus \succsim_i \tag{4b}$$

$$\overline{\left((X_i^0)^2 \setminus \succsim_i^0\right)} \times \left((X_i^1)^2 \setminus \succsim_i^1\right) \subset (X_i)^2 \setminus \succsim_i \tag{4c}$$

where $(X_i^k)^2$ is the set of all comparable pairs of sub-bundles.

$$e_i = (e_i^0, e_i^1), \; e_i^0 = e_i^1 \in R_+^H \tag{5}$$

where $e_i^k$ is the component endowment of $i$ in period $k$, $k = 0, 1$.

$$Y_j = Y_j^0 \times Y_j^1, \; Y_j^0, \; Y_j^1 \subset R^H \tag{6}$$

where $Y_j^k$ is the component production set of firm $j$ for period $k$, $k = 0, 1$.

$$Y_j^1 = Y_j^0 \cup (d)Y_j^\Delta, \; Y_j^0 \cap Y_j^\Delta = \varnothing, \; d \in \{0, 1\} \tag{7}$$

where $Y_j^\Delta$ is the set of additional production vectors which may be available to firm $j$ and $d$ is the community's decision parameter ($d = 0$ if the addition to the production set is rejected, $d = 1$ if the addition is accepted).

$$Y_j^\Delta \neq \{0\} \text{ for } j \in J' \subset J,\ Y_j^\Delta = \{0\} \text{ for } j \in J\backslash J' \qquad (8)$$

A few explanatory remarks are offered concerning specifications (2)–(8). Thus (2) states that what is consumable in one period is consumable in the other. (3) and (4) provide a partially specified standard for the evaluation of two-period prospects. According to (3), the consumption bundles of each period are ranked by the same criterion. Thus if the ordered pair $(a, b)$ is in $\succsim^k$ for period $k$ then $a$ is "not worse than" $b$ in a sense to be completed only by (4). (4) specifies intertemporal independence of preferences in terms of the orthogonality of the one-period "orderings." Thus $a$ is said to be "not worse than" $b$ if, for any $c$ from the other period, $a$ paired with $c$ is not worse than $b$ paired with $c$. Moreover, (4a) specifies that if $a$ is "not worse than" $b$ and, in the other period, $c$ is "not worse than" $d$ then $a$ paired with $c$ is not worse than $b$ paired with $d$; and (4b–c) require that if $a$ is "worse than" $b$ and $c$ is "not better than" $d$ then $a$ paired with $c$ is worse than $b$ paired with $d$. (Figure 12.1 parts (a) and (b) illustrates (4) when $H = 1$ and preferences are insatiable.) Conditions (4) provide only a partial specification; they leave open the ordering of $a$ paired with $c$ and $b$ paired with $d$ when in one-period comparisons $a$ is "better than" $b$ and $c$ "worse than" $d$. However they suffice for our purposes. (5) needs no explanation. The orthogonal form of $Y_j$ in (6) implies that no activity today can affect the supply possibilities of tomorrow. For example, the constrution and operation of artesian wells today has no bearing on the level of tomorrow's water table or on tomorrow's water pressure. (7) specifies the expansion of the individual firm's production set while (8) states that not all firms need participate in the economy's expansion.

Having specified the physical conditions which must be satisfied by an ERE, we must make precise the institutional framework within which the economy operates.

The only markets are spot markets for commodities. (9)

Thus at the end of period 0 there can be no outstanding commitments or indebtedness.

All profits earned during period 0 are distributed and spent during that period. (10)

We now have two period-specific component economies, say $\varepsilon^0$ and $\varepsilon^1$. Let $Y_j' = Y_j^0 \cup Y_j^\Delta$. Then we may specify that $\varepsilon^1 = \varepsilon^0$ if $d = 0$ and $\varepsilon^1 = \varepsilon^\Delta \equiv ((X_i^1, \succsim_i^1, e_i^1)_{i\in I}, (Y_j')_{j\in}, (\theta_{ij})_{i\in I, j\in_J})$ if $d = 1$. Thus $\varepsilon^\Delta$ differs from $\varepsilon^0$ only in the expansion of the production sets of some firms. $\varepsilon^0$ and $\varepsilon^1$ are completely isolated from each other, except that in period 1 the *equilibrium attainable state* of period 0 will be known. In particular, it is *not* known in period 0

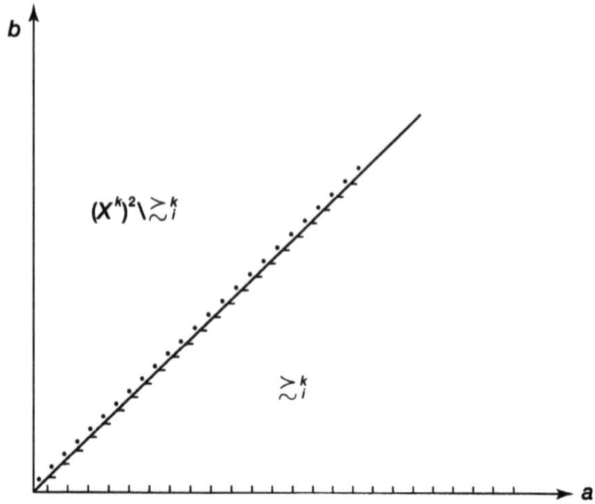


*Figure 12.1a* Period $k$.

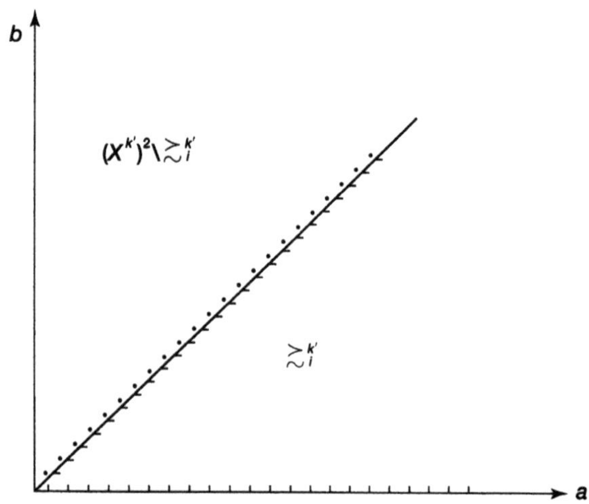


*Figure 12.1b* Period $k'$.

that the production sets will expand in period 1. Let $t_{ik}^0$ denote the amount of commodity $k$ purchased by individual $i$ in period 0. Then an equilibrium attainable set of period 0 is an array of $(m + n)H$ numbers

$$\begin{pmatrix} t_{11}^0 \cdots t_{m1}^0; & y_{11}^0 \cdots y_{n1}^0 \\ \vdots \quad\quad \vdots & \vdots \quad\quad \vdots \\ t_{1H}^0 \cdots t_{mH}^0; & y_{1H}^0 \cdots y_{nH}^0 \end{pmatrix} \equiv (t_1^0, \ldots, t_m^0; y_1^0, \ldots, y_n^0) \equiv a^0$$

which satisfies the conditions

$$e_i^0 + t_i^0 \in X_i^0 \ (i \in I)$$
$$y_j^0 \in Y_j^0 \ (j \in J) \qquad \text{(micro-physical attainability)} \qquad (11)$$

$$\sum_{i \in I} t_i^0 = \sum_{i \in I} y_j^0 \qquad \text{(macro-physical attainability)} \qquad (12)$$

Let $\wp$ be the $(H - 1)$-dimensional natural simplex, and let

$$p^0 = (p_1^0, \ldots, p_H^0) \in \wp \qquad (13)$$

be an $H$-dimensional vector such that

$$\text{for all } i, \ p^0 \cdot t_i^0 \leq \sum_{j \in J} \theta_{ij} p^0 \cdot y_j^0 \qquad \text{(micro-fiscal attainability)} \qquad (14)$$

$$\text{for all } i, \ e_i^0 + t_i^0 \gtrsim_i^0 e_i^0 + t^0 \text{ for all } t^0 \in \left\{t^0 \colon t^0 + e_i^0 \in X_i^0, \ p^0 \cdot t^0 \leq \sum_{j \in J} \theta_{ij} p^0 \cdot y_j^0\right\}$$
$$\text{(micro-optimality for consumers)} \qquad (15)$$

$$\text{for all } j, \ p^0 \cdot y_j^0 \geq p^0 \cdot y^0 \text{ for all } y^0 \in Y_j^0 \qquad \text{(micro-optimality for firms)} \qquad (16)$$

Any array $a^0$ that satisfies conditions (11)–(16) is a *market equilibrium* of $\varepsilon^0$. A market equilibrium of $\varepsilon^\Delta$ is similarly defined. Shortly, we shall introduce sufficient conditions for the existence of market equilibrium.

### *Grandmont–McFadden–Grinols compensation*

First, however, we must formally introduce, and establish some of the properties of, GMG compensation.

**Definition** The *GMG scheme of lumpsum compensation* $\sigma^\#$ assigns

(i) to each individual $i$, $\sigma_h^\#(p^1, i) = p^1 \cdot t_i^0$
(ii) to each firm $j$, $\sigma_f^\#(p^1, j) = -p^1 \cdot y_j^0$

Thus the GMG scheme gives each individual a cost-of-living adjustment and takes from each firm its "base period" profits indexed by "current period" prices.

**Proposition 1** *The GMG scheme of lumpsum compensation* $\sigma^\#$ *has the following properties*

(i) *It is* Pareto non-deteriorating, *that is, it ensures that in the new situation* ($d = 1$) *each individual can afford a consumption bundle "not inferior to" that chosen in the old situation* ($d = 0$).
(ii) *It is* self-financing, *that is,* $\sum_{i \in I} \sigma_h^\#(p^1, i) + \sum_{j \in J} \sigma_f^\#(p^1, j) = 0$.
(iii) *Both* $\sigma_f^\#(p^1, j)$ *and* $\sigma_h^\#(p^1, i)$ *are* continuous *in* $p^1$.
(iv) *It is* privacy-preserving, *in the sense that* $\sigma_h^\#(., j)$ *and* $\sigma_f^\#(., j)$ *are determined by past choices as reflected in the array* $a^0$, *not by* $\varepsilon^\Delta$.

**Proof** (i) The income of $i$ under $p^1$ is

$$w_i(p^1, \sigma^\#) = p^1 \cdot \left(e_i^1 + \sum_{j \in J} \theta_{ij} y_j^1\right) + p^1 \cdot \left(x_i^0 - e_i^0 - \sum_{j \in J} \theta_{ij} y_j^0\right)$$

(from the definitions of $\sigma^\#$ and $t_i^0$)

$$= p^1 \cdot x_i^0 + \sum_{j \in J} \theta_{ij} \left(\max_{y \in Y_j^1} p^1 \cdot y - p^1 \cdot y_j^0\right)$$

(since $y_j^1$ is profit maximizing and $e_i^0 = e_i^1$)

$$\geq p^1 \cdot x_i^0 \qquad \text{(since, for all } j, y_j^0 \in Y_j^0 \subseteq Y_j^1) \qquad (17)$$

Hence $x_i^1 \succsim_i^1 x_i^0$ for any $x_i^1$ chosen at prices $p^1$ and income $w_i(p^1, \sigma^\#)$.

Parts (ii)–(iv) are obvious. Q.E.D.

## *Existence of market equilibrium*

To ensure that $\varepsilon^0$ has a market equilibrium we simply adopt the assumptions made by Debreu (1959) for his Theorem 5.7(1), with the exception of his (c), which will be modified to accommodate the possibility of compensation in kind. Debreu's assumptions are as follows. For every individual $i$,

(a) $X_i^1$ is closed, convex and has a lower bound for $\leqq$,
(b.1) there is no saturation consumption in $X_i^1$,
(b.2) for every $x_i'$ in $X_i^1$, the sets $\{x_i \in X_i^1 : x_i \succsim_i^1 x_i'\}$ and $\{x_i \in X_i^1 : x_i \precsim_i^1 x_i'\}$ are closed in $X_i^1$,
(b.3) if $x_i^1$ and $x_i^2$ are two points in $X_i^1$ and if $\lambda$ is a real number in (0, 1) then $x_i^2 \succ_i^1 x_i^1$ implies $\lambda x_i^2 + (1 - \lambda) x_i^1 \succ_i^1 x_i^1$,
(c) there is an $\hat{x}_i$ in $X_i^1$ such that $\hat{x}_i << e_i^1$;

moreover,

(d.1) for every firm $j$, $0 \in Y_j^1$,
(d.2) $Y^1 = \sum_{j \in J} Y_j^1$ is closed and convex,
(d.3) $Y^1 \cap (-Y^1) \subseteq \{0\}$,
(d.4) $Y^1 \supseteq (-R_+^H)$

To ensure that $\varepsilon^\Delta$ has a market equilibrium, assumption (c) must be slightly modified to allow for compensation in kind. Specifically, it is required not that there is an $\hat{x}_i$ in $X_i^1$ such that $\hat{x}_i << e_i^1$ but that

(c′) there is an $\hat{x}_i$ in $X_i^1$ such that $\hat{x}_i << e_i^1 + t_i^0$.

To make clear the need to vary Debreu's assumption (c), we modify a diagram devised by Koopmans (1957: 30). In Figure 12.2, $\hat{x}_i << e_i^1$, so Debreu's (c) is satisfied. However our (c′) is not satisfied. After compensation in kind of $t_i^0$, the "virtual endowment" becomes $\hat{x}_i$. As the price line sweeps from $p^0$ to $\tilde{p}$, the intersection of the budget set and the consumption set is steadily compressed until the price line coincides with the linear edge of $X_i^1$. Implosion then occurs and the point chosen jumps from $x_i^0 = e_i^0 + t_i^0$ to $\tilde{x}$; both upper and lower hemi-continuity are lost.

**Proposition 2** *$\varepsilon^0$ has an equilibrium, and $\varepsilon^\Delta$ supplemented by the GMG scheme of lumpsum compensation $\sigma^\#$ has an equilibrium.*

**Proof** In view of Proposition 1(iii), we can apply Theorem 5.7(1) of Debreu (1959). Q.E.D.

It is not assumed that the equilibrium is unique, either in $\varepsilon^0$ or in $\varepsilon^1$. However it is assumed that if $\varepsilon^1 = \varepsilon^0$ then any realised equilibrium from period 0 will be replicated in period 1.

**Assumption** *All individuals share the common belief that if $\varepsilon^1 = \varepsilon^0$ then the attainable substate $a^0$ will recur under market coordination.*

**Proposition 3** *If*

$$y^0 \text{ is in the interior of } Y^1 = \sum_{i \in J} Y_j^1 \tag{18}$$

*then the new equilibrium is Pareto-superior to the old.*

**Proof** By construction, $p^1 \cdot y_j^1 > p^1 \cdot y_j^0$ for some $j$, say $j = 1$. Moreover $\theta_{ij} > 0$ for some $i$, say $i = 1$. From (17), therefore, $w_1(p^1, \sigma^\#) > p^1 \cdot x_1^0$. From Debreu's assumption (b.1), which rules out saturation consumption in $X_1^1$, $x_1^1 \succ_1^1 x_1^0$.

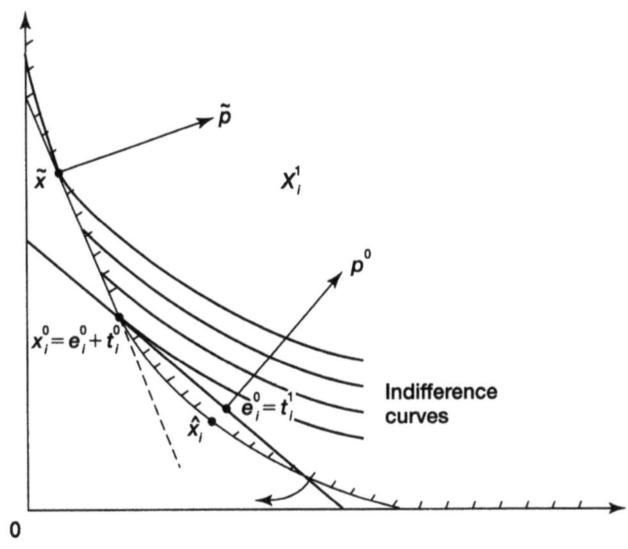


*Figure 12.2*

Hence, from (4a) individual 1 is strictly better off in the new equilibrium. (Q.E.D.)

**Remark 1** It has been assumed that the community must choose between two production sets, one of which is included in the other ($Y^0 \subset Y^0 \cup Y^\Delta$); and in proving Proposition 3 use has been made of that relationship. However the assumption of inclusion is not necessary to the proof. Outside a neighbourhood of the equilibrium production of period 0, any amount of technical regress or amnesia can be allowed; in short, only (18) is needed.

Figure 12.3, which is based on the assumptions that there are just two produced goods, both consumable, and that primary factors are not consumable and therefore are inelastically supplied, establishes the plausibility of that assertion. The upper boundary of the aggregate production set of period 0 is represented by the curve ABC; the upper boundary of the alternative production set for period 1 is represented by A′B′C′; and the period 0 (period 1) equilibrium is represented by point B (point B′), where the Scitovsky indifference curve SS (S′S′) forms a tangent with ABC (A′B′C′). Since SS and S′S′ cannot intersect, B′ must lie between D and E.

**Remark 2** In the GMG-compensated equilibrium of period 1, some individuals are better off, and none is worse off, than in the equilibrium of period 0. However, without more restrictive assumptions about preferences, or redistribution beyond that implicit in GMG compensation, there is no assurance that every individual, or even a majority of individuals, is better off in the GMG-compensated equilibrium. Thus GMG compensation alone

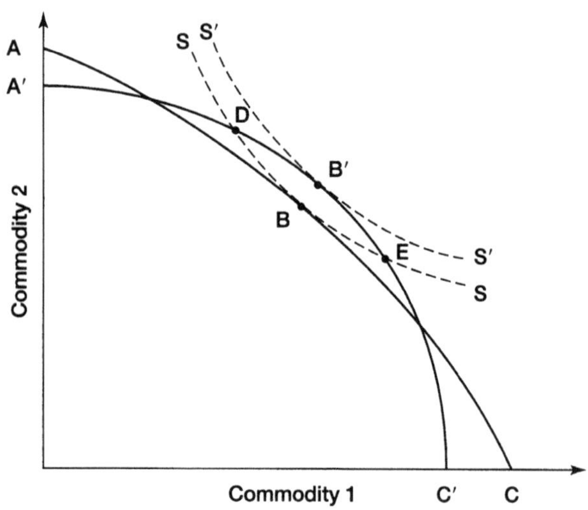


*Figure 12.3*

does not ensure that a majority would be in favour of accepting the additional technical possibilities.

To ensure that *all* individuals are better off in the compensated equilibrium, it suffices that the government engage in lumpsum redistribution of the type dubbed "sagacious" by Grandmont and McFadden (1972). The latter may be financed from the profit, max $p^1 Y^{\Delta}$. To verify that the profit is positive, notice that there exists $\delta > 0$ such that $y^0 + \delta(1, 1, \ldots, 1) \equiv (y^0 + y^{\delta}) \in Y^{\Delta}$ and that, for any $p^1 \in \wp$,

$$\begin{aligned} \max p^1 Y^{\Delta} &\geq p^1 \cdot y^{\delta} \\ &= \delta(p_1^1 + p_2^1 + \ldots + p_H^1) \\ &= \delta \end{aligned}$$

Alternatively, by restricting preferences and production sets, we can ensure that no individual is able to predict that $p^1 = p^0$ or that $p^1 \neq p^0$ and, therefore, that all individuals will be in favour of accepting the additional technical possibilities. For example, attention might be restricted to smooth economies in which (i) the preferences of each individual $i$ are represented by a smooth utility function $u_i$ with strictly positive first derivatives and a strictly quasi-concave bordered Hessian

$$\begin{bmatrix} \partial^2 u_i / \partial x_{ij} \partial x_{ik} & \partial u_i / \partial x_{ij} \\ \partial u_i / \partial x_{ik} & 0 \end{bmatrix}$$

and in which (ii) for each firm $j$, the relative interior of the set of efficient production points, say

$$(Y_j \cup Y_j^{\Delta})_{\text{eff}}$$

is an open smooth surface embedded in $R^H$ with Gaussian curvature everywhere non-zero; see Balasko (1988: 45–48, 202). This specification rules out the possibility that $Y^{\Delta}$ contains a linear (Ricardian) facet which might be decisive in determining $p^1$. Moreover, no individual knows the preferences of other individuals; hence no individual can predict that $p^1 = p^0$ or that $p^1 \neq p^0$. However, no individual is worse off if $p^1 = p^0$ and, in view of (i) above, all individuals are better off if $p^1 \neq p^0$. It follows that all individuals will be in favour of accepting the additional technical possibilities. It is worth emphasizing that the foregoing argument does not require that individuals assess the likelihood that $p^1 = p^0$. Finally, the assumption of smoothness [(i) and (ii)] is sufficient but not necessary; an alternative sufficient condition consists of (i) and the strict convexity of $Y^0 \cup Y^{\Delta}$.

**Remark 3** Suppose that $y^0$ is in $Y^0 \cup Y^{\Delta}$ but not in the interior of $Y^0 \cup Y^{\Delta}$. Then it is not generally true that the GMG-compensated equilibrium of period 1 is Pareto-preferred to the equilibrium of period 0. Thus in the example of Figure 12.4, which incorporates preferences which are smooth and of full dimensionality, there is no compensated equilibrium that is Pareto-preferred to the period 0 equilibrium at Q. In that equilibrium, land is a free good. This suggests that by imposing suitable restrictions on $p^0$ one might ensure that the compensated equilibrium is Pareto-preferred to the equilibrium of period 0 even when $y^0$ is in the boundary of $Y^0 \cup Y^\Delta$. Let $H^0$ denote the preferred open half-space defined by the hyperplane through $y^0$ with normal $p^0$, and let $R^c$ denote the commodity subspace for consumables. Then the condition

$$R^c \cap (H^0 \cap Y^\Delta) \neq \varnothing \tag{19}$$

added to the requirement that preferences be smooth and of full dimensionality, ensures that the GMG-compensated equilibrium of period 1 is Pareto-preferred to the equilibrium of period 0. It should be noted that (18) implies (19) and that (19) is equivalent to max $p^0 Y^\Delta > 0$.

At this point we draw the reader's attention to Appendix B which contains a simple worked example. The example is designed to clarify the role and properties of GMG compensation.

### *An allocation mechanism*

Finally, we can consider a mechanism which encompasses the social decision to accept or reject the additional production possibilities $Y_j^\Delta, j \in J$, as well

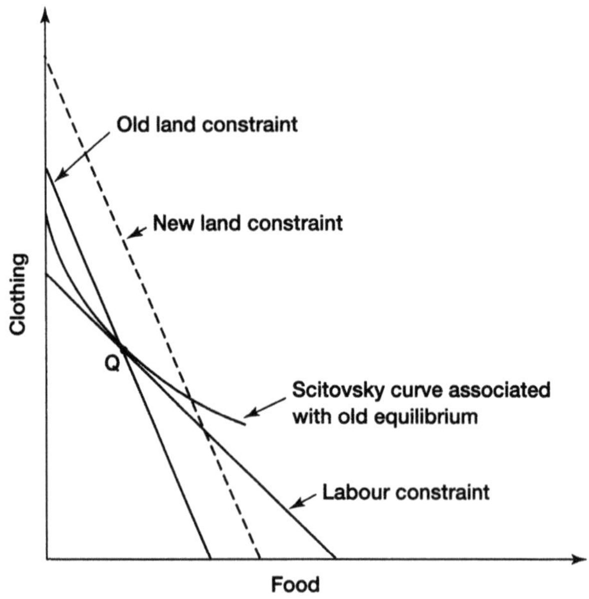


*Figure 12.4*

as the allocation of resources subsequent to that decision. Following Hurwicz (1979) and Green and Laffont (1979), the mechanism combines a game and a quasi-game, played in sequence.

In the first stage, which is completed in period 0, each individual has a yea-or-nay choice: $d_i = 0$ or 1 for each $i$, with the understanding that 0 is for the status quo, that is, the repetition in period 1 of the allocation of period 0, and 1 is for supply augmentation with a GMG-compensated Walrasian allocation. In the absence of a veto, the additional production possibilities are accepted. Thus the *social choice function* is

$$d = f(d_i, d_{)i(}) \\ = \prod_{j \in J} d_j$$

where $d_{)i(} \equiv (d_1, \ldots, d_{i-1}, d_{i+1}, \ldots, d_n)$ and where $d = 1$ means that the compensated supply augmentation is to be implemented and $d = 0$ means that the status quo is to be preserved. It is worth emphasizing that in the foregoing account it is *not* assumed that $\varepsilon^0$ has a unique equilibrium. However it *is* assumed that if $d = 0$ then any realised equilibrium from period 0 will be replicated in period 1; see the "Assumption" of the previous subsection.

Let us pass to the second stage, which occupies period 1. If $d = 0$, the period 0 allocation is re-established, with individual $i$ enjoying the status quo consumption $x_i^0$; and, if $d = 1$, individual $i$ participates in the quasi-game defined by Hurwicz (1979, Section 4) in which $Y^1 = Y^0 \cup Y^\Delta$ and the GMG scheme of compensation $\sigma^\#$ is in force. In the latter case, the economy will reach one of the set of compensated Walrasian allocations $W(a^0, \varepsilon^\Delta)$, which one depending on the coordination provided by the market. However, for all possible $i$ and for all possible equilibria in $W(a^0, \varepsilon^\Delta)$, $x_i^1 \succsim_i^1 x_i^0$ but not necessarily $x_i^0 \succsim_i^1 x_i^1$. The *outcome function* can be rendered in tabular form: see Table 12.1 below.

Suppose that $\varepsilon^1 = \varepsilon^\Delta$ and let $A(\varepsilon^\Delta)$ be the set of substates attainable in a GMG-compensated equilibrium, with the generic element $a^k = (t_1^k, \ldots, t_m^k; y_1^k, \ldots, y_n^j)$, $k = 1, \ldots, K \geq 1$.

**Proposition** 4 *$d = 1$ is a dominant-strategy equilibrium.*

*Table 12.1* The outcome function

| *Choices of individual i* | *Choices of other individuals* $d_{)i(} = (1, 1 \ldots, 1)$ | $d_{)i(} \neq (1, 1 \ldots, 1)$ |
|---|---|---|
| $d_i = 1$ | $d = 1$<br>$\varepsilon^1 = \varepsilon^\Delta$<br>compensation | $d = 0$<br>$\varepsilon^1 = \varepsilon^0$ |
| $d_i = 0$ | $d = 0$<br>$\varepsilon^1 = \varepsilon^0$ | $d = 0$<br>$\varepsilon^1 = \varepsilon^0$ |

**Proof** Let the preferences of individual $i$ be represented by the utility function $u^i$. Suppose that $a^k \in A(\varepsilon^\Delta)$ prevails. From Proposition 3,

$$(u_i(e_i^0 + t_i^0, e_i^0 + t_i^k))_{i\in I} \geq (u_i(e_i^0 + t_i^0, e_i^0 + t_i^0))_{i\in I} \text{ for all } k$$

From Table 12.1, then, $(d_i)_{i\in I} = (1, 1, \ldots, 1)$ is the dominant-strategy equilibrium, notwithstanding the fact that the value of the utility allocation cannot be known to any individual, even in a probabilistic sense. Q.E.D.

### *A generalization*

In the last subsection we studied an economy the population of which has the option of accepting or rejecting an increase in its productive capacity. We now modify the context by supposing that the enlarged capacity is conditional on the provision of a public or semi-public good the availability of which benefits some producers. It will be shown that our earlier analysis continues to apply.

Suppose that, to produce the public good, the authorities must choose a vector $y^- \in Y^- \subset R^H$, where the set $Y^-$ is closed and bounded for $\leq$. If the public good is provided, $Y_j^1 = Y_j' = Y_j^0 \cup Y_j^\Delta$ for all $j \in J' \subset J$ while $Y_j^1 = Y_j^0$ for $j \in J\backslash J'$. Thus, if the public good is provided, $Y' \equiv \sum_{j\in J} Y_i'$ describes the gross productive capacity of the private sector and $Y' - Y^-$ describes the net productive capacity. If, on the other hand, the public good is not provided, $Y_j^1 = Y_j^0$ for all $j \in J$. Suppose further that the authorities know with certainty that

$$y^0 \equiv \sum_{j\in J} y_i^0 \in Y' - Y^- \tag{20}$$

Formally, then, the community is in the same situation as in earlier subsections. (There, it was presented by Nature with the option of accepting or rejecting an enlargement of its overall productive capacity; here, it is presented by Nature with the option of embarking on an activity which will enlarge its net productive capacity.) Given (19), individual $i$ will choose the strategy $d_i = 1$, and the community will produce the public good at minimum cost ex post

$$y^{-*} \equiv \arg\min p^1 Y^- \tag{21}$$

and then supplement the economy $\varepsilon^\Delta$ with a GMG scheme of lumpsum compensation.

## Reformulation in terms of overlapping generations

Throughout the last section it was assumed that there are just two periods of time and that the lifetime of each individual coincides with the lifetime of the economy. However by viewing the population as a set of partially overlapping generations it is possible to reformulate the model without these limiting features. Moreover the introduction of overlapping generations allows us to relax the assumption that each individual has the same endowment and preferences in each period of this life; and it allows us to accommodate foreseen technical expansion without creating an incentive for compensation-seeking individuals to manipulate their pre-disturbance choices.

In each period $k$, $k = 0, 1, 2, \ldots, m$ individuals are born and $n$ firms are established by them. Each individual and each firm survives for two periods. Associated with each period there are $H$ goods. The index sets for individuals and firms are, respectively, $I = \{(i', k)\}_{i'=1,\ldots,m; k=0,1,2,\ldots}$ and $J = \{(j', k)\}_{j'=1,\ldots,n; k=0,1,2,\ldots}$. A technical disturbance occurs at the end of period 1. Our overlapping-generations economy is then an array like (1). However the following changes are needed to accommodate individuals and firms of generation 0, that is, individuals $i = (i', 0)$, $i' = 1, \ldots, m$, and firms $j = (j', 0)$, $j' = 1, \ldots, n$:

$$X_{(i',0)} \subset R_+^H,\ \gtrsim_{(i',0)} \subset R_+^H \times R_+^H,\ e_{(i',0)} \in R_+^H,\ Y_{(j',0)} \subset R^H$$

Specifications (2)–(5) of the last section then apply only to $(i', k)$, $k > 0$. However we no longer need insist that $X_i^0 = X_i^1$ in (2), that $\gtrsim_i^0 = \gtrsim_i^1$ in (3), or that $e_i^0 = e_i^1$ in (5), where superscripts 0 and 1 now denote the young [individual $(i', k)$ during period $k$] and the old [individual $(i', k)$ during period $k + 1$]. Moreover (6) must be replaced by

$$\begin{aligned} &\text{for all } j' = 1, \ldots, n, \\ &Y_{(j',0)} = Y_{j'}^0,\ Y_{(j',1)} = Y_{j'}^0 \times Y_{j'}^1 \\ &Y_{(j',k)} = Y_{j'}^1 \times Y_{j'}^1 \text{ for } k > 1 \\ &Y_{j'}^0,\ Y_{j'}^1 \subset R^H \end{aligned} \tag{6'}$$

and, in (7) and (8), the subscript $j$ should be replaced by $j'$ and the set $J$ by the set $\{1, \ldots, n\}$. Finally, we rule out indebtedness between contemporaries, as in (9) and (10); borrowing and lending across generations is, of course, incompatible with the overlapping structure of the population.

Our story starts at the beginning of period 1, when individual $i = (i', 0)$ is already old. At the end of that period a technical improvement becomes available. Depending on the public choice between $d = 0$ and $d = 1$, $Y_{j'}^1 = Y_{j'}^0$ for all $j'$ or $Y_{j'}^1 = Y_{j'}^0 \cup Y_{j'}^\Delta$ for all $j'$. Thus we are confronted with two alternative sequence economies, each with an overlapping-generations structure and differing from each other during and after period 2. Each such economy operates like a countable sequence of one-period economies. Thus in period $k$, $k \geq 1$, all individuals $(i', k - 1)$ and $(i', k)$ behave as if they live during that period only; they achieve a momentary equilibrium which, for period 1, resembles the equilibrium of the period 0 component economy of ERE, described by (11)–(16).[4]

The critical flow matrix is

$$a^0 \equiv (t^0_{(1,0)}, \ldots, t^0_{(m,0)}, t^0_{(1,1)}, \ldots, t^0_{(m,1)}; y^0_{(1,0)}, \ldots, y^0_{(n,0)}, y^0_{(1,1)}, \ldots, y^0_{(n,1)})$$

$$\equiv \begin{pmatrix} t^0_{(1,0),1}, \ldots, t^0_{(m,0),1}, t^0_{(1,1),1}, \ldots, t^0_{(m,1),1}; y^0_{(1,0),1}, \ldots, y^0_{(n,0),1}, y^0_{(1,1),1}, \ldots, y^0_{(n,1),1} \\ \vdots \\ t^0_{(1,0),H}, \ldots, t^0_{(m,0),H}, t^0_{(1,1),H}, \ldots, t^0_{(m,1),H}; y^0_{(1,0),H}, \ldots, y^0_{(n,0),H}, y^0_{(1,1),H}, \ldots, y^0_{(n,1),H} \end{pmatrix}$$

where, for any $j'$, $y^0_{(j',0)} = y^0_{(j',1)} \equiv y^0_{j'}$, say. Thus, in period $k$, $k = 2, 3, \ldots$, GMG compensation assigns

to each individual $i = (i', k - 1)$, $\sigma^{\#}_b(p^1, i) = p^1 \cdot t^0_{(i',0)}$
to each individual $i = (i', k)$, $\sigma^{\#}_b(p^1, i) = p^1 \cdot t^0_{(i',1)}$
to each firm $j = (j', k - 1)$, $\sigma^{\#}_f(p^1, j) = - p^1 \cdot y^0_{j'}$
to each firm $j = (j', k)$, $\sigma^{\#}_f(p^1, j) = -p^1 \cdot y^0_{j'}$

The self-financing property of GMG compensation [Proposition 1(ii)] now takes on the special meaning of *contemporaneous* self-financing. Thus, for all $k \geq 2$,

$$\sum_{i'=1}^{m} \sigma^{\#}_b(p^1, (i', k-1)) + \sum_{i'=1}^{m} \sigma^{\#}_b(p^1, (i', k)) + \sum_{j'=1}^{n} \sigma^{\#}_f(p^1, (j', k-1)) + \sum_{j'=1}^{n} \sigma^{\#}_f(p^1, (j', k)) = 0$$

Existence can be established if (c′) is replaced by the Gale–McKenzie assumption of irreducibility, in the form given it by Balasko and Shell (1980) in a context of overlapping generations. It can then be shown that, for the overlapping-generations economy, $d = 1$ is a dominant-strategy equilibrium. Moreover, this is so whether or not the expansion of production opportunities is expected, for no individual agent can profitably manipulate his choices in period 1, the base period for GMG compensation: No member of generation 0 has the motivation to manipulate his choices because the GMG scheme of compensation does not apply to that generation; nor will any member of generation 1 manipulate his choices because his manipulation affects only generations not yet born.

The equilibrium is not coalition-proof, since generation 1 can bribe generation 0. However one can imagine the economy growing in scale, with an unchanging list of types in each generation and with compensation based on group data, that is, on generation-specific, type-specific averages. Then, as each individual recedes into insignificance, any coalition for the manipulation of choices must grow in size or lose effectiveness. One may suppose that the larger the economy the less likely is the coalition issue to arise.

## Summary and prospect

We have sought to demonstrate that lumpsum compensation of the GMG type is both more powerful and less demanding of unattainable information than any of its lumpsum or non-lumpsum competitors and, basing ourselves on that finding, we have suggested that the recent tendency to focus on non-lumpsum compensation in theoretical welfare economics should be reversed. Of greater importance, we have argued that the applicability and policy relevance of post-Paretian comparative statical welfare economics, including the compensation principle, is confined to the highly restricted class of essentially repetitive economies and to the only slightly less restricted class of stationary economies with overlapping generations.

Throughout the Analysis section it was assumed that the disturbance is unexpected. The assumption was convenient for it deprived households of the incentive to manipulate their pre-disturbance choices. However the assumption is unnecessarily strong. There is an incentive to manipulate choices only if the disturbance is foreseen with some degree of confidence and if it is known that compensation will be computed on the basis of choices made after the point of time at which the disturbance is first anticipated. For a more thorough discussion of the possibility of choice manipulation, the reader is referred to Kemp and Wan (1995, Chapter 3).[5]

Our discussion has been thoroughly traditional in its assumption that all costs of adjusting to technical change and compensation are negligible. The assumption is unrealistic. Typically, the processes of hiring and firing divert resources from their productive uses both in the expanding sector and in the contracting; see Kemp and Wan (1973). Thus it is conceivable that during the process of adjustment there will be a decline in the outputs of all final goods. In that event, GMG compensation cannot be always self-financing.

Evidently there is need of a more capacious theory. One might try to make do with present-value compensation. However the relevant rates of time preference may be known only to the agents in question; if so, the issue of manipulation must be faced again. Moreover, in a context of overlapping generations, it is necessary to compensate individuals during their lifetimes.

An alternative approach is more promising. It begins with the recognition that costs of adjustment depend on the rate of which the disturbance takes place and that the rate of disturbance is often under the control of the authorities. It is then noted that the choice facing the community is between alternative time paths of technical change, each of them compatible with sustained GMG compensation. Of course, public choice must now be exercised not over two alternatives but over many. Can one devise sagacious redistributions or restrictions on preferences and technologies which ensure that a unanimous choice is made? This issue, and others like it, deserve further study.

# APPENDIX A

## A comment on Hammond and Sempere (1995)

Hammond and Sempere (1995: 1191) have suggested that the DN scheme of compensation discussed in the Introduction be modified by the introduction of poll subsidies. The latter mop up excess supplies of goods and thus render the Weymark condition unnecessary. (In ancient correspondence with the authors, Bill Ethier proposed a similar modification of the DN scheme.) However the modified scheme involves the freezing of consumer prices by means of commodity taxes of some specific structure, and this requires unattainable global information about preferences and other family characteristics. If, lacking such information, the authorities were to impose taxes which fail to freeze prices, they would find themselves locked into a sequential process of tinkering with real prices (not just the price quotations of an auctioneer). In contrast, GMG compensation never requires the authorities to trade out of equilibrium.

Hammond and Sempere (1995: 1191) have suggested also that if under autarky household earnings are stochastic then the objective of even GMG compensation is unclear. This suggestion is based on a serious misunderstanding of the nature of GMG compensation. If there is a market for every commodity, with commodities differentiated by place and time of delivery, and also by the state of nature at the place and time of delivery, then, clearly, mere randomness of earnings creates no problems for GMG compensation in the sense of *expected* utility. Moreover it is now known that, even if markets are incomplete, free trade is potentially gainful in terms of *expected* utility; see Kemp and Wong (1995).

In short, the Hammond–Sempere modification of the DN scheme of non-lumpsum compensation is vulnerable to objections similar to those directed in the Introduction to the DN scheme itself; and the Hammond–Sempere criticism of the GMG scheme of lumpsum compensation is without foundation.

# APPENDIX B

## A numerical example

Consider a farm economy in which a single crop is produced in amount $y_1$ by means of labor and land inputs $-y_2$ and $-y_3$, respectively. For convenience only, it is assumed that there is a single price-taking worker, a single price-taking landlord, and a single farm. The farm is owned by the landlord. The commodity endowment of the worker is

$$e_w = (e_{w1}, e_{w2}, e_{w3}) = (0, 8/27, 0)$$

and that of the landlord is

$$e_1 = (e_{t1}, e_{t2}, e_{t3}) = (0, 0, 8/27)$$

The production function is

$$y_1 = (-y_2)^{2/3}\,(-y_3)^{1/3} \text{ before the disturbance}$$
$$y_1 = (-y_2)^{1/3}\,(-y_3)^{1/3} \text{ after the disturbance}$$

where the distubance is the adoption of a technical improvement which reduces the dependence of output on labor. Finally, the common utility index is

$$u = y$$

In the absence of compensation, the competitive equilibrium quantities, before and after the disturbance, are as shown in Table 12.2. Thus

$$t_w^0 = (16/81,\ -8/27,\ 0)$$

$$t_1^0 = (8/81,\ 0,\ -8/27)$$

$$y^0 = (8/27,\ -8/27,\ -8/27)$$

Computed at the post-disturbance, cum-compensation equilibrium prices

$$p^1 = (1,\ 1/2,\ 1/2)$$

the GMG transfer to the worker is

$$(16/81,\ -8/27,\ 0) \boxdot (1,\ 1/2,\ 1/2) = 4/81$$

and the GMG transfer to the landlord is

$$(8/81,\ 0,\ -8/27) \boxdot (1,\ 1/2,\ 1/2) = -4/81$$

The net post-disturbance income of the worker, after compensation, is therefore

$$(4/27) + (4/81) = 16/81$$

*Table 12.2* Compensation not paid

| | *Before disturbance* | *After disturbance* | *Gain* |
|---|---|---|---|
| Output | 8/27 | 4/9 | |
| Share of labor | 2/3 | 1/3 | |
| Share of land | 1/3 | 1/3 | |
| Share of profit | 0 | 1/3 | |
| Worker's share | 2/3 | 1/3 | |
| Landlord's share | 1/3 | 2/3 | |
| Worker's income | 16/81 | 4/27 | −4/81 |
| Landlord's income | 8/81 | 8/27 | +16/81 |

which is equal to his pre-disturbance income; and the net post-disturbance income of the landlord, after compensation, is

$$(8/27) - (4/81) = 20/81$$

which exceeds his pre-disturbance income of 8/21.

## Notes

1 We recall with pleasure the stimulation provided by a series of articles, on post-Paretian welfare economics and the compensation principle in particular, written in the 1970s by John Chipman, usually in collaboration with James Moore. We have in mind Chipman and Moore (1971, 1972, 1973, 1978) and Chipman (1976).

For helpful comments we are grateful to Jürgen Eichberger and Kar-yiu Wong, and to participants in the conference in honor of John Chipman, held at the University of Minnesota, September 25 and 26, 1992.

Our paper has appeared, in essentially its present form, as Chapter 24 of M.C. Kemp (1995) *The Gains from Trade and the Gains from Aid*. London: Routledge.

2 Recently, Hammond and Sempere (1992) have reviewed some of the above issues and have arrived at conclusions which differ in essentials from ours. Their paper is discussed in Appendix A and in Wan (1997), both of which focus on crucial and hitherto neglected issues and, in our opinion, resolve the debate with finality.

3 Alternatively, it might have been shown that if the endowments of some households unexpectedly expand, and that of no household contracts, then GMG compensation is feasible.

4 A formal definition of a competitive equilibrium can be obtained by extending the definition of Balasko and Shell (1980: 285) to cover production.

5 Households might misrepresent their actual choices, whether or not those choices have been manipulated. However the possibility of false reporting is not peculiar to lumpsum compensation; it dogs all branches of economic policy. Moreover GMG compensation is partially protected against false reporting by the "double entry" property of transactions: each transaction involves at least two parties with opposing interests in overstating or understating the extent of the transaction.

## Bibliography

Atkinson, A.B. and Stiglitz, J.E. (1980) *Lectures on Public Economics*. New York: McGraw-Hill.

Balasko, Y. (1988) *Foundations of the Theory of General Equilibrium*. Boston: Academic Press.

Balasko, Y. and Shell, K. (1980) "The Overlapping-Generations Model, I: The Case of Pure Exchange Without Money," *Journal of Economic Theory* 23: 281–306.

Chipman, J.S. (1976) "The Paretian Heritage," *Revue Européenne de Sciences Sociales et Cahiers Vilfredo Pareto* 14: 65–71.

Chipman, J.S. and Moore, J.C. (1971) "The Compensation Principle in Welfare

Economics," in A.M. Zarley (ed.) *Papers in Quantitative Economics*, volume 1. Lawrence, Manhattan and Wichita, KS: The University Press of Kansas.

—— (1972) "Social Utility and the Gains from Trade," *Journal of International Economics* 2: 157–172.

—— (1973) "Aggregate Demand, Real National Income, and the Compensation Principle," *International Economic Review* 14: 153–181.

—— (1978) "The New Welfare Economics, 1939–1974," *International Economic Review* 19: 547–584.

Debreu, G. (1959) *Theory of Value*. New York: John Wiley & Sons 61: 8–27 and 261–278.

Diamond, P.A. and Mirrlees (1971) "Optimal Taxation and Public Production, I and II," *American Economic Review*.

Dixit, A.K. and Norman, V.D. (1980) *Theory of International Trade*. Cambridge: Cambridge University Press.

Grandmont, J.M. and McFadden, D. (1972) "A Technical Note on Classical Gains from Trade," *Journal of International Economics* 2: 109–125.

Green, J.R. and Laffont, J.-J. (1979) *Incentives in Public Decision-Making*. Amsterdam: North-Holland.

Grinols, E.L. (1981) "An Extension of the Kemp–Wan Theorem on the Formation of Customs Unions," *Journal of International Economics* 11: 259–266.

—— (1984) "A Thorn in the Lion's Paw: Has Britain Paid Too Much for Common Market Membership?" *Journal of International Economics* 16: 271–293.

Hammond, P.J. and Sempere, J. (1995) "Limits to the Potential Gains from Market Integration and Other Supply-Side Policies," *Economic Journal* 105: 1180–1204.

Hurwicz, L. (1979) "On Allocations Attainable Through Nash Equilibria," *Journal of Economic Theory* 21: 140–165.

—— (1986) "On Informational Decentralisation and Efficiency in Resource Allocation Mechanisms," in S. Reiter (ed.) *Studies in Mathematical Economics*. Volume 25 of The Mathematical Association of America, Studies in Mathematics.

Kemp, M.C. and Wan, H.Y., Jr (1972) "The Gains from Free Trade," *International Economic Review* 13: 509–522.

—— (1973) "Hysteresis of Long-Run Equilibrium from Realistic Adjustment Costs," in G. Horwich and P.A. Samuelson (eds) *Trade, Stability and Macroeconomics. Essays in Honor of Lloyd A. Metzler*. New York: Academic Press.

—— (1993) *The Welfare Economics of International Trade*. Chur, London, Paris, New York, Melbourne: Harwood Academic Publishers.

Kemp, M.C. and Wong, K.-Y. (1995) "The Gains from Trade when Markets are Possibly Incomplete," Chapter 5 in M.C. Kemp (ed.) *The Gains from Trade and the Gains from Aid*. London: Routledge.

Koopmans, T.C. (1957) *Three Essays on the State of Economic Science*. New York: McGraw-Hill.

Vanek, J. (1965) *General Equilibrium of International Discrimination*. Cambridge, MA: Harvard University Press.

Wan, H.Y., Jr (1995) "A Note on Compensation Schemes," *Japanese Economic Review* 48: 147–155.

Weymark, J.A. (1979) "A Reconciliation of Recent Results in Optimal Taxation Theory," *Journal of Public Economics* 12: 171–189.

13

# A RESULT ON LARGE ANONYMOUS GAMES: AN ELEMENTARY AND SELF-CONTAINED EXPOSITION

*M. Ali Khan*

In this chapter, I view a theorem on the existence of Cournot–Nash equilibrium of a large anonymous game from a vantage point furnished by point-set topology, and by a 1970 paper of John Chipman's.

## Introduction

This chapter is an essay in honor of John Chipman and it has two basic objectives: first, to provide an exposition of a particular theorem on large anonymous games; and second, to view this theorem from the lens provided by Chipman's 1970 paper on *External Economies of Scale and Competitive Equilibrium*. Since the bulk of my essay – nine out of twelve sections – is devoted to the first objective, I spend most of this introduction on justifying the second; why I celebrate this particular paper, and that too, given current norms, at what some would regard its relatively advanced age of almost twenty-five years.

It is not that this 1970 paper is a synecdoche of Chipman's writings in economics. There is no econometrics or "raw" institutional detail in it,[1] and it belongs to a genre Chipman had already delineated about twenty years earlier as "entirely theoretical in nature."[2] Indeed, Chipman's writings are wide-ranging enough that there may be an existence issue here; there is possibly no paper in the *oeuvre*, at least as it is constituted at the present, that may stand up to the task of summarizing the whole. Nevertheless, the 1970 work does give visibility to several aspects of Chipman's writings.[3] It shows the reliance on, and the respect for, the inheritance;[4] the use of necessary mathematics without any trace of self-consciousness;[5] the disregard of subject boundaries in choice of material;[6] the use of explicit functional forms and parameter values;[7] the emphasis on characterization for questions of existence;[8] the meticulous textual analysis;[9] the care and concern towards exposition;[10] the recognition that the opposite of pure theory is not applied theory;[11] self-criticism[12] and, I am sure, other facets which have escaped my observation and appreciation.

This is an overview of his 1970 text from the point of view of method, but microscopically conceived. In a more macroscopic vein, the paper is a useful teaching and learning aid for blunting some possibly false and misleading dichotomies, and for not allowing them to gain currency unquestioningly. I have in mind attitudes which force one to choose between general equilibrium and game theory;[13] between the old and the new trade theory;[14] between macroeconomics and general equilibrium theory;[15] between cooperative and non-cooperative game theory;[16] between statics and dynamics, or more fashionably, one-shot and repeated games;[17] between the normative and the positive;[18] between the computational and the conceptual.[19] Of course, any study is circumscribed by boundaries peculiar to itself,[20] and it goes without saying that when one falls under a branch of any of these dichotomies, one need not necessarily and simultaneously be falling under the other. My point is simply that these labels ought not to become so hard and fast as to constitute the *only* definitions of the identity and *type* of a researcher and his or her scholarship, stereotypes if one prefers, and so unyielding as not to recognize that progress in one subject is achieved from, and by, the light of the other. Originality frequently consists precisely in delineating this "other."[21] This is especially so, it seems to me, when the subject is "progressing" so fast, say relative to when Chipman was writing in 1970, that myopia becomes a prerequisite for research prowess and more comprehensive views are obscured. Uncontested boundaries may be useful for allocating resources within the academy, but may not be optimally, or even equally, suited for the development of the subject. Chipman's work as a whole, and his 1970 paper as an important element of that whole, allows one to appreciate, in the economist's jargon, the "gains from arbitrage" obtained without putting a priori restrictions on the "markets" one can arbitrage between. To the extent that the 1970 paper shows by example the gains from this cross-fertilization within theory (now to take a metaphor from outside economics), and mathematical theory at that, it is not dated at all and well worth a careful reading.[22]

I turn next to my own exposition and to the plan of this chapter. I try to develop a self-contained language so that the statement of an existence theorem – both the assertion and the conditions for its validity – can be elucidated. In this, I explicate the basic vocabulary of game theory by defining the terms *agent*, *actions*, *preferences*, *interdependence*, *large society*, *summary of societal actions*, *equilibrium*. In my treatment, I try to see how far I can proceed from the English phrase "the smallest topology containing an arbitrary collection of sets." I try to give a self-contained explanation of the phrase, as well as of all the terms in it; and in the subsequent development, do not even assume familiarity with the notion of a function or that of a set. I do, however, primarily for reasons of space, leave the proof of a particular result, Lemma 5.1 below, to the reader. She will have to decide for herself the extent to which I have, or have not, been successful in trying to measure up to the Bourbaki rules of the game.[23]

I learn two lessons from this exercise; first, the statement of my result requires no mention of linearity[24] and therefore of convexity; and second, even though the theorem has the appearance of far-reaching generality, it still fails to be fully adequate to Chipman's 1970 setting, circumscribed as it is by its "very stringent assumptions."[25] As regards the first point, it is not to say that linearity is not everywhere lurking in the background,[26] but only that the statement of the result does not require this vocabulary to be made explicit. This raises the interesting question as to whether there are alternative proofs, or indeed other structures also lurking around, which when made explicit would allow a different treatment and give different, but still valuable, insights. My second point is simply a restatement of the rather trite but sometimes neglected observation that generality is always relative to the question that is posed and the results that are obtained.

This chapter then can be read in at least two ways: as an exposition of a piece of pure mathematics, particularly point-set topology; and second, as an exploration of the applicability of the theory of large anonymous games to imperfect competition. Whether it can also be read as an exemplar, for or against, of the teaching/research and original/expository dichotomies, I leave to my reader. I have already indulged myself long enough with questions of method; it is time to get to substance and to work.

## Functional analysis: prerequisites

I begin with Halmos' description of the basic idea of a set.

> A pack of wolves, a bunch of grapes, or a flock of pigeons are all examples of a set of things. Sets, as they are usually conceived, have *elements* or *members*. An element of the set may be a wolf, a grape or a pigeon. It is important to know that a set itself may be an element of another set. A line, for instance, is a set of points; the set of all lines in the plane is a natural example of a set of sets (of points).[27]

It is of interest that Halmos does not give a formal definition of a *set*, but draws a parallel with Euclidean geometry; like "that approach," he will simply "describe what it is that one can do with these objects."

I shall specify my generic notation of a set by considering the *product* of two sets $X$ and $Y$, denoted by $X \times Y$, and the *complement* of any subset $B$ of $X$, denoted by $B^c$. The former is simply the collection of all pairs $(x, y)$, the first coordinate $x$ of which belongs to $X$ and the second $y$ belongs to $Y$, and is written as

$$X \times Y = \{(x, y) : x \in X, y \in Y\},$$

while the latter is

$$B^c = \{x \in X : x \notin B\}.$$

## *Topological space*

Next, I discuss the notion of a *topological* structure on an arbitrary set. A *topology* on a set $A$ is simply a particular set of subsets of $A$. For concreteness, I shall find it useful to think of a topology on $A$ as a "bag" containing all kinds of subsets of $A$ that satisfy some particular restrictions. It is these restrictions which give topology its defining characteristic; in other words, make a topology into a topology. These restrictions on the set of subsets of $A$, or on the "bag" that I am working with, are easily stated. $A$ and the empty set $\emptyset$ belong to the bag; the *intersection* of any finite number of sets chosen from the bag belongs to the bag, the *union* of an arbitrary collection of sets chosen from the bag belongs to the bag. Note that an arbitrary collection need not be countable; the number of drops in a glass of milk or the number of points constituting a circle are hardly countable.[28]

A topology helps me to formalize the meaning of "closeness." Two points are "arbitrarily close" from the viewpoint of a particular topology, if any set in that topology, or to continue the metaphor, any element in the corresponding bag, which contains one of those points also contains the other. Thus, my conception of what is close and what is not, is solely and completely dependent on the *topology* that I am endowed with or the bag that I work with. The greater the number of sets in my bag, the finer my measures of *closeness*.

Thus a bag consisting only of the "fullset" $A$ and the empty set $\emptyset$ is a topology on A. This is the so-called *indiscrete* topology. It is a topology because the set of these two elements satisfy all the restrictions that make a topology into a topology. It is, of course, a very *coarse* or *rough* topology – indeed the *coarsest*. Put another way, it is the "smallest" topology that exists on the set $A$. A candidate for a "smaller" topology would be a single set, $A$ or $\emptyset$, and this would not be a topology. In summary, the indiscrete topology treats every point in $A$ as arbitrarily close to every other point in $A$. All points are neighbors; all natives alike.

On the other hand, a bag consisting of all subsets of $A$ is a very *fine* topology indeed. It is the "largest" topology that exists on the set $A$ – the so-called *discrete* topology. The only point that is arbitrarily close to another point is the point itself. One now sees so clearly that one can even distinguish raindrops; a notion of *neighborliness* or of *similarity* based on the *discrete* topology is very demanding – everybody in the world is unique.

Thus, any arbitrary set of points can be endowed with at least two topologies – the *discrete* and the *indiscrete*, the finest and the coarsest. For example, the set of all baseball players in Minnesota is a topological space when endowed with either of these two topologies. Of course, there may be a lot of other topologies on this (or any other) set. In particular, the subset of all players excluding your favorite player is another topology on this set – this is the so-called *excluded point* topology.[29] More generally, it is good to keep in mind that an *intersection* of any two topologies on a set is also a topology. This intersection is simply the collection of all elements that are common to *both* bags. Indeed, the intersection of any *arbitrary* collection of topologies on a set is also a topology.

Now consider an arbitrary collection of subsets of a set. Such a collection need not be a topology – indeed this is precisely the force of the word *arbitrary*. Next, consider the collection or, if you like, set of all topologies containing this arbitrary collection of subsets. This set of topologies is certainly not empty – the discrete topology for one belongs to it. Now consider the intersection of all of these topologies. This topology contains the original collection of subsets – indeed this is playing precisely on the meaning of the word *intersection*. This intersection – or the topology that is obtained by the intersection of all of them – formalizes the phrase "the *smallest* topology containing the given arbitrary collection of subsets."

A note on terminology. Rather than specify that a particular set belongs to a topology – an element of the corresponding bag – I shall simply refer to it as an *open* set. I shall also refer to a complement of an *open* set as a *closed* set. The adjectives *open* and *closed* mean nothing more and nothing less than this. It goes without saying that a particular subset of $A$ may or may not be in the bag, or indeed, the latter may be rich enough so as to contain a set as well as its complement. All this is simply to say that an element of a topological space can be *open* or *closed* or both or neither.

I now present two basic concepts. First, a topological space is said to be *Hausdorff* if corresponding to any two points in the set, there exist two disjoint open sets, each containing the given point. Second, a subset of a topological space is said to be *compact* if any collection of open sets, namely sets chosen from the bag, that cover the set (which is to say that the set is contained in the union of the elements of this collection), has a finite subcollection which also covers the set. More colloquially, I can say that a set is *compact* if every open cover has a finite subcover. In the sequel I shall be working with *compact Hausdorff* topological spaces.

I now end this subsection by showing how one can manufacture new topological spaces from old.[30] Consider a subset $Y$ of a topological space $(X, \tau)$. I can endow $Y$ with a topology derived from the original topology $\tau$, the so-called *relative* topology $\tau_Y$, by focusing on the intersections of all open sets with $Y$. In terms of notation,

$$\tau_Y = \{(O \cap Y) \subseteq X : O \in \tau\}.$$

Thus[31] the new topology, or the new bag, is simply constituted by taking the intersections of all elements of the old bag with $Y$.

Next, I turn to the so-called *product* topology – I shall confine myself to the products of only two elements in which case it can also be referred to as the *box* topology.[32] For any two topological spaces $(X, \tau_X)$ and $(Y, \tau_Y)$, the *product* topology is a topology on the product $X \times Y$ and simply consists of arbitrary unions of the products of sets in the two topologies. In terms of set-theoretic notation, the new bag[33] $\tau_{X \times Y}$ is constituted from unions of sets chosen from the bag

$$\{(U \times O) \subseteq (X \times Y) : U \in \tau_X, O \in \tau_Y\},$$

which is simply the product of elements taken from the two initially-given bags.

## *Measurable space*

I now change gears, and discuss another structure on an arbitrary set. This is a *measurable* structure and it too consists of subsets of a given set. Just as for a topology, I shall also find it useful to think of a $\sigma$-*algebra* on $A$ as a bag containing all kinds of subsets of $A$ that satisfy some restrictions. It is these restrictions which give a $\sigma$-*algebra* its defining characteristic; in other words make a $\sigma$-*algebra* a $\sigma$-*algebra*. These restrictions are also easily stated. First, $A$ belongs to the bag; second, the complement of any set chosen from the bag belongs to the bag; and finally, the union of any countable collection of sets chosen from the bag also belongs to the bag. The set of integers is countable whereas the set of real numbers, or indeed, all the aforementioned drops in a glass of milk, are not.

I need a $\sigma$-algebra because I am going to draw on some ideas from probability theory; in particular, I am going to focus on subsets of agents in a "large" society and try to determine the "size" of these subsets relative to that of the society from which they are chosen. In probability theory, one attaches non-negative real numbers less than or equal to unity, to particular events rather than to particular coalitions. A $\sigma$-algebra helps me to formalize the notion of an event space or, in the context of this chapter, the space of coalitions.

A set equipped with a $\sigma$-algebra is termed a *measurable* space, and I invite the comparison between a *measurable* space and a *topological* space. There are obvious analogs of discrete and indiscrete topologies. The intersection of an arbitrary collection of $\sigma$-algebras on a set is also a $\sigma$-algebra on the set. Thus, one can give meaning to the phrase, "the *smallest* $\sigma$-algebra containing a given arbitrary collection of sets." At this stage, however, one can go a little further. A particular topological space $(A, \tau)$, can be made into a measurable space by endowing it with the "smallest" σ-algebra containing the given topology. This is an important σ-algebra and I shall refer to it as the *Borel σ-algebra* and denote it by $\mathcal{B}(A)$.

Just as I did for topological spaces, I can also manufacture new σ-algebras from old – the *restricted* σ-algebra is an analogue of the *relative* topology and defined in an identical way. However, if I define the *product* σ-algebra in the way that I did a *product* topology, I get into difficulties. If $\mathcal{X}$, $\mathcal{Y}$ denote σ-algebras on the spaces $X$ and $Y$, the set

$$\mathcal{X} \times \mathcal{Y} = \{(U \times O) \subseteq (X \times Y) : U \in \mathcal{X}, O \in \mathcal{Y}\}$$

is *not* a σ-algebra – the restriction of *complementation* makes itself felt. However, I can consider the "smallest" σ-algebra containing $\mathcal{X} \times \mathcal{Y}$, and refer to it as the *product* σ-algebra and denote it by $\mathcal{X} \otimes \mathcal{Y}$. In conclusion, note the curiosum that the Borel σ-algebra corresponding to the product topology on $X$ and $Y$, if these happen to be topological spaces, of course, is *not* the same as the σ-algebra $\mathcal{B}(X) \otimes \mathcal{B}(Y)$.

### *Function*

I turn next to the idea of a *function*. This is simply an association between two sets with the important proviso that for any particular element in the first set, which I shall call the *domain* of the function, there is only one element in the other set, which I shall call the *range* of the function. Thus a function, in order to make sense, presupposes what is its domain and its range.

I can take the set of all economists in Minnesota as a domain, the set of all universities as a range, and the association of an economist with a particular university where he or she obtained her degree as an example of a function, provided every economist has only one degree. On substituting flowers for economists and colors for the names of universities, I have another example of a function provided I rule out multi-colored flowers. Of course, a function may have all elements of its domain associated with only one point in the range; as indeed in my horticultural example, all flowers may be identically and singly colored.

In keeping with the two spaces that I have discussed, I shall be interested in two properties of a function. The first is referred to as *continuity* and simply requires that a "slight perturbation of an element in the domain leads to a slight perturbation in the corresponding element in the range." This can be put in an alternative and better-phrased way if I take a global point of view. A *continuous* function is simply one that "brings back open sets into open sets." In symbols, a function $f$ from a topological space

$(X, \tau_X)$ into $(Y, \tau_Y)$ is *continuous* if for any $W \in \tau_Y$, there exists $V \in \tau_X$ such that $f(V) \subseteq W$. This can be equivalently expressed[34] as

$$f^{-1}(W) \in \tau_X \text{ for all } W \in \tau_Y,$$

where the notation $f^{-1}(W)$ simply means $\{x \in X : f(x) \in W \subseteq Y\}$.

The other property I am interested in is that of *measurability*. Having developed the notion of *continuity* and continuing to draw on the analogy between topological and measurable structures, the definition of measurability is identical to my last definition provided I think of $\tau_X$ and $\tau_Y$ as $\sigma$-algebras. The following nice result brings out this intimate connection between the two kinds of structures.

**Lemma 1** *Every continuous function from one topological space to another is Borel measurable.*

**Proof of Lemma 1** Consider a bag of sets with the property that the inverse image under $f$ of any of these sets is in the Borel $\sigma$-algebra of the domain of $f$. Since $f$ is continuous, the said bag contains all open sets.[35] But then this $\sigma$-algebra certainly contains the "smallest" $\sigma$-algebra containing the open sets, namely the Borel $\sigma$-algebra. I am done.

I shall have occasion to look at this result again in the context of real-valued functions.[36]

## *Measure*

A *measure* is a function from a $\sigma$-algebra to the set of non-negative real numbers such that the *measure* of the set of a countable union of mutually disjoint elements from the $\sigma$-algebra is the sum of the measures of the individual elements. This is a mouthful, and some notation will facilitate the description.

Let $(X, \mathcal{X})$ be a measurable space. Then $\mu$ is a measure on $(X, \mathcal{X})$ if

$$\mu : \mathcal{X} \to \mathbb{R}_+ \text{ such that } \mu\left(\bigcup_{i=1}^{i=\infty} A_i\right) = \sum_{i=1}^{i=\infty} \mu(A_i)\ ;\ A_i \cap A_j = \emptyset;\ i \neq j.$$

It bears emphasis that *measures* are functions, but defined on sets rather than on points – on elements of the $\sigma$-algebra $\mathcal{X}$ rather than[37] those of $X$. If the value of the measure on the whole space is unity, I shall refer to it as a probability measure and denote the set of all such measures by $\mathcal{M}_+^1(X)$. I shall limit myself to probability measures in this exposition.[38]

I shall end this section by considering a *marginal* measure corresponding to a *measure* $\mu$ defined on a measurable space $(X \times Y, \mathcal{X} \otimes \mathcal{Y})$. The *marginal* of $\mu$, say on $X$, is denoted by $\mu_X$, and is a measure[39] that gives the value $\mu_X(W) = \mu(W \times Y)$ to any arbitrary element $W$ chosen from the $\sigma$-algebra $\mathcal{X}$.

## An agent

By now, I have already said enough to develop the notion of an agent. "Economists" typically add the adjective "economic" but this is redundant for my exposition. Furthermore, my notion of an agent derives from the social context in which that agent operates – as I shall show, there is no circularity in such a conception.

To emphasize what is different in my exposition, I begin with the following assertion.

> There is no such thing as an abstract biological personality, this biological individual that has become the alpha and the omega of contemporary ideology. There is no human being outside society, and therefore not outside objective socioeconomic conditions.[40]

A "cultural anthropologist," rather than a "literary critic," puts the idea this way.

> In order to know what another is like it is not enough to use terms and concepts that speak of a basic psychic structure; a description is also needed of what the other has been reliably reported to have said and done in a host of particular interactions. It is context that reveals persons, not the other way around.[41]

In order to develop this "description" of an agent, I begin with a basic domain of choice, $A$. I shall also refer to it as the space of possible actions, and assume it to be a *compact Hausdorff* topological space. Note that this is a "large" space.[42] I emphasize both the purity and the structural paucity of this choice space. It has a topology on it, and in principle, need have no other structures. Thus, the result that I am in the process of developing does not require me, for example, to add elements chosen from $A$, or to measure the distance between them.

Now consider the Borel $\sigma$-algebra, $\mathcal{B}(A)$, on[43] $A$. Next, consider the space of all probability measures $\mathcal{M}^1_+(A)$ on $A$. This set, an object in itself, denotes a set or collection of objects, each of which is a *summary of societal actions*. Thus, for any $\mu$ picked from $\mathcal{M}^1_+(A)$, and any set of actions $W$ chosen from $\mathcal{B}(A)$, $\mu(W)$ represents the proportion of the agents of the society whose actions lie in the set $W$.

A basic expositional point ought to be brought out here. I am trying to develop the notion of an *agent* from which I shall construct the notion of a *society*. However, through the object $\mathcal{M}^1_+(A)$, I am already presupposing what a "summary of societal actions" is and therefore presumably what a society is. To cut through this uneasiness, simply think of $\mathcal{M}_+^1(A)$ as a mathematical object for whose definition I only need $A$ and the topology on $A$, and whose interpretation will develop in due course.

Now remain with the topological space $A$ and consider the product space $A \times A$ endowed with its product topology. I shall denote this topological space simply by $A^2$. Accordingly, when I pick an element of $A^2$, I am picking an element from the topology on $A \times A$ rather than an arbitrary subset of $A \times A$. Note that this is simply a piece of notation which I have now defined precisely.[44]

I am now ready to develop the notion of *preferences* or *tastes* of an *agent* as based on the elements in $A$. A *system of preferences* is simply a complement $P^c$ of a subset $P$ chosen from the space $A^2$. Since both $P$ and $P^c$ are subsets of a product space $A \times A$, any generic element of $P$ will be written as a pair $(x, y)$. At the beginning of the previous section, I defined the notion of a *product* of two sets. I now define what I mean by the *multiple* of two subsets but of a product space. First, however, the notion of a *diagonal* of a product space. This is denoted by $\Delta$ and is simply the set $\{(x, x) : x \in A\}$. The *multiple* of two subsets, $X$ and $Y$, of $A \times A$ is noted by $X \circ Y$ and is given by

$$\{(x, z) \in A \times A : (x, y) \in X ; (y, z) \in Y\}.$$

If there exist points in $X$ and $Y$ whose second and first coordinates are identical, the point constituted by the first and second coordinates belongs to $X \circ Y$. It goes without saying that $X \circ Y$ is not necessarily equal to $Y \circ X$ and that it may be empty. I can now define the basic space

$$\mathcal{P}(A) = \{P^c \subseteq A \times A : P \in A^2; \Delta \subseteq P^c; P \circ P \subseteq P\}.$$

*Preferences* or *tastes* of an agent are represented by $P$, or equally adequately, by $P^c$. In order to interpret this, consider any element, a point or a pair $(x, y)$, chosen from $A \times A$. There are several possibilities. Either $(x, y)$ is an element of $P$ in which case, it has the interpretation that "$x$ is preferred to $y$;" or it is an element of $P^c$ in which case, it has the interpretation that "$x$ is not preferred to $y$;" or finally, $(x, y)$ is an element neither of $P$ nor of $P^c$ in which case, it has the interpretation that the agent cannot say anything about the desirability of $x$ as compared to $y$, one way or another. Note the word "finally" in the above sentence; $(x, y)$ cannot be an element of both $P$ and $P^c$. Thus, by formalizing *preferences* in the way that I do, I do not assume that preferences have to be *complete* in the sense that any element of the action set can be compared or ranked by the said agent with respect to any other.[45] However, I do assume that *preferences* have to satisfy the technical requirement of *continuity*. This is formalized by the requirement that $P^c$ is *closed*, a consequence of the fact that it is a complement of a set belonging to the topological space $A^2$, and hence of a set that is *open*. Furthermore, I assume that *preferences* are *irreflexive* ($\Delta \subseteq P^c$ and hence $\Delta \not\subseteq P$), and *transitive* ($P \circ P \subseteq P$).

Now focus on the fact that $\mathcal{F}(A)$ is a set – forget, at least for the moment, the description of the elements of this set. Consider also the set $\mathcal{M}_+^1(A)$ simply as a collection of objects in the abstract way that I discussed in the beginning of the previous section. I can now describe an agent simply as a function from the space $\mathcal{M}_+^1(A)$ to the space $\mathcal{F}(A)$. In terms of notation, I can say that an agent is represented as follows

Agent: Summary of Societal Actions → Preferences.

Thus, an agent is a functional relationship or a description that relates a particular summary of societal actions to preferences.

> The crucial move in this reinterpretation is to think [a] person just *is* [a] network, as for purposes of ballistics she is a point mass, or for purposes of chemistry a linkage of molecules. She is a network that is constantly reweaving itself . . . [and] rational behavior is just adaptive behavior of a sort which roughly parallels the behavior, in similar circumstances, of the other members of some relevant community.[46]

I want to ignore, for the moment the question of "rational" behavior and focus on the "network," in particular, on the "reweaving" that this implies. But first, a few more technicalities.

## Functional analysis: a first pass

Consider the space $C(A; \mathbb{R})$ of continuous functions from $A$ to the set of real numbers $\mathbb{R}$; $\mathbb{R}$ is endowed with the "smallest" topology containing the sets $\{B_{\in}(x)\}_{\varepsilon>0; x\in\mathbb{R}}$ where $B_\varepsilon(x)$ is the set of points whose distance[47] from $x$, say in absolute value, is less than $\varepsilon$, namely $\{y \in \mathbb{R} : | y - x | < \varepsilon\}$. This is the so-called *Euclidean* topology. I shall abbreviate $C(A; \mathbb{R})$ to $C(A)$.

I turn next to the notion of an *integral* of an arbitrary element chosen from $C(A)$ with respect to an arbitrary element chosen from $\mathcal{M}_+^1(A)$. I begin with a special case of Lemma 1.

**Lemma 2** *Every element of $C(A)$ is a Borel measurable function.*

The set of Borel measurable functions is, in general, strictly larger than that of continuous functions. In order to see this, let $A$ be the unit interval $[0, 1]$ endowed with the *excluded point* topology, 1/2 being the point excluded. It is easy to see that the smallest $\sigma$-algebra containing this topology contains the singleton set $\{1/2\}$. The real-valued function $f$ which takes the value of unity at $\{1/2\}$ but zero everywhere else is not continuous. For any positive $\varepsilon$, say less than (1/20), there does not exist a set $V$ in the topology on $[0, 1]$ such that $f(V) \subseteq \{x \in \mathbb{R} : 1/2 - \varepsilon < x < 1/2 + \varepsilon\}$.

However, $f$ is Borel measurable. For any positive $\varepsilon$ less than 1, $V$ in the sentence above can be chosen to be $\{1/2\}$; while for any $\varepsilon$ greater than or equal to 1, $V$ can be chosen to be $[0, 1]$.

**Lemma 3** *A compact subset S of* $\mathbb{R}$ *is bounded in the sense that there exists a positive number M such that the absolute value of any element in S is less than M.*

**Proof of Lemma 3** For any $s \in S$ consider the set $S_s = \{x \in \mathbb{R}: s - 1/2 < x < s + 1/2\}$. Certainly $S \subseteq \bigcup_{s\in S} S_s$. Since $S$ is compact, there exists a finite positive integer $k$ such that $S \subseteq \bigcup_{i=1}^{i=k} S_{s_i}$. Since a set of finite real numbers has a largest and a smallest element, let $\bar{s} = \text{Max}_{i=1}^{i=k} s_i$, and $\underline{s} = \text{Min}_{i=1}^{i=k} s_i$. The $M$ we are looking for is given by $1 + \text{Max}(\bar{s}, \underline{s})$.

**Lemma 4** *The range of a real valued continuous function f on a compact set A is bounded.*

**Proof of Lemma 4** Once I show that a continuous function takes a compact set into a compact set, I can apply the above lemma to complete the proof of the claim. Towards this end, pick any arbitrary open cover of the range of a continuous function $f$. This means that I pick an arbitrary index set $I$ and open sets $R_i$, $i \in I$, in $\mathbb{R}$ such that $f(A) \subseteq \bigcup_{i\in I} R_i$. Since $f$ is continuous, $f^{-1}(R_i)$ is open for each $i \in I$. $f^{-1}(R_i)$, $i \in I$, is an open cover of $A$. (Pick any $x \in A$. There exists $j \in I$ such that $f(x) \in R_j$. But then $f^{-1}(R_j)$ contains $x$.) Since $A$ is compact, there exists a finite positive integer $k$ such that $A \subseteq \bigcup_{j=1}^{j=k} R_{i_j}$. But then it is easy to check that $R_{i_j}$, $j = 1, \ldots k$, cover the range of $f$.

I shall now appeal to a lemma for which I offer no proof.

**Lemma 5** *Corresponding to every real valued measurable function f with a bounded range, there exists a sequence of simple real valued measurable functions* $\{f_n\}_{n\in\mathbb{N}}$ *such that for almost any x in the domain of f,* $f_n(x)$ *converges to* $f(x)$.

Colloquially, I am saying that every bounded real valued measurable function is the *pointwise limit* of a sequence of simple real valued measurable functions.[48]

I shall develop the notion of an integral of a real valued continuous function in two steps. I first show how to integrate *simple* real-valued measurable functions, and then extend the procedure to bounded real-valued Borel measurable functions. Since Lemma 2 guarantees that every *continuous* real-valued function is Borel measurable, and Lemma 3 that it is bounded, I would be done.

Towards this end, consider a function $f$ defined on $A$ which is Borel measurable and which takes only a finite set of values, say $r_1, \ldots, r_k$. Since $f^{-1}(r_i) \in \mathcal{B}(A)$ for each $i$, $\mu(f^{-1}(r_i))$ is well-defined. I can now define[49] the integral of $f$ with respect to the measure $\mu$ as

$$\int_A f\, d\mu = \sum_{i=1}^{i=k} r_i \mu(f^{-1}(r_i)).$$

I turn next to the extension to bounded, real-valued measurable functions. From Lemma 5, I know that corresponding to any such function $f$, there exists a sequence of real-valued measurable simple functions $\{f_n\}_{n \in \mathbb{N}}$ which converges to $f$ *pointwise*, which is to say, in the manner described in Lemma 5. I can now give meaning to each of the terms $\int_A f_n\, d\mu \equiv s_n$ and manufacture a new sequence $\{s_n\}_{n \in \mathbb{N}}$. Since $\mu$ is a probability measure, and since $f$ is bounded, there exists a real number greater than all of the $s_n$. I can now define

$$\int_A f\, d(\mu) = \sup_{n \in \mathbb{N}} s_n = \sup_{n \in \mathbb{N}}\{\int_A f_n\, d(\mu)\},$$

where sup simply denotes the least upper bound.

There is still a loose end which I shall not tie. I have not shown, and cannot show, that the convergent sequence of simple functions that corresponds to a given bounded measurable function, is unique. Thus, there may be several sequences $\{s_n\}_{n \in \mathbb{N}}$. The point is that the supremum of all these sequences is the same number, or to put the matter another way, the value of the integral is invariant with respect to the approximating sequence of simple functions.[50]

## An agent as a continuous function

So far I have developed the notion of an agent as a function from the space of summaries of societal actions to the space of preferences, both defined on an action set $A$. For technical reasons I now want to limit myself to agents who respond to "small" changes in societal actions, or more precisely "small" changes in the statistics summarizing these societal changes, by "small" changes in their preferences. In other words, I want to focus on agents whose relationship to society is summarized by continuous, rather than arbitrary functions. In Rorty's terms, I want the "reweaving" to be a smooth and continuous process, rather than one which is abrupt and discontinuous. Changes in the "societal environment" do not lead to brusque changes in personalities, "brusque" being measured by the underlying topology. To the obvious question as to why I limit myself by such a constraint of continuity, a simple but not very satisfying answer is that I can prove the theorem that I report here under this limitation. But then subsidiary questions arise. Is this a hypothesis which can be tested? Are agents in the "real world" better captured by arbitrary or by measurable functions rather than by continuous functions? More broadly, do these symbols, and the mathematics that they represent, have any empirical counterpart. I shall keep such questions hanging.

Once I decide to go with continuous functions, I need topologies on both the range and the domain of such functions. But these can be developed with a few more technicalities.

## Functional analysis: a second pass

This section is divided into two subsections – each devoted to a particular topology.

### *A topology on the space of preferences*

Consider a topological space $X$ and focus on all of the *closed* subsets of $X$; namely, on all those subsets of $X$ which have as their complements, sets in the particular bag that I begin with. The set of all of these closed subsets is of course another set of objects – in particular, two of the elements of such a set are the empty set $\emptyset$ and the "fullset" $X$. I can say this much without even specifying any more details about the particular bag that I am working with. Denote this set by $\mathcal{H}(X)$. I now consider putting a topology on $\mathcal{H}(X)$, which is to say the possibility of endowing the "points" of $\mathcal{H}(X)$ with a structure that allows me to make precise the statement that "one element of $\mathcal{H}(X)$ is arbitrarily close to another." I want to give one particular answer to the question as to when is one *closed* set arbitrarily "close" or "near" to another closed set?

Towards this end, for any arbitrary pair of subsets of $X$, $(K, O)$, where $K$ is compact and $O$ is open (since there is a topology on $X$, these adjectives makes sense), consider

$$\mathcal{T}_K = \{F \in \mathcal{H}(X) : F \cap K = \emptyset\} \text{ and } \mathcal{T}_O = \{F \in \mathcal{H}(X): F \cap O \neq \emptyset\}.$$

$\mathcal{T}_K$ contains all closed sets which do not intersect with the arbitrarily chosen compact set $K$. Similarly, $\mathcal{T}_O$ contains all closed sets which intersect with the arbitrarily chosen open set $O$. Note, yet again, that these are sets of sets. Now consider the "smallest" topology containing the collections, or simply the sets, given by

$$\{\mathcal{T}_K\}_{K \text{ compact}} \text{ and } \{\mathcal{T}_O\}_{o \text{ open}}$$

Since I have already given meaning to the phrase "the smallest topology containing a given set of subsets," such a topology is well-defined and I shall refer to it as the *Choquet–Kuratowski* topology.[51]

I now have all the machinery that I need to endow the space of *preferences* with a topology. Consider the topological space $A^2$ and endow $\mathcal{H}(A^2)$ with the *Choquet–Kuratowski* topology. For this operation, the fact that $A^2$ is a product space with a product topology is entirely irrelevant; what is solely of consequence is that $A^2$ is a topological space. Since $\mathcal{P}(A)$ is a subset of $\mathcal{H}(A^2)$, it can be endowed with the *relative Choquet–Kuratowski* topology. I have a topology on the range space of the functions which are to "stand in" for agents.

Next, I turn to a topology on the domain space $\mathcal{M}^1_+(A)$ of such functions.

### *A topology on the space of societal actions*

Consider an arbitrary positive integer $k$, $k$ arbitrary positive real numbers $\varepsilon_i$, and $k$ arbitrary continuous[52] real-valued functions on $A$, $f_i$. Thus, in terms of symbols, I pick an arbitrary element $\pi$ from the set $\Pi$, where

$$\pi = (k, (\varepsilon_1, \ldots, \varepsilon_k), (f_1, \ldots, f_k)) \in (\mathbb{N}, (\underbrace{\mathbb{R}, \ldots, \mathbb{R}}_{k \text{ times}})), (\underbrace{C(A), \ldots, C(A)}_{k \text{ times}})) = \Pi.$$

$\pi$ is simply a parameter that I shall use to define a topology on $\mathcal{M}^1_+(A)$, very much in the same spirit that I used the pair $(K, O)$ to define the Choquet–Kuratowski topology on $A^2$.

For an arbitrary $\pi$, consider the following subset of $\mathcal{M}^1_+(A)$.

$$\mathcal{T}_\pi = \{\mu \in \mathcal{M}^1_+(A) : \left|\int_A f_i \, d\mu \right| < \varepsilon_i \text{ for all } i = 1, \ldots, k\}.$$

This is simply the set of all probability measures on $A$ such that when the $k$ test-functions $f_i$ are integrated with respect to them, I obtain real numbers which are respectively less than the test-numbers $\varepsilon_i$. For different choices of $\pi$, I can generate different such subsets of $\mathcal{M}^1_+(A)$. Now consider the "smallest" topology containing the sets

$$\{\mathcal{T}_\pi\}_{\pi \in \Pi}.$$

Since I have given meaning to the phrase "the smallest topology containing a given set of subsets," ad nauseam, I certainly have a topology on the space of probability measures acting on a topological space. I shall refer to this topology as the *weak★topology*.[53]

## Space of agents

In terms of the vocabulary that I have developed so far, an agent is a "linkage" between summaries of society's actions and preferences and desires, and as a particular summary changes, these preferences and desires change, and this "reweaving" is done in a way that is not "abrupt." However, an agent has a distinct identity and this consists in the particular way that the two spaces are "linked." An agent is a continuous function, and his or her distinction is contained in and specified by the particular function that proxies and stands for him or her. There is a sense of *self*, and this consists not necessarily being independent of a particular community, but in the way that one responds to that community.

I can now ask as to the extent of the difference between any two agents –

how does one measure the uniqueness of one particular agent relative to that of another? How "close" is one to another? In terms of symbols, an agent is an element of $C(\mathcal{M}^1_+(A); \mathcal{F}(A))$, the set of continuous functions from $\mathcal{M}^1_+(A)$ to $\mathcal{F}(A)$, and I have been naturally led to the question of what it means for one continuous function being "close" to another. But $C(\mathcal{M}^1_+(A); \mathcal{F}(A))$ is another set of objects – the description of these objects notwithstanding – and I can endow this set of objects, as indeed any set of objects, with a topology. Such a topology, in the context that I am working with, would measure how distinct one agent is from another; in the phrase of Debreu's,[54] it would delineate the "neighborliness" of *neighboring economic agents*.

But, of course, there are many topologies on the space of continuous functions, as indeed on the space of closed subsets of a topological space, or on the space of probability measures on a topological space. The choice of topology has to be dictated by its utility for the problem at hand and in terms of the interpretation that it offers. I shall not explore these questions, but shall turn to the specification of the topology that allows me to prove the theorem that I report here.

Towards this end, for any arbitrary pair of subsets of $\mathcal{M}^1_+(A)$, and of $\mathcal{F}(A)$, $(K, O)$, $K$ compact in the weak★topology and $O$ open in the Choquet–Kuratowski topology, consider

$$\mathcal{T}_{(K,\,O)} = \{f \in C(\mathcal{M}^1_+(A), \mathcal{F}(A)) : f(K) \subset O\}.$$

Note that $\mathcal{T}_{(K,\,O)}$ contains all those continuous functions which "take the set $K$ into the set $O$." By now the routine is familiar; indeed, this entire chapter could be entitled "an explication and exemplification of the phrase *the smallest topology containing an arbitrary set of subsets of a set*." I shall refer to the "smallest" topology containing the sets.

$$\{\mathcal{T}_{(K,\,O)}\}_{K \text{ compact},\, O \text{ open}}$$

as the *compact–open* topology, and I shall denote the topological space of agents, the set $C(\mathcal{M}^1_+(A); \mathcal{F}(A))$ endowed with the compact–open topology, by the abbreviated symbol $\mathcal{U}_A$.

## A society or a large game

Let me summarize the argument as I have developed it so far. I am given an action set $A$ equipped with a topology. With such a set, or better still, with such a topological space, I can manufacture two other topological spaces. One is a space each of whose elements are summaries of societal actions, while the other is a space each of whose elements represent a system of preferences on the action set $A$. The first space is equipped with the *weak★topology* and the second with the *Choquet–Kuratowski* toplogy. An agent is simply a continuous function from one space to another. With these two topological spaces, however, I need to manufacture yet another one. This is the space of agents equipped with the *compact–open* topology. The question that I can now finally pose and answer is what is a society? or, in more fashionable terminology, what is a game?

A "society" or a "nation" or a "community" is constituted by a set of agents – this set consists of different proportions of different kinds or "types" of agents. Since the space $\mathcal{U}_A$ is the totality of all possible kinds of agents, albeit a totality restricted by the requirement of *continuity*, a "society" can be formalized as a probability measure on $\mathcal{U}_A$, and as such, may be seen simply as an element of $\mathcal{M}^1_+(\mathcal{U}_A)$. Such a *measure* would measure, for example, the proportion of *priests*, *warriors*, *traders* and *others* that constitute a particular society, these four kinds of agent being proxied by four different functions chosen from $\mathcal{U}_A$. However, the technical problem is that for me to be able to discuss the space of probability measures on $\mathcal{U}_A$, I need a σ-algebra on it, which is possibly to say, the space of coalitions that can be formed from the elements in it.

However, $\mathcal{U}_A$ is already a topological space and I know how to manufacture a σ-algebra from a topology – the so-called Borel σ-algebra, $\mathcal{B}(\mathcal{U}_A)$. Of course, I could have defined a σ-algebra directly without reference to any topology, and here again, the choice of σ-algebra is dictated by its utility for the problem at hand and in terms of the interpretation that it offers. In any case, I shall remain with $\mathcal{B}(\mathcal{U}_A)$, and regard a particular "society" or a particular "game" as an element of the space of probability measures defined on the measurable space $(\mathcal{U}_A, \mathcal{B}(\mathcal{U}_A))$, or in terms of my earlier notation, $(C(\mathcal{M}^1_+(A); \mathcal{F}(A)), \mathcal{B}(C(\mathcal{M}^1_+(A); \mathcal{F}(A))))$. A particular measure specifies for any particular set chosen from my σ-algebra, the proportion of "society" whose members constitute that set. Note that in this specification, I have not specified the number of agents in the society, only proportions. It is in this sense that I am formalizing a "large" society or a "large" game.

However, for the theorem that I am in the process of reporting, I cannot work with an arbitrary probability measure on the space $\mathcal{U}_A$ – the society that such a measure represents is "too diverse," and I need a limitation on this diversity. Such a limitation is captured by restricting attention to *Radon* probability measures on the space $\mathcal{U}_A$. These are probability measures "most of whose mass" is constrained to lie in a compact set. To expand on this, a measure is Radon if for any $\varepsilon > 0$, however small, there exists a compact subset $K$ of $(C(\mathcal{M}^1_+(A); \mathcal{F}(A)))$ whose measure is greater than $(1 - \varepsilon)$. Since there is a topology on $(C(\mathcal{M}^1_+(A); \mathcal{F}(A)))$, the adjective *compact* makes sense. Furthermore, since singleton sets are compact, the example of a society classified into four, or indeed finitely many, types of agents is one that is represented by a Radon measure. In the sequel, I shall limit myself to societies formalized as Radon measures.

## An equilibrium

Let me return to the notion of a *preference* on $A$ as I developed it in the third section. Recall that it is simply an element $P^c$ of the topological space $\mathcal{F}(A)$. I now want to focus on the set of elements in $A$ that are *maximal* with respect to $P$. *Maximal* is a difficult word with different shades of meaning – here I shall mean it with reference to the set (!) $P$ and define it as

$$M(P^c) = \{a \in A\text{: For all } b \in A, (b, a) \notin P\} = \{a \in A\text{: For all } b \,\varepsilon\, A, (b, a) \in P^c\}.$$

Thus, in terms of the interpretation that I have given to $P$, $M(P)$ simply represents all those actions to which no other action is "preferred," where the preferences are given by $P$. Of course, in simply defining such a set, I am saying nothing about whether it is nonempty or not. This is yet another reason why the words *maximum* or *best* need to be used with some caution.

Now consider the product space constituted by the space of actions and the space of players, namely the space $(A \times \mathcal{U}_A)$. Endowed with its product topology, this is a topological space. Endowed with the product $\sigma$-algebra $\mathcal{B}(A) \otimes \mathcal{B}(\mathcal{U}_A)$, it is a measurable space. Think of this measurable space as a bag which contains sets; each such set consists of pairs of objects, an action $a$ and a player $f$. I am interested in a particular subset of this product space. As it happens, this subset is also an element of the $\sigma$-algebra $\mathcal{B}(A) \otimes \mathcal{B}(\mathcal{U}_A)$, but this is something that has to be proved. But then I run ahead of my story. The set I am interested in depends on a particular summary of society's actions, say same $\rho \in \mathcal{M}^1_+(A)$, and is given by

$$B_\rho = \{(a, f) \in (A \times \mathcal{U}_A)\text{: } a \in M(f(\rho))\}.$$

This is an important set for the result that I am attempting to develop. I begin my description of it by observing that my notation for it emphasizes the fact that it depends on the summary of society's actions, $\rho$. To see why, pick any element $(a, f)$ from the bag $(A \times \mathcal{U}_A)$. One would like to check if for this *action–agent* pair, the action $a$ represents a *best* or *maximal* element for the agent $f$. It is important to see that this question is ill-posed. The agent represented by $f$ cannot determine an answer to this question simply because he or she "has not found his or her bearings." It is only after one has specified how society behaves, that an agent's personality, in this case his or her *preferences*, will be determined. To put the matter another way, I have defined *maximal* elements with respect to elements of $\mathcal{F}(A)$, rather than with respect to elements in $C(\mathcal{M}^1_+(A), \mathcal{F}(A))$. However, once I know society's actions, or more precisely, a summary of such actions, as represented by an element $\rho$ of $\mathcal{M}^1_+(A)$, I can determine the corresponding "system of preferences", namely $f(\rho)$ (recall that this is an element of $\mathcal{F}(A)$), and only then, the corresponding set of *maximal* elements $M(f(\rho))$.

Continuing my narrative as regards the set $B_\rho$, I can now say that given a particular $\rho$ in $\mathcal{M}^1_+(A)$, the set $B_\rho$ represents *maximal* action–agent pairs.

Thus, when I pick an element $(a, f)$ from the bag $(A \times \mathcal{U}_A)$, I already have given to me a $\rho$, and therefore the set $M(f(\rho))$. I need only check whether $a$ belongs to it or not. All those pairs $(a, f)$ such that $a$ belongs to $M(f(\rho))$ constitute the set $B_\rho$.

Note that I have stuck in here a basic behavioral hypothesis. Given an agent's perception of how "everybody is behaving in a society in which s/he is a member," s/he picks actions which are best for him or her in so far as s/he has an identity represented by a particular function $f$. Every agent is following his or her self-interest but this self-interest is tempered both by society's actions and by the restrictions that go into the formalization of an *agent* and his or her *preferences*. The fewer the restrictions – in the exposition here *continuity* and the Radon assumption for the former, and *reflexivity*, *transitivity* and *continuity* for the latter – the less of a parody it is.

Finally, I turn to the notion of equilibrium, a notion that goes back to Cournot (1838), Nash (1951), and in the formulation directly antecedent to mine, to Mas-Colell (1984). Consider a process in which every agent forms an expectation of society's actions, and then acts. I can now pose the question as to whether there is a "rest point" to this process? Is there a summary of society's actions, which in motivating the entire society to choose its actions, leads to a configuration of actions which are themselves summarized by the summary of actions one began with? Is there a measure $\tau$ on the product space $A \times \mathcal{U}_A$ such that its marginal $\tau_{\mathcal{U}_A}$ on the player space $\mathcal{U}_A$ is equal to the game $\mu$ and such that it gives "full measure" to the set $B_{\tau_A}$; which is to say $\tau(B_{\tau_A}) = 1$? $\tau_A$ being the marginal of $\tau$ on the action space $A$. I collect the answer in a separate section.

## A result

**Definition 1** *A Cournot–Nash equilibrium $\tau$ of a society $\mu$ is a measure on the product of the space of actions A and the space of agents $\mathcal{U}_A$ such that (i) it gives full measure to the set of all maximizing action–agent pairs conditioned with respect to society's actions, such actions being summarized by its marginal on the action space A; and such that (ii) its marginal on the player space equals the given society $\mu$.*

I can now present the long-awaited result.

**Theorem 1** *Any society represented by a Radon measure has a Cournot–Nash equilibrium.*

Given any Cournot–Nash equilibrium $\tau$, I can determine the equilibrium summary of society's actions, $\tau_A$, as well as an equilibrium configuration of preferences, $\psi(\tau) \in \mathcal{M}^1_+(\mathcal{F}(A))$. This object represents a mouthful and relies on the function

$$ev : \mathcal{U}_A \times \mathcal{M}^1_+(A) \to \mathcal{F}(A) \text{ where } ev(f, \rho) = f(\rho),\ f \in \mathcal{U}_A,\ \rho \in \mathcal{M}^1_+(A).$$

The function *ev* is the so-called *evaluation mapping*, and it is one of the important properties of the compact–open topology that it is continuous.[55] If I pick a particular element, say $\tau_A$ in $\mathcal{M}^1_+(A)$, I can use it to convert a function of two variables into that of a single variable. I shall denote such a converted function by $ev_{\tau_A}$. Note that,

$$ev_{\tau_A} : \mathcal{U}_A \rightarrow \mathcal{F}(A) \text{ where } ev_{\tau_A}(f) = ev(f, \tau_A) = f(\tau_A), f \in \mathcal{U}_A.$$

But now, I have all the symbols that I need to define the object $\psi(\tau)$. The narrative behind the following equality

$$\psi(\tau) = \tau_{\mathcal{U}A} \circ (ev_{\tau_A})^{-1}, \psi(\tau) \in \mathcal{M}^1_+(\mathcal{F})$$

is as follows. Pick any configuration of preferences, namely an element $W$ in the Borel σ-algebra $\mathcal{B}(\mathcal{F}(A))$. If the function $ev_{\tau_A}$ is Borel measurable, it brings back measurable sets into measurable sets, and thus $(ev_{\tau_A})^{-1}(W) \in \mathcal{B}(\mathcal{U}_A)$. But then I can measure this set by the Radon measure $\mu = \tau_{\mathcal{U}_A}$ representing the *society* I am working with. I am thus *inducing* the measure $\mu$ on to the space $\mathcal{F}(A)$ through the evaluation map[56] *ev* and the equilibrium summary of society's actions $\tau_A$. I call this *induced* measure $\psi(\tau)$, and it represents the equilibrium configuration of preferences. In conclusion, I can say

> what makes the mosaic work is the confidence that one can be as totally pragmatic, adaptive, opportunistic, and generally ad hoc in one's relations with others – a fox among foxes, a crocodile among crocodiles – as one wants without any risk of losing one's sense of who one is.[57]

## A suggested application

I now turn to the question whether Theorem 1 can be applied to Chipman's 1970 setting to show the existence of competitive equilibrium with external economies of scale. Chipman begins with named agents, *m* consumers and $N_i$ firms, *i* running over *n* industries,[58] and the first step is to see whether his non-anonymous set-up can be described as a game, conventionally and simply understood: names of players, action sets which are subsets of an ambient space, and payoffs defined on the products of these action sets.[59] The second step is to translate this into the setting of a large anonymous game, and hence into that of Theorem 1.

Chipman works in $(n + 1)$-dimensional Euclidean space, $\mathbb{R}^{n+1}$, and uses the input–output classification for commodities. The first *n* commodities are demanded by the consumers and supplied by the firms, whereas the $(n + 1)$th commodity, labor, is supplied by the consumers and demanded by the firms. There is no joint production, and the production plan of each firm consists only of labor–output pairs,[60] with the technology (production functions) formalized by an input–output coefficient. Since each firm maximizes profits, these coefficients play a crucial role in the specification of the payoff function of each firm.

The input–output coefficients available to a particular firm depend on aggregate industrial output. This leads Chipman to write that "The crucial concept . . . developed here is that of *parametric external economies of scale*" (p. 349) – to his distinctions (p. 353) between *objective* and *subjective* production functions, or under an alternative interpretation, between the *long-run* and the *short* – and it is this dependence that basically introduces "game theory" into the problem of the general allocation of resources. The payoffs of the consumers, on the other hand, are all determined from a given positively homogeneous and strictly quasi-concave function.[61] This allows the analysis to be conducted in terms of a single consumer, and furthermore, given the explicit funcitonal form, to the derivation of demands as a constant proportion of income. It has the additional consequence that the distribution of the endowment of labor, $Z$, among the $m$ consumers need not be specified.

The parameters, then, are the aggregate quantity of labor $Z$, the utility function proxied by $\theta_i$, and the production functions by $(\kappa_i, \rho_i)$, $i$ ranging over the $n$ industries, or equivalently, over the $n$ outputs. The unknowns to be determined are the output prices $p_i$, the wage rate $w$, the output levels $y_{ij}$, and the allocation of labor over all the firms, and hence over industries.[62]

> The main results may be summarized as follows: There exists a unique full employment equilibrium with positive wages. If production functions are homogeneous of the same degree in each industry, this equilibrium is also Pareto optimal. On the other hand, . . . "ideal" output [is] greater or smaller than laissez-faire output as $\rho_i$ is greater or smaller than the weighted average $\rho' = \Sigma_{i=1}^{n} \theta_i \rho_i$ where the weights are the proportions of the consumers' budgets devoted to the respective commodities. (p. 351)

In addition to this theorem on the existence and characterization of equilibrium – really Cournot–Nash equilibrium – there is a result on the asymptotic stability of a particular adjustment process, and a further analysis of "taxes, bounties and optimality rules."[63]

Chipman's theorem on dynamic stability suggests a precisely formulated open question for my setting; namely, conditions on $Q$, and hence on the parameters of my model, under which $\tau_t$ converges to a rest point of the differential inclusion

$$\tau_{t+1} \in Q(\tau_t), \text{ where } Q(\tau_t) \equiv \{\nu \in \mathcal{M}_+^1(A \times \mathcal{U}_A)\colon \nu_{\mathcal{U}_A} = \mu;\ \nu \in \mathcal{B}_{(\tau_A)t}\},$$

where $t$ can be interpreted either as "real" or as "computer" time. At the end of the "Equilibrium" section, I had already posed the question of the existence of equilibrium as the rest point of a dynamic process; and indeed, the proof of Theorem 1 is nothing more and nothing less than an argument guaranteeing the existence of a fixed point of the correspondence $Q$. My 1970 text also suggests two other (open) questions. First, the characterization of equilibrium; more specifically, the isolation of sufficient conditions under which some or all of the Cournot–Nash equilibria are Pareto optimal. This is another way of asking, in a specific context, for conditions under which competition leads to cooperation. Second, conditions for uniqueness, or at least generic local uniqueness, with all of the formalizations that these words entail.[64] My intention in this subsection, however, is to go the other way; to see whether my Theorem 1 has anything to say on the existence of *competitive equilibrium with external economies of scale.*

For the translation of Chipman's finite game into a large anonymous game, let the action set of any firm in a particular industry $i$ be $A_i \subseteq \mathbb{R}$, and the action set of a consumer be a product of these $n$ individual action sets, $\Pi_{i=1}^{n} A_i \equiv A \subseteq \mathbb{R}^n$. A firm in a particular industry $i$ is a continuous function from $\mathcal{M}_+^1(A)$, in fact the marginal of the measures on $A_i$, to the space $C(A_i)$. A consumer's preferences do not depend *directly* on the actions of the firms or on those of other consumers – there are no externalities in this sector – and are simply represented by the space $C(A)$. The space of agents then is the space $C(\mathcal{M}_+^1(A); C(A))$, with explicit recognition given to the fact that consumer characteristics, $C(A)$, as well as firm characteristics, $C(\mathcal{M}_+^1(A_i); C(A_i))$, are all elements of this ambient space. A *game* is simply a measure concentrated on $(n + 1)$ atoms in this characteristic space.

Before proceeding further, three points ought to be noted. First, in this reformulation, I have given up on questions of the cardinality of the set of agents; all I can furnish are the proportions in which a firm of a particular type, or the (identical) consumers, constitute the economy. Second, parametric external economies are formalized as distributions of industrial output levels, rather than their integral, average or some other summary statistic.[65] Finally, note that I have suppressed labor from the analysis – it can be obtained once the equilibrium output levels are determined – as well as the fictitious player.[66]

The remaining question is whether the game, so formalized, satisfies the hypotheses of Theorem 1. The compactness of the individual action sets follows from the fact that $Z$ is exogenously given; this puts bounds both on the labor that can be supplied by the consumers and employed by the firms, and hence on consumer income and firm output levels. Given the continuity assumptions on consumer preferences and on production functions, the hypotheses on preferences is no problem; indeed, there is a lot of "give" on this score. Finally, the game is clearly a Radon measure, concentrated as it is on a finite number of types. All of this notwithstanding, the point is that Theorem 1 *cannot* be applied in its present form to yield a competitive equilibrium.

The problem is one of long standing in the subject, and it is simply that the consumers' action sets, rather than their payoffs, respond to the actions of the other players.[67] In the context that I describe, these actions are given by the industry's marginal costs which equal the average costs.[68] There are at least two ways of dealing with this difficulty. The first is to view changes in action sets as changes in payoffs by considering extended real-valued upper semicontinuous functions, which take negatively infinite values off a particular (budget) set.[69] The other way is simply to redefine $\mathcal{F}(A)$ so that it now equals

$$\bigcup_{B \in \mathcal{H}(A);\ B \neq \phi} \mathcal{F}_B(A), \text{ where } \mathcal{F}_B(A) \equiv \{P^c \subseteq B \times B : P \in B^2;\ \Delta \subseteq P^c;\ P \circ P \subseteq P\}.$$

Under this extension, a change in preferences incorporates changes in their domain.[70]

This subsection would be even more incomplete if I did not draw attention to the work of Roberts and Sonnenschein (1977) and of Pascoa (1993a). Roberts and Sonnenschein emphasize the ad hoc nature of the assumption of convexity or single-valuedness of firm responses in the literature on the existence of monopolistically competitive equilibrium. It would be interesting to see how Chipman's particular assumptions, especially his formalization of "parametric" external economies, allows him to "skirt" the slippery slope identified by them. Second, and in the same vein, Pascoa is as clearly a follower of the 1970 paper as he is a precursor to the attempt here. Again, it would be interesting to make the interconnections precise.

## Concluding remarks

I end this chapter with two remarks which pertain both to Theorem 1 and to the suggested application. The first of these is motivated by the extensions of Theorem 1 that are suggested by the application. There seems little doubt that such extensions are feasible; what is more problematic is the altered meaning that is taken on by the technical assumptions when they are stretched to the competitive context. As an example of this sensitivity, consider the definition of an agent as a continuous function when the set of actions is finite. The *discrete* and the *Euclidean* topologies are "natural" ones on the range and domain of such a function – societal responses are now simply elements of finite–dimensional simplices – but the continuity assumption then allows only constant functions. A "natural" assumption has ruled out precisely that which is to be analyzed! More concretely, the application pointed to upper semicontinuous functions; the economic implications of the continuity hypotheses concerning spaces of such functions remain to be carefully examined.

My second remark is also motivated by the application, and it concerns *symmetric* equilibria. The translation of Chipman's 1970 model into the setting of a large anonymous game asks for sufficient conditions under which identical firms, or identical consumers, behave identically in equilibrium. Do the Cournot–Nash equilibria exhibit the equal treatment property? What was taken for granted in Chipman's analysis now becomes a question, and a difficult one at that,[71] in mine.

There seems to be no getting away from the fact that a lot of work remains to be done; as any "economist" knows, there are costs of arbitrage.[72]

## Notes

Some of the material presented in this chapter was delivered as invited lectures at The Research Centre for Mathematical and Physical Sciences in Chittagong in December 1990; and at the Institute of Economics, Academia Sinica in Taipei in July 1992. I am grateful to Jim Moore for his invitation to write, and for his agreement to my collecting these ideas, for the Chipman *festschrift*. I have benefited from conversations with Rolph Trouillot in the Fall of 1993; the encouragement and careful reading of earlier drafts by Saleha Jilani, Edi Karni and Shinji Yamashige; and by the comments of Shapan Adnan, Ismet Beg, Jamal Nazrul Islam, James Mirrlees, Asghar Quader and Yeneng Sun. Errors, particularly those arising from ambiguity and imprecision, are solely mine.

1 See, as examples, Chipman (1976, 1979a) and Chipman et al. (1976) on the one hand, and Chipman (1981 and 1985) on the other.

2 See Chipman's (1951: 10–11) PhD dissertation where he writes, "The development of [a] theoretical framework is a large enough task in itself to justify independent treatment, [and] many useful conclusions can be drawn from [a] purely theoretical discussion without recourse to extensive empirical research." For a less optimistic, and more guarded and resigned tone, see Khan (1993a and b, 1994).

3 I emphasize again the qualifying phrase, given the form of the *oeuvre* as it currently exists; how it will evolve in the future is anyone's guess.

4 In the 1970 paper that I take as my text (henceforth a lack of explicit reference and floating page numbers will refer to Chipman (1970)), Chipman writes that his "formulation makes possible a rehabilitation of the doctrine evolved by Marshall, Pigou and R.F. Kahn" (p. 351). There are copious references to Pigou's work of 1912 and 1920 (see footnote 9 on p. 351), to Marshall's *Principles*, and to a 1935 paper of Kahn. The last author serves as a pervasive interlocutor; see p. 366 and the footnote therein. All of this, of course, is in keeping with Chipman's interests in the history of economic thought; in addition to Chipman (1965–66), the reader can sample Chipman (1979b).

5 He quotes without reference the well-known theorem that [in Euclidean space] a maximum of a continuous function on a closed, bounded set is attained in the set (p. 362); also uses Jensen's inequality (p. 381) and that between arithmetic and geometric means (p. 363); Laplace transforms (p. 384); and Knopp's theorem (p. 385). Geometry is also not slighted (see the italicized statement on p. 361). Already in his dissertation he had "employ[ed] a considerable amount of mathematics," and had squarely faced the fact that "few economists today are equipped with this mathematical knowledge;" see Chipman (1951: 11).

6 Irreversibilities and learning by doing (pp. 350–351); aggregation and the Gorman–Nataf theorem (p. 356); public goods (and bads) (p. 350); classical

and Keynesian economics (Footnote 7 on p. 348, Footnote 1 on p. 359, Footnote 7 on p. 383); customs unions and trade theory (Footnotes 4, 5 and 6 on p. 348, Footnote 3 on p. 379); and, most interestingly from the point of view of this essay, a continuum of firms (p. 349).

7 See pp. 377 and 380 and equations 2.1, 2.6, 3.6, 3.7 in particular. As another example, see Chipman (1971, Section 10.6).

8 By using his assumptions to characterize the equilibrium, Chipman whittles down the existence issue to complete decomposability and towards obtaining the solution "industry by industry"; see the last paragraph on p. 361.

9 I will simply refer the reader to the 64 footnotes, not counting the acknowledgement. Arguably, for the paper I use as my text, Footnote 9 on p. 351 makes my point best.

10 I find interesting the following statements in Chipman (1951: 10–11), "It is difficult, in a study of this sort, to describe precise concepts in language that was devised for other purposes. I hope the reader will be forgiving, therefore, if the style is in places pedantic and clumsy . . . To those who may suggest that some of my conclusions were too obvious to require mathematical proof, I can only reply that they were not obvious to me, and that some propositions which I thought to be obvious . . . do not necessarily hold in the real world."

11 Even though the 1970 paper is an exercise in "pure theory", Chipman draws many policy conclusions from it. In any case, applied theory may simply be an oxymoron.

12 Referring to his celebrated survey of the theory of international trade, Chipman writes "The treatment of optimality given on those pages is off the mark, and superseded by that of the present paper. I . . . hope that the present contribution may serve as a rigorous foundation for this" (Footnote 7, p. 351).

13 Chipman puts this point with characteristic insight: "There is no logical contradiction involved in the notion that economic agents do not perceive things as they actually are, and while the idea of treating production functions parametrically may be more subtle and unusual than that of treating market prices this way, both ideas are of the same logical order" (p. 349). Also sees the prerequisites demanded by Debreu (1952), available in Debreu (1983).

14 Chipman (1970), in arguing for intervention with *laissez faire*, albeit in a closed economy, is an important precursor of the so-called new trade theory, in so far as it has as its principal preoccupation the assertion that imperfect competition may dictate the interference with free trade; see Krugman (1987), Corden (1990), Jones (1993). In his *Palgrave* entry on international trade Chipman (1987: 923) writes, "However these latter models have so far not been successfully formulated as general-equilibrium models. It goes without saying that, in the nature of the case, a partial equilibrium model is incapable of explaining or predicting trade patterns or analysing the effects on prices and resource allocation of trade restrictions and transfers."

15 There is no money in the 1970 analysis (in spite of the reference to Footnote 7 on p. 348), but Chipman rules out zero wage unemployment equilibria as uninteresting (p. 371) and comments on Walras' law (pp. 382–383); also Footnote 1 on p. 359.

16 See the fifth paragraph in the section below on "A suggested application".

17 Chipman writes "No discussion of competitive equilibrium under increasing returns would be complete without a discussion of dynamic stability" (p. 381). In my 1970 text, the two subjects flow together. To get an idea of

Chipman's deep interests in dynamics, the reader can sample Chipman (1977b).

18 The normative analysis on "ideal output" is conducted on, and after the identification of, the positive model. It is difficult to argue that this identification is not itself based on normative criteria.

19 It is the computations with explicit functional forms that lead to conceptual simplifications in the analysis of equilibrium. Computational interests go to the very beginning of the career; see Chipman (1953).

20 As my own second sentence in the paragraph above makes abundantly clear.

21 See Trouillot (1991) for a discussion of the issues underlying this statement. Also Pocock (1993) in another context.

22 It is an interesting exercise for me, and possibly for the reader, to test my hypotheses about Chipman's writing (stated in the above two paragraphs) on his 1965–1966 *magnum opus* "A Survey of the Theory of International Trade." If these three articles, or one three-part article, are a large mural painting, then the 1970 paper is clearly a miniature which both illuminates, and is illuminated by, it.

23 From Bourbaki (1966), "In principle, it requires no particular knowledge of mathematics on the reader's part, but only a certain familiarity with mathematical reasoning and a certain capacity for abstract thought." Also see Debreu (1959).

24 It is a good exercise for the reader to track and identify all of the linear functions and linear spaces that are interspersed in this exposition.

25 See the third paragraph on p. 348.

26 Integration is essential and the proof on which I am silent, requires the Fan–Glicksberg fixed point theorem.

27 See Halmos (1960: 1). He writes further that "the mathematical concept of a set can be used as the foundation for all known mathematics," and that in his book, he will study "sets, and sets of sets, and similar towers of sometimes frightening height and complexity, . . . [and] nothing else."

28 The reader whose susceptibilities to rigor are offended by the use of the word "hardly" may substitute "not" for it.

29 It is useful to check out the validity of this statement and the others that follow it.

30 In a sense, this entire chapter can be seen as exemplifying this, but let us leave this aside for the moment.

31 I leave it to the reader to check that this new bag is indeed a topology, and warn him or her not to proceed further if he or she cannot do this to his or her satisfaction.

32 I refer the interested reader to look at Bourbaki (1966) if he or she is curious as to why two different words are being used for the same concept.

33 I leave it to the reader to check that this new bag is not a topology, and that the qualifer "arbitrary union" is needed.

34 I leave it to the reader to check out how the second statement is a formalization of the first intuitive one, and also to try to reconcile both statements with the $\varepsilon - \delta$ definition of *continuity* if he or she is aware of it.

35 I leave it to the reader to check that this bag is "closed under complementation and countable intersections" – which is to say that it is a $\sigma$-algebra.

36 See Lemma 2 below.

37 Except in so far as the elements of $X$ are also elements of $\mathcal{X}$.

38 As the more mature (!) reader may have guessed by now, a measure simply formalizes the notion of a *probability* on an *event* space $\mathcal{X}$.

39 I leave it to the reader to check that a *marginal* measure is indeed a measure.
40 Quoted in Todorov (1984: 30–31). Also paragraphs 8–15 in Kelly (1992).
41 See Rosen (1989: 14). For similar remarks from Adam Smith and Schumpeter, see Khan (1991, Section 2).
42 The fact that compact subsets of a finite-dimensional Euclidean space are "small" is a reflection of the space rather than of the notion of "compactness."
43 Recall that this is simply the $\sigma$-algebra generated by the elements of the topology on $A$.
44 In particular, the notation does not mean that I am "squaring" the space in any of the arithmetical senses that the reader may give to the term "squaring."
45 The reader should note that at this stage in my formalization of *preferences*, I have avoided any mention of *utility* or *payoff* functions (*continuous*, *quasi-concave* or otherwise) defined on the action set $A$. I simply have no need for them. Indeed, there will be no such functions defined on $A$ which represent *preferences* that are not *complete*. In the "suggested application" section, however, I shall return to such functions.
46 Rorty (1991: 199).
47 I am not assuming that the reader knows the abstract definition of a distance, but simply that she or he is comfortable with manipulation of absolute values of the real numbers.
48 For a simple proof, see for example Rudin (1966: 16). This is the weak link in the characterization of "self-contained" that I referred to in the introduction.
49 With the help of simple drawings, the reader can convince him or herself that this is a very simple way of calculating the "area under the curve" represented by the graph of the function $f$. This simple "observation" is of course one of the immortal contributions of Lebesgue to analysis.
50 I leave this too to the interested reader.
51 Professor Edi Karni asked for examples to illustrate preferences that are considered "near" under this topology. This question is very well taken not only in this context but also in terms of the theorem that I am in the process of developing. Also see the "concluding remarks" below.
52 Since there is a topology on $A$, the adjective *continuous* makes sense.
53 I depart from standard terminology here. What I am calling the weak★ topology is really a *relative* topology, relative with respect to what is conventionally termed the weak★topology by functional analysts, and the weak topology by probabilists.
54 See Chapter 13 in Debreu (1983).
55 Indeed it is the "smallest" topology on $\mathcal{U}_A$ such that the *evaluation mapping* is continuous; see, for example, Bourbaki (1966).
56 The reader should note that this entire procedure revolves around the Borel measurability of the mapping $ev_{\tau_A}$; look again at Lemma 1 above.
57 Geertz (1983: 68).
58 Thus in terms of cardinality of the set of agents, there are $m + \Sigma_{i=1}^{n} N_i$ agents in the economy or, in the terminology of this essay, *society* or *game*. This cardinality will be dispensed with in the sequel.
59 For the initiatied purist, I am describing a "game in normal form."
60 Hence the relation between the number of industries and the number of commodities.
61 Chipman writes that this can be dispensed with and that all he needs to assume are the conditions for the validity of the Gorman–Nataf theorem; Footnote 7 on p. 356. These conditions "yield demand functions which, for

each set of prices are linear in income with the same slope (propensity to consume) for each individual."

62 It is interesting to reflect on the extent to which this conception is driven by Ricardian trade theory.

63 In particular, a proof of what Chipman terms the *Marshall's conjecture* guarantees the fulfillment of the government budget constraint (p. 377).

64 See Chapters 19 and 14 in Debreu (1983).

65 For the structural identity of the formulations with distributions and integrals in a setting with a *finite* number of actions, see Khan and Sun (1993b).

66 This is a time-honored way of converting equilibria of games to equilibria of economies; see Chapter 4 in Debreu (1983); also Shafer and Sonnenschein (1976).

67 This is precisely the import of Debreu's 1952 extension of Nash (1951); see Chapter 2 in Debreu (1983).

68 The Ricardian assumptions again! In disequilibrium, the budget sets could be defined on the basis of the average of these industrial average costs. There may, however, be some problems concerning symmetric equilibria here; see the "concluding remarks" section.

69 See the extension of Khan (1989) in Rath (1992). Also see Pascoa (1993b).

70 This is precisely the way preferences are defined in Khan and Sun (1990) but see the first "concluding remark" below.

71 See Theorem 2 in Mas-Colell (1984), and the counterexamples in Rath and Yamashige (1993); also Yamashige (1992).

72 These paragraphs draw heavily, as indeed does much of this chapter, on my joint work with Yeneng Sun.

## Bibliography

### *Selected works of John S. Chipman*

1951 *The Theory of Inter-sectoral Money Flows and Income Formation*. Baltimore: The Johns Hopkins Press. Reprinted from The Johns Hopkins University *Studies in Historical and Political Science* LXVIII (1950) No. 2.

1953 "Computational problems in linear programming," *Review of Economics and Statistics* 35: 342–359.

1965–66 "A survey of the theory of international trade," *Econometrica* 33: 477–519, 685–760 and 34, 18–76.

1969 "Factor price equalization and the Stolper–Samuelson theorem," *International Economic Review* 10: 399–406.

1970 "External economies of scale and competitive equilibrium," *Quarterly Journal of Economics* LXXXIV: 347–385.

1971 "International trade with capital mobility: a substitution theorem," in J.N. Bhagwati, R.W. Jones, R.A. Mundell and J. Vanek (eds) *Trade, Balance of Payments and Growth: Papers in International Economics in Honor of Charles P. Kindleberger*. Amsterdam: North Holland.

1972 "The theory of exploitative trade and investment policies: a reformulation and a synthesis," in L.E. Di Marco (ed.) *International Economics Development: Essays in Honour of Raúl Prebisch*. New York: Academic Press.

1973 "The ordering of portfolios in terms of mean and variances," *Review of Economic Studies* 40: 167–190.
1976 "Estimation and aggregation in econometrics: an application of the theory of generalized inverses," in M.Z. Nashed (ed.) *Generalized Inverses and Applications*. New York: Academic Press.
1977a "An empirical implication of Auspitz–Lieben–Edgeworth–Pareto complementarity," *Journal of Economic Theory* 14: 228–231.
1977b "A renewal model of economic growth: the continuous case," *Econometrica* 45: 295–316.
1979a "Efficiency of least squares estimation of linear trend when residuals are auto-correlated," *Econometrica* 47: 115–128.
1979b "Mill's 'superstructure': how well does it stand up?" *History of Political Economy* 11: 477–500.
1981 "Internal–external price relationships in the West German economy," *Zeitschrift fur die Gasamte Staatswissenschaft* 137: 612–637.
1982 "Capital movement as a substitute for technology transfer: a comment," *Journal of International Economics* 1982: 107–109.
1985 "Relative prices, capital movements, and sectoral technical change: theory and an empirical test," in K. Jungenfelt (ed.) *Structural Adjustment in Developing Open Economies*. New York: St Martin's Press.
1987 "International trade," in J. Eatwell, P.K. Newman and M. Milgate (eds) *The New Palgrave*. London: Macmillan.
1990 "Marshall's consumer's surplus in modern perspective," in J.K. Whitaker (ed.) *Centenary Essays on Alfred Marshall*. Cambridge: Cambridge University Press.
with K.R. Kadiyala, A. Madansky and J.W. Pratt, 1976 "Efficiency of the sample mean when residuals follow a first-order stationary Markoff process," *Journal of the American Statistical Association* 62: 1237–1246.
with J.C. Moore, 1978 "The new welfare economics 1939–1974," *International Economic Review* 19: 547–584.
with J.C. Moore, 1979 "On social welfare functions and the aggregation of preferences," *Journal of Economic Theory* 21: 111–139.

## *Other references*

Bourbaki N. (1966) *Elements of Mathematics: General Topology*. Reading, MA: Addison-Wesley.
Cournot, A.A. (1838) *Researches into the Mathematical Principles of the Theory of Wealth*. N.T. Bacon (trans.) (1929) London: Macmillan.
Corden, W.M. (1990) "Strategic trade policy: how new? how sensible?," *World Bank Working Paper* No. 396.
Debreu, G. (1959) *Theory of Value*. New Haven, CT: Yale University Press.
Debreu, G. (1983) *Mathematical Economics: Twenty Papers of Gerard Debreu*. Cambridge: Cambridge University Press.
Eatwell, J., Milgate, M. and Newman, P.K. (eds) (1987) *The New Palgrave*. New York: Macmillan.
Geertz, C. (1983) *Local Knowledge*. New York: Basic Books.

Halmos, P.R. (1960) *Naive Set Theory*. Berlin: Springer-Verlag edition dated 1974.

Jones, R.W. (1993) "The new protectionism and the nature of world trade," *Pakistan Development Review* 32: 389–408.

Kelly, A. (1992) "Revealing Bakhtin," *New York Review of Books* 39: 44–48.

Khan, M. Ali (1989) "On Cournot–Nash equilibrium distributions for games with a non-metrizable action space and upper semicontinuous payoffs," *Transactions of the American Mathematical Society* 315: 127–146.

Khan, M. Ali (1991) "On the languages of markets," *Pakistan Development Review* 30: 503–549.

Khan, M. Ali (1993a) "The irony in/of economic theory," *Modern Language Notes* 108: 759–803.

Khan, M. Ali (1993b) "On economics and language," *Journal of Economic Studies* 20: 51–69.

Khan, M. Ali (1993c) "On education as a commodity," *Pakistan Development Review* 32: 541–579.

Khan, M. Ali and Sun, Y. (1990) "On a reformulation of Cournot–Nash equilibria," *Journal of Mathematical Analysis and Applications* 146: 442–460.

Khan, M. Ali and Sun, Y. (1993a) "Extremal structures and symmetric equilibria with countable actions," *Johns Hopkins Working Paper* No. 316.

Khan, M. Ali and Sun, Y. (1993b) "On large games with finite actions: a synthetic treatment," in W. Takahashi (ed.) *Nonlinear and Convex Analysis in Economic Theory*. Berlin: Springer-Verlag. Japanese translation forthcoming in *Mita Journal of Economics*.

Krugman, P. (1987) "Is free trade passé?," *Journal of Economic Perspectives* 1: 131–144.

Mas-Colell, A. (1984) "On a theorem of Schmeidler," *Journal of Mathematical Economics* 13: 201–206.

Nash, J. (1951) "Non-cooperative games," *Annals of Mathematics* 54: 289–295.

Pascoa, M.R. (1993a) "Noncooperative equilibrium and Chamberlinian monopolistic competition," *Journal of Economic Theory* 60: 335–353.

Pascoa, M.R. (1993b) "Approximate equilibrium in pure strategies for non-atomic games," *Journal of Mathematical Economics* 22: 223–242.

Pocock, J.G.A. (1993) "Nature and history, self and other: European perceptions of world history in the age of encounter," mimeo.

Rath, K. (1991) "Essays in Game Theory," unpublished Johns Hopkins PhD dissertation.

Rath, K. (1992) "Existence and representation results for large games with discontinuities," University of Notre Dame, mimeo.

Rath, K. and Yamashige, S. (1993) "On the non-existence of symmetric equilibria," mimeo.

Roberts, D.J. and Sonnenschein, H. (1977) "On the foundations of the theory of monopolistic competition," *Econometrica* 45: 101–113.

Rosen, L. (1989) *The Anthropology of Justice*. Cambridge: Cambridge University Press.

Rorty, R. (1991) *Essays on Heidegger and Others*. New York: Cambridge University Press.

Rudin, W. (1966) *Real Analysis*. New Jersey: McGraw-Hill.

Schmeidler, D. (1973) "Equilibrium points of non-atomic games," *Journal of Statistical Physics* 7: 295–300.

Shafer, W. and Sonnenschein, H. (1976) "Equilibrium with externalities, commodity taxation and lump sum transfers," *International Economic Review* 17: 601–611.

Trouillot, M. (1991) "Anthropology and the savage slot: the poetics and politics of otherness," in R.G. Fox (ed.) *Recapturing Anthropology*. New York: School of American Research Press.

Todorov, T. (1984) *Mikhail Bakhtin: The Dialogical Principle*. Minneapolis: University of Minnesota Press.

Yamashige, S. (1992) "Large Games and Large Economies with Incomplete Information, unpublished Johns Hopkins PhD dissertation.

# 14

# COMPLICATED BEHAVIOR IN MODELS WITH TWO COMMODITIES: A REVIEW

*Mukul Majumdar*

## 1. Introduction

In his *New Palgrave* essay, John Chipman remarked that "a good definition of international-trade theory as it has evolved would be 'general equilibrium theory with structure'". The need for "additional structures" arose out of the emphasis on developing Samuelsonian "comparative statics": meaningful theorems on the qualitative behavior of variables with respect to changes in parameters. "To obtain unambiguous qualitative results, one needs fairly drastic simplifications", noted Chipman, and among such simplifications is the restriction on the number of agents and commodities. "The number 'two' is undoubtedly encountered more frequently in the theory of international trade than in any other field of economics" (Jones 1977) and the appropriateness of "two-by-two" models has been much discussed. One can question the significance of a proposition that does not generalize to higher dimensions in any meaningful way. One can also think of economic problems that cannot even be posed in such a framework. On the other hand, such models can be useful points of departure in research, and can "present a standard of comparison against which truly multi-dimensional results can be appreciated" (Jones 1977).

In the literature on the "pure" theory of trade comparisons of two equilibrium situations have given us valuable insights. However, the underlying adjustments should not be taken for granted. Both *convergence* and its *speed* may be critical for the success of a policy prescription derived from a comparative static exercise. This, of course, is not an original observation. One of the themes of Samuelson's *Foundations* was that "in order for comparative static analysis to yield fruitful results, we must first develop a theory of dynamics". Following his lead, writers in the trade literature have not hesitated to invoke a "stability condition" to assign an appropriate sign to the "denominator" (and invoke the "special structures" to control the "numerator") while studying the derivative of a relevant "variable" with respect to some "parameter" in the model. Early formal expositions (see, for example, Kemp (1964)) recognized some of the difficulties underlying the *correspondence principle*: associated with a particular equilibrium configuration, there may be alternative adjustment processes ("Marshallian" versus "Walrasian") that yield different "stability conditions". By far the dominant practice, however, is to keep such questions in the background and derive some "local" stability conditions in terms of *continuous time* adjustment systems describing the "disequilibrium". Yet, it should not be forgotten that there was already an explicit recognition in the *Foundations* that discrete time models cast in terms of difference equations "were perhaps of even greater importance in economic theory", and that a *non-linear* first order difference equation was "richer" in opening up possibilities of alternative behavior (see Samuelson's (1974) discussion of twenty-four equilibrium points on pages 303–307).

In this chapter, I plan to draw attention to some relatively recent developments in mathematics on the qualitative behavior of dynamical systems. These have led to a better understanding of global stability (or lack of it), cycling and bifurcation properties. The distinction between discrete and continuous time specifications of dynamical systems has also been reiterated. One of the primary lessons to be learned from the mathematics literature is that even *simple* dynamical systems may behave extremely *unpredictably. Complicated behavior* of a dynamic process is due to *non-linearity* rather than complexity of formal specifications. A two commodity model provides in some sense the simplest scenario for an understanding of the complexities of the dynamic process that I review. As Richard Goodwin (1990) put it: "the weird and wonderful world that non-linear dynamics opens up is so complicated that it is highly desirable to keep to low dimensional models" and this is exactly what I do – keeping the tradition of pure theory of international trade in mind – with the belief if complexities are present and are perhaps pervasive in models with two goods, there is no reason why these should disappear in more general frameworks.

In his classic *Survey*, Chipman (1965b) assessed some developments of Walrasian equilibrium theory and their various links to the evolution of ideas in the pure theory of international trade. He felt that "few subjects have been so controversial as the question of stability of equilibrium in international trade". As he put it:

> what we are more interested in now is the stability of a *process*. An adjustment process is (globally) stable if from any given point, every solution path through that point converges to *some* equilibrium. A process is globally unstable if it is not globally stable. It

> is of great interest to know under what conditions the competitive economy is globally stable (in the sense of the "process" being stable); it is also interesting to inquire whether equilibrium is globally stable . . ., in which case the process is stable and equilibrium is unique. This latter is not generally to be expected; but stability of the competitive *process* is usually believed to prevail. However, this is such a subtle and controversial question that we must examine it in detail.

In their well-known paper, Arrow and Hurwicz (1958) established the stability of the tatonnement *process* (formulated in terms of a differential equation) in a two commodity model. Subsequently Scarf's example (1960) of lack of global stability of the tatonnement *process* involved three goods. However, even with two goods an interesting point was made in an example due to Gale (1963) that was used by Chipman (1965b) in the context of international trade. When cast in a discrete time difference equation form even the simple tatonnement process may generate more subtle complications. This has been the subject of Saari's important contributions (1985, 1987). Explicit derivation of *chaotic* behavior of such processes has appeared in Day and Pianigiani (1991) who (like Saari) focused on *topological* or Li–Yorke (1975) chaos, and Bala and Majumdar (1992) who studied *ergodic* chaos. These new results throw light on the nature of cycles, the question of sensitivity of qualitative behavior with respect to variations in parameters like initial conditions, as well as on the possibility of aperiodic, unpredictable trajectories of a dynamical system. Instead of looking at a small neighborhood of a particular *equilibrium* or steady state, we are offered a broader perspective of the entire *process* and the scope of comparative dynamics.

To proceed more formally, suppose that one has a discrete time *non-linear* dynamic model described as

$$x_{t+1} = f(x_t) \tag{1.1}$$

where – it should perhaps be stressed – $f$ is a "relatively simple" ("innocent") real valued continuous function from a non-degenerate compact interval $X$ of reals into itself. Here are two of the theoretical issues:

- What exactly is meant by *chaotic* or *complicated* behavior and how *pervasive* is such behavior in economic models?
- Given an example of a particular type of chaotic behavior, how *robust* is the example?

The first issue has been probed rather deeply in descriptive and optimizing models, both in equilibrium and disequilibrium frameworks.[1] Complex behavior, according to Day and Pianigiani (1991):

> arises in economic processes as a generic consequence of inherent non-linearity. This fact is by now well-known. Its relevance has been explored in models of consumer behavior, business fluctuations, stock market behavior, population dynamics, growth cycles, competitive market mechanisms and optimal intertemporal equilibrium theory.

Alternative definitions of chaos have been examined, with the Li–Yorke or "topological" chaos being the most common.

The question of *robustness* has also been stressed by Day, BenHabib, Grandmont and others. But precise results here are much harder to come by.[2] The problem can be formalized in at least two ways. One can think of varying the function "$f$" over a set in an appropriate function space. Or, one can, in the spirit of Samuelson's comparative dynamics, explicitly introduce a parameter "$\mu$" in some set $\Theta$ and study a *family* of dynamic processes of the form

$$x_{t+1} = f_{\mu}(x_t) \tag{1.2}$$

After agreeing upon a particular definition of chaotic behavior, one can then attempt to show that the set of those parameter values in $\Theta$ that generate such behavior is in a precise sense *non-negligible*. This question of robustness assumed particular importance when it was observed that for a particular $\mu$ in (1.2) a process may be chaotic in some sense, but the "typical" behavior from "almost all" initial conditions can still be very regular (see the remark following Theorem 3). Similarly, if the set of parameter values $\mu$ for which complexities persist in (1.2) is itself "negligible" one can argue that a "typical" model is "regular" or "well-behaved".

To keep the exposition self-contained, some basic definitions and mathematical theorems are summarized in Section 2. The scope of the chapter is restricted to topological as well as ergodic chaos. In Section 3 I take up the question of chaotic behavior of the tatonnement *process* in economies with two commodities. In view of Warlras' law such an economy can be described by a single excess demand function. The first result (due to Bala and Majumdar (1992)) asserts the existence of an excess demand function such that a corresponding discrete time tatonnement process displays both topological and ergodic chaos. In addition, there is a neighborhood of this function such that topological chaos is generated by each tatonnement process for which the excess demand function belongs to this neighborhood. The demonstration is of independent interest since it provides an example of a *computer assisted analytical proof*. Moreover, we can identify a parametric family of excess demand functions (i.e. economies) such that for a non-negligible subclass of this family (i.e. for a subclass of parameter values with positive Lebesgue measure) all the excess demand functions lead to (discrete time) tatonnement processes displaying ergodic chaos. So far it has not been possible to link chaos to specific properties of utility functions and/or endowment patterns.[3] In Section 4 a family of Cobb–Douglas economies is considered following Day and Pianigiani (1991). While they established the presence of (topologically) chaotic behavior for an uncountable set of parameter values, it is shown that such behavior holds for an open set of parameters defining the family of economies.

## 2. Technical preliminaries

Given a map $f$: $X \rightarrow X$, and any $x \in X$ we define $f^0(x) \equiv x$, and for any integer $k \geq 1$,

$$f^k(x) = f(f^{k-1}(x))$$

A point $x \in X$ is a *fixed* point of $f$ if $f(x) = x$. For any integer $k \geq 2$, a point $x \in X$ is a *periodic point of period k* if $f^k(x) = x$, and $f^j(x) \neq x$ for all $j = 1, \ldots, k - 1$. We denote the set of periodic points in $X$ (i.e. points which have period $k$ for some $k \geq 2$) by $\mathscr{P}(X)$. Its complement in $X$, the set of non-periodic points, is denoted by $\mathscr{N}(X)$.

Consider a dynamical system described as $x_{t+1} = f(x_t)$ for $t = 0, 1, 2, \ldots$, where $x_0 \in X$ is the initial position of the system. For characterizing the behavior of this dynamical system we recall the basic Li–Yorke result (see Day and Pianigiani (1991, Theorem 2)):

**Theorem 1** Existence of Topological Chaos. Let $X = [\hat{\alpha}, \hat{\beta}]$ be a non-degenerate compact interval and let f: $X \rightarrow X$ be continuous. Suppose there exist points $a$, $b$, $c$, $d$ in $X$ such that either

$$d \leq a < b < c, \text{ and } f(a) = b, f(b) = c, f(c) = d \qquad \text{(LY)}$$

or

$$d \geq a > b > c, \text{ and } f(a) = b, f(b) = c, f(c) = d. \qquad \text{(LY)}'$$

Then,

(1) for each integer $k \geq 2$ there exists $x_k \in X$ such that $x_k$ is a periodic point of period k for the function $f$.

(2) there is an uncountable set $W \subset \mathscr{N}(X)$ satisfying the following conditions:

(2a) If $p$, $q \in W$ with $p \neq q$ then

$$\limsup_{k\to\infty}|f^k(p) - f^k(q)| > 0, \liminf_{k\to\infty}|f^k(p) - f^k(q)| = 0$$

(2b) $p \in W$ and $q \in \mathscr{P}(X)$ implies

$$\limsup_{k\to\infty}|f^k(p) - f^k(q)| > 0.$$

Theorem 1 provides us with sufficient conditions ((LY) or (LY)′) for a particular type of "turbulent" or "chaotic" behavior. The property (2a) says that there are pairs of initial positions arbitrarily near each other such that the sequences of iterates move apart and return close to each other infinitely often. Furthermore, as (2b) states, if the initial point is in the set $W$, then the system does not tend to any periodic point. Formally,

**Definition 1** $f$ is said to exhibit *topological chaos* on the set $X$ if (1) and (2) hold.

The following result due to Kloeden (1976) indicates that chaotic functions are not isolated. In what follows, when we consider the space $C(X)$ of bounded continuous functions on $X$, we use the usual "sup" norm[4] to define a distance on $C(X)$.

**Theorem 2** Pervasiveness of Topological Chaos. Let $X = [\hat{\alpha}, \hat{\beta}]$ and $f: X \rightarrow X$ be continuous. Given any $\varepsilon > 0$, there is a continuous $g: X \rightarrow X$ such that

$$\|f - g\| < \varepsilon$$

and $g$ exhibits topological chaos.

Roughly speaking, for any continuous $f: X \rightarrow X$, there is some continuous $g: X \rightarrow X$ sufficiently close to $f$ which displays topological chaos. Next, we identify circumstances under which chaos prevails in an open neighborhood containing a continuous $f: X \rightarrow X$. The following result (Bala and Majumdar (1992, Corollary 3.1)) gives conditions under which the Li–Yorke topological chaos is robust with respect to perturbations of the function $f$ (defining the dynamical system) in the space $C(X)$.

**Theorem 3** Robustness of Topological Chaos. Let $X = [\hat{\alpha}, \hat{\beta}]$ and $f: X \rightarrow X$ satisfy (LY) in Theorem 1 with the strict inequality $d < a$ or (LY)′ with strict inequality $d > a$. In addition, suppose $\hat{\alpha} < r(X,f) < R(X,f) < \hat{\beta}$, where $R(X,f)$ and $r(X,f)$ are the maximum and minimum respectively of $f$ on the interval $X$. Then, there exists an open neighborhood $H \subset C(X)$, containing $f$, such that $g \in \mathrm{H}$ implies that (1) and (2) of Theorem 1 hold with $g$ in place of $f$.

It has been argued that the Li–Yorke topological chaos may be "unobservable" since the uncountable set $W$ may have Lebesgue measure zero.[5] A different notion of "complicated" behavior has been formalized by using concepts from ergodic theory. Consider a probability space $(X, \Sigma, \upsilon)$ and a $\Sigma$-measurable map $f: X \rightarrow X$; $\upsilon$ is *invariant under* $f$ if $\upsilon(E) = \upsilon(f^{-1}(E))$ for all $E$ in $\Sigma$; $\upsilon$ is *ergodic* if "$E \in \Sigma, f^{-1}(E) = E$" implies "$\upsilon(E) = 0$ or $\upsilon(E) = 1$". Take $X = [\hat{\alpha}, \hat{\beta}]$ and $\Sigma$ to be the Borel $\sigma$-field of $[\hat{\alpha}, \hat{\beta}]$. We introduce formally the definition of *ergodic chaos*:

**Definition 2** A Borel measurable $f$: $[\hat{\alpha}, \hat{\beta}] \rightarrow [\hat{\alpha}, \hat{\beta}]$ exhibits *ergodic chaos* if there is an ergodic invariant measure $\upsilon$ that is absolutely continuous with respect to the Lebesgue measure.

Roughly speaking, if $f$ exhibits ergodic chaos, then for $\upsilon$-almost every initial point $x \in X$ (hence, from a set of initial conditions with positive Lebesgue measure), the sequence of iterates $\{f^k(x)\}$ will "fill up" the support of the measure $\upsilon$; consequently, the dynamics of the system $(X, f)$ will be complicated.

We first state a result (Misiurewicz (1981), see also Grandmont (1988), Collet and Eckmann (1980), Ruelle (1989: 58)) giving sufficient conditions for ergodic chaos. First we introduce the notion of a Schwarzian derivative. Let $X = [\hat{\alpha}, \hat{\beta}]$ and $f$: $X \rightarrow R$ be of class $C^3$. The Schwarzian derivative $Sf(x)$ is given by

$$Sf(x) \equiv f'''(x)/f'(x) - (3/2)\{f''(x)/f'(x)\}^2, \; x \in X, \; f'(x) \neq 0$$

**Theorem 4** Existence of Ergodic Chaos. Let $f$: $X \rightarrow X$ satisfy:

(i) $f$ is of class $C^3$, and there exists $x^* \in (\hat{\alpha}, \hat{\beta})$ such that $f'(x^*) = 0$, $f'(x) > 0$ for $x < x^*$, $f'(x) < 0$ for $x > x^*$, $f''(x^*) < 0$.
(ii) $f(x) > x$ for all $x \in (\hat{\alpha}, x^*)$, $f(x^*) \in (x^*, \hat{\beta})$, $Sf(x) < 0$ for all $x \in X$ except $x = x^*$.
(iii) There exists $k \geq 2$ such that $y = f^k(x^*)$ is an unstable fixed point of $f$, i.e. satisfies $f(y) = y$, $|f'(y)| > 1$.

Then $f$ exhibits ergodic chaos.

Let us now turn to the robustness question for ergodic chaos. Here, a fundamental result characterizes a particular class of functions that has played a special role in the development of the theory of dynamical systems.

Let $X = [0, 1]$. Consider the parametric family $\mathscr{F}$ of maps $f_\mu$: $[0, 1] \times [2, 4] \rightarrow [0, 1]$ defined as

$$\mathscr{F} = \{f_\mu : f_\mu(x) = \mu x(1 - x), \; x \in [0, 1] \text{ and } \mu \in [2, 4]\}$$

The following result due to Jakobson (1981) (see also Benedicks and Carleson (1985)) throws light on the issue of robustness of ergodic chaos from a measure theoretic point of view. We shall use it in conjunction with the result of Debreu (1974) to develop "robust" examples of price adjustment processes that display ergodic chaos.

**Theorem 5** Robustness of Ergodic Chaos over $\mathscr{F}$. There is a set $M \subset [2, 4]$ with positive Lebesgue measure that if $\mu \in M$ then $f_\mu \equiv \mu x(1 - x)$, $x \in [0, 1]$ exhibits ergodic chaos.

## 3. Robust chaos

To start out with a historical note, let me quote from Chipman (1965a):

> The laws of adjustment specified by Walras were described as trials or *tatonnements*. Curiously enough, he described the process in words, but did not include it in his mathematics; it remained for Samuelson (1948, Chapters 9–11) to do so. The principle is very simple: when the demand for a commodity exceeds the supply, its price will rise, and when the demand falls short of the supply, its price will fall. This is an old principle, described by Mill (1848, pp. 549–552 of 1895 edition) and Smith (1776, pp. 48–56) and which undoubtedly can be traced back farther still.

The limitations of tatonnement as an adjustment process have been discussed in Arrow and Hahn (1971). Notwithstanding the difficulties, the Arrow and Hurwicz result (1958) on the ("system") stability of the *process* gives a simple example of how a price mechanism responding to the forces of excess demand or supply can lead to some equilibrium. Since economic theory also has a tradition of "period" analysis, it is natural to inquire whether such a result carries over to discrete time formulation. The work of Saari (1985, 1987) led to the recognition that "positive" results may not be obtainable for a large class of adjustment processes (including tatonnement). Recall that two variants of the tatonnement have received attention. I shall use examples of both: the "normalized" process, in which the price of one of the two goods – that of the "numéraire" is fixed, and the "non-normalized" process in which all goods are treated symmetrically.

Let us consider first the possibilities of chaos in a competitive economy with two commodities where the discrete time tatonnement is non-normalized. Ideally, one would like to start with the characteristics of individual agents and derive the relevant market excess demand functions. It was easier, however, to deal directly with the excess demand functions (assuming Walras' law) and not to treat the agents explicitly.

Let $I^0 \equiv (0, 1)$, and for $\varepsilon < {}^1\!/_2$ let $I_\varepsilon \equiv [\varepsilon, 1 - \varepsilon]$. $I_\varepsilon$ may be regarded as the projection of the set $S_\varepsilon$ onto its first coordinate, where $S_\varepsilon$ is defined as:

$$S_\varepsilon \equiv \{(p, q){:}p^2 + q^2 = 1, p \geq \varepsilon, q \leq \sqrt{2\varepsilon - \varepsilon^2}\}.$$

For any continuous, real-valued function $\phi$ on $I^0$, there exists a continuous function $\hat{\phi}$ on $I^0$, obtained via Walras' Law:

$$\hat{\phi}(p) \equiv -(1 - p^2)^{-1/2} p\phi(p), p \in I^0.$$

Now, Debreu's theorem implies that for any continuous function $\phi$ on $I^0$, and for any $\varepsilon$ in (0, 1/2), there exists a two-agent, two-commodity exchange economy with each agent having strictly convex, continuous and monotone preferences, whose excess demand functions agree with $(\phi, \hat{\phi})$ on the set $I_\varepsilon$. In what follows, $I$ represents an economy $\mathscr{E}$ by its excess demand function.

In the tatonnement process, prices are raised (resp. lowered) in response to positive (resp. negative) excess demand and left unchanged at the competitive equilibrium. Thus, for the excess demand function $Z(p)$, given an initial condition $p_0 \in I_\varepsilon$, we have for each $t \geq 0$:

$$p_{t+1} = \begin{cases} p_t + \lambda Z(p_t), & \text{if } p_t + \lambda Z(p_t) \in I_\varepsilon \\ 1 - \varepsilon, & \text{if } p_t + \lambda Z(p_t) > 1 - \varepsilon \\ \varepsilon, & \text{if } p_t + \lambda Z(p_t) < \varepsilon \end{cases} \tag{3.1}$$

where $\lambda > 0$ is a "speed of adjustment" parameter. For the excess demand functions we shall deal with, the sequence $(p_t)$ satisfying (3.1) will stay in $I_\varepsilon$ if it starts in $I_\varepsilon$, so the second and third cases of (3.1) are written out to complete the formality.

We can now discuss a result that establishes simultaneous occurrence of topological and ergodic chaos, where the topological chaos, in fact, is also "robust".

**Proposition 1** Consider an open interval $J = (0, 0.01)$. For every $\varepsilon \in J$, there exists an economy $\zeta_\varepsilon \in C(I_\varepsilon)$ such that:

(3.1a) There is some $\bar{p}$, $\varepsilon < \bar{p} < 1 - \varepsilon$, with $\zeta_\varepsilon(\bar{p}) = 0$. In addition,
(3.1a′) for a neighborhood $(\bar{p} - \eta, \bar{p} + \eta) \subset I_\varepsilon$, the excess demand function $\zeta_\varepsilon$ is strictly decreasing
(3.1b) the tatonnement process

$$p_{t+1} = p_t + \lambda\zeta_\varepsilon(p_t)$$

exhibits ergodic chaos on $I_\varepsilon$.

Furthermore, there exists an open neighborhood $\Gamma$ (depending on $\varepsilon$) of $\zeta_\varepsilon$ such that if $\phi \in \Gamma$, then (3.1a, a′, b) above holds for $\phi$ in place of $\zeta_\varepsilon$, and

(3.1c) the tatonnement process

$$p_{t+1} = p_t + \lambda\phi(p_t)$$

exhibits topological chaos on $I_\varepsilon$.

*Some remarks on the proof* I want to indicate the unusual computation that was needed to invoke Theorem 4 in order to assert the presence of ergodic chaos. First, we start with the family

$$h_\mu(p) = \mu p(1 - p),\ 3 < \mu < 4,\ p \in (0, 1). \tag{3.2}$$

Note that $h'(p^*) = 0$ where $p^* = 1/2$. Also $h_\mu(\bar{p}) = \bar{p}$ at $\bar{p} = (\mu - 1)/\mu$, and

$|h'_\mu(\bar{p})| > 1$. In order to verify the condition (iii) of Theorem 4, we require for some $k \geqq 2$ and some $\mu \in (3, 4)$

$$h_\mu^{\,k}(p^*) - (1 - 1/\mu) = 0. \tag{3.3}$$

Using integer arithmetic on the computer, the roots of equation (3.3) can be shown to be the same as the roots to the 32-degree equation:

$$\begin{aligned} P(\mu) = {} & (4294967296 - 4294967296\mu + 1073741824\mu^6 - 268435456\mu^7 - \\ & 268435456\mu^8 - 134217728\mu^9 - 150994944\mu^{10} + 251658240\mu^{11} + \\ & 16777216\mu^{12} + 41943040\mu^{13} - 77594624\mu^{14} - 67108864\mu^{15} + \\ & 76546048\mu^{16} + 5177344\mu^{17} - 14745600\mu^{18} - 6684672\mu^{19} + \\ & 3342336\mu^{20} + 5341184\mu^{21} - 3891200\mu^{22} - 8192\mu^{23} + 954368\mu^{24} - \\ & 406016\mu^{25} + 27136\mu^{26} + 35840\mu^{27} - 16128\mu^{28} + 3520\mu^{29} - 448\mu^{30} + \\ & 32\mu^{31} - \mu^{32})/(4294967296\mu). \end{aligned}$$

To show that there exists a root between 3.92 and 3.93, we evaluate the above equation at $\mu_1 = (392/100)$ and $\mu_2 = (393/100)$. Again, computer calculations show that:

$$P(392/100) = -\frac{92981404266896745193936775546482577362649088}{10625181290357943453273037448525428771972656 25}$$

and

$$P(393/100) = \frac{4242302387981546296165032618431388061333325990582938391445071455429193599}{168792214732800000000000000000000000000000000000000000000000000000000000000}$$

Since $P(\mu)$ changes sign, the intermediate value theorem ensures the result. We shall denote the root lying in (3.92, 3.93) as $\mu^*$. Likewise, we shall write

$$h^*(p) \equiv h_{\mu^*}(p) = \mu^* p(1 - p).$$

We require a restriction on $\varepsilon$ which ensures that $p_{t+1} = h^*(p_\varepsilon)$ remains in $I_\varepsilon$ for every initial $p_0 \in I_\varepsilon$. This leads to the restriction $\varepsilon$ must be in the interval $J = (0, 0.01)$. Now Theorem 4 can be invoked to prove (3.1a–b). Theorem 3 is used to get (3.1c). See Bala and Majumdar (1992) for details. Q.E.D.

**Remark 1** Convergence problems of more general iterative processes have been considered by Saari (1985). We are alerted by Theorem 2 that difficulties are likely to persist even when more general schemes are proposed. An interesting mathematical result due to Yamaguti and Matano (1979) on the speed of adjustment is as follows. Consider the difference equation: $x_{t+1} = x_t + (\Delta t)f(x_t)$ where $f$ satisfies (i) continuity, (ii) $f(0) = f(\bar{u}) = 0$ for some $\bar{u} > 0$, (iii) $f(u) > 0$ $(0 < u < \bar{u})$, $f(u) < 0$ $(\bar{u} < u < k$, $k$ may be plus infinity). There is some $c_1 > 0$ such that for all $\Delta t > c_1$, this difference equation is Li–Yorke chaotic.

Can one invoke appropriate "special structures" to rule out the possibilities exposed by Proposition 1? It is useful to elaborate on this point. We shall see that as long as such "special structures" admit a particular family (see equation (3.4) below) of excess demand functions, non-normalized price adjustment processes displaying even ergodic chaos can always be constructed, and such ergodic chaos is a "non-negligible" part of this family. To proceed more formally, let $\{b_n\}$ be a strictly increasing sequence of real numbers such that (i) for all $n \geq 1$, $b_n \in [2, 4)$ and (ii) $b_n \uparrow 4$.

Consider sets of the form $M \cap [2, b_n]$, where $M$ is the set in Theorem 5. Clearly there exists some $n'$ such that $M \cap [2, b_{n'}]$ has positive Lebesgue measure. Let $\Lambda \equiv M \cap [2, b_{n'}]$. We fix attention on the family of functions $\hat{\mathcal{F}}$ given by:

$$\hat{\mathcal{F}} = \{f_\mu | f_\mu(x) = \mu x(1 - x) \text{ where } 2 \leq \mu \leq b_{n'}\}.$$

Since $b_{n'} < 4$, it is easy to see that every member $f_\mu$ in $\hat{\mathcal{F}}$ is bounded above by $b_{n'}/4 < 1$. Fix $\varepsilon$ sufficiently small and $0 < \varepsilon < 1 - b_{n'}/4$. It is not difficult to show that for all $\mu \in [2, b_{n'}]$, $f_\mu$ maps $I_\varepsilon$ back into itself. Hence each $f_\mu$ in $\hat{\mathcal{F}}$ can be regarded as defining a dynamical system on $I_\varepsilon$. Now fix the adjustment parameter $\lambda$ in the tatonnement process. For each $\mu \in [2, b_{n'}]$ let $\mathcal{E}_\mu$ be the economy defined as

$$\zeta_\mu(p) = \lambda^{-1} \{(\mu - 1)p - \mu p^2\}, p \in I_\varepsilon. \tag{3.4}$$

It is easily shown that each economy $\mathcal{E}_\mu$ has a unique competitive equilibrium $\bar{p}(\mu) = (\mu - 1)/\mu$ which lies in the interior of $I_\varepsilon$.

The tatonnement process applied to the economy $\mathcal{E}_\mu$ generates the corresponding dynamical system $f_\mu$ in $\hat{\mathcal{F}}$. From Theorem 5 and the above discussion, it follows that:

**Proposition 2** There exists a set of positive Lebesgue measure $\Lambda \equiv M \cap [2, b_{n'}]$ such that if $\mu \in \Lambda$ then the tatonnement process exhibits ergodic chaos for the economy $\mathcal{E}_\mu$. The economy $\mathcal{E}_\mu$ has a unique equilibrium $\bar{p}$ which lies in the interior of $I_\varepsilon$ and the excess demand function is strictly decreasing in a neighborhood of $\bar{p}$.

## 4. Chaos in Cobb–Douglas economies

Reflection on the two formal results may alert the reader that there are unresolved issues related to the pervasiveness of complicated behavior. For example, in Proposition 1, there seems to be no "natural" way to identify a measure theoretic size of the neighborhoods $\Gamma$ in the function space on which topological chaos persists. Secondly, one can question why a family like equation (3.4) is of intrinsic interest to economists. Surely, a non-negligible subclass of the quadratic family may still be negligible in a wider class of economies. The point that does seem to emerge is that examples of chaotic behavior are by no means isolated, and (uncountably) many economies (in some sense close to each other) generate such behavior if a tatonnement is used.

It should be recalled that some "troubles" with the tatonnement were earlier linked to the dominance of income effects. So far we have not been able to identify similar "sources" for complications. Efforts to describe families like equation (3.4) in terms of utility functions and endowments have not yet led to any striking insights or intuitive results. However, significant progress has been made in another direction. Studies of economies where the utility functions are Cobb–Douglas, have led to examples of (topologically) chaotic tatonnement. In what follows, I shall sketch how the earlier results of Day and Pianigiani (1991) can be refined to assert "robustness" in a precise sense. To facilitate computations, we use "normalized" price adjustment processes.

Consider an exchange economy with two (price taking) agents and two commodities. Denote the two agents by $i = 1, 2$ and the goods by $x$ and $y$. Agent 1 has an initial endowment $w^1 = (4, 0)$ while agent 2 has $w^2 = (0, 2)$. Let $\alpha$, $\beta$ be two real numbers in the interval $(0, 1)$. The utility function of agent 1 is $u^1(x, y) = x^{\alpha}y^{1-\alpha}$ and that of agent 2 is $u^2(x, y) = x^{\beta}y^{1-\beta}$ for $(x, y)$ in the consumption space $R^2_+$; a typical economy $e$ can thus be described by the pair $(\alpha, \beta)$ which refers to the exponents of the utility functions of the agents. We shall denote the space of Cobb–Douglas economies defined in this manner by $\mathscr{E}_{\mathrm{CD}} \equiv (0, 1) \times (0, 1)$. Of particular interest for our purposes is the economy $\bar{e} = (3/4, 1/2)$.

Fixing the price of good $y$ as 1, and that of $x$ as $p \geq 0$, the excess demand function for good $x$ is denoted by $z(p; e)$ and is given by:

$$z(p; e) = 2\beta/p - 4(1 - \alpha), e = (\alpha, \beta). \tag{4.1}$$

For every $e \in \mathrm{E}_{\mathrm{CD}}$ there is a unique competitive equilibrium $p^*(e)$ given by:

$$p^*(e) = \beta/2(1 - \alpha). \tag{4.2}$$

In particular, for $\bar{e} = (3/4, 1/2)$, $p^*(\bar{e}) = 1$.

The tatonnement process is described by $p_{t+1} = T(p_t, e, \lambda)$ where

$$T(p_t, e, \lambda) = p_t + \lambda z(p_t; e), \tag{4.3}$$

and $\lambda > 0$ is a "speed of adjustment" parameter. Of particular interest for our purpose is the case where $\lambda = 361/100$. We denote this value as $\bar{\lambda}$.

Substituting equation (4.1) in equation (4.3) we get

$$p_{t+1} = T(p_t, e, \lambda) = p_t + \lambda[2\beta/p_t - 4(1 - \alpha)]. \tag{4.4}$$

Equation (4.4) is a dynamical system parameterized by $e = (\alpha, \beta)$ and $\lambda \in R_{++}$. We then have:

**Proposition 3** There exist open sets $N \subset \mathscr{E}_{\mathrm{CD}}$ and $\mathrm{V} \subset R_{++}$ such that if $e = (\alpha, \beta) \in N$ and $\lambda \in \mathrm{V}$ then the process (4.4) exhibits topological chaos.

**Proof** Let $\mathrm{K} \subset \mathscr{E}_{\mathrm{CD}}$ and $\Lambda \subset R_{++}$ be compact sets containing $\bar{e} = (3/4, 1/2)$

and $\bar{\lambda} = 361/100$ in their respective interiors. For $e = \bar{e}$ and $\lambda = \bar{\lambda}$ equation (4.4) becomes

$$P_{t+1} = T(p_t, \bar{e}, \bar{\lambda}) = p_t + 361/(100p_t) - 361/100. \tag{4.5}$$

For convenience, we shall write $T(p, \bar{e}, \bar{\lambda})$ simply as $T(p)$. Let $X$ denote the interval [0.18, 17]. If $p_t \in X$ then $p_{t+1} \in X$ as well. This follows because the global minimum of $T$ is at 1.9 (from the first and second order conditions) where $T$ takes the value $0.19 > 0.18$. Likewise the maximum value of $T$ is at 0.18 where it takes the value $16.63 < 17$. Hence $T$ maps the interval $X$ strictly into the interior of $X$.

It is then easy to verify that $T$ satisfies condition (LY) on the interval $X$, i.e. that there are points $a$, $b$, $c$, $d$ in X such that $c < b < a < d$ and $T(a) = b$, $T(b) = c$, $T(c) = d$. Specifically, let $a = 3.75$. Then $b = T(a) = 1.9$, $c = T(b) = 0.19$ and $d = T(c) = 15.58 > a$. Thus the process (4.5) exhibits topological chaos on $X$.

Clearly, the conditions of Theorem 3 are satisfied by the map $T$ (regarded as a function from $X$ to $X$). Hence, there exists some $\varepsilon > 0$ such that if $g \in C(X)$ satisfies

$$\sup_{p \in X} |T(p) - g(p)| < \varepsilon \tag{4.6}$$

then $g$ also exhibits topological chaos on $X$.

Recall that $T(p) \equiv T(p, \bar{e}, \bar{\lambda})$, where $\bar{e}$ lies in the interior of the compact set $K \subset \mathscr{E}_{CD}$ and $\bar{\lambda}$ is in the interior of the compact set $\Lambda$. Now, for $e = (\alpha, \beta) \in K$ and $\lambda \in \Lambda$ the map $T(p, e, \lambda)$ given by equation (4.6) above is clearly jointly continuous on the compact set $X \times K \times \Lambda$. Let $e'$ be another economy in $K$ and $\lambda' \varepsilon \Lambda$. By uniform continuity, there exists $\delta > 0$ such that if the (four-dimensional) Euclidean distance

$$d((p, e, \lambda), (p', e', \lambda')) < \delta \tag{4.7}$$

then

$$|T(p, e, \lambda) - T(p', e', \lambda')| < \varepsilon. \tag{4.8}$$

Let $N \times V$ be an open set in the interior of $K \times \Lambda$ containing $(\bar{e}, \bar{\lambda})$ and having radius less than $\delta$. If $e \in N$ and $\lambda \in V$ then for each $p \in X$,

$$d((p, \bar{e}, \bar{\lambda}), (p, e, \lambda)) < \delta$$

and, hence,

$$|T(p, \bar{e}, \bar{\lambda}) - T(p, e, \lambda)| < \varepsilon. \tag{4.9}$$

Taking the supremum over all $p \in X$ we note that $(e, \lambda) \in N \times V$ implies $T(\bullet, e, \lambda)$ is within $\varepsilon$ sup norm distance of $T(\bullet, \bar{e}, \bar{\lambda})$. Since the relation (4.6) is satisfied by every mapping $T(\bullet, e, \lambda)$ with $(e, \lambda) \in N \times V$, the tatonnement process exhibits topological chaos on an open set of

Cobb–Douglas economies, for an open set of "rate of adjustment" parameters $\lambda$. Q.E.D.

## Concluding remarks

If one is interested in the stability or global behavior of an *adjustment process*, complicated behavior emerges in examples that are by no means pathological or isolated. The results reviewed above may lead one to ask "where do we go from here?"

Let me conclude by quoting yet another thoughtful passage from Chipman (1987):

> The fact that national governments act independently leads to the need to analyze the effects of country-specific shocks, which take the form of intensification or liberalization of restrictions on trade or capital movements, unilateral transfers such as reparation payments, gifts or loans and disparities in monetary and fiscal policies. For this reason the emphasis in international trade theory has from the beginning been on comparative statics. One wants to ascertain the qualitative, if not quantitative, effect of a tariff or quota or transfer on the various quantities involved. To obtain unambiguous qualitative results one needs fairly drastic simplifications and strong assumptions. On the other hand, the emphasis in general equilibrium theory has been on proving the existence, stability and Pareto optimality of competitive equilibrium for which much milder assumptions are required . . . The requirements of "simplicity" in a theory are not absolute, but vary with the goals of the theory and the technical resources available to researchers at the time. With the increasing possibilities of handling large-scale models and data sets and estimating their parameters numerically, it is natural to expect a movement of both general-equilibrium traditions towards each other.

## Notes

This chapter is dedicated with affection and respect to Professor John S. Chipman on his sixty-fifth birthday. He was the guru to many of us studying the pure theory of international trade as graduate students in the sixties. I am particularly indebted to Professor Venkatesh Bala of McGill University for his help in completing the proofs and for graciously permitting me to report on our collaborative efforts. Thanks are also due to Professors David Easley, Don Saari, Richard Day, Tapan Mitra, and Henry Wan for many helpful discussions. In preparing this version, I have benefited from the detailed comments of Professors Debraj Ray and Manjira Datta on stylistic as well as substantive issues.

1 Several excellent surveys from different perspectives are already available. As a "random" sample, see Baumol and BenHabib (1989), Day and Pianigiani (1991), Grandmont (1985), Brock and Dechert (1990), Saari (1991).

2 See Day and Shafer (1987), Bala and Majumdar (1992), and Majumdar and Mitra (1994a–b).

3 After the completion of this paper Tapan Mitra showed me an example of a class of exchange economies in which the tatonnement (normalized) process is represented by the quadratic family. This example is discussed in detail in Bala, Majumdar and Mitra (1995).

4 For any function $f$ in $C(X)$, define the norm $\|f\| = \sup_{x \in X} |f(x)|$. Of course, if $X$ is a compact nondegenerate real interval, continuity implies boundedness.

5 Consider the map $f(x) = \mu x(1-x)$ defined on [0, 1]. For a value of $\mu$ near 3.83 it can be shown that $f^3(1/2) = 1/2$. As $^1/_2$ is a periodic point of period 3 (by the Sarkovski–Li–Yorke result) there are periodic points of every prime period and there is an uncountable set $W$ from which we have chaotic dynamics. Nevertheless, it is possible to show that the orbit of $^1/_2$ is "asymptotically stable" and attracts (Lebesgue) almost all points of [0, 1].

## Bibliography


Arrow, K.J. and Hurwicz, L. (1958) "On the Stability of Competitive Equilibrium, I," *Econometrica* 26: 522–552.

Arrow, K.J. and Hahn, F. (1971) *General Competitive Analysis*. San Francisco: Holden Day.

Bala, V. and Majumdar, M. (1992) "Chaotic Tatonnement," *Economic Theory* 2: 437–445.

Bala, V., Majumdar, M. and Mitra, T. (1995) "Controlling Chaos: Some Analytical Results and Applications to Tatonnement," presented at the Fifth Viennese Workshop on Advances in Nonlinear Dynamics.

Baumol, W.J. and BenHabib, J. (1989) "Chaos: Significance, Mechanism and Economic Applications," *Journal of Economic Perspectives* 3: 77–105.

Benedicks, M. and Carleson, L. (1985) "On Iteration of $1 - ax^2$ on $(-1, 1)$," *Annals of Mathematics* 122: 1–25.

Brock, W.A. and Dechert, W.D. (1990) "Nonlinear Dynamical Systems: Instability and Chaos in Economics," in W. Hildenbrand and H. Sonnenschein (eds) *Handbook of Mathematical Economics*, 4: 2209–2235.

Chipman, J.S. (1965a) "The Nature and Meaning of Equilibrium in Economic Theory," in D. Martindale (ed.) *Functionalism in Social Sciences*. Reprinted in H. Townsend (ed.) (1971) *Price Theory*. Harmondsworth, UK: Penguin Books Ltd.

Chipman, J.S. (1965b) "A Survey of the Theory of International Trade: Part 2, The Neoclassical Theory," *Econometrica* 23: 685–760.

Chipman, J.S. (1987) "International Trade" in J. Eatwell, M. Milgate, and P. Newman (eds) *The New Palgrave*, pp. 922–954. London: Macmillan.

Collet, P. and Eckmann, J.P. (1980) *Iterated Maps on the Interval as Dynamical Systems*. Boston: Birkhauser.

Day, R.H. and Pianigiani, G. (1991) "Statistical Dynamics and Economics," *Journal of Economic Behavior and Organization* 16 (1–2): 37–84.

Day, R.H. and Shafer, W. (1987) "Ergodic Fluctuations in Deterministic Economic Models," *Journal of Economic Behavior and Organizations* 8: 339–361.

Debreu, G. (1974) "Excess Demand Functions," *Journal of Mathematical Economics* 1: 15–23.

Gale, D. (1963) "A Note on the Global Instability of Competitive Equilibrium," *Naval Research Logistics Quarterly* 10: 81–87.

Goodwin, Richard M. (1990) *Chaotic Economic Dynamics*. Oxford: Clarendon Press.

Grandmont, J.M. (1985) "On Endogenous Competitive Business Cycles," *Econometrica* 53(5): 995–1046.

Grandmont, J.M. (1988) "Non-linear Difference Equations, Bifurcations and Chaos: an Introduction," *CEPREMAP* Working Paper, no. 8811, Paris.

Jakobson, M.V. (1981) "Absolutely Continuous Invariant Measures for One-Parameter Families of One-Dimensional Maps," *Communications in Mathematical Physics* 81: 39–88.

Jones, R.W. (1977) "'Two-Ness' in Trade Theory: Costs and Benefits," Special Papers in International Economics, No. 12, International Finance Section, Department of Economics, Princeton University.

Kemp, M.C. (1964) *The Pure Theory of International Trade*. New Jersey: Prentice-Hall.

Kloeden, P.E. (1976) "Chaotic Difference Equations are Dense," *Bulletin of the Australian Mathematical Society* 15: 371–379.

Li, T. and Yorke, J.A. (1975) "Period Three Implies Chaos," *American Mathematical Monthly* 82: 985–992.

Majumdar, M. and Mitra, T. (1994a) "Periodic and Chaotic Programs of Optimal Intertemporal Allocation in an Aggregative Model with Wealth Effects," *Economic Theory*: 649–676.

Majumdar, M. and Mitra, T. (1994b) "Robust Ergodic Chaos in Discounted Dynamic Optimization Models," *Economic Theory* 4: 677–688.

Mill, J.S. (1848) *Principles of Political Economy*, 1. Appleton-Century-Crofts, 5th edition, 1895.

Misiurewicz, M. (1981) "Absolutely Continuous Measures for Certain Maps of an Interval," *Publications Mathematiques* 53: 17–51.

Neary, J.P. (1985) "Two-by-two International Trade Theory with Many Goods and Factors," *Econometrica* 53: 1233–1248.

Ruelle, D. (1989) *Chaotic Evolution and Strange Attractions*. Cambridge: Cambridge University Press.

Saari, D.G. (1985) "Iterative Price Mechanisms," *Econometrica* 53: 1117–1131.

Saari, D.G. (1987) "Some Informational Requirements for Convergence," *Journal of Complexity* 3: 302–311.

Saari, D.G. (1991) "Erratic Behavior in Economic Models," *Journal of Economic Behavior and Organization* 16(1–2): 3–36.

Samuelson, Paul A. (1947) *Foundations of Economic Analysis*. Cambridge, MA: Harvard University Press.

Scarf, H. (1960) "Some Examples of Global Instability of Competitive Equilibrium," *International Economic Review* 1: 157–172.

Smith, A. (1933) *An Inquiry into the Nature and Causes of the Wealth of Nations*, vol. 1 (1776). London: Dent.

Yamaguti, Masay and Matano, Hiroshi (1979) "Euler's Finite Difference Scheme and Chaos," *Proceedings of Japan Academy* 55(A): 78–80.

# 15

# COMPUTING WILLINGNESS-TO-PAY IN RANDOM UTILITY MODELS

*Daniel McFadden*

Welfare evaluation of a policy that alters the resource allocation can often be cast as the problem of calculating mean *Willingness to Pay* (WTP) in a population of consumers with a distribution of utilities induced by varying tastes and budgets. This interpretation is particularly useful when some of the components of choice at the level of the individual are discrete. This chapter reviews the theory of WTP measurement, and provides easily computed WTP bounds. If preferences satisfy the *parallel Engle curve condition* of Chipman and Moore, so indirect utility is linear in income with a coefficient that does not vary with consumer, alternative, or allocation, then mean WTP can be characterized as the compensating variation for a *representative consumer* who has the *expected* utility function. Absent the parallel condition, compensating variations in the expected utility function do not in general yield mean WTP. The chapter reviews *generalized extreme value* (GEV) random utility models, which yield an analytic expression for expected utility, and when the parallel Engle curve condition holds, an analytic *log sum* formula for mean WTP coincides with the compensating variation that keeps expected utility constant. An example shows that when utility is nonlinear in income, so the parallel Engle curve condition does not hold, compensating variation calculated from expected utility can give substantially biased estimates of mean WTP. Finally, the chapter describes a Monte Carlo Markov Chain (MCMC) simulation method that can be used to obtain accurate estimates of mean WTP in GEV random utility models that do not satisfy the parallel Engle curve condition. This procedure is of independent interest as a method for obtaining random draws from a GEV density.

## Introduction

Welfare evaluation of a policy that alters the quality of a resource can often be cast as the problem of calculating mean *consumer surplus*, or *Willingness to Pay* (WTP), in a population of consumers with varying tastes and budgets. This interpretation is particularly useful when some of the components of choice at the level of the individual are discrete. There are special circumstances under which the mean WTP can be calculated *as if* there were a single representative consumer; these coincide with the conditions under which individual preferences can be aggregated into a social preference order. However, in general it is necessary to develop procedures for explicit aggregation of the WTP of the individual consumers.

The next section reviews the theory of mean WTP in *random utility models* (RUM), and gives some easily computed bounds. The section that follows considers indirect utility functions that are additively separable in unobserved effects and in (linear or nonlinear) functions of income. The fourth section reviews the theory of WTP in *generalized extreme value* (GEV) random utility models, where analytic formulas for WTP result when indirect utility satisfies the *parallel Engle curve condition* of Chipman and Moore (1980); see also Deaton and Muellbauer (1980: 149). The fifth section considers a representative consumer approximation to WTP for a GEV model that is nonlinear in income, and shows that it can be substantially biased. And the sixth section describes a simulation method that can be used to obtain an accurate estimate of mean WTP in GEV random utility models that are nonlinear in income.

## Equivalent variation in random utility models

Suppose consumers face $i = 1, \ldots, J$ mutually exclusive and exhaustive discrete alternatives.[1] The consumer has income $y$. If alternative $i$ is chosen, there is an "access charge" ($t_i$); a "user fee" per unit of consumption ($p_i$), which may be zero; and a vector of other attributes ($x_i$). There may be other commodity prices in the background. If restricted to alternative $i$, the consumer will maximize preferences subject to this restriction and subject to the constraints imposed by the availability of time and income. The result will be a level of satisfaction that can be characterized by an *indirect utility* function $U(y - t_i, p_i, x_i, \varepsilon_i)$ that is homogeneous of degree zero and quasi-convex in income and prices (including those in the background), increasing in income, and non-increasing in prices; see, for example, Diamond and McFadden (1974) and Varian (1984). Consumers are heterogeneous in unobserved factors that influence their behaviour (e.g. tastes). The effects of these unobserved factors are summarized by $\varepsilon_i$. Let $\boldsymbol{t} = (t_1, \ldots, t_J)$, $\boldsymbol{p} = (p_1, \ldots, p_J)$, $\boldsymbol{x} = (x_1, \ldots, x_J)$. Consumers choose $i$ to maximize

$U(y - t_i,p_i,x_i,\varepsilon_i)$. The proportion $P_i(y,\boldsymbol{t},\boldsymbol{p},\boldsymbol{x})$ of consumers choosing $i$ is given by the probability of the event

$U(y - t_i,p_i,x_i,\varepsilon_i) > U(y - t_j,p_j,x_j,\varepsilon_j)$ for $j \neq i$.

A typical application of this setup is choice of recreational fishing trips, with the alternatives $i$ distinguished by fishing site and duration of trip. The access charge $t_i$ will be transportation and living expenses for the trip, including opportunity cost of time; $p_i$ will be charges associated with intensity of use of the site chosen, such as fees and equipment costs; and $x_i$ will include the observed site attributes that matter to anglers, such as site size measured by the number of accessible fishing spots, ease of access, fish abundance, facilities at the site, and aesthetics.[2] The basic ideas of applying the random utility model to transportation decisions, and its use in benefit-cost analysis, were introduced by McFadden (1973, 1974, 1981), Domencich and McFadden (1975), and Diamond and McFadden (1974). Hanemann (1985) provides the foundation for resource valuation applications.

Suppose a policy is adopted that raises the quality of some alternatives from *injured* to *restored* conditions. In the recreational fishing example, this might be a damage remediation program that increases fish abundance. Use the notation $\boldsymbol{x}' = (x_1', \ldots, x_J')$ for the attributes of sites in the *as is* case with injury, and the notation $\boldsymbol{x}'' = (x_1'', \ldots, x_J'')$ for the attributes of sites in the *but for* case with restoration. The *principle of compensating variation* is that the *as is* income of *each* consumer is *lowered* in the *but for* case with restoration so that maximum utility *after* the quality improvement equals maximum utility *before* the quality improvement. Then, *mean WTP per consumer* is the *average* of these compensating variation income reductions in the target population.[3]

For *any* pair of alternatives $j,m$, define $C_{jm}$ to be the *net* reduction in income combined with the quality improvement that equates the utility from alternative $j$ with injury and the utility from alternative $m$ without injury; i.e.

$$U(y - t_j,p_j,x_j',\varepsilon_j) = U(y - t_m - C_{jm},p_m,x_m'',\varepsilon_m).$$

Define $C = C(y,\boldsymbol{t},\boldsymbol{p},\boldsymbol{x}',\boldsymbol{x}'',\varepsilon)$ to be the income adjustment $C$ that equates *maximum* utility at injured conditions to *maximum* utility at restored conditions:

$$\text{Max}_j\, U(y - t_j,p_j,x_j',\varepsilon_j) = \text{Max}_m\, U(y - t_m - C,p_m,x_m'',\varepsilon_m).$$

Define $\boldsymbol{B}_{ik}$ to be the event that with the income adjustment $C = C(y,\boldsymbol{t},\boldsymbol{p},\boldsymbol{x}',\boldsymbol{x}'',\varepsilon)$, alternative $i$ is chosen under injury conditions and alternative $k$ is chosen under restored conditions. Then $\boldsymbol{B}_{ik}$ is the set of $\varepsilon$'s such that for all $j,m$,

$$U(y - t_j,p_j,x_j',\varepsilon_j) \leq U(y - t_i,p_i,x_i',\varepsilon_i), \text{ and}$$

$$U(y - t_m - C(y,\boldsymbol{t},\boldsymbol{p},\boldsymbol{x}',\boldsymbol{x}'',\varepsilon),p_m,x_m'',\varepsilon_m) \leq U(y - t_k - C(y,\boldsymbol{t},\boldsymbol{p},\boldsymbol{x}',\boldsymbol{x}'',\varepsilon),p_k,x_k'',\varepsilon_k).$$

The probability of the event $\boldsymbol{B}_{ik}$ will depend on the economic variables of the problem, $(y,\boldsymbol{t},\boldsymbol{p},\boldsymbol{x}',\boldsymbol{x}'')$, through these defining inequalities.[4] It is possible that the ε's are correlated with some of the economic variables. However, for the welfare impact of the quality improvement to be well defined and identifiable, it is critical that a consumer's unobserved ε's *not* shift when the quality improvement occurs. This implies that the distribution of the ε's must be *invariant* with respect to policy that alters $\boldsymbol{x}$ or adjusts income.

Suppose the event $\boldsymbol{B}_{ik}$. Then, $C(y,\boldsymbol{t},\boldsymbol{p},\boldsymbol{x}',\boldsymbol{x}'',\varepsilon) = C_{ik}$. Utility maximization and the monotonicity of the indirect utility function imply the following result:

> *Lemma* In the event $\boldsymbol{B}_{ik}$ where the consumer maximizes utility at alternative $i$ before the quality improvement and at alternative $k$ after the quality improvement and income compensation, one has
>
> $\text{Max}_m\, C_{im} = C(y,\boldsymbol{t},\boldsymbol{p},\boldsymbol{x}',\boldsymbol{x}'',[\varepsilon) = \text{Min}_j\, C_{jk}$.

In particular, $\boldsymbol{B}_{ik}$ implies $C_{ii} \leq C(y,\boldsymbol{t},\boldsymbol{p},\boldsymbol{x}',\boldsymbol{x}'',\varepsilon) \leq C_{kk}$. Thus, the income compensation actually required to keep a consumer's maximum utility constant is bracketed by the income compensation required to keep the utility of the *original* alternative constant and the income compensation required to keep the utility of the *final* alternative constant. The intuition for these bounds is that the ability of the consumer to substitute away from $i$ under restored conditions may increase final utility, requiring additional income reduction to equate final utility to the initial utility level, while the ability of the consumer to substitute away from $k$ under injury conditions may increase initial utility, requiring less income reduction to equate final utility to the initial utility level.

No alternative becomes less desirable as a result of the quality improvement, so that $C_{ii} \geq 0$. If alternative $k$ is *unaffected* by the quality improvement, then $C_{kk} = 0$. Together, these conditions imply that a consumer whose final choice $k$ is *not* affected by the quality improvement must have $C(y,\boldsymbol{t},\boldsymbol{p},\boldsymbol{x}',\boldsymbol{x}'',\varepsilon) = 0$.

The income reduction $C_{jj}$ for an alternative $j$ depends on $\varepsilon_j$ *only* if this unobserved factor interacts with income. In most random utility model applications, the assumption is made that the ε's enter the indirect utility function *additively*, so that $U(y - t_j,p_j,x_j,\varepsilon_j) = V(y - t_j,p_j,x_j) + \varepsilon_j$ and there is *no* interaction between income and the unobservable ε's. In this case, *the income reduction $C_{jj}$ for a fixed alternative $j$ satisfies $V(y - t_j,p_j,x_j') = V(y - t_j - C_{jj},p_j,x_j'')$* and *does not depend on* ε.

The distribution of the unobserved ε's in the target population will induce a distribution of income compensation levels $C(y,\boldsymbol{t},\boldsymbol{p},\boldsymbol{x}',\boldsymbol{x}'',\varepsilon)$. The mean of this distribution will be mean willingness to pay for the quality improvement. Then, *expected income compensation* (or mean WTP) satisfies

$$EC(y,t,p,x',x'',\varepsilon) = \sum_{i=1}^{J}\sum_{k=1}^{J} \text{Prob}(B_{ik})\cdot E\{C_{ik}|B_{ik}\}.$$

The distribution of ε's also induces the choice probabilities $P_j(y,t,p,x)$. Let $P_j' = P_j(y,t,p,x')$ denote the injury case probability of alternative $j$, and $P_j'' = P_j(y,t,p,x'')$ denote the restored case probability of this alternative. Define

$B_i' = \bigcup_{m=1}^{J} B_{im}$ and $B_k'' = \bigcup_{j=1}^{J} B_{jk}$.

Then

$$P_i' = \text{Prob}(B_i') \equiv \sum_{m=1}^{J} \text{Prob}(B_{im}) \text{ and } P_k'' = \text{Prob}(B_i'') \equiv \sum_{j=1}^{J} \text{Prob}(B_{jk})$$

are the *injury* and *restored* probabilities, respectively, when compensation is actually paid.

Direct evaluation of $EC(y,t,p,x',x'',\varepsilon)$ is often difficult, because $C_{ik}$ may depend nonlinearly on the ε's, making $E\{C_{ik}|B_{ik}\}$ difficult to compute. In addition, the probabilities $\text{Prob}(B_{ik})$ may be difficult to calculate. Exceptions where there are accurate practical approximations to $EC(y,t,p,x',x'',\varepsilon)$ are discussed in the next two sections. However, bounds for $EC(y,t,p,x',x'',\varepsilon)$ may suffice for many policy purposes. One has

$$EC(y,t,p,x',x'',\varepsilon) = \sum_{i=1}^{J}\sum_{k=1}^{J} \text{Prob}(B_{ik})\cdot E\{C_{ik}|B_{ik}\}$$
$$\leq \sum_{i=1}^{J}\sum_{k=1}^{J} \text{Prob}(B_{ik})\cdot E\{C_{kk}|B_{ik}\} = \sum_{k=1}^{J} P_k''\cdot E\{C_{kk}|B_k''\}$$

and

$$EC(y,t,p,x',x'',\varepsilon) = \sum_{i=1}^{J}\sum_{k=1}^{J} \text{Prob}(B_{ik})\cdot E\{C_{ik}|B_{ik}\}$$
$$\geq \sum_{i=1}^{J}\sum_{k=1}^{J} \text{Prob}(B_{ik})\cdot E\{C_{ii}|B_{ik}\} = \sum_{i=1}^{J} P_k'\cdot E\{C_{ii}|B_k'\}.$$

Then, in the case of additive disturbances where the income reductions $C_{jj}$ required to keep the indirect utility of each fixed alternative $j$ do *not* depend on the unobserved ε's, one has the bounds

$$\sum_{j=1}^{J} P_j'\cdot C_{jj} \leq EC(y,t,p,x',x'',\varepsilon) \leq \sum_{j=1}^{J} P_j''\cdot C_{jj}.$$

These bounds provide a convenient check on exact computations of population mean WTP. In applications where the quality improvement induces little substitution among alternatives, the brackets may be sufficiently narrow to provide an adequate approximation to *EC* without further calculation. If the choice probabilities $P_j(y,t,p,x)$ do *not* depend on income $y$, then computation of the upper bound is straightforward. However, if the choice probabilities do depend on income, then the restored choice probabilities $P_j''$ depend on the compensating income reduction, and will themselves have to be bounded.

It is sometimes useful to calculate the *rate* of change in WTP as quality improves. An infinitesimal change from $x'$ to $x'' = x' + \Delta x$ results in an infinitesimal change $P_j'' = P_j' + \Delta P_j$ in the choice probabilities. Suppose the unobserved factors are additive, $U(y - t_j,p_j,x_j,\varepsilon_j) = V(y - t_j,p_j,x_j) + \varepsilon_j$. From the formula for the compensating income reduction for a fixed alternative $j$,

$$C_{jj} = \frac{\partial V(y - t_j,p_j,x_j')/\partial x_j}{\partial V(y - t_j,p_j,x_j')/\partial y}\Delta x_j + \sigma(\Delta x),$$

where the last term is an infinitesimal of higher order. Substituting this expression into the bounds above yields

$$EC(y,t,p,x',x'+dx,\varepsilon) \approx \sum_{j=1}^{J} P_j' \frac{\partial V(y-t_j,p_j,x_j')/\partial x_j}{\partial V(y-t_j,p_j,x_j')/\partial y} \Delta x_j.$$

For small quality improvements, this formula will approximate closely the target population WTP.

## Mean WTP for additively separable indirect utility

Consider random utility models in which the indirect utility function is additively separable in the unobserved ε's, characteristics of alternatives, and linear or nonlinear functions of income:

$$U(y-t_i,p_i,x_i,\varepsilon_i) = f_i(y-t_i) - \beta_i p_i + \gamma x_i + \varepsilon_i.$$

The $f_i$ are increasing functions. While $f_i$ may depend on the choice alternative $i$, common formulations of the consumer's overall preference maximization problem often yield $f_i$ that do not depend on $i$. A leading practical case is the *parallel Engle curve condition* of Chipman and Moore (1980) or Deaton and Muellbauer (1980), where the indirect utility function is *linear* in income with a *constant* coefficient that does not vary by consumer, income level, or alternative: $f_i(y-t_i) = \alpha(y-t_i)$, with α a constant. (The coefficient α may vary with background prices that are unchanged by the policychange.)Aqualityimprovementmakes$\gamma(x_i''-x_i')\geq 0$ for all $i$.

When the indirect utility function satisfies the parallel Engle curve condition, the income compensation $C(y,t,p,x',x'',\varepsilon)$ for a consumer who chooses alternative $i$ before the quality improvement and alternative $k$ after the quality improvement and income adjustment satisfies

$$C(y,t,p,x',x'',\varepsilon) = \frac{1}{\alpha}\cdot\left\{\alpha(t_i-t_k) + \beta_i p_i - \beta_k p_k + \gamma x_k'' - \gamma x_i' + \varepsilon_k - \varepsilon_i\right\}.$$

Then, the expected income compensation satisfies

$$\begin{aligned} EC(y,t,p,x',x'',\varepsilon) &= \frac{1}{\alpha}\cdot\sum_{i=1}^{J}\sum_{k=1}^{J}\mathrm{Prob}(B_{ik})\cdot\left\{\alpha(t_i-t_k) + \beta_i p_i - \beta_k p_k + \gamma(x_k''-x_i') + \right. \\ &\qquad\left. E\{\varepsilon_k-\varepsilon_i|B_{ik}\}\right\} \\ &= \frac{1}{\alpha}\cdot\sum_{i=1}^{J}P_i'\cdot\left\{\alpha t_i + \beta_i p_i - \gamma x_i' - E\{\varepsilon_i|B_i'\}\right\} - \frac{1}{\alpha}\cdot\sum_{k=1}^{J}P_k''\cdot\left\{\alpha t_k + \beta_k p_k - \gamma x_i'' - E\{\varepsilon_k|B_k''\}\right\} \\ &= \frac{1}{\alpha}\cdot\left\{E\ \mathrm{Max}_i\ U(y-t_i,p_i,x_i'',\varepsilon_i) - E\ \mathrm{Max}_i\ U(y-t_i,p_i,x_i',\varepsilon_i)\right\}. \end{aligned}$$

The last equality holds *only* when the indirect utility function satisfies the parallel Engle curve condition.

Computation of the expected income compensation requires analytic or numerical calculation of the expectations $E\{\varepsilon_i|B_i'\}$ and $E\{\varepsilon_i|B_i''\}$, or equivalently of the expected utilities $E$ Max$_i$ $U(y-t_i,p_i,x_i'',\varepsilon_i)$ and

$\boldsymbol{E}$ Max$_i$ $U(y - t_i,p_i,x_i'',\varepsilon_i)$. When the indirect utility function satisfies the parallel Engle curve condition, the solution above is identical to the solution $C = \boldsymbol{EC}(y,\boldsymbol{t},\boldsymbol{p},\boldsymbol{x}',\boldsymbol{x}'',\varepsilon)$ to the equation

$$\boldsymbol{E}\ \text{Max}_i\ U(y - t_i,p_i,x_i'',\varepsilon_i) = \boldsymbol{E}\ \text{Max}_i\ U(y - t_i - C,p_i,x_i',\varepsilon_i).$$

It is possible in the last formula to interpret $C$ as the income reduction that keeps constant the expected indirect utility function of a *representative* consumer. This interpretation is a consequence of the fact that when indirect utility functions satisfy the parallel Engle curve condition, it is possible to aggregate preferences into a social preference that generates the market demand functions using Roy's identity; see Chipman and Moore (1980, 1990).

The income reduction $C_{ii}$ in the case of the linear indirect utility function satisfies $C_{ii} = \gamma(x_i'' - x_i')/\alpha$. Then, the bounds on mean WTP derived earlier specialize for the indirect utility function that is *linear* in income:

$$\sum_{j=1}^{J} P_j' \cdot \gamma(x_j'' - x_j')/\alpha \leq \boldsymbol{EC}(y,\boldsymbol{t},\boldsymbol{p},\boldsymbol{x}',\boldsymbol{x}'',\varepsilon) \leq \sum_{j=1}^{J} P_j'' \cdot \gamma(x_i'' - x_i')/\alpha.$$

These bounds provide a convenient check even when $\boldsymbol{EC}$ has an analytic formula, and in some applications will be tight enough to answer policy questions without more detailed analysis that depends on further assumptions on preferences.

Next consider more general nonlinear dependence of indirect utility on income, via functions $f_i(y - t_i)$ that are not all linear, or vary by alternative. The income compensation for a consumer who chooses $i$ in the injury case and $k$ in the restored case satisfies $C_{ik} = y - t_k - f_k^{-1}(f_i(y - t_i) - \beta_i p_i + \beta_k p_k - \gamma(x_k'' - x_i') + \varepsilon_i - \varepsilon_k)$. Unlike the linear in income case, $C_{ik}$ *cannot* be written as a difference of utilities normalized by the marginal utility of income, so the formula for expected WTP *cannot* be expressed in terms of a difference in expected utilities in the injury and restored cases. In particular, because expectations are not preserved by nonlinear transformations, one *cannot* calculate $\boldsymbol{EC}(y,\boldsymbol{t},\boldsymbol{p},\boldsymbol{x}',\boldsymbol{x}'',\varepsilon)$ by solving for the income reduction that equates *expected* utility before and after the quality improvement. One can still define expected utility, but it will *not* be a social utility function that generates the market demand functions via Roy's identity, and the value $C$ of an income reduction that keeps expected utility constant will *not* coincide with the WTP $\boldsymbol{EC}(y,\boldsymbol{t},\boldsymbol{p},\boldsymbol{x}',\boldsymbol{x}'',\varepsilon)$ derived by averaging the equivalent variation income reductions for each individual.

Calculation of $\boldsymbol{EC}(y,\boldsymbol{t},\boldsymbol{p},\boldsymbol{x}',\boldsymbol{x}'',\varepsilon)$ will in general require explicit consideration of the distribution of income compensations induced by the nonlinear transformation, with simultaneous or iterative solution of the random utility model for $C(y,\boldsymbol{t},\boldsymbol{p},\boldsymbol{x}',\boldsymbol{x}'',\varepsilon)$ and the events $\boldsymbol{B}_{ik}$. This calculation is in most cases analytically intractable; the sixth section provides a simulation method for one class of models that is asymptotically unbiased and can be made as accurate as is needed. The general bounds on mean WTP given earlier can be specialized to the case of indirect utility functions that are linear in the disturbance and a (nonlinear) function of income. The income compensation $C_{jj}$ that equates the utility of alternative $j$ before and after the quality improvement satisfies $f_j(y - t_j) - f_j(y - t_j - C_{jj}) = \gamma(x''_j - x'_j)$. Using the theorem of the mean, $\alpha_j C_{jj} = \gamma(x''_j - x'_j)$, where $\alpha_j$ is the marginal utility of income $df_j(y)/dy$ evaluated at some intermediate point between $y - t_j$ and $y - t_j - C_{jj}$. If $f_j$ is convex, so that marginal indirect utility is nondecreasing in income, then $\dfrac{df_j(y - t_j)}{dy} \geq \alpha_j \geq \dfrac{df_j(y - t_j - C_{jj})}{dy}$. If $f_j$ is concave, a shape that may be inconsistent with the theoretical requirement that the indirect utility function be quasi-convex in income and prices, then these inequalities are reversed. Substituting the expression for $C_{jj}$ in the earlier general bounds on mean WTP, one obtains

$$\sum_{j=1}^{J} P'_j \cdot \gamma(x''_j - x'_j)/\alpha_j \leq EC(y,\mathbf{t},\mathbf{p},\mathbf{x}',\mathbf{x}'',\varepsilon) \leq \sum_{j=1}^{J} P''_j \cdot \gamma(x''_j - x'_j)/\alpha_j.$$

Then, substituting upper and lower bounds, respectively, on $\alpha_j$, one can use these inequalities to bound mean WTP when the dependence of the indirect utility function on income is nonlinear or varies by alternative. Again, for small quality improvements, the bounds are narrow, and establish that WTP in the target population is approximately equal to the sum over alternatives of the choice probabilities times the quality improvement for an alternative, divided by the marginal utility of income *for this alternative*.

## WTP in generalized extreme value models

Assume that the indirect utility can be written

$$U(y - t_i,p_i,x_i,\varepsilon_i) = V(y - t_i,p_i,x_i) + \varepsilon_i,$$

where $\varepsilon_i$ is a part that varies randomly across consumers and $v_i = V(y - t_i,p_i,x_i)$ is a systematic part, common across consumers. This will usually be specialized either to the parallel Engle curve condition case $v_i = \alpha(y - t_i) - \beta_i p_i + \gamma x_i$, or to the nonlinear in income case $v_i = f_i(y - t_i) - \beta_i p_i + \gamma x_i$. The terms $\alpha$, $\beta_i$, $\gamma$ are parameters. Assume that the $\varepsilon$'s have a joint cumulative distribution function (CDF) of *generalized extreme value* (GEV) form:

$$F(\varepsilon_1, \ldots, \varepsilon_J) = \exp(-H(e^{-\varepsilon_1}, \ldots, e^{-\varepsilon_J})),$$

where $H(w_1, \ldots, w_J)$ is (i) a non-negative linear homogeneous function of $w \geq 0$, satisfying the properties (ii) if any argument goes to $+\infty$, then $H$ goes to $+\infty$ and (iii) the mixed partial derivatives of $H$ exist, are continuous, and alternate in sign, with non-negative odd mixed derivatives. A function $H$ with these properties will be termed a *GEV generating function*. McFadden (1978, Theorem 1, p. 80), shows that when the function H is a GEV generating function, the function $F(\varepsilon_1, \ldots, \varepsilon_J)$ is a multivariate cumulative distribution function, and that its one-dimensional marginals are extreme value distributions. The following result summarizes the argument:

*Theorem 1* Suppose $H(w)$ for $w = (w_1, \ldots, w_J)$ has the properties

(i) $H$ is homogeneous of degree one in $w \geq 0$;
(ii) If $w_i \to +\infty$, then $H \to +\infty$;
(iii) The mixed partial derivatives of $H$ alternate in sign:

$$(-1)^k \cdot H_{1 \ldots k} \equiv (-1)^k \cdot \frac{\partial^k H}{\partial w_1 \ldots \partial w_k} \leq 0;$$

Then, $F(\varepsilon) = \exp(-H(e^{-\varepsilon_1}, \ldots, e^{-\varepsilon_J}))$ is a CDF with Extreme Value Type I univariate marginals. Further the random utility model $u_i = v_i + \varepsilon_i$ with $\varepsilon$ distributed $F(\varepsilon)$ satisfies $\boldsymbol{E} \max_i u_i = \log H(e^{v_1}, \ldots, e^{v_J}) + E$, where $E = 0.5772156649$ is Euler's constant, and the choice probabilities satisfy

$$P_i = e^{v_i} \cdot H_i(e^{v_1}, \ldots, e^{v_J}) / H(e^{v_1}, \ldots, e^{v_J}).$$

**Proof** Condition (ii) implies that if $\varepsilon_i \to -\infty$, then $F(\varepsilon) \to 0$. Condition (i) implies that if $\varepsilon \to +\infty$, then $F(\varepsilon) \to 1$. Setting $\varepsilon_j = +\infty$ for $j \neq 0$, condition (i) yields $F = \exp(-H(1, 0, \ldots, 0)e^{-\varepsilon_1})$, and similarly for other indices, so that the univariate marginals are Extreme Value Type I distributed. Consider the mixed partial derivatives of $F$. Note that $F_1 = F \cdot H_1 \cdot e^{-\varepsilon_1} \geq 0$. Proceed by induction. Suppose one has established that $F_{1 \ldots k} = F \cdot e^{-\varepsilon_1} \ldots e^{-\varepsilon_k} \cdot \{\sum_j A_{kj}\} \geq 0$, with the $A_{kj}$ non-negative terms involving products of mixed derivatives of $H$ with the property the sum of the orders of the derivatives equals $k$. Then,

$$F_{1 \ldots k,k+1} = F \cdot e^{-\varepsilon_1} \ldots e^{-\varepsilon_k} e^{-\varepsilon_{k+1}} \{\sum_j \underbrace{[A_{kj} H_{k+1} - \partial A_{kj} / \partial w_{k+1}]}_{A_{k+1,j}}\}.$$

But $\partial A_{kj} / \partial w_{k+1}$ is a sum of terms, each of which increases the order of one derivative of $H$ by one degree, and condition (iii) implies $-\partial A_{kj} / \partial w_{k+1} \geq 0$. This implies $A_{k+1,j} \geq 0$, completing the induction step. Therefore, $F_{1 \ldots m} \geq 0$, establishing that $F$ is the CDF of a non-negative density.

Let $\eta = \max_i(v_i + \varepsilon_i)$. The CDF of this random variable is

$$F(\eta - v_1, \ldots, \eta - v_m) = \exp(-H(e^{v_1 - \eta}, \ldots, e^{v_J - \eta})) = \exp(-e^{-\eta} \cdot H(e^{v_1}, \ldots, e^{v_J})).$$

This is an Extreme Value Type I cumulative distribution function, shifted in mean, so that this class of random utilities is closed under maximization. The expected value of maximum utility is

$$\boldsymbol{E}\,\eta = \int_{-\infty}^{+\infty} \eta \cdot e^{-\eta} H \cdot \exp(-e^{-\eta} \cdot H) \cdot d\eta = \log H + \underbrace{\int_{-\infty}^{+\infty} \zeta \cdot e^{-\zeta} \cdot \exp(-e^{-\zeta}) \cdot d\zeta}_{E}.$$

Finally, integration yields

$$P_i = \text{Prob}(v_j + \varepsilon_j \leq v_i + \varepsilon_i) = \int_{-\infty}^{+\infty} F_i(\varepsilon_i + v_i - v_1, \ldots, \varepsilon_i + v_i - v_J)\cdot d\varepsilon_i$$

$$= \frac{e^{v_i}\cdot H_i(e^{v_1}, \ldots, e^{v_J})}{H(e^{v_1}, \ldots, e^{v_J})}.$$

The linear function $H = \sum_{i=1}^{J} w_i$ is a GEV generating function which yields the multinomial logit (MNL) model. A three-level nested MNL model is generated by a function $H$ of the form

$$H = \sum_{m=1}^{M} \left[ \sum_{k=1}^{K} \left[ \sum_{i \in A_{mk}} w_i^{S'_m S_k} \right]^{\frac{1}{S_k}} \right]^{\frac{1}{S'_m}},$$

where the $A_{mk}$ partition $\{1, \ldots, J\}$ and $s_k, s'_m \geq 1$. This form corresponds to a tree in which $m$ indexes major branches, $k$ indexes limbs from each branch, and $i$ indexes the final twigs. The larger $s_k$ or $s'_m$, the more substitutable the alternatives in $A_{mk}$. The following theorem can be applied recursively, starting from linear functions, to establish that $H$ above is a GEV generating function and the nested MNL model with $0 \geq s'_m, s_k \geq 1$ is a GEV random utility model.

> *Theorem 2* If sets $A,B$ satisfy $A \cup B = \{1, \ldots, J\}$, $H^A(w_A)$ and $H^B(w_B)$ are GEV generating functions in $w_A$ and $w_B$, respectively, and if $s \geq 1$, then $H(w) = H^A(w_A{}^s)^{1/s} + H^B(w_B)$ is a GEV generating function in $(w_1, \ldots, w_J)$.

**Proof** It is immediate from the construction that $H(w)$ satisfies conditions (i) and (ii) in Theorem 1. Consider condition (iii). Since cross-derivatives between $A$ and $B$ are zero, it is necessary to establish only that $H^A(w_A{}^s)^{1/s}$ satisfies (iii). Assume $w_A = (w_1, \ldots, w_k)$ and observe that $H_1 = w_1^{s-1}\cdot(H^A)^{1/s-1}\cdot H_1^A \geq 0$. Now proceed by induction. Suppose one has established

$$H_{12\ldots i} = (-1)^{i-1}\cdot w_1^{s-1}\ldots w_i^{s-1}\cdot\sum_J Q_{ij},$$

with each term $Q_{ij} \geq 0$ consisting of a product of $H^A$ raised to a power $1/s-k$, for an integer $k > 0$, and one or more mixed partial derivatives of $H^A$, with the property that the sum of the order of the derivatives is $i$. Then,

$$H_{12\ldots i,i+1} = (-1)^{i-1}\cdot w_i^{s-1}\ldots w_1^{s-1}\cdot w_{i+1}^{s-1}\cdot\sum_J \underbrace{\partial Q_{ij}/\partial w_{i+1}}_{-Q_{i+1,j}}.$$

But each derivative $-Q_{i+1,j} = \partial Q_{ij}/\partial w_{i+1}$ is a sum in which each term increases the order of a mixed derivative of $H^A$ by one, resulting in a change of sign, *or* adds a first derivative of $(H^A)^{1/s-k}$, which again results in a change of sign since $s \geq 1$. Therefore, each $Q_{i+1,j}$ is non-negative, establishing the induction step. This proves that the mixed derivatives $H_{12\ldots i}$ alternate in sign, as required by (iii). This argument applies to the components of $w_A$ indexed in any order.

I will not comment on the assumptions leading to GEV models other than to note that writing $U$ as a sum of systematic and random terms is not particularly restrictive, requiring only that a representation of utility be chosen that admits moments. However, the assumption that the random components are in a parametric family that does not depend on the variables of the problem is quite restrictive. The assumption of linearity of the indirect utility function in attributes of alternatives is a reasonable approximation if the variations between alternatives are small or if a flexible linear approximation is adopted.

I next calculate the mean WTP in the target population when the unobserved ε's have a generalized extreme value distribution and the indirect utility function satisfies the parallel Engle curve condition: $U(y - t_i,p_i,x_i,\varepsilon_i) = v_i + \varepsilon_i$ with $v_i = \alpha(y - t_i) - \beta_i p_i + \gamma x_i$. Let $v_i' = \alpha(y - t_i) - \beta_i p_i + \gamma x_i'$ and $v_i'' = \alpha(y - t_i) - \beta_i p_i + \gamma x_i''$. Using the formula for mean WTP derived earlier for the linear in income case,

$$EC(y,t,p,x',x'',\varepsilon) = \frac{1}{\alpha}\cdot\left\{E\ \mathrm{Max}_i U(y - t_i,p_i,x_i'',\varepsilon_i) - E\ \mathrm{Max}_i U(y - t_i,p_i,x_i',\varepsilon_i)\right\}.$$

Combine this with the result from Theorem 1 that $E \max_i u_i = \log H(e^{v_1}, \ldots, e^{v_J}) + E$. Then one has

$$EC(y,t,p,x',x'',\varepsilon) = \frac{1}{\alpha}\cdot\left\{\log H(e^{v_1''}, \ldots, e^{v_J''}) - \log H(e^{v_1'}, \ldots, e^{v_J'})\right\}.$$

This is the "log sum" formula first developed by Ben Akiva (1973), McFadden (1973), and Domencich and McFadden (1975) for the multinomial logit model, and by McFadden (1978, 1981) for the nested logit model. This formula is valid *only* when the indirect utility function satisfies the parallel Engle curve condition.

The log sum formula has a geometric interpretation that coincides with the traditional geometry of consumer surplus. The total differential of this expression is

$$d \log H(e^{v_1}, \ldots, e^{v_J}) = \sum_{j=1}^{J} \frac{e^{v_j}\cdot H_j(e^{v_1}, \ldots, e^{v_J})}{H(e^{v_1}, \ldots, e^{v_J})}\cdot dv_j = \sum_{j=1}^{J} P_j(v)\cdot dv_j.$$

Then, integrating over any (rectifiable) path $v(t)$, $0 \leq t \leq 1$, from $v'$ to $v''$,

$$EC(y,t,p,x',x'',\varepsilon) = \frac{1}{\alpha}\cdot\left\{\sum_{j=1}^{J}\int_{t=0}^{1} P_j(v)\cdot\frac{dv(t)}{dt}\cdot dt\right\}.$$

But this is the sum over commodities of the areas behind the demand curves for the alternatives, normalized by the marginal utility of income; the integral is independent of path. Thus, in the linear in income case, the analytic formula for mean WTP coincides with the traditional Hicksian (= Marshallian) definition of consumer surplus as the sum of the areas behind the affected demand curves.

## A representative consumer approximation to WTP in GEV models

Consider the case of a random utility model with generalized extreme value disturbances and a *nonlinear* dependence on income,

$$U(y - t_i, p_i, x_i, \varepsilon_i) = v_i + \varepsilon_i \text{ and } v_i = f_i(y - t_i) - \beta_i p_i + \gamma x_i.$$

One can calculate expected utility. Consider interpreting it as the utility of a "representative" consumer and solving for the *expected utility equivalent variation* $C$ that equates *expected* utility before and after the quality improvement, so that $\log H(e^{v''_1}, \ldots, e^{v''_J}) = \log H(e^{v'_1}, \ldots, e^{v'_J})$, where $v'_j = f_j(y - t_j) - \beta_j p_j + \gamma x'_j$ and $v''_j = f_j(y - t_j - C) - \beta_j p_j + \gamma x''_j$. Morey has proposed this value $C$ as an approximation to mean WTP (Morey, Rowe and Watson 1993). However, this solution does *not* coincide with the mean of the individual-by-individual equivalent income reductions when the indirect utility function is nonlinear in income. An example shows that the expected utility equivalent variation $C$ differs from the theoretically correct measure of WTP when the indirect utility function is nonlinear in income. To make the example simple, I assume there are two alternatives, indexed 1 and 2, with injury only to alternative 1. The indirect utilities are assumed to be $u_1 = \sqrt{y} + x_1 + \varepsilon_1$, and $u_2 = \sqrt{y} + \varepsilon_2$, with zero travel costs to either alternative, no use charges, and zero site attributes at site 2. I assume that $x'_1 = 0$ and $x''_1 \equiv x > 0$. I assume that $\varepsilon_1$ and $\varepsilon_2$ are independently Extreme Value Type I distributed; then $\nu = \varepsilon_1 - \varepsilon_2$ has a logistic cumulative distribution function, $G(\nu) = 1/(1 + e^{-\nu})$. Choice behavior is then described by a binomial logit model, a special case of a generalized extreme value model, with $P_1 = 1/(1 + e^{-x_1})$. Then, $P'_1 = 1/2$ and $P''_1 = 1/(1 + e^{-x})$.

The Morey method solves for $C$ that equates *expected* utility before and after the quality improvement. In this simple example, $C$ can be obtained analytically, and satisfies $C = 2\cdot\sqrt{y}\cdot\log[(1 + e^{x})/2] - \{\log[(1 + e^{x})/2]\}^2$. This value is to be compared with the exact calculation of compensating income, which proceeds as follows. First, a consumer who chooses alternative 2 after the improvement sees no change in utility, and requires zero income adjustment. Second, a consumer who chooses 1 before the improvement requires the reduction $C$ that satisfies $C = 2\cdot\sqrt{y}\cdot x - x^2$. Finally, a consumer who switches from 2 to 1 as a result of the quality improvement satisfies $\sqrt{y} + \varepsilon_2 = \sqrt{y - C} + x + \varepsilon_1$, or $C = 2\cdot\sqrt{y}\cdot(x + \nu) - (x + \nu)^2$. The consumer will fall into the three cases above when $\nu < -x$, $\nu > 0$, and $-x < \nu < 0$, respectively. Then,

$$EC(y,t,p,x',x'',\varepsilon) = \{2\cdot\sqrt{y}\cdot x - x^2\}\cdot[1 - G(0)] + \int_{-x}^{0}\{2\cdot\sqrt{y}\cdot(x + \nu) - (x + \nu)^2\}\cdot G'(\nu)d\nu$$
$$= (2\sqrt{y} - x)\cdot x + 2(\sqrt{y}\cdot\log(1 + e^{-x}) - 2(\sqrt{y} - x)\cdot\log 2 - 2\sum_{k=1}^{\infty}(-1)^{k+1}(1 - e^{-kx})/k^2.$$ [5]

The Morey method and exact mean WTP can also be compared to the bounds

$$C_{11}\cdot P_1' \equiv \frac{2\cdot\sqrt{y}\cdot x - x^2}{2} \leq EC(y,t,p,x',x'',\varepsilon) \leq \frac{2\cdot\sqrt{y}\cdot x - x^2}{1+e^{-x}} \equiv C_{11}\cdot P_1''.$$

The table below gives the percentage error in WTP estimated by the Morey method for this example when $y = 1$ and $0 < x < 1$. For very small improvements, the exact and Morey method calculations both increase from zero at the rate given by the derivative of exact WTP with respect to $x$. For larger improvements, there is increasing bias.

| Improvement x | 0.1 | 0.4 | 0.7 | 1.0 |
|---|---|---|---|---|
| Exact mean WTP | 0.097 | 0.354 | 0.547 | 0.659 |
| Percent error in Morey approximation | 2.5% | 10.4% | 19.2% | 29.9% |
| Percent error in lower bound | −2.5% | −9.7% | −16.8% | −24.1% |
| Percent error in upper bound | 2.4% | 8.1% | 11.2% | 11.0% |
| Percent error in average of bounds | −0.0% | −0.8% | −2.8% | −6.6% |

Thus, the Morey method is seriously biased for large improvements in $x$. For all $x$, the simple, easily computed bounds on WTP are at least as accurate as the Morey approximation, and the average of these bounds is an order of magnitude more accurate. The Morey method can be reasonably accurate in situations where the mean of a nonlinear transformation equals the nonlinear transformation of the mean. However, the example suggests that it will usually be more accurate, and more reliable, to employ an average of the upper and lower bounds.

## A Markov chain Monte Carlo (MCMC) simulation estimator of WTP

Consider the random utility model with generalized extreme value disturbances and nonlinear income effects, $U(y - t_i,p_i,x_i,\varepsilon_i) = f_i(y - t_i) - \beta_i p_i + \gamma x_i + \varepsilon_i$. The analytic intractability of the expression for exact mean WTP in this case, and the inaccuracy of Morey approximation to mean WTP for moderate quality changes, suggest a need for a better estimation method.[6]

The simulation procedure described below has the advantage that it can be made as accurate as one needs, and that its degree of accuracy can be assessed statistically. I first describe the procedure, expand on some of its computational elements, and finally give practical comments and examples. Let $H(w_1, \ldots, w_J)$ denote a GEV generating function, $F(\varepsilon) = \exp(-H(e^{-\varepsilon_1}, \ldots, e^{-\varepsilon_J})$ the associated GEV distribution, and $f(\varepsilon)$ its density. Let $g(\varepsilon) = \prod_{j=1}^{J} e^{-\varepsilon_j} \cdot \exp(-e^{-\varepsilon_j})$ denote the density of an i.i.d. Extreme Value vector.

### *Simulation procedure*

1 Given an estimated GEV choice model with GEV generating function $H(w_1, \ldots, w_J)$, distribution $F(\varepsilon)$, and density $f(\varepsilon)$, construct vectors $\varepsilon^t$ recursively from an arbitrary starting vector $\varepsilon^{\circ}$ for $t = 1, \ldots, T$, as follows: At step $t$, draw (0,1) uniformly distributed random variables $\eta^t$ and $\zeta_j^t$ for $j = 1, \ldots, J$. Define $\varepsilon_j^{\sim t} = -\log(-\log(\zeta_j^t))$, $g_t = \Pi_{j=1}^{J}(-\zeta_j^t \cdot \log(\zeta_j^t))$, and $f_t = \partial^J F(\varepsilon^{\sim t})/\partial\varepsilon_1^t \ldots \partial\varepsilon_J^t$. Define a Markov chain

$$\varepsilon^t = \begin{cases} \tilde{\varepsilon}^t & \text{if } \eta^t \le f_t \cdot g_{t-1}/f_{t-1} \cdot g_t \\ \varepsilon^{t-1} & \text{otherwise} \end{cases}.$$

Call the vectors $\varepsilon^t$ obtained in this manner a GEV sampler.

2 For each $\varepsilon^t$, find $u_t^* = \max_j \{f_j(y - t_j) - \beta_j p_j + \gamma x_j' + \varepsilon_j^t\}$.

3 For each $\varepsilon^t$ and $u_t^*$, search iteratively to find the income reduction $C_t$ that satisfies $u_t^* = \max_m \{f_m(y - t_m - C_t) - \beta_m p_m + \gamma x_m'' + \varepsilon_m^t\}$.

4 Approximate $EC(y,t,p,x',x'',\varepsilon)$ by the average $\text{WTP}_T \equiv \frac{1}{T} \cdot \sum_{t=1}^{T} C_t$.

Steps (2)–(4) in this procedure are computationally simple and can be done quickly. A fast one-dimensional iterative search is required in Step (3). Initial upper and lower bounds on $C_t$ can be obtained from the general bounds given in the fourth section; these need not be very tight. Step (1), approximating a sample from the GEV distribution, is the major computational task. The GEV Sampler in Step (1) is a Markov Chain Monte Carlo (MCMC) method for constructing draws from GEV distributions that uses an independence Metropolis–Hastings (MH) kernel and an i.i.d. Extreme Value Type I proposal density, with draws made using the inverse transform method; see Chib and Greenberg (1995), and also Roberts and Smith (1994), Tierney (1994), Chib and Greenberg (1994, 1996), and McFadden (1997). Because the GEV density is everywhere positive, the MCMC process is irreducible and Harris recursive; this implies that the GEV sampler displays strong ergodicity. Strong ergodicity also applies to the approximation in step (4) above for $EC(y,t,p,x',x'',\varepsilon)$, since the functions $f_m$ are continuous and increasing, making the transformations in steps (2) and

(3) continuous, and the values $C_t$ are contained in an interval between zero and an upper bound on consumer's income.

The general MCMC method can have a rate of convergence lower than any geometric rate. However, a modification of the GEV sampler that corresponds to computational practice yields stronger results. Let $M$ denote a large number, say the largest number representable in standard floating point computer calculations, and define $\mathbf{X} = \{\varepsilon| -M \leq \varepsilon \leq M\}$. Construct the quantities $\tilde{\varepsilon}_j^t$, $g_t$, and $f_t$ as in the simulation procedure described above, but now define the Markov chain as

$$\varepsilon^t = \begin{cases} \tilde{\varepsilon}^t & \text{if } \tilde{\varepsilon}^t \in \mathbf{X} \text{ and } \eta^t \leq f_t \cdot g_{t-1}/f_{t-1} \cdot g_t \\ \varepsilon^{t-1} & \text{otherwise} \end{cases}.$$

This is now an independence Metropolis–Hastings sampler on the compact set $\mathbf{X}$; its invariant is the truncated GEV density $1(\varepsilon \in \mathbf{X}) \cdot f(\varepsilon)/\int_{\mathbf{X}} f(y)\, d\mu(y)$. Note that the sampler requires only the ratio of this density at two arguments, so that the normalizing denominator does not appear. To the level of practical computer accuracy, this density will be indistinguishable from the untruncated GEV density. On the compact set $X$, there is a lower bound $1 - \rho > 0$ on $w(\varepsilon,y)/f(y) = \text{Min}\{g(y)/f(y), g(\varepsilon)/f(\varepsilon)\}$, implying the probability of event $B$ following a vector $\varepsilon$ is bounded below by a positive constant $K$ times the GEV probability of $B$. Consider the continuous bounded function $C(y,\boldsymbol{t},\boldsymbol{p},\boldsymbol{x}',\boldsymbol{x}'',\varepsilon)$ for $\varepsilon \in \mathbf{X}$ that is defined by simulation steps (2) and (3). Then, there exists $K' > 0$ such that the bias in the modified GEV sampler goes away at a $1/T$ rate; specifically

$$|E\{\text{WTP}_T - \boldsymbol{E}_{\mathbf{X}} C(y,\boldsymbol{t},\boldsymbol{p},\boldsymbol{x}',\boldsymbol{x}'',\varepsilon)\}| \leq 2K'/(1-\rho)T,$$

where $K'$ is a product of $K$ and the bound on $C(y,\boldsymbol{t},\boldsymbol{p},\boldsymbol{x}',\boldsymbol{x}'',\varepsilon)$; here, $\boldsymbol{E}_{\mathbf{X}}$ denotes expectation with respect to the computationally indistinguishable truncated GEV distribution. An alternative to constructing $\text{WTP}_T$ as an average of $C_t$ over all draws $t = 1, \ldots, T$ is to burn in the GEV sampler by discarding the first $T_0$ draws, and calculating the average of $C_t$ for the remaining $(T - T_0)$ draws. The magnitude of bias will be minimized when the number of draws retained is roughly the last $-1/\log(\rho)$. However, for large $T$, the mean square error of the approximation will decrease when the sampler is burned in only if $\rho$ is sufficiently small relative to the variance of the process. Then, as a practical matter, there is no clear a priori argument for burning in the GEV process before estimating WTP.

McFadden (1997) establishes that $\sqrt{T}(\text{WTP}_T - \boldsymbol{E}_{\mathbf{X}} C(y,\boldsymbol{t},\boldsymbol{p},\boldsymbol{x}',\boldsymbol{x}'',\varepsilon))$ is asymptotically normal with a variance of $\sigma^2$. To estimate $\sigma^2$, consider $r = 1, \ldots, R$ independent repetitions of the Markov chain of length $T$, with realizations $\varepsilon^{tr}$, and define

$$\mathrm{WTP}_{TR} \equiv \frac{1}{TR}\sum_{r=1}^{R}\sum_{t=1}^{T} C(y,\boldsymbol{t},\boldsymbol{p},\boldsymbol{x}',\boldsymbol{x}'',\varepsilon^{tr})$$

and

$$\hat{\sigma}^2 = \frac{1}{R}\sum_{r=1}^{R}\left[\frac{1}{T}\sum_{t=1}^{T} C(y,\boldsymbol{t},\boldsymbol{p},\boldsymbol{x}',\boldsymbol{x}'',\varepsilon^{tr}) - \mathrm{WTP}_{TR}\right]^2.$$

These estimators are consistent when $R,T \to +\infty$.

While the last results guarantee rapid asymptotic convergence, they do not establish the rate $\rho$ or the constant $K$. Roberts (1992) and Zellner and Min (1995) propose convergence criteria that may be useful. A practical graphical method is to run the sampler until there is no visible drift or variance in $\mathrm{WTP}_T$ at the relevant economic scale. The statistical properties of the sampler can be estimated by constructing $r = 1, \ldots, R$ independent chains with stopping times $T_r$. Let $\mathrm{WTP}_{(r)}$ denote the estimate of $\boldsymbol{E}_{\mathbf{X}}C(y,\boldsymbol{t},\boldsymbol{p},\boldsymbol{x}',\boldsymbol{x}'',\varepsilon)$ obtained from chain $r$. Then, a regression

$$\mathrm{WTP}_{(r)}\cdot\sqrt{T_r} = \beta_0\cdot\sqrt{T_r} + \beta_1/\sqrt{T_r} + \xi_r$$

will provide an "accelerated" estimate $\hat{\beta}_0$ of the almost sure limit $\boldsymbol{E}_{\mathbf{X}}C(y,\boldsymbol{t},\boldsymbol{p},\boldsymbol{x}',\boldsymbol{x}'',\varepsilon)$ of the sampler. The estimate of $\beta_0$ will be consistent for exact WTP as $R$ and $\min_r T_r$ approach infinity.

To illustrate the use of the MCMC method and give an indication of the magnitudes of the convergence parameters, I apply it to a three-alternative example with a GEV generating function $H(w_1,w_2,w_3) = [w_1^s + w_2^s]^{1/s} + w_3$. The utility functions are assumed to be $u_i = y + x_i + \varepsilon_i$ for $i = 1,2,3$. I take these to satisfy the parallel Engle curve property, so that the analytic value of WTP calculated by the log sum formula, or equivalently by the Morey method, is available for comparison. Assume $x_i' = 0$ for all $i$, and $x_1'' \geq 0$, $x_2'' = x_3'' = 0$. Table 15.1 gives the exact WTP, and also the bounds on WTP from the third section, for several values of the parameter $s$ that determines the correlation of $\varepsilon_1$ and $\varepsilon_2$. Unless $s$ is large, the simple bounds are moderately accurate, and might suffice for a policy decision. The bounds are least accurate when one of two very close substitutes is improved, inducing a large shift in population shares for these substitutes, as in the third case in Table 15.1. When the attributes of alternatives 1 and 2 improve together, the bounds are quite accurate even for $s$ large. The bounds in this example are superfluous since exact WTP is easy to compute, but the point is that the average of the bounds will often provide a simple and relatively accurate approximation to mean WTP.

Table 15.2 summarizes the results of using the GEV sampler to approximate WTP for the cases $s = 1$, 2, and 10. In the $s = 1$ case, the model is MNL, and the GEV sampler is unbiased. In the $s = 10$ case, alternatives 1 and 2 are close substitutes, so that remediation that improves only alternative 1 leads to a large shift in the shares of these alternatives. In each case, 1,000 repetitions of a chain of length 10,000 were calculated, and results

*Table 15.1* Exact WTP and bounds

| | *Parameters and attributes* | | | | | | | | | | | |
|---|---|---|---|---|---|---|---|---|---|---|---|---|
| *Inclusive value parameters* | 1 | 2 | 10 | 1 | 2 | 10 | 1 | 2 | 10 | 1 | 2 | 10 |
| *Restored case attributes* | | | | | | | | | | | | |
| Alternative 1 | 0.2 | 0.2 | 0.2 | 0.1 | 0.1 | 0.1 | 0.2 | 0.2 | 0.2 | 0.1 | 0.1 | 0.1 |
| Alternative 2 | 0.0 | 0.0 | 0.0 | 0.1 | 0.1 | 0.1 | 0.1 | 0.1 | 0.1 | 0.0 | 0.0 | 0.0 |
| *Injury probabilities* | | | | | | | | | | | | |
| Alternative 0 | 0.333 | 0.414 | 0.483 | 0.333 | 0.414 | 0.465 | 0.333 | 0.414 | 0.497 | 0.333 | 0.414 | 0.465 |
| Alternative 1 | 0.333 | 0.293 | 0.259 | 0.333 | 0.293 | 0.267 | 0.333 | 0.293 | 0.252 | 0.333 | 0.293 | 0.267 |
| Alternative 2 | 0.333 | 0.293 | 0.259 | 0.333 | 0.293 | 0.267 | 0.333 | 0.293 | 0.252 | 0.333 | 0.293 | 0.267 |
| *Restored probabilities* | | | | | | | | | | | | |
| Alternative 0 | 0.310 | 0.388 | 0.447 | 0.311 | 0.390 | 0.441 | 0.301 | 0.378 | 0.450 | 0.322 | 0.402 | 0.451 |
| Alternative 1 | 0.379 | 0.367 | 0.487 | 0.344 | 0.305 | 0.280 | 0.367 | 0.342 | 0.546 | 0.356 | 0.329 | 0.341 |
| Alternative 2 | 0.310 | 0.246 | 0.066 | 0.344 | 0.305 | 0.280 | 0.332 | 0.280 | 0.004 | 0.322 | 0.269 | 0.207 |
| Exact WTP | 0.071 | 0.066 | 0.077 | 0.068 | 0.060 | 0.055 | 0.103 | 0.092 | 0.098 | 0.034 | 0.031 | 0.030 |
| Lower bound on WTP | 0.067 | 0.059 | 0.052 | 0.067 | 0.059 | 0.053 | 0.100 | 0.088 | 0.076 | 0.033 | 0.029 | 0.027 |
| Percent error | −6.6% | −11.7% | −39.4% | −1.6% | −2.0% | −2.3% | −3.3 | −4.7% | −26.2% | −3.3% | −5.9% | −13.0% |
| Upper bound on WTP | 0.076 | 0.073 | 0.097 | 0.069 | 0.061 | 0.056 | 0.107 | 0.096 | 0.110 | 0.036 | 0.033 | 0.034 |
| Percent error | 6.3% | 10.7% | 23.9% | 1.6% | 2.0% | 2.2% | 3.2% | 4.6% | 11.1% | 3.2% | 5.7% | 11.5% |
| Average of bounds | 0.0712 | 0.0659 | 0.0746 | 0.0678 | 0.0598 | 0.0547 | 0.1033 | 0.0922 | 0.0926 | 0.0345 | 0.0311 | 0.0304 |
| Percent error | −0.1% | −0.5% | −7.8% | −0.0% | −0.0% | −0.0% | −0.1% | −0.1% | −7.5% | −0.0% | −0.1% | −0.7% |

are tabulated for $T$ = 500, 1,000, 10,000, and 50,000. The results in Table 15.2 show that feasible, but large, values of $T$ are required for high precision. There is a gain from "acceleration" of the WTP estimator by extrapolation of the asymptotic formula for bias correction. The regression $\mathrm{WTP}_{(r)}\cdot\sqrt{T_r} = \beta_0\cdot\sqrt{T_r} + \beta_1 + \beta_2/\sqrt{T_r} + \zeta_r$ yields an estimate $\hat{\beta}_0$ of "bias-corrected" mean WTP. One can calculate root mean square error and predict the sample size required for a specified level of precision. When $s$ = 10, a sample size of $T \approx 51{,}250$ is required to achieve one percent relative accuracy, a feasible but intensive computation.

A final example corresponds to a circumstance that arises frequently in

*Table 15.2* GEV sampler estimates of WTP

| | *Examples* | | |
|---|---|---|---|
| *Inclusive value coefficients* | 1 | 2 | 10 |
| *Restored case attributes* | | | |
| Alternative 1 | 0.2 | 0.2 | 0.2 |
| Alternative 2 | 0.0 | 0.0 | 0.0 |
| Exact WTP | 0.07120 | 0.06585 | 0.07673 |
| Regression accelerated est of WTP | 0.07123 | 0.06576 | 0.07689 |
| Percent bias | 0.04% | −0.14% | −0.21% |
| *Results at T = 500* | | | |
| Empirical bias in sampler | 0.00007 | −0.00086 | 0.00125 |
| Percent of exact WTP | 0.10% | −1.31% | 1.64% |
| Empirical root mean square error | 0.00115 | 0.00276 | 0.00777 |
| Percent of exact WTP | 1.62% | 4.20% | 10.12% |
| *Results at T = 1,000* | | | |
| Empirical bias in sampler | 0.00005 | −0.00061 | 0.00089 |
| Percent of exact WTP | 0.07% | −0.93% | 1.16% |
| Empirical root mean square error | 0.00080 | 0.00192 | 0.00549 |
| Percent of exact WTP | 1.13% | 2.91% | 7.16% |
| *Results at T = 10,000* | | | |
| Empirical bias in sampler | 0.00002 | −0.00019 | 0.00028 |
| Percent of exact WTP | 0.02% | −0.29% | 0.37% |
| Empirical root mean square error | 0.00025 | 0.00061 | 0.00174 |
| Percent of exact WTP | 0.36% | 0.92% | 2.26% |
| *Results at T = 50,000* | | | |
| Empirical bias in sampler | 0.00001 | −0.00009 | 0.00013 |
| Percent of exact WTP | 0.01% | −0.13% | 0.16% |
| Empirical root mean square error | 0.00011 | 0.00027 | 0.00078 |
| Percent of exact WTP | 0.16% | 0.41% | 1.01% |
| Sample size $T$ to achieve 1% error | 1,271 | 8,350 | 51,247 |
| Acceptance rate | 1.000 | 0.556 | 0.121 |
| Serial correlation | 0.000 | 0.444 | 0.883 |

applications, indirect utility functions that are additive linear in income, but with coefficients that differ across alternatives. Such models allow alternative shares to vary with income. Assume two alternatives with utilities $u_1 = y + x_1 + \varepsilon_1$ and $u_2 = \varepsilon_2$, where $\varepsilon_1$ and $\varepsilon_2$ are i.i.d. Extreme Value Type I disturbances. Assume $y = 1, x_1' = 0$ with injury, and $x_1'' = x > 0$ with restoration. Alternative 1 with injury is chosen if $\nu = \varepsilon_2 - \varepsilon_1 < y$; the probability of this event is $P_1' = 1/(1 + e^{-y})$. Alternative 1 with restoration is then also chosen, and the equivalent variation is $C_{11} = x$. Alternative 2 with restoration and compensation $C$ is chosen if $\nu > y - C + x$; the probability of this event is $1 - P_1''$, with $P_1'' = 1/(1 + e^{-y-x+2C})$. Alternative 2 with restoration is then also chosen, and the equivalent variation is $C_{22} = 0$. Finally, alternative 2 with injury and alternative 1 with restoration and compensation are chosen if $y < \nu < y - C_{21} + x$, and the equivalent variation is $C_{21} = y + x - \nu$ The exact mean WTP can be calculated for this example, and is

$$EC(y,t,p,x',x'',\varepsilon) = \int_{-\infty}^{y} C_{11}\cdot f(\nu)\, d\nu + \int_{y}^{y+x} C_{21}(\nu)\cdot f(\nu)\, d\nu = \log(1+e^{y+x}) - \log(1+e^{y}).$$

The simple bounds are $x/(1 + e^{-y}) \equiv x \cdot P_1' \leq EC(y,t,p,x',x'',\varepsilon) \leq x \cdot P_1'' \leq x/(1+e^{-y-x})$. The Morey approximation finds the equivalent variation $C$ that keeps expected utility constant: $\boldsymbol{E} \max u_i = \log(1 + e^{y+x_1})$ and $\log(1 + e^{y}) = \log(1 + e^{y-C+x})$, or $C = x$. The MCMC procedure in this example is unbiased, and estimates mean WTP as an average of the equivalent variations for individuals at i.i.d. draws of $\nu$. For $y = 1$ and various $x$, Table 15.3 below gives the exact mean WTP, the percentage errors in the Morey approximation, the lower and upper bounds and their average, and the MCMC sample sizes necessary to provide an estimate of mean WTP that has a root mean square error of one percent or less.

The Morey approximation is badly biased, even for small $x$ values, and clearly inferior to the simple bounds. The bounds are moderately accurate, and the average of the bounds is quite accurate for all $x$ values. The MCMC method is computationally straightforward, and at feasible sample sizes yields results that are more accurate with a RMSE that is one percent of the exact mean WTP. Because the MCMC method in this example reduces

*Table 15.3* Estimates of mean WTP when income coefficient varies by alternative

| Improvement x | 0.1 | 0.4 | 0.7 | 1.0 |
|---|---|---|---|---|
| Exact mean WTP | 0.0741 | 0.3072 | 0.5545 | 0.8137 |
| Percent error in Morey approximation | 35.0% | 30.2% | 26.2% | 22.9% |
| Percent error in lower bound | −1.3% | −4.8% | −7.7% | −10.2% |
| Percent error in upper bound | 1.3% | 4.5% | 6.7% | 8.3% |
| Percent error in average of bounds | −0.0% | −0.2% | −0.5% | −1.0% |
| GEV sampler size for 1% RMSE | 3433 | 2816 | 2325 | 1920 |

to i.i.d. sampling from extreme value distributions, it gives too optimistic a picture of the simulation sample sizes needed to achieve RMSE targets for more general GEV disturbances. The average bound will suffice for many policy applications, and the simulation method can be used as a cross-check on these bounds and to estimate mean WTP with whatever precision is needed.

## Conclusions

This chapter has established (1) general bounds on WTP that hold whenever consumers are choosing among discrete alternatives and there is a distribution of tastes in the population, and (2) simpler bounds and closed formulas for WTP in cases where the indirect utility function satisfies the parallel Engle curve condition of linear dependence on income, with a coefficient that does not vary by consumer, alternative, or resource allocation condition. For the case of utilities whose unobserved components have a GEV distribution in the population, an analytic formula is given for expected utility equivalent variation. When the indirect utility function satisfies the parallel Engle curve condition, this provides a representative consumer interpretation of expected utility, and an analytic form for WTP. However, when the indirect utility function does not satisfy the parallel Engle curve condition, the expected utility equivalent variation does not coincide with the consumer surplus definition of mean WTP, and an analytic expression is generally unavailable. The chapter gives a Monte Carlo Markov Chain simulation method that can be used in this case to estimate true WTP.

Mean WTP in this chapter is conditioned on observed values of income, user fees, prices, and alternative attributes under injury and restored conditions. For a population in which these variables are heterogeneous, mean WTP and its bounds are simply the expressions in the chapter, averaged with respect to the (empirical) distribution of these variables. One can extend this analysis to include unobserved heterogeneity in the population, by forming expectations of the formulas in the chapter with respect to the distribution of the unobserved variables. For example, suppose choice can be described by a multinomial logit model with random coefficients, and conditioned on these coefficients, indirect utility satisfies the parallel Engle curve condition. Then mean WTP conditioned on these coefficients is given by an analytic log sum formula. Averaging this mean WTP formula with respect to the distribution of the random coefficients then gives the true population mean WTP. If the parallel Engle curve condition is not satisfied, then the MCMC procedure described above, with additional simulation of the random coefficients, can be used to estimate mean WTP.

## Notes

This research was supported by the E. Morris Cox endowment at the University of California, Berkeley, and by the Atlantic Richfield Company. The sponsors are not responsible for the conclusions I draw in this chapter. In developing Section VI of the chapter, I have benefited from discussions with John Geweke, Vassilis Hajivassiliou, Reed Johnson, Tony Lancaster, Peter Rossi, Kenneth Train, and Steve Waters, and from the comments of two anonymous referees at the *Energy and Resources Journal*.

1 For current discussion, treat the consumer as making a single decision. For applications where multiple decisions are made over a "season", one can either interpret alternative $i$ as a "portfolio" of decisions made in sequence, or as one of the multiple decisions. In the first interpretation, the WTP to be calculated will be the overall compensation required for the "season". In the second interpretation, the WTP from this analysis will be an input to a higher-level model that puts together the individual decisions.

2 One of the alternatives will typically be "no trip", so that WTP calculations will take account of both trip substitution and trip generation.

3 This chapter deals with WTP *given* $y,t,p,x',x''$. Applications require unconditional WTP, obtained by averaging conditional WTP over the target population distribution of $y,t,p,x',x''$. A simple unweighted average corresponds to a particular "market-dictated" judgment that the social value of an additional dollar is the same for every individual, irrespective of income or utility level. This is the *de facto* standard used in benefit-cost analysis. However, it will not correspond to a social optimum unless redistribution policy is already non-distortionary and socially optimal. In general, a *weighted* average of individual WTP would be required to reach a (second-best) socially optimal decision.

4 Assume that the probability of ties between alternatives is zero; sufficient conditions for this are that the $\varepsilon$ vector has a continuous density whose support is $\mathbb{R}^J$, and that the vector of utility functions provides a one-to-one continuous mapping from $\varepsilon \in \mathbb{R}^J$ on to $\mathbb{R}^J$.

5 I used integration by parts, and the series expansion $\log(1 + e^{\nu}) = \sum_{k=1}^{\infty}(-1)^{k+1} \cdot e^{k\nu}/k$ for $\nu \leq 0$, to obtain the formulas $\int_{-x}^{0} \nu \cdot G'(\nu)\, d\nu = \frac{x}{1 + e^{x}} + \log[(1 + e^{x})/2]$ and $\int_{-x}^{0} \nu^2 \cdot G'(\nu)\, d\nu = \frac{-x^2}{1 + e^{x}} - 2 \cdot x \cdot \log(1 + e^{-x}) + 2 \sum_{k=1}^{\infty}(-1)^{k+1}(1 - e^{-kx})/k^2$.

6 In a recent paper, Karlström (1998) gives an ingenious argument showing for RUM of the form $U(y-t_i,p_i,x_i,\varepsilon_i) = V(y-t_i,p_i,x_i) + \varepsilon_i$ that each term on the right-hand side of the formula $EC(y,t,p,x',x'',\varepsilon) = \sum_{i=1}^{J} \sum_{k=1}^{J} \text{Prob}(B_{ik})E(C_{ik}B_{ik})$ can be written as a one-dimensional integral over an income interval of an expression involving a derivative of the choice probability $P_i$ with respect to the systematic part of the utility of alternative $k$, evaluated at particular income arguments. When it is feasible to calculate the choice probabilities analytically or numerically, it is also easy to calculate these one-deminsional integrals numerically. For the purpose of approximating WTP in GEV models, this approach appears to be clearly preferable to the MCMC method described in this section. For other policy purposes such as assessment of the distributional implications of a policy change, where one would like to recover the full distribution of compensating variations, the MCMC method that follows provides a general purpose, albeit computationally burdensome, method for simulating draws from the GEV distribution.

## Bibliography

Ben-Akiva, M. (1973) "Structure of passenger travel demand models," PhD dissertation, MIT.

Chib, S. and Greenberg, E. (1994) "Bayes inference in regression models with ARMA (*p*,*q*) errors," *Journal of Econometrics* 64: 183–206.

Chib, S. and Greenberg, E. (1995) "Understanding the Metropolis–Hastings Algorithm," *American Statistician* 49: 327–335.

Chib, S. and Greenberg, E. (1996) "Markov Chain Monte Carlo simulation methods in econometrics," *Econometric Theory* 12: 409–431.

Chipman, J. and Moore, J. (1980) "Compensating Variation, Consumer's Surplus, and Welfare," *American Economic Review* 70: 933–949.

Chipman, J. and Moore, J. (1990) "Acceptable Indicators of Welfare Change," in J Chipman, D. McFadden, and K. Richter (eds) *Preferences, Uncertainty, and Optimality*. Westview Press.

Diamond, P. and McFadden, D. (1974) "Some uses of the expenditure function in public finance," *Journal of Public Economics*: 3–21.

Deaton, A. and Muellbauer, J. (1980) *Economics and Consumer Behavior*. Cambridge: Cambridge University Press.

Domencich, T. and McFadden, D. (1975) *Urban Travel Demand: A Behavioral Analysis*, Amsterdam: North-Holland.

Hanemann, W.M. (1985) "Applied welfare analysis with discrete choice models," working paper, Department of Agricultural and Resource Economics, University of California.

Karlström, A. (1998) "Hicksian welfare measures in a nonlinear random utility framework," working paper, Department of Infrastructure and Planning, Royal Institute of Technology, Stockholm.

McFadden, D. (1973) "Conditional logit analysis of qualitative choice behavior," in P. Zarembka (ed.) *Frontiers in Econometrics*. New York: Academic Press.

McFadden, D. (1974) "The measurement of urban travel demand," *Journal of Public Economics*: 303–328.

McFadden, D. (1978) "Qualitative methods for analyzing travel behaviour of individuals," in D. Hensher and P. Stopher (eds) *Behavioural Travel Modelling*, pp. 279–318. London: Croom Helm.

McFadden, D. (1981) "Econometric models of probabilistic choice," in C. Manski and D. McFadden (eds) *Structural Analysis of Discrete Data with Econometric Applications*. Cambridge, MA: MIT Press.

McFadden, D. (1997) *Lectures in Simulation-Assisted Statistical Inference*. Berlin: Springer-Verlag.

Morey, E. Rowe, R. and Watson, M. (1993) "A repeated nested-logit model of Atlantic salmon fishing," *American Journal of Agricultural Economics* 75: 578–592.

Roberts, G. (1992) "Convergence diagnostics of the Gibbs sampler," in J. Bernardo et al. (eds) *Bayesian Statistics 4*, pp. 775–782. Oxford: Oxford University Press.

Roberts, G. and Smith, A. (1994) "Simple conditions for the convergence of the Gibbs sampler and Metropolis-Hastings algorithms," *Stochastic Processes and their Applications* 49: 207–216.

Tierney, L. (1994) "Markov chains for exploring posterior distributions," *Annals of Statistics* 22: 1701–1762.

Varian, H. (1984) *Microeconomic Analysis*, second edn. New York: Norton.

Zellner, A. and Min, C. (1995) "Gibbs Sampler convergence criteria," *Journal of the American Statistical Association* 90: 921–927.

# 16

# THE CORE AND COMPETITIVE EQUILIBRIA IN FINITE ECONOMIES[1]

*Lionel W. McKenzie*

The approach to competitive markets by way of bargaining among traders was developed by Edgeworth (1881). Walras (1874–77) considered markets led by market managers. In these markets, prices are announced which lead to offers to buy and sell, which are aggregated over the market. Then price lists are revised in the light of supply and demand, upward for an excess demand, downward for an excess supply. Trades are carried out when demand and supply are in balance. On the other hand, Edgeworth considered bargaining between individual traders in which no bargains are final until a point is reached where no group of traders can conclude a new bargain which they prefer to their existing bargains. Edgeworth showed in the simplest case of trading in two goods that such a situation, in which no new bargains are possible which are preferred by some participants, will approach a competitive equilibrium as the number of traders increases indefinitely. This result has been generalized to the case of many goods and to production economies in recent years. The path breaking paper was that of Debreu and Scarf (1963). Most of the results described in this chapter may be found in McKenzie (1988, 1990) and McKenzie and Shinotsuka (1991). There are also similar theorems in Hildenbrand and Kirman (1988). My purpose here is to show precisely where assumptions must be strengthened or may be weakened in establishing the major theorems of the subject for the case of economies with a finite number of agents and a finite number of goods.

## Core allocations which are competitive allocations

Consider an economy where the consumption sets $C^h \subset \boldsymbol{R}^n$, $h = 1, \ldots, H$, represent the sets of net possible trades by consumers. $C = \Sigma_{h=1}^{H} C^h$ is the set of possible net trades by all consumers together. Positive quantities represent amounts received by the consumer and negative quantities represent quantities provided by the consumer. A strictly preferred set $P^h(x)$ contains all commodity bundles preferred to $x$. A weakly preferred set $R^h(x)$ contains all commodity bundles to which $x$ is not preferred. $P^h$ is irreflexive if $x \notin P^h(x)$. From the interpretation of $P^h$ is clear that it is irreflexive. We will also use the expression $xP^hy$ for $x \in P^h(y)$ and correspondingly for $R^h$. That is, $P^h$ or $R^h$ may denote a relation or a correspondence determined by the relation. There is a production possibility set $Y \subset \boldsymbol{R}^n$. We will use the activities model of production, so $Y$ will be a convex cone with vertex at the origin. However diminishing returns can be accommodated by introducing entrepreneurial factors (McKenzie 1959). These activities are available to all consumers. An allocation of trades $\hat{x}$ is a list $(x^1, \ldots, x^H)$ such that $x^h \in C^h$ for all $h$. We may also write $\{x^h\}$ for an allocation when no confusion will result. A feasible allocation is an allocation that satisfies $\Sigma_1^H x^h \in Y$. If $x \in C^h$ then the $h$th consumer is locally not satiated at $x$ if an arbitrary neighborhood $U$ of $x$ contains $y \in U \cap C^h$ with $y \in P^h(x)$. The economy $E_1$ is given by the list $(C^1, \ldots, C^H, P^1, \ldots, P^H, Y)$.

In this section we make two assumptions on preferences.

1 $C^h$ is convex and not empty for all $h$.

2 For all $h$, $P^h$ is open valued relative to $C^h$. If $\hat{x}$ is feasible, the $h$th consumer is locally not satiated at $x^h$.

We also make two assumptions on production possibilities.

3 The production set $Y$ is a convex cone with vertex at the origin.

4 $Y \cap \boldsymbol{R}^n_+ = \{0\}$.

Finally two assumptions relate consumption sets and production sets. Let $x_S = \Sigma_{h \in S} x^h$ and $C_S = \Sigma_{h \in S} C_S^h$ where $S$ is a subset of consumers. An economy is said to be irreducible if for every nontrivial partition of the set of consumers into two subsets $S_1$ and $S_2$ the following condition holds. If $(x^1, \ldots, x^H)$ is a feasible allocation then there is $w \in C_{S_2}$ and $y' \in Y$ such that $z_{S_1} = y' - \alpha w$ for some $\alpha > 0$ and $z^h \in P^h(x^h)$ for all $h \in S_1$.

5 $Y \cap C^h \neq \varnothing$ and relative interior $Y \cap$ relative interior $C \neq \varnothing$.

6 The economy $E_1$ is irreducible.

Assumption 3 implies that production processes are independent and divisible. Assumption 4 is only a convenience since goods produced out of nothing need not be economized.

Irreducibility means that, given any feasible allocation of trades, if the consumers are divided into two nonempty sets each set will have a possible trade some multiple of which, together with a possible output variation, improves the allocation to the members of the other set. This idea and assumptions like 5 and 6 will play important roles whenever the existence of a competitive equilibrium is to be proved. The first part of Assumption 5 is a survival assumption for isolated individuals. The second part of Assumption 5 guarantees that there is $z \in C^h$ with $pz < 0$ for some $h$. Then Assumption 6 provides that if one consumer satisfies this condition all do. Assumption 6 together with Assumption 5 will imply that prices which support preferred sets together with the production set will be competitive equilibrium prices. We will mean by the relative interior of a set $V \subset \mathbf{R}^n$ the interior of $V$ relative to the smallest affine subspace containing $V$. We use this notion only with reference to convex sets. If a convex set is not empty, its relative interior is not empty.

The central idea leading to the concept of the core is that of an improving coalition. Given an allocation $(x^1, \ldots, x^H)$, an improving coalition is a subset of consumers $B$ such that for each $h \in B$ there is $z^h \in C^h$ with $\Sigma_{h \in B} z^h \in Y$ and $z^h \in P^h(x^h)$ for all $h$. Then the core of the economy is defined as the set of all feasible allocations for which there is no improving coalition. This concept corresponds to Edgeworth's idea of equilibrium since if an allocation is in the core there will be no group of traders who can negotiate a new bargain among themselves, taking account of their production possibilities, which will improve the position of all the traders in the group. We will show that when the consumers are duplicated without limit any allocation that remains in the core indefintely can be realized as a competitive equilibrium. Also the part of the core that assigns the same allocation to the replicas of each person will shrink to the set of competitive equilibria of the original economy.

Under these assumptions there is not a set of firms which exist independently of the choices of the agents. Rather there is a set of production possibilities, which are generated by activities available to any subset of agents that chooses to use them. For this reason the profit condition of competitive equilibrium will require that no profits are available and the demand condition will assume that households receive no income net of their sales of goods and services. However the conditions for competitive equilibrium will be equivalent under the present assumptions to the usual ones. We will say that $\{x^h\}$ is a competitive allocation if there is a price vector $p$ and an output $y$ such that

I $px^h \leq 0$, and $z \in P^h(x^h)$ implies $pz > 0$, for all $h$.
II $y \in Y$ and $py = 0$, while $z \in Y$ implies $pz \leq 0$.
III $\Sigma_{h=1}^{H} x^h = y$.

Since an activity can operate at any positive level, a positive profit is inconsistent with profit maximization. Since an activity can operate at zero level, a negative profit is also inconsistent with profit maximization. This leads to Condition II. Thus in equilibrium profits are zero and household income is 0 for all $h$. Zero income, along with maximization of preference within budget constraints, leads to Condition 1. Condition III is the balance of supply and demand.

Local nonsatiation alone implies that a competitive allocation lies in the core. In a Pareto improvement it is only required that some consumers benefit, not necessarily all consumers, while none suffers. The stronger criterion for improving coalitions may be defended as providing all members of an improving coalition with an incentive to act. Also the weaker definition is not sufficient for our proof that the equal treatment core is closed. This result is needed to prove that the equal treatment core converges to the set of competitive equilibria of the original economy as the economy is replicated and also to prove existence of equilibrium.

**Theorem 1** Local nonsatiation implies that a competitive allocation for $E_1$ is in the core.

*Proof* Let $\{x^h\}$ be a competitive allocation. It is implied by local nonsatiation that $px^h = 0$. Suppose $B$ is an improving coalition by means of the allocation $\{z^h\}_{h \in B}$ where $\Sigma_{h \in B}\, z^h = z \in Y$. Then $z^h \in P^h(x^h)$ for all $h \in B$. However $z^h \in P^h(x^h)$ implies that $pz^h > px^h$ from the demand condition of competitive equilibrium. Therefore $\Sigma_{h \in B}\, pz^h > \Sigma_{h \in B}\, px^h = 0$. But $z \in Y$ implies $pz \leq 0$ by condition II of competitive equilibrium. Thus no such improving coalition $B$ can exist and $\{x^h\}$ lies in the core. (Q.E.D.)

For each $h$ let the number of consumers identical to the consumer with index $h$ be increased to $r$ by adding new consumers and index the expanded set by $hs$ where $h = 1, \ldots, H$ and $s = 1, \ldots, r$. The economy that is replicated $r$ times will be referred to as $E_r$. The economy $E_r$ for $r > 1$ is given by the list $(C^{11}, \ldots, C^{1r}, \ldots, C^{H1}, \ldots, C^{Hr}, P^{11}, \ldots, P^{Hr}, Y)$. Allocations for $E_r$ may be written $\{x^{hs}\}$. We will consider allocations $\{x^{hs}\}$ in the core in which $x^{h1} = x^{hs}$ for $s = 1$ to $r$. These allocations form the equal treatment core. That is, the replicas of a given consumer receive the same allocation that he or she does. There will be no ambiguity if equal treatment allocations are indicated by the expression $\{x^h\}_r$.

**Lemma 1** As $r$ increases, the allocations $\{x^h\}_r$ in the equal treatment core of $E_r$ form a non-increasing sequence of nested sets.

*Proof* If $B$ is an improving coalition for the allocation $\{x^h\}_r$ when $r = s$, it is also an improving coalition when $r = s + 1$. Therefore as $r$ increases no new allocations $\{x^h\}_r$ can appear in the equal treatment core. (Q.E.D.)

The basic result is:

**Theorem 2** Under Assumptions 1–6 if $\{x^h\}_r$ is in the equal treatment core of $E_r$ for all $r$ as $r \to \infty$ then $\{x^h\}$ is a competitive allocation for $E_1$.

*Proof* Assume that $\{x^h\}_r$ is an allocation in the equal treatment core for all values of $r$. For any $x \geq 0$ let $P^h(x)$ be the set of trades preferred to the trade $x$ by consumers who are duplicates of the original consumer with index $h$. We may refer to them as consumers of the $h$th type. By Assumption 2, $P^h(x)$ is not empty and $P^h(x)$ is open relative to $C^h$. Let $P(x^1, \ldots, x^H) = P(\hat{x})$ be the convex hull of the $P^h(x^h)$.

Suppose $Y \cap P(\hat{x}) \neq \varnothing$. Then there is a set of consumers $B$ and weights $\alpha_i$ such that $\Sigma_{i \in B}\, \alpha_i z^i = y \in Y$, $\alpha_i > 0$, $\Sigma_{i \in B}\, \alpha_i = 1$, and $z^i \in P^{h(i)}(x^{h(i)})$ where the $i$th consumer of the set $B$ is a replica of the $h(i)$th original consumer. The consumers may be chosen so that the number of consumers in $B$ is less than or equal to $n + 1$ (Fenchel 1953: 37). For any positive integer $s$ let $a_i^s$ be the smallest integer greater than or equal to $s\alpha_i$. By the first part of Assumption 5, for each $i \in B$ there is $y^i \in C^{h(i)} \cap Y$. Let $w_s^i = (s\alpha_i / a_i^s)(z^i - y^i) + y^i$. Since $w_s^i$ is a convex combination of $z^i$ and $y^i$ it lies in $C^{h(i)}$ by Assumption 1. Moreover $w_s^i \to z^i$ as $n \to \infty$. It is this argument that requires the convexity of $C_h$ and the survival assumption for isolated individuals.

Since the preferred sets are open relative to the $C^{h(i)}$ by Assumption 2, we have $w_s^i \in P^{h(i)}(x^{h(i)})$ for all $i$ for some number $s$ which is large enough.

Also

$$\sum_{i \in B} a_i^s w_s^i = \sum_{i \in B} (s\alpha_i z^i - s\alpha_i y^i + a_i^s y^i) = sy + \sum_{i \in B} (a_i^s - s\alpha_i) y^i.$$

The fact that $0 \leq a_i^s - s\alpha_i$ and $y^i \in Y$ implies that $\Sigma_{i \in B}\, a_i^s w_s^i \in Y$, since $Y$ is a convex cone by Assumption 3. Let $T = \{\tau | h(i) = \tau$ for some $i \in B\}$. Let $B_\tau = \{i \in B | h(i) = \tau\}$. Put $r = \max_{\tau \in T}(\Sigma_{i \in B_\tau}\, a_i^s)$. If the economy has been replicated $r$ times there are enough traders of each type $\tau$ in $T$ to offer the net trade $\Sigma_{i \in B_\tau}\, a_i^s w_s^i$ needed from the $\tau$th type to achieve the improved allocation for all $i \in B$. Then the improving coalition can be formed if the original economy has been replicated $r$ times. This contradicts the hypothesis. Therefore $Y \cap P(x^1, \ldots, x^H) = \varnothing$. In other words $\{x^h\}_r$ in the core for all $r$ implies that the production set $Y$ intersected with the convex hull of the $P^h(x^h)$, the sets of preferred trades of the original consumers, is empty.

Consider $P(\hat{x})$ and $Y$ in the smallest linear subspace $L$ that contains both $C$ and $Y$. By a separation theorem for convex sets (Berge 1963: 162) there is a vector $p \in L$, $p \neq 0$, such that $pz \geq 0$ for all $z \in P(x^1, \ldots, x^H)$ and $pz \leq 0$ for all $z \in Y$. Since $P^h(x^h) \subset P(x^1, \ldots, x^H)$, $pz \geq 0$ for all $z \in P(x^h)$. By Assumption 2 there is a point $z \in P^h(x^h)$ in every neighborhood of $x^h$. Thus $px^h \geq 0$ must hold for all $h$. Since $(x^1, \ldots, x^h)$ is an allocation it is also true that $\Sigma_{h=1}^H\, x^h = y \in Y$. Therefore $p \cdot \Sigma_{h=1}^H\, x^h \leq 0$. This implies that $px^h = 0$ must hold for all $h$.

To complete the proof it is necessary to show that in fact $pz > 0$ for any $z \in P_h(x^h)$ for all $h$. We first prove two lemmas.

**Lemma 2** Let sets $A$ and $B$ be convex sets in $R^n$. Suppose $0 \in A$. If relative interior $A \cap$ relative interior $B \neq \emptyset$ there is no hyperplane which separates $A$ and $B$ in the smallest linear subspace containing both.
*Proof* Let $L$ be the smallest linear subspace containing $A$ and $B$. If $H$ is a hyperplane separating $A$ and $B$ in $L$ then there is $q \in L$, $q \neq 0$, such that $H = \{z \in L | qz = \mu\}$ and $H$ separates $A$ and $B$ in $L$. However, $q$ may be chosen so that $qz \leq \mu$ for all $z \in A$ and $qz \geq \mu$ for all $z \in B$. Then $y \in A \cap B$ implies $qy = \mu$. But $y \in$ relative interior $A$ implies $qz = \mu$ for all $z \in A$. Similarly $qz = \mu$ for all $z \in B$. Then $0 \in A$ implies $\mu = 0$. Since $A$ and $B$ span $L$ this implies $qz = 0$ for all $z \in L$. Then $q \in L$ implies that $q = 0$. Since this is a contradiction of the choice of $q$, no such separation is possible. (Q.E.D.)

**Lemma 3** If $pz \geq 0$ for all $z \in P^h(x)$ where $x \in C^h$, and there is $w \in C^h$ such that $pw < 0$, then $pz > 0$ holds for all $z \in P^h(x)$.
*Proof* Assume there is $z \in P^h(x)$ where $pz = 0$. Since $P^h$ is open in $C^h$ and $C^h$ is convex by Assumption 1, there is $z' \neq z$ on the line segment from $w$ to $z$ and close to $z$ such that $z' \in P^h(x)$. But $pz' < 0$ in contradiction to the hypothesis. Thus $pz > 0$ holds for all $z \in P^h(x)$. (Q.E.D.)

The vector $p$ supports $Y$. Thus $pz \leq 0$ for all $z \in Y$. Since relative interior $Y \cap$ relative interior $C$ contains a point $w$ by the second part of Assumption 5, and $0 \in Y$, it is implied by Lemma 2 that $pw < 0$. Therefore $pw^h < 0$ for some $w^h \in C^h$ for some $h$. Let $pw^h < 0$ hold for $h \in S_1$ and $pw^h \geq 0$ hold for $h \in S_2$ where $S_2$ and $S_1$ partition the set of consumers. Lemma 3 implies that $pz > 0$ holds for all $z \in P^h(x^h)$ for $h \in S_1$. However by irreducibility there is $w \in C_{S_2}$ and $y' \in Y$ such that $z_{s_1} = y' - \alpha w$ for $\alpha > 0$ and $z^h \in P^h(x^h)$ for all $h \in S_1$. Since $py' \leq 0$ and $pz_{S_1} > 0$, we have $pw < 0$ in contradiction to the definition of $S_2$. Therefore $S_2$ must be empty. Then $S_1 = (1, \ldots, H)$ and $pz > 0$ for $z \in P(x^h)$ for all $h$. Thus the demand condition of competitive equilibrium is met. Since $px^h = 0$ and $y = \Sigma_{h=1}^{H} x^h$ we have $py = 0$. But $pz \leq 0$ for all $z \in Y$ by the support property. Therefore the profit condition is met. The balance condition is implied by the definition of a feasible allocation. Thus $\{x^h\}_1$ is a competitive allocation for $E_1$. (Q.E.D.)

## Convergence of the equal treatment core to the set of equilibria

With somewhat strengthened assumptions it is possible to go further and prove convergence of the set of allocations in the equal treatment core to the set of competitive allocations. We introduce

1′ $C^h$ is convex and not empty, and *closed and bounded from below*, for all $h$.
2′ Relative to $C^h$, $P^h$ is open valued with *open lower sections* for all $h$. If $\hat{x}$ is feasible, the $h$th consumer is locally not satiated at $x^h$.
3′ The production set $Y$ is a *closed* convex cone with vertex at the origin.

The new assumptions are in italics.

Let $K_r$ be the set of allocations $\{x^h\}_r$ in the equal treatment core of $E_r$ where there are $r$ members of each type and let $W$ be the set of competitive allocations $\{x^h\}$ in $E_1$. Let the distance $d(K_r, W)$ of the equal treatment core to the set of competitive allocations in $E_1$ be given by

$$d(K_r, W) = \max_{x \varepsilon K_r} \min_{z \varepsilon W} |x - z| + \max_{z \varepsilon W} \min_{x \varepsilon K_r} |x - z|.$$

Convergence of the equal treatment core to the set of competitive allocations of $E_1$ is defined by $d(K_r, W) \to 0$ as $r \to \infty$.

Let $T$ be the set of equal treatment allocations which are feasible, that is, $T = \{\{x^h\}_r | \Sigma_{h=1}^{H} x^h \in Y\}$. Because of equal treatment and Assumption 3, that $Y$ is a cone, the index $r$ is irrelevant to feasibility. We first prove:

**Lemma** 4 With Assumptions 1′ and 3′ the set $T$ is compact.

*Proof* Since $T$ lies in a metric space, to prove compactness it suffices to show that every infinite sequence of feasible allocations has a point of accumulation which is contained in $T$ (Berge 1963: 90). Let $\hat{x}^s = (x^{1s}, \ldots, x^{Hs})$, $s = 1, 2, \ldots$, be a sequence of allocations with $\Sigma_{h=1}^{H} x^{hs} = y^s \in Y$. I claim that $\hat{x}^s$ is bounded. If not, since the $C^h$ are bounded below it must be that $x_i^{hs} \to \infty$ for some $h$ and $i$. But for a subsequence (retain notation) $y^s/|y^s| \to y \geq 0$ and $\neq 0$. Since $Y$ closed implies that $y \in Y$ Assumption 4 is violated. This shows that $x^{hs}$ is bounded for each $h$. Since $C^h$ is closed there is a point of accumulation $(\bar{x}^1, \ldots, \bar{x}^H)$ for the sequence $(x^{1s}, \ldots, x^{Hs})$, $s = 1, 2, \ldots$, with $\bar{x}^h \in C^h$ for all $h$. The point $(\bar{x}^1, \ldots, \bar{x}^H)$ represents a feasible allocation and lies in $T$. (Q.E.D.)

The new closedness and boundedness assumptions were needed for Lemma 4.

We may now prove:

**Theorem 3** Give Assumptions 1′, 2′, 3′, 4, 5, 6, if the equal treatment core of $E_r$ is not empty, as the number of replications increases without limit, the equal treatment core of $E_r$ converges to the set of competitive allocations of the original economy $E_1$.

*Proof* From the definition of a competitive allocation the competitive allocations of the original economy are the competitive allocations with equal treatment in the replicated economy. Since by Theorem 1 competitive allocations are always in the core, the second term of the distance formula is 0 for all $r$. Thus the theorem requires that the first term be shown to converge to 0. Suppose that $\{z^h\}_r$ is an allocation for which there is an improving coalition $B$. Recall $T$ is the set of equal treatment allocations which are feasible. Let the allocation to the replicas of the $h$th consumer be perturbed by $\Delta x^h$ where $\Sigma_{h=1}^{H} \Delta x^h = 0$, $|\Delta x^h| < \varepsilon > 0$, and $x^h + \Delta x^h \in C^h$, for all $h$. By Assumption 2′ the preference correspondences $P^h$ have open lower sections relative to $C^h$. Thus if $\varepsilon$ is sufficiently small the new allocation $\{x^h + \Delta x^h\}_{h \in B}$ is still dominated by the same net trades achievable within $B$ alone that dominated $\{x^h\}_{h \in B}$. Note that this argument uses the strong definition of an improving coalition. Then the set of allocations $T \backslash K_r$ for which there is an improving coalition is open relative to the set of feasible allocations. Also the set $T$ of feasible equal treatment allocations is closed in $\boldsymbol{R}^n$ by Lemma 4. Therefore the set of allocations $K_r$ is closed in $\boldsymbol{R}^n$. This is the argument that requires open lower sections for the preference correspondences $P^h$.

By Lemma 1 an allocation in the equal treatment core for the $s$th replica economy is in the core for all $r < s$. Suppose there are allocations $\{w^h\}_r$ in $K_r$ and at a distance of at least $\varepsilon > 0$ from any allocation in $W$ for indefinitely large $r$. Since $T$ is compact by Lemma 4, there would be an accumulation point $\{z^h\}$ of the sequence $\{w^h\}_r$ where $\{z^h\}$ lies at least $\varepsilon$ from any allocation in $W$. But Lemma 1 implies that a subsequent $\{w^h\}_r$ (save notation) which converges to $\{z^h\}$ as $r \to \infty$ provides for any $s$ a subsequence (save notation) along which $r > s$ holds which converges to $\{z^h\}$ as $r \to \infty$ and which is contained in $K_s$. Since $K_s$ is closed $\{z^h\}$ lies in $K_s$ for all $s$. Therefore $\{z^h\}$ is a competitive allocation of $E_1$ by Theorem 2, contradicting the inference from the definition of the sequence $\{w^h\}_r$ that $\{z^h\}$ lies at least $\varepsilon$ from the set of competitive allocations of $E_1$. Thus no such sequence can exist and it must be that $K_r$ converges to $W$ as $r \to \infty$. (Q.E.D.)

The Pareto optimum is an allocation for which the coalition of the whole is not an improving coalition, even in a weak sense. No other improving coalitions are considered, in particular not the coalitions composed of single consumers. On the other hand the competitive equilibrium does not allow any improving coalition. Moreover competitive equilibrium requires that each consumer's allocations have zero value at some price vector. In a sense the core is an intermediate notion, especially if we take a weaker definition of an improving coalition and thus a stronger definition of the core. This definition would serve for the proof of Theorem 2 with no major change, but not for the proof of Theorem 3. Let a weakly improving coalition $B$ for an allocation $\{x^h\}$ be a coalition for which there is an allocation $\{z^h\}$ with $\Sigma_{h \in B}\, z^h = \Sigma_{h \in B}\, x^h$ such that $x^h \notin P^h(z^h)$ for any $h \in B$ and $z^h \in P^h(x^h)$ for some $h \in B$. Then the strong core is the set of allocations for which there is no weakly improving coalition. If an allocation is in the strong core then for any coalition there is no allocation within its feasible set which is a Pareto improvement over its core allocation. The analogous relation holds between the ordinary core allocation and the weak Pareto optimum, defined as an allocation such that no reallocation can improve the position of every consumer.

The set of competitive equilibrium allocations is the subset of the strong core in which the core allocations have a zero value at a supporting price vector. Thus although a limit of equal treatment allocations in the strong core as the number of replications increases without limit is a competitive equilibrium, it is not clear that this limit lies in the strong core. However we will find that a slight strengthening of the irreducibility assumption, which we need for proving that the equal treatment core is not empty, will imply that the strong and weak cores coincide.

## Nonemptiness of the core

It has been proved that every competitive equilibrium is in the core. We will show that the existence of an allocation in the core may be proved independently of the existence of equilibrium allocations. Then the existence of an allocation in the equal treatment core can be used together with Theorem 2 to prove the existence of a competitive equilibrium for $E_1$. The economy $E_1$ is defined, as described, by means of consumption sets $C^h \subset \boldsymbol{R}^n$, strict preference correspondences $P^h$, for $h = 1, \ldots, H$, and a production set $Y$. $C = \Sigma_{h=1}^{H} C^h$. The assumptions are strengthened in some respects and weakened in others. Assumptions 1′, 3′, and 4 are retained. The graph of $P^h$ is the set $\{(x, y) \in C^h \times C^h | y \in P^h(x)\}$. Assumption 2′ is replaced by the slightly stronger assumption:

2″ For all $h$, *$P^h$ is convex valued. The graph of $P^h$ is open relative to $C^h \times C^h$.*

Assumption 6 is not needed and Assumption 5 is replaced by the weaker assumption:

5′ For all $h$, $C^h \cap Y$ is not empty.

It will be noted that $P^h$ is now assumed to be convex valued although this assumption was not needed in Theorem 3 to prove convergence of the equal treatment core to the set of competitive equilibria for $E_1$. This assumption is also critical for the existence of competitive equilibrium. On the other hand irreducibility, interiority, and local nonsatiation are not needed here. The assumption that the graph of $P^h$ is open is a slight strengthening of the assumption in 2′ that $P^h$ is open valued and has open lower sections. On the other hand, irreducibility and interiority assumptions are important for the existence of a competitive equilibrium but not for the existence of a point in the core.

We first record some properties of the set of feasible allocations $F_S$ where $S \subset (1, \ldots, H)$. Let $x_S = (x^h)_{h \in S}$. $F_S = \{(x^h)_{h \in S} | x^h \in C^h$ for all $h \in S$ and $\Sigma_{h \in S} x^h \in Y\}$.

**Lemma 5** $F_S$ is nonempty, compact, and convex.

*Proof* Assumption 5′ and the fact that $Y$ is a cone imply that $F_S$ is not empty. $F_S$ is compact by the argument of the proof of Lemma 4. Convexity of $F_S$ follows from the convexity of the $C^h$ and $Y$. (Q.E.D.)

Let $\mathcal{B}$ be a nonempty family of subsets of $\{1, \ldots, H\}$. Define $\mathcal{B}_h = \{S \in \mathcal{B} | h \in S\}$. A family $\mathcal{B}$ is balanced if there exist nonnegative weights $\{\lambda_S\}$ with $\Sigma_{S \in \mathcal{B}_h} \lambda S = 1$ for all $h$. Let $I = \{1, \ldots, H\}$. The economy is said to be $0$-balanced, if for any balanced family $\mathcal{B}$ with balancing weights $\{\lambda_S\}$ which satisfies $x_S \in F_S$ for all $S \in \mathcal{B}$, it follows that $x_I \in F_I$ where $x_I^h = \Sigma_{S \in \mathcal{B}_h} \lambda_S x_S^h$.

**Lemma 6** The economy $E_1$ is $0$-balanced.
*Proof* To show that $x_I$ is feasible it is necessary and sufficient to show that $x_I^h \in C^h$ for all $h$ and $\Sigma_{h \in S} x_I^h \in Y$. Since $x_S^h \in C^h$ for each $S \in \mathcal{B}_h$ by the feasibility of $x_S$ and $x_I^h$ is a convex combination of the $x_S^h$ for $S \in \mathcal{B}_h$, $x_I^h$ lies in $C^h$ by the convexity of $C^h$. On the other hand, since $Y$ is a cone with vertex at the origin $\Sigma_{h \in S} x_S^h \in Y$ implies that $\Sigma_{h \in S} \lambda_S x_S^h \in Y$ and $\Sigma_{S \in \mathcal{B}} \Sigma_{h \in S} \lambda_S x_S^h \in Y$. But $\Sigma_{S \in \mathcal{B}} \Sigma_{h \in S} \lambda_S x_S^h = \Sigma_{h \in I} \Sigma_{S \in \mathcal{B}_h} \lambda_S x_S^h = \Sigma_h x_I^h$. This completes the proof. (Q.E.D.)

The following theorem is from Border (1985). It is rephrased to accord with our terminology.

**Theorem (Border)** Let $E$ be an economy given by the list $(C^1, \ldots, C^H, P^1, \ldots, P^H, Y)$ satisfying:

1 For each $h = 1, \ldots, H$, $C^h$ is a nonempty convex subset of $\boldsymbol{R}^n$.
2 For any $S \subset I$, $F_S$ is a nonempty compact subset of $\Pi_{h \in S} C^h$.
3 For each $h$, (a) $P^h$ has an open graph in $C^h \times C^h$, (b) $x \notin P^h(x)$, (c) $P^h$ is convex valued (but possibly empty).
4 $E$ is $0$-balanced.

Then the core of $E$ is not empty.

We may now assert:

**Theorem 4** Under Assumptions 1′, 2″, 3′, 4, and 5′ the economy $E$ has a nonempty core.
*Proof* Condition 1 in Border's theorem is contained in Assumption 1. Lemma 5 implies Condition 2. Condition 3 is implied by Assumption 2″ and the definition of $P^h$. Condition 4 is provided by Lemma 6. Applying Border's theorem the conclusion follows. (Q.E.D.)

## Existence of competitive equilibrium

We have proved the core not to be empty under assumptions which are weaker in some respects and stronger in other respects than the assumptions used to show that allocations that remain in the equal treatment cores of replicated economies are competitive allocations. We also found that the equal treatment core converges to the set of competitive allocations. This suggests that if the nonemptiness of the core can be extended to the equal treatment core, it will be possible to prove that a competitive equilibrium exists by using the strongest form of each assumption from earlier sections. However to prove that the equal treatment core is not empty it is necessary to strengthen the irreducibility assumption although no irreducibility assumption was needed to prove the core nonempty.

If $C$ is a convex set, $x \in C$ is an extreme point of $C$ if $x$ is not a convex combination of two points of $C$ distinct from $x$. We will say that the economy is strongly irreducible if it is irreducible and, whenever $S_1$, $S_2$ is a nontrivial partition of $\{1, \ldots, H\}$, and $x_{S_1} + x_{S_2} \in Y$ where $x_{S_2}$ is not an extreme point of $C_{S_2}$, there are $z_{S_1} + z_{S_2} \in Y$ with $z^h P^h x^h$ for $h \in S_1$. Another version of this concept was introduced in Boyd and McKenzie (1993).

By Theorem 2 we have found that under weak conditions the equal treatment core $K_r$ converges to the set of competitive equilibria $W$ of $E_1$. Bounding and closing $C^h$ and closing $Y$, and introducing convexity of preference with an open graph, it was possible to prove that the core of $E_r$ is not empty. This result did not require irreducibility. However in order to obtain the existence of competitive equilibrium we will require stronger forms of both Assumptions 2″ and 6.

**Assumption** 2‴ For all $h$, $P^h$ is convex valued *and transitive. For all* $x \in C^h$, $R^h(x)$ *is the closure of* $P^h(x)$. The graph of $P^h$ is open relative to $C^h \times C^h$.
**Assumption** 6′ The economy is *strongly* irreducible.

Recall that $x$ is indifferent with $y$, $xI^hy$, if $xR^hy$ and $yR^hx$ where $xR^hy$ means not $yP^hx$. We define $I^h(x) = \{y | yI^hx\}$. Thus $y \in I^h(x)$ means $x \notin P^h(y)$ and $y \notin P^h(x)$. The strengthening of the assumption on preferences in 2‴ and the introduction of strong irreducibility in 6′ are needed to prove that equal treatment allocations in the core for replicates of a given consumer are indifferent. This result is needed in turn to show that $K_r$ is not empty if $E_r$ is not empty.

**Lemma 8** For $x \in C^h$, $x$ is locally nonsatiated for all $h$.
*Proof* Since $x^h \in R^h(x^h)$ Assumption 2‴ implies there is $z$ in every neighborhood of $x^h$ with $z \in P^h(x^h)$. (Q.E.D.)

Lemma 8 allows us to appeal to results which depend on local nonsatiation.

**Lemma 9** If $x \in P^h(z)$ and $z \in R^h(y)$ then $x \in P^h(y)$.
*Proof* Since $R^h(y)$ is the closure of $P^h(y)$ there is $z^\nu \to z$ where $z^\nu \in P^h(y)$. Since the graph of $P^h$ is open, for $\nu$ large enough $x \in P^h(z^\nu)$. Thus by transitivity $x \in P^h(y)$. (Q.E.D.)

Lemma 9 allows us to prove:

**Lemma 10** Under Assumptions 1′, 2′′′, and 6′, suppose $\{x^{hk}\}_r$, $h = 1, \ldots, H$, and $k = 1, \ldots, r$, is an allocation in the core of $E_r$. Then for given $h$, $x^{hk} I^h x^{hk'}$ holds for all $k$ and $k'$.

*Proof* Let the allocation $\{x^{hk}\}_r$ where $h = (1, \ldots, H)$ and $k = (1, \ldots, r)$ lie in the core for the economy $E_r$. I claim that $x^{hk} I^h x^{hj}$ for all $h, k, j$. Suppose not. Consider a replica with index $hj(h)$, for each original consumer with index $h$, where $hj(h)$ satisfies $x^{hk} R^h x^{hj(h)}$ for all $k = 1, \ldots, r$. That is, $hj(h)$ has an allocation which is no better, and perhaps poorer, than the allocation of any other replica of $h$. The existence of $hj(h)$ is guaranteed by the irreflexivity and transitivity of preference, and it is for this reason that transitivity is introduced. Consider the coalition $B = \{1j(1), \ldots, Hj(H)\}$ and the allocation to the member of $B$ with index $hj(h)$ of $(1/r)\,\Sigma_{k=1}^{r} x^{hk} = x^h$. Since $R^h$ is the closure of $P^h$ by Assumption 2′′′, $R^h$ is convex valued. Therefore for each $h$ we have $x^h R^h x^{hj(h)}$. Also if $x^{ik} P^i x^{ij(i)}$ for some $i, k$, then $x^i$ is a convex combination which includes an interior point of $R^i(x^{ij(i)})$, so $x^i$ cannot lie on the boundary of $R^i(x^{ij(i)})$ relative to $C^h$. Therefore $x^i P^i x^{ij(i)}$ holds.

Now $\Sigma_{h=1}^{H} x^h = (1/r)\,\Sigma_{k=1}^{r} \Sigma_{h=1}^{H} x^{hk}$ which lies in $Y$ since $\{x^{hk}\}$ is feasible and $Y$ is a cone. Thus $\{x^h\}_1$ is a feasible allocation. By strong irreducibility and convexity we will see that it is possible to spread the gain received by $i$ from the allocation $\{x^h\}_1$ to all $h$. Let $S_1 = \{h | h \neq i\}$ and $S_2 = \{i\}$. Since $x^i$ is not an extreme point of $C^i$, strong irreducibility implies that there is a feasible allocation $\{z^h\}$ with $z^h P^h x^h$ for $h \in S_1$. Take the convex combination $w^h = \{\lambda x^h + (1 - \lambda) z^h\}$ for $0 \leq \lambda \leq 1$. $\{w^h\}_{h=1}^{H}$ is a feasible allocation. Moreover $w^h$ is preferred by all $h \in S_1$ to $x^h$ and, using Lemma 9, to $x^{hj(h)}$ as well. Since $x^i P^i x^{ij(i)}$ and the graph of $P^i$ is open, for $\lambda$ sufficiently close to 1, $w^i$ is preferred by $i$ to $x^h$. Thus $B$ is an improving coalition and $\{x^{hk}\}_r$ is not an allocation in the core of $E_r$ contrary to the assumption. Therefore $x^{hk} I^h x^{hk'}$ must hold for all $k, k'$. (Q.E.D.)

Note that Lemma 10 implies that the weak and strong cores coincide under strong irreducibility.

**Lemma 11** Under the assumptions of Lemma 10 the equal treatment core $K_r$ of $E_r$ is nonempty if the core of $E_r$ is nonempty.

*Proof* According to Lemma 10, for any allocation in the core the allocations received by the replicas of a given $h$ in the original economy are indifferent. By the convex valuedness of the correspondence $R^h$ the equal treatment allocation in which each replica of $h$ receives $x^h$, as defined in the proof of Lemma 10, satisfies $x^h R^h x^{hk}$ for all $h, k$. Then by Lemma 9 there is no improving coalition for the allocation $\{x^{hk}\}_r$. There is also no improving coalition for the allocation $\{y^{hk}\}_r$ in which $y^{hk} = x^h$ for all $h, k$. Therefore $\{y^{hk}\}_r$ is in the core of $E_r$. (Q.E.D.)

**Lemma 12** Under Assumptions 1′, 2‴, 3′, 4, 5′, 6′, the equal treatment core $K_r$ of $E_r$ is not empty.

*Proof* By Theorem 4 the core of $E_r$ is not empty. By Lemma 11 this implies that the equal treatment core $K_r$ of $E_r$ is not empty. (Q.E.D.)

We may now prove:

**Theorem 5** Under Assumptions 1′, 2‴, 3′, 4, 5, and 6′ the economy $E_1$ has a competitive equilibrium, and $K = W$.

*Proof* The assumptions imply the assumptions of the previous section, so by Theorem 4 the core of $E_r$ is not empty for any $r$. Since the assumptions also imply the assumptions of Lemma 12, the set of equal treatment allocations in the core is not empty for any $E_r$. From the proof of Theorem 3 the set $K_r$ is closed. Also the $K_r$ are nested by Lemma 1. Therefore $K = \bigcap_{r=1}^{\infty} K_r$ is not empty. But the assumptions imply the assumptions in the first section, so, by Theorem 2, $K$ is included in the set of competitive allocations for $E_1$. Indeed, by Theorem 3 the equal treatment core of $E_r$ converges to the set of competitive allocations of $E_1$ as $r \to \infty$. Since both sets are closed $K$ is precisely the set $W$ of competitive allocations. Finally the proof of Theorem 2 provides a price vector $p$ which supports the allocations of $K$ in a competitive equilibrium given by $(p, y, \hat{x})$ where $y = \Sigma_{h=1}^{\infty} x^h$. (Q.E.D.)

Once transitivity is introduced, the Scarf theorem (1967) becomes available for proving that the core is not empty, so it would be enough to stay with open lower sections and open values, rather than requiring an open graph. On the other hand, use of the weak core requires strong irreducibility, which is needed in the proof that the equal treatment core is closed. However we know from the theorem of Gale and Mas-Colell (1975) that existence of competitive equilibrium can be proved without transitivity. Indeed we know from Moore (1975) and McKenzie (1981) that the survival of isolated individuals is also not needed for proving the existence of competitive equilibrium. Indeed individual survival, convexity of $R^h$, and transitivity may be dispensed with together (see McKenzie (1981)).

The line of proof that we have followed is that used by Boyd and McKenzie (1993) to prove a theorem for the case of an infinite number of goods, except that they assume transitivity already at the stage where it is proved that the core is not empty. This is to allow the use of Scarf theorem for a nonempty core, which is proved in the utility space, rather than the Border (1985) theorem, which is proved in the goods space. The Border proof makes essential use of the finite dimensionality of the goods space (see Yannelis (1991)). Yannelis provides a proof of nonemptiness of the core for the case of a goods space with infinite dimension. However the proof of existence is still blocked by need for transitivity to establish that consumers of the same type have allocations in the core which are indifferent. Whether the line of proof we have used here for the finite case can be improved to match the results of Gale and Mas-Colell, Moore, and McKenzie, is an open question so far as I know.

A further strengthening of the assumptions can reduce the core of $E_r$ to the equal treatment core. Assume that preferences are strictly convex in the sense that $xI^hy$ and $z = \alpha x + (1 - \alpha)y$, for $x, y \in C^h$ and $0 < \alpha < 1$ implies $zP^hx$. Then we may prove a result used by Debreu and Scarf (1963).

**Lemma 13** Assume $P^h$ is strictly convex, $R^h(x^h)$ is the closure of $P^h(x^h)$ when $\hat{x}$ is feasible, and $E_1$ is strongly irreducible. Then all allocations in the core of $E_r$ are equal treatment allocations.

*Proof* The conclusion of the lemma is equivalent to the statement that an allocation in the core of $E_r$ has $x^{hk} = x^{hk'}$ for all $k, k' = 1, \ldots, r$. Suppose not. For any $h$ let $x^{hj(h)}$ satisfy $x^{hk}R^hx^{hj(h)}$ for all $k$. Then the consumer with index $hj(h)$ is a worse off consumer among the replicates of the $h$th original consumer. By strict convexity of preference $(1/r)\ \Sigma_{k=1}^{r}\ x^{hk}R^hx^{hj(h)}$ for $h = 1, \ldots, H$ with $P^h$ in place of $R^h$ at least once. Strong irreducibility implies that $P^h$ can be realized for all $hj(h) \in B = (1j(1), \ldots, Hj(H))$. But $\bar{x}^h = (1/r)\ \Sigma_{k=1}^{r}\ x^{hk} \in C^h$ by convexity of $C^h$ and $(1/r)\ \Sigma_{h=1}^{H}\ \Sigma_{k=1}^{r}\ x^{hk} \in Y$ since $Y$ is a cone. Thus $B$ is an improving coalition with the allocation $\{\bar{x}^h\}$, so $\{x^{hk}\}_r$ is not in the core of $E_r$, contrary to assumption. This implies that $x^{hk} = x^{hk'}$ for all $k, k' = 1, \ldots, r$, and all allocations in the core of $E_r$ are equal treatment allocations. (Q.E.D.)

## Notes

1 I am grateful to John Boyd and Tomoichi Shinotsuka for their assistance.

## Bibliography


Berge, Claude (1963) *Topological Spaces*. New York: Macmillan.

Border, Kim C. (1985) *Fixed Point Theorems with Applications to Economics and Game Theory*. Cambridge: Cambridge University Press.

Boyd, John H., III and McKenzie, Lionel W. (1993) "The Existence of Competitive Equilibrium over an Infinite Horizon with Production and General Consumption Sets," *International Economic Review* 34: 1–20.

Debreu, Gerard and Scarf, Herbert (1963) "A Limit Theorem on the Core of an Economy," *International Economic Review* 4: 235–246.

Edgeworth, Francis Y. (1881) *Mathematical Psychics*. London: Kegan Paul.

Fenchel, W. (1951) *Convex Cones, Sets, and Functions*. Mathematics Department, Princeton University (mimeographed).

Gale, David and Mas-Colell, Andreu (1975) "An Equilibrium Existence Theorem for a General Model without Ordered Preferences," *Journal of Mathematical Economics* 2: 9–16.

Hildenbrand, W. and Kirman, Alan (1988) *Equilibrium Analysis, Variations on a Theme by Edgeworth and Walras*. New York: North-Holland.

McKenzie, Lionel W. (1959) "On the Existence of General Equilibrium for a Competitive Market," *Econometrica* 27: 54–71.
McKenzie, Lionel W. (1981) "The Classical Theorem on Existence of Competitive Equilibrium," *Econometrica* 49: 819–841.
McKenzie, Lionel W. (1988) "A Limit Theorem on the Core," *Economics Letters* 27: 7–9.
McKenzie, Lionel W. (1990) "A Limit Theorem on the Core, Addendum," *Economics Letters* 32: 109–110.
McKenzie, Lionel, and Shinotsuka, Tomoichi (1991) "A Limit Theorem on the Core, Addendum II," *Economics Letters* 37: 331.
Moore, James (1975) "The Existence of 'Compensated Equilibrium' and the Structure of the Pareto Efficient Frontier," *International Economic Review* 15: 267–300.
Scarf, Herbert (1967) "The Core of an *n*-Person Game," *Econometrica* 35: 50–69.
Yannelis, Nicholas C. (1991) "The Core of an Economy without Ordered Preferences," in M. Ali Khan and N.C. Yannelis (eds) *Equilibrium Theory in Infinite Dimensional Spaces*. Berlin: Springer-Verlag.
Walras, Leon (1874–77) *Eléments d'Economie Politique Pure*. Lausanne: Corbaz. Trans. by W. Jaffe from the 1926 definitive edition as *Elements of Pure Economics* (1954). New York: Orion; London: George Allen and Unwin.

# 17

# QUASI-EQUIVALENT VARIATION ANALYSIS IN THE GORMAN POLAR CASE

*James C. Moore*

## Introduction

For some time I have thought that I would like to try to write a simple expository development of the method of "quasi-equivalent variation analysis" for the case of the Gorman Polar Form which John Chipman and I introduced in Chipman and Moore (1990) (I will refer to this article as "CM90" hereafter). In the earlier work, John and I were interested in developing a number of ideas other than quasi-equivalent variation analysis per se; and, as a result, one must read through a great deal of technical material before getting to a discussion of this technique. Moreover, some problems with the word processing software which was used for the production of the volume in which the 1990 article appears resulted in such a large number of "typos" that CM90 is extremely difficult to read. Consequently, it would seem that a simplified version of the paper itself would be useful; but, in fact, in this chapter I will develop a somewhat simplified version of the technique of "quasi-equivalent variation analysis" itself. Moreover, I will present a slightly different argument as to why such analysis should be of interest than is done in CM90, as well as a discussion of how and why such a method should be used. In the context of some examples, I will also explore the simplifications which are possible in the situation in which a subset of prices remains fixed throughout the analysis. A complete exploration of this case will have to await a later work, however.[1]

In CM90, we developed what we call "quasi-equivalent variation" analysis for the Gorman Polar case. While we differentiate our analysis from "equivalent variation," I should emphasize at the outset that we do so only because the technique we develop slightly (but we believe, significantly) extends the domain of applicability of equivalent variation analysis for the Gorman case. The difference, essentially, is that our method avoids some troublesome ambiguities in the domain of the income compensation function, which we replace with the "income equivalence function" in our analysis. The latter function will coincide with the former on part of its domain, but will have the Gorman form over a larger domain than does the income compensation function. The main innovation in the work cited is that we show that our modified equivalent variation analysis can be done almost as easily as (the theoretically incorrect) Marshallian consumer surplus analysis. In this chapter, I will show that our techniques can be simplified still more; and I will present a number of examples showing how the technique works in some simple cases. In fact, I will show that this technique can be used as easily, or nearly so, as the theoretically indefensible Marshallian consumer's surplus analysis.

While I have not specifically discussed the material developed here (except for parts of a couple of examples) with John, all of the material in this chapter is inspired by, and developed from, our joint work. Consequently, it seems particularly appropriate to me that I should contribute this article to a volume in honor of John Chipman. If this is deemed to be a good piece, much of what is good in it is certainly due to John.

## Preliminaries

With apologies to those who may have read our 1990 article, I should note at the outset that, in order to adhere to what appears to be standard notation in the literature, I will not adhere to the notation of CM90; although I will make use of the preliminary definitions of that article. I will denote Euclidean $n$-space by "$\mathbf{R}^n$," let "$\mathbf{R}^n_+$" denote the nonnegative orthant in $\mathbf{R}^n$, and define the strictly positive orthant, $\mathbf{R}^n_{++}$, for this space by:

$$\mathbf{R}^n_{++} = \{\mathbf{x} \in \mathbf{R}^n \mid \mathbf{x} >> 0\};$$

where, for $\mathbf{x},\mathbf{y} \in \mathbf{R}^n$, we define $\mathbf{x} >> \mathbf{y}$ by:

$$x >> y \Leftrightarrow x_i > y_i \text{ for } i = 1, \ldots, n.$$ [2]

I will assume throughout this chapter that $G$, the consumer's preference relation, is a weak order on the set $\mathbf{R}^n_+$, and generates a single-valued demand function, $\mathbf{h}\colon \Omega^* \to \mathbf{R}^n_+$, where we define $\Omega^*$ by:

$$\Omega^* = \{(\mathbf{p},m) \in \mathbf{R}^{n+1}_+ \mid \mathbf{p} \in \mathbf{R}^n_{++} \;\&\; m \in \mathbf{R}_+\} = \mathbf{R}^n_{++} \times \mathbf{R}_+;$$

and that $\mathbf{h}$ satisfies the **budget balance condition**:

$$(\forall(\mathbf{p},m) \in \Omega^*)\colon \mathbf{p} \cdot \mathbf{h}(\mathbf{p},m) = m.$$

The **indirect preference relation, $G^*$, generated by G** is then defined by:

$$(\mathbf{p},m)G^*(\mathbf{p}',m') \Leftrightarrow \mathbf{h}(\mathbf{p},m)\, G\mathbf{h}(\mathbf{p}',m');$$

and I shall assume throughout that $G^*$ is continous.[3]

If $\Omega$ is a subset of $\Omega^*$, I will say that a function, $V: \Omega \to \mathbf{R}$ is an **indirect utility function for G***, or is an **indirect utility function representing G* on $\Omega$** iff

$$(\forall(\mathbf{p},m),(\mathbf{p}',m') \in \Omega): [V(\mathbf{p},m) \geq V(\mathbf{p}',m')] \Leftrightarrow [(\mathbf{p},m)G^*(\mathbf{p}',m')].$$

Under the assmptions being employed here, it follows from Debreu (1959: 56–59) that, if $\Omega$ is a connected subset of $\Omega^*$, then there exists a continuous indirect utility function representing $G^*$ on $\Omega$.[4] We note also that if $V(\cdot)$ is an indirect utility function representing $G^*$ on a subset, $\Omega$, of $\Omega^*$, then $V$ must be positively homogeneous of degree zero in $(\mathbf{p},m)$ on $\Omega$; and that, if $\Omega$ is an open set, and $V$ is differentiable on $\Omega$, then $V$ must satisfy the Antonelli–Allen–Roy equations: [5]

$$V_j(\mathbf{p},m) = -V_m(\mathbf{p},m)h_j(\mathbf{p},m) \text{ for } j = 1, \ldots, n; \text{ and all } (\mathbf{p},m) \in \Omega; \tag{1}$$

where "$V_j(\mathbf{p},m)$" and "$V_m(\mathbf{p},m)$" denote the partial derivative of $V(\cdot)$ with respect to the $j$th price and $m$, respectively, evaluated at $(\mathbf{p},m)$.

It is common in works dealing with compensating and equivalent variation to define these concepts with the use of the so-called minimum expenditure (cost) function:

$$e(\mathbf{p},u) = \min\{\mathbf{p} \cdot \mathbf{x} \mid \mathbf{x} \in \mathbf{R}^n_+ \;\&\; u(\mathbf{x}) \geq u\}; \tag{2}$$

where $u(\cdot)$ is a utility function representing $G$ on $\mathbf{R}^n_+$. For a variety of reasons, not the least of which is that we would like our work to depend only upon the concept of indirect preferences, as defined above, Chipman and I have preferred to work with the **income compensation function**,[6] if originally developed in Hurwicz and Uzawa (1971) and McKenzie (1957), and which is defined on $\mathbf{R}^n_{++} \times \Omega^*$ by

$$\mu(\mathbf{q};\mathbf{p},m) = \min\{m' \in \mathbf{R} \mid (\mathbf{q},m')G^*(\mathbf{p},m)\}; \tag{3}$$

and I will continue this tradition here. It is well-known that, if we hold $\mathbf{q}$ fixed, and consider the function $\mu(\mathbf{q}\,;\cdot)$ as a function of $(\mathbf{p},m)$ on $\Omega^*$, then the resultant function is, under the assumptions being employed here, an indirect utility function for $G^*$; and we have, for all $(\mathbf{p}',m'), (\mathbf{p}'',m'') \in \Omega^*$:

$$(\mathbf{p}',m')I^*(\mathbf{p}'',m'') \Leftrightarrow m' = \mu(\mathbf{p}';\mathbf{p}'',m''); \tag{4}$$

where the relation $I^*$ is defined on $\Omega^*$ by:

$$(\mathbf{p}',m')I^*(\mathbf{p}'',m'') \Leftrightarrow [(\mathbf{p}',m')G^*(\mathbf{p}'',m'') \;\&\; (\mathbf{p}'',m'')G^*(\mathbf{p}',m')]. \tag{5}$$

It should also be mentioned that the income compensation function is positively homogeneous of degree one in the base price, $\mathbf{q}$ and positively homogeneous of degree zero in $(\mathbf{p},m)$; that is, for all $(\mathbf{q};\mathbf{p},m) \in \mathbf{R}^n_{++} \times \Omega^*$, and all $\lambda > 0$,

$$\mu(\lambda\mathbf{q};\mathbf{p},m) = \lambda\mu(\mathbf{q};\mathbf{p},m) \;\&\; \mu(\mathbf{q};\lambda\mathbf{p},\lambda m) = \mu(\mathbf{q};\mathbf{p},m). \tag{6}$$

## Consumer's surplus: initial considerations

Following CM90, we shall be interested in the following definition in connection with the evaluation of economic welfare of the consumer.

**Definition 1** *Let* $\Xi \subseteq \Omega^* \times \Omega^*$, *and let* $W: \Xi \to \mathbf{R}$. *We shall say that* $W(\cdot)$ *is an* **acceptable indicator of welfare change (for G*) on** $\Xi$ *iff, for each* $(\mathbf{p}_1,m_1), (\mathbf{p}_2,m_2) \in \Xi$: [7]

$$W[(\mathbf{p}_1,m_1), (\mathbf{p}_2,m_2)] \geq 0 \Leftrightarrow (\mathbf{p}_2,m_2)G^*(\mathbf{p}_1,m_1)$$

Notice that if $V: \Omega \to \mathbf{R}$ is any indirect utility function representing $G^*$ on a set $\Omega \subseteq \Omega^*$, then the function $W$ defined on $\Omega \times \Omega$ by:

$$W[(\mathbf{p}_1,m_1), (\mathbf{p}_2,m_2)] = V(\mathbf{p}_2,m_2) - V(\mathbf{p}_1,m_1), \tag{7}$$

is an acceptable indicator of welfare change for $G^*$ on $\Omega \times \Omega$. An acceptable indicator of welfare change does not necessarily take the form (7); however, let's take note of the following fact, which is worth stating formally because of the frequency with which we shall refer to it.

**Proposition 1** (Chipman and Moore (1976, 1990)). *If* $\Xi$ *is of the form* $\Xi = \Omega \times \Omega$, *for some subset,* $\Omega$, *of* $\Omega^*$, *and if* $W: \Xi \to \mathbf{R}$ *is an acceptable indicator of welfare change on* $\Xi$ *which takes the form*

$$W[(\mathbf{p}_1,m_1), (\mathbf{p}_2,m_2)] = F(\mathbf{p}_2,m_2) - F(\mathbf{p}_1,m_1),$$

*for all* $(\mathbf{p}_1,m_1), (\mathbf{p}_2,m_2) \in \Xi$, *then F is an indirect utility function for* $G^*$ *on* $\Omega$.

If a function $W$ is an acceptable indicator of welfare change, then it can be used to evaluate the desirability of a change from $(\mathbf{p}_1,m_1)$ to $(\mathbf{p}_2,m_2)$; with the change a desirable one if, and only if, $W[(\mathbf{p}_1,m_1), (\mathbf{p}_2,m_2)]$ is non-negative. Notice, however, that this is a very weak requirement; in fact we can both illustrate this fact and show that an acceptable indicator of welfare change need not take the form (7) as follows. We first define the function $\chi: \mathbf{R} \to \mathbf{R}$ by:

$$\chi(x) = \begin{cases} 1 & \text{if } x > 0, \\ 0 & \text{if } x = 0, \text{ and} \\ -1 & \text{if } x < 0. \end{cases} \tag{8}$$

The proof of the following result is again more or less immediate, but it will be sufficiently valuable in our further work to justify a formal statement none the less.

**Proposition 2** *If* $\Xi$ *is a nonempty subset of* $\Omega^* \times \Omega^*$, *and* $W: \Xi \to \mathbf{R}$ *is an acceptable indicator of welfare change on* $\Xi$, *then the function* $W^*$ *defined on* $\Xi$ *by*

$$W^*[(\mathbf{p}_1,m_1), (\mathbf{p}_2,m_2)] = \chi(W[\mathbf{p}_1,m_1),(\mathbf{p}_2,m_2)]),$$

*with $\chi$ defined in (8), above, is also an acceptable indicator of welfare change on $\Xi$.*

Notice that Proposition 2 establishes the fact that an acceptable indicator of welfare change need not take the form (7). It also shows that an acceptable indicator of welfare change need only provide trinary information. Thus it is all the more remarkable that there are no conditions under which standard Marshallian surplus provides an acceptable indicator of welfare change on any set $\Xi$ of the form

$$\Xi = \Omega \times \Omega, \tag{9}$$

with $\Omega$ a non-empty open set; as was established in Chipman and Moore (1976). Proposition 2 also effectively establishes the fact that an acceptable indicator of welfare change need not be useful for a ranking of projects; a fact which is of particular interest in connection with the idea of compensating variation. Consider the following defintion.

**Definition 2** *Let* $\Omega \subseteq \Omega^*$, *let* $(\mathbf{p}_0,m_0) \in \Omega^*$, *and let* $v\colon \Omega \to \mathbf{R}$. *We shall say that* $v$ **is an acceptable indicator of welfare improvement (for G*) from** $(\mathbf{p}_0,m_0)$ **on** $\Omega$ *iff for all* $(\mathbf{p},m) \in \Omega$,

$$v(\mathbf{p},m) \geq 0 \Leftrightarrow (\mathbf{p},m)G^*(\mathbf{p}_0,m_0).$$

Notice that in the special case where $\Xi$ is of the form $\Xi = \{(\mathbf{p}_0,m_0)\} \times \Omega$, for some $\Omega \subseteq \Omega^*$, a function $W\colon \Xi \to \mathbf{R}$ is essentially a mapping from $\Omega$ to the reals. Moreover, given a set $\Xi$ of this form, $W(\cdot)$ is an acceptable indicator of welfare change (for $G^*$) on $\Xi$ if, and only if, it is an acceptable indicator of welfare improvement (for $G^*$) from $(p_0,m_0)$ on $\Omega$. In fact, I have introduced Definition 2 as something of a "straw man;" to show that Definition 1 is sufficiently broad to incorporate this second notion. In particular, notice that the **compensating variation function**, which can be defined, on

$$\Xi_{\omega_0} \stackrel{\text{def}}{=} \{(\mathbf{p}_0,m_0)\} \times \Omega^*$$

for any $\omega_0 = (\mathbf{p}_0,m_0)$, by:

$$C[(\mathbf{p}_0,m_0),(\mathbf{p},m)] = m - \mu(\mathbf{p};\mathbf{p}_0,m_0),$$

is an acceptable indicator of welfare change (for $G^*$) on $\Xi_{\omega_0}$.

In fact, as is easy to see, the compensating variation function is easily extended to the domain $\Omega^* \times \Omega^*$ via:

$$W^c[(\mathbf{p}_1,m_1),(\mathbf{p}_2,m_2)] = m_2 - \mu(\mathbf{p}_2;\mathbf{p}_1,m_1);$$

and *is* an acceptable indicator of welfare change on $\Omega^* \times \Omega^*$, as is easily seen. Thus, compensating variation can be used to (a) eliminate undesirable projects, and (b) calculate potential damages after an undesirable change, or (c) calculate how much could be spent on a public project (ignoring the aggregation problems present when there is more than one consumer in the economy) while still resulting in a net welfare gain. However, what is often needed is a method of ranking projects, from most to least desirable; presumably with the object of undertaking the $m$ best projects out of $n$ available (with, of course, $n > m$). Here the following is a minimal requirement. Suppose we are currently at the price-income state $(\mathbf{p}_0, m_0)$, and are contemplating Policies One and Two, which will result in price-income states $(p_1, m_1)$ and $(p_2, m_2)$, respectively. We would like to be able to infer from the fact that:

$$W^c[(\mathbf{p}_0,m_0),(\mathbf{p}_1,m_1)] \geq W^c[(\mathbf{p}_0,m_0),(\mathbf{p}_2,m_2)]$$

that Policy One is more desirable than Policy Two; that is, that:

$$(\mathbf{p}_1,m_1)G^*(\mathbf{p}_2,m_2).$$

However, at this point the whole method goes awry, in the case of Compensating Variation analysis; for obviously:

$$W^c[(\mathbf{p}_0,m_0),(\mathbf{p}_1,m_1)] \geq W^c[(\mathbf{p}_0,m_0),(\mathbf{p}_2,m_2)],$$
$$\Leftrightarrow m_1 - \mu(\mathbf{p}_1;\mathbf{p}_0,m_0) \geq m_2 - \mu(\mathbf{p}_2;\mathbf{p}_0,m_0).$$

It is then easy to show, as was noted in Chipman and Moore (1992), and elaborated somewhat in Chipman and Moore (1980) and CM90,[8] that this inference will be correct, given any $(\mathbf{p}_1,m_1),(\mathbf{p}_2,m_2) \in \Omega \subseteq \Omega^*$ iff the function $\nu: \Omega \rightarrow \mathbf{R}$ defined by:

$$\nu(\mathbf{p},m) = m - \mu(\mathbf{p};\mathbf{p}_0,m_0),$$

is an indirect utility function representing $G^*$ on $\Omega$. However, an indirect utility function must be positively homogeneous of degree zero in its arguments; whereas the function $\nu$ is positively homogeneous of degree one. Consequently, it follows that, if $\Omega$ is an open set, then the function $W^c$ cannot be used to rank projects on $\Omega$, starting from a given base budget (for details, see CM90, and Chipman and Moore (1980) and (1992)).

In order to consider this issue further, let's set out a formal definition, as follows.

**Definition 3** *Let* $\Xi \subseteq \Omega^* \times \Omega^*$, *suppose* $W: \Xi \rightarrow \mathbf{R}$ *is an acceptable indicator of welfare change (for* $G^*$*)* on $\Xi$, *and suppose* $(\mathbf{p}_0,m_0)$ *and* $\Omega \subseteq \Omega^*$ *are such that:*[9]

$$(\mathbf{p}_0,m_0) \in \Omega \;\&\; \{(\mathbf{p}_0,m_0)\} \times \Omega \subseteq \Xi.$$

*We shall say that* $W$ **provides a valid ranking on** $\Omega$ *(for* $G^*$*)*, **given the base state** $(\mathbf{p}_0,m_0)$ *iff, for each* $(\mathbf{p}_1,m_1)$, $(\mathbf{p}_2,m_2) \in \Omega$:

$$W[(\mathbf{p}_0,m_0),(\mathbf{p}_1,m_1)] \geq W[(\mathbf{p}_0,m_0),(\mathbf{p}_2,m_2)]$$
$$\Leftrightarrow (\mathbf{p}_1,m_1)G^*(\mathbf{p}_2,m_2).$$

Upon reflection, it is easily seen that $W$ provides a valid ranking on $\Omega$, given the base state $(\mathbf{p}_0, m_0)$, iff the function $V: \Omega \to \mathbf{R}$ defined by:

$$V(\mathbf{p},m) = W[(\mathbf{p}_0,m_0), (\mathbf{p},m)] + \alpha; \tag{10}$$

where $\alpha$ is an arbitrary constant, is an indirect utility function representing $G^*$ on $\Omega$. Whatever value we choose for $\alpha$, notice that, since we have required $W$ to be an acceptable indicator of welfare change,[10] we will have:

$$V(\mathbf{p}_0,m_0) = \alpha. \tag{11}$$

More importantly, however, it now follows that the function $W^*: \Omega \times \Omega \to \mathbf{R}$ defined by:

$$W^*[(\mathbf{p}_1,m_1), (\mathbf{p}_2,m_2)] = V(\mathbf{p}_2,m_2) - V(\mathbf{p}_1,m_1), \tag{12}$$

is an acceptable indicator of welfare change on $\Xi \equiv \Omega \times \Omega$. It is also true, as was noted earlier, that a function of the form (12), where $V: \Omega \to \mathbf{R}$ is an indirect utility function representing $G^*$ on $\Omega$, is an acceptable indicator of welfare change. Moreover, it is now also easy to see that such a function provides a valid ranking on $\Omega$, given any base state $(\mathbf{p}_0,m_0) \in \Omega$. Consequently, in the remainder of this chapter, we shall develop and analyze only functions $W$ which can be written in the form (12).

In connection with these latter considerations, let $\mathbf{q} \in \mathbf{R}^n_{++}$ be arbitrary. It follows from the discussion of the previous section that the function $v: \Omega \to \mathbf{R}$ defined by:

$$v(\mathbf{p},m) = \mu(\mathbf{q};\mathbf{p},m), \tag{13}$$

is an indirect utility function representing $G^*$ on $\Omega^*$. Thus, defining $\Xi^* = \Omega^* \times \Omega^*$, the function $W^e: \Xi^* \to \mathbf{R}$ given by:

$$W^e[(\mathbf{p}_1,m_1),(\mathbf{p}_2,m_2)] = v(\mathbf{p}_2,m_2) - v(\mathbf{p}_1,m_1), \tag{14}$$

is not only a valid indicator of welfare change on $\Xi^*$; it also provides a valid ranking on $\Omega^*$. If, in fact, $(\mathbf{p}_0,m_0) \in \Omega^*$ is interpreted to be the current price-income state, and we let $\mathbf{q} = \mathbf{p}_0$, then $W^e[(\mathbf{p}_0,m_0),(\mathbf{p}_1,m_1)]$ can be interpreted as the minimum amount which could be added to the consumer's income, $m_0$, in order to induce him or her *not* to vote for the change to the price-income state $(\mathbf{p}_1,m_1)$; for here we have:

$$m_0 + W^e[(\mathbf{p}_0,m_0),(\mathbf{p}_1,m_1)] = \mu(\mathbf{p}_0;\mathbf{p}_1,m_1).$$

In other words, for this special case, $W^e[(\mathbf{p}_0,m_0),(\mathbf{p}_1,m_1)]$ becomes the equivalent variation measure.

From this discussion, however, we can see that equivalent variation can be used as a measure of compensation for a change which is *not* made; for example, compensation for an uncorrected pollution or noise problem. It can also be used to eliminate undesirable projects from consideration; moreover, in stark contrast to compensating variation, it *can* be used to rank projects.

In the remainder of this chapter, we will, essentially, be considering equivalent variation analysis for indirect utility functions of the "Gorman Polar Form;" or more exactly, a variant thereof which Chipman and I have called "quasi-equivalent variation analysis." The essential idea of the analysis is simply to develop a method of estimation of the income compensation function, which will then be used for equivalent variation analysis, in essence. The only thing that makes our method slightly different has to do with the fact that our analysis effectively extends the domain over which the income compensation function can be taken to be of the Gorman form. I will explain this idea more fully in the next section.

## The income equivalence function and the "Gorman Polar Form"

As was pointed out by Gorman himself (Gorman 1961), an indirect utility function cannot generally be of the "Gorman Polar Form" over all of $\Omega^*$. Thus, in formulating a workable definition of indirect preferences of the Gorman form, one must begin with a definition of the type of domain over which one will be assuming the Gorman form to hold. We will simplify and specialize the treatment of CM90 somewhat by utilizing the following.

**Definition 4** *We will say that* $\Omega \subseteq \Omega^*$ *is a* **budget domain** *iff there exists a function* $\eta$: $\mathbf{R}^n_{++} \rightarrow \mathbf{R}_+$ *which is positively homogeneous of degree one and satisfies:*

$$\Omega = \{(\mathrm{p},m) \in \mathbf{R}^n_{++} \times \mathbf{R}_+ \mid m \geq \eta(\mathrm{p})\};$$

*and in this case we shall say that* $\Omega$ **is determined by** $\eta$.

In CM90, we showed that several apparently different definitions of indirect preferences of the "Gorman form" were all equivalent; and were all equivalent to something we called the "measurability condition." For our present purposes, the most convenient of the definitions of the "Gorman form" is the following.[11]

**Definition 5** *We will say that* $G^*$ *is of the* **Gorman form** *on the budget domain* $\Omega$ *iff there exist positively homogeneous of degree one functions* $\alpha$: $\mathbf{R}^n_{++} \rightarrow \mathbf{R}_{++}$ *and* $\gamma$: $\mathbf{R}^n_{++} \rightarrow \mathbf{R}_+$ *such that the function* $V$: $\Omega \rightarrow \mathbf{R}$ *defined by:*

$$V(\mathrm{p},m) = \frac{m - \gamma(p)}{\alpha(\mathrm{p})}, \tag{15}$$

*represents* $G^*$ *on* $\Omega$.

Given our definition of a budget domain, we see that $G^*$ is of the Gorman form on $\Omega$ iff it has a representation of the form (15) (with $\alpha$ and $\gamma$ both positively homogeneous of degree one), for $m \geq \eta(p)$. If we mechanically set about the task of finding the value of the income compensation function at $(\mathbf{q};\mathbf{p},m) \in \mathbf{R}^n_{++} \times \Omega$ by equating

$$V(\mathbf{q},m') = \frac{m' - \gamma(\mathbf{q})}{\alpha(\mathbf{q})} = \frac{m - \gamma(\mathbf{p})}{\alpha(\mathbf{p})} = V(\mathbf{p},m), \tag{16}$$

and solving for $m'$, we obtain:

$$m' = a(\mathbf{q},\mathbf{p}) + b(\mathbf{q},\mathbf{p})m; \tag{17}$$

where $a(\cdot)$ and $b(\cdot)$ are given by:

$$a(\mathbf{q},\mathbf{p}) = \frac{\alpha(\mathbf{p}) \cdot \gamma(\mathbf{q}) - \alpha(\mathbf{q}) \cdot \gamma(\mathbf{p})}{\alpha(\mathbf{p})} \text{ and } b(\mathbf{q},\mathbf{p}) = \frac{\alpha(\mathbf{q})}{\alpha(\mathbf{p})}, \tag{18}$$

respectively. Given equation (4) in the "Preliminaries" section, one is then tempted to infer from this that the income compensation function takes the form:

$$\mu(\mathbf{q};\mathbf{p},m) = a(\mathbf{q},\mathbf{p}) + b(\mathbf{q},\mathbf{p})m \text{ for } (\mathbf{q};\mathbf{p},m) \in \mathbf{R}^n_{++} \times \Omega. \tag{19}$$

Unfortunately, this inference is not correct; and (19) is not a valid representation of the income compensation function on $\mathbf{R}^n_{++} \times \Omega$! The problem is that equation (17) yields a value of $m'$ such that $(\mathbf{q},m')I^*(\mathbf{p},m)$ if and only if $m' \geq \eta(\mathbf{q})$. Since this may not be the case, the income compensation function does not generally take the form indicated by (19) on all of $\mathbf{R}^n_{++} \times \Omega$. It is probably time to take a quick look at an example. The following is an abridged version of Example 3.5, pp. 88–92.

**Example 1** We consider the weak order, $G$, representable on $\mathbf{R}^2_+$ by:

$$u(x_1,x_2) = x_1 + 2\sqrt{x_2}. \tag{20}$$

This function is a very frequently-used member of the Gorman class, being of the quasi-linear form. It is fairly easily shown that the demand function generated by $G$ is given by:

$$\mathbf{h}(\mathbf{p},m) = \begin{cases} (0,m/p_2) & \text{for } m < (p_1)^2/p_2 \\ \left(\frac{m}{p_1} - \frac{p_1}{p_2}, \left[\frac{p_1}{p_2}\right]^2\right) & \text{for } m \geq (p_1)^2/p_2. \end{cases}$$

If we define the function $\eta$ on $\mathbf{R}^2_{++}$ by:

$$\eta(\mathbf{p}) = (p_1)^2/p_2,$$

$G^*$ can be represented on the budget domain determined by $\eta$ by the function:

$$V(\mathbf{p},m) = m/p_1 + p_1/p_2 = \frac{m + [(p_1)^2/p_2]}{p_1};$$

which is of the Gorman form, with

$$\gamma(\mathbf{p}) = -(p_1)^2/p_2 \text{ and } \alpha(\mathbf{p}) = p_1.$$

However, the income compensation function is a complicated four-branch expression which is of the form (19) over only one branch of its domain. For details, see CM90, p. 89. □

Suppose we return to the general situation in which $G^*$ is of the Gorman form on the budget domain $\Omega$, where $\Omega$ is determined by $\eta$; and suppose $G^*$ is representable on $\Omega$ by a function $V(\cdot)$ of the form (15). The function $\nu: \mathbf{R}^n_{++} \times \Omega \to \mathbf{R}_+$ given by: [12]

$$\nu(\mathbf{q};\mathbf{p},m) = a(\mathbf{q},\mathbf{p}) + b(\mathbf{q},\mathbf{p})m; \tag{21}$$

where the functions $a$ and $b$ are given by (18), above, we have called the **income equivalence function** in CM90. As already noted, this function is generally not synonymous with the income-compensation function over all of its domain.[13] However, it is shown in CM90 that (a) if we fix $\mathbf{p}_0 \in \mathbf{R}^n_{++}$, and define $v: \Omega \to \mathbf{R}$ by:

$$v(\mathbf{p},m) = \nu(\mathbf{p}_0;\mathbf{p},m) = \alpha(\mathbf{p}_0,\mathbf{p}) + b(\mathbf{p}_0,\mathbf{p})m, \tag{22}$$

is an indirect utility function representing $G^*$ on all of $\Omega$, and (b) if, for a given $(\mathbf{p},m) \in \Omega$ we have:

$$\nu(\mathbf{p},m) \geq \eta(\mathbf{p}), \tag{23}$$

then:

$$\nu(\mathbf{p}_0;\mathbf{p},m) = \mu(\mathbf{p}_0;\mathbf{p},m). \tag{24}$$

In CM90 we also showed, in effect, that if a function of the form (21) exists which is such that the function $v(\cdot)$ defined in (22) represents $G^*$ on a budget domain $\Omega$, then $G^*$ is of the Gorman form on $\Omega$. Moreover, we also showed that the income equivalence function corresponding to an indirect preference relation, $G^*$, if one exists, is *unique*.

Now suppose that $G^*$ admits of an income equivalence function of the form (21), and fix $\mathbf{q} \in \mathbf{R}^n_{++}$ at any desired vector. If we define the set $\Xi = \Omega \times \Omega$, and the function $w: \Xi \to \mathbf{R}$ by:

$$w[(\mathbf{p}_0,m_0),(\mathbf{p}_1,m_1)] = \nu(\mathbf{q};\mathbf{p}_1,m_1) - \nu(\mathbf{q};\mathbf{p}_0,m_0), \tag{25}$$

it follows from the discussion of the previous section that $w(\cdot)$ is an acceptable indicator of welfare change, and provides a valid ranking of projects on $\Omega$. Chipman and I have called the use of this function "quasi-equivalent variation analysis" because if we think of $(\mathbf{p}_0,m_0) \in \Omega$ as the current price-income state, and set $\mathbf{q} = \mathbf{p}_0$ in (25), then it is easily shown from the properties of the function $a(\cdot)$ that $\nu(\mathbf{p}_0,\mathbf{p}_0,m_0) = m_0$, and thus with this convention (that is, with $\mathbf{q} = \mathbf{p}_0$), $w$ takes the form:

$$w[(\mathbf{p}_0,m_0),(\mathbf{p}_1,m_1)] = \nu(\mathbf{p}_0;\mathbf{p}_1,m_1) - m_0. \tag{26}$$

If we also have:

$$\nu(\mathbf{p}_0;\mathbf{p}_1,m_1) = \mu(\mathbf{p}_0;\mathbf{p}_1,m_1),$$

then (26) is exactly the equivalent variation measure of a change from $(\mathbf{p}_0,m_0)$ to $(\mathbf{p}_1,m_1)$.

In the next section we will investigate the problem of estimating the function $w$ in applied analysis.

## A simplified method of quasi-equivalent variation analysis

In this section, we shall consider the welfare analysis of a single consumer; proceeding, in effect, as if we are analyzing a one-consumer economy, so that the consumer's income is synonymous with the aggregate income for the economy. We shall suppose that we are evalauting projects which will involve a change away from $(\mathbf{p}_0,m_0)$ to another price-income state for the consumer; and we will use the current price vector, $\mathbf{p}_0$, as the base price in our analysis.

Suppose that the consumer's demand function is of the Gorman form:

$$\mathbf{h}(\mathbf{p},m) = \mathbf{f}(\mathbf{p}) + \mathbf{g}(\mathbf{p})m, \tag{27}$$

on the budget domain, $\Omega$ defined by the positively homogeneous of degree one function $\eta$: $\mathbf{R}^n_{++} \rightarrow \mathbf{R}_+$; so that the demand function is of the form (27) for any $\mathbf{p} \in \mathbf{R}^n_{++}$ and $m \geq \eta(\mathbf{p})$.

If the consumer's demand function is given by (27) on $\Omega$, then, among other things, it must be the case that $\mathbf{f}$ is positively homogeneous of degree zero, that $\mathbf{g}$ is positively homogeneous of degree minus one, and that $\mathbf{f}$ and $\mathbf{g}$ satisfy the identities:

$$\mathbf{p}\cdot\mathbf{f}(\mathbf{p}) = 0 \ \& \ \mathbf{p}\cdot\mathbf{g}(\mathbf{p}) = 1. \tag{28}$$

Moreover, from the symmetry of the Slutsky matrix, it follows that for all $\mathbf{p} \in \mathbf{R}^n_{++}$:

$$f^j_k(\mathbf{p}) + f^k(\mathbf{p})g^j(\mathbf{p}) = f^k_j(\mathbf{p}) + f^j(\mathbf{p})g^k(\mathbf{p}) \text{ for } j,\ k = 1, \ldots, n, \tag{29}$$

and:

$$g^j_k(\mathbf{p}) = g^k_j(\mathbf{p}) \text{ for } j,k = 1, \ldots, n, \tag{30}$$

where, for example, "$f^j_k(\mathbf{p})$" denotes the $k$th partial derivative of $f^j$, the $j$th coordinate function of $\mathbf{f}$, evaluated at $\mathbf{p}$. In CM90 it is shown that under these conditions, the system of partial differential equations:

$$G_j(\mathbf{p}) = g^j(\mathbf{p}) \text{ for } j = 1, \ldots, n, \tag{31}$$

has a unique solution, $G$, satisfying the initial condition:

$$G(\mathbf{p}_0) = \delta, \tag{32}$$

for any $\delta > 0$ (CM90, pp. 105–6). Moreover, it is also shown in CM90 that, under these conditions, there exists a function $\gamma: \mathbf{R}^n_{++} \rightarrow \mathbf{R}_+$ which is positively homogeneous of degree one, and satisfies, for all $\mathbf{p} \in \mathbf{R}^n_{++}$:

$$f^j(\mathbf{p}) = \gamma_j(\mathbf{p}) - g^j(\mathbf{p})\gamma(\mathbf{p}) \text{ for } j = 1, \ldots, n. \tag{33}$$

It is then shown in CM90 (Theorem 4.2, p. 115) that, if we are given a demand function of the form (27), and which satisfies the restrictions (28)–(30), we can obtain the corresponding income-equivalence function as follows. Letting $G(\cdot)$ be any solution of the differential equation system (31), we define[14] $b: \mathbf{R}^n_{++} \times \mathbf{R}^n_{++} \rightarrow \mathbf{R}_{++}$ by:

$$b(\mathbf{q},\mathbf{p}) = \exp[G(\mathbf{q})]/\exp[G(\mathbf{p})]. \tag{34}$$

Next, given any positively homogeneous of degree one function, $\gamma: \rightarrow \mathbf{R}_+$ satisfying (33),[15] we define $a: \mathbf{R}^n_{++} \times \mathbf{R}^n_{++} \rightarrow \mathbf{R}$ by:

$$a(\mathbf{q},\mathbf{p}) = \gamma(\mathbf{q}) - b(\mathbf{q},\mathbf{p})\gamma(\mathbf{p}). \tag{35}$$

Of course, since we are interested in conducting a quasi-equivalent variational analysis with base price $\mathbf{p}_0$, the indirect utility function of interest is given by:

$$v(\mathbf{p},m) = \mathrm{V}(\mathbf{p}_0;\mathbf{p},m) = \gamma(\mathbf{p}_0) - \gamma(\mathbf{p}) \exp[G(\mathbf{p}_0)]/\exp[G(\mathbf{p})] + (\exp[G(\mathbf{p}_0)]/\exp[G(\mathbf{p})])m. \tag{36}$$

While the above derivations are at least nearly as easily carried out as in the usual development of the theoretically incorrect Marshallian consumer's surplus analysis,[16] we have developed the steps for the case in which we supppose the investigator has somehow been presented with the correct demand function for the consumer, but does not know the form of the corresponding income-equivalence function. In practice, of course, an investigator will specify the form of the demand function and then estimate the parameters of the function. Typically the parameter values for the demand function will completely determine the income-equivalence function as well, and usually the form of the income-equivalence function will be known to the investigator; so that once the parameters of the demand function are estimated, the estimate of the income-equivalence function will be immediately available. In this situation, the procedure needed to obtain the indirect utility function in (36) is greatly simplified, as is illustrated by the following examples.

**Example 2** Suppose the direct preference relation, $G$, is representable on $\mathbf{R}^n_+$ by the utility function

$$U(\mathbf{x}) = \Pi^n_{j=1} (x_j + c_j)^{\theta_j} \text{ for } \mathbf{x} \in \mathbf{R}^n_+; \tag{37}$$

where

$$c_j \geq 0 \text{ and } \theta_j > 0 \text{ for } j = 1, \ldots, n, \text{ and } \Sigma^n_{j=1} \theta_j = 1. \tag{38}$$

In this case, it is easy to show that the corresponding demand functions take the form:

$$h^j(\mathbf{p},m) = \frac{\theta_j(m + \mathbf{p}\cdot\mathbf{c})}{p_j} - c_j \tag{39}$$

for

$$m \geq \max_j \left(\frac{p_j c_j}{\theta_j}\right) - \mathbf{p}\cdot\mathbf{c},\ \text{and } j = 1, \ldots, n.$$

In this example, we will first explore the workings of the derivation just developed, and then look at the simplifications possible when we take advantage of the fact that the form of the income-equivalence function is known in this case before the parameters of the demand function are estimated.

Now, equation (39) is of the form

$$h^j(\mathbf{p},m) = f^j(\mathbf{p}) + g^j(\mathbf{p})m; \tag{40}$$

where

$$f^j(\mathbf{p}) = (\theta_j\mathbf{p}\cdot\mathbf{c})/p_j - c_j \tag{41}$$

and

$$g^j(\mathbf{p}) = \theta_j/p_j. \tag{42}$$

Since $f^j(\cdot)$ takes the form

$$f^j(\mathbf{p}) = g^j(\mathbf{p})\mathbf{p}\cdot\mathbf{c}/p_j - c_j \tag{43}$$

we see that if we define the function $\gamma(\mathbf{p})$ by

$$\gamma(\mathbf{p}) = -\mathbf{p}\cdot\mathbf{c} \tag{44}$$

we can express $f^j$ as:

$$f^j(\mathbf{p}) = \gamma_j(\mathbf{p}) - g^j(\mathbf{p})\gamma(\mathbf{p}). \tag{45}$$

Thus the function $\gamma(\cdot)$ defined in (44) can be used in the formula in equation (35) in this case. Consequently, the system of partial differential equations to be solved is, in this case, given by

$$G_j(\mathbf{p}) = \theta_j/p_j \text{ for } j = 1, \ldots, n; \tag{46}$$

which is easily solved to obtain:

$$G(\mathbf{p}) = \Sigma_{j=1}^{n}\ \theta_j \log p_j. \tag{47}$$

Substituting the formulas obtained in (44) and (47) into the formula in equation (36), above, we obtain in this case:

$$v(\mathbf{p},m) = \mathrm{v}(\mathbf{p}_0;\mathbf{p},m) = \left[\frac{\Pi_{j=1}^{n} (p_{0j})^{\theta_j}}{\Pi_{j=1}^{n} (p_j)^{\theta_j}}\right] \cdot [m + \mathbf{p} \cdot \mathbf{c}] - \mathbf{p}_0 \cdot \mathbf{c}. \tag{48}$$

Notice also that in the special (standard Cobb–Douglas) case in which $\mathbf{c} = \mathbf{0}$, our formula in (48) simplifies to:

$$v(\mathbf{p},m) = \mathrm{v}(\mathbf{p}_0;\mathbf{p},m) = \left[\frac{\Pi_{j=1}^{n} (p_{0j})^{\theta_j}}{\Pi_{j=1}^{n} (p_j)^{\theta_j}}\right] \cdot m.$$

Now suppose that only the first $m$ ($1 \leq m < n$) prices will be changed as a result of the policies being investigated. If one assumes that the last $n - m$ prices are equal in the price vectors $\mathbf{p}_0$ and $\mathbf{p}$, the formula in (48) simplifies to:

$$v(\mathbf{p},m) = \left[\frac{\Pi_{j=1}^{m} (p_{0j})^{\theta_j}}{\Pi_{j=1}^{m} (p_j)^{\theta_j}}\right] \cdot [m + \mathbf{p} \cdot \mathbf{c}] - \mathbf{p}_0 \cdot \mathbf{c}. \tag{49}$$

Consequently, it can be seen that in this situation, only the values of $\theta$ corresponding to the commodities whose prices will change need to be estimated. Thus one can proceed by specifying values for $c_j$ for $j = m + 1, \ldots, n$, and estimating the parameters for just the first $m$ demand functions. Of course, if this shortcut procedure is adopted, one would want to evaluate $v(\cdot)$ for several different values of $c_{m+1}, \ldots, c_n$ in order to get some idea of how sensitive the welfare results were to the specification of these parameters. □

In the following examples, I will leave it to the interested reader to develop the simplifications possible in the estimation of $v(\mathbf{p},m)$ for the situation in which only a subset of the prices will be changed. Generally the simplifications made possible are quite similar to those just discussed for Example 2.

**Example 3** Suppose the direct preference relation, $G$, is representable on $\mathbf{R}_{+}^{n}$ by the utility function

$$U(\mathbf{x}) = -\log\left[\Sigma_{j=1}^{n} \exp(-x_j/d_j)\right]; \tag{50}$$

where

$d_j > 0$ for $j = 1, \ldots, n$.

If, for each $\mathbf{p} \in \mathbf{R}_{++}^{n}$, we define $\varepsilon(\mathbf{p})$ by

$$\varepsilon(\mathbf{p}) = \max_j\{\log(p_j d_j)\} - \min_i\{\log(p_i d_i)\}, \tag{51}$$

then it is easy to show that $h(\cdot)$ is given by

$$h^j(\mathbf{p},m) = d_j\left[\frac{\Sigma_{i=1}^n p_i d_i \log(p_i d_i)}{\mathbf{p}\cdot\mathbf{d}} - \log(p_j d_j) + \frac{m}{\mathbf{p}\cdot\mathbf{d}}\right]$$
$$\text{for } (\mathbf{p},m) \in \Omega,\ j = 1, \ldots, n; \tag{52}$$

where $\Omega$ is defined by:

$$\Omega = \{(\mathbf{p},m) \in \mathbf{R}^{n+1}_{++} \times \mathbf{R}_+ \mid m > \mathbf{p}\cdot\varepsilon(\mathbf{p})\}. \tag{53}$$

Following the procedure set out at the beginning of this section, we first consider the system of differential equations:

$$G_j(\mathbf{p}) = d_j/\mathbf{p}\cdot\mathbf{d} \text{ for } j = 1, \ldots, n. \tag{54}$$

Since

$$G(\mathbf{p}) = \log(\mathbf{p}\cdot\mathbf{d})$$

is obviously a solution of the system, equation (34), above, yields

$$b(\mathbf{q},\mathbf{p}) = \mathbf{q}\cdot\mathbf{d}/\mathbf{p}\cdot\mathbf{d} \text{ for } (\mathbf{q},\mathbf{p}) \in \mathbf{R}^n_{++} \times \mathbf{R}^n_{++}. \tag{55}$$

Next we note that (52) is of the form

$$h^j(\mathbf{p},m) = f^j(\mathbf{p}) + g^j(\mathbf{p})m;$$

where

$$g^j(\mathbf{p}) = d_j/\mathbf{p}\cdot\mathbf{d} \tag{56}$$

and

$$f^j(\mathbf{p}) = -d_j\log(p_j d_j) + (d_j/\mathbf{p}\cdot\mathbf{d})\,\Sigma_{i=1}^n p_i d_i \log(p_i d_i);$$

or, upon adding and subtracting the product $d_j \log(\mathbf{p}\cdot\mathbf{d})$ from the right-hand-side of the latter expression:

$$f^j(\mathbf{p}) = d_j[\log(\mathbf{p}\cdot\mathbf{d}) - \log(p_j d_j)] - [d_j/\mathbf{p}\cdot\mathbf{d}]$$
$$\times [(\mathbf{p}\cdot\mathbf{d})\log(\mathbf{p}\cdot\mathbf{d}) - \Sigma_{i=1}^n p_i d_i \log(p_i d_i)]. \tag{57}$$

From (56) and (57) we see that $f^j(\mathbf{p})$ is of the form

$$f^j(\mathbf{p}) = \gamma_j(\mathbf{p}) - g^j(\mathbf{p})\cdot\gamma(\mathbf{p});$$

where

$$\gamma(\mathbf{p}) = (\mathbf{p}\cdot\mathbf{d})\log(\mathbf{p}\cdot\mathbf{d}) - \Sigma_{i=1}^n p_i d_i \log(p_i d_i). \tag{58}$$

From equations (35) and (54), we obtain:

$$a(\mathbf{q},\mathbf{p}) = [\mathbf{q}\cdot\mathbf{d}]\cdot[\log(\mathbf{q}\cdot\mathbf{d}/\mathbf{p}\cdot\mathbf{d})] - \Sigma_{i=1}^n q_i d_i \log(q_i d_i)$$
$$+ [\mathbf{q}\cdot\mathbf{d}/\mathbf{p}\cdot\mathbf{d}]\cdot[\Sigma_{i=1}^n p_i d_i \log(p_i d_i)]; \tag{59}$$

and thus the income-equivalence function, $v(\cdot)$, is in this case given by:

$$v(\mathbf{q};\mathbf{p};m) = [\mathbf{q}\cdot\mathbf{d}]\cdot[\log(\mathbf{q}\cdot\mathbf{d}/\mathbf{p}\cdot\mathbf{d})] - \Sigma_{i=1}^n q_i d_i \log(q_i d_i)$$
$$+ [\mathbf{q}\cdot\mathbf{d}/\mathbf{p}\cdot\mathbf{d}]\cdot[m + \Sigma_{i=1}^n p_i d_i \log(p_i d_i)]. \ \square$$

**Example 4** Let $X = \{\mathbf{x} \in \mathbf{R}^n_+ \mid \mathbf{x} \geq \mathbf{z}\}$, where $\mathbf{z} \in \mathbf{R}^n_+$, and suppose that $G$ is representable on $X$ by the utility function

$$U(x) = \min\left\{\frac{x_1 - c_1}{d_1}, \frac{x_2 - c_2}{d_2}, \ldots, \frac{x_n - c_n}{d_n}\right\}; \tag{60}$$

where $\mathbf{c} \in \mathbf{R}^n$ and $\mathbf{d} \in \mathbf{R}^n_{++}$. Then, defining

$$\zeta = \max_i \left\{\frac{z_i - c_i}{d_i}\right\}$$

and

$$\Omega = \{(\mathbf{p},m) \in R^n_{++} \times \mathbf{R}_+ \mid m > \mathbf{p} \cdot \mathbf{c} + \zeta\mathbf{p} \cdot \mathbf{d}\},$$

it is easy to show that, for $(\mathbf{p},m) \in \Omega$, we have:

$$h^j(\mathbf{p},m) = c_j + d_j(m - \mathbf{p} \cdot \mathbf{c})/\mathbf{p} \cdot \mathbf{d} \text{ for } j = 1, \ldots, n. \tag{61}$$

Proceeding as before, we first must solve the system of differential equations:

$$G_j(\mathbf{p}) = d_j/\mathbf{p} \cdot \mathbf{d} \text{ for } j = 1, \ldots, n; \tag{62}$$

which clearly has as a solution,

$$G(\mathbf{p}) = \log(\mathbf{p} \cdot \mathbf{d}). \tag{63}$$

From inspection of equation (61) we also see that in this case the function $\gamma(\cdot)$ can be taken to be

$$\gamma(\mathbf{p}) = \mathbf{p} \cdot \mathbf{c}.$$

Thus in this case, our formula (36) becomes (for arbitrary $\mathbf{q}$):

$$v(\mathbf{q};\mathbf{p},m) = \mathbf{q} \cdot \mathbf{c} + \left(\frac{\mathbf{q} \cdot \mathbf{d}}{\mathbf{p} \cdot \mathbf{d}}\right)(m - \mathbf{p} \cdot \mathbf{d}). \ \square$$

**Example 5**[17] Suppose $\mathbf{z},\mathbf{c} \in \mathbf{R}^n_+$ and $\mathbf{d} \in \mathbf{R}^n_{++}$ satisfy

$$\Sigma^n_{i=1} c_i = 1 = \Sigma^n_{i=1} d_i,$$

define

$$\eta(\mathbf{p}) = \max_j \left\{\frac{p_j z_j + (d_j - c_j) \Pi^n_{i=1} p_i^{c_i}}{d_j}\right\} \tag{64}$$

and

$$\Omega = \{(\mathbf{p},m) \in \mathbf{R}^n_{++} \times \mathbf{R}_+ \mid m > \eta(\mathbf{p})\};$$

and consider the demand function, $\mathbf{h}(\cdot)$ given by:

$$h^j(\mathbf{p},m) = \frac{(c_j - d_j \Pi^n_{i=1} p_i^{c_i} + d_j m}{p_j} \text{ for } (\mathbf{p},m) \in \Omega, j = 1, \ldots, n. \tag{65}$$

In this case, if we proceed as per the method developed above, we begin by considering the system of differential equations:

$G_j(\mathbf{p}) = d_j/p_j$ for $j = 1, \ldots, n$;

which obviously has, as a solution,

$$G(\mathbf{p}) = \Sigma_{j=1}^{n} d_j \log(p_j). \qquad (66)$$

An inspection of the demand functions in (65) also yields the conclusion that in this case, we can take the function $\gamma(\cdot)$ to be given by:

$\gamma(\mathbf{p}) = \Pi_{i=1}^{n} p_i^{c_i}$.

Thus in this case our formula (36) becomes:

$$v(\mathbf{q};\mathbf{p},m) = \prod_{i=1}^{n} q_i^{c_i} + \left(\frac{\Pi_{i=1}^{n} q_i^{d_i}}{\Pi_{i=1}^{n} p_i^{d_i}}\right) \cdot \left(m - \prod_{i=1}^{n} p_i^{c_i}\right) \cdot \square$$

## Notes

I have had many helpful and stimulating conversations on the general subject of this chapter with my colleague, William Novshek, whose help is gratefully acknowledged.

1 Some of the theoretical underpinnings for such an investigation have already been completed by other authors. See Epstein (1982), LaFrance and Hanemann (1989), LaFrance (1991), and Hanemann and Morey (1992).

2 As is more or less standard notation, I shall write '$x \geq y$' to mean $x_1 \geq y$, for $i = 1, \ldots, n$, and '$x > y$' to mean $x \geq y$ and $x \neq y$.

3 As will become more apparent as we proceed, essentially everything which we shall be doing in this chapter can be formulated in terms of, and will depend only upon assumptions concerning, the indirect preference relation, $G^*$.

4 It is, in fact, easy to see that $\Omega^*$ itself is a connected set, and thus that there exists a continuous indirect utility function representing $G^*$ on $\Omega^*$. Notice, however, that *there may exist no direct utility function* representing $G$ under these circumstances (see Chipman and Moore (1976: 74)). Therefore, the conventional method of obtaining an indirect utility function by defining

$$V(\mathbf{p},m) = U[\mathbf{h}(\mathbf{p},m)]$$

is inadmissible here.

5 For a proof of the result in the generality stated here, and a further discussion of the result, see CM90, p. 71.

6 The strongest reason for this preference stems from the considerations discussed in n. 4, above; however, it is also true that the domain of the function defined in equation (2) is a bit ambiguous even if the direct utility function exists and is well-behaved. Moreover, it will also be possible to define equivalent and compensating variation somewhat more directly by using the income-compensation function rather than the expenditure function.

7 We shall often deal with a finite sequence (most often two) of price-income pairs, $(\mathbf{p}_t,m_t)$. Where this is the case, we shall denote the coordinates of $\mathbf{p}_t$ by "$p_{ti}$," for $i = 1, \ldots, n$.

8 The 1992 paper was actually presented, in essentially the published form, at an

NBER/NSF conference on "Theoretical Industrial Organization" at the University of Illinois in the fall of 1976.

9 The assumption that $(\mathbf{p}_0, m_0) \in \Omega$ is made essentially for the sake of convenience here; and could easily be dispensed with at the cost of some awkward terminology later on.

10 Therefore, we must have $W[(\mathbf{p}_0, m_0), (\mathbf{p}_0, m_0)] = 0$, since by assumption $(\mathbf{p}_0, m_0) \in \Omega$.

11 See also Gorman (1961), and Blackorby, Boyce, and Russell (1978), and Pollak (1971).

12 I have perhaps confused readers familiar with CM90 here, because I have reversed the order of **q** and **p** in the definition. This has been done to mimic the notation I have been using (and which is standard) in connection with the income-compensation function.

13 Except in the case where $G^*$ is homothetic; in which case, the income-equivalence and income-compensation functions are identical. In this case it is also true that $a(\mathbf{q}, \mathbf{p})$ is identically zero.

14 There is a bit of a goof in CM90 at this point. In the initial development of this method (pp. 105–9 of CM90), we indicate that we wish to deal with the unique solution of the differential equation system (31) satisfying $G(\bar{\mathbf{p}}) = 0$. This is redundant, as it turns out, and *any* solution of (33) can be used to define $b(\cdot)$ via equation (34) of the present text.

15 In CM90, it is also shown how to obtain such a function. See pp. 113–114.

16 After all, evaluating a line integral also involves solving a system of partial differential equations.

17 I believe this demand function was invented by John Chipman, for an as-yet-unwritten joint paper he and I plan to write on Gorman Polar Form utility functions.

## Bibliography


Blackorby, Charles, Boyce, R. and Russell, R.R. (1978) "Estimation of Demand Systems Generated by the Gorman Polar Form: A Generalization of the S-Branch Utility Tree," *Econometrica* 46: 345–63.

Chipman, John S. and Moore, J.C. (1976) "The Scope of Consumer's Surplus Arguments," in A. Tang, F. Westfield, and J. Worley (eds) *Evolution, Welfare and Time in Economics: Essays in Honor of Nicholas Georgescu-Roegen*. New York: D.C. Heath.

Chipman, John S. and Moore, J.C. (1980) "Compensating Variation, Consumer's Surplus, and Welfare," *The American Economic Review* 70: 933–49.

Chipman, John S. and Moore, J.C. (1990) "Acceptable Indicators of Welfare Change, Consumer's Surplus Analysis and the Gorman Polar Form," in J.S. Chipman, D. McFadden, and M.K. Richter (eds) *Preferences, Uncertainty, and Optimality: Essays in Honor of Leonid Hurwicz*. Denver: Westview Press.

Chipman, John S. and Moore, J.C. (1992) "Compensating Variation as a Measure of Welfare Change," in W. Neuefeind and R. Riezman (eds) *Economic Theory and International Trade: Essays in Memoriam, J. Trout Rader*. Berlin: Springer-Verlag.

Debreu, Gerard (1959) *Theory of Value*. New York: Wiley.

Epstein, Larry G. (1982) "Integrability of Incomplete Systems of Demand Functions," *Review of Economic Studies* 49: 411–25.

Gorman, W.M. (1961) "On a Class of Preference Fields," *Metroeconomica* 13: 53–6.
Hanemann, Michael and Morey, E. (1992) "Separability, Partial Demand Systems, and Consumer's Surplus Measures," *Jnl of Environ. Economics and Management* 22: 241–58.
Hurwicz, Leonid and Uzawa, H. (1971) "On the Integrability of Demand Functions," in J. S. Chipman, L. Hurwicz, M.K. Richter, and H.F. Sonnenschein (eds) *Preferences, Utility, and Demand.* New York: Harcourt Brace Jovanovich.
LaFrance, Jeffrey T. (1991) "Consumer's Surplus versus Compensating Variation Revisited," *Amer. Jnl. of Agr. Economics* 73: 1496–1507.
LaFrance, Jeffrey T. and Hanemann, W.M. (1989) "The Dual Structure of Incomplete Demand Systems," *Amer. Jnl. of Agr. Economics* 71: 262–74.
McKenzie, Lionel W. (1957) "Demand Theory Without a Utility Index," *Review of Economic Studies* 24: 185–89.
Pollak, Robert (1971) "Additive Utility Functions and Linear Engel Curves," *Review of Economic Studies* 38: 401–14.

# 18

# MARSHALLIAN DEMONSTRATION OF TAX-SUBSIDY SCHEME UNDER VARIABLE RETURNS TO SCALE

*Takashi Negishi*[1]

Marshall proposed that diminishing returns industries should be taxed and increasing returns industries should be subsidized. This proposition has been misunderstood by modern scholars on the basis that Marshall forgot to consider the changes in producers' surplus in his demonstration. We vindicate Marshall as that criticism by modern scholars is based on their confusion of particular expenses curves and supply curves, which Marshall correctly distinguished. It is suggested that Marshall's proposition can also be applied to the case of variable returns due to internal economies through his life-cycle theory of firms.

## Introduction

Among many important contributions made by Professor Chipman to economic science, particularly interesting to me are those to the history of economic thoughts, which consider the classical problems in the light of modern theory. They are really the products of a rare combination of historical and theoretical talents and insights. Chipman himself included two of such contributions in the five articles of his own which he considered most important (Blaug and Sturges 1983: 66–67). They are (1) "A survey of the theory of international trade," *Econometrica*, 1965, 1966 and (2) "External economies of scale and competitive equilibrium," *Quarterly Journal of Economics*, 1970.

The latter contribution deals with Marshall's famous proposition that optimality would require taxation of industries operating under decreasing returns and subsidization of industries under increasing returns. Against Samuelson's scorn (1947: 196), Chipman demonstrated rigorously that the proposition, as well as Marshall's arguments in its support, is correct in a simplified general equilibrium model, if variable returns are due to the so-called Marshallian external economies to scale (Chipman 1990: 282–283).[2] After twenty years, however, standard textbooks of the history of economic thoughts still "have little reason for confidence in the Marshallian Theorem that the state can increase economic welfare by taxing increasing cost industries and subsidizing decreasing cost industries" (Blaug 1985: 387–388; Ekelund and Hébert 1990: 399).

The aim of this chapter is, therefore, to revisit Marshall's own demonstration in his *Principles*, and to consider how and why it was misunderstood by many eminent modern writers in the fields of economic theory and the history of economic thought. We start with the case of a tax on an industry of decreasing returns and modern writers' criticism that Marshall forgot to consider the producers' surplus. The next section is devoted to an examination of Marshall's concept of producers' surplus and particular expenses curve. After this, Marshall's tax proposal is vindicated for a manufacturing industry of diminishing returns caused by Marshallian external diseconomies, while his correct analysis of the case of agriculture is explained in the following section. The sixth section vindicates Marshall's proposal of bounties on industries of increasing returns due to Marshallian external economies. Finally, we consider in the last two sections the case of industries of increasing returns caused by internal economies which are compatible with competition.

## Producers' surplus

In Book V, chapter XIII, section 4, of his *Principles*, Marshall considered "the effects which a change in the conditions of supply may exert on consumers' surplus or rent" (Marshall 1961, vol. 1: 467). It is true, however, that in Figures 30–32 of *Principles*,[3] Marshall merely compared changes in consumers' surplus with the receipts from a tax or the cost of a bounty, and no consideration was given to changes in rent or producers' surplus before he concluded that "these results throw light on the doctrine of *maximum satisfaction*," i.e. "the general doctrine that a position of (stable) equilibrium of demand and supply is a position also of *maximum satisfaction*" (1961, vol. 1: 470).

For example, Figure 18.1 is a reproduction of part of Marshall's Figure 31, where the level of output is measured horizontally, and the price and cost vertically. Curve DD′ is the demand curve for the industry, and curve SS′ is the supply curve of the industry, which obeys the law of diminishing returns. Suppose that the imposition of a tax raises SS′ to ss′ and the old equilibrium A is shifted to the new equilibrium a. The rate of tax is aE on each unit of the product and the gross receipts of the tax will be cFEa, since Oh, that is CK, units are produced in the new equilibrium. Marshall argued that, the loss of consumers' surplus being cCAa, the gross receipts from the tax will be greater or less than the loss of consumers' surplus as CFEK is greater or less than aKA. In the case of Figure 18.1, as in Marshall's Figure 31, it is much greater.

Even so, however, it is hardly possible to persuade those who know the fundamental theorem of welfare economics that this implies the non-optimality of the competitive equilibrium A. If the production possibility set is strictly convex, so that the supply curve is rising as is SS′, there exists producers' surplus SAC, which is reduced by the imposition of the tax to SEF. The combined loss of consumers' and producers' surplus is, then, greater than the tax receipt by AaE. Why did Marshall not consider such a loss of producers' surplus and argue for taxes upon industries of diminishing returns?

This is exactly Samuelson's view, which represents modern economists' interpretations and criticism of Marshall's proposals.

> Because Marshall (*Principles*, Book V, Ch. XIII, pp. 467–470) made an elementary mistake in his graphical reckoning of consumers' surplus, forgetting to take into account producers' surplus . . . an odd omission for a chap who always insisted correctly that there are two blades in the scissors of supply and demand . . . he came up with what seems like an exciting policy theorem: *Tax to contract increasing cost industries: subsidize to expand decreasing cost industries.*[4]

The argument that we have outlined is directly drawn from Marshall's text. It is apparent, however, that it is incomplete

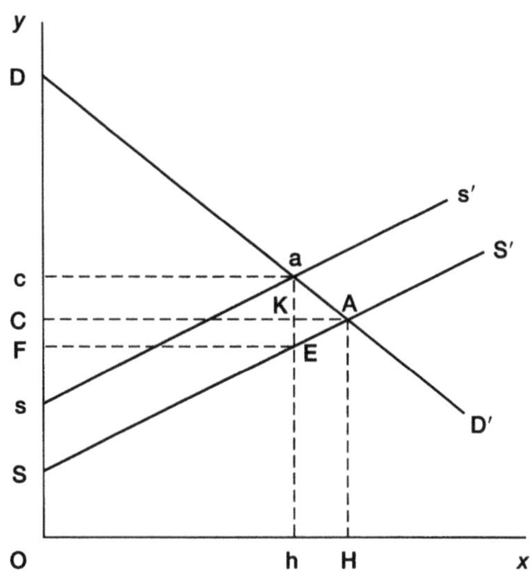


*Figure 18.1*

> because it fails to take into account the change in producers' as well as consumers' surplus resulting from a tax or subsidy. Marshall deals with the problem of producers' surplus in Appendix H to the *Principles* but with considerable confusion.[5]

Can you believe that Marshall was such a careless "chap" who forgot to consider changes in producers' surplus? Was he so stubborn to insist on such a "false theorem" (Samuelson 1967: 113) throughout so many editions of *Principles*? There must be some difference between what Marshall really meant and what latter day economists believe Marshall did.

## Particular expenses curve

As a matter of fact, Marshall clearly recognized the existence of producers' surplus and considered its significance very deliberately in his *Principles*. For example, see Appendix H in *Principles*, which is apparently attached to Book V, chapter XIII, where Marshallian tax-bounty proposal is discussed. Figure 18.2 is an exact reproduction of Marshall's Figure 39 in Appendix H (1961, vol. 1: 811). The area AFS is called producers' surplus by Marshall himself.

As in the case of Figure 18.1, the product of an industry is measured along O*x*, and its price along O*y*. The curve DD′ is, of course, the demand curve for the industry. Thus, Figure 18.2 seems similar to Figure 18.1 and we are tempted to consider that the area ACS in Figure 18.1 corresponds to the area AFS in Figure 18.2. There is, however, a very important difference

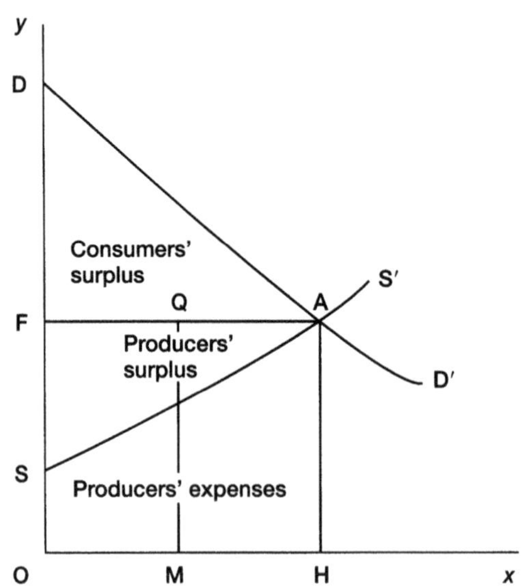


*Figure 18.2*

between the two figures. While the curve SS′ in Figure 18.1 is called the supply curve, SS′ in Figure 18.2 is what Marshall called the particular expenses curve.

> Now the difference between the particular expense curve and a normal supply curve lies in this, that in the former we do, and in the latter we do not, take the general economies of production as fixed and uniform throughout. The particular expenses curve is based throughout on the assumption that the aggregate production is OH, and that all the producers have access to the internal and external economies which belong to this scale of production; and, these assumptions being carefully borne in mind, the curve may be used to represent a particular phase of any industry, whether agricultural or manufacturing: but they cannot be taken to represent its general conditions of production. That can be done only by the normal supply curve, in which PM represents the normal expenses of production of the OMth unit on the supposition that OM units (not any other amounts, as OH) are being produced; and that the available economies of production external and internal are those which belong to a representative firm where the aggregate volume of production is OM.
>
> (Marshall 1961, vol. 1: 811)

Marshall distinguished workers' surplus and savers' (waiters') surplus, which are included in the area SAHO in Figure 18.2 as producers' expenses, from "the excess of earning of an appliance of production over the prime cost of its work" (1961, vol. 1: 830–832). The latter surplus is, of course, due to the limited supply of such an appliance used by producers. Since Marshall is concerned with a long-run equilibrium, only where producers have full access to the external economies, however, may the rent of land used by producers be left to be shown as the area AFS in Figure 18.2.

> All appliances of production, whether machinery, or factories with the land on which they are built, or farms, are alike in yielding large surpluses over the prime costs of particular acts of production to a man who owns and works them: also in yielding him normally no special surplus in the long run above what is required to remunerate him for his trouble and sacrifice and outlay in purchasing and working them (no special surplus, as contrasted with his general worker's and waiter's surplus). But there is this difference between land and other agents of production, that from a social point of view land yields a permanent surplus, while perishable things made by man do not.[6]

## Manufacturing industry

Let us consider the case of a manufacturing industry, in which the effect of land used by producers is negligible. Suppose that there exist Marshallian external diseconomies and that cost curves of individual producers are raised by the general expansion of the industry as a whole. Then the industry is subject to diminishing returns to scale and the long-run supply curve of the industry is upward sloping. To demonstrate this, it is convenient to work with the representative firm, which is a small replica or miniature of the industry and whose cost of production is a function of its level of output as well as the level of output of the industry.[7]

In Figure 18.3, both the output of the representative firm and the corresponding output of the industry are measured horizontally along O*x*, with, of course, different scales, and costs and prices are measured vertically along O*y*. Curves DD′ and dd′ are demand curves for the industry, and curve SS′ is the supply curve of the industry in the long run. Curves SMC and SAC are, respectively, the short-run marginal cost curve and the short-run average cost curve of the representative firm. SMC plays also the role of the short-run supply curve of the industry.

Suppose the demand curve is DD′, which intersects with SS′ at point A. Point A signifies the long-run equilibrium of the industry with free entry. Curve SAC of the representative firm, which corresponds to the industrial output OM, reaches the minimum at point A, so that point A is also on the curve SMC. Since "the normal supply price of any amount of the commodity may be taken to be its normal expenses of production (including *gross*

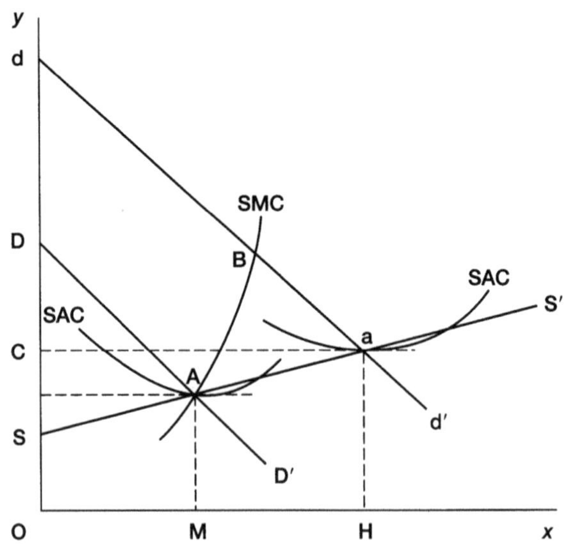


*Figure 18.3*

earnings of management)" (Marshall 1961, vol. 1: 342–343), the representative firm is earning the normal profit included in the cost at point A, and the volume of the industrial output remains unchanged.[8]

> In a rigidly stationary state in which supply could be perfectly adjusted to demand in every particular, the normal expenses of production, the marginal expenses, and the average expenses (rent being counted in) would be one and the same thing, for long periods and for short.
>
> (Marshall 1961, vol. 1: 497)

If the demand curve is shifted to dd′, the equilibrium is shifted to point B, at which dd′ intersects with SMC. Gradually, however, the cost curves of the representative firm are shifted upward by the external diseconomies caused by the expansion of industrial output due to the price being higher than the normal supply price at point B. The long-run equilibrium is again established at point a. The rising supply curve SS′ passes equilibrium points like A, a, etc. It is, however, different from the particular expenses curve. If the level of industrial output is OH, the latter curve is a dotted horizontal line Ca.

If we interprete that the curve SS′ in Figure 18.1, i.e. curve SS′ in Marshall's Figure 31, is the curve SS′ in Figure 18.3, then, the area SAC in Figure 18.1 is not the producers' surplus. Since the particular expenses curve corresponding to the industrial output OH is the dotted line AC, there exists no producers' surplus in this case. Marshall did not forget "to take into account producers' surplus." He was right to point out the possibility that point A is not optimal when the industry is subject to diminishing returns caused by external diseconomies, like the congestion in the free use of specific natural resources or specific public factors of production.

It is necessary to make these free resources or public factors *specific* to the industry in question, since, as was pointed out by Sraffa, we are assuming "that the conditions of production and the demand for a commodity can be considered, in respect to small variations, as being practically independent, both in regard to each other and in relation to the supply and demand of all other commodities" (Sraffa 1926: 538). In his famous criticism on Marshall, Sraffa concluded that "the imposing structure of diminishing returns is available only for the study of that minute class of commodities in the production of which the whole of a factor of production is employed" (1926: 539). In the case of free resources or public factors, however, we are not sure whether such a class of commodities is minute or not.

## Agriculture

If we consider the case of an agricultural industry, however, there is a possibility that the area SAC in Figure 18.1 represents producers' surplus which has to be taken into consideration. Suppose there are no Marshallian external economies or diseconomies, but the industry is subject to diminishing returns caused by the limited supply of land adapted for use in only this industry. Then, curve SS′ in Figure 18.1 is the supply curve as well as the particular expenses curve, exclusive of rent for the owners of land. The area SAC represents landlords' rent as producers' surplus.

As a matter of fact, Marshall considered this case in his *Principles*, in Figure 33, which is a reproduction of his Figure 31, a partial reproduction of which is our Figure 18.1.

> SS′ being the supply curve before the imposition of a tax, landlords' rent is represented by CSA. After the tax has been imposed and the supply curve raised to ss′ the landlords' rent becomes the amount by which cOha, the total price got for Oh produce sold at the rate ha, exceeds the total tax cFEa, together with OhES the total expenses of production, exclusive of rent, for Oh produce: that is, it becomes FSE. Thus the loss of landlords' rent is CFEA; and this added to cCAa the loss of consumers' surplus, makes up CFEAa, which exceeds the gross tax by aAE.
>
> (Marshall 1961, vol. 1: 473–474)

In spite of Blaug (1985: 387), therefore, we cannot call the conclusion "anti-Marshallian," even if it implies "that the combined loss in consumers' and producers' surplus from a tax actually exceeds the amount of tax receipts." Far from "forgetting to take into account producers' surplus," Marshall considered it deliberately when it was necessary to do so, and rightly pointed out an exception to his proposal of a tax upon industries of diminishing returns. But why is this the only case where Marshall did take into account producers' surplus? In the long run, surplus in the production accrues only to the primary factors of production, i.e. labor and land. Why, then, did Marshall consider only the landlords' rent?

Let us recall the basic assumption in the application of consumers' surplus analysis; that the marginal utility of money is constant and identical for all the consumers. Here money represents all the goods which can be bought by money, except the product of the industry in question. Labor service is also represented by money, so that its marginal disutility (marginal utility of leisure) and its marginal productivity in other industries remain unchanged, irrespective of the level of output in the industry in question. What remains to be considered as producers' surplus is, then, the rent for land which is assumed to have no direct utility and not to be used in other industries.

## External economies

Marshall recommended a bounty on a commodity which obeys the law of increasing return.

> A bounty on such a commodity causes so great a fall in its price to the consumer, that the consequent increase of consumers' surplus may exceed the total payments made by the State to producers; and certainly will do so in case the law of increasing return acts at all sharply.
>
> (1961, vol. 1: 469)

He demonstrated this by using Figure 32 in his *Principles*, which we partly reproduce here as Figure 18.4. As in the case of Figure 18.1, the output of the industry is measured along O*x*, and prices and cost O*y*. The position of the supply curve before the granting of the bounty is ss′ while the position after it is SS′. The increase of consumers' surplus is cCAa, and the direct payments made by the State under the bounty are represented by RCAT. In the case of Figure 18.4, the former is larger than the latter. (See Marshall 1961, vol. 1: 469–470.)

Again no explicit mention is made of producers' surplus and Marshall emphasized "the fact that a fall in price due to improvements benefits consumers without injuring producers" and "the doctrine of maximum satisfaction assumes that every fall in the price which producers receive

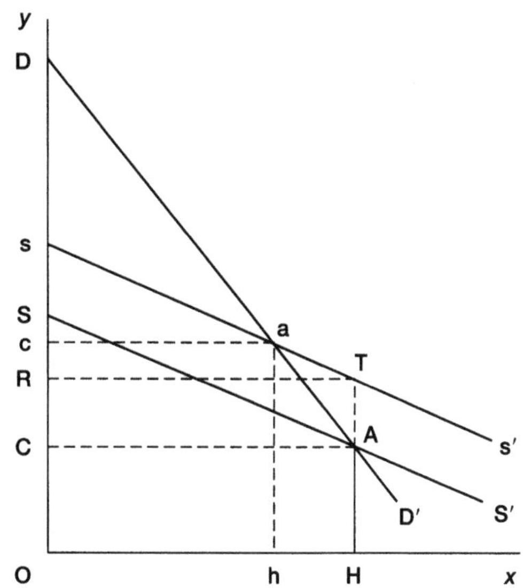


*Figure 18.4*

for the commodity, involves a corresponding loss to them; and this is not true of a fall in price which results from improvements in industrial organization" (1961, vol. 1: 472).

Marshall can be vindicated by the consideration of an industry of increasing returns caused by Marshallian external economies. Consider the representative firm as in Figure 18.3. Suppose that the long-run equilibrium a is located below the long run equilibrium A, since cost curves of individual firms are shifted downwards by the general expansion of the industry. Then, the supply curve SS′ which passes equilibrium points such as A, a, etc. is downward sloping, as curve ss′ in Figure 18.4.

Although the supply curve ss′ is downward sloping in Figure 18.4, the particular expenses curve is horizontal, since the representative firm on the supply curve yields only the normal profit which is included in the cost. If point a is a long-run equilibrium, the particular expenses curve is ac, since firms are enjoying external economies corresponding to the industrial output O. There exists no producers' surplus to be taken into account, and Marshall was right to point out the possibility that point a is not optimal when the industry is subject to increasing returns caused by external economies.

## Internal economies (1)

In spite of Samuelson who argued that "it was a *competitive* decreasing cost industry we were talking about, a contradiction in terms if the increasing returns are *internal* to the firm. So Marshallians hasten to say that it must be, of course, decreasing cost due to *external* economies that we meant, and which ought to be subsidized" (1967: 113), it is well known that Marshall insisted on a possibility of the compatibility of increasing returns due to internal economies and competitive equilibrium. It is based on his life-cycle theory of private firms. Internal economies may not be fully exploited by an individual firm, since its life-span is limited. Like an individual tree in a forest, an individual firm in an industry grows and decays, although the forest and industry remain stationary.

> Rapid growth of firms in some trade which offer great economies to production on a large scale . . . But long before this end [monopoly] is reached, his [a new businessman's] progress is likely to be arrested by the decay, if not of his faculties, yet of his liking for energetic work.[9]

In Figure 18.5, where output is measured along O*x* and prices and costs, along O*y*, the curve SAC is the short-run average cost curve of a firm with a plant of a given scale. The curve SAC is shifted downward to the right by investment and upward to the left by disinvestment. The dotted curve LAC is the envelope of the short-run average cost curves at different scales of the plant. Since the long-run average cost curve LAC is downward sloping, there exist internal economies. According to the life-cycle theory of firms, a young firm's SAC is located below, relative to the price of the product, but is shifted above as it gets older.

Young firms are expanding the scale of their plants, since the price is higher than SAC including the normal profit at the level of output, where the short run marginal cost, SMC, is equal to the price of the product, while old firms are reducing the scale of their plants, since the price is lower than SAC at the level of output where SMC is equal to the price. The aggregate output of the industry remains, however, stationary and the representative firm is at equilibrium A in Figure 18.5, yielding just the normal profit.

To see this, let us denote SAC of a firm in short-run equilibrium by $x$ and the price of the product of the industry by $p$.[10] It is assumed that the rate of change in output caused by the changes in the scale of the plant is proportional to the difference between $p$ and $x$. Let $y(x)$ be the total output of the firms with the value of the same $x$. Furthermore, let $D(x)$ denote changes in $y$. Then,

$$D(x)/y(x) = p - x. \qquad (1)$$

Since the industrial output remains unchanged, i.e.

$$\int y(x)\,dx = \text{constant}, \qquad (2)$$

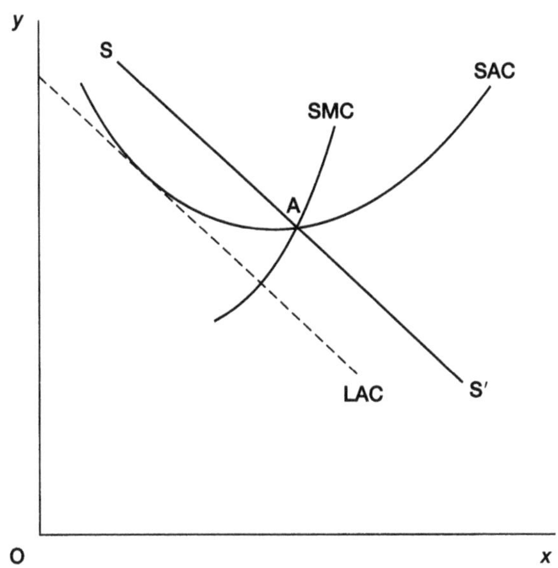


*Figure 18.5*

from (1),

$$\int D(x)\,dx = \int (p - x)y(x)\,dx = 0. \tag{3}$$

From the right-hand side of (3), we have

$$p = \int xf(x)\,dx \tag{4}$$

where $f(x) = y(x)/\int y(x)\,dx$.

Since (4) implies that the value of the total sales of the industry is equal to its total cost including normal profit, the representative firm as the miniature of the industry is at A in Figure 18.5, yielding just the normal profit, when the expansion of young firms is balanced by the contraction of old firms. The expansion of young firms does not last long, since they soon become old firms. If curve ss′ in Figure 18.4 is interpreted as curve SS′ in Figure 18.5, Marshall was right to point out the possibility that point a is not optimal when the industry is subject to increasing returns caused by internal economies.

## Internal economies (2)

Although Marshall's life-cycle theory of firm gives a realistic picture of nineteenth-century industry, however, the question remains as to its relevancy after the great development of joint-stock companies. Marshall himself was well aware of this problem.

> As with the growth of trees, so was it with the growth of business as a general rule before the great recent development of vast joint-stock companies, which often stagnate, but do not readily die. Now that rule is far from universal.[11]

To get rid of this difficulty, we may consider that a capital asset with embodied technology has a limited life, since wages rise as a result of technical progress, instead of Marshall's supposition that the life-span of an individual firm is limited. In other words, we may replace Marshall's theory of the life-cycle of a firm in a stationary equilibrium with a theory of the life-cycle of technology in a balanced growth equilibrium. While Marshall considered economic growth with both population and wealth growing proportionally as a "modification of the fiction of a stationary state" (1961, vol. 1: 368), we are going to consider the growth of physical wealth with technical progress and unchanged population. In view of the so-called stylized facts of economic growth that real wage and capital–labor ratio are rising while the relative shares of capital and labor remain unchanged,[12] however, it is evident which plan will "bring us nearer to real life and help to break up a complex problem" (Marshall 1961, vol. 1: 368).[13]

In Figure 18.5, let us suppose that SAC is the short-run average cost curve of a plant of the given scale composed of capital assets in which today's technology is embodied. Although its LAC is downward sloping and SAC can be shifted downward by enlarging the plant, the scale of the plant would remain limited, since SAC will be shifted upward in the future when the real wage is raised by the dominance in the economy of newer capital assets embodied with more efficient technology of the future. Consider a competitive firm with several plants of different vintages. While the profit from new plants with new technology is much higher than the normal profit, profit from old plants with old technology falls short of the normal. At equilibrium, the firm's position is indicated by point A in Figure 18.5, yielding only the normal profit which is included in its SAC.

If the firm is the representative firm of the industry, and its SS′ curve of Figure 18.5 is considered as curve ss′ in Figure 18.4, we can vindicate Marshall's proposal of bounties on industries of increasing returns due to internal economies, without assuming that the life-span of an individual firm is limited.

It was often argued that "truly reversible decreasing cost industries associated with external economies are perhaps a *curiosum*" (Samuelson 1967: 115) and that "those economies which are external from the point of view of the individual firm, but internal as regards the industry in its aggregate, constitute precisely the class which is most seldom to be met with" (Sraffa 1926: 540). If so, we must admit that the only remaining case worth considering is the case of industries of increasing returns due to economies which are internal from the point of view of individual firms. Provided that this case is compatible with the competition, however, we need not admit "supply curves showing decreasing costs are not to be found more frequently than their opposite" (Sraffa 1926: 540).

## Notes

1 I am highly grateful to Professor P.A. Samuelson for his comments on the earlier version.

2 However, Samuelson was of course not against a subsidy to increasing returns activities. See, for example, Samuelson 1982: 173–174.

3 See Marshall 1961, vol. 1: 467–469. Figures 30, 31, and 32 correspond, respectively, to the cases of constant returns, diminishing returns and increasing returns.

4 See Samuelson 1967: 112. See also Ellis and Fellner 1943: 494, who may perhaps be the first to express such an interpretation of Marshall.

5 See Blaug 1985: 368, and Ekelund and Hébert 1990: 399.

6 See Marshall 1961, vol. 1: 832 and also 1961, vol. 1: 499, 501–502.

7 For the representative firm, see Frisch 1956 and Negishi 1989: 352–354, 365–367.

8 Gross earnings of management is defined by Marshall as the sum of "the supply price of business ability and energy" and "the supply price of that organization

by which the appropriate business ability and the requisite capital are brought together" (Marshall 1961, vol. 1: 313).

9 See Marshall 1961, vol. 1: 285–286, and Marshall 1921: 315–316.

10 For the details, see Negishi 1989: 367.

11 See Marshall 1961, vol. 1: 316. It was in the sixth edition of *Principles* (1910) that Marshall first added a reservation clause on joint-stock companies (1961, vol. 11: 343). See also Marshall 1921: 316.

12 The stylized facts are originally due to Kaldor (1961). See Burmeister 1980: 46, 291.

13 For the details of the following arguments, see Negishi 1985: 45–56; 1989: 369–375.

## Bibliography


Blaug, M. (1985) *Economic Theory in Retrospect*. Cambridge: Cambridge University Press.

Blaug, M. and Sturges, P. (eds) (1983) *Who's Who in Economics*. Brighton, Sussex: Wheatsheaf Books Ltd.

Burmeister, D. (1980) *Capital Theory and Dynamics*. Cambridge: Cambridge University Press.

Chipman, J.S. (1990) "Marshall's Consumer's Surplus in Modern Perspective," in J.K. Whitaker (ed.) *Cenetary Essays on Alfred Marshall*. Cambridge: Cambridge University Press.

Ekelund, R. Jr and Hébert, R.F. (1990) *A History of Economic Theory and Method*. New York: McGraw-Hill.

Ellis, H.S. and Fellner, W. (1943) "External Economies and Diseconomies," *American Economic Review* 33: 493–511.

Frisch, R. (1956) "Alfred Marshall's Theory of Value," *Quarterly Journal of Economics* 64: 495–524.

Kaldor, N. (1961) "Capital Accumulation and Economic Growth," in F.A. Lutz and D.C. Hague (eds) *Theory of Capital*. London: Macmillan.

Marshall, A. (1921) *Industry and Trade*. London: Macmillan.

—— (1961) *Principles of Economics*. London: Macmillan.

Negishi, T. (1985) *Economic Theories in a Non-Walrasian Tradition*. Cambridge: Cambridge University Press.

—— (1989) *History of Economic Theory*. Amsterdam: North-Holland.

Samuelson, P.A. (1947) *Foundations of Economic Analysis*. Cambridge, MA: Harvard University Press.

—— (1967) "The Monopolistic Competition Revolution," in R.E. Kuenne (ed.) *Monopolistic Competition Theory: Studies in Impact*. New York: John Wiley.

—— (1982) "A Chapter in the History of Ramsey's Optimal Feasible Taxation and Optimal Public Utility Prices," in S. Anderson, K. Larsen, P.N. Rusmussen and J. Vibe-Pedersen (eds) *Economic Essays in Honour of J.H. Gelting*. Copenhagen: Danish Economic Association.

Sraffa, P. (1926) "The Laws of Returns under Competitive Conditions," *Economic Journal* 36: 535–550.

19

# THE ENVELOPE THEORY IN A SMOOTH CONSTRAINED OPTIMIZATION PROBLEM WITH APPLICATIONS IN ECONOMICS

*Yoshihiko Otani*

## Introduction

The behavior of an individual agent in economics is often formulated as a solution to a constrained optimization problem with economic parameters. In this formulation, properties of the behavior of an economic agent are obtained by examining how the optimizing solution will respond to changes in economic parameters. This is called a comparative static analysis of the agent's optimizing behavior. These comparative static results are known to be very closely related to properties of an optimum value function.

In this chapter, we would like to examine the geometric structure and its properties associated with the optimum value function of a constrained optimization problem. In particular, we shall first reformulate the classical definition of an envelope and then show that the surface generated by the optimum value function defines an envelope of a family of surfaces generated by the objective function for the optimization problem parametrized by variables to be optimized. Then we shall show that both Samuelson's envelope theorem and the LeChatelier–Samuelson principle are closely related to properties of the optimum value function. We shall also examine the manifold structure of the envelope and then the surface generated by the optimum parametrized solutions. Finally we shall show how our formulation can be applied to characterize the set of Pareto efficient allocations in an exchange economy.

## The model, definitions and assumptions

Let $f$: $\mathbf{R}^n \times \tilde{\mathbf{A}} \to \mathbf{R}$, $g$: $\mathbf{R}^n \times \tilde{\mathbf{A}} \to \mathbf{R}^m$ be both smooth functions where $\tilde{\mathbf{A}}$ is an open subset of $\mathbf{R}^r$. We shall consider a family of maximization problems parametrized by $\alpha \in \tilde{\mathbf{A}}$, i.e. $\max_x\{f(x, \alpha) \mid g(x, \alpha) = 0_m\}$ where $0_m$ denotes an $(m \times 1)$ vector of zeros.

Define $F$: $\mathbf{R}^n \times \mathbf{A} \to \mathbf{R}$ and $\mathbf{M}$, a subset of $\mathbf{R}^n \times \mathbf{A}$ where $\mathbf{A} = \tilde{\mathbf{A}} \times \mathbf{R}$ by:

$F(x, a) \equiv [f(x, \alpha) - \beta, (g(x, \alpha))']'$ and

$\mathbf{M} = \{(x, a) \mid F(x, a) = 0_{m+1}\}$,

where $a \equiv (\alpha, \beta)$. We shall assume that the following rank condition on the constraint function holds on $\mathbf{M}$.

**Assumption 1**: The rank of the matrix $d_x g(x, \alpha)$ is $m$ for every $(x, \alpha, \beta) \in \mathbf{M}$ where $d_x g$ indicates the derivative of $g$ with respect to $x$.

By Assumption 1, the constraint $g(x, \alpha) = 0_m$ can be uniquely solved locally for $m$ coordinates of $x$. It will be notationally convenient if for every $(x, \alpha)$, we can use the same $m$ coordinates of $x$. For example, suppose that we can write $x = (y, z)$, $y \in \mathbf{R}^m$, $z \in \mathbf{R}^q$, and $\operatorname{rank}[d_y g(x, \alpha)] = m$ for every $(x, \alpha)$ where $q = n - m$. This assumption will not necessarily be needed for our analysis, but it will be notationally rather cumbersome without this. So we will strengthen Assumption 1 to the following.

**Assumption 1′** For every $(x, \alpha, \beta) \in \mathbf{M}$, $\operatorname{rank}[d_y g(x, \alpha)] = m$ where $x = (y, z)$, $y \in \mathbf{R}^m$, $z \in \mathbf{R}^q$, and $q = n - m$.

The $(m + 1) \times (n + r + 1)$ Jacobian matrix of the mapping $F$ is given as follows:

$$dF(x, \alpha, \beta) = \begin{bmatrix} d_x f & d_\alpha f & -1 \\ d_x g & d_\alpha g & 0_m \end{bmatrix}.$$

Thus, by Assumption 1, the rank of $dF(x, \alpha, \beta)$ is $(m + 1)$ for every $(x, \alpha, \beta) \in \mathbf{M}$. Hence $\mathbf{M} = F^{-1}(0_{m+1})$ is a smooth manifold of dimension $n + r + 1 - (m + 1) = (n - m) + r = q + r$. Since $\operatorname{rank}[d_y g(y, z, \alpha)] = m$ and $d_\beta F(x, \alpha, \beta) = [-1(0_m)']'$ we have that:

$$\operatorname{rank}[d_y F(x, \alpha, \beta), d_\beta F(x, \alpha, \beta)] = m + 1.$$

Thus given $(x^0, a^0) \in \mathbf{M}$ where $a^0 = (\alpha^0, \beta^0)$, there exists a local diffeomorphism $h$: $\mathbf{M} \cap U(x^0, a^0) \to U(z^0, \alpha^0)$ where $U(x^0, a^0)$ is an open neighborhood of $(x^0, a^0)$ in $\mathbf{R}^n \times \mathbf{R}^{r+1}$, $a^0 = (\alpha^0, \beta^0)$, and $U(z^0, \alpha^0)$ is an open neighborhood of $(z^0, \alpha^0)$ in $\mathbf{R}^q \times \mathbf{R}^r$. In other words, we can use $(z, \alpha)$ as a local coordinate system of the manifold $\mathbf{M}$. In fact this is through a unique smooth map $\tilde{y}$: $U(z^0, \alpha^0) \to U(y^0)$ obtained by the implicit function theorem such that $g(\tilde{y}(z, \alpha), z, \alpha) \equiv 0_m$ on $U(z^0, \alpha^0)$ and a smooth map $\tilde{\phi}$: $U(z^0, \alpha^0) \to U(\beta^0)$ defined by $\tilde{\phi}(z, \alpha) = f(\tilde{y}(z, \alpha), z, \alpha)$ so that $\beta = \tilde{\phi}(z, \alpha)$ where $U(y^0)$ and $U(\beta^0)$ are open neighborhoods of $y^0$ in $\mathbf{R}^m$ and $\beta^0$ in $\mathbf{R}$ respectively. Thus for a given $(z, \alpha) \in U(z^0, \alpha^0)$,

$$h^{-1}(z, \alpha) = [\tilde{y}(z, \alpha), z, \alpha, \tilde{\phi}(z, \alpha)] \in \mathbf{M} \cap U(x^0, a^0).$$

Note that $\tilde{y}(z, \alpha)$ and $\tilde{\phi}(z, \alpha)$ are defined on some neighborhood $U(z^0, a^0)$ of $(z^0, \alpha^0)$ for each $(z^0, \alpha^0)$ such that $(x^0, \alpha^0) \in \mathbf{M}$. Thus it will be more precise to write $\tilde{y}(z, \alpha; z^0, \alpha^0)$ and $\tilde{\phi}(z, \alpha; z^0, \alpha^0)$. But to avoid cumbersome notations, we will simply write $\tilde{y}(z, \alpha)$ and $\tilde{\phi}(z, \alpha)$.

Regarding $z$ as a parameter vector, let $F_z(y, a) = F(y, z, a)$ be a family of functions parametrized by $z$ and then define $\mathbf{M}_z$, a family of subsets of $\mathbf{R}^m \times \mathbf{A}$ parametrized by $z$, as follows:

$$\mathbf{M}_z = \{(y, a) \mid (F_z(y, a) = 0_{m+1}\} = F_z^{-1}(0_{m+1}).$$

Since $\text{rank}[d_yF_z(y, a), d_\beta F_z(y, a)] = \text{rank}[d_yF(x, \alpha, \beta), d_\beta F(x, \alpha, \beta)] = m + 1$ and $m + r + 1 - (m + 1) = r$, $\mathbf{M}_z$ is an $r$-dimensional smooth manifold. In fact $\mathbf{M}_z \cap U(y^0, a^0)$ is locally diffeomorphic to $U(\alpha^0)$, since locally $y = \tilde{y}(z, \alpha)$. Let $\mathbf{A}_z$ be the projection of $\mathbf{M}_z$ on to the $a$-space, i.e.

$$\mathbf{A}_z = \{a \mid (y, a) \in \mathbf{M}_z \text{ for some } y\}.$$

$\mathbf{A}_z$ is an $r$-dimensional smooth manifold. Indeed if we define $\tilde{\phi}_z(\alpha) = \tilde{\phi}(z, \alpha)$ for $(z, \alpha) \in U(z^0, \alpha^0)$, then we can write: for $z \in U(z^0)$,

$$\mathbf{A}_z \cap U(a^0) = \{a \mid a = (\alpha, \beta) \in U(a^0), \text{ and } \tilde{\phi}_z(\alpha) - \beta = 0\}$$

where $U(a^0)$ and $U(z^0)$ are some appropriate neighborhoods of $a^0$ and $z^0$ respectively. $\mathbf{A}_z$ defines a family of surfaces parametrized by $z$ and we will be interested in the envelope of this family.

## Critical points of a projection and the envelope

Since $\text{rank}[d_xg(x, \alpha)] = m$, we note that if there exists $\eta \in \mathbf{R}^{m+1}$, $\eta = (\lambda_0, \lambda) \neq 0_{m+1}$, $\lambda_0 \in \mathbf{R}$, and $\lambda \in \mathbf{R}^m$ such that $\eta \cdot d_xF(x, a) = \lambda_0 d_xf(x, \alpha) + \lambda \cdot d_xg(x, \alpha) = (0_n)'$, then $\lambda_0 \neq 0$. Thus we may take $\lambda_0 = 1$. Define $\Sigma$, a subset of $\mathbf{R}^m \times \mathbf{R}^n \times \mathbf{A}$ as follows:

$$\Sigma = \{(\lambda, x, a) \mid (F(x, a) = 0_{m+1}, (1, \lambda) \cdot d_xF(x, a) = d_xf(x, \alpha) + \lambda \cdot d_xg(x, \alpha) = (0_n)'\}.$$

Let $\pi_a$: $\mathbf{R}^m \times \mathbf{R}^n \times \mathbf{A} \to \mathbf{A}$ and $\pi_x$: $\mathbf{R}^m \times \mathbf{R}^n \times \mathbf{A} \to \mathbf{R}^n$ be respectively projections to the $a$-space $\mathbf{A}$ and the $x$-space $\mathbf{R}^n$. Define $\varepsilon = \pi_a(\Sigma)$. $\varepsilon$ will be called *the (image) envelope of the family of surfaces* $\mathbf{A}_z$. $\Sigma$ is sometimes called *the source envelope*. In order to compare the above definition with the standard definition of an envelope, define:

$$\tilde{\Sigma} \cap U(z^0, a^0) = \{(z, a) = (z, \alpha, \beta) \mid \tilde{\phi}(z, \alpha) - \beta = 0, \text{ and } d_z\tilde{\phi}(z, \alpha) = (0_q)'\}.$$

We may call $\tilde{\Sigma} \cap U(z^0, a^0)$ the reduced source envelope. Then $\varepsilon$, the envelope of $\mathbf{A}_z$, is in fact the projection of $\tilde{\Sigma} \cap U(z^0, a^0)$ to the $a$-space and this will turn out to agree with the standard definition of an envelope. We can see that our definition is equivalent to the standard definition as follows. Since $\tilde{\phi}(z, \alpha) = f(\tilde{y}(z, \alpha), z, \alpha)$, we have that

$$d_z\tilde{\phi} = (d_y f)(d_z\tilde{y}) + d_z f.$$

But $d_z\tilde{y} = -(d_y g)^{-1}(d_z g)$. Hence

$$d_z\tilde{\phi} = -(d_y f)(d_y g)^{-1}(d_z g) + d_z f.$$

Define $\lambda \equiv -(d_y f)(d_y g)^{-1}$. Then we get that: $d_z\tilde{\phi} = 0$ if and only if

$$d_y f + \lambda \cdot d_y g = 0 \text{ and } d_z\tilde{\phi} = d_z f + \lambda \cdot d_z g = 0.$$

Thus we may conclude that under Assumption 1′, $d_z\tilde{\phi}(z, \alpha) = 0$ if and only if there exists $\lambda$ such that $d_x f(x, \alpha) + \lambda \cdot d_x g(x, \alpha) = 0$. For the standard definition and analysis of envelope, see Bruce and Giblin 1984: 99–132. In the standard definition of an envelope, the parameter space is usually taken to be one dimensional, but we are allowing an arbitrary, but finite, dimensional parameter space (the space of $z$ in the above formulation). Furthermore we are allowing the presence of side constraints so that we can discuss an envelope associated with a constrained optimization problem.

You may notice that we have used an argument similar to the one used in justifying the Lagrangean method for a constrained optimization problem. In fact we can utilize the same analogy as follows. Define the Lagrangean function by:

$$L(\lambda, x, \alpha) = f(x, \alpha) + \lambda \cdot g(x, \alpha).$$

Then define $G$: $\mathbf{R}^m \times \mathbf{R}^n \times \mathbf{A} \to \mathbf{R}^{m+n+1}$ by:

$$G(\lambda, x, a) = (L(\lambda, x, \alpha) - \beta, d_\lambda L(\lambda, x, \alpha), d_x L(\lambda, x, \alpha))'.$$

We note that $G(\lambda, x; a) = 0_{m+n+1}$ if and only if $f(x, \alpha) - \beta = 0$, $g(x, \alpha) = 0_m$ and $d_x f(x, \alpha) + \lambda \cdot d_x g(x, \alpha) = (0_n)'$. Therefore $\Sigma = G^{-1}(0_{m+n+1})$.

Given $(x^0, a^0) \in \mathbf{M}$, there exists a local chart $h$: $\mathbf{M} \cap U(x^0, a^0) \to U(z^0, \alpha^0)$. The projection map $\pi_a$ is said to be *a submersion at* $(x^0, a^0) \in \mathbf{M}$ if $\pi_a \circ h^{-1}$: $U(z^0, \alpha^0) \to \mathbf{A}$ is a submersion at $(z^0, \alpha^0)$ where $h(x^0, a^0) = (z^0, \alpha^0)$, i.e. the rank of $d(\pi_a \circ h^{-1})(z^0, a^0)$ is $r + 1$.

**Theorem 1** $\pi_a$ is a submersion at $(x^0, a^0) \in \mathbf{M}$ if and only if $F_{a^0}$ is a submersion at $x^0$ where $F_a(x) = F(x, a)$, a family of functions parametrized by $a$.

*Proof* Let $\gamma = h^{-1}$ and write $d\gamma(z^0, \alpha^0) = \begin{bmatrix} \mathrm{A} \\ \mathrm{B} \end{bmatrix}$ where $A$ is an $n \times (q + r)$

matrix and $B$ is an $(r + 1) \times (q + r)$ matrix. Note that $\text{rank}[d\gamma(z^0, \alpha^0)] = q + r$ and $d(\pi_a \circ \gamma)(z^0, a^0) = B$. Let $K$ be the tangent space of $\mathbf{M}$ at $(x^0, a^0)$. Then we have that:

$$K \equiv T_{(x^0, a^0)}[M] = T_{(x^0, a^0)}[F^{-1}(0_{m+1})] = \ker[dF(x^0, a^0)]$$
$$= \ker[d_xF(x^0, a^0), d_aF(x^0, a^0)].$$

On the other hand, since $h$: $U(x^0, a^0) \to U(z^0, \alpha^0)$ gives a local chart of the manifold $\mathbf{M}$, $K$ can be expressed through $\gamma = h^{-1}$ as follows:

$$K = d\gamma(z^0, \alpha^0)(\mathbf{R}^{q+r}) = \begin{bmatrix} A \\ B \end{bmatrix}(\mathbf{R}^{q+r}) = \begin{bmatrix} A(\mathbf{R}^{q+r}) \\ B(\mathbf{R}^{q+r}) \end{bmatrix}.$$

Also the tangent space of $F_a^{-1}(0_{m+1})$ at $x^0$ can be expressed as follows:

$$T_{x^0}[Fa^{-1}(0_{m+1})] = \ker[dF_{a^0}(x^0)] = \ker[d_xF(x^0, a^0)] = d\pi_x(K) = A(\mathbf{R}^{q+r}),$$

where $\pi_x$ is a projection of $\mathbf{R}^n \times \mathbf{A}$ to the $x$-space $\mathbf{R}^n$.

Now the rank of $dF_{a^0}(x^0)$ equals $m + 1$ if an only if $\dim\{\ker[dF_{a^0}(x^0)]\} = n - (m + 1) = q - 1$. On the other hand, $\dim\{\ker[dF_{a^0}(x^0)]\} = \dim\{A(\mathbf{R}^{q+r})\} = q - 1$ if and only if $\dim\{B(\mathbf{R}^{q+r})\} = q + r - (q - 1) = r + 1$. Thus we can conclude that the rank of $dF_{a^0}(x^0)$ is $m + 1$ if and only if the rank of $d(\pi_a \circ \gamma)(z^0, a^0) = B$ is $r + 1$, i.e. $F_{a^0}$ is a submersion at $x^0$ if and only if $\pi_a \circ \gamma$ is a submersion at $(z^0, \alpha^0)$. □

*A critical point of the projection* $\pi_a$ is a point $(x, a) \in \mathbf{M}$ such that $\pi_a$ is not regular at $(x, a)$, or $\text{rank}[dF_a(x)] = \text{rank}[d_xF(x, a)] < m + 1$. *A critical value of the projection* $\pi_a$ is a point $a = (\alpha, \beta)$ for which $(x, a) \in \mathbf{M}$ is a critical point for some $x$. Thus by Theorem 1 the projection of $\Sigma$ to the $(x, a)$-space is the set of critical points of $\pi_a$. We state this as a corollary.

**Corollary** $(x, a) \in \mathbf{M}$ is a critical point of the projection $\pi_a$ if and only if there exists $\lambda \in \mathbf{R}^m$ such that $(\lambda, x, a) \in \Sigma$.

The Jacobian matrix of the mapping $G$ is given as follows:

$$dG(\lambda, x, a) = \begin{bmatrix} (g)' & d_xf + \lambda \cdot d_xg & d_\alpha f + \lambda \cdot d_\alpha g & -1 \\ 0_{m\times m} & d_xg & d_\alpha g & 0_m \\ (d_xg)' & d_{xx}f + \lambda \cdot d_{xx}g & d_{x\alpha}f + \lambda \cdot d_{x\alpha}g & 0_n \end{bmatrix}$$

where $0_{m\times m}$ denotes an $(m \times m)$-matrix of zeros. Define the $(n + m) \times (n + m)$ bordered Hessian denoted by $H(\lambda, x, a)$ by:

$$H(\lambda, x, a) = \begin{bmatrix} 0_{m\times m} & d_xg \\ (d_xg)' & d_{xx}f + \lambda \cdot d_{xx}g \end{bmatrix}.$$

**Assumption 2** (The second-order regularity condition). For every $(\lambda, x, a) \in \Sigma$, $d_{xx}L(x, \alpha) = d_{xx}f(x, \alpha) + \lambda \cdot d_{xx}g(x, \alpha)$ is negative definite on the kernel of $d_xg(x, \alpha) = \{v \in \mathbf{R}^n \mid d_xg(x, \alpha)(v) = 0_m\} = [d_xg(x, \alpha)]^\perp$.

By the above second-order regularity condition, the rank of the matrix $H(\lambda, x, a)$ is well-known to be $(n + m)$. Thus $\text{rank}[dG(\lambda, x, a)] = n + m + 1$. Therefore $\dim(\Sigma) = \dim[G^{-1}(0_{m+n+1})] = n + m + r + 1 - (n + m + 1) = r$. Hence $\Sigma$ is an $r$-dimensional smooth manifold.

Consider the following system of equations with variables $(\lambda, x)$ and a parameter vector $\alpha$,

$$\Phi(\lambda, x, \alpha) \equiv [(g(x, \alpha))', d_x f(x, \alpha) + \lambda \cdot d_x g(x, \alpha)]' = 0_{m+n}.$$

The Jacobian matrix of this system with respect to $x$ is the bordered Hessian $H(\lambda, x, \alpha) \equiv d_x\Phi(\lambda, x, \alpha)$ which has the full rank on $\Sigma$ by Assumption 2. Thus by the implicit function theorem, given $(\lambda^0, x^0, a^0) \in \Sigma$, there exists a pair of mappings $(\lambda(\cdot), x(\cdot))$ from an open neighborhood $U(\alpha^0)$ of $\alpha^0$ to an open neighborhood $U(\lambda^0, x^0)$ of $(\lambda^0, x^0)$ such that for every $\alpha \in U(\alpha^0)$, $\Phi(\lambda(\alpha), x(\alpha), \alpha) \equiv 0_{m+n}$, i.e.

$$g(x(\alpha), \alpha) \equiv 0_m \text{ and}$$

$$d_x f(x(\alpha), \alpha) + \lambda(\alpha) \cdot d_x g(x(\alpha), \alpha) \equiv (0_n)'.$$

We can also define $\varphi: U(\alpha^0) \to U(\beta^0)$ for some open neighborhood $U(\beta^0)$ of $\beta^0$ by

$$\varphi(\alpha) \equiv f(x(\alpha), \alpha).$$

We shall call this mapping $\varphi: U(\alpha^0) \to U(\beta^0)$ *the (local) optimum value function*. Hence we can assert that $(\lambda, x, a) = (\lambda, x, \alpha, \beta) \in \Sigma \cap U(\lambda^0, x^0, a^0)$ if and only if $(\lambda, x, \alpha, \beta) = (\lambda(\alpha), x(\alpha), \alpha, \varphi(\alpha))$. Therefore $\Sigma \cap U(\lambda^0, x^0, a^0)$ is diffeomorphic to $U(\alpha^0)$ and $\alpha$ provides a local coordinate system for $\Sigma \cap U(\lambda^0, x^0, a^0)$. In fact the local diffeomorphism is given by the following mapping:

$$\psi(\lambda, x, \alpha, \beta) = (\lambda - \lambda(\alpha), x - x(\alpha), \alpha, \beta - \varphi(\alpha))$$

sending $(\lambda, x, \alpha, \beta) \in \Sigma \cap U(\lambda^0, x^0, a^0)$ to $(0_m, 0_n, \alpha, 0)$. The inverse mapping of $\psi$ is clearly given by $\psi^{-1}(\lambda, x, \alpha, \beta) = (\lambda + \lambda(\alpha), x + x(\alpha), \alpha, \beta + \varphi(\alpha))$.

Since $\varepsilon = \pi_\alpha(\Sigma)$, we can use the above mapping $\varphi: U(\alpha^0) \to U(\beta^0)$ to assert that:

$$\varepsilon \cap U(\alpha^0, \beta^0) = \{(\alpha, \beta) \in U(\alpha^0, \beta^0) \mid \varphi(\alpha) - \beta = 0\}$$

where $U(\alpha^0, \beta^0) = U(\alpha^0) \times U(\beta^0)$. Clearly $\varepsilon \cap U(\alpha^0, \beta^0)$ is diffeomorphic to $U(\alpha^0)$. Without loss of generality, we may suppose that $\pi_a[U(\lambda^0, x^0, a^0)] = U(\alpha^0, \beta^0)$. Then we have that $\varepsilon \cap U(\alpha^0, \beta^0) = \pi_\alpha[\Sigma \cap U(\lambda^0, x^0, a^0)]$ and $U(\alpha^0) = \pi_\alpha[\Sigma \cap U(\lambda^0, x^0, \alpha^0, \beta^0)]$ where $\pi_\alpha$ is a projection of $(\lambda, x, \alpha, \beta)$ to the $\alpha$-space.

Define a mapping $\xi: U(\alpha^0) \to \Sigma \cap U(\lambda^0, x^0, a^0)$ by $\xi(\alpha) = (\lambda(\alpha), x(\alpha), \alpha, \varphi(\alpha))$. Then clearly we have that $\xi \circ \pi_\alpha = \text{id}[\Sigma \cap U(\lambda^0, x^0, a^0)]$ and $\pi_\alpha \circ \xi = \text{id}[U(\alpha^0)]$. Therefore both $\Sigma \cap U(\lambda^0, x^0, a^0)$ and $\varepsilon \cap U(\alpha^0, \beta^0)$ are diffeomorphic to $U(\alpha^0)$. (See Balasko 1988: 72.) Hence the envelope $\varepsilon$ is an $r$-dimensional submanifold of **A** which itself is an $(r+1)$-dimensional manifold since it is an open subset of $\mathbf{R}^{r+1}$. Therefore this result shows that when the second-order regularity condition holds, then the envelope $\varepsilon$ of the family of surfaces $\mathbf{A}_z$ is in fact the set of fold points of $\Sigma$. We state this result as follows.

**Proposition 1** $\Sigma$ and $\varepsilon = \pi_\alpha(\Sigma)$ are both $r$-dimensional smooth manifolds locally diffeomorphic to each other and $\varepsilon$ is the set of fold points of $\Sigma$.

## The tangent space of the envelope and properties of the optimum value function

The tangent space of the source envelope $\Sigma$ at $(\lambda, x, a)$, denoted by $T_{(\lambda,x,a)}[\Sigma]$, is the kernel of the linear map $dG(\lambda, x, a)$, i.e. $T_{(\lambda,x,a)}[\Sigma] = \ker[dG(\lambda, x, a)]$. By the definition of the mapping $G$, $(\bar{\lambda}, \bar{x}, \bar{a}) \in \ker[dG(\lambda, x, a)]$ if and only if $(\bar{\lambda}, \bar{x}, \bar{a})$ satisfies

$$-\bar{\beta} + (d_\alpha f + \lambda \cdot d_\alpha g)\bar{\alpha} = 0 \text{ and}$$

$$\begin{bmatrix} d_\alpha g \\ d_{x\alpha} f + \lambda \cdot d_{x\alpha} g \end{bmatrix} \bar{\alpha} + H \begin{bmatrix} \bar{\lambda} \\ \bar{x} \end{bmatrix} = 0_{m+n}.$$

Since $H$ is nonsingular by the second-order regularity condition, the second system of equations above uniquely determines $(\bar{\lambda}, \bar{x})$ for a given $\bar{\alpha}$. Therefore $(\bar{\alpha}, \bar{\beta}) \in T_a[\varepsilon] = T_a[\pi_a(\Sigma)] = d\pi_a[T_{(\lambda,x,a)}(\Sigma)]$ if and only if $(\bar{\alpha}, \bar{\beta})$ satisfies

$$-\bar{\beta} + (d_\alpha f + \lambda \cdot d_\alpha g)\bar{\alpha} = -\bar{\beta} + [d_\alpha L(\lambda, x, \alpha)]\bar{\alpha} = 0,$$

i.e. $(\bar{\alpha}, \bar{\beta}) \in \ker[d_{(\alpha,\beta)}\{L(\lambda, x, \alpha) - \beta\}]$.

In a neighborhood of $(\alpha^0, \beta^0)$, the image envelope can be expressed by means of the optimum value function as follows:

$$\varepsilon \cap U(\alpha^0, \beta^0) = \{(\alpha, \beta) \in U(\alpha^0, \beta^0) \mid \varphi(\alpha) - \beta = 0\}.$$

Thus the tangent space of $\varepsilon$ at $(\alpha, \beta) \in U(\alpha^0, \beta^0)$ is the kernel of the derivative map of $\{\varphi(\alpha) - \beta\}$ with respect to $(\alpha, \beta)$, i.e. $(\bar{\alpha}, \bar{\beta}) \in T_a[\varepsilon]$ if and only if $[d\varphi(\alpha)]\bar{\alpha} - \bar{\beta} = 0$. Hence we have obtained that: for $(\lambda, x, a) \in \Sigma \cap U(\lambda^0, x^0, a^0)$,

$$\bar{\beta} = [d\varphi(\alpha)]\bar{\alpha} = [d_\alpha L(\lambda, x, \alpha)]\bar{\alpha}.$$

Since $\varepsilon$ is an $r$-dimensional manifold, the tangent space $T_a[\delta]$ is an $r$-dimensional real vector space. Thus $[d\varphi(\alpha)]\bar{\alpha} = [d_\alpha L(\lambda, x, \alpha)]\bar{\alpha}$ for every $\bar{\alpha} \in R^r$. Therefore we can conclude that $d\varphi(\alpha) = d_\alpha L(\lambda, x, \alpha)$. This is called the envelope theorem in economics due to Samuelson (1947). (See also Otani (1982), and Otani and El-Hodiri (1987: 94–101.) Note that

$$A_z \cap U(\alpha^0, \beta^0) = \{(\alpha, \beta) \mid \bar{\varphi}_z(\alpha) - \beta = 0\} \text{ and}$$

$\varepsilon \cap U(\alpha^0, \beta^0) = \{(\alpha, \beta) | \varphi(\alpha) - \beta = 0\}.$

Since $\tilde{\phi}(z, \alpha) \equiv f(\tilde{y}(z, \alpha), z, \alpha)$ and $g(\tilde{y}(z, \alpha), z, \alpha) \equiv 0$ for $(z, \alpha) \in U(z^0, \alpha^0)$, we have that for $(z, \alpha) \in U(z^0, \alpha^0)$,

$$d_\alpha \tilde{\phi} = (d_y f)(d_\alpha \tilde{y}) + d_\alpha f \text{ and } d_\alpha \tilde{y} = -(d_y g)^{-1}(d_\alpha g).$$

Hence

$$d_\alpha \tilde{\phi} = d_\alpha f - (d_y f)(d_y g)^{-1}(d_\alpha g) = d_\alpha f + \lambda \cdot d_\alpha g = d_\alpha L(\lambda, x, \alpha),$$

where $\lambda = -(d_y f)(d_y g)^{-1}$. Thus we have shown that: for $(\lambda, x, a) \in \Sigma \cap U(\lambda^0, x^0, a^0)$,

$$d\varphi(\alpha) = d_\alpha \tilde{\phi}(z, \alpha) = dL_\alpha(\lambda, x, \alpha).$$

We state these results as Theorem 2 with is a restatement of Samuelson's envelope theorem in the framework of differential geometry.

**Theorem 2** (Samuelson's envelope theorem). For $(\lambda, x, a) \in \Sigma \cap U(\lambda^0, x^0, a^0)$,

(i) $(\bar{\alpha}\, \bar{\beta}) \in T_a[\varepsilon]$ if and only if $\bar{\beta} = [d\varphi(\alpha)]\bar{\alpha} = [d_\alpha \tilde{\phi}(z, \alpha)]\bar{\alpha} = [d_\alpha L(\lambda, x, \alpha)]\alpha$ and
(ii) $d\varphi(\alpha) = d_\alpha \tilde{\phi}(z, \alpha) = d_\alpha L(\lambda, x, \alpha)$.

Remember that $\varepsilon \cap U(a^0)$ can be considered as the projection of $\tilde{\Sigma} \cap U(z^0, a^0)$ to the $a$-space where

$$\tilde{\Sigma} \cap U(z^0, a^0) = \{(z, a) | \tilde{\phi}(z, \alpha) - \beta = 0, \text{ and } d_z \tilde{\phi}(z, \alpha) = (0_q)'\}.$$

Thus for every $\alpha \in U(\alpha^0)$, $d_z \tilde{\phi}(z(\alpha), \alpha) \equiv (0_q)'$. If we differentiate $d_z \tilde{\phi}(z(\alpha), \alpha) \equiv (0_q)'$ with respect to $\alpha$, we can obtain that:

$$(d_{zz} \tilde{\phi})(dz) + (d_{z\alpha} \tilde{\phi}) = 0_{q \times r}.$$

Now since $d_{zz} \tilde{\phi}$ is symmetric, we must have that:

$$(dz)'(d_{zz} \tilde{\phi})(dz) = -(dz)'(d_{z\alpha} \tilde{\phi}) = -(d_{\alpha z} \tilde{\phi})(dz).$$

Since $d\varphi(\alpha) = d_\alpha \tilde{\phi}(z(\alpha), \alpha)$ by Theorem 2, the second derivative of $\varphi$ can be written as follows:

$$d^2\varphi(\alpha) = d_{\alpha z} \tilde{\phi}(z(\alpha), \alpha)\, dz(\alpha) + d_{\alpha\alpha} \tilde{\phi}(z(\alpha), \alpha)$$

$$= d_{\alpha\alpha} \tilde{\phi}(z(\alpha), \alpha) - (dz(\alpha))'[d\tilde{\phi}_{zz}(z(\alpha), \alpha)](dz(\alpha)).$$

Thus in particular the second partial derivative with respect to $\alpha_k$ becomes:

$$\partial^2 \varphi / \partial^2 \alpha_k = \partial^2 \tilde{\phi} / \partial^2 \alpha_k - (\partial z / \partial \alpha_k)'[d_{zz} \tilde{\phi}](\partial z / \partial \alpha_k).$$

We claim that $(\partial z / \partial \alpha_k)'[d_{zz} \tilde{\phi}](\partial z / \partial \alpha_k) < 0$ provided that $\partial z / \partial \alpha_k \neq 0$. This can be seen by going through some tedious computation to obtain the following.

$$(\partial z/\partial \alpha_k)'[d_{zz}\tilde{\phi}](\partial z/\partial \alpha_k) = \eta' d_{xx}L(\lambda, x, a)\eta,$$

where

$$\eta = \begin{bmatrix} d_z\tilde{y} \\ I_q \end{bmatrix} (\partial z/\partial \alpha_k).$$

Since $g(\tilde{y}(z, \alpha), z, \alpha) \equiv 0$, we have that:

$$(d_y g)(d_z\tilde{y}) + d_z g = (d_y g, d_z g)\begin{bmatrix} d_z\tilde{y} \\ I_q \end{bmatrix} = (d_x g)\begin{bmatrix} d_z\tilde{y} \\ I_q \end{bmatrix} = 0_{m\times q}.$$

Thus $\eta \in [d_x g]^{\perp}$ and $\eta \neq 0_n$ provided that $\partial z/\partial \alpha_k \neq 0$. Therefore by the second-order regularity condition, $\eta' d_{xx}L(\lambda, x, a)\eta < 0$. We state these results as follows:

**Theorem 3** (A generalized LeChatelier–Samuelson principle). For every $\alpha \in U(\alpha^0)$,

(i) $d^2\varphi(\alpha) = d_{\alpha\alpha}\tilde{\phi}(z(\alpha), \alpha) - (dz(\alpha))'[d\tilde{\phi}_{zz}(z(\alpha), \alpha)](dz(\alpha))$,

(ii) $\partial^2\varphi/\partial^2\alpha_k - \partial^2\tilde{\phi}/\partial^2\alpha_k = -(\partial z/\partial \alpha_k)'[d_{zz}\tilde{\phi}](\partial z/\partial \alpha_k) > 0$

provided that $\partial z/\partial \alpha_k \neq 0$ for every $k = 1, 2, \ldots, r$.

The above result can be regarded as a general form of the so-called LeChatelier–Samuelson principle. (See Samuelson 1947; Otani 1982; Otani and El-Hodiri 1987: 97–101, for example.) In the case of the standard LeChatelier–Samuelson principle, the objective function has a special form:

$$f(x, \alpha) = (-\alpha)\cdot x = (-\alpha_y)\cdot y + (-\alpha_z)\cdot z$$

and the constraint is independent of $\alpha$ as in the case of a cost minimization problem. Then

$\partial\varphi(\alpha)/\partial\alpha_{yk} = -y_k(\alpha)$ and

$\partial\tilde{\phi}(z, \alpha)/\partial\alpha_{yk} = -\tilde{y}_k(z, \alpha)$.

Then the above theorem gives us that:

$$\partial\tilde{y}_k(z, \alpha)/\partial\alpha_{yk} - \partial y_k(\alpha)/\partial\alpha_{yk} = -(\partial z/\partial\alpha_{yk})'[d_{zz}\tilde{\phi}](\partial z/\partial\alpha_{yk}) > 0, \text{ i.e.}$$

$$\partial\tilde{y}_k(z, \alpha)/\partial\alpha_{yk} > \partial\tilde{y}_k(z, \alpha)/\partial\alpha_{yk} + (\partial z/\partial\alpha_{yk})'[d_{zz}\tilde{\phi}](\partial z/\partial\alpha_{yk}) = \partial y_k(\alpha)/\partial\alpha_{yk}.$$

Since $\partial\tilde{y}_k(z, \alpha)/\partial\alpha_{yk}$ is known to be negative for an input demand, the above result shows that the input demand responds more in the absolute value to a change in its own input price if more inputs become variable. See Otani

(1982), and Otani and El-Hodiri (1987) for more details of the standard case.

When the objective function is nonlinear and the constraint is not independent of a parameter vector $\alpha$, it is difficult to obtain clear analogous properties on optimizing solutions as functions of a parameter vector. (See Kusumoto 1976; Silberberg 1971, for example.) But if we regard the LeChatelier–Samuelson principle as a second derivative property of the optimum value function, then a clear general statement as above becomes possible.

## A structure of the set of optimizing solutions

Sometimes we will be interested in the set $\pi_x[\Sigma]$ of optimizing solutions as parameters vary where $\pi_x$ denotes the projection to the $x$-space. In this section, we shall further assume the following.

**Assumption 3** (i) $n \geq r$; and (ii) for every $(\lambda, x, a) \in \Sigma$, $x = (v, w)$, $v \in \mathbf{R}^{n-r}$, and $w \in \mathbf{R}^r$, the rank of $d_{(\lambda,\, v,\, \alpha)}\Phi(\lambda, v, w, \alpha)$ is $(n + m)$ where

$$\Phi(\lambda, x, \alpha) \equiv [(g(x, \alpha))', d_x f(x, \alpha) + \lambda \cdot d_x g(x, \alpha)]'.$$

First note that $(\lambda, x, \alpha)$ is an $(n + m) \times 1$ vector and $w$ is an $(r \times 1)$ vector. Thus under the above assumption, we can apply the implicit function theorem to the system of equations $\Phi(\lambda, v, w, \alpha) = 0_{m+n}$ for a given $(\lambda^0, x^0, a^0) \in \Sigma$. Then we can assert that there exists a unique map $(\hat{\lambda}(\ ), \hat{v}(\ ), \hat{\alpha}(\ ))$: $U(w^0) \rightarrow U(\lambda^0, v^0, \alpha^0)$ such that

$$\Phi(\hat{\lambda}(w), \hat{v}(w), w, \hat{\alpha}(w)) \equiv 0_{m+n}$$

for every $w \in U(w^0)$ where $U(w^0)$ and $U(\lambda^0, v^0, \alpha^0)$ are some open neighborhoods of $w^0$ and $(\lambda^0, v^0, \alpha^0)$ respectively. We can also obtain $\beta = \hat{\phi}(w) \equiv f(\hat{v}(w), w, \hat{\alpha}(w))$ for $w \in U(w)$ and $\hat{\phi}$: $U(w^0) \rightarrow U(\beta^0)$ for some neighborhood $U(\beta^0)$ of $\beta^0$. Hence as in the "critical points" section, the mapping from $(\lambda, v, w, \alpha, \beta)$ to $(\lambda - \hat{\lambda}(w), v - \hat{v}(w), w, \alpha - \hat{\alpha}(w), \beta - \hat{\phi}(w))$ which sends $(\lambda, v, w, \alpha, \beta) \in \Sigma \cap U(\lambda^0, x^0, a^0)$ to $(0_m, 0_{n-r}, w, 0_r, 0)$ provides a (local) diffeomorphism between $\Sigma \cap U(\lambda^0, x^0, a^0)$ and $U(w^0)$. What we have done here is to switch local coordinates from $\alpha$ in the previous sections to $w$ in this section.

Let $\pi_w$ be the projection of $(\lambda, v, w, a)$ to $w$ and without loss of generality suppose that $\pi_x[\Sigma \cap U(\lambda^0, x^0, a^0)] = \pi_x(\Sigma) \cap U(x^0)$ and $\pi_w[\Sigma \cap U(\lambda, x^0, a)] = U(w^0)$. Let $\psi$: $U(w^0) \rightarrow \Sigma \cap U(\lambda^0, x^0, a^0)$ be defined by $\psi(w) = (\hat{\lambda}(w), \hat{v}(w), w, \hat{\alpha}(w), \hat{\phi}(w))$. Then $\psi \circ \pi_w = \mathrm{id}[\Sigma \cap U(\lambda^0, x^0, a^0)]$ and $\pi_w \circ \psi = \mathrm{id}[U(w^0)]$. Thus both $\Sigma \cap U(\lambda^0, x^0, a^0)$ and $\pi_x(\Sigma) \cap U(x^0)$ are diffeomorphic to $U(w^0)$. Therefore we can conclude the following.

**Proposition 2** The set $\pi_x(\Sigma)$ of optimizing solutions is a smooth manifold of dimension $r$ and it is locally diffeomorphic to $\Sigma$.

## An application to Pareto efficiency in an exchange economy

In this section, we shall show that our results can be applied nicely to characterize the structure of Pareto efficient allocations in an exchange economy. The differentiable structure of Pareto efficient allocations has been investigated initially by Smale (1981) and more extensively by Balasko (1988), and Mas-Colell (1985).

We shall consider an exchange economy with $I$ agents and $l$ commodities in which agent $i$ ($i = 1, \ldots, I$) is characterized by a $C^2$ utility function $u^i$: $R^l_+ \to R$ and the total endowment available to the economy is given by $\omega \in R^l_{++}$. We shall also assume a differentiable strong monotonicity condition on utility functions such that for every $x_i >> 0_l$, $du^i(x_i) >> 0_l$.

Let $x = (x_1, \ldots, x_I) \in R^n_+$ where $n \equiv lI$ denote an allocation. Then an allocation $x$ is said to be feasible if $\Sigma^I_{i=1}\, x_i = \omega$. Let us write $U(x) = (u^1(x_1), \ldots, u^I(x_I))$. Then a feasible allocation $x^0$ is said to be *Pareto efficient* if there does not exist a feasible allocation $x^1$ such that $U(x^1) > U(x^0)$, i.e. $u^i(x^1_i) \geq u^i(x^0_i)$ for every $i$ and $u^i(x^1_i) > u^i(x^0_i)$ for at least one $i$. Let $P(\omega)$ be the set of interior Pareto efficient allocations, i.e. $x \in P(\omega)$ if $x >> 0_n$ and $x$ is Pareto efficient. We shall assume that $P(\omega) \neq \varnothing$. Under a suitable boundary condition on utility functions, it can be shown that $P(\omega) \neq \varnothing$. But we will not pursue it in this chapter. (See Smale (1981) and Dierker (1974) on the existence of an interior equilibrium.)

Let $x^0 \in P(\omega)$. Then for each $i = 1, \ldots, I$, $x^0_i$ maximizes $u^i(x_i)$ subject to

$$u^j(x_j) - v_j \geq 0 \;(j \neq i) \text{ and}$$

$$\omega - \sum_{j=1}^{I} x_j \geq 0,$$

where $v_j = u^j(x^0_j)$. (See Otani and El-Hodiri 1987: 254.) Let us call this maximization problem $M(i)$. Then for the problem $M(I)$, the Jacobian matrix of the constraint denoted by $g(x, \tilde{v})$ with respect to $x$ where $\tilde{v} = (v_1, \ldots, v_{I-1})$ is given as follows.

$$d_x g(x, \tilde{v}) = \begin{bmatrix} du^1 & 0_l & \cdots & 0_l \\ 0_l & \ddots & \ddots & \vdots \\ \vdots & \ddots & du^{I-1} & 0_l \\ -I_l & \cdots & -I_l & -I_l \end{bmatrix}$$

Clearly the above matrix has the rank $m \equiv (I - 1) + l$. In fact the rank condition holds for every $M(i)$. We will choose $M(I)$ for our analysis. Then the Lagrangean function for $M(I)$ with $\tilde{\nu}$ as a parameter vector can be written as follows.

$$L(\lambda, \mu, x, \tilde{\nu}) = u^I(x_I) + \sum_{i=1}^{I-1} \lambda_i\{u^i(x_i) - \nu_i\} + \mu \cdot (\omega - \sum_{i=1}^{I} x_i).$$

Since the rank condition holds for every $M(i)$ and the differentiable strong monotonicity condition on utility functions is assumed, there exists $(\lambda^0, \mu^0) \in \mathbf{R}^{I-1+l}$ such that

(i) $d_x L(\lambda^0, \mu^0, x^0, \tilde{\nu}) = (0_n)'$,

(ii) $\lambda^0 \gg 0$, $\mu^0 \gg 0$, $u^i(x_i^0) - \tilde{\nu} = 0$, and $\omega - \sum_{i=1}^{I} x_i^0 = 0_l$.

The second-order regularity condition for $M(I)$ becomes that

$$d_{xx}L(\lambda^0, \mu^0, x^0) = \sum_{i=1}^{I} \lambda_i^0 d^2 u^i(x_i^0)$$

be negative definite on the kernel of $d_x g(x^0, \tilde{\nu})$ or on $\ker[d_x g(x^0, \tilde{\nu})]$ where $\lambda_I = 1$. Note that $(\bar{x}_1, \ldots, \bar{x}_I) \in \ker[d_x g(x^0, \tilde{\nu})]$ if and only if $du^i(x_i^0)(\bar{x}_i) = 0$ $(i = 1, \ldots, I-1)$ and $\Sigma_{i=1}^{I} \bar{x}_i = 0_l$.

Then

$$du^I(x_I^0)(\bar{x}_I) = -du^I(x_I^0)(\bar{x}_1 + \ldots + \bar{x}_{I-1}) = -\mu^0(\bar{x}_1 + \ldots + \bar{x}_{I-1})$$
$$= -\sum_{i=1}^{I-1} \lambda_i^0 du^i(x_i^0)(\bar{x}^i) = 0.$$

Thus the second-order regularity condition becomes that for every $i$ (i = 1, ..., $I$), $d^2u(x_i^0)$ be negative definite on $\ker[du^i(x_i^0)]$.

The source envelope for this case can be defined as follows:

$$\Sigma = \{(\lambda, \mu, x, \nu) \mid x \in \mathbf{R}^n_{++}, u^i(x_i) - \nu_i = 0 \ (i = 1, \ldots, I), \omega - \sum_{i=1}^{I} x_i = 0_l,$$
$$\lambda_i du^i(x_i) - \mu' = (0_l)' \ (i = 1, \ldots, I), \lambda_I = 1, \lambda' = (\lambda_1, \ldots, \lambda_{I-1})\},$$

where $\nu \equiv (\tilde{\nu}, \nu_I)$. Note that this case corresponds to the general case in previous sections with $n = lI$, $m = (I-1) + l$, $q = n - m = (l-1)(I-1)$, and $r = I - 1$. Then the image envelope is given by $\varepsilon = \pi_\nu(\Sigma)$. In order to make the analysis more concrete, let us define for $i = 1, \ldots, I-1$, $x_{il} = f^i(z_i, \nu_i)$ implicitly by

$$u^i(z_i, f^i(z_i, \nu_i)) = \nu_i.$$

where $z_i = (x_{i1}, \ldots, x_{i(l-1)})$. Then we can define

$$\tilde{\varphi}(z, \tilde{\nu}) = u^I(\tilde{\omega} - z_1 - \ldots - z_{I-1}, \omega_l - f^1(z_1, \nu_1) - \ldots - f^{I-1}(z_{I-1}, \nu_{I-1})),$$

where $z = (z_1, \ldots, z_{I-1})$ and $\tilde{\omega} = (\omega_1, \ldots, \omega_{l-1})$. $\tilde{\varphi}(z, \tilde{v})$ is nothing but the reduced form utility level of agent $m$ obtained by solving the constraint $g(x, \tilde{v}) = 0_m$ for $x_I$ and $x_{il}$ $(i = 1, \ldots, I - 1)$ and substituting them into $u^I(x^I)$. Then we can define a reduced form manifold and a family of parametrized surfaces parametrized by $z$ respectively by:

$\tilde{\mathbf{M}} = \{(z, v) \mid \tilde{\varphi}(z, \tilde{v}) - v_I = 0\}$ and

$A_z = \{v \mid \tilde{\varphi}_z(\tilde{v}) - v_I = 0\}$,

where $\tilde{\varphi}_z(\tilde{v}) = \tilde{\varphi}(z, \tilde{v})$ and $v \equiv (\tilde{v}, v_I)$. A reduced form source envelope can also be defined by:

$\tilde{\Sigma} = \{(z, v) \mid \tilde{\varphi}(z, \tilde{v}) - v_I = 0, \text{ and } d_z\tilde{\varphi}(z, \tilde{v}) = (0^q)'\}$.

Then $\varepsilon = \pi_v(\tilde{\Sigma})$. The envelope can also be defined through the optimum value function. By the second-order regularity condition, the system of equations

$\Phi(\lambda, \mu, x, \tilde{v}) = [(g(x, \tilde{v}))', d_xL(\lambda, \mu, x, \tilde{v})]' = 0_{m+n}$

can be solved locally and uniquely to obtain $(\lambda(\tilde{v}), \mu(\tilde{v}), x(\tilde{v}))$. Or equivalently, the second-order regularity condition guarantees that $d_z\tilde{\varphi}(z, \tilde{v}) = 0_q$ can be solved locally and uniquely to obtain $z = z(\tilde{v})$. Then the optimum value function can be defined by: $\varphi(\tilde{v}) = \tilde{\varphi}(z(\tilde{v}), \tilde{v})$. Then we can express the envelope $\varepsilon$ locally be means of the optimum value function $\varphi(\tilde{v})$ as follows:

$\varepsilon = \{v \mid \varphi(\tilde{v}) - v_I = 0\}$.

In the language of economics, the envelope $\varepsilon$ is nothing but the utility possibility frontier. By Proposition 1, $\Sigma$ and $\varepsilon$ are both $(I - 1)$-dimensional smooth manifolds locally diffeomorphic to each other and $\varepsilon$ is the set of fold points of $\Sigma$.

**Example** In order to see how the envelope is generated for this case, suppose that $I = 2$ and $l = 2$. Then our economy becomes the case of an Edgeworth box on a plane. The mapping $\tilde{\varphi}$ is defined by: $\tilde{\varphi}(x_{11}, v_1) = u^2(\omega_1 - x_{11}, \omega_2 - f^1(x_{11}, v_1))$. Thus we have that:

$\mathbf{A}_z = \{(v_1, v_2) \mid \tilde{\varphi}(x_{11}, v_1) - v_2 = 0\}$

where $z = x_{11}$. Hence $\mathbf{A}_z$ describes the utility possibilities along a fixed $x_{11}$. Let $(x_1^0, x_2^0)$ be the intersection of the contract curve and the vertical line at $x_{11}$. If we let $v_1^0 = u^1(x_1^0)$, and $v_2^0 = u^2(x_2^0)$, then $v_2^0 = \tilde{\varphi}(x_{11}^0, v_1^0) = \tilde{\varphi}(x_{11}(v_1^0), v_1^0) = \varphi(v_1^0)$. Then the envelope $\varepsilon$ will be the utility possibility frontier as the envelope of a parametrized family of utility possibilities $v_2 = \tilde{\varphi}(x_{11}, v_1)$ with $x_{11}$ as the parameter.

The set $P(\omega)$ of interior Pareto efficient allocations is the projection of $\Sigma$ to the $x$-space, i.e. $P(\omega) = \pi_x(\Sigma)$. We can employ the same approach as in the last section to obtain a characterization of $P(\omega)$. But in this case, a more direct approach is possible. This is because if $x \in P(\omega)$, then $\nu$ and Lagrange multipliers $(\mu, \lambda)$ can be uniquely determined by:

$$\nu = \hat{\nu}(x) \equiv (u^1(x^1), \ldots, u^I(x_I)),$$

$$\mu = \hat{\mu}(x) \equiv du^I(x_I), \text{ and } \lambda_i = \hat{\lambda}_i(x) \equiv (\partial u^I/\partial x_{I1})/(\partial u^i/\partial x_{i1}) \ (i = 1, \ldots, I - 1).$$

Then define $\psi: P(\omega) \to \mathbf{R}^{I-1} \times \mathbf{R}^l \times \mathbf{R}^{lI} \times \mathbf{R}^I$ by $\psi(x) = (\hat{\lambda}(x), x, \hat{\mu}(x), \hat{\nu}(x))$. Then $\psi \circ \pi_x = id(\Sigma)$ and $\pi_x \circ \psi = id[P(\omega)]$. Therefore $\Sigma$ and $P(\omega)$ are diffeomorphic and $P(\omega)$ is an $(I - 1)$-dimensional manifold. Also from our previous result, we can assert that $P(\omega)$ and $\varepsilon$ are locally diffeomorphic and $(\nu_1, \ldots, \nu_{I-1})$ provides a local chart of $P(\omega)$.

## Conclusion

In this chapter, we have reformulated the classical concept of an envelope allowing an arbitrary, but finite, dimensional parameter space and the presence of side constraints so that it can fit well with constrained optimization problems which arise, particularly, in economics. We have shown that a source envelope can be characterized as a set closely associated with the set of critical points of a projection. Under the second-order regularity condition, the envelope becomes the set of fold points of the source envelope and it becomes an $r$-dimensional smooth manifold. The envelope can also be expressed by means of the optimum value function of a constrained maximization problem. The so-called envelope theorem of Samuelson is indeed due to a property of the tangent space of the envelope and the LeChatelier–Samuelson principle can also be shown to be due to a second derivative property of the optimum value function. We can use the same framework of this chapter in analyzing the structure of the set of optimizing solutions as parameters vary. Finally we have shown that our results in this chapter can be applied fairly nicely to characterize the structure of Pareto efficient allocations. In particular we can assert that the utility possibility frontier provides the parametrization of the set of Pareto efficient allocations.

## Bibliography


Balasko, Y. (1988) *Foundation of the Theory of General Equilibrium*. New York: Academic Press.

Bruce, J.W. and Giblin, P.J. (1984) *Curves and Singularities*. Cambridge: Cambridge University Press.

Dierker, E. (1974) *Topological Methods in Walrasian Economics*. Berlin: Springer-Verlag.

Kusumoto, S. (1976) "Extensions of the LeChatelier–Samuelson Principle and their Applications to Analytical Economics – Constraints and Economic Analysis," *Econometrica* 44: 509–536.

Mas-Colell, A. (1985) *The Theory of General Economic Equilibrium: A Differentiable Approach*. Cambridge: Cambridge University Press.

Otani, Y. (1982) "A Simple Proof of the LeChatelier–Samuelson Principle and the Theory of Cost and Production," *J. Econ. Theory* 27: 430–438.

Otani, Y. and El-Hodiri, M. (1987) *Microeconomic Theory*. Berlin: Springer-Verlag.

Samuelson, P. (1947) *Foundations of Economic Analysis*. Cambridge, MA: Harvard University Press.

Silberberg, E. (1971) "The LeChatelier Principle as a Corollary to a Generalized Envelope Theorem," *J. Econ. Theory* 3: 146–155.

Smale, S. (1981) "Global Analysis and Economics," in K.J. Arrow and M.D. Intriligator (eds) *Handbook of Mathematical Economics*, Vol. I pp. 331–370. Amsterdam: North-Holland.

# 20

# A CLASSICAL THEOREM FOR JOHN CHIPMAN: MAXIMAL AND MINIMAL MALTHUSIAN POPULATION; A SWEEPING NON-SUBSTITUTION THEOREM AT THE CORE OF THE CANONICAL CLASSICAL MODEL

*Paul A. Samuelson*

## Summary

Pre-1870 classical economics had as its core a subsistence wage and a limited supply of land. Surprisingly, the pre- and post-Malthus writers failed to articulate how the long-run population level had to be endogenously affected by the composition of landowners' demand for luxury consumptions. It is proved here that population is *maximal* (*minimal*) when consumption concentrates on good(s) with maximum (minimum) ratio of *augmented embodied labor* relative to *augmented embodied land* – where "augmented" means we count in for each good both *its* required direct and indirect primary inputs and those same primary inputs required for the subsistence fodder of *its* labor inputs. There results for the pre-neoclassical world a basic Cantillon–Samuelson Non-Substitution Theorem of post-neoclassical type.

When Thomas Carlyle called economics "the dismal science," he had in mind the classical Malthusian prophecy that population would always expand to offset any technological progress and to thwart any rise in real wages above a definable minimum of subsistence level. So to speak, the ultimate real wage rate was exogenously set by man's biological superfecundity. And just as rabbits grow up to the determinate carrying capacity of Darwin's jungle, so will there be for each stage of technology an asymptotic population level in classical economic theory.

My present little theorem demonstrates what may not have been explicitly noted in the writings of David Ricardo, Adam Smith, Stuart Mill, Karl Marx, or Malthus himself:

> Namely, that variations in tastes of landowners and capitalists toward wanting to spend on luxury goods that are land intensive (directly and indirectly) will *lower* the steady-state equilibrium population. Contrariwise, and this may have been vaguely glimpsed at places in the classical literature, if landowners and other possessors of discretionary income alter their tastes in direction toward goods of little ultimate land content, there will be a release of scarce acres to the production of more subsistence wage goods that will keep alive a larger population.
>
> A corollary of the theorem, and one that will seem intuitively plausible, is that discovery of new subsistence wage-goods that economize in all the many stages of their production on land-inputs – as for example when the potato could substitute for grain as human fodder in eighteenth-century Europe – will increase the long-run equilibrium population.

Also, in terms of post-neoclassical economic theory, I am propounding a new Non-Substitution Theorem valid for a land-labor technology.

To sum up, I shall deduce that the size of equilibrium population is an *endogenous* variable in the 1959 Ricardo–Cantillon–Samuelson *land*-theory-of-value system – (Samuelson 1959: 7–18), which is dependent on the composition of non-laborers' demands.

> The range within which population can fall is not unlimited: a *maximal population* would obtain when all discretionary consumption consisted of the good(s) that are "relatively most land sparing;" a *minimal* population would obtain when all such consumption was directed toward good(s) "most land requiring;" and of course anything that reduces the land embodied in the Malthusian market-basket of subsistence wage goods would be conducive toward a higher equilibrium population level.

The first section describes the properties of the canonical classical equilibrium of Malthus *et al.* in the simplest corn-and-cloth scenario *sans* positive long-run profits and ignoring time-phasing.

The second section sketches the general case of many goods. Its exposition is primarily verbal and graphic, leaving to the Mathematical Appendix detailed derivations.

The third section establishes that the present theorem(s) essentially encompass the canonical classical system of Smith, Malthus, Ricardo,

Mill, and Marx – or, for that matter, Cantillon and pre-Smith writers. Surprisingly the complete picture seems never to have been written down in the pre-1870 literature, even though aspects of it can be pretty clearly recognized in various Smith–Ricardo–Mill passages. It is less strange that neoclassical writers such as Jevons, Menger, Walras, Marshall, Clark, Pareto, and Wicksell never completed the classical picture. (They had newer fish to fry!)

But I do confess to some surprise that modern historians of economic analysis – Schumpeter, Cannan, two Hollanders, Taussig, Seligman, Viner, Sraffa, Stigler, Blaug, and other stalwarts – never paused to dig out the full classical corpus in its interconnected whole. (I had wrongly thought from the account of Thomas Chalmer's work given by A.M.C. Waterman (1991) that Chalmers (1808, 1832) had enunciated the theorem about dependence of Malthusian population level on composition of demand for luxuries. Alas, Professor Waterman in personal communication dashes my hopes in this regard.)

Only in the Mathematical Appendix have I faced up to capital theory aspects, which arise in time-phased systems involving produced inputs and a positive long-run interest rate in the steady state. This discussion spells out how to define goods' "augmented embodied land contents."

## Proof in a corn–cloth model

To warm up the fingers, consider a sonata in which corn alone is the subsistence wage good. It is produced (timelessly) by homogeneous labor and land. Cloth is produced (timelessly) by labor alone. Land is homogenous; and its fixed supply = $\bar{A} = 1$. For this scenario Ricardo's numerical examples with their numerous alternative techniques can come close to the content of J.B. Clark's neoclassical paradigms of marginal cost and marginal products. As the Mathematical Appendix illustrates, even if every good could be produced out of land, labor, and produced goods by a single technique or by only a few techniques, the same endogenous determination of population involving non-workers' tastes does apply.

### *Simplest population case: corn-only in both subsistence and luxury demand*

Here landowners eschew cloth as part of their luxury expenditure. They choose to spend their *rent* income exclusively on corn itself, competing, so to speak, with the needs of workers for subsistence corn.

Figure 20.1 shows (for a continuum-of-land or continuum-of-technology model) the long-run population equilibrium measured at $ON_1^*$. Here we can define our corn units so that each day's subsistence wage of $\bar{w}$ exactly

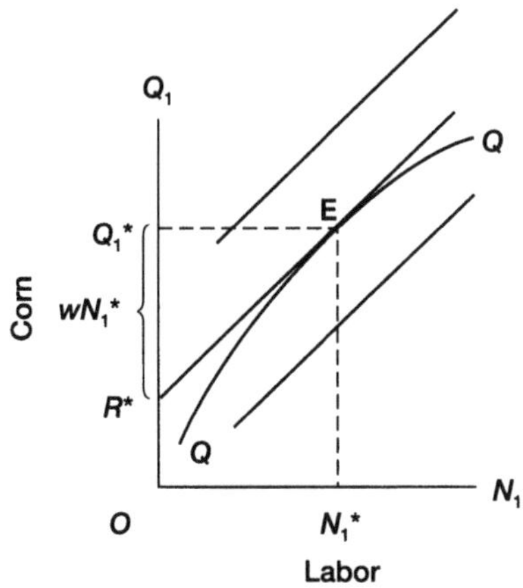


*Figure 20.1*

*Note*: When landowners consume only land-intensive corn, population is *minimal* at $R^*Q_1^*$ or $ON_1^*$. When they consume only land-sparing cloth, population is *maximal* at $OQ_1^*$. When they consume both, equilibrium population is inbetween.

equals unity. This motivates drawing the diagram's parallel lines with a slope of unity or 45°. There is one $E$ point defined on the $QEQ$ output locus where the curve's slope (its "marginal product in corn") is just tangential to one of the 45° lines. Directly below $E$ is $N_1^*$, the equilibrium level of corn labor (and, in this first scenario, the ultimate level of *total* population $N^*$).

The workers receive as their $\bar{w}N^*$ wages the upper line-segment of corn, $R^*Q_1^*$. The residual line segment of $OR^*$ represents landowners' rent. It is received and paid in kind in this no-cloth scenario.

If *all* of the gross corn output $ON_1^*$ were available to support labor supply enhanced above $N_1^*$, we would see $O(N_1^* + N_2^*) = OQ_1^*$ of population, which is $OQ_1^*/R^*Q$ bigger than $N_1^*$. The next section shows how that will come to pass when landowners shift all their consumption to cloth instead of corn.

## *Maximal population case*

Now assume landowners eschew *all* corn consumption. Where will their $OR^*$ corn rent now have to go? It must go somewhere. It will go into the bellies of new to-be-born workers, who will produce no corn at all but who will be bribed by corn wage payments to work at cloth. How much cloth can be produced? How many $N_2^*$ workers will come into existence permanently, now that $N^*$ exceeds $N_1^*$? Their incremental number is limited only by the measure of $OR^*$ corn that landlords do not want to consume.

In the present extreme case where none of the corn rent is wanted as landowner consumption, *all* of the $OQ^*$ interval is available for population support.

**Theorem** The *maximal* population exceeds the *minimal* as $OQ^*$ exceeds $R^*$.

### *General case*

If landowners spend one-half, one-third, or two-thirds of their Rent income on cloth, then one-half, one-third, or two-thirds of the "*potential* (surplus) population" will come into permanent existence.

If Say's Law is a doctrine that there is a conserved total of something that must get itself spent in one direction if not in another, then it is the wrong image for the present phenomenon.

Here we face something like "The Widow's Cruse" or like the Balanced-Budget Theorem in effective-demand macroeconomics. Ask for more milk from the pitcher and more will bubble out!

However, a bootstrap operation is not possible here. By diddling their luxury demands, competitive landlords cannot add one cubit to their rent *rate* per acre or alter in any way their *total* residual rent! Nor can landlords diddle down the Malthusian iron wage rate of $\bar{w}$.

## Multi-good Malthusian equilibrium

Now adhere to homogeneous labor but shift to homogeneous land that is fixed in supply (at unity) so that our theorem will remain valid no matter how many goods there are. (Warning: We do ignore *joint* products and do assume constant returns to scale.) Also, we do permit the subsistence market basket of wage goods to involve any number of goods or even all of them. Thus, the vector of per capita wage-goods needed to keep the population supply intact can be written as $0 \neq (m_1 m_2 \ . \ . \ . \ m_n) \geq 0$. At least one of the goods is assumed to need (directly or indirectly) some land for its production; also, every good (luxury or not) is assumed to need (directly or indirectly) some of land or of labor, or of both.

We can write the *real* wage rate at time $t$ as

$$w(t) = W(t)/\sum_{1}^{n} P_j(t)m_j. \qquad (1)$$

Here the subsistence-basket provides our real metric.

As in the Canonical Classical (growth) Model of Malthus et al., described in Samuelson (1978), strength of population growth, $(dN/dt)/N = \dot{N}/N$, is posited to depend on the excess of actual $w(t)$ over the $\bar{w}$ subsistence rate.[1] Under the present deflation technique of (1), $\bar{w}$ is by definitional convention to be unity:

$$\dot{N}/N = S[w(t) - \bar{w}] = S[w(t) - 1] \qquad (2)$$

$$S[0] = 0; \ 0 < (w - \bar{w}) \ S[w - \bar{w}] \text{ for } w \neq \bar{w}. \qquad (3)$$

Reference can be made to Samuelson (1980, Fig. 1(b): 575–576) for the Fundamental Factor-Price Frontier Theorem giving a trade-off between real wage and real rent rates when the profit rate is zero (or constant). Figure 20.2 shows how its convex frontier permits us to deduce (from Malthus's constancy of $\bar{w}$) the real rent rate and rent total enjoyed by landowners, and the unique $(R/W)^*$ that predetermines the optimal input/output techniques that can be competitively viable.

Figure 20.2 plots the convex *FEF* Factor-Price Frontier 'twixt Real Wage and Real Rent Rates ($w = W/\Sigma_1^n P_j m_j$ and $R/\Sigma_1^n P_j m_j$).

Malthus's iron law of wages pins our equilibrium at *E*, which is the point on *FEF* due north of $\bar{w}$. The *R*/*W* slope of *OE* is thus pinned down and that pins down our relevant $a_{ij}\{R^*/W^*\}$, $b_{Nj}\{R^*/W^*\}$, $b_{Aj}\{R^*/W^*\}$ input/output techniques as discussed in Mathematical Appendix §2.

Along the *FEF* trade-off frontier, the higher *R*/*W* ratios occur near the top and the lower ones near the bottom. Malthus's iron law of final real wage picks for us the point *E* (and its appropriate techniques in the background). In pinning $\bar{w}$ at one, it pins down real rent rate at $R^*$.

Landlords can spend their determinate $R^*$ on the corn–cloth menu of goods shown in Figure 20.3. Of course, with three goods and $n = 3$, a plane in three dimensions would be the menu; and for general $n \geq 3$, the picture would have to be in *n*-dimensional space. The slopes of the respective pairs of goods will be determined not by their embodied *labor* contents as defined in the conventional Labor Theory of Value. (Nor will they be determined by the conventionally computable embodied *land* contents.)

Instead, as shown in the present Mathematical Appendix, and in Samuelson (1959), the $P_i/P_j$ slopes in Figure 20.3 depend upon "*augmented*" land contents of goods (inclusive of lands needed directly or indirectly to produce subsistence fodder for all needed laborer inputs!).

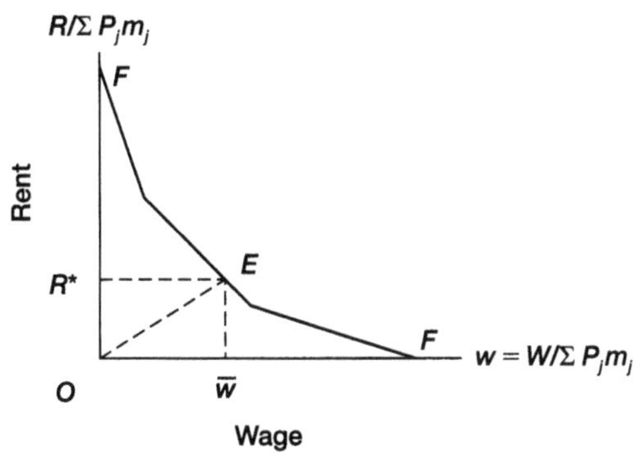


*Figure 20.2*
*Note*: Once the subsistence wage is specified at $\bar{w}$, rent and $R^*/W^*$ are pinned down.

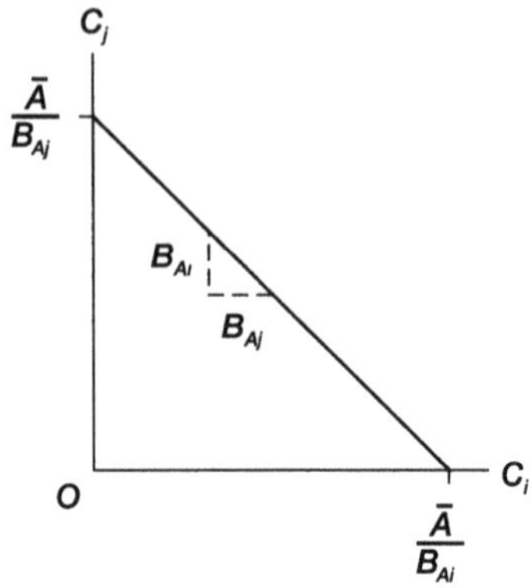


*Figure 20.3*
*Note*: Landowners have $R^*\bar{A}$ to spend on consumption goods, each priced in proportion to its *augmented land content*.

## Conclusion

What unified the pre-1870 "classical" writings was their subsistence theory of the wage rate (and, later, of the profit or interest rate). It was this hypothesis that made their system manageable by scholars in their early stages of economic science.

In the last half of the twentieth century, I find it naive to put much credence in a subsistence-wage model for the sixteenth to nineteenth centuries in western Europe. And indeed the classical writers without exception spend many of their pages – consciously or tacitly – on processes that involve short- and intermediate-run divergences from alleged subsistence wage rates. Good sense often broke in!

Also, in the Age After Newton, real wages were palpably rising: therefore, to save the face of the subsistence-wage paradigm, the iron basket of subsistence rations was opportunistically divorced from physiological content and subtly transmuted from an exogenous datum to an endogenous fudge factor which accommodated to whatever happened to the time series of wage rates.

I would make the aesthetic point that, one who professes to have subsistence theories ought (if only for once) to work out just what are their dynamic and comparative-statical properties.

As homage to John Chipman, the present analysis is devoted to that task.

## MATHEMATICAL APPENDIX

1 Let $(N_1, \ldots, N_j, \ldots, N_n)$ be the amounts of labor devoted to goods $1, \ldots, j, \ldots, n$. The amounts of land those goods use is written as

$(A_1, \ldots, A_j, \ldots, A_n)$. To achieve $Q_j$ of the $j$th good may also require some of the $i$th good as input, $Q_{ij}$.

The technical coefficients of production as defined by Walras, Leontief, and Sraffa can then be defined for $i, j=1, \ldots, n$,

$$a_{ij} = Q_{ij}/Q_j,\ b_{Nj} = N_j/Q_j,\ b_{Aj} = A_j/Q_j. \tag{A1}$$

These could be constants. Or there may be alternative vectors of $(b_{Nj}, b_{Aj}, a_{ij}, \ldots, a_{nj})$ to produce a unit of $Q_j$. So long as time-phasing can be ignored and/or the profit rate is $r = 0$, we know that ruthless competition will select an optimal input vector that depends only on the specified Rent/Wage ratio of $R/W$. At (generically rare!) switchpoints there will be inessential ties rather than unique $(a^*, b_N^*, b_A^*)$ choices; for brevity I can delay treating these ambiguities. (When positive $r$ is in the picture, the elements of the optimal vector will depend on both $R/W$ and $r$ – entailing $[b_{Aj}\{r;R/W\} \ldots, a_{ij}\{r;R/W\}]$ best choices; or, since $R/W$ is endogenous for specified $\bar{r}$, entailing $[b_{Aj}\{1+\bar{r}\} \quad b_{Nj}\{1+\bar{r}\}, a_{ij}\{1+\bar{r}\}]$ best choices.)

2 Figure 20.2 in the text shows how to find the unique $R^*/W^*$ ratio imposed by Malthus's subsistence real wage rate.

See Samuelson (1980: 575–576) for a heuristic statement of the fundamental Factor Price Frontier between the real wage and real rent rate (each expressed in terms of the Malthusian market-basket of subsistence goods). Write this Factor Price Frontier as

$$R/\sum_1^n P_j m_j = \Psi(W/\sum_1^n P_j m_j) \text{ for } \bar{r} = 0. \tag{A2}$$

$\Psi(w)$, a convex, monotone-decreasing function.

Since real $w$ must equal $\bar{w}$ of unity, we have

$$R^*/W^* = \Psi(1)/(1) = \Psi(1). \tag{A3}$$

Unless otherwise specified, when I write $[a_{ij}; b_{Nj}; b_{Aj}]$, this is to be understood to mean the optimal coefficients for Malthus's $R^*/W^*$.

3 The next problem is to show how to compute each and every good's Cantillon–Samuelson *augmented land content* (inclusive of land needed to produce the subsistence goods required by needed labor).

The following row vector gives these augmented embodied land contents:

$$0 < [B_{A1} \ldots B_{An}] = [b_{A1} \ldots b_{An}]\,[I - a_{ij} - m_i b_{Nj}]^{-1}. \tag{A4}$$

The square inverse matrix on the right embodies the ingenious concept of "feeding coefficients" used by Francis Seton (1957) in his definitive disposal of Marx's "transformation problem." (Explanation: Suppose a unit of $C_2$ luxury cloth directly uses $b_{A2}$ of land: that is in the $b_{Aj}$ row vector. Suppose cloth needs some corn as raw material: that is in the $a_{21}$

term. Suppose cloth needs labor and labor must have $m_1$ of corn as subsistence: then the $m_1 b_{N2}$ term takes care of that. The matrix geometric progression created by expanding out the $[I - a - mb_N]^{-1}$ inverse accumulates in a convergent sum the land needed to produce the needed corn and cloth in an infinity of earlier generations.)

4 How much $(C_1, \ldots, C_n)$ can all the landowners consume? Owning $\bar{A}$ acres in all, they can enjoy whatever vector of consumptions with *augmented land contents* that add up to the $\bar{A}$ total supply of land – no more and no less.

Figure 20.3's menu of luxury consumption is thus finally defined by

$$B_{A1}C_1 + B_{A2}C_2 + \ldots + B_{An}C_n = \bar{A} > 0. \qquad \text{(A5)}$$

5 When more $C_1$ is consumed and less $C_n$, that will generally alter the population of labor needed by the system. To see why and by how much, we must now compute the total *augmented labor requirement* for each unit of $C_j$. We can call it $B_{Nj}$.[2]

The following relations – which allocate each $Q$ to luxury consumption + needed produced inputs + needed subsistence wage goods – verify its calculation:

$$\begin{aligned}[Q_i] &= [C_i + \sum_1^n a_{ij}Q_j + \sum_1^n m_i b_{Nj} Q_j] \\ &= [I - a - mb_N]^{-1}C.\end{aligned} \qquad \text{(A6)}$$

Combining (A4) and (A6), we derive

$$\begin{aligned}\sum_1^n b_{Nj}Q_j &= b_N Q = b_N[I - a - mb_N]^{-1}C \\ &= B_N C = \sum_1^n B_{Nj}C_j\end{aligned} \qquad \text{(A7a)}$$

$$B_N = [B_{N_1} \ldots B_{Nn}], \text{ augmented labor contents.} \qquad \text{(A7b)}$$

The reader must be reminded that, where there are choices among more than one feasible technique, in all of our formulas we must understand that the coefficients are those viable ones that do give minimum real prices $[P_j/R]$. Strictly speaking, to indicate this I should write out each $[b_{Aj}\ b_{Nj}\ a_{ij}\ B_{Aj}]$ vector as having elements that are competitively viable with the ultimate endogenous $W^*/R^*$; and, when $r$ is specified as $\bar{r} \geq 0$, their choice will depend on $1 + \bar{r}$ also. That is why, later in (13), I write $[B_{Aj}\quad B_{Nj}]$ as $[B_{Aj}\{1 + \bar{r}\}\quad B_{Nj}\{1 + \bar{r}\}]$. In (A4) and (A7), this would be $[B_{Aj}\{1 + 0\}\quad B_{Nj}\{1 + 0\}]$.

6 Our *maximal* and *minimal* populations result from the following standard linear programming problems. First, subject to

$$\sum_1^n B_{Aj}C_j \leq \bar{A} > 0,\ C_j \geq 0,\ B_{Aj} > 0,\ B_{Nj} \geq 0 \qquad \text{(A8a)}$$

$$\begin{aligned}\text{Maximal } N^* &= \underset{C_j}{\text{Max}} \sum_1^n B_{Nj}C_j \\ &= \bar{A}\,\text{Max}[B_{N1}/B_{A1}, \ldots, B_{Nn}/B_{An}] < \infty\end{aligned} \qquad \text{(A8b)}$$

Second, subject to (8a)

$$\text{Minimal } N^* = \underset{C_i}{\text{Max}} \sum_1^n B_{Nj} C_j$$
$$= \bar{A}\text{Min}[B_{N1}/B_{A1}, \ldots, B_{Nn}/B_{An}] > 0 \quad \text{(A8c)}$$

This demonstrates my main Theorem.[3] Only in the singular case where all $B_{Ni}/B_{Ai}$ rations happen to be identical will the *minimal* and maximal $N^*$ be the same for Malthus. Note that the percentages spent on $C$'s can, for fixed $F$, have no effect on ($\bar{w}$, $R^*$, $R^*\bar{A}$, $P_1^*/P_j^*$, $W^*/P_i^*$, $R^*/P_i^*$), a neat (Cantillon–Samuelson) Non-Substitution Theorem constraining long-run equilibrium.

7 When workers get educated to require more of the ($m_j$) subsistence amounts, the effective $(W/R)^*$ must rise: real $w^*$ rises and real $R^*$ falls. Hurrah for "preventive checks" to population. (Paradoxically, Ricardo's Neat Product falls and so does *his* Gross Product inclusive of sterile workers' fodder – and a jolly good thing too, as ethical do-gooders such as Stuart Mill and Harriet Taylor will say. In Figure 20.1, $E$ moves to the southwest.) The total of real wages can rise or fall when the workers' per capita wage is elevated by their becoming educated to insist on higher living standards before they reproduce. Among neo-classical writers, impressed with Cobb–Douglas images and with high elasticities of substitution, the marginal product curve is usually specified to be elastic: for these cases, the total of wages falls as the drop in population percentage-wise outweighs the rise in wage per person. For the Stigler–Malthus logarithmic production function (M's geometric and arithmetic progressions), the total of wages is a constant. For CES functions with low $\sigma$, when the rent share is high a rise in every ($m_j$) should raise $W^*N^*/\Sigma_1^n P_i^*m_i$.

Here is the comparative-statistics sign pattern when $w^*$ rises with $\bar{A}$ land supply constant (and, of course, with technology unchanged):

$$\text{sign}[\partial N^*/\partial w^* \quad \partial R^*/\partial w^* \quad \partial(\bar{A}R^*)/\partial w^* \quad \partial(w^*N^*)/\partial w^*]$$
$$= [- \; - \; - \; \overset{\circ}{\pm}]. \quad \text{(A9)}$$

8 There remains the case where time-phasing matters and where the long-run profit rate is positive: $r^* > 0$. Now rentier-capitalists as well as landowners exert a relevant demand to consume luxuries. It is still true that the ultimate Malthusian population of $N^*$ can be maximal or minimal or inbetween. But now our *augmented land contents* must take into account "*dated* accumulations of inputs."

Now we must alter Figure 20.2 to show a *family* of (convex) Factor-Price Frontier contours. The higher the profit rate $r$ the lower the convex trade-off contour – as in Figure 20.4. As before, $\bar{w}$ is at unity; but now a lower $R^*$ emerges when the vertical line at $\bar{w}$ intersects a positive-$r^*$ contour that is lower down. Most authorities take for

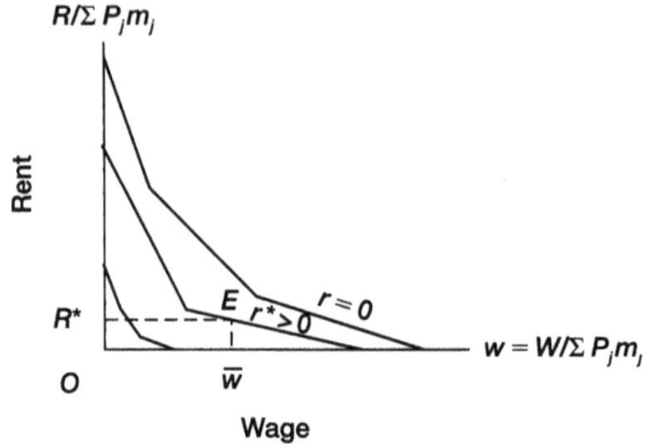


*Figure 20.4*
*Note*: Each higher positive $r^*$ profit rate generates a lower convex (real wage, real rent) contour. For $\bar{w}$ and $r^*$ specified, where the vertical through $\bar{w}$ intersects the contour of $r^*$ at $E$, that pins down $R^*$ and $R^*/W^*$.

granted that the existence of positive profit will kill off or abort some equilibrium population. However, when labor and capital are substitutes rather than complements, a rise in $r^*$ can raise $N^*$!

For any specified long-run $\bar{r}$, equilibrium steady-state competitive prices are defined by the matrix relations:

$$P = [P_j] = [Rb_{Aj} + Wb_{Nj} + \sum_{i+1}^{n} P_i a_{ij}](1 + \bar{r}) \qquad \text{(A10a)}$$

$$= [(Rb_{Aj} + Wb_{Nj})(1 + \bar{r})]\,[I - a_{ij}(1 + \bar{r})]^{-1}, \qquad \text{(A10b)}$$

where in (A10a) $[b_N \quad b_A \quad a]$ are understood to be competitively viable (and optimal) techniques. Strictly speaking, we should write them as dependent on $(1 + \bar{r})$, namely as $[b_N\{1 + \bar{r}\} \quad b_A\{1 + \bar{r}\} \quad a\{1 + \bar{r}\}]$.

Substitute

$$W = \sum_{i=1}^{n} \mathrm{P_i m_i}$$

into (A10a) to get

$$P = [Rb_{Aj}](1 + \bar{r}) + \sum_{i=1}^{n} P_i(a_{ij} + m_i b_{Nj})(1 + \bar{r}) \qquad \text{(A10c)}$$

$$= [Rb_{Aj}](1 + \bar{r})[I - a_{ij}(1 + \bar{r}) - m_i b_{Nj}(1 + \bar{r})]^{-1} \qquad \text{(A10d)}$$

$$\equiv [Rb_{Aj}](1 + \bar{r})[I - \alpha_{ij}(1 + \bar{r})]^{-1}, \text{ definition of } \alpha_{ij} \qquad \text{(A10e)}$$

$$\equiv Rb_A\{1 + \bar{r}\}(1 + \bar{r})[I - \alpha\{1 + \bar{r}\}(1 + \bar{r})]^{-1} \qquad \text{(A10f)}$$

$$\equiv R[B_{A1}\{1 + \bar{r}\} \ldots B_{An}\{1 + \bar{r}\}], \text{ by def. of } B_{Aj}\{1 + \bar{r}\}. \qquad \text{(A10g)}$$

The $[P_1/R \ldots P_n/R]$ or $[B_{A1}\{1 + \bar{r}\} \ldots \mathrm{B}_{An}\{1 + \bar{r}\}]$ are the *natural* prices, the only ones, embedded in the classical system and the following *convergent infinite* matrix series interprets them as Dated Augmented Land contents:

$$B_A\{1 + \bar{r}\} = b_A\{1 + \bar{r}\}(1 + \bar{r})[I + \alpha\{1 + \bar{r}\}(1 + \bar{r}) + \alpha\{1 + \bar{r}\}^2(1 + \bar{r})^2 + \ldots + \alpha\{1 + \bar{r}\}^t(1 + \bar{r})^t + \ldots]. \tag{A11}$$

By the notations $[b_A\{1 + \bar{r}\} \quad b_N\{1 + \bar{r}\} \quad \alpha\{1 + \bar{r}\}]$, we mean of course that, for each specified $r$ when there is a choice among alternative techniques, competitive arbitrage will rule out any such that do not simultaneously minimize *all* of $[P_1/R \ldots P_n/R]$ ratios. Adam Smith's Invisible Hand again is producing visible Pareto-optimal results!

As in Figures 20.2 and 20.4, once $(\bar{w} \quad \bar{r})$ are specified by a Malthusian, $(R/W)^*$ is determined along with $[W/\Sigma P_jm_j \quad R/\Sigma P_jm_j]$ – and this independently of $C_i/C_j$ taste ratios. Now (A2) and (A3) are modified by positive $\bar{r}$ to become

$$R/\sum_1^n P_jm_j = \Psi(W/\sum_1^n P_jm_j;r) \equiv \Psi(w;\bar{r}) \tag{A12a}$$

$\Psi$ monotone-decreasing in $(w;r)$ and convex in $(w)$ (A12b)

$$R^*/W^* = \Psi(1;\bar{r})/(1) = \Psi(1;\bar{r}). \tag{A12c}$$

9 When the long-run profit rate is positive, $\bar{r} > 0$, capitalists participate in distribution along with wage earners and landowners. Total luxury consumptions, $[C_1 \ldots C_N]$, now come from spending out of rent incomes, $R^*A$; and out of interest earned on capitalists' outlays for produced inputs and for advances to workers' wages, $\bar{r}\bar{w}N^* + \bar{r}\Sigma_i \Sigma_j p_ia_{ij}\{1 + \bar{r}\}Q_j^*$. Whether $\bar{r} > 0$ or $= 0$, Malthus's subsistence $(\bar{w},\bar{r})$ parameters do determine the real total of rent income independently of the composition of luxury demands, $(C_i/C_j)$. But $(C_i/C_j)$ does affect the endogenous variable of capitalists' *total* profit income.

Still it remains the case that there is a *maximal* and a *minimal* Malthusian population level. Much as before we contemplate the Max or Min problem. Subject to

$$\sum_1^n B_{Aj}\{1 + \bar{r}\}C_j \le \bar{A},\ C_j \ge 0,\ B_{Nj}\{\quad\} > 0 \tag{A13a}$$

$$\underset{C_j}{\text{Max}} \sum_1^n B_{Nj}\{1 + \bar{r}\}C_j = \bar{A}\text{Max}[\ldots, B_{Nj}\{1 + \bar{r}\}/B_{Aj}\{1 + \bar{r}\}, \ldots]. \tag{A13b}$$

Alternatively, subject to (13a),

$$\underset{c_j}{\text{Min}} \sum_1^n B_{Nj}\{1 + \bar{r}\}C_j = \bar{A}\underset{c_j}{\text{Min}} \sum_1^n[\ldots, B_{Nj}\{1 + \bar{r}\}/B_{Aj}\{1 + \bar{r}\}, \ldots]. \tag{A13c}$$

Notice that it is now goods' "*dated* augmented land and dated augmented labour requirements" that determine whether a shift in pattern of luxury demands will raise or lower the Malthusian population. (Warning: Note 3 on p. 351 covers the singular case where $B_{Nj}\{1 + \bar{r}\}$ can be a set correspondence rather than a unique function of $\{1 + \bar{r}\}$.)

10 With time-phasing and positive profits in the picture, the comparative statics given in (A9) for $r^* = 0$ now becomes more complicated.

For technology unchanged, the General Factor-Price Frontier theorem tells us that if one of (real wage rate, real rent rate, uniform profit rate) rises, some other one or both other ones must fall. More specifically, in a specified technology, a rise in one or both of $(\bar{w},\bar{r})$ must lower real rent rate. This denies validity to what Samuel Hollander (1987) alleges to be David Ricardo's fundamental profit rate–wage rate tradeoff relation.

As mentioned just before (A13a) above, a rise in $\bar{r}$ alone could itself induce a *rise* in Malthusian population level rather than a fall!

When invention forces into use new competitive techniques, this must improve one or more of (real wage, real rent, profit rate). Therefore, until Karl Marx brought scarce land and positive rent into his competitive scenario, he could not validly proclaim both a fall in the rate of profit and in the rate of real wage. A fall in one would mandate a rise in the other! As 1999 counsel for Marx, I would have to inform him and the jury that only in the context of *rent-raising* change could both dire Marxian laws be valid under Darwinian competition.

11 Readers are reminded that this analysis has ruled out joint production[4] and increasing returns to scale incompatible with pure competition. Also, heterogeneity of lands can be shown to complicate somewhat the beautiful simplicities of the Malthusian paradigm. On the other hand, all complications entailed by heterogeneity of capital goods have been carefully addressed by my circumspect exposition. (Example: when I spoke of a case where "capital and labor are *substitutes* rather than *complements*," it was not necessary to worry about what this would mean in a multi-good input/output model with Wicksell effects and possible reswitchings. It would be enough to give one valid counterexample to refute the notion that $\partial N^*/\partial r^*$ had to be negative.)

Note finally that the present analysis is robust and covers neoclassical smoothness with an infinity of alternative techniques – as in Figure 20.1; and as well it covers Sraffa–von Neumann discrete technologies with only a finite number of alternative techniques – as in Figures 20.2 and 20.4.

## Notes

I owe thanks for partial support to my Gordon Y Billard Postdoctoral Fellowship at the MIT Sloan School of Management, and for editorial assistance to Janice M. Murray.

1 When time-phasing and produced inputs are brought into the model, the (algebraic) excess of the actual interest or profit rate over a posited subsistence rate, $\bar{r}$, will drive capital accumulation forward or backward. I skip writing for

$r(t)$ a relation like that for $\dot{N}/N$ and $w(t)$. Later I show how time-phasing modifies the exposition.

2 Warning: a luxury good's *total augmented labor requirement* is not at all the same thing as the Locke–Smith–Ricardo–Marx *embodied labor content* of that good in the traditional *labor theory of value* – which is given by $b_N[I - a]^{-1}$, something definitely less than $b_N[I - a - mb_N]^{-1}$. This last includes the labor needed to produce workers' subsistence goods on top of the labor needed to produce the goods that the landowners consume. Similarly, the Cantillon–Samuelson *augmented land* content exceeds the $b_A[I - a]^{-1}$ land content of goods calculated while ignoring labor as an input requirement. In Samuelson (1959), I propounded for Ricardo a Physiocratic Land Theory of Value, not knowing that Cantillon had had similar notions two centuries before. As the present Appendix §3 describes, this theory required that I reckon in the (augmented) land needed to feed laborer inputs along with direct and indirect lands.

3 For any specified $\bar{r}$, each $B_{Aj}\{1 + \bar{r}\}$ is uniquely minimal. But at "switch points" $[b'_{Aj} \;\; b'_{Nj} \;\; a'_{ij}]$ can be indifferently tied with $[b''_{Aj} \;\; b''_{Nj} \;\; a''_{ij}]$. Therefore the ultimately observed $[B'_{Nj}]$ and $[B''_{Nj}]$ vectors could well be unequal; and, as we'll see, that means that even for specified $[C_j/C_1]$ spending there can be a whole *interval* of resulting $N^*/\bar{A}$ equilibria. Always there will be a *maximal* feasible $N^*/\bar{A}$ ratio and a minimal one, but at generically rare switch points it will be indeterminate where the equilibrium will fall on the admissible interval of $B_{Nj}/B_{Aj}$ ambiguity.

4 Fixed capital, or durable capital goods, does by definition involve certain jointness of production: cloth and *used* machines as joint outputs. My analysis can easily handle the exponential-depreciation case where $d_{ij}$ fraction of $Q_{ij}$ input is used up in each production cycle: merely replace $a_{ij}(1 + r)$ wherever it occurs by $a_{ij}(d_{ij} + r)$, where $0 \leq d_{ij} \leq 1$. The circulating capital case is when $d_{ij} = 1$. We now see easily that Ricardo's third edition chapter of 1821 on how invention can hurt the demand for labor has no deep connection with a shift from circulating to fixed capital. With no change in any $d_{ij}$, the effect can happen. Example: an invention that solely halves *all* $b_{Nj}$! And it can happen when the invention increases all $d_{ij}$, provided it involves decreases in $(b_{Nj}, b_{Aj}, a_{ij})$ enough to be viable and such as to reduce the new ultimate $N^*$. Since Ricardo's long-run profit rate and real wage are unchangeable by the invention, a viable invention must, if anything, raise land rent.

## Bibliography


Chalmers, Thomas (1808) *An Enquiry into the Nature and Stability of National Resources*. Edinburgh: Oliphant and Brown.

—— (1832) *On Political Economy in Connexion with the Moral State and Moral Prospects of Society*. Glasgow: Collins.

Hollander, Samuel (1987) *Classical Economics*. Oxford and New York: Basil Blackwell.

Pasinetti, Luigi (1960) "A Mathematical Formulation of the Ricardian System," *Review of Economic Studies* 27: 78–98.

Samuelson, Paul A. (1959) "A Modern Treatment of the Ricardian Economy: I. The Pricing of goods and Labor and Land Services," *Quarterly Journal of Economics* 73: 1–35. Reproduced as Chapter 31 in Joseph E. Stiglitz (ed.) (1966) *The Collected Scientific Papers of Paul A. Samuelson*, vol. 2. Cambridge, MA: The MIT Press.

—— (1978) "The Canonical Classical Model of Political Economy," *Journal of Economic Literature* 16: 1415–34. Reproduced as Chapter 340 in Kate Crowley (ed.) (1986) *The Collected Scientific Papers of Paul A. Samuelson*, vol. 5. Cambridge: MA: The MIT Press.

—— (1980) "Noise and Signal in Debates Among Classical Economists: A Reply," *Journal of Economic Literature* 18: 575–78. Reproduced as Chapter 341 in Kate Crowley (ed.) (1986) *The Collected Scientific Papers of Paul A. Samuelson*, vol. 5. Cambridge, MA: The MIT Press.

—— (1992) "Marx on Rent: a Failure to Transform Correctly," *Journal of the History of Economic Thought* 14: 143–67.

Seton, Francis (1957) "The 'transformation problem'," *Review of Economic Studies* 24: 149–60.

Waterman, A.M.C. (1991) "'The Canonical Classical Model of Political Economy' in 1808, as Viewed from 1825: Thomas Chalmers on the 'National Resources'," *History of Political Economy* 23: 221–41.

# 21

# EXTERNAL DISECONOMIES IN THE COMMONS

*Joaquim Silvestre*

## Parametric economies and diseconomies of scale

John Chipman (1965, 1970) pioneered the modelling of economies and diseconomies of scale that are external to the firm, which he called parametric external economies or diseconomies of scale. His formalization is based on the following idea: firm $i$ uses labor $L_i$, and takes the output/labor ratio parametrically, i.e. it perceives a linear production function $y_i = \bar{k}L_i$. In fact, the output–labor ratio depends on the aggregate level of activity, represented by the aggregate amount $L$ of labor applied, or by the aggregate amount $y$ of output obtained: we can formalize it as a function $a(L, y)$ which is increasing in $L$ or $y$ (or both), i.e. $y/L = k(a(L, y))$. As an example, we have a one-input production function often used in economics, $y = f(L)$, where $k(\cdot)$ can be equivalently written as $f(L)/L$ or as $y/f^{-1}(y)$.[1] There are parametric external *diseconomies* of scale if $a$ is decreasing, or, in other words, if the aggregate technology displays decreasing output–labor ratios. Conversely, there are parametric external *economies* of scale if $a$ is increasing.

John Chipman's 1970 paper was motivated by external *economies* of scale due to increasing specialization. In his words (p. 349):

> The concept may be illustrated in terms of Adam Smith's pin factory [fn: *Wealth of Nations*, ch. 1]. If a particular firm expands, some of the work can be divided and specialities will develop. Such specialized labor becomes available, at least part-time, to other firms in the industry. However, only a substantial expansion in the industry will provide enough openings for a pool of labor to develop with a specialized skill, and the contribution of a single firm to this process will be so imperceptible that it will be neglected by the entrepreneur. The change in the character of the labor force will be regarded as exogenous by all firms, even though each firm (by the laws of arithmetic) necessarily contributes to the process.

Accordingly, he chose a formulation with only one input and full reversibility of the production technology. This chapter extends his approach to parametric external diseconomies in a common pool resource exploited by many independent firms. The chapter can be placed at the intersection of two traditions: the analysis of returns to scale in theoretical production economies (see Gerard Debreu 1959; Tjalling C. Koopmans 1957) on the one hand, and, on the other, dynamic models of renewable resources, as in the literature on fisheries (see Colin Clark 1976 and references therein). The general question is: in which ways does the use by many firms of a common pool, renewable resource generate parametric external diseconomies of scale?

Parametric external diseconomies of scale are present if the output–labor ratio goes down with increases in the total activity level. What is at the root of this phenomenon? The established view in economics is that, as long as all productive inputs are explicitly listed, one should expect production processes to be additive, because an exact clone of a given production process should have the same output. Diseconomies of scale violate additivity, and, thus, they suggest that not all production inputs have been recognized: there must be an additional input, implicit in the background. Lionel McKenzie (1959) interpreted it as an "entrepreneurial input," and viewed it as constant. But the obvious interpretation of the implicit input in the exploitation of a natural resource is the resource itself (the stock of fish, say). On the other hand, the constancy of the quantity of the implicit input reflects a short-term view, whereas external economies and diseconomies often reflect longer run phenomena. John Chipman refers in the above quotation to the "change in the character of the labor force," something that would take time. Similarly, in natural resources the diseconomy may operate through changes in the amount of the resource. The implicit input relevant for external diseconomies is, in general, not constant.

## The model

### *The production function*

The technology is assumed to involve two inputs: an explicit one, called labor, and an implicit one, denoted by $S$. The production function $F: R^2_+ \to R: (L, S) \to F(L, S)$, is continuous on the nonnegative orthant and twice differentiable on its interior. Write $\frac{\partial F(L, S)}{\partial L} = F_L(L, S)$ and $\frac{\partial F(L, S)}{\partial S} = F_S(L, S)$. We assume that $F(0, S) = F(L, 0) = 0$.

The following two assumptions are maintained throughout the chapter.

*Assumption 1: positive marginal product of the implicit input* If $L$ and $S$ are positive, then $F_S(L, S) > 0$.

The main text compares points with positive $F_L(L, S)$, but Appendix 1 covers the case where $F_L(L, S)$ is negative for large $L$. This case is more relevant here, where the aggregate technology is subject to external diseconomies of scale, than in the standard formulation where the aggregate production set is simply the sum of the individual ones, and individual profit maximization carries over to the aggregate.

"Large" is understood as relative to the level of the implicit input. Formally, a continuous, nondecreasing function $L^+: R_{++} \rightarrow R_{++}$ is postulated such that, for all $S > 0$, the marginal product of labor $F_L(L, S)$ is positive when $L < L^+(S)$ and negative when $L > L^+(S)$. We admit the notational abuse "$L^+(S) = \infty$" to cover the standard case where $F_L(L, S)$ is positive over the positive orthant.

*Assumption 2: nonincreasing average product of labor* If $L^0$, $L^1$ and $S^0$ are positive and if $L^1 > L^0$, then $\dfrac{F(L^0, S^0)}{L^0} \geq \dfrac{F(L^1, S^0)}{L^1}$.

Note that $\dfrac{F(L, S)}{L}$ is, in fact, strictly decreasing in $L$ whenever $F$ displays nonincreasing returns to scale and Assumption 1 holds.[2,3]

### *The law of motion*

We postulate that $dS/dt$ depends on the activity level $a$ and the existing level of $S$. The implicit input $S$ should not be interpreted as produced capital, and we do not allow for "depreciation," i.e. for decreases in $S$ that depend only on the passage of time, irrespective of activity. Accordingly, the general form of the law of motion is:[4]

$$\frac{dS}{dt} = G(a(L, F(L, S)), S). \tag{1}$$

The control variable is labor; we denote an exogenous path of labor by $\tilde{L}: R_+ \rightarrow R_+: t \rightarrow \tilde{L}(t)$, where $R_+$ denotes the nonnegative halfline. (But for other variables we abuse notation and write the same, untilded symbol for a time path and for a real number.) Given a path $\tilde{L}$ and an initial condition $S(0)$, we solve (1) to get $S(t \mid \tilde{L}, S(0))$. This gives a path $k(t \mid \tilde{L}, S(0))$ for the output–labor ratio, namely:

$$k(t \mid \tilde{L}, S(0)) = \frac{F(\tilde{L}(t), S(t \mid \tilde{L}, S(0)))}{\tilde{L}(t)}.$$

### *The McKenzie case (constant S) and the conventional properties*

We look at the constant $S$ case as a benchmark. The function $G$ is identically zero, and the amount of the implicit input $S$ is fixed. If $\dfrac{F(L, S)}{L}$ is strictly decreasing in $L$, then this case displays the following conventional properties.

*Conventional Property 1 The higher the amount of input, the lower the output–labor ratio.*

Conventional Property 1 captures the idea of parametric external diseconomies. Yet, the diseconomies are not so pronounced in the McKenzie case as to cause a decrease in the absolute amount of output as labor increases, so that the following property holds.

*Conventional Property 2 Provided that* $F_L(L, S) > 0$, *the higher the amount of input, the higher the amount of output.*

## *The renewable resource case*

The paradigm is the fishery, studied by an extensive literature, with $S$ interpreted as the stock of fish, and $L$ sometimes called "effort." The law of motion (1) is now derived as follows. In the absence of production (fishing), the stock of fish would grow according to a natural "growth function:" $H$: $R_+ \rightarrow$: $R$: $S \rightarrow H(S)$. We assume, as is customary, that $H(0) = 0$ (a population with zero fish has zero population growth), that $H$ is twice differentiable, and that there exist values $S^a$, $S^*$ and $S^b$ such that:

$S^a \geq 0$,
$S^b > S^* > S^a$,
$H(S)$ is positive and has a positive derivative for $S \in (S^a, S^*)$.
$H(S)$ is positive and has a negative derivative for $S \in (S^*, S^b)$, and
$H(S)$ is negative for $S$ positive and either greater than $S^b$ or less than $S^a$.[5]

Hence, $H$ attains a maximum at $S^*$. The value $y^* = H(S^*)$ is called the *maximum sustainable yield.* If $S^a > 0$, then the growth function is said to exhibit a *critical depensation.*

If there is fishing, and $y(t) \geq 0$ denotes the instantaneous catch at time $t$, then the law of motion of the stock of fish is:

$$\frac{dS}{dt} = H(S(t)) - y(t),$$

which given our assumption on the underlying technology, can be written:

$$\frac{dS}{dt} = H(S(t)) - F(L(t), S(t)). \tag{2}$$

The following example illustrates this point.

*Example 1* Production Function: $F(L, S) = 2\ L^{0.5}\ S^{0.5}$.

Growth Function: $H(S) = 20\ S\ (1 - \frac{S}{200}) - 100$.

This growth function, illustrated in Figure 20.1(a), is typical in the literature on fisheries. Note that $S^a$ is positive (critical depensation). The production function displays constant returns to scale.[6]

A *steady state* is defined as a triple $(L, S, y)$, where $S$ is a constant stock, $L$ is a constant flow of labor and $y$ is a constant flow of output such that $y = H(S)$ (i.e. the dynamic system defined by (2) is stationary), and $y = F(L, S)$.

One should note that (as long as there can be no fishing without fish, i.e. $F(L, 0) = 0$, for all $L \geq 0$), for any $L \geq 0$ we have that $(L, 0, 0)$ is a steady state, associated with *extinction*. Zero output is also a steady state at the positive stock level $S^b$, as well as, under a critical depensation, at the positive stock level $S^a$. It is also clear that no steady state flow of output can exceed $y^*$.

Any point on the graph of $H$ with nonnegative vertical coordinate depicts the $(S, y)$ coordinates of steady state $(L, S, y)$. The $(L, y)$ projection is represented in Figure 21.1(b) (Clark 1976, 1990): the graph can be obtained by elminating $S$ in the equations "$y = H(S)$" and "$y = F(L, S)$." I have added Figure 21.1(c), which is an isoquant map for $F(L, S)$, with flags indicating some output levels. Of course, the function $H$ of Figure 21.1(a) and the isoquant map, with flags, of Figure 21.1(c) are the primitives of the model: Figure 21.1(b) and the steady-state locus of Figure 21.1(c) are derived from them. Points labeled $A$ and $B$ in each figure are the respective projections of the same point in the 3-dimensional space with coordinates $(L, S, y)$.

## The conventional properties when the resource is renewable: dynamic paths and steady states

Because $S$ now varies, the behavior of the system is more complex than in the McKenzie case. A higher activity level dynamically induces a lower $S$, which in turn depresses output. This implies that, as long as $F_L(L, S) > 0$, if we compare two dynamic paths that start at the same $S(0)$ and such that the flow of labor is always lower in the second one than in the first one, then the output–labor ratio will always be higher in the first one, in line with Conventional Property 1.[7] Moreover, the depressive effect may be strong enough as to eventually result in a lower amount of output for the path with higher labor, so that Conventional Property 2 fails.[8]

The level of $S$ may be significantly increased by refraining from production early on, and the system may then be led to a steady state with a high $S$. In fact, the long-run output and labor values of steady states may be more relevant for policy purposes than the comparison of two dynamic paths, one having a consistently higher labor flow than the other one, that start at the same initial value of $S$: the literature on fisheries has accordingly emphasized

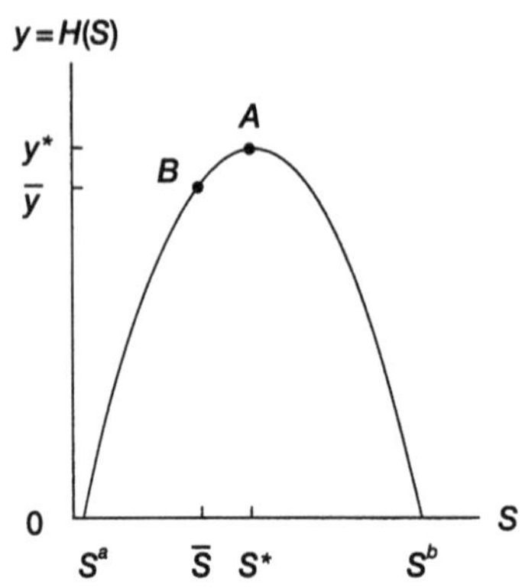


*Figure 21.1a* Growth function

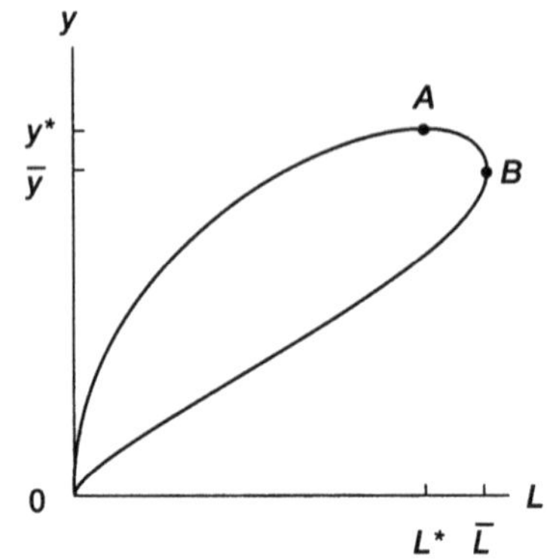


*Figure 21.1b* Yield correspondence

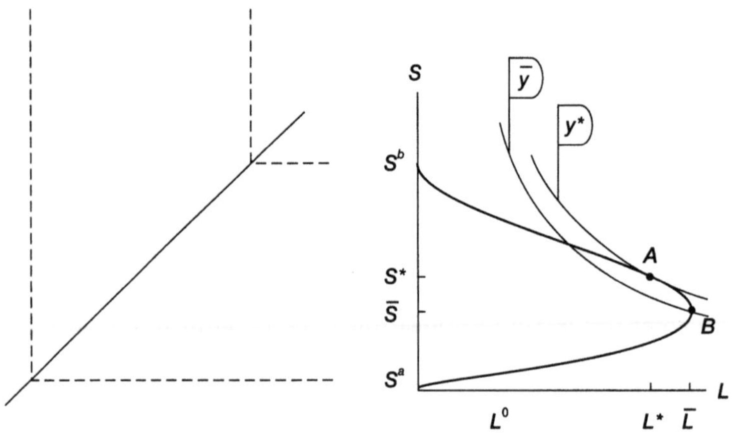


*Figure 21.1c* Isoquants; steady-state input pairs

*Note*: Figures 21.1a–c: Example 1, computed values: $S^a = 5.1$, $S^b = 194.9$, $y^* = 900$, $L^* = 2025$, $S^* = 100$, $\bar{y} = 818$, $\bar{L} = 2344$, $\bar{S} = 71.3$.

the labor–output pairs that can be achieved as steady states. It is clear from Figure 21.1(b) that Conventional Properties 1 and 2 do not hold for steady states. First, one can choose, in the lower branch, two steady states $(L^1, S^1, y^1)$ and $(L^0, S^0, y^0)$ so that $L^1 > L^0$ yet $y^1/L^1 > y^0/L^0$, i.e. the first steady state has both a higher level of labor and a higher output–labor ratio than the second one, negating Conventional Property 1. Second, one can choose, in the segment of the graph between points A and B, two steady states $(L^1, S^1, y^1)$ and $(L^0, S^0, y^0)$ so that $L^1 > L^0$ yet $y^1 < y^0$, negating Conventional Property 2. Moreover, comparing a steady state with positive $y$ with an "extinction" one with $L > \bar{L}$ provides another negation of Property 2.

Thus, the comparison of steady states does not display Conventional Properties 1 and 2. In a sense, anything can happen: output–labor ratios may be larger for larger amounts of labor, but they may be lower, and this with a vengeance: the absolute amount of output may actually be lower for higher levels of labor.

But perhaps the violations of Conventional Properties 1 and 2 involve peculiar or anomalous steady states. Consider, for instance, steady states in the lower branch of Figure 21.1(b). On the one hand, they are socially inefficient in a strong sense, because, by letting the stock of fish grow early, one could approach steady states on the upper branch yielding higher output for the same labor input. On the other hand, they turn out to be locally unstable for simple out-of-steady-state paths. The remainder of the chapter studies the manner in which the conventional properties can be recovered by restricting attention to some "well behaved" subsets of steady states.

## The maximum-yield function

The graph of Figure 21.1(b) is that of the *yield correspondence*, defined as:

$\varphi$: $R_+ \rightarrow R_+$: $\varphi(L) = \{y \in R_+$: there exists an $S$ such that $y = H(S) = F(L,S)\}$.[9]

As just argued, some of the steady states involve unnecessarily low yields for the amount of labor spent. This motivates defining a selection of the yield correspondence by its maximum values. Formally, define the *maximum-yield function* by:

$\tilde{f}$: $R_+ \rightarrow R_+$: $\tilde{f}(L) = \max\{y\text{: } y \in j(L)\}$.

Because $F(L, 0) = 0$ for all $L \geq 0$, and extinction is a steady state, the maximum-yield correspondence is well defined, i.e. $\varphi(L) \neq \in$ for any $L \geq 0$. Clearly, $\varphi(L) \subset [0, y^*]$, i.e. the yield correspondence is bounded. Moreover, for all $L \geq 0$, the set $\varphi(L)$ is closed.[10] It follows that $\varphi(L)$ is compact and, thus, that the maximum-yield function $\tilde{f}$ is well defined.

It turns out that the maximum-yield function may display increasing output–labor ratios at points where $F_L(L, S) < 0$: an example is offered in Appendix 1 below. But as long as $F_L(L, S) > 0$ and all variables are positive, Conventional Property 1 necessarily holds. Formally:

*Theorem 1 If* $0 < L^0 < L^1$ *and if, for* $i = 0,1$, "$\tilde{f}(L^i) > 0$" *implies* "$F_L(L^i,S^i) > 0$ *at the corresponding steady-state value* $S^i$," *then either* $\tilde{f}(L^0) = \tilde{f}(L^1) = 0$ *or*

$$\frac{\tilde{f}(L^0)}{L^0} > \frac{\tilde{f}(L^1)}{L^1}$$

*Proof* Appendix 2.

On the other hand, Conventional Property 2 does not hold for the maximum-yield function, as is obvious from Figure 21.1(b) (segment between points $A$ and $B$).

## Stability with constant input flows

Whether a steady state is stable or unstable depends on the postulated behavior of $\tilde{L}(t)$ out of steady state, which in turn determines the qualitative features of the law of motion (2). A case often studied by the literature on fisheries is that of a constant $\tilde{L}$: $\tilde{L}(t) = L^0$, for all $t$, and $y(t)$ adjusts so as to always satisfy the equation "$y(t) = F(L^0, S(t))$." Substituting into (2), the law of motion becomes:

$$\frac{dS}{dt} = H(S(t)) - F(L^0, S(t)).$$

We say that a steady state is *input-stable* if it is (locally) stable under this law of motion. The eigenvalue condition for (local) input stability is:

$$H'(S) - F_S(L, S) < 0. \tag{3}$$

Restricting attention to steady states that are input-stable leads to the *input-stable yield correspondence*:

$$\varphi_I: R_+ \to R_+: \varphi_I(L) =$$
$$\{y \in R_+: \text{there exists an } S \text{ such that } y = H(S) = F(L, S) \text{ and } H'(S) - F_S(L, S) < 0\},$$

and to the *input-stable maximum-yield function*:

$$\tilde{f}_I: R_+ \to R_+: \tilde{f}_I(L) = \max\{y: y \in j_I(L)\}.$$

Input stability can be visualized in Figure 21.1(c), reproduced in Figure 21.2 as a phase diagram for constant input flows. Steady states in the

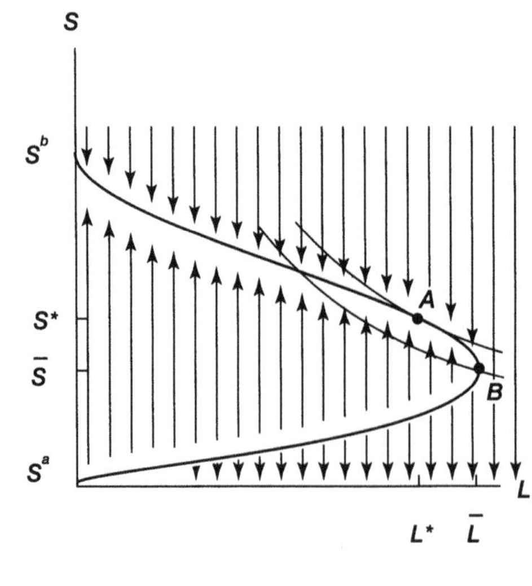


*Figure 21.2*
*Note*: The input-stable steady states are those in the segment ($S^b$, $B$) (through $A$), plus extinction steady states (on horizontal axis).

segment $(S^b, B)$ of Figure 21.2 (or 21.1(a)–(c)) are input stable, whereas the ones on the segment $(S^a, B]$ are not.

Does the input-stable yield correspondence satisfy Conventional Property 1? In other words, if $0 < L^0 < L^1$ and if $y^0 \in j_I(L^0)$ and $y^1 \in j_I(L^1)$, is it necessarily true that $\frac{y^0}{L^0} > \frac{y^1}{L^1}$ ?

The following example demonstrates that the answer is negative.

*Example 2* The production function is $F(L, S) = 2\,L^{0.5}\,S^{0.5}$. For simplicity, the growth function is presented as a step-linear function instead of a smooth function. It is clear that all kinks can be smoothed out without changing the substantive features of the example.

Consider the growth function:

$$H(S) = \begin{cases} -1.5S, & \text{for } S \in [0,0.5], \\ -1.5+1.5S, & \text{for } S \in [0.5,2], \\ \in 1.25+(1/8)S, & \text{for } S \in [2,6], \\ -4+S, & \text{for } S \in [6,7], \\ 10-S, & \text{for } S > 7. \end{cases}$$

Figure 21.3(a) graphs the growth function, and Figure 21.3(b) the yield correspondence. The input-stable yield correspondence is the union of the curves (0, A) and (B, C) of Figure 21.3(b). Point $E$ has a larger amount of labor than $D$, yet the output–labor ratio is higher at E than at D, negating Conventional Property 1.

Yet, a "local" version of the property holds, namely, when one restricts the comparison to points $(L^0, y^0)$ and $(L^1, y^1)$ on the same branch of the graph of the correspondence. Indeed, (3) permits the application of the Implicit Function Theorem at any input-stable steady state and the local solution of (3) for $y$ in terms of $L$, with the derivative:

$$\frac{dy}{dL} = \frac{H' \cdot F_L}{H' - F_S}\ .$$

See the argument in the proof of Theorem 3 in Appendix 2. The arguments in the proofs of Proposition 1 and Theorem 3 of Appendix 2 show that, if $\frac{dy}{dL} > 0$, then $\frac{d\frac{y}{L}}{dL} < 0$. Because "$\frac{dy}{dL} \leq 0$" implies that "$\frac{d\frac{y}{L}}{dL} < 0$," it follows that the output–labor ratio is decreasing within each branch.

The analysis of Conventional Property 1 for the input-stable maximum-yield function is harder because $H'(S) - F_S(L, S)$ could in principle be zero at a point where the steady state function is decreasing, in which case the input-stable maximum-yield function would be discontinuous and the output–labor ratio would be increasing at the point of discontinuity. I

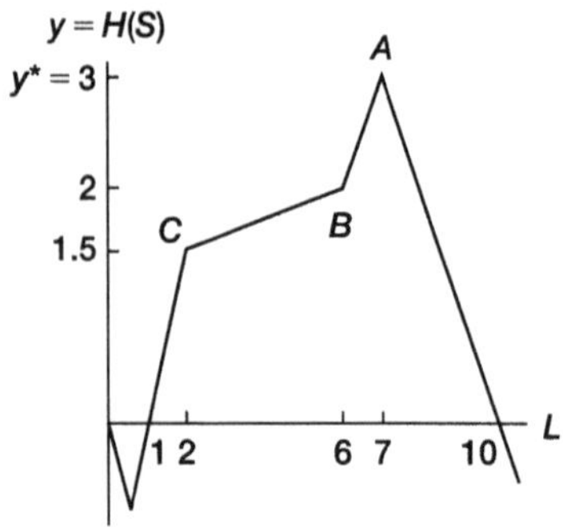


*Figure 21.3a* Growth function

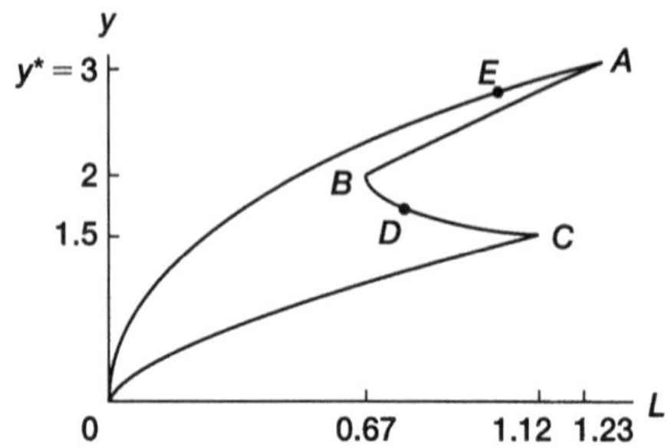


*Figure 21.3b* Yield correspondence

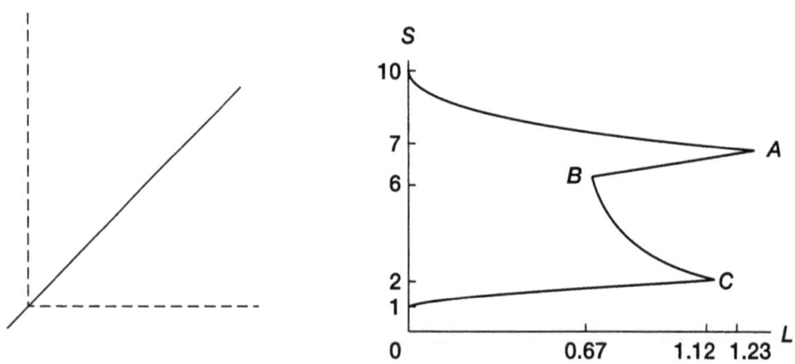


*Figure 21.3c* Steady-state input pairs
*Note*: Figures 21.3a–c: Example 2, the output–labor ratio is higher at $E$ than at $D$.

conjecture that such an example can indeed be found, but that it would fail to be robust.

Now we turn to Conventional Property 2. It is clear from the segment ($A$, $B$) in Figure 21.1(b) that the property is satisfied neither by the input-stable correspondence, nor by the input-stable maximum-yield function.

## Stability with constant output flows

Alternatively, consider the case where $y$ is fixed at, say, $y^0$, and $\tilde{L}(t)$ adjusts so as to always satisfy the equation "$y^0 = F(\tilde{L}(t), S(t))$." Substituting into (2), the law of motion becomes:

$$\frac{dS}{dt} = H(S(t)) - y^0.$$

We say that a steady state is *output-stable* if it is (locally) stable under this law of motion. The eigenvalue condition for (local) output stability is:

$$H'(S) < 0, \tag{4}$$

independent of the production function $F$. Note that this yields a stricter stability criterion, because (4) implies (3).

Figure 21.1(a), reproduced in Figure 21.4 as a phase diagram for constant output flows, provides a visualization of output stability. Note that only the segment $(S^b, A)$ is output stable with positive output: the segment $[A, B)$ is input stable, but not output stable. The extinction steady states (projected on to the origin in Figures 21.1(a) and 21.4, and on to the horizontal axis in Figures 21.1(b)–(c)) are output stable if and only if there is a critical depensation with $H'(0) < 0$, as is clear from Figure 21.4.

Restricting attention to steady states that are output-stable leads to the *output-stable yield correspondence*:

$\varphi_y: R_+ \rightarrow R_+$:
$\varphi_y(L) = \{y \in R_+$: there exists an $S$ such that $y = H(S) = F(L, S)$ and $H'(S) < 0\}$, and to the *output-stable maximum-yield function*:

$\tilde{f}_y: R_+ \rightarrow R_+: \tilde{f}_y(L) = \max\{y: y \in \varphi_y(L)\}$.

Conventional Property 1 holds for the output-stable maximum-yield function. Formally:

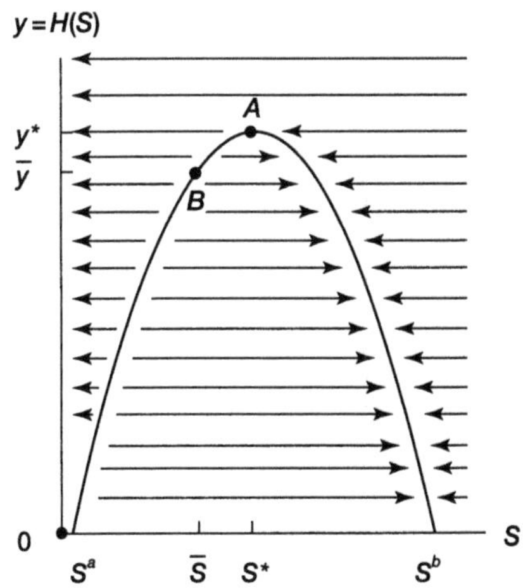


*Figure 21.4*
*Note*: The output-stable steady states are those in the segment $(A, S^b)$, plus extinction (origin).

*Theorem 2* *If* $0 < L^0 < L^1$ *and if, for* $i = 0,1$, "$\tilde{f}_y(L^i) > 0$" *implies* "$F_L(L^i,S^i) > 0$ *at the corresponding steady-state value* $S^i$," *then either* $\tilde{f}_y(L^0) = \tilde{f}_y(L^1) = 0$ *or* $\dfrac{\tilde{f}y(L^0)}{L^0} > \dfrac{\tilde{f}y(L^1)}{L^1}$.

*Proof* Appendix 2.

For the output-stable yield correspondence, Conventional Property 1 may fail if one compares $y^0 = 0 \in \varphi_y(L^0)$ with a positive $y^1$ in $\varphi_y(L^1)$, $0 < L^0 < L^1$. (Consider, for instance, a point in the extinction branch of Figure 21.1(b) and another one with slightly higher labor input on the positive-output, output-stable branch.) But it follows from Theorem 2 and Lemma 9 in Appendix 2 that the answer is affirmative as long as a positive $y^0$ is used in the comparison.

We now consider Conventional Property 2: can aggregate yields be decreasing in the labor input? A discontinuous fall to the zero yield of the extinction steady state, as in Figure 21.1(b), is a form of decrease. But, except for a fall to extinction, Conventional Property 2 holds for the output-stable yield correspondence and maximum-yield function. Formally:

*Theorem 3* *If* $0 < L^0 < L^1$, *and if, for* $i = 0, 1$, $y^i \in \varphi_y(L^i)$, $y^i > 0$ *and* $F_L(L^i, S^i) > 0$ *at the corresponding steady-state value* $S^i$, *then* $y^1 > y^0$.

*Proof* Appendix 2.

Figures 21.1(b) and 21.3(b) illustrate: in accordance with Theorem 3, the non-extinction branch of the output-stable yield correspondence is increasing.

## Conclusion

Parametric diseconomies of scale can often be explained by the presence of an implicit, nonmarketed input, jointly used by firms. The McKenzie tradition views the quantity of the implicit input as constant. Parametric diseconomies of scale then appear: this I call Conventional Property 1. But they are not so severe as to induce decreasing absolute amounts of output: this is Conventional Property 2.

Many cases of external diseconomies of scale involve nonconstant amounts of the implicit input. This chapter has focused on the implicit input as renewable resource, subject to natural growth laws, and has enquired about the ways in which Conventional Properties 1 and 2 are preserved when comparing steady states. As a first observation, neither property is preserved if the comparison can be made between any pair of steady states.

Our results, in a nutshell, show that Conventional Property 1 is recovered, at least in a local form, if we rule out grossly inefficient or unstable steady states. Conventional Property 2, on the other hand, is recovered only (and in a qualified form, due to the possibility of extinction) for a particular selection of steady states that requires local stability relative to constant output paths.

## APPENDIX 1: THE CASE $F_L(L, S) < 0$

If there is a region where the production function displays decreasing negative marginal product of labor, then, given a value for $S \in (S^a, S^b)$, the same level of output is typically achievable both at a low value of $L$, in the region where $F_L(L,S) > 0$, and a high value of $L$, in the region where $F_L(L, S) < 0$. In particular, there are typically two steady states $(L^0, S, H(S))$ and $(L^1, S, H(S))$ for each given $S \in (S^a, S^b)$. The graphs corresponding to Figures 21.1(b) and 21.1(c) above then display two branches, not necessarily disconnected. A first branch picks up the steady states in the "$F_L(L, S) > 0$" region, and looks like the ones in Figures 21.1(b) and 21.1(c), but there is a second branch, for steady states in the "$F_L(L, S) < 0$" region. Of course, steady states in the "$F_L(L, S) < 0$" region are socially inefficient, because the same output yield can be achieved at lower levels of labor and the same amount of input $S$. The following example illustrates a typical case where the two branches are disconnected.[11]

*Example 3* We take:

$$H(S) = 0.5\, S \left(1 - \frac{\bar{S}}{200}\right) - 10,$$

$$F(L, S) = \begin{cases} 0.005L\, S, \text{ for } S \geq L, \\ 0.005((S - 0.1L)/0.9)^2, \text{ for } S \in [0.1\, L, L], \\ 0, \text{ for } S \geq 0.1\, L. \end{cases}$$

Figure 21.5 illustrates that Theorems 1 and 3 above cannot be extended to the "$F_L(L, S) < 0$" region. For Theorem 1, observe that the slope of the maximum-yield function is infinite at point $C$, and thus the output–labor ratio is increasing in a right neighborhood of $\bar{L}$. For Theorem 3, note that the output-stable correspondence is decreasing to the right of point $D$: this is actually a general fact. Formally:

*Theorem 4 Let* $(L^0, S^0, y^0)$ *and* $(L^1, S^1, y^1)$ *be output-stable steady states satisfying:* (i) $L^1 > L^0$; (ii) $y^0 > 0$; (iii) $F_L(L^0, S^0) \leq 0$; (iv) $F_L(L^1, S^1) \leq 0$; *then* $y^0 > y^1$.

*Proof* Appendix 2.

But Theorem 2 does extend to the "$F_L(L, S) < 0$" region. Formally:

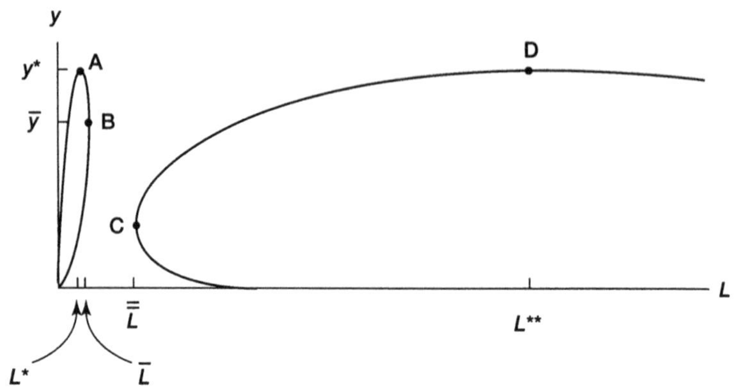


*Figure 21.5a* Yield correspondence.

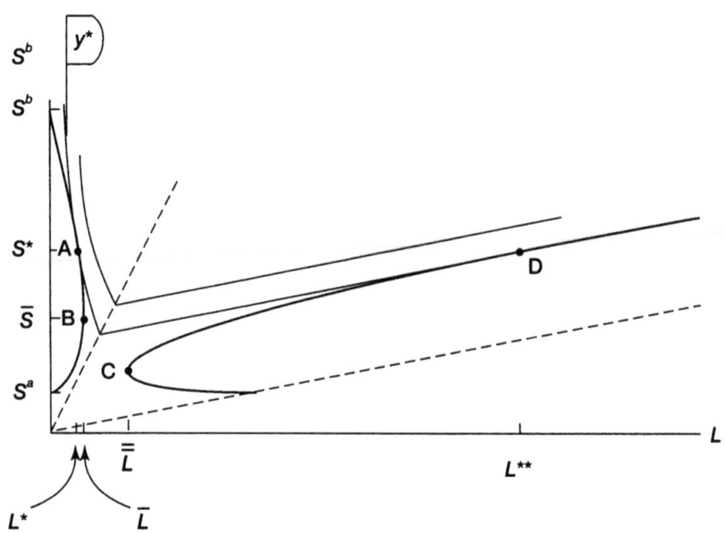


*Figure 21.5b* Isoquants; steady-state input pairs

*Note*: Figures 21.5a–b: Example 3:

Input-stable branches: segment ($S^b$, *B*) in Figure 21.5b, or (O, *B*) in Figure 21.5a (through point *A*); segment (*C* ∞) in Figures 21.5a–b (through point *D*) (plus extinction)

Output-stable branches: segment ($S^b$, *A*) in Figure 21.5b, or (O, *A*) in Figure 21.5a (not through point B); segment (*D* ∞) in Figures 21.5a–b; (plus extinction)

Computed values: $S = 22.45$, $S^b = 177.4$, $y^* = 15$, $L^* = 30$, $S^* = 100$, $\bar{L} = 36.7$, $\bar{S} = 65.9$, $\bar{y} = 12.1$, $\bar{\bar{L}} = 81.7$, $L^{**} = 507$.

*Theorem 5* *Let* $(L^0, S^0, y^0)$ *and* $(L^1, S^1, y^1)$ *be output-stable steady states satisfying: (i)* $L^1 > L^0$; *(ii)* $y^0 > 0$; *(iii)* $F_L(L^1, S^1) < 0$; *then* $\frac{y^0}{L^0} > \frac{y^1}{L^1}$ .

*Proof* Appendix 2.

## APPENDIX 2: PROOFS

Define: $\xi$: $R^2{}_+ \rightarrow R$: $\xi(L, S) = H(S) - F(L, S)$.
Write: $\xi_L(L, S) = - F_L(L, S)$ and $\xi_S(L, S) = H'(S) - F_S(L, S)$.

*Lemma 1*

(a) *If* $0 < L^0 < L^1$, $\varphi(L^0) = \{0\}$ *and* $(L^1, S^1, y^1)$ *is a steady state for some* $S^1$ *and* $y^1$, $y^1 > 0$, *then* $F_L(L^1, S^1) < 0$.
(b) *If* $0 < L^0 < L^1$, $\varphi_y(L^0) = \{0\}$ *and* $(L^1, S^1, y^1)$ *is an output-stable steady state for some* $S^1$ *and* $y^1$, $y^1 > 0$, *then* $F_L(L^1, S^1) < 0$.

*Proof* The same argument proves (a) and (b). Because $L^0 > 0$ and $F_S > 0$ in the interior of $R^2{}_+$, we have that $F(L^0, S^b) > 0$, which in turn implies that $\xi(L^0, S^b) < 0$. Because $y^1 > 0$, we must have that $S^1 \in (S^a, S^b)$. I claim that $\xi(L^0, S^1) < 0$. Suppose not. Then either $\xi(L^0, S^1) = 0$ or, by the Intermediate Value Theorem, $\xi(L^0, S) = 0$ for some $S \in (S^1, S^b)$ (which, in case (b), would satisfy $H'(S) < 0$, because $H'(S^1) < 0$). Either way, $\varphi(L^0)$ (resp. $\varphi_y(L^0)$) would own a positive element, contrary to assumption.Thus, $\xi(L^0, S^1) < 0$. If $F_L(L^1, S^1) \geq 0$, then $F_L(L, S^1) > 0$ for $L \in (L^0, L^1)$, implying that $F(L^1, S^1) > F(L^0, S^1)$, and, thus, that $\xi(L^1, S^1) < \xi(L^0, S^1) < 0$, contradicting the hypothesis that $(L^1, S^1, y^1)$ is a steady state. Q.E.D.

*Lemma 2* *If* $L > 0$, *then there is a unique* $S$ *such that* $(L, S, \tilde{f}(L))$ *is a steady state.*

*Proof* Existence has been argued in the third paragraph of the section on the maximum-yield function. Uniqueness is immediate from the assumption that $F_S > 0$ on $R^2{}_{++}$. Q.E.D.

Write $\tilde{S}(L)$ for the $S$ defined in the statement of Lemma 2.

*Lemma 3* *If* $\tilde{S}(L^1) \in (S^*, S^b)$, *if* $F_L(L^1, \tilde{S}(L^1)) > 0$ *and if* $L^0 \in (0, L^1)$, *then* $\tilde{S}(L^0) \in (\tilde{S}(L^1), S^b) \subset (S^*, S^b)$.

*Proof* Because $H(\tilde{S}(L^1)) > 0$ and $F_L(L^1, \tilde{S}(L^1)) > 0$, Lemma 1(a) guarantees that $H(\tilde{S}(L^0)) > 0$. Moreover, $F_L(L, \tilde{S}(L^1)) > 0$ for all $L \in (0, L^1)$. Thus,

$\xi(L^0, \tilde{S}(L^1)) = H(\tilde{S}(L^1)) - F(L^0, \tilde{S}(L^1)) > \xi(L^1, \tilde{S}(L^1)) = 0$. On the other hand, $\xi(L^0, S^b) = 0 - F(L^0, S^b) < 0$. By the Intermediate Value Theorem, there is an $S^2 \in (\tilde{S}(L^1), S^b)$ such that $\xi(L^0, S^2) = 0$. I claim that $S^2 = \tilde{S}(L^0)$. Because $H$ is decreasing on $(S^*, S^b)$, $H(S) < H(S^2)$ for $S \in (S^2, S^b)$. Moreover, because $F$ is increasing in $S$, $F(L^0, S) < F(L^0, S^2)$ for $S \in (0, S^2)$. Thus, $S^2 = \tilde{S}(L^0) \in (\tilde{S}(L^1), S^b) \subset (S^*, S^b)$. Q.E.D.

Define:

$\bar{S} = \inf\{S: S = \tilde{S}(L)$ for some $L$ such that $H(\tilde{S}(L)) > 0$ and $F_L(L, \tilde{S}(L)) > 0\}$.

Clearly, $\bar{S} \geq S^a$.

*Proposition 1 Let* $\bar{S} \geq S^*$. *If* $0 < L^0 < L^1$, *and if, for* $i = 1, 2$, "$\tilde{f}(L^i) > 0$" *implies* "$F_L(L^i, \tilde{S}(L^i)) > 0$," *then either* $\tilde{f}(L^0) = \tilde{f}(L^1) = 0$ *or* $\dfrac{\tilde{f}(L^0)}{L^0} > \dfrac{\tilde{f}(L^1)}{L^1}$.

*Proof* The statement is true if $\tilde{f}(L^1) = 0$. By Lemma 1(a), we cannot have $0 = \tilde{f}(L^0) < \tilde{f}(L^1)$. So we only need to consider the case where $\tilde{f}(L^0) > 0$ and $\tilde{f}(L^1) > 0$, which, by hypothesis, implies that $F_L(L^1, \tilde{S}(L^1)) > 0$. Because $\bar{S} \geq S^*$, we have that $\tilde{S}(L^1) \in [S^*, S^b)$ and thus, by Lemma 3, $\tilde{S}(L) > S^*$ and $H(\tilde{S}(L)) > 0$ for all $L \in (0, L^1)$. Hence, $L \in (0, L^1)$ implies that $H'(\tilde{S}(L)) < 0$ and, thus that

$$H^1(\tilde{S}(L)) - F_S(L, \tilde{S}(L)) < 0. \tag{A.1}$$

Therefore, by the Implicit Function Theorem, the function $\tilde{S}(L)$ is differentiable on $(0, L^1)$, and its derivative is:

$$\tilde{S}' = \frac{F_L}{H' - F_S}. \tag{A.2}$$

Assumption 2 yields:

$$0 \geq \frac{d\dfrac{F(L, S)}{L}}{dL} = \frac{F_L \cdot L - F}{L^2}. \tag{A.3}$$

Clearly, $\tilde{f}(L) = F(L, \tilde{S}(L))$ for $L \in (0, L^1)$. Hence, using (A.2):

$$\frac{d\dfrac{\tilde{f}(L)}{L}}{dL} = \frac{d\dfrac{F(L, \tilde{S}(L))}{L}}{dL} = \frac{[F_L + F_S \cdot \tilde{S}']L - F}{L^2} = \frac{[F_L + F_S \dfrac{F_L}{H' - F_S}]L - F}{L^2}$$

$$= \frac{F_L \cdot L - F}{L^2} + \frac{F_S \dfrac{F_L}{H' - F_S} L}{L^2},$$

the sum of a nonpositive term (by A.3) and a negative term (by A.1).
Q.E.D.

*Lemma 4 If, for given* $S^0$ *and for* $i = 0, 1$, $L^i$ *satisfies*:

(a) $\xi(L^i, S^0) = 0$,
(b) $F_L(L^i, S^0) > 0$,
(c) $F(L^i, S^0) > 0$,

*then* $L^0 = L^1$.

*Proof* Suppose not: without loss of generality, let $L^0 < L^1$. Note that $S^0 > 0$ because $H(S^0) > 0$ by (a) and (c). By (b), $L^0 < L^1 < L^+(S^0)$, and, therefore, $F(L^0, S^0) < F(L^1, S^0)$, because $F_L(L, S^0) > 0$ at $L \in (L^0, L^1)$. But this contradicts (a), according to which both $F(L^0, S^0)$ and $F(L^1, S^0)$ must equal $H(S^0)$. Thus, the solution to the equation in $L$ "$\xi(L, S^0) = 0$" is unique in the region where the marginal product of labor is positive. Q.E.D.

*Lemma 5 Let* $\bar{S} < S^*$. *There exists a differentiable function*

$\Lambda: (\bar{S}, S^b) \rightarrow R$,

*such that, for* $S^0 \in (\bar{S}, S^b)$:

(a) $H(S^0) = F(\Lambda(S^0), S^0) > 0$,
(b) $F_L(\Lambda(S^0), S^0) > 0$.

*Proof* Let $S^0 \in (\bar{S}, S^b)$. Then, there is a $(L^1, S^1)$ such that $S^1 = \tilde{S}(L^1)$, $S^1 < S^0$, $H(\tilde{S}(L^1)) > 0$ and $F_L(L^1, S^1) > 0$. Clearly, $\xi(L^1, \tilde{S}(L^1)) = 0$, and $S^0 \in (\tilde{S}(L^1), S^b)$. I claim that $\xi(L^1, S^0) < 0$. Suppose not. Then, either $\xi(L^1, S^0) = 0$, in which case $(L^1, S^0, H(S^0))$ would be a steady state, or $\xi(L^1, S^0) > 0$, in which case, given that $\xi(S^b, L^1) = 0 - F(L^1, S^b) < 0$, there would exist an $S^2 \in (S^0, S^b)$ with $\xi(L^1, S^2) = 0$. In either case, there would be a steady state involving $L^1$ and a level of $S$ higher than $\tilde{S}(L^1)$, and hence, a level of $y$ greater than $\tilde{f}(L^1)$, a contradiction. Thus, $\xi(L^1, S^0) < 0$.

Because $\xi(0, S^0) = H(S^0) - 0 > 0$, the Intermediate Value Theorem guarantees the existence of a positive solution $L^0$ to the equation "$\xi(L, S^0) = 0$." Because $(L^0, S^0)$ lies northwest of $(L^1, \tilde{S}(L^1))$ and $F_L(L^1, \tilde{S}(L^1)) > 0$, we have that $F_L(L^0, S^0) > 0$. Moreover, $F(L^0, \tilde{S}(L^0)) > 0$, because both $L^0$ and $\tilde{S}(L^0)$ are positive. By Lemma 4, $L^0$ is the unique solution to the equation "$\xi(L, S^0) = 0$." Define $\Lambda(S^0)$ to be such a unique solution. The differentiability of $\Lambda$ follows from the Implicit Function Theorem applied to the equation "$\xi(L, S) = 0$" by noting that $\xi_L(\Lambda(S), S) = F_L(\Lambda(S), S) > 0$ for all $S \in (\bar{S}, S^b)$. Q.E.D.

Recall that $y^* = H(S^*)$. In the case where $\bar{S} < S^*$, write: $\bar{y} = H(\bar{S})$.

*Lemma 6 Let* $\bar{S} < S^*$. *There exist two continuous functions*

$\hat{L}:(\bar{y}, y^*] \rightarrow R,$
$\hat{S}:(\bar{y}, y^*] \rightarrow (\bar{S}, S^*),$

*such that, for* $y \in (\bar{y}, y^*]$:

(a) $H(\hat{S}(y)) = F(\hat{L}(y), \hat{S}(y)) = y,$
(b) $F_L(\hat{L}(y), \hat{S}(y)) > 0.$

*Proof* Because $\bar{S} \geq S^a$, we have that $H'(S) > 0$ on $(\bar{S}, S^*)$. Moreover, $H$ is continuous on $(\bar{S}, S^*]$. Thus, the function $H$ is continously invertible on $(\bar{S}, S^*]$. Write $\hat{S}$ for the inverse of $H$ and define $\hat{L}$ by $\hat{L}(y) = \Lambda(\hat{S}(y))$. It follows that $\hat{L}$ is continuous on $(\bar{y}, y^*]$ by virtue of being the composition of $\Lambda$ (a differentiable function by Lemma 5) and the continuous function $\hat{S}$. Q.E.D.

Write: $Y = \{y^0 \in (\bar{y}, y^*: \hat{L}(y^0) > \hat{L}(y)$ for all $y \in (y^0, y^*]\}$.
Clearly, $y^* \in Y$.

*Lemma 7 Let* $\bar{S} < S^*$. *The restriction of* $\hat{L}$ *to* $Y$ *is a decreasing function* (i.e. *if both* $y^0$ *and* $y^1$ *belong to* $Y$ *and* $y^0 < y^1$, *then* $\hat{L}(y^0) > \hat{L}(y^1)$).

*Proof* Immediate. Q.E.D.

If $\bar{S} < S^*$, then define $L^* = \tilde{L}(y^*)$.

*Lemma 8 Let* $\bar{S} < S^*$. *If* $L^0 \geq L^*$, $y^0 = \tilde{f}(L^0) > 0$ *and* $F_L(L^0, \tilde{S}(L^0)) > 0$, *then* $y^0 \in Y \cup \{\bar{y}\}$. *If, moreover,* $y^0 > \bar{y}$, *then* $L^0 = \hat{L}(y^0)$.

*Proof* I first show that $\tilde{S}(L^0) \in [\bar{S}, S^*]$. The fact that $\tilde{S}(L^0) \geq \bar{S}$ is implied by the definition of $\bar{S}$. It is also clear that $\tilde{S}(L^0) \leq S^*$ (otherwise, because $F_L(L^0, S) > 0$ for $S \geq \tilde{S}(L)$, one would have that $F(L^0, \tilde{S}(L^0)) > F(L^*, S^*) = y^*$, a contradiction). Thus, $\tilde{S}(L^0) \in [\bar{S}, S^*]$. Because $y^0 = H(\tilde{S}(L^0))$, and because $H$ is increasing on $[\bar{S}, S^*]$, this in turn implies that $y^0 \in [\bar{y}, y^*)$.

Let $y^0 > \bar{y}$. By Lemma 6, $\hat{L}(y^0)$ solves the equation in $L$: "$\xi(L, S^0) = 0$," where $S^0$ is fixed at $S^0 = \hat{S}(y^0)$. By Lemma 4, such a solution is unique in the region where $F_L(L,S) > 0$. Thus, $L^0 = \hat{L}(y^0)$.

It remains to be shown that, if $y^0 > \bar{y}$, then $y^0 \in Y$. If $L^0 = L^*$, then $\tilde{f}(L^0) = y^* \in Y$. So let $L^0 > L^*$, and suppose that $y^0 \notin Y$, i.e. let there be a $y^1 \in (y^0, y^*]$ such that $\hat{L}(y^1) \geq \hat{L}(y^0)$. Because $L^0 > L^* = \hat{L}(y^*)$ and $\hat{L}$ is a continuous function, the Intermediate Value Theorem implies the existence of a $y^2 \in [y^1, y^*] \subset (y^0, y^*]$ such that $L^0 = \hat{L}(y^2)$. But then $(L^0, \hat{S}(y^2), y^2)$ is a steady state with $y^2 > y^0$, contradicting the assumption that $y^0 = \tilde{f}(L^0)$. Q.E.D.

*Lemma 9 If* $\bar{y} = \tilde{f}(\bar{L})$ *for some* $\bar{L} > L^*$, *then* $\bar{L} > L$ *for all* $L$ *in the image of* $(\bar{y}, y^*]$ *under* $\hat{L}$.

*Proof* Suppose not, i.e. let there be an $(L^0, y^0)$ such that $L^0 > \bar{L}$, $L^0 = \hat{L}(y^0)$ and $y^0 \; \varepsilon \; (\bar{y}, y^*]$. Because $\hat{L}(y^*) = y^*$, the Intermediate Value Theorem guarantees the existence of a $y^1 \; \hat{L}(y^0, y^*]$ such that $\hat{L}(y^1) = \bar{L}$. Because $y^1 > \bar{y}$, this contradicts the assumption that $\bar{y} = \tilde{f}(\bar{L})$. Q.E.D.

*Proposition 2 Let* $\bar{S} < S^*$. *If* $0 < L^0 < L^1$, *and if, for* $i = 0, 1$, "$\tilde{f}(L^i) > 0$" *implies* "$F_L(L^i, \tilde{S}(L^i)) > 0$," *then either* $\tilde{f}(L^0) = \tilde{f}(L^1) = 0$ *or* $\dfrac{\tilde{f}(L^0)}{L^0} > \dfrac{\tilde{f}(L^1)}{L^1}$.

*Proof* As in Proposition 1, we only need to consider the case where $\tilde{f}(L^0) > 0$ and $\tilde{f}(L^1) > 0$. The argument in the proof of Proposition 1 yields the result for $L^1 \leq L^*$. Thus, it suffices to prove the assertion for $L^0$ and $L^1$ satisfying $L^* \leq L^0 < L^1$.

By Lemma 8, $\tilde{f}(L^i) \geq \bar{y}$ for $i = 0, 1$. The desired inequality clearly holds if $\tilde{f}(L^0) = \tilde{f}(L^1) = \bar{y}$. So let $\tilde{f}(L^i) > \bar{y}$ for $i = 0$ or $i = 1$. I claim that $\tilde{f}(L^0) > \bar{y}$. Suppose, on the contrary, that $\tilde{f}(L^0) = \bar{y}$. Then $\tilde{f}(L^1) > \bar{y}$ which, by Lemma 8, implies that $L^1 = \hat{L}(\tilde{f}(L^1))$, contradicting the fact that, by Lemma 9, $L^0$ must be greater than $\hat{L}(y)$ for all $y \in (\bar{y}, y^*]$. Thus, $\tilde{f}(L^0) > \bar{y}$. If $\tilde{f}(L^1) = \bar{y}$, then trivially $\tilde{f}(L^0) > \tilde{f}(L^1)$, and the desired inequality follows.

So let $\tilde{f}(L^1) > \bar{y}$. Then, by Lemma 8, $\tilde{f}(L^0) \in Y$ and $\tilde{f}(L^1) \in Y$. It follows from Lemmas 7 and 8 that $\tilde{f}(L^0) > \tilde{f}(L^1)$, which again yields the desired inequality. Q.E.D.

*Proof of Theorem 1* Immediate from Propositions 1 and 2. Q.E.D.

*Lemma 10 If* $y^0 \in \varphi_y(L^0)$ *and* $y > 0$, *then* $y^0 = \tilde{f}_y(L^0) = \tilde{f}(L^0)$.

*Proof* By assumption, there is an $S^0 \in (S^*, S^b)$ such that $y^0 = F(L^0, S^0) = H(S^0)$. It suffices to show that there does not exist an $S^1$ such that $H(S^1) = F(L^0, S^1) > F(L^0, S^0)$. Suppose that such an $S^1$ exists. Then $S^1 \in (S^0, S^b)$, and, because $S^0 \in (S^*, S^b)$, $H'(S)$ would be negative for all $S \in (S^0, S^1)$, i.e. $H(S^1) < H(S^0)$. Contradiction. Q.E.D.

*Proof of Theorem 2* The statement is true if $\tilde{f}_y(L^1) = 0$. By Lemma 1(b), we cannot have $0 = \tilde{f}_y(L^0) < \tilde{f}_y(L^1)$. So we only need to consider the case where $\tilde{f}_y(L^0) > 0$ and $\tilde{f}_y(L^1) > 0$. Recalling the stability condition (4) and using Lemma 10, the proof of Proposition 1 applies without modification.

Q.E.D.

*Proof of Theorem 3* By Lemmas 1(b) and 10, $\tilde{f}_y(L) > 0$ for $L \in (L^0, L^1)$. Thus, $(L, \tilde{S}(L), \tilde{f}_y(L))$ is a strictly positive vector that satisfies the system of equations:

$$y - F(L, S) = 0,$$
$$y - H(S) = 0.$$

The Jacobian of the system, writing the partial derivatives with respect to $y$ and $S$ in the first and second column respectively, is:

$$\begin{bmatrix} 1 & -F_S & -F_L \\ 1 & -H' & 0 \end{bmatrix}.$$

Because $H'(\tilde{S}(L)) < 0$ and $F_S > 0$, we have that $\begin{vmatrix} 1 & -F_S \\ 1 & -H' \end{vmatrix} > 0$. The fact that $\tilde{f}_y(L)$ has a positive derivative in the interval $(L^0, L^1)$ follows from the Implicit Function Theorem after computing:

$$\begin{bmatrix} \tilde{f}'_y \\ \tilde{S}' \end{bmatrix} = \frac{1}{H' - F_S}\begin{bmatrix} -H' & F_S \\ -1 & 1 \end{bmatrix}\begin{bmatrix} -F_L \\ 0 \end{bmatrix} = \frac{1}{H' - F_S}\begin{bmatrix} H'. F_L \\ F_L \end{bmatrix}. \qquad \text{Q.E.D.}$$

*Proof of Theorem 4* Suppose not, i.e. let $y^0 \leq y^1$. Because $y^0 > 0$ and $F(L, 0) = 0$, we must have $S^0 > 0$, and $S^1 > 0$. Thus, $y^0 = F(L^0, S^0) > F(L^1, S^0)$, because $L^0 \geq L^+(S^0)$ and $L^1 > L^0$. If $S^0 \geq S^1$, then $F(L^1, S^0) \geq F(L^1, S^1) = y^1$. Putting the two inequalities together we get $y^0 > y^1$, contrary to hypothesis. Thus, "$y^0 \leq y^1$" implies "$S^0 < S^1$." But because of output stability, "$S^0 < S^1$" implies that, for $i = 0, 1$, $H'(S^i) < 0$ and, thus, $S^i \in [S^*, S^b]$. But $H$ is decreasing on $[S^*, S^b]$, and, hence, $y^0 > y^1$. Contradiction. Q.E.D.

*Proof of Theorem 5* If $F_L(L^0, S^0) \leq 0$, then the result follows from Theorem 4: we are left with the case where $F_L(L^0, S^0) > 0$. The result is trivial if $y^0 \geq y^1$. Thus, let $y^0 < y^1$, which in particular implies that $S^1 > 0$, and, therefore, that $L^1 > L^+(S^1)$. Define $f^1$: $[0, L^1] \rightarrow R^+$: $f^1(L) = F(L, S^1)$. Because of our assumptions, $f^1$ is continuous on $[0, L^1]$, increasing on $[0, L^+(S^1)]$ and decreasing on $[L^+(S^1), L^1]$. Thus, $f^1(L^+(S^1)) > f^1(L^1) = y^1$. Moreover, $f^1(0) = 0$. Thus, the Intermediate Value Theorem implies that there is a $L^2 \in (0, L^+(S^1))$ such that $f^1(L^2) = f^1(L^1) = y^1$, i.e. $(L^2, S^1, y^1)$ is an output-stable steady state, with $F_L(L^2, S^1) > 0$ (because $L^2 < L^+(S^1)$) and:

$$\frac{y^1}{L^2} > \frac{y^1}{L^1}. \tag{A.4}$$

If $L^2 \geq L^0$, then, by Theorem 2, $y^1/L^2 < y^0/L^0$, which together with (A.4), implies that $y^1/L^1 < y^0/L^0$, as claimed. If $L^2 < L^0$, then by Theorem 3, $y^0 > y^1$, i.e. $y^0/L^0 > y^1/L^1$. Q.E.D.

## Notes

1 See, for example, the formalization of a fishery by Martin Weitzman (1974).

2 *Proof* Write $\lambda = (L^1/L^0) > 1$, i.e. $L^1 = \lambda L^0$. Because $F$ displays nonincreasing returns to scale, we have that $F(\lambda L^0, \lambda S^0) \leq \lambda F(L^0, S^0)$. Assumption 1 implies that $F(\lambda L^0, S^0) < F(\lambda L^0, \lambda S^0)$. Putting the two inequalities together we obtain:

$$F(\lambda L^0, S^0) < \lambda F(L^0, S^0), \text{ i.e. } \frac{F(\lambda L^0, S^0)}{\lambda L^0} < \frac{F(L^1, S^0)}{L^1} \qquad \text{Q.E.D.}$$

3 Clearly, Assumption 2 is also satisfied whenever $F$ is of the type: "$F(L, S) = \gamma(L)\psi(S)$", and $\gamma(L/L)$ is nonincreasing in $L$, as, e.g., in the Cobb–Douglas form $F(L,S) = L^{\alpha}S^{\beta}$, for $\beta > 0$ and $\alpha \in (0, 1]$. Functions of this type have been extensively used in the literature on fisheries.

4 By letting $G$ be an increasing function of $i$, and by interpreting $S$ as "knowledge," this formulation could also be applied to the external economies of scale that have become popular in the theory on endogenous growth (Paul Romer 1986).

5 These assumptions rule out an "exhaustible resource," for which $H$ is identically zero.

6 It is often assumed in the literature on fisheries that $F(L, S) = LS$, a homogeneous of degree two Cobb–Douglas, with the following justification (see Clark 1990, ch. 7): output actually depends on labor and the average density of fish, equal to the stock divided by the relevant surface area. If $F(L, S) = LS$, then the output per hour is proportional to the density of fish. Because the surface area is fixed, doubling both labor and stock more than doubles the catch. Of course, if the three inputs, labor, stock and surface area (or, better, its reciprocal) were explicitly listed, then doubling the three of them would leave the density of fish unchanged and, thus, exactly double the amount of output.

7 *Proof* Let $\tilde{L}^1(t) > \tilde{L}^0(t)$, $\forall\ t$. For $i = 0,1$, write $S^i(t) \equiv S(t \mid \tilde{L}^i, S(0))$, and $y^i(t) \equiv F(\tilde{L}^i(t), S^i(t))$. We first show that $S^0(t) > S^1(t)$, $\forall\ t$. Because $y^0(0) < y^1(0)$, we must have that $\dot{S}^0(0) = H(S(0)) - y^0(0) > H(S(0)) - y^1(0) = \dot{S}^1(0)$, and thus $S^0(t) > S^1(t)$ in a neighborhood of $t = 0$. Suppose that there exists a $\bar{\bar{t}}$ such that $S^0(\bar{\bar{t}}) \leq S^1(\bar{\bar{t}}$: then $\bar{\bar{t}} \equiv \min\{t \geq 0 \mid S^0(t) = S^1(t)\}$ exists and is positive. But because $S^0(t) > S^1(t)$, $\forall\ t < \bar{\bar{t}}$, we must have that $0 \geq \dot{S}^0(\bar{\bar{t}}) - \dot{S}^1(\bar{\bar{t}}) = -F(\tilde{L}^0(\bar{\bar{t}}), S^0(\bar{\bar{t}})) + F(\tilde{L}^1(\bar{\bar{t}})), S^0(\bar{\bar{t}}))$, contradicting the fact that $\tilde{L}^1(\bar{\bar{t}}) > \tilde{L}^0(\bar{\bar{t}})$. Thus, $S^0(t) > S^1(t)$, $\forall\ t$. If follows that

$$\frac{y^0(t)}{\tilde{L}^0(t)} \geq \frac{F(\tilde{L}^0(t), S^1(t))}{\tilde{L}^0(t)} \geq \frac{F(\tilde{L}^1(t), S^1(t))}{\tilde{L}^1(t)},$$

the last inequality being implied by Assumption 2. Q.E.D.

8 Consider constant-input paths in the interval $(L^*, \bar{L})$ of Figures 21.1(b)–(c) and see the dynamic analysis of the section on stability with constant input flows.

9 It is sometimes called the "yield function;" but I prefer to call it "correspondence" because it is typically multi-valued.

10 *Proof.* Let $\{y^n\} \to y$, where $y^n \in \varphi(L)$ for all $n$, i.e. there exists a $S^n \leq S^b$ such that $y^n = H(S^n) = F(L, S^n)$, for all $n$. Taking a subsequence if necessary, $\{S^n\}$ converges to, say, $S$. By the continuity of $H$ and $F$, $\{y^n\} = \{H(S^n)\} \to H(S)$, $\{y^n\} = \{F(L, S^n)\} \to F(L, S)$. Thus, $y = H(S) = F(L, S)$. Q.E.D.

11 It turns out that the disconnectedness is related to the possibility of achieving the maximum sustainable yield $y^*$ with the technology $F(S, L)$ for some $S \in (S^a, S^b)$ and some $L$. This is possible in Example 3: see Figure 21.5(b). But if

one changes the parameters so that $F$ is less productive in such a way that $F(S, L) < y^*$, for all $S \in (S^a, S^b)$ and all $L$, then the branches corresponding to the two regions meet.

## Bibliography

Chipman, John S. (1965) "A Survey of the Theory of International Trade: Part 2, The Neo-Classical Theory," *Econometrica* 33: 685–760.

—— (1970) "External Economies of Scale and Competitive Equilibrium," *Quarterly Journal of Economics* 84(3): 347–385.

Clark, Colin W. (1976, 1990) *Mathematical Bioeconomics: The Optimal Management of Renewable Resources* (first edition: 1976, second edition: 1990). New York: John Wiley.

Debreu, Gerard (1959) *Theory of Value*. New York: Wiley.

Koopmans, Tjalling C. (1957) *Three Essays on the State of Economic Science*. New York: McGraw-Hill.

McKenzie, Lionel (1959) "On the Existence of General Equilibrium for a Competitive Market," *Econometrica* 27: 54–71.

Romer, Paul M. (1986) "Increasing Returns and Long-Run Growth," *Journal of Political Economy* 94: 1002–1037.

Weitzman, Martin (1974) "Free Access vs. Private Ownership as Alternative Systems for Managing Public Property." *Journal of Economic Theory* 8(2): 225–234.

# INDEX

For Product Safety Concerns and Information please contact our EU
representative GPSR@taylorandfrancis.com
Taylor & Francis Verlag GmbH, Kaufingerstraße 24, 80331 München, Germany

www.ingramcontent.com/pod-product-compliance
Ingram Content Group UK Ltd.
Pitfield, Milton Keynes, MK11 3LW, UK
UKHW020023200926
475702UK00014B/2028
*9781138985933*